## PART II.—FOREIGN COUNTRIES.

# STANLEY GIBBONS,

### INCORPORATED,

## Priced Catalogue

OF

## ❖ STAMPS ❖

OF

# FOREIGN COUNTRIES

## (1904).

### SIXTEENTH EDITION.

**COPYRIGHT.**

### STANLEY GIBBONS, INCORPORATED,

STAMP IMPORTERS, DEALERS, & PHILATELIC PUBLISHERS

**167, BROADWAY, NEW YORK, U.S.A.**

HEAD OFFICE:—391, STRAND, LONDON, W.C., ENGLAND.

# INTRODUCTION.

———◆———

THE chief feature of a dealer's Priced Catalogue of Postage Stamps is that of *prices*. Prices in the stamp business must be regulated exactly as they are in every other business—by "supply and demand."

A careful examination of the various Stock Books of all countries—which are compiled from time to time, and which contain the bulk of the stock held by the firm—shows that whereas those books which contain the stamps of Great Britain and her possessions, dealt with in Part I. of the Catalogue, are often practically depleted within a few months of compilation, those which contain the stamps of "Foreign Countries" have been "picked over" to a very much smaller extent, even when they have been made up for a twelvemonth or a longer period.

The obvious inference to be drawn from these facts is that in proportion to the stamps of the British Empire those of Foreign Countries must have been priced too high, and consequently collectors will find a very GREAT REDUCTION in the prices of the stamps in Part II.

By bringing into line the prices in this part, it is anticipated that a revived popularity and greater demand will be created for the stamps of this section, which will probably necessitate *rises* at no very distant date, but until that takes place the new prices will generally hold good until the publication of a succeeding edition.

The chief alteration of the text in Part II. is the rearrangement of the lists of Portugal and Colonies, a task which has been lightened by the co-operation of several specialist collectors of this group, to whom we take this opportunity of expressing our cordial thanks.

Many inquiries have been received from collectors whether it is intended to publish new editions of the Catalogues of

**LOCAL POSTAGE STAMPS,**

and of

**ENVELOPES, POST CARDS, AND WRAPPERS,**

but, as we announced some time since, we have been compelled, owing to the increase in the business of postage stamps, to relinquish importing in these branches of our business. It is *not* our present intention to reissue the two Catalogues above named.

An important point to remember is that *all prices* quoted in our Catalogue are in every case based upon *stock in hand* at the time of going to press. We do not believe in "guess-work prices," or those based upon the average of other Catalogues.

### SPECIAL TERMS FOR LARGE PURCHASES.

The terms for all small orders are nett as quoted, but we have decided to allow a discount of *10 % for cash purchases* of a minimum amount of £10 at one time. This discount will not apply to "Current Issues." *Special terms* will be quoted to those desirous of making really important purchases. These will vary according to the amount, the country, and class of stamps required.

STANLEY GIBBONS, LIMITED,
391, STRAND, LONDON, W.C.

# INDEX.

# ABBREVIATIONS USED IN THIS PART.

| | | |
|---|---|---|
| B. . . . . | denotes | Barred (as in Spain). |
| F. C. . . . | ,, | Fiscal Cancellation. |
| Imp., Imperf. | ,, | Imperforate (not Perforated). |
| Mm. . . . | ,, | Millimètres. |
| O. . . . . | ,, | Circular hole in Stamp (Spain). |
| P. . . . . | ,, | Pen-cancelled. |
| Perf., Pf. . . | ,, | Perforated. |
| *Percé en arc*. | ,, | Perforated in curves. |
| *Percé en scie*. | ,, | Perforated with a saw-edge. |
| Pin-Perf. . . | ,, | Perforated without removing any paper. |
| Roul. . . . | ,, | Rouletted—a broken line of cuts. |
| S. . . . . | ,, | SPECIMEN (surcharge). |
| T. C. . . . | ,, | Telegraph Cancellation. |
| Un. . . . . | ,, | Unused. |
| Us. . . . . | ,, | Used. |
| Wmk. . . . | ,, | Watermark. |

COLOURS.—Bwn., brn. (brown); car., carm. (carmine); blk. (black); gn. (green); pur. (purple); rd. (red); vio. (violet); yell. (yellow).

NOTE.—Stamps in the Catalogue not described as "*imperf.*" or "*perf.*" are to be taken as imperforate.

# STANLEY GIBBONS, INCORP.,

4h Edition, 1904.  **PRICED CATALOGUE**  16th Edition, 1904.

OF

# 𝔘sed and 𝔘nused ℘ostage 𝔖tamps.

## PART II.

## ADHESIVE STAMPS OF

# FOREIGN COUNTRIES.

| o. Type. | | Un. | Used. |
|---|---|---|---|

### ABYSSINIA.
King Menelik II., 1889.

1      2

**44.** Types 1 (¼ *to* 2 guerche) *and* 2 (4 *to* 16 guerche). *Perf.* 14×13½.

| | Un. | Used. |
|---|---|---|
| ½ g., green | .. | .. |
| ½ g., red /. | .. | .. |
| 1 g., blue | .. | .. |
| 2 g., brown | .. | .. |
| 4 g., claret | .. | .. |
| 8 g., lilac | .. | .. |
| 16 g., black | .. | .. |

Set of 7, unused, 36 c.

#### 1901.

*amps of* 1894 *overprinted* **Ethiopi** *in* violet.

| | Un. | Used. |
|---|---|---|
| ½ g., green | .. | .. |
| ½ g., red.. | .. | .. |
| 1 g., blue | .. | .. |
| 2 g., brown | .. | .. |
| 4 g., claret | .. | .. |
| 8 g., lilac | .. | .. |
| 16 g., black | .. | .. |

*As last, but overprint in* blue.

| | Un. | Used. |
|---|---|---|
| ½ g., green | .. | .. |
| ½ g., red.. | .. | .. |
| 1 g., blue | .. | .. |
| 2 g., brown | .. | .. |

| No. | | Un. | Used. |
|---|---|---|---|
| 19 | 4 g., claret | .. | .. |
| 20 | 8 g., lilac | .. | .. |
| 21 | 16 g., black | .. | .. |

*Similar to last, but* "Ethiopie" *in script type, in* blue-black (Bb.) *or* violet (V.).

| 22 | ½ g., green (Bb.) | .. |
|---|---|---|
| 23 | ½ g., red (Bb.) .. | .. |
| 24 | 1 g., blue (Bb.).. | .. |
| 25 | 2 g., brown (Bb.) | .. |
| 26 | 4 g., claret (Bb.) | .. |
| 27 | 8 g., lilac (V.) .. | .. |
| 28 | 16 g., black (Bb.) | .. |

### ሰበጣ፡ መልእት።
3      4

1 APRIL, **1902**. *Same types overprinted in Amharic characters,* Type **3**, "bosata" *or* "posta", *in* blue-black, violet, *or* black (Bk.).

| 29 | ½ g., green (Bb.) | .. |
|---|---|---|
| 30 | ½ g., red (Bb.) .. | .. |
| 31 | 1 g., blue (V.) .. | .. |
| 32 | 2 g., brown (V.) | .. |
| 33 | 4 g., claret (Bb.) | .. |
| 34 | 8 g., lilac (Bb.) | .. |
| 35 | 16 g., black (Bb.) | .. |

**1903.** *Same types overprinted in Amharic characters,* Type **4**, "malekathe," i.e. Ethiopia.

| 36 | ½ g., green (Bb.) | .. |
|---|---|---|
| 37 | ½ g., red (Bb.) .. | .. |
| 38 | 1 g., blue (Bb.) | .. |
| 39 | 2 g., brown (Bb.) | .. |
| 40 | 4 g., claret (Bk.) | .. |
| 41 | 8 g., lilac (Bk.) | .. |
| 42 | 16 g., black (Bk.) | .. |

We give the above list of the different varieties chronicled from time to time, but are unable to vouch for its accuracy.

B

No.          *Un.*    *Used.*

### UNPAID LETTER STAMPS.

**3**

**1896.**   Type **1** *surcharged with* Type **3**.

(*a*) *In* black.

| | | | |
|---|---|---|---|
| 101 | ½ guerche, | green | .. |
| 102 | ⅓   ,, | rose | .. |
| 103 | 4   ,, | lilac-brown. | |
| 104 | 8   ,, | violet | .. |

(*b*) *In* red.

| | | | |
|---|---|---|---|
| 105 | 1 guerche, | pale blue | .. |
| 106 | 2   ,, | brown | |
| 107 | 16   ,, | black | .. |

Set of 7, unused, 36 c.

*Errors.*   Surcharge omitted.

| | | | |
|---|---|---|---|
| 108 | 4 guerche, | claret | .. |
| 109 | 8   ,, | lilac | .. |
| 110 | 16   ,, | black | .. |

## AFGHANISTAN.

Shahi. Sunar. Abasi. ½ rupee. 1 rupee.

The illustrations above show the characters denoting the values, which in Types **2–16a** are inside the inner circle and above or below the Tiger's head, and in Types **17–37** are in the outer circle, below the Tiger's head.

Numerals used for the date.

| 1 | 2 | 3 | 4 | 5 | 6 |
|---|---|---|---|---|---|
| 7 | 8 | 9 | 0 | | |

All the stamps of Afghanistan are imperf. The arrows indicate the position of the date on each type.

**1**

**1868.**   Type **1**.   *White laid paper.*

' | No value, violet    ..   —   75.00

---

No. Type.          *Un.*    *Used.*

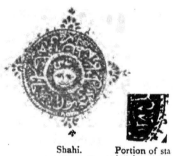

Shahi.        Portion of sta
**2**          showing the d.

Sunar.
**3**

**1870-71.**   Dated 1288.

(i.) Plate A.

*Outer circle measures* 30 mm. *in diameter.*

| | | | | | |
|---|---|---|---|---|---|
| 2 | 2 | Shahi, black | .. | 8.75 | 3.75 |

Abasi.
**4**

(ii.) Plate B.

*Outer circle* 28 mm. *in diameter.*

| | | | | | |
|---|---|---|---|---|---|
| 2a | 2 | Shahi, black | .. | — | 3.75 |
| 3 | 3 | Sunar ,, | .. | 15.00 | 7.50 |

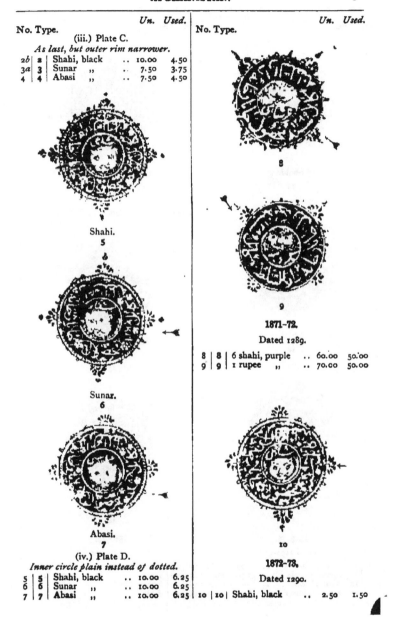

| No. Type. | | | Un. | Used. |
|---|---|---|---|---|

**(iii.) Plate C.**

*As last, but outer rim narrower.*

| 2b | 2 | Shahi, black | .. | 10.00 | 4.50 |
|---|---|---|---|---|---|
| 3a | 3 | Sunar | " | .. | 7.50 | 3.75 |
| 4 | 4 | Abasi | " | .. | 7.50 | 4.50 |

Shahi.
5

Sunar.
6

Abasi.
7

**(iv.) Plate D.**

*Inner circle plain instead of dotted.*

| 5 | 5 | Shahi, black | .. | 10.00 | 6.25 |
|---|---|---|---|---|---|
| 6 | 6 | Sunar | " | .. | 10.00 | 6.25 |
| 7 | 7 | Abasi | " | .. | 10.00 | 6.25 |

| No. Type. | | | Un. | Used. |
|---|---|---|---|---|

8

9

**1871-72.**

Dated 1289.

| 8 | 8 | 6 shahi, purple | .. | 60.00 | 50.00 |
|---|---|---|---|---|---|
| 9 | 9 | 1 rupee | " | .. | 70.00 | 50.00 |

10

**1872-73.**

Dated 1290.

| 10 | 10 | Shahi, black | .. | 2.50 | 1.50 |
|---|---|---|---|---|---|

| No. Type. | Un. | Used. | No. Type. | Un. | Used. |
|---|---|---|---|---|---|

Shahi.

11

1 rupee.

14

15 | 14 | 1 rupee, black .. 8.75 7.50

Abasi.

12

Sunar.

15

½ rupee.

13

Abasi.

16

**1873-74.**

Dated 1290–91.

**1874-75.**

Dated 1292.

| No. | Type No. | Type | Un. | Used | No. | Type No. | Type | Un. | Used |
|---|---|---|---|---|---|---|---|---|---|
| 1 | 11 | Shahi, black | .. 75 | 62 | 16 | 15 | Sunar, purple | .. 6.25 | 6.25 |
| | ,, | Shahi, purple | .. 37.50 | 22.50 | 17 | 16 | Abasi ,, | .. 12.50 | 12.50 |
| | 12 | Abasi, black | .. — | 10.00 | 18 | 15 | Sunar, black | .. 17.50 | 12.50 |
| 13 | ½ rupee, black | | .. 8.75 | 7.50 | 19 | 16 | Abasi ,, | .. 35.00 | |

No. Type.    *Un.*   *Used.*

16a

*Variety with wide outer circle.*

| | | | | *Un.* | *Used.* |
|---|---|---|---|---|---|
| 19a | 16a | Sunar, purple | .. | 31.25 | 25.00 |
| 19b | " | " black | .. | | |

Shahi.
17

Sunar.      Abasi.
18      19

½ rupee.      1 rupee.
20      21

**1875-76.** Dated 1293.

| | | | | *Un.* | *Used.* |
|---|---|---|---|---|---|
| 20 | 17 | Shahi, black | .. | — | 35.00 |
| 21 | 18 | Sunar " | .. | — | 50.00 |
| 22 | 19 | Abasi " | .. | — | 75.00 |
| 23 | 20 | ½ rupee " | .. | | |
| 24 | 21 | 1 " " | .. | | |

No. Type.    *Un.*   *Used.*

| | | | | *Un.* | *Used.* |
|---|---|---|---|---|---|
| 25 | 17 | Shahi, purple | .. | — | 35.00 |
| 26 | 18 | Sunar " | .. | — | 60.00 |
| 27 | 19 | Abasi " | .. | | |
| 28 | 20 | ½ rupee " | .. | 50.00 | |
| 29 | 21 | 1 " " | .. | 60.00 | |

*Varieties on thick card-paper.*

| | | | |
|---|---|---|---|
| 20a | 17 | Shahi, black | .. |
| 21a | 18 | Sunar " | .. |
| 22a | 19 | Abasi " | .. |
| 23a | 20 | ½ rupee " | .. |
| 24a | 21 | 1 " " | .. |

Shahi.      Sunar.
22      23

Abasi.      ½ 1upee.
24      25

1 rupee.
26

**1875-76.** Dated 1293.

*Five series for different districts.*

| | | | | *Un.* | *Used.* |
|---|---|---|---|---|---|
| 30 | 22 | Shahi, grey | .. | 2.50 | 1.25 |
| 31 | 23 | Sunar " | .. | 2.50 | 2.00 |
| 32 | 24 | Abasi " | .. | 3.75 | 3.75 |
| 33 | 25 | ½ rupee " | .. | 6.25 | 6.25 |
| 34 | 26 | 1 " " | .. | 6.25 | 7.50 |
| 35 | 22 | Shahi, purple | .. | — | 3.75 |
| 36 | 23 | Sunar " | .. | — | 6.25 |
| 37 | 24 | Abasi " | .. | — | 12.50 |
| 38 | 25 | ½ rupee " | .. | — | 18.75 |
| 39 | 26 | 1 " " | .. | — | 20.00 |

| No. | Type. | | Un. | Used. |
|---|---|---|---|---|
| 40 | 22 | Shahi, black | .. | |
| 41 | 23 | Sunar ,, | .. | |
| 42 | 24 | Abasi ,, | .. | |
| 43 | 25 | ½ rupee ,, | .. | |
| 44 | 26 | 1 ,, ,, | .. | |
| 45 | 22 | Shahi, green | .. 12.50 | 2.50 |
| 46 | 23 | Sunar ,, | .. — | 6.25 |
| 47 | 24 | Abasi ,, | .. — | 12.50 |
| 48 | 25 | ½ rupee ,, | .. | |
| 49 | 26 | 1 ,, ,, | .. | |
| 50 | 22 | Shahi, brown | .. — | 3.75 |
| 51 | 23 | Sunar ,, | .. | |
| 52 | 24 | Abasi ,, | .. | |
| 53 | 25 | ½ rupee ,, | .. | |
| 54 | 26 | 1 ,, ,, | .. | |

*Varieties on thick card-paper.*

| | | | Un. | |
|---|---|---|---|---|
| 41a | 23 | Sunar, black | .. | |
| 42a | 24 | Abasi ,, | .. | |
| 43a | 25 | ½ rupee ,, | .. | |
| 44a | 26 | 1 ,, ,, | .. | |

| No. | Type. | | Un. | Used. |
|---|---|---|---|---|
| 65 | 27 | Shahi, purple | .. 1.25 | 1.00 |
| 66 | 28 | Sunar ,, | .. 2.50 | 1.50 |
| 67 | 29 | Abasi ,, | .. 5.00 | 3.75 |
| 68 | 30 | ½ rupee ,, | .. 10.00 | 7.50 |
| 69 | 31 | 1 ,, ,, | .. 10.00 | 7.50 |
| 70 | 27 | Shahi, green | .. 2.50 | 1.25 |
| 71 | 28 | Sunar ,, | .. 3.75 | 2.00 |
| 72 | 29 | Abasi ,, | .. 7.50 | 7.50 |
| 73 | 30 | ½ rupee ,, | .. 15.00 | 15.00 |
| 74 | 31 | 1 ,, ,, | .. 17.50 | 17.50 |
| 75 | 27 | Shahi, yellow | .. 2.00 | 1.25 |
| 76 | 28 | Sunar ,, | .. 5.00 | 7.50 |
| 77 | 29 | Abasi ,, | .. 15.00 | 15.00 |
| 78 | 30 | ½ rupee ,, | .. 17.50 | |
| 79 | 31 | 1 ,, ,, | .. 20.00 | |

Shahi. 27    Sunar. 28

Abasi. 29    ½ rupee. 30

Shahi. 32    Sunar. 33

Abasi. 34    ½ rupee. 35

1 rupee. 36

1 rupee. 31    Portion of stamp showing the date.

**1876–77. Dated 1294.**

| No. | Type. | | Un. | Used. |
|---|---|---|---|---|
| 55 | 27 | Shahi, grey | .. 2.00 | 1.25 |
| 56 | 28 | Sunar ,, | .. 3.75 | 2.50 |
| 57 | 29 | Abasi ,, | .. 7.50 | 6.25 |
| 58 | 30 | ½ rupee ,, | .. 12.50 | |
| 59 | 31 | 1 rupee ,, | .. 12.50 | 10.00 |
| 60 | 27 | Shahi, black | .. 5.00 | 2.50 |
| 61 | 28 | Sunar ,, | .. 5.00 | 2.50 |
| 62 | 29 | Abasi ,, | .. 25.00 | 15.00 |
| | 30 | ½ rupee ,, | .. 25.00 | |
| | 31 | 1 ,, ,, | .. 25.00 | |

**1878 (April). Dated 1295.**

| No. | Type. | | Un. | Used. |
|---|---|---|---|---|
| 80 | 32 | Shahi, grey | .. 1.00 | 75 |
| 81 | 33 | Sunar ,, | .. 1.00 | 75 |
| 82 | 34 | Abasi ,, | .. 2.50 | 2.50 |
| 83 | 35 | ½ rupee ,, | .. 5.00 | 4.00 |
| 84 | 36 | 1 ,, ,, | .. 5.00 | 5.00 |
| 85 | 32 | Shahi, black | .. 1.00 | 1.00 |
| 86 | 33 | Sunar ,, | .. 1.50 | 1.50 |
| 87 | 34 | Abasi ,, | .. 3.75 | |
| 88 | 35 | ½ rupee ,, | .. 10.00 | |
| 89 | 36 | 1 ,, ,, | .. 12.50 | |
| 90 | 32 | Shahi, purple | .. 75 | 75 |
| 91 | 33 | Sunar ,, | .. 1.25 | 1.00 |
| 92 | 37 | Abasi ,, | .. 2.50 | 2.50 |
| 93 | 35 | ½ rupee ,, | .. 5.00 | 4.50 |
| 94 | 36 | 1 ,, ,, | .. 6.25 | 6.25 |

| No. | Type. | | | Un. | Used. |
|---|---|---|---|---|---|
| 95 | 32 | Shahi, green | .. | — | 75 |
| 96 | 33 | Sunar ,, | .. | 2.50 | 90 |
| 97 | 34 | Abasi ,, | .. | 5.00 | 3.75 |
| 98 | 35 | ½ rupee ,, | .. | 10.00 | 8.00 |
| 99 | 36 | 1 ,, ,, | .. | 10.00 | 8.00 |
| 100 | 32 | Shahi, brn.-yellow | | — | 75 |
| 101 | 33 | Sunar ,, | | 1.50 | 1.25 |
| 102 | 34 | Abasi ,, | | 3.75 | |
| 103 | 35 | ½ rupee ,, | | 7.50 | |
| 104 | 36 | 1 ,, ,, | | 7.50 | |

37

**1878 (JUNE). Type 37. Dated 1295.**

| 105 | Shahi, grey .. | .. | 75 | 50 |
|---|---|---|---|---|
| 106 | Shahi, purple .. | .. | 90 | 75 |
| 107 | Shahi, green .. | .. | 75 | 62 |
| 108 | Shahi, yellow .. | .. | 75 | 62 |
| 109 | Shahi, black .. | .. | | |

1 abasi.
38

2 abasi.
39

**1880-90. Types 38-40. Dated 1298.**
The value is shown by the characters within the inner circle.

*On thin laid bâtonné paper.*

| 110 | 1 abasi, violet (1880) . | 1.25 | 1.25 |
|---|---|---|---|
| 111 | 2 ,, ,, ( ,, ) . | 3.75 | 2.50 |
| 112 | 1 rupee ,, ( ,, ) . | — | 3.75 |
| 113 | 1 a., violet-blk. (1882) | 2.00 | 1.50 |
| 114 | 2 a. ,, ( ,, ) | 2.50 | 2.50 |
| 115 | 1 rupee ,, ( ,, ) | 3.00 | 2.50 |
| 115a | 1 a., black .. | .. | 3.75 | 6.25 |
| 115b | 2 a. ,, | .. | .. |

1 rupee.
40

| 115c | 1 rupee, black.. | .. | | |
|---|---|---|---|---|
| 115d | 1 abasi, purple | .. | 1.50 | 75 |
| 115e | 2 ,, ,, | .. | 2.50 | 1.00 |
| 115f | 1 rupee ,, | .. | 2.50 | 1.25 |
| 116 | 1 abasi, pink (1883) .. | 1.00 | 1.00 |
| 117 | 2 ,, ,, { ,, } .. | | |
| 118 | 1 rupee ,, { ,, } .. | | |

*Wove bâtonné paper.*

| 119 | 1 a., orange-red (1884) . | | |
|---|---|---|---|
| 120 | 2 a. ,, { ,, } . | 1.25 | 1.25 |
| 121 | 1 rupee ,, { ,, } . | 2.50 | |

**1884. Thin white wove paper.**

| 122 | 1 abasi, purple | .. |
|---|---|---|
| 123 | 2 ,, ,, | .. |
| 124 | 1 rupee ,, | .. |
| 125 | 1 abasi, rose | .. |
| 125a | 1 ,, black | .. |
| 125b | 2 ,, ,, | .. |

**1884-85. Thin coloured wove paper.**

| 126 | 1 a., purple on green | .. |
|---|---|---|
| 127 | 1 a., red on blue | .. |
| 128 | 1 a., red on green | .. |

*Coloured laid bâtonné paper.*

| 129 | 1 a., purple on yellow. | | |
|---|---|---|---|
| 129a | 1 a., red on green | .. | |
| 130 | 1 a., red on yellow | .. | |
| 130a | 2 a. ,, ,, | .. | 2.50 | |
| 130b | 1 rupee, red on ,, | .. | 7.50 | 2.50 |
| 130c | 1 a., red on pale grey. | — | 10.00 |
| 130d | 1 a., red on lilac | .. | — | 10.00 |

*Coloured wove bâtonné paper.*

| 130e | 1 a., purple on grey .. |
|---|---|
| 130f | 2 a. ,, ,, .. |
| 130g | 1 a., orange ,, .. |
| 130h | 1 a., claret on yellow. |
| 130i | 1 a., violet on green.. |
| 130j | 1 a., red ,, .. |
| 130k | 1 a., orange on blue.. |

**1886. White laid bâtonné paper.**

| 131 | 1 abasi, orange-brown | 75 | 75 |
|---|---|---|---|
| 132 | 2 ,, ,, | 2.00 | 2.00 |
| 133 | 1 rupee ,, | 3.00 | |
| 134 | 1 abasi, carmine | .. | 1.50 | 1.00 |
| 134a | 1 a., rose-carmine | .. | 1.25 | 1.00 |
| 135 | 2 abasi, carmine | .. | |
| 135a | 2 a., rose-carmine | .. | 1.50 | 1.50 |
| 136 | 1 rupee, carmine | .. | |
| 136a | 1 r., rose-carmine | .. | 1.75 |

| No. | | Un. | Used. |
|---|---|---|---|

*Thin coloured wove paper.*

| No. | | Un. |
|---|---|---|
| 137 | 1 a., red on *yellow* .. | 1.50 |
| 138 | 2 a. ,, ,, .. | 5.00 |
| 139 | 1 rupee ,, ,, .. | 5.00 |
| 143 | 1 a., red on *orange* .. | 1.25 |
| 144 | 2 a. ,, ,, .. | 5.00 |
| 145 | 1 rupee ,, ,, .. | 5.00 |
| 145*a* | 1 a., carmine on rose . | |
| 145*b* | 1 a., lilac on rose .. | |
| 145*c* | 2 a., violet on pale blue | |

It appears doubtful whether all the
varieties of this set were issued

*Coloured ribbed paper.*

| 146 | 1 a., carmine on *green* | 1.25 |
|---|---|---|
| 147 | 2 a. ,, ,, | 5.00 |
| 148 | 1 rup. ,, ,, | 5.00 |
| 150 | 1 a. ,, *lilac*. | 3.75 |
| 151 | 2 a. ,, ,, . | 5.00 |
| 152 | 1 rup. ,, ,, . | 5.00 |
| 152*a* | 1 a. ,, *orange* | 7.50 |
| 152*b* | 1 a. ,, *rose* .. | 1.50 |
| 152*c* | 2 a. ,, ,, .. | 5.00 |
| 152*d* | 1 r. ,, ,, .. | 5.00 |
| 152*e* | 1 r., purple on orange | 12.50 |
| 152*f* | 1 a., red on yellow .. | |
| 152*g* | 2 a. ,, ,, | |
| 152*h* | 1 r., carmine ,, .. | |

**1888.** *Thin wove paper.*

| 153 | 1 a., black on *magenta*. | |
|---|---|---|
| 154 | 1 a., claret on *orange* .. | |

*Laid bâtonné paper.*

| 155 | 1 a., black on *lavender* | |
|---|---|---|
| 156 | 1 a., puce on *green* .. | |
| 157 | 1 a., black on *pink* .. | |
| 158 | 2 a. ,, ,, .. | |
| 159 | 1 r. ,, ,, .. | |

*Thin laid paper.*

| 160 | 1 a., black on *pink* .. | |
|---|---|---|
| 161 | 2 a. ,, ,, .. | |
| 162 | 1 rup. ,, ,, .. | |
| 163 | 1 a., brown on *yellow* . | |
| 164 | 2 a. ,, ,, . | |
| 165 | 1 rup. ,, ,, . | |
| 166 | 1 a., blue on *green* .. | |
| 167 | 2 a. ,, ,, .. | |
| 168 | 1 rup. ,, ,, .. | |
| 168*a* | 2 a., purple on *lavender* | |

*Ordinary white laid paper.*

| 169 | 1 a., lake .. .. | |
|---|---|---|
| 169*a* | 1 a., purple .. .. | |
| 169*b* | 1 a., brown-orange .. | |
| 169*c* | 2 a., lake-red.. .. | 3.75 |
| 169*d* | 2 a., purple .. .. | |

*Ordinary wove paper.*

| 9*e* | 1 a., deep violet on salmon | |
|---|---|---|
| 9*f* | 1 a., green on salmon . | |

| No. | | Un. | Used. |
|---|---|---|---|

1 abasi.
40*a*

**1889-90.** Type 38 *redrawn, wide
outer circle.* Type 40*a*.

| 170 | 1 a., purple .. .. | 1.25 | 1.00 |
|---|---|---|---|
| 170*a* | 1 a., vermilion .. | | |
| 171 | 1 a., carmine-rose .. | 1.00 | 1.00 |
| 172 | 1 a., purple on *yellow* | | |

**1891.** Types **38, 39,** *and* **40.**

| 173 | 1 a., green on *rose wove* | 7.50 |
|---|---|---|
| 174 | 2 a., black on *white laid* | 6.25 |
| 175 | 1 r., purple on *green*
bâtonné .. .. | |

| 1 abasi. | 2 abasi. |
|---|---|
| 41 | 42 |

1 rupee.
43

**1892.** Types **41** *to* **43.** *Pelure paper.*

| 176 | 1 abasi, slate .. .. | 2.50 | 1.25 |
|---|---|---|---|
| 177 | 2 ,, ,, .. .. | — | 3.75 |
| 178 | 1 rupee ,, .. .. | — | 5.00 |

44

| No. | | | Un. | Used. |
|---|---|---|---|---|

Portion of the stamp showing the date.

**1893-99.** Type 44, dated 1310.
Black *impression on coloured papers.*

| 179 | 1 a., yellow-green | .. | 90 | 62 |
|---|---|---|---|---|
| 180 | 1 a., green | .. | — | 1.25 |
| 180a | 1 a., blue-green | .. | — | 62 |
| 180b | 1 a., greenish-blue | .. | | . |
| 181 | 1 a., yellow | .. | 90 | 90 |
| 182 | 1 a., orange | .. | 1.00 | 1.00 |
| 183 | 1 a., salmon | .. | — | 50 |
| 184 | 1 a., lilac-rose | .. | 1.25 | 1.00 |
| 185 | 1 a., pale rose | .. | 1.25 | 90 |
| 186 | 1 a., deep ,, | .. | — | 90 |
| 187 | 1 a., magenta | .. | — | 75 |
| 188 | 1 a., blue .. | .. | | |
| 188a | 1 a., deep dull blue | .. | | |
| 189 | 1 a., violet | .. | — | 1.25 |
| 189a | 1 a., scarlet | .. | | |
| 189b | 1 a., brick-red | .. | — | 1.25 |

45

46

**1894.** Types 45 and 46.

| 190 | 2 a., black on green | .. | — | 1.25 |
|---|---|---|---|---|
| 191 | 1 r. ,, ,, | .. | 2.00 | 2.00 |

**1900.** Type 44, dated 1316.
Black *impression on coloured paper.*

| 192 | 2 a., dull pink .. | .. | | |
|---|---|---|---|---|
| 193 | 2 a., magenta .. | .. | | |

| No. | | | Un. | Used. |
|---|---|---|---|---|

REGISTRATION STAMP.

51

**1894.** Type 51.

| 301 | 2 a., black on green | . | 1.25 | 1.25 |
|---|---|---|---|---|

*Similar to* Type 44, *but without the long character across the middle.* Thin *wove paper.* Dated 1311.

| 301a | 1 r., black on green .. | | | |
|---|---|---|---|---|

**1898.** *Similar to* Type 44, *but wider.*

| 302 | 2 a., black on deep rose | — | 1.25 |
|---|---|---|---|---|
| 303 | 2 a. ,, orange .. | 2.00 | |
| 304 | 2 a. ,, yellow .. | | |
| 305 | 2 a. ,, green .. | — | 1.00 |

NOTE.—We have nearly all the rarities of this country in stock, both used and unused, and selections can be sent to advanced collectors. Prices vary so much, according to condition, that we omit them in many cases. Most *used* Afghan stamps have a piece cut or torn out of them.

## ARGENTINE REPUBLIC.

1                    2

**1858.** Type 1. *Small figure of value.*

| 1 | 5 centavos, red | .. | 8 | 50 |
|---|---|---|---|---|
| 2 | 10 ,, green | .. | 12 | 1.25 |
| 3 | 15 ,, blue | .. | 12 | 1.25 |

There are nine varieties of each value, of which the principal is—

*Variety* "5 :", *with colon.*

| 4 | 5 centavos, red.. | .. | 62 |
|---|---|---|---|

|  | Un. | Used. |
|---|---|---|
| No. | | |

**1861.** Type **2.** *Large figure of value.*

| 5 | 5 centavos, red | .. | 18 | 1.50 |
|---|---|---|---|---|

Nos. 1-5 were issued by the Argentine Confederation; those that follow by the Argentine Republic.

3          4

(a)        (b)

**1862.** Type 3. *Small "5," large "C" in* "CENTAVOS." (a).

| 6 | 5 c., rose | .. | .. | 1.00 | 36 |
|---|---|---|---|---|---|
| 7 | 5 c., deep rose | .. | .. | 1.00 | 36 |
| 8 | 10 c., green | .. | .. | — | 3.00 |
| 9 | 15 c., blue | .. | .. | | |

*With accent over* "Ú" *of* "REPUBLICA."

| 10 | 5 c., rose | .. | .. | 5.00 | 1.00 |
|---|---|---|---|---|---|
| 11 | 10 c., green | .. | .. | 5.00 | 2.50 |
| 12 | 10 c., deep green | .. | 7.50 | 3.75 |
| 13 | 15 c., pale blue | .. | .. | 11.25 | 5.00 |
| 13a | 15 c., deep ,, | .. | .. | | |

The 15 c. is known *tête-bêche.*

**1862.** Type 4. *Large "5," small "C" in* "CENTAVOS." (b).

| 14 | 5 c., rose | .. | .. | — | 2.50 |
|---|---|---|---|---|---|
| 15 | 5 c., rose-red | .. | .. | — | 1.00 |

Numerous reprints exist of this stamp in many shades of *red* and *rose*, but the paper is usually thicker than that of the issued stamps. There are also bogus varieties of 10 c. and 15 c. of this type of the 5 c.

5          6

**1864.** Types 5 to 7. *Portrait of Rivadavia.* Wmk. Type 8. *Imperf.*

| | 5 c., rose-red | .. | .. | — | 3.75 |
|---|---|---|---|---|---|
| | 10 c., green | .. | .. | — | 30.00 |
| | 15 c., blue | .. | .. | — | 40.00 |

|  | Un. | Used. |
|---|---|---|
| No. | | |

7          8

**1864.** *The same.* Perf. 11½.

| 19 | 5 c., rose-red | .. | .. | 7.50 | 50 |
|---|---|---|---|---|---|
| 20 | 5 c., brown-rose | .. | 1.00 | 25 |
| 21 | 5 c., carmine | .. | .. | 1.25 | 90 |
| 22 | 10 c., green | .. | .. | 1.50 | 1.00 |
| 23 | 15 c., blue | .. | .. | 2.10 | 2.10 |

**1867.** *The same. No. wmk.*

| 24 | 5 c., carmine (perf. 11½) | | |
|---|---|---|---|
| 25 | 5 c.  ,,  (imperf.). | 6.25 | 1.50 |

(Rivadavia.)      (Belgrano.)
9          10

(San Martin.)
11

A

**1867.** Types 9 *to* 11. *No wmk.* Perf. 12.
(a) *Head on ground of horizontal lines.*

| 26 | 5 c., vermilion (A) | .. | 1.25 | 62 |
|---|---|---|---|---|
| 28 | 15 c., blue | .. | .. | 1.85 | 75 |

No. Un. Used.

No. Un. Used.

B

*(b) Ground of crossed lines.*

| 29 | 5 c., vermilion (B) | .. | 12 | 2 |
| 29a | 10 c., green | .. .. | 25 | 12 |
| 30 | 15 c., blue | .. | 75 | 25 |

No. 29 (B) differs from No. 26 (A) in having the head entirely redrawn, the most noticeable difference being in the outline of the collar above the "AR" of "ARGENTINE." In No. 26 it is rounded, in No. 29 nearly straight.

*Variety, on laid paper.*

| 31 | 10 c., green | .. .. | 12.50 | 2.50 |

(Balcarce.) (Moreno.)
12 13

(Alvear.) (Posadas.)
14 15

**1873.** Types **12** to **16.** *Perf.* 12.

| 32 | 1 c., violet | .. .. | 25 | 2 |
| 33 | 1 c., mauve | .. .. | 4 | 4 |
| 34 | 4 c., brown | .. .. | 6 | 6 |
| 34a | 4 c., chestnut | .. .. | 50 | 6 |
| 35 | 4 c., sepia .. | .. .. | 6 | 2 |
| 36 | 30 c., orange | .. .. | 2.50 | 62 |
| 37 | 60 c., black | .. .. | 75 | 6 |

(Saavedra.)
16

| 38 | 90 c., blue | .. .. | 1.85 | 8 |

**1876.** Type 9. *Rouletted.*

| 39 | 5 c., vermilion .. | .. | 3.15 | 2.50 |

# 1 2 8

17 18 19

**1877.** Types 9 *and* 10 *surcharged in* black *with* Type 17, 18, *or* 19. *Perf.* 12.

| 40 | 1 on 5 c., vermilion | .. | 62 | 62 |
| 41 | 2 on 5 c. | ,, | 3.15 | 3.15 |
| 42 | 8 on 10 c., green | .. | 1.25 | 75 |

*On* No. 31, *laid paper.*

| 43a | 8 on 10 c., green | .. |

*Varieties. Surcharge inverted.*

| 43 | 1 on 5 c., vermilion | .. |
| 44 | 2 on 5 c. | ,, |
| 45 | 8 on 10 c., green | .. |

Nearly all the specimens of Nos. 43 to 45 which we have seen have forged surcharges.

(Rivadavia.) (Belgrano.)
20 21

(Saarsfield.) (San Martin.)
22 23

**1877-78.** Types **20** to **23.** *Rouletted.*

| 47 | 8 c., lake | .. .. | 16 | 6 |
| 48 | 16 c., green | .. .. | 12 | 2 |
| 49 | 20 c., pale blue .. | .. | 62 | 16 |
| 50 | 24 c., deep blue .. | .. | 30 | 4 |

| No. | *Un.* | *Used.* |
|-----|------|--------|

(Lopez.)

24

**1877-87.** *Perf.* 12.

| 51 | 2 c., green | | | 4 | 2 |
|----|-------------|---|---|---|---|
| 52 | 8 c., lake | .. | .. | 12 | 2 |
| 53 | 24 c., deep blue (1887) | .. | 36 | 6 |
| 54 | 25 c., rosy lake (14) | .. | 62 | 50 |

½

( PROVISORIO)

26

**FEB., 1882.**

Type 9 *surcharged in* black *with* Type 26, *and perf. across centre.*

| 55 | ½ on 5 c., vermilion | .. | 25 | 25 |
|----|---------------------|----|----|----|

½      ½

PROVISORIO?   PROVISORIO?

(*a*)       (*b*)

MARCH, 1882. *Surcharged with* Type 26.

| 56 | ½ on 5 c., vermilion (*a*). | 36 | 36 |
|----|----------------------------|----|----|
| 56a | ½ on 5 c. | „ | (*b*). | 8 | |

*Surcharge inverted.*

| 57 | ½ on 5 c., vermilion | .. |
|----|---------------------|----|

*Double surcharge.*

57a| ½ on 5 c., vermilion (*a*).

There are numerous varieties of this surcharge.

27

**1882.** Type 27. *Typographed.*

(*a*) *Perf.* 12.

| | ½ c., brown | .. | .. | 4 | 8 |
|---|------------|----|----|---|---|
| | ½ c., pale brown | | | | |
| | 1 c., rose-red | .. | .. | 6 | 8 |
| | 2 c., ultramarine | .. | 2.00 | 18 |

| No. | *Un.* | *Used.* |
|-----|------|--------|

(*b*) *Perf.* 14.

| 62 | ½ c., brown | .. | .. |
|----|------------|----|----|
| 63 | 1 c., scarlet | .. | .. | 4 | 8 |
| 64 | 12 c., ultramarine | .. | 36 | 12 |

**1883.** *Typographed. Perf.* 14.

| 65 | 12 c., Prussian blue | .. | — | 62 |
|----|---------------------|----|---|----|

**1884**  **½**   **1 C 1884**   **CUATRO Centavos 1884**

28      29      30

**1884.** Types 9 *and* 11 *surcharged with* Types 28, 29, *and* 30.

(*a*) *Ground of horizontal lines.*

| 66 | ½ (*red*) on 15 c., blue | .. | | |
|----|-------------------------|----|---|---|
| 67 | ½ (*black*) on 15 c., blue | . | 1.50 | |
| 68 | 1 (*red*) on 15 c., blue | .. | 62 | 1.00 |

*Inverted surcharges.*

| 69 | ½ (*red*) on 15 c., blue | .. |
|----|-------------------------|----|
| 70 | ½ (*black*) on 15 c., blue | .. |
| 71 | 1 (*red*) on 15 c., blue | .. |

(*b*) *Ground of crossed lines.*

| 72 | ½ (*black*) on 5 c., vermil. | 8 | 25 |
|----|-----------------------------|---|----|
| 73 | ½ (*red*) on 15 c., blue | .. | 25 | 12 |
| 74 | ½ (*black*) on 15 c., blue. | 50 | 62 |
| 75 | 1 (*red*) on 15 c., blue | .. | 50 | 62 |
| 76 | 4 (*black*) on 5 c., vermil. | 25 | 25 |

*Inverted surcharges.*

| 76a | ½ (*black*) on 5 c., vermil. | | |
|-----|-----------------------------|---|---|
| 77 | ½ (*red*) on 15 c., blue | .. | 2.10 |
| 78 | ½ (*black*) on 15 c., blue. | |
| 79 | 1 (*red*) on 15 c., blue . | |
| 80 | 4 (*black*) on 5 c., vermil. | 1.50 |

31

**1884.** Type 31. *Engraved.*

*Perf.* 12.

| 81 | ½ c., brown | .. | .. | 2 | 2 |
|----|------------|----|----|---|---|
| 82 | 1 c., rose-red | .. | .. | 2 | 2 |
| 83 | 12 c., Prussian blue | .. | 62 | 4 |
| 84 | 12 c., ultramarine | .. | 36 | 6 |
| 85 | 12 c., greenish blue | .. | 2.50 | 25 |

Un.  Used.

No.

(Urquiza.)
3²

(Lopez.)
33

(Celman.)
34

(Sarmiento.)
3⁶

A

B

Un.  Used.

No.

(Avellaneda.)
37

(San Martin.)
3⁸

(Roca.)
39

(Belgrano.)
40

(Dorrego.)
41

(Moreno.)
4²

| 92 | 10 c., brown | .. | .. | 25 | 2 |
| 93 | 15 c., orange | .. | .. | 18 | 4 |
| 94 | 20 c., green | .. | .. | 18 | 4 |
| 95 | 25 c., violet | .. | .. | 36 | 12 |
| 96 | 30 c., brown | .. | .. | 30 | 12 |
| 97 | 40 c., slate | .. | .. | 1.10 | 12 |
| 98 | 50 c., blue | .. | .. | 1.25 | 12 |

There are several varieties in many of the values, consisting in the different distances of the top of the head from the frame.

(Mitre.)
43

(Paz.)
44

**1889-90.** Types 45 to 55.  *Perf.* 11½, 12.

| 99 | ½ c., green | .. | .. | 2 | 2 |
| 100 | ½ c. blue | .. | .. | 62 | 4 |

**1888-90.**  Types 5 *and* 3² *to* 43.
*Perf.* 11½.

| 86 | ½ c., blue | .. | .. | 2 | 2 |
| 87 | 2 c., yellow-green | .. | 18 | 12 |
| 88 | 3 c., blue-green | .. | 8 | 4 |
| 89 | 5 c., rose-red, collar on one side (A) .. | .. | 1.00 | 25 |
| 90 | 5 c., rose-red, collar on both sides (B). | .. | 18 | 2 |
| 91 | 6 c., dull red | .. | .. | 50 | 62 |

| No. | Un. | Used. |
|---|---|---|

(Urquiza.)
45

(Saarsfield.)
46

(Derqui.)
47

(Celman.)
48

(Rivadavia.)
49

(Sarmiento.)
50

(Avellaneda.)
51

(Alberdi.)
52

| No. | | Un. | Used. |
|---|---|---|---|
| 101 | ½ c., ultramarine .. | 2 | 2 |
| 102 | 1 c., sepia .. .. | 4 | |
| 103 | 1 c., brown .. .. | 2 | 2 |
| 104 | 2 c., violet .. .. | 2 | 2 |
| 104a | 2 c., slate-violet .. | 12 | 2 |
| 105 | 2 c., purple .. .. | 4 | 6 |
| | 2 c., dull mauve .. | 4 | 6 |
| | 3 c., blue-green .. | 4 | 2 |
| | 5 c., rose-red .. .. | 8 | 2 |
| | 6 c., slate-blue .. | 8 | 4 |
| | c., indigo .. .. | 36 | |
| | c., dark brown .. | 8 | 2 |
| | c., deep blue .. | 12 | 4 |

| No. | | Un. | Used. |
|---|---|---|---|

(Dorrigo.)
53

(Mitre.)
54

(Posadas.)
55

| | | Un. | Used. |
|---|---|---|---|
| 112 | 40 c., olive-grey .. .. | 50 | 2 |
| 113 | 50 c., orange .. .. | 50 | 4 |
| 114 | 60 c., blue-black .. | 75 | 8 |

56

1890. Type 52 *surcharged with* Type 56.
| 115 | ¼, in black, on 12 c.. .. | 2 | 4 |
| 116 | ¼, in red, on 12 c.. .. | 2 | 2 |

(Saarsfield.)
57

(Rivadavia.)
58

1890-92. Types 57 *and* 58. *Types re-drawn. Same perf.*
| 117 | 1 c., brown .. .. | 2 | 2 |
| 118 | 5 c., dull scarlet .. | 4 | 2 |

(Rivadavia.)
59

(San Martin.)
60

1891. Types 59 *to* 62. *Perf.* 11½.
| 119 | 8 c., rose-carmine .. | 8 | 6 |
| 120 | 1 p., deep blue .. | 2.50 | 62 |

No. | Un. | Used. | | No. | | Un. | Used.

(La Madrid.)
61

(W. Brown.)
62

| 121 | 5 p., ultramarine | .. | 10.00 | 3.15 |
| 122 | 20 p., green | .. | 25.00 | 12.50 |

(Rivadavia.)
63

(Belgrano.)
64

(San Martin.)
65

66

**1892-95.** *Wmk.* Type 66. *Small Sun.*
*Perf.* 11½.
Type 63.

| 123 | ½ c., blue | .. | .. | 2 | 2 |
| 124 | ½ c., slate-blue | .. | .. | 2 | 4 |
| 125 | 1 c., brown | .. | .. | 2 | 2 |
| 126 | 2 c., green | .. | .. | 4 | 2 |
| 127 | 3 c., orange | .. | .. | 12 | 2 |
| 128 | 5 c., rose-red | .. | .. | 6 | 2 |

Type 64.

| 129 | 10 c., dull red | .. | .. | 8 | 2 |
| 130 | 12 c., deep blue | .. | .. | 12 | 2 |
| 131 | 16 c., slate | .. | .. | 25 | 4 |
| 132 | 24 c., sepia | .. | .. | 18 | 4 |
| 133 | 50 c., deep green | .. | 1.00 | 6 |

Type 65.

| 134 | 1 p., dull red | .. | .. | 6.25 | 36 |
| 135 | 1 p., lake | .. | .. | 2.50 | 12 |
| 136 | 2 p., deep green | .. | 3.15 | 18 |
| 137 | 5 p., deep indigo | .. | 5.00 | 36 |

*Error of colour.*

| 137a | 5 c., green | .. | .. |

66*

**1896-97.** *Wmk.* Type 66.* *Sun larger*
(6 mm. *instead of* 4½ mm. *in diameter*).
*Perf.* 11½.
Type 63.

| 138 | ½ c., slate | .. | .. | 2 | |
| 138a | ½ c., deep blue | | 12 | |
| 139 | ½ c., indigo | .. | .. | 2 | |
| 140 | 1 c., brown | .. | .. | 2 | 2 |
| 141 | 2 c., blue-green | .. | 6 | 2 |
| 141a | 2 c., deep yellow-green | 4 | 2 |
| 142 | 3 c., orange | .. | .. | 8 | 2 |
| 143 | 5 c., rose-carmine | .. | 4 | 2 |

Type 64.

| 144 | 10 c., rose-red | .. | .. | 8 | 2 |
| 145 | 12 c., deep blue | .. | 16 | 2 |
| 146 | 16 c., slate | .. | .. | 16 | 4 |
| 147 | 24 c., sepia | .. | .. | 25 | 6 |
| 148 | 30 c., orange | .. | .. | 25 | 4 |
| 149 | 50 c., deep green | .. | 50 | 6 |
| 150 | 80 c., deep lilac | .. | 62 | 18 |

Type 65.

| 151 | 1 p., lake | .. | .. | 90 | 12 |
| 152 | 1 p. 20 c., black | .. | 90 | 36 |
| 153 | 2 p., deep green | .. | — | 62 |
| 153a | 5 p., deep indigo | .. |

67

**1892.** Type 67. *Columbian issue.* *Wmk.*
*Small Sun,* Type 66. *Perf.* 11½.

| 154 | 2 c., pale blue | .. | .. | 12 | 12 |
| 155 | 5 c., deep ,, | .. | .. | 12 | 16 |

68

69

**1899-1900.** Type 68. *Perf.* 12.

| 156 | ½ c., brown | .. | .. | 2 | 2 |
| 157 | 1 c., bluish green | .. | 2 | 2 |

|  |  | Un. | Used. |
|---|---|---|---|
| **No.** |  |  |  |
| 158 | 2 c., dark indigo .. .. | 2 | 2 |
| 159 | 5 c., carmine .. .. | 4 | 2 |
| 160 | 10 c., deep green .. | 8 | 2 |
| 161 | 12 c., sky-blue .. .. | 10 | |
| 161a | 12 c., bright blue .. | 8 | 8 |
| 161b | 12 c., slate-blue .. | | |
| 162 | 16 c., orange .. .. | | |
| 163 | 20 c., lake .. .. | 12 | 4 |
| 164 | 24 c., violet .. .. | 14 | 8 |
| 165 | 30 c., carmine .. .. | 50 | 12 |
| 166 | 50 c., bright blue .. | 36 | 18 |

Type 69.  *Central design in black.*

| | | | |
|---|---|---|---|
| 167 | 1 p., deep blue .. | 62 | 25 |
| 168 | 5 p., brown-orange .. | 2.50 | 1.25 |
| 169 | 10 p., deep green .. | 5.00 | 3.15 |
| 170 | 20 p., carmine .. .. | 10.00 | 6.25 |

*Error.   Centre inverted.*

| | | | |
|---|---|---|---|
| 171 | 1 p., deep blue | | |
| 171a | 20 p., carmine .. | | |

**1901.**  Type 68.  *Same types, wmk., and perf.*

| | | | |
|---|---|---|---|
| 172 | 3 c., orange .. .. | 2 | 2 |
| 173 | 12 c., olive-green .. | 10 | 8 |
| 174 | 15 c., slate-blue .. .. | 10 | 4 |
| 175 | 30 c., scarlet .. .. | 25 | 6 |
| 176 | 30 c., vermilion .. .. | 25 | 6 |

70

Oct. 26, **1902.**  Type 70.  *Commemorative stamp.  Perf. 11½.*

| | | | |
|---|---|---|---|
| 177 | 5 c., deep blue .. | 4 | |

81                    8a

**1886.**  Type 81.  *Postal Fiscal.  Perf.*

| | | | |
|---|---|---|---|
| 201 | 5 c., red .. .. | | |

**1890.**  Type 8a.  *Postal Telegraphs. Perf. 11½.*

| | | | |
|---|---|---|---|
| 221 | 10 c., rose-red (Type I.).. | 18 | |
| 222 | 10 c.  „   ( „ II.).. | — | 12 |
| 223 | 40 c., blue  ( „ I.).. | 36 | 62 |
| 224 | 40 c.  „   ( „ II.).. | — | 62 |

|  |  | Un. | Used. |
|---|---|---|---|
| **No.** | | | |

OFFICIAL STAMPS.

# OFICIAL
91

**1884.**  *Surcharged in black with Type 91.*
(a) *Horizontal surcharge.*

| | | | |
|---|---|---|---|
| 301 | 1 c., scarlet (No. 82) .. | 2.50 | 2.50 |
| 302 | 2 c., green (No. 51) .. | — | 3.00 |
| 303 | 4 c., brown (No. 34) .. | 2.50 | 2.50 |
| 304 | 8 c., lake (No. 52) .. | 3.00 | 3.00 |
| 305 | 12 c., ultramar. (No. 61) | 2.50 | 2.50 |

(b) *Diagonal surcharge.*

| | | | |
|---|---|---|---|
| 306 | 2 c., green (No. 51) .. | — | 2.50 |
| 307 | 24 c., blue (No. 50) .. | — | 1.85 |
| 308 | 60 c., black (No. 37) .. | 3.15 | 2.50 |

*Varieties.*  (1) *Surcharge inverted.*

| | | | |
|---|---|---|---|
| 309 | 24 c., blue (No. 50) .. | | |

(2) *Surcharge double.*

| | | | |
|---|---|---|---|
| 310 | 24 c., blue (No. 50) .. | | |

9a

**1884.**
*Surcharged with Type 9a diagonally.*
(1) *In black.*

| | | | |
|---|---|---|---|
| 311 | ½ c., brown (No. 81) .. | | |
| 312 | 1 c., scarlet (No. 63) .. | 62 | 90 |
| 313 | 1 c., rose-red (No. 82).. | 8 | 12 |
| 314 | 2 c., green (No. 51) .. | 8 | 12 |
| 315 | 4 c., brown (No. 34) .. | 50 | |
| 316 | 4 c., sepia (No. 35) .. | 12 | 18 |
| 317 | 8 c., lake (No. 52) .. | 12 | 6 |
| 318 | 10 c., green (No. 27) .. | | |
| 319 | 12 c., ultramar. (No. 61) | 50 | 62 |
| 320 | 12 c., Prussian blue (No. 83) .. .. | 18 | 25 |
| 321 | 16 c., green (No. 49) .. | 25 | 25 |
| 322 | 20 c., blue (No. 49) .. | 50 | 50 |
| 323 | 24 c., blue (No. 50) .. | 50 | 50 |
| 324 | 24 c., blue (No. 53) .. | 1.25 | 1.25 |
| 325 | 25 c., rosy lake (No. 54) | 1.25 | 1.25 |
| 326 | 30 c., orange (No. 36) .. | 3.75 | 3.00 |
| 327 | 60 c., black (No. 37) .. | 1.50 | 1.50 |
| 328 | 90 c., blue (No. 38) .. | 1.25 | 1.25 |

*Surcharge inverted.*

| | | | |
|---|---|---|---|
| 328a | 1 c., scarlet (No. 63) .. | 7.50 | |
| 329 | 1 c., rose-red (No. 82) .. | 25 | |
| 330 | 2 c., green (No. 51) .. | | |
| 331 | 4 c., brown (No. 34) .. | — | 2.50 |
| 331a | 12 c., Prussian blue (No. 83) .. .. | | |
| 332 | 24 c., blue (No. 50) .. | 75 | 75 |
| 332a | 24 c.  „   (No. 53) .. | 50 | |
| 333 | 60 c., black (No. 37) .. | | |
| 334 | 90 c., blue (No. 38) .. | | |

No.                  *Un.*  *Used.*

**(2)** *In* red.

| | | | | Un. | Used. |
|---|---|---|---|---|---|
| 335 | 2 c., green (No. 51) | .. | | 12 | 18 |
| 336 | 4 c., brown (No. 34) | .. | | 12 | 18 |
| 337 | 24 c., blue (No. 50) | .. | | 1.50 | 1.25 |
| 338 | 60 c., black (No. 37) | .. | | 7.50 | 3.00 |
| 339 | 90 c., blue (No. 38) | .. | | 12.50 | 7.50 |

*Surcharge inverted.*

340 | 2 c., green (No. 51) .. |

The existence of genuine specimens of Nos. 311, 318, and 339 is considered doubtful.

Two sets of official stamps of Type 92 may be made, having the word *OFICIAL* inclined at different angles.

**93**

DEC., 1901. Type 93. *Perf.* 11½.

| | | | | | |
|---|---|---|---|---|---|
| 341 | 1 c., grey | .. | .. | — | 6 |
| 342 | 2 c., brown | .. | .. | — | 6 |
| 343 | 5 c., red .. | .. | | — | 8 |
| 344 | 10 c., deep green | .. | .. | — | 8 |
| 345 | 30 c., blue | .. | .. | | |
| 346 | 50 c., orange | .. | .. | | |

Set of six, unused, 62 c.

## BUENOS AYRES.

**1**

APRIL, 1858. Type 1. *Imperf.*

| | | | Un. | Used. |
|---|---|---|---|---|
| 1 | DOS PS. (2 p.), blue | .. | 22.50 | 8.75 |
| 2 | DOS PS. (2 p.), deep blue | — | | 8.75 |
| 3 | TRES PS. (3 p.), yellow-green | .. | 50.00 | 35.00 |
| 4 | TRES PS. (3 p.), deep grn. | — | | 40.00 |
| 5 | TRES PS. (3 p.), blue-grn. | 45.00 | | 30.00 |
| 6 | CUATO PS. (4 p.), scarlet | — | | 90.00 |
| 7 | CUATO PS. (4 p.), rose-red | — | | 90.00 |
| 8 | CINCO PS. (5 p.), orange | — | | 100.00 |
| 9 | CINCO PS. (5 p.), ochre . | — | | 100.00 |
| 10 | CINCO PS. (5 p.), olive-yel. | — | | 125.00 |

Reprints are known of the 3 pesos, including *tête-bêche* pairs.

No.                  *Un.*  *Used.*

### Nov., 1858.

*The plates of the above stamps used, and in some cases altered, to print other values.*

*(a) The plate of the 4 pesos used to print stamps which were sold at 4 reales.*

| | | Un. | Used. |
|---|---|---|---|
| 11 | CUATO PS. (4 r.), choc.-bn. | 17.50 | 11.25 |
| 12 | CUATO PS. (4 r.), sepia.. | 17.50 | 12.50 |
| 13 | CUATO PS. (4 r.), grey-bn. | — | 15.00 |
| 14 | CUATO PS. (4 r.), yell.-bn. | | |

*(b) The plate of the 5 p., altered by partially erasing the first "C" and the final "CO" in "CINCO."*

| | | Un. | Used. |
|---|---|---|---|
| 15 | IN PS. (1 peso), brown.. | 17.50 | 8.75 |
| 16 | IN PS. (1 ,, ), yell.-bn. | 17.50 | 10.00 |

### JAN., 1859.

*(c) Stamps printed from the last plate as altered, but the colour changed.*

| | | Un. | Used. |
|---|---|---|---|
| 17 | IN PS. (1 peso), blue | 7.50 | 3.75 |
| 18 | IN PS. (1 ,, ), deep blue | 13.75 | 5.00 |
| 19 | IN PS. (1 ,, ), dp. indigo | 15.00 | 5.00 |

*(d) The plate of the 4 p., altered by erasing the "CUA" of "CUATO."*

| | | Un. | Used. |
|---|---|---|---|
| 20 | TO PS. (1 peso), blue .. | 17.50 | 11.25 |
| 21 | TO PS. (1 ,, ), dk. blue | — | 12.50 |

Several varieties may be found in these latter stamps, owing to the careless way in which the alteration of value was made. We know that at least one stamp on the plate had the original value left in; and we thus find the error "CUATO PS.," *blue*, while other stamps show only "T PS." There are, in fact, 48 varieties of this stamp. The "IN PS.," *blue*, is known printed on both sides.

The "IN PS." and "TO PS." stamps have been reprinted. These reprints are also found in pairs *tête-bêche.*

**2**

JAN., 1860. Type 2. *Imperf.*

*(a) Printed in Paris; sharp, clear impressions, with lines in background clear and well defined.*

| | | Un. | Used. |
|---|---|---|---|
| 22 | 4 reales, green on bluish | | |
| 23 | 4 ,, deep green on bluish | .. | .. |
| 24 | 1 peso, pale blue | .. | 3.15 | 1.25 |
| 25 | 1 ,, deep blue | .. | 3.15 | 1.25 |
| 26 | 2 pesos, vermilion | .. | |
| 27 | 2 ,, red | .. | |

|  | *Un.* | *Used.* |
|---|---|---|
| No. |  |  |

*(b) Locally printed from the same plates; blurred impressions, with lines of background more or less broken.*

| 28 | 4 reales, green on bluish | 5.00 | 2.50 |
| 29 | 4 „ deep green on bluish .. .. | — | 3.00 |
| 30 | 1 peso, pale blue .. | 2.50 | 1.25 |
| 31 | 1 „ deep blue .. | 2.50 | 75 |
| 32 | 1 „ indigo .. .. | 2.00 | 1.25 |
| 33 | 2 pesos, vermilion .. | — | 3.15 |
| 34 | 2 „ red .. | | |

**Nov., 1862.** *Locally printed; colours changed.*

| 35 | 1 peso, pale rose .. | 3.00 | 2.00 |
| 36 | 1 „ deep rose .. | — | 3.75 |
| 37 | 2 pesos, blue .. .. | — | 1.85 |
| 38 | 2 „ deep blue .. | 4.35 | 2.50 |

**3**

**1859.**

Stamps of the above type, consisting of 4 reales, yellow, 6 r., green, 8 r., violet, and 10 r., blue, are often met with, but are only essays, and were never in use.

## CORDOBA.

**1**

**1860.** Type 1. *Wove paper. Imperf.*

| 1 | 5 c., blue | .. | .. |
| 2 | 10 c., black | .. | .. |

*Variety. Stop after "CEN."*

| 3 | 5 c., blue | .. | .. |
| 3a | 10 c., black | .. | .. |

*The same, on laid.*

| 4 | 5 c., blue | .. | .. | 1.00 |
| 5 | 10 c., black | .. | .. | |

*Variety. Stop after "CEN."*

| | 5 c., blue | .. | .. | 6.25 |
| | 10 c., black | .. | .. | 18.75 |

|  | *Un.* | *Used.* |
|---|---|---|
| No. |  |  |

## CORRIENTES.

**1**          **2**

**1856.** Type 1. Black *on colour. Imperf.*

| 1 | 1 r. M.C., blue.. .. | — | 3.75 |

*Value pen-cancelled.*

| 2 | (3 c.), blue | .. | .. |

**1864-75.** Type 2. *Value erased.*

| 3 | (3 c.), blue .. .. | 25 | 36 |
| 4 | (2 c.), blue-green (1864) | 1.25 | 1.50 |
| 5 | (2 c.), yellow (1867) .. | 50 | 50 |
| 6 | (2 c.), dark blue (1871). | 75 | 75 |
| 7 | (2 c.), rose (1873) .. | 1.00 | 1.00 |
| 8 | (2 c.), magenta (1875).. | 62 | 75 |
| 9 | (5 c.), yell.-green (1864) | 75 | 1.25 |

The plate consists of two rows of four stamps, all different, giving eight types.

Reprints have been made of all the above stamps and on other coloured papers besides those used for postal issues. In the reprint of No. 1 the value "UN REAL M. C." differs in type from that on the originals.

# AUSTRO-HUNGARIAN MONARCHY.

Francis Joseph, Emperor of Austria (1848) and King of Hungary (1867).

## AUSTRIA.

**1**

**1850.** Type 1. *Thin paper. Three varieties of the* 9 kr.

| 1 | 1 kr., orange .. | .. | 15.00 | 1 |
| 2 | 1 kr., yellow .. | .. | — | 1. |
| 3 | 2 kr., grey-black | .. | 3.75 | |
| 4 | 2 kr., black .. | .. | 3.75 | 8 |
| 5 | 3 kr., pale red .. | .. | 3.75 | 2 |
| 6 | 3 kr., deep „ .. | .. | 5.00 | . |
| 7 | 6 kr., brown .. | .. | 6.25 | |
| 8 | 6 kr., red-brown | .. | 7.50 | |
| 9 | 9 kr., blue (A) .. | .. | 10.00 | 2 |

| | | | | Un. | Used. |
|---|---|---|---|---|---|
| No. | | | | | |

A

B

C

| 10 | 9 kr., pale blue (A) | .. | 10.00 | 2 |
| 11 | 9 kr.   "    (B) | .. | — | 4 |
| 11a | 9 kr.   "    (C) | .. | | |

*Printed on both sides.*

| 12 | 1 kr., yellow | .. | .. | — | 62 |

*Thick paper.*

| 13 | 1 kr., orange | .. | .. | 18.75 | 12 |
| 14 | 1 kr., yellow | .. | | 12.50 | 12 |
| 15 | 2 kr., grey-black | | .. | 3.75 | 8 |
| 16 | 2 kr., black | .. | .. | 3.75 | 8 |
| 17 | 3 kr., pale red | .. | | 1.85 | 2 |
| 18 | 3 kr., deep ,, | .. | | 1.85 | 2 |
| 19 | 6 kr., pale brown | | | 2.50 | 4 |
| 20 | 6 kr., deep ,, | | | 2.50 | 4 |
| 21 | 9 kr., pale blue (A) | | .. | 10.00 | 2 |
| 22 | 9 kr., blue (A) | .. | .. | 8.75 | 2 |

*Ribbed paper.*

| 23 | 3 kr., red | .. | .. | — | 62 |

This issue was reprinted in 1865, 1871, and 1885, and the 1 kr. (in both colours) and 2 kr. again in 1889. All the reprints are on medium thick paper, and the colours are brighter and fresher than those of the original stamps. The reprints are for the most part more clearly printed.

2

3

4

5

No.

I.

II.

**1858–59.** Types 2, 3 (2 *and* 5 kr.), 4 *and* 5.
*Perf.* 15.

There are two varieties of the head. In Var. I. the loops of the bow at the back of the head are broken, forming a resemblance to a figure "3." In Var. II. the loops are complete, and the ribbon is thicker. In addition to this the profile of the wreath at the top of the head, and the lock of hair over the forehead, are more prominent.

| 24 | 2 kr, yellow | .. | .. | 7.50 | 18 |
| 25 | 2 kr., orange | .. | .. | 50.00 | 2.50 |
| 26 | 3 kr., black (I.) | | .. | 6.25 | 75 |
| 27 | 3 kr.   ,,   (II.) | | .. | 6.25 | 75 |
| 28 | 3 kr., green (II.) | | .. | 2.00 | 90 |
| 29 | 3 kr., blue-green (II.) | | .. | 2.50 | 90 |
| 30 | 5 kr., red (I.) | .. | .. | — | 4 |
| 31 | 5 kr.   ,,   (II.) | .. | | 5.00 | 2 |
| 32 | 5 kr., deep red (II.) | | .. | 11.25 | 4 |
| 33 | 10 kr., brown (I.) | | .. | 15.00 | 12 |
| 34 | 10 kr., pale brown (I.) | | .. | — | 12 |
| 35 | 10 kr., brown (II.) | | .. | — | 4 |
| 36 | 10 kr., pale brown (II.) | | .. | 12.50 | 4 |
| 37 | 15 kr., blue (I.) | .. | | — | 10 |
| 38 | 15 kr., pale blue (I.) | | .. | — | 12 |
| 39 | 15 kr.. blue (II.) | | .. | 15.00 | 6 |
| 40 | 15 kr., pale blue (II.) | | .. | 15.00 | 6 |

All the stamps of this issue were reprinted in 1865, 1871, and 1885, and the 2 k. and 3 k. (each in both colours) in 1889. All the reprints are of the second type. Those of 1865 are perf. 12, those of 1871 perf. 11, those of 1884 perf. 13, and those of 1889 perf. 12½, varying to 12.

|  | | | | *Un.* | *Used.* |
|---|---|---|---|---|---|
| No. | | | | | |

6

**1861.** Type 6.
*Perf.* 14.

| 41 | 2 kr., yellow | .. | .. | 90 | 8 |
| 42 | 3 kr., pale green | | .. | 75 | 8 |
| 43 | 3 kr., deep „ | | .. | 1.00 | 8 |
| 44 | 5 kr., pale red | .. | .. | 62 | 2 |
| 45 | 5 kr., deep „ | .. | .. | 75 | 2 |
| 46 | 10 kr., pale brown | | .. | 1.50 | 2 |
| 47 | 10 kr., deep „ | | .. | 1.50 | 2 |
| 48 | 15 kr., pale blue | .. | | 1.50 | 2 |
| 49 | 15 kr., deep „ | .. | | 2.00 | 2 |

Reprints of all the above values were
made in 1865, 1871, and 1884, and the
2 kr. in 1889. Those of 1865 are perf. 12,
those of 1871 perf. 11, those of 1884
perf. 13, and that of 1889 perf. 12.

7

**1863.** Type 7. *Perf.* 14.

| 50 | 2 kr., yellow | .. | .. | 2.50 | 25 |
| 51 | 3 kr., green | .. | .. | 1.50 | 16 |
| 52 | 5 kr., pale rose | .. | | 1.85 | 2 |
| 53 | 5 kr., deep „ | .. | | 1.85 | 2 |
| 54 | 10 kr., blue | .. | | 3.75 | 6 |
| 55 | 15 kr., stone-brown | | .. | 6.25 | 6 |

**1865.** *The same, but perf.* 9½.

| 56 | 2 kr., yellow | .. | .. | 18 | 4 |
| 57 | 2 kr., orange-yellow | .. | | 12 | 4 |
| 58 | 3 kr., pale blue-green | .. | | 36 | 8 |
| 59 | 3 kr., pale yell.-green | .. | | 50 | 8 |
| 60 | 5 kr., pale rose | .. | | 18 | 2 |
| 61 | 5 kr., deep „ | .. | | 36 | 4 |
| 62 | 10 kr., pale blue | | .. | 62 | 2 |
| 63 | 10 kr., deep „ | .. | | 36 | 2 |
| 64 | 15 kr., pale stone-brown | | | 50 | 2 |
| 65 | 15 kr., deep „ | | | 62 | 2 |

All five values were reprinted in 1884,
rf. 13, and the 2 kr., 3 kr., and 15 kr. in
9, the first two being perf. 10½, and the
perf. 11½.

|  | | | | *Un.* | *Used.* |
|---|---|---|---|---|---|
| No. | | | | | |

8

9

A

B

C

**1867.** Type 8. *Perf.* 9½.

| 66 | 2 kr., yellow | .. | .. | 4 | 2 |
| 67 | 2 kr., orange-yellow | .. | | 8 | 2 |
| 68 | 3 kr., green | .. | .. | 6 | 2 |
| 69 | 3 kr., deep green | | .. | 12 | 4 |
| 70 | 5 kr., rose (A) | .. | | 36 | 2 |
| 71 | 10 kr., blue | .. | | 18 | 2 |
| 72 | 10 kr., deep blue | | .. | 12 | 2 |
| 73 | 15 kr., deep brown | | .. | 1.25 | 2 |
| 74 | 15 kr., bistre | .. | | 1.25 | 4 |
| 75 | 15 kr., deep bistre | | .. | 75 | 6 |
| 76 | 15 kr., bistre-brown | | .. | 62 | 4 |
| 77 | 25 kr., purple | .. | | 1.50 | 12 |
| 78 | 25 kr., deep lilac | | | 62 | 2 |
| 79 | 25 kr., grey-lilac | | .. | 25 | 2 |

Type 9. *Perf.* 12.

| 80 | 50 kr., pink-brown | | .. | 1.85 | 7½ |
| 81 | 50 kr., brown | .. | | 2.50 | 2½ |

**1872.** *Altered dies. Perf.* 9½. (B) *differ*
*from* (A) *in the shape of the curve*
*opposite the figure* "5," *and in* (C)
*the line within the foliate orna*
*ment in the upper part of th*
*spandrel on the left is produced int*
*the curved end.*

| 82 | 5 kr., rose-red (B) | .. | 8 | |
| 83 | 5 kr. „ (C) | .. | 8 | |
| 84 | 5 kr., rose (C) .. | .. | — | 1 |

**1877.** *Types of* 1867 *and* 1872.
(i.) *Perf.* 10½, 11.

| 85 | 2 kr., yellow | .. | .. | 3.75 | 1 |
| 86 | 3 kr., green | .. | .. | — | 1 |
| 87 | 5 kr., rose-red (B) | .. | | — | |
| 88 | 5 kr. „ (C) | .. | | — | |
| 89 | 10 kr., blue | .. | | — | 2 |
| 90 | 15 kr., bistre-brown | | .. | — | 1. |

No. | | Un. | Used.
---|---|---|---

**(ii.) *Perf.* 12.**

| No. | | Un. | Used. |
|---|---|---|---|
| 91 | 2 kr., yellow .. .. | | |
| 92 | 3 kr., green .. .. | — | 25 |
| 93 | 5 kr., rose-red (B) .. | | |
| 94 | 5 kr. ,, (C) .. | — | 18 |
| 95 | 10 kr., blue .. .. | — | 3.75 |
| 96 | 15 kr., bistre-brown .. | — | 50 |

**(iii.) *Perf.* 13.**

| | | | |
|---|---|---|---|
| 97 | 2 kr., yellow .. .. | | |
| 98 | 3 kr., green .. .. | 12.50 | 62 |
| 99 | 5 kr., rose-red (B) .. | 6.25 | |
| 100 | 5 kr. ,, (C) .. | 7.50 | 12 |
| 101 | 10 kr., blue .. .. | 8.75 | |
| 102 | 15 kr., bistre-brown .. | | |
| 103 | 50 kr., brown .. .. | 6.25 | 1.50 |

**(iv.) *Perf. compound of* 9½ *with* 10½.**

| | | | |
|---|---|---|---|
| 103a | 10 kr., blue .. .. | | |

**(v.) *Perf. compound of* 10½ *with* 12 *or* 13.**

| | | | |
|---|---|---|---|
| 104 | 2 kr., yellow .. .. | | |
| 105 | 3 kr., green .. .. | — | 50 |
| 106 | 5 kr., rose-red .. .. | — | 1.25 |
| 106a | 10 kr., blue .. .. | — | 3.15 |

**(vi.) *Perf. compound of* 10½ *with* 8½, 9.**

| | | | |
|---|---|---|---|
| 106b | 5 kr., rose-red (C) .. | | |

The perforations of these two sets are very complicated, and many other combinations can be found. See *Monthly Journal*, May, 1903.

**10**

**1883.**

Type 10. *Inscription and figures in* black.

**(i.) *Perf.* 9½.**

| | | | |
|---|---|---|---|
| 107 | 2 kr., brown .. .. | 4 | 2 |
| 108 | 3 kr., emerald-green .. | 4 | 2 |
| 109 | 5 kr., carmine .. .. | 8 | 2 |
| 110 | 10 kr., ultramarine .. | 12 | 2 |
| 111 | 20 kr., greenish grey .. | 50 | 2 |
| 112 | 50 kr., red-lilac .. .. | 45 | 12 |

**(ii.) *Perf.* 10, 10½.**

| | | | |
|---|---|---|---|
| 113 | 2 kr., brown .. .. | 6 | 2 |
| 114 | 3 kr., emerald-green .. | 6 | 2 |
| 115 | 5 kr., carmine .. .. | 8 | 2 |
| 116 | 10 kr., ultramarine .. | 12 | 2 |
| 117 | 20 kr., greenish grey .. | 16 | 4 |
| 118 | 50 kr., red-lilac .. .. | 55 | |

**(iii.) *Perf.* 12.**

| | | | |
|---|---|---|---|
| 119 | 5 kr., carmine .. .. | 1.25 | 1.00 |

**(iv.) *Perf.* 13.**

| No. | | Un. | Used. |
|---|---|---|---|
| 120 | 2 kr., brown .. .. | 7.50 | |
| 121 | 3 kr., green .. .. | 7.50 | |
| 122 | 5 kr., carmine .. .. | 3.15 | 1.25 |
| 123 | 10 kr., ultramarine .. | 7.50 | |

The 5 kr. was reprinted in 1895, perf. 10½.

**11** **12**

**1890-91.** Type 11. *Granite paper.*
*Numerals in* black.

**(i.) *Perf.* 9, 9½.**

| | | | |
|---|---|---|---|
| 124 | 1 kr., slate .. .. | 5.00 | 12 |
| 125 | 2 kr., brown .. .. | | |
| 126 | 3 kr., green .. .. | — | 12 |
| 127 | 5 kr., rose-carmine .. | — | 8 |
| 128 | 10 kr., blue .. .. | — | 1.00 |
| 129 | 12 kr., lake .. .. | — | 8 |
| 130 | 15 kr., mauve .. .. | — | 12 |
| 131 | 20 kr., olive .. .. | — | 12 |
| 132 | 24 kr., grey-blue .. | — | 12 |
| 133 | 30 kr., brown .. .. | 5.00 | 8 |
| 134 | 50 kr., red-lilac .. .. | 4.35 | 62 |

**Type 12.**

| | | | |
|---|---|---|---|
| 135 | 1 g., deep blue .. .. | — | 16 |
| 136 | 2 g., carmine .. .. | — | 18 |

**(ii.) *Perf.* 10, 10½.**

| | | | |
|---|---|---|---|
| 137 | 1 kr., slate .. .. | 4 | 2 |
| 138 | 2 kr., brown .. .. | 8 | 2 |
| 139 | 3 kr., green .. .. | 8 | 2 |
| 140 | 5 kr., rose-carmine .. | 6 | 2 |
| 141 | 10 kr., blue .. .. | 8 | 2 |
| 142 | 12 kr., lake .. .. | 30 | 2 |
| 143 | 15 kr., mauve .. .. | 25 | 2 |
| 144 | 20 kr., olive .. .. | 36 | 2 |
| 145 | 24 kr., grey-blue .. | 36 | 4 |
| 146 | 30 kr., brown .. .. | 50 | 2 |
| 147 | 50 kr., red-lilac .. .. | 62 | 12 |
| 148 | 1 g., deep blue .. .. | 3.75 | 8 |
| 149 | 2 g., carmine .. .. | — | 12 |

*Same types.* **(iii.) *Perf.* 11½, 12.**

| | | | |
|---|---|---|---|
| 150 | 1 kr., slate .. .. | 6 | 2 |
| 151 | 2 kr., brown .. .. | 6 | 2 |
| 152 | 3 kr., green .. .. | 4 | 2 |
| 153 | 5 kr., rose-carmine .. | 12 | 2 |
| 154 | 10 kr., blue .. .. | 12 | 2 |
| 155 | 12 kr., lake .. .. | 12 | 2 |
| 156 | 15 kr., mauve .. .. | — | 2 |
| 157 | 20 kr., olive .. .. | 25 | 6 |
| 158 | 24 kr., grey-blue .. | 50 | 4 |
| 159 | 30 kr., brown .. .. | 50 | 4 |
| 160 | 50 kr., red-lilac .. .. | — | 10 |

|  |  | Un. | Used. |
|---|---|---|---|
| No. |  |  |  |

**Type 12.**

| 161 | 1 g., deep blue.. | .. | 1.25 | 6 |
|---|---|---|---|---|
| 162 | 2 g., carmine .. | .. | 1.85 | 12 |

*Same types.* (iv.) *Perf.* 13.

| 163 | 1 kr., slate | .. | .. | 2 | 2 |
|---|---|---|---|---|---|
| 164 | 2 kr., brown | .. | .. | 2 | 2 |
| 165 | 3 kr., green | .. | .. | 4 | 2 |
| 166 | 3 kr., blue-green | .. | — | 12 |
| 167 | 5 kr., rose-carmine | .. | 4 | 2 |
| 168 | 10 kr., blue | .. | .. | 8 | 2 |
| 169 | 12 kr., lake | .. | .. |
| 170 | 15 kr., mauve | .. | .. | 12 | 2 |

**Type 12.**

| 171 | 1 g., deep blue | .. | 5.00 | 8 |
|---|---|---|---|---|
| 172 | 2 g., carmine .. | .. | — | 10 |

(v.) *Compound perfs.*

| 173 | 1 kr. (9½ × 11½) | .. |
|---|---|---|
| 173a | 3 kr. (13½ × 10½) | .. | 1.00 |
| 173b | 5 kr. (10 × 13½) | .. | 1.25 |
| 173c | 10 kr. (11 × 10½) | .. |
| 173d | 12 kr. (10½ × 12) | .. |
| 173e | 20 kr. (10½ × 13) | .. |
| 173f | 30 kr. (11½ × 10½) | .. | — | 1.85 |
| 174 | 1 g. (11½ × 10½) | .. | — | 2.50 |
| 174a | 1 g. (12 × 11) | .. |
| 175 | 2 g. (11½ × 13) | .. | 6.25 | 2.50 |
| 175a | 2 g. (10½ × 11½) | .. |

The whole series is said to be known
without the figures in the corners, and the
3 kr. and 1 and 2 gulden are known printed
in other colours, but such copies are probably only proofs.

**13**

**1891.** Type **13.** *Numerals in black.*

(i.) *Perf.* 9½.

| 183 | 20 kr., green | .. | .. |
|---|---|---|---|
| 184 | 24 kr., dull blue.. | .. |
| 185 | 30 kr., brown | .. | — | 90 |
| 186 | 50 kr., red-lilac .. | .. |

(ii.) *Perf.* 10, 10½.

| 190 | 20 kr., green | .. | .. | 18 | 2 |
|---|---|---|---|---|---|
| 191 | 24 kr., dull blue.. | .. | 36 | 2 |
| 192 | 30 kr., brown | .. | .. | 36 | 2 |
| 193 | 50 kr., red-lilac .. | .. | 50 | 2 |

(iii.) *Perf.* 11½.

| 4 | 20 kr., green | .. | .. | 25 | 4 |
|---|---|---|---|---|---|
| 7 | 24 kr., dull blue.. | .. | — | 2 |
|  | 30 kr., brown | .. | .. | 1.00 | 2 |
|  | 50 kr., red-lilac .. | .. | 1.25 | 8 |

| No. |  |  | Un. | Used. |
|---|---|---|---|---|

(iv.) *Perf.* 13.

| 198 | 20 kr., green | .. | .. | 18 | 2 |
|---|---|---|---|---|---|
| 199 | 24 kr., dull blue.. | .. | 25 | 5 |
| 200 | 30 kr., brown | .. | .. | 36 | 2 |
| 201 | 50 kr., red-lilac .. | .. | 36 | 12 |

(v.) *Compound perfs.*

| 202 | 20 kr. (11½ × 10½) . | .. |
|---|---|---|
| 203 | 24 kr. (13 × 10½) .. | .. | — | 1.00 |
| 204 | 30 kr. (10½ × 13) .. | .. | — | 1.00 |
| 205 | 30 kr. (11½ × 10½) | .. |

**1896.** Type **12.** *Colours changed.*

(i.) *Perf.* 10, 10½.

| 206 | 1 g., lilac | .. | .. | 2.00 | 4 |
|---|---|---|---|---|---|
| 207 | 2 g., green | .. | .. | 1.25 | 36 |

(ii.) *Perf.* 11½.

| 208 | 1 g., lilac | .. | .. | — | 2 |
|---|---|---|---|---|---|
| 209 | 2 g., green | .. | .. | 2.50 | 25 |

(iii.) *Perf.* 13.

| 210 | 1 g., lilac | .. | .. | 75 | 65 |
|---|---|---|---|---|---|
| 211 | 2 g., green | .. | .. |

**14**    **15**

**1899-1902.** *Change of currency. New
types. Granite paper. Figures in black.*

(i.) *Perf.* 12½, 13. Type **14.**

| 212 | 1 h., lilac | .. | .. | 2 | 2 |
|---|---|---|---|---|---|
| 213 | 2 h., grey | .. | .. | 2 | 2 |
| 214 | 3 h., brown | .. | .. | 2 | 2 |
| 215 | 5 h., deep green | .. | 2 | 2 |
| 216 | 6 h., orange | .. | .. | 2 | 2 |

**Type 15.**

| 217 | 10 h., rose | .. | .. | 4 | 2 |
|---|---|---|---|---|---|
| 218 | 20 h., brown | .. | .. | 6 | 4 |
| 219 | 25 h., ultramarine | .. | 8 | 2 |
| 220 | 30 h., mauve | .. | .. | 10 | 4 |

**Type 13.**

| 221 | 40 h., pale green | .. | 12 |
|---|---|---|---|
| 222 | 50 h., pale blue .. | .. | 16 | 6 |
| 223 | 60 h., pale brown | .. | 18 |

**Type 12.**

| 224 | 1 kron., rose | .. | .. | 30 | 6 |
|---|---|---|---|---|---|
| 225 | 2 ,, lavender | .. | 55 | 4 |
| 226 | 4 ,, pale green | .. | 1.00 |

*Error. Corner figures inverted.*

| 226a | 1 h., lilac | .. | .. |
|---|---|---|---|

(ii.) *Perf.* 10½.

| 226b | 1 h., lilac | .. | .. |
|---|---|---|---|
| 227 | 2 h., grey | .. | .. | 6 |

| No. | | Un. | Used. |
|---|---|---|---|
| 228 | 3 h., brown .. .. | — | 36 |
| 228a | 5 h., green .. .. | | |
| 229 | 6 h., orange .. .. | 4 | 4 |
| 230 | 20 h., brown .. .. | 1.25 | 10 |
| 231 | 25 h., ultramarine .. | 12 | 8 |
| 232 | 30 h., mauve .. .. | 14 | 10 |
| 233 | 40 h., pale green .. | 18 | 12 |
| 234 | 50 h., pale blue .. | 20 | 10 |
| 235 | 1 kron., rose .. .. | 40 | 12 |
| 236 | 2 ,, lavender .. | 1.10 | 12 |
| 237 | 4 ,, pale green .. | 1.30 | |

(iii.) *Perf.* 10½ *and* 12½ *compound.*

| 237a | 2 h., grey .. .. | 1.85 | 1.85 |
|---|---|---|---|
| 238 | 5 h., deep green .. | 12 | 6 |
| 239 | 20 h., brown .. .. | | |
| 240 | 30 h., mauve .. .. | 7.50 | |
| 241 | 50 h., pale blue .. | 50 | |
| 242 | 60 h., pale brown .. | | |

There are also other varieties of compound perforation.

**1902.** *With bars of shiny varnish, about 2 mm. wide and about 7 mm. apart, diagonally downwards from left to right. Perf.* 12½, 13.

| 243 | 1 h., lilac .. .. | 2 | |
|---|---|---|---|
| 244 | 2 h., grey .. .. | 2 | |
| 245 | 3 h., brown .. .. | 2 | |
| 246 | 5 h., deep green .. | 2 | |
| 247 | 6 h., orange .. .. | 2 | |
| 248 | 10 h., rose .. .. | 4 | |
| 249 | 20 h., brown .. .. | 6 | 4 |
| 250 | 25 h., ultramarine .. | 8 | 2 |
| 251 | 30 h., mauve .. .. | 10 | |
| 252 | 35 h., bright green .. | 12 | 6 |
| 253 | 40 h., pale green .. | 12 | 2 |
| 254 | 50 h., pale blue .. .. | 16 | 6 |
| 255 | 60 h., yellow-brown .. | 18 | 2 |

### NEWSPAPER STAMPS.

21

**1851–56.** Type **21.** *Thin paper. Two varieties* (I. *and* II.) *of the* 1 kr.

| 301 | (1 kr.), pale blue (I.). | 1.25 | |
|---|---|---|---|
| 301a | (1 kr.) ,, (II.). | | |
| 302 | (1 kr.), deep blue (I.). | | |
| 302a | (1 kr.) ,, (II.) | | |
| 303 | (6 kr.), dull yellow .. | — | 30.00 |
| 304 | (30 kr.), rose .. .. | | |

*Thick paper.*

| 305 | (1 kr.), pale blue (I.). | 50 | 12 |
|---|---|---|---|
| 305a | (1 kr.) ,, (II.). | 36 | 12 |

| No. | | Un. | Used. |
|---|---|---|---|
| 306 | (1 kr.), deep blue (I.). | 50 | |
| 306a | (1 kr.) ,, (II.) | 36 | 18 |
| 307 | (6 kr.), dull yellow .. | | |
| 308 | (6 kr.), red (1856) .. | | |
| 309 | (30 kr.), rose .. .. | | |

*Ribbed paper.*

| 310 | (1 kr.), pale blue .. | 1.85 | 62 |
|---|---|---|---|
| 311 | (1 kr.), blue .. .. | 3.00 | 75 |

All four stamps were reprinted in 1865, 1871, 1884, 1889, and 1894. The colours are for the most part brighter and fresher than those of the original stamps, and all are of Var. I.; *i.e.* with the "G" of "ZEITUNGS" like a "C," and the "S" of "STEMPEL" badly formed.

22          23

**1858–59.** Type **22.**

| 312 | (1 kr.), blue (A) .. | 2.50 | 1.00 |
|---|---|---|---|
| 313 | (1 kr.), lilac (B) .. | 62 | 50 |
| 314 | (1 kr.), grey-lilac (B) .. | 75 | 50 |

The varieties (A) and (B) are the same as those given under the general issues as (I.) and (II.) respectively.

Reprints in both blue and lilac were made in 1865, 1871, 1884, 1889, and 1894. Those of 1871 are Var. (A), the others are Var. (B).

**1861.** Type **23.**

| 315 | (1 kr.), grey-lilac .. | 1.00 | 18 |
|---|---|---|---|
| 316 | (1 kr.), lilac .. .. | 36 | |

This stamp was reprinted five times, at the same dates as those of the previous issues.

24

**1863.** Type **24.**

| 317 | (1 kr.), pale lilac .. | 4 | 4 |
|---|---|---|---|

Reprints of this stamp were made in 1871 and 1884. The latter is on the paper wmkd. "Zeitungs-Marken" in the sheet.

| No. | | Un. | Used. |
|---|---|---|---|

**25**

**26**

**1867. Type 25.**

| | | | |
|---|---|---|---|
| 318 | (1 kr.), purple .. .. | 6 | 2 |
| 319 | (1 kr.), lilac .. .. | 4 | 2 |
| 320 | (1 kr.), brown-lilac .. | 12 | 4 |
| 321 | (1 kr.), red-lilac .. | 2 | 2 |
| 322 | (1 kr.), grey .. .. | 4 | 2 |

There are three varieties of type of this stamp, probably due to the die having been twice retouched.

**1880. Type 26.**

| | | | |
|---|---|---|---|
| 323 | ½ kr., grey-green .. | 2 | 2 |
| 324 | ½ kr., sea-green .. | 2 | 2 |

No. Type. *Perf. unofficially.*

| | | | | |
|---|---|---|---|---|
| 325 | 26 | ½ kr., green .. | 8 | 6 |
| 326 | 25 | (1 kr.), lilac .. .. | 8 | 6 |

**27**

**1900. Type 27.**
*Granite paper. Imperf.*

| | | | |
|---|---|---|---|
| 327 | 2 (h.), deep blue .. | 2 | 2 |
| 328 | 6 (h.), orange .. .. | 2 | 2 |
| 329 | 10 (h.), brown .. .. | 4 | 2 |
| 330 | 20 (h.), pink .. .. | 8 | 4 |

**IMPERIAL JOURNAL STAMPS.**

These stamps did not pay postage, but represented a tax, collected by the Post Office, on newspapers coming from foreign countries.

**31**

**32**

⁊ Type 31. Rosettes *in the corners.*

| | | |
|---|---|---|
| 2 kr., pale green .. | 1.85 | 25 |
| 2 kr., deep ,, .. | — | 36 |

| No. | | Un. | Used. |
|---|---|---|---|

**1858. Type 32. Balls *in the corners.***

| | | | | |
|---|---|---|---|---|
| 353 | 1 kr., pale blue .. | 2 | 2 |
| 354 | 1 kr., deep ,, .. | 4 | 2 |
| 355 | 2 kr., dull brown .. | 1.25 | 25 |
| 356 | 2 kr., brown .. | 1.25 | 25 |
| 357 | 2 kr., red-brown .. | — | 25 |
| 358 | 4 kr., dull brown .. | 10.00 | 5.00 |
| 359 | 4 kr., brown .. .. | — | 7.50 |

The 4 kr. of the above issue, and the 2 kr. of 1850, were reprinted in 1873.

The stamps with wmk. large letters are omitted as these are stamps from the same sheets as those above, but showing the wmk. in the whole sheet.

**1878. *Larger shield in centre.***

| | | | |
|---|---|---|---|
| 363 | 1 kr., pale blue.. | — | 2 |
| 364 | 2 kr., pale brown .. | 4 | |

**33**

**34**

No. Type. **1890.** *Arms in a circle.*

| | | | | |
|---|---|---|---|---|
| 365 | 33 | 1 kr., brown (imperf.) | 2 | 2 |
| 366 | ,, | 2 kr., green ( ,, ) | 2 | 2 |
| 367 | 34 | 25 kr., carm. (perf. 13) 1.50 | 25 |

**UNPAID LETTER STAMPS.**

**51**

**1894-95. Type 51. (i.) *Perf.* 10, 10½.**

| | | | | |
|---|---|---|---|---|
| 401 | 1 kr., brown .. .. | 2 | |
| 402 | 2 kr. ,, .. .. | 2 | 2 |
| 403 | 3 kr. ,, .. .. | 4 | 2 |
| 404 | 5 kr. ,, .. .. | 16 | 12 |
| 405 | 6 kr. ,, .. .. | 8 | |
| 406 | 7 kr. ,, .. .. | 25 | |
| 407 | 10 kr. ,, .. .. | 8 | 7 |
| 408 | 20 kr. ,, .. .. | — | 12 |
| 409 | 50 kr. ,, .. .. | 62 | 50 |

**(ii.) *Perf.* 11½.**

| | | | | |
|---|---|---|---|---|
| 410 | 1 kr., brown .. .. | — | 4 |
| 411 | 2 kr. ,, .. .. | — | |
| 412 | 3 kr. ,, .. .. | | |
| 413 | 5 kr. ,, .. .. | 4 | 4 |
| 414 | 6 kr. ,, .. .. | — | 2 |
| 415 | 7 kr. ,, .. .. | | |
| 416 | 10 kr. ,, .. .. | | |
| 417 | 20 kr. ,, .. .. | 50 | 12 |
| 418 | 50 kr. ,, .. .. | 1.00 | 10 |

| No. | | | Un. | Used. |
|---|---|---|---|---|
| | *(iii.) Perf. 12½, 13.* | | | |
| 419 | 1 kr., brown | .. .. | — | 4 |
| 420 | 2 kr. ,, | .. .. | — | 4 |
| 421 | 3 kr. ,, | .. .. | — | 4 |
| 422 | 5 kr. ,, | .. .. | — | 4 |
| 423 | 10 kr. ,, | .. .. | — | 4 |

52

| No. | | | Un. | Used. |
|---|---|---|---|---|
| | **1900.** Type 52. *(i.) Perf. 12½, 13.* | | | |
| 431 | 1 h., brown | .. .. | 2 | 2 |
| 432 | 2 h. ,, | .. .. | 2 | |
| 433 | 3 h. ,, | .. .. | 2 | 2 |
| 434 | 4 h. ,, | .. .. | 2 | 4 |
| 435 | 5 h. ,, | .. .. | 2 | 4 |
| 436 | 6 h. ,, | .. .. | 4 | 4 |
| 437 | 10 h. ,, | .. .. | 4 | 4 |
| 438 | 12 h. ,, | .. .. | 6 | 6 |
| 439 | 15 h. ,, | .. .. | 8 | 8 |
| 440 | 20 h. ,, | .. .. | — | 8 |
| 441 | 40 h. ,, | .. .. | | |
| 442 | 100 h. ,, | .. .. | | |
| | *(ii.) Perf. 10½.* | | | |
| 443 | 2 h., brown | .. .. | 6 | |
| 444 | 3 h. ,, | .. .. | | |
| 445 | 5 h. ,, | .. .. | | |
| 446 | 100 h. ,, | .. .. | | |
| | *Varieties. Imperf.* | | | |
| 451 | 1 h., brown | .. .. | 2 | 4 |
| 452 | 2 h. ,, | .. .. | 4 | 2 |
| 453 | 3 h. ,, | .. .. | 4 | 4 |
| 454 | 4 h. ,, | .. .. | 6 | 6 |
| 455 | 5 h. ,, | .. .. | 6 | 6 |
| 456 | 6 h. ,, | .. .. | 8 | 8 |
| 457 | 10 h. ,, | .. .. | 6 | 12 |
| 458 | 12 h. ,, | .. .. | 6 | 16 |
| 459 | 15 h. ,, | .. .. | 8 | 16 |
| 460 | 20 h. ,, | .. .. | 8 | 12 |
| 461 | 40 h. ,, | .. .. | 16 | 16 |
| 462 | 100 h. ,, | .. .. | 30 | 18 |

Some values are found pin-perf (semi-officially).

## AUSTRIAN ITALY.

1

**1850.** Type 1. *Thin paper.*
*Two varieties of the 15 c. and 45 c.*

| | | | | |
|---|---|---|---|---|
| 5 c., orange | .. | .. | 20.00 | 75 |
| 5 c., yellow | .. | .. | — | 36 |

| | A | | B |
|---|---|---|---|

| | A | | B |
|---|---|---|---|

| No. | | | Un. | Used. |
|---|---|---|---|---|
| 3 | 10 c., grey-black | .. | 6.25 | 36 |
| 4 | 10 c., black | .. | — | 36 |
| 5 | 15 c., dull red (A) | .. | 5.00 | 4 |
| 6 | 15 c., red (A) | .. | 6.25 | 4 |
| 7 | 15 c., dull red (B) | .. | — | 2 |
| 8 | 15 c., red (B) | .. | — | 2 |
| 9 | 30 c., pale brown | .. | — | 4 |
| 10 | 30 c., deep ,, | .. | — | 4 |
| 11 | 45 c., pale blue (A) | .. | — | 8 |
| 12 | 45 c., blue (A) | .. | — | 8 |
| 13 | 45 c., pale blue (B) | .. | — | 6 |
| 14 | 45 c., blue (B) | .. | — | 6 |
| | *Printed on both sides.* | | | |
| 15 | 5 c., yellow | .. | — | 3.75 |
| | *Thick paper.* | | | |
| 16 | 5 c., orange | .. | — | 1.85 |
| 17 | 5 c., yellow | .. | — | 1.25 |
| 18 | 10 c., grey-black | .. | 11.25 | 50 |
| 19 | 10 c., black | .. | — | 50 |
| 22 | 15 c., dull red (B) | .. | 3.75 | 2 |
| 23 | 15 c., bright red (B) | .. | — | 2 |
| 24 | 30 c., pale brown | .. | 10.00 | 2 |
| 25 | 30 c., deep ,, | .. | 7.50 | 2 |
| 28 | 45 c., pale blue (B) | .. | — | 6 |
| 29 | 45 c., blue (B) | .. | — | 4 |
| | *Ribbed paper.* | | | |
| 30 | 15 c., red (A) | .. | — | 50 |
| 31 | 15 c. ,, (B) | .. | — | 62 |
| 32 | 30 c., brown | .. | — | 50 |
| 33 | 45 c., blue | .. | — | 50 |
| | *Laid paper.* | | | |
| 33a | 15 c., red.. | .. | | |

All five values were reprinted in 1865, 1871, and 1884, and the 5 c. (in two colours), another 10 c., in 1889. The colours of the reprints are brighter and fresher than those of the original stamps, and for the most part they are more clearly printed.

**1858–59.** *Perf.* 15.

*Types and varieties as in issue of Austria of the same date.*

| No. | | | Un. | Used. |
|---|---|---|---|---|
| 34 | 2 sld., yellow (I.) | .. | | |
| 35 | 2 sld. ,, (II.) | .. | 1.25 | 30 |
| 36 | 3 sld., black (I.) | .. | 3.15 | 75 |
| 37 | 3 sld. ,, (II.) | .. | — | 50 |
| 37a | 3 sld., green (I.) | .. | | |
| 38 | 3 sld. ,, (II.) | .. | 1.85 | 36 |
| 39 | 3 sld., blue-green (II.). | | 5.00 | 1.25 |

|  |  | *Un.* | *Used.* |
|---|---|---|---|
| No. | | | |
| 40 | 5 sld., red (I.) .. .. | 36 | 2 |
| 41 | 5 sld. ,, (II.).. .. | 30 | 2 |
| 42 | 10 sld., brown (I.) .. | 1.25 | 6 |
| 43 | 10 sld. ,, (II.) .. | 1.50 | 6 |
| 44 | 15 sld., blue (I.).. .. | 2.00 | 8 |
| 45 | 15 sld. ,, (II.) .. | 2.00 | 6 |

Reprints of all six values were made in 1865 (perf. 12), 1871 (perf. 11), 1884 (perf. 13), and of the 2 sld. and 3 sld. (each in both colours) in 1889 (perf. 12½ to 12). All the reprints are of Type II.

**1861.** Austria Type 6. *Perf.* 14.

| 46 | 5 sld., dull red .. .. | 5.00 | 2 |
| 47 | 10 sld., brown .. .. | 7.50 | 12 |

These two values were reprinted in 1865 (perf. 12), 1871 (perf. 11), and 1884 (perf. 13). With these reprints were also struck off impressions of the 2 sld., 3 sld., and 15 sld. values, which were prepared but never issued.

**1863.** Type 2. *Wmk. "* BRIEFMARKEN *" in double-lined capitals horizontally across the sheet. Perf.* 14.

| 48 | 2 sld., yellow .. .. | 18 | 25 |
| 49 | 3 sld., yellow-green .. | 1.50 | 30 |
| 50 | 5 sld., dull rose .. | 2.50 | 2 |
| 51 | 5 sld., bright rose .. | — | 4 |
| 52 | 10 sld., dull blue .. | 10.00 | 12 |
| 53 | 15 sld., stone-brown .. | 5.00 | 25 |

**1864.** *The same, but perf.* 9½.

| 54 | 2 sld., yellow .. .. | 18 | 90 |
| 55 | 3 sld., yellow-green .. | 8 | 8 |
| 56 | 3 sld., blue-green .. | — | 12 |
| 57 | 5 sld., dull rose .. | 6 | 2 |
| 58 | 5 sld., deep ,, .. | 8 | 2 |
| 59 | 10 sld., dull blue .. | 18 | 2 |
| 60 | 10 sld., deep blue .. | 8 | 2 |
| 61 | 15 sld., pale stone-brown | 12 | 8 |
| 62 | 15 sld., deep ,, | 25 | 8 |

All five values were reprinted in 1884 (perf. 13), and the 2 sld. and 3 sld. in 1889 (perf. 10½).

IMPERIAL JOURNAL STAMPS.
**1858.** Austria Type 31.

| 81 | 1 kr., black .. .. | 3.75 | |
| 82 | 2 kr., dull red .. .. | 75 | 8 |
| 83 | 2 kr., red .. .. | | |
| | 4 kr. ,, .. .. | — | 10.00 |

The three values were reprinted in 1870. The 1 kr. can be found with different types the figure " 1."

|  | *Un.* | *Used.* |
|---|---|---|
| No. | | |

**AUSTRIAN POST OFFICES IN THE TURKISH EMPIRE.**

61      62

**1867.** Type 61. *Wmk. as in* 1863. *Perf.* 9½.

| 601 | 2 sld., yellow .. .. | 6 | 12 |
| 602 | 2 sld., orange .. .. | 18 | 12 |
| 603 | 3 sld., pale green .. | 8 | 4 |
| 604 | 3 sld., green .. .. | 6 | 6 |
| 605 | 5 sld., rose .. .. | 75 | 4 |
| 606 | 5 sld., rose-red .. | 12 | 1 |
| 607 | 10 sld., blue .. .. | 25 | 2 |
| 608 | 10 sld., deep blue .. | 25 | 2 |
| 609 | 15 sld., bistre .. .. | 75 | 4 |
| 610 | 15 sld., deep bistre .. | 2.50 | 12 |
| 611 | 15 sld., reddish brown . | 25 | 6 |
| 612 | 25 sld., purple .. .. | 1.25 | 25 |
| 613 | 25 sld., slate .. .. | 90 | 25 |
| 613a | 25 sld., brown-lilac .. | 36 | 12 |

Type 62. *(a) Perf.* 9½.

| 613b | 50 sld., pale brown .. | | |

*(b) Perf.* 12.

| 614 | 50 sld., pink-brown .. | 3.75 | 7 |
| 614a | 50 sld., pale brown .. | | |

*The same, but perf.* 10½.

| 615 | 10 sld., blue .. .. | — | 5 |
| 615a | 15 sld., bistre .. .. | | |
| 616 | 50 sld., pale brown .. | 1.25 | 5 |

The 10 sld. was reprinted in 1895, perf. 10½, in a deep dull blue.

*Variety of perf.*

| 616a | 10 sld., blue (10½ × 9½) . | | |
| 616b | 50 sld., pale brn. (10½ × 9½) | | |

63

**1883.** Type 63. *Inscription and figures in* black. *Perf.* 9½.

| 617 | 2 sld., brown .. .. | 4 | 4 |
| 618 | 3 sld., emerald-green . | 16 | 10 |
| 618a | 3 sld., yellow-green .. | 8 | |
| 619 | 5 sld., rose .. .. | 6 | 4 |
| 619a | 5 sld., rose-red .. | — | 6 |
| 620 | 10 sld., ultramarine .. | 25 | 2 |

|  | | *Un.* | *Used.* |
|---|---|---|---|
| **No.** | | | |
| 620a | 10 sld., dull blue .. | 18 | 2 |
| 621 | 20 sld., greenish grey.. | 25 | 10 |
| 622 | 50 sld., red-lilac .. | 50 | 25 |

## 10 PARA 10    10 PARA 10
    *a*              *b*

**1886.** Type 63 *surcharged in* black.
(a) *Printed at Constantinople, surcharge* 16 mm. *across the middle, space between* "10" *and* "P" 2 mm., "PARA" *above base line of* "10."
(b) *Printed at Vienna, surcharge* 15½ mm. *across the middle, space between* "10" *and* "P" 1½ mm., "PARA" *on the line with* "10."

| 623 | 10 p. on 3 sld. (a) | .. | 6.25 | |
| 624 | 10 p. on 3 sld. (b) | .. | 8 | 8 |

## 1 PIASTER 1
65

**1888.** Austria Type 10 *surcharged as* Type 65, *in* black. *Perf.* 10½.

| 625 | 10 pa. on 3 kr., green .. | 2 | 2 |
| 626 | 20 pa. on 5 kr., rose .. | 4 | 4 |
| 627 | 1 pi. on 10 kr., blue .. | 12 | 2 |
| 628 | 2 pi. on 20 kr., grey .. | 25 | 6 |
| 629 | 5 pi. on 50 kr., violet .. | 62 | 25 |

**1890–92.**
*Austrian types with lower figures of value removed similarly surcharged at foot.*
No. Type.    (a) *Perf.* 9½.

| 629a | 11 | 8 pa. on 2 kr., brown | — | 1.85 |
| 629b | " | 2 pi. on 20 kr., olive | | |

(b) *Perf.* 10½.

| 630 | 11 | 8 pa. on 2 kr., brown | 2 | 2 |
| 631 | " | 10 pa. on 3 kr., green | 4 | 4 |
| 632 | " | 20 pa. on 5 kr., carm. | 6 | 4 |
| 633 | " | 1 pi. on 10 kr., blue | 8 | 2 |
| 634 | 13 | 2 pi. on 20 kr., olive | 18 | 6 |
| 635 | " | 5 pi. on 50 kr., red-lilac | 30 | 8 |

(c) *Perf.* 11 to 12.

| 636 | 11 | 10 pa. on 3 kr., green | — | 6 |
| 637 | " | 20 pa. on 5 kr., carm. | | |
| 638 | " | 1 pi. on 10 kr., blue | — | 4 |
| 639 | " | 2 pi. on 20 kr., olive | 25 | 25 |
| 640 | 13 | 2 pi. on 20 kr. ,, | — | 25 |
| 640a | " | 5 pi. on 50 kr., red-lilac .. | — | 12 |

(d) *Perf.* 12½ to 13½.

| 641 | 11 | 10 pa. on 3 kr., blue-green | 4 | 4 |
| 642 | " | 20 pa. on 5 kr., carm. | 4 | 4 |
| 643 | " | 1 pi. on 10 kr., blue | 8 | 4 |
| 644 | " | 2 pi. on 20 kr., olive | 36 | 18 |
| 644a | 13 | 2 pi. on 20 kr. ,, | 30 | 30 |
| 644b | 11 | 5 pi. on 50 kr., red-lilac | 62 | 50 |
| 644c | 13 | 5 pi. on 50 kr., red-lilac .. | 1.25 | |

---

|  | | *Un.* | *Used.* |
|---|---|---|---|
| **No.** | | | |

## 20 PIASTER 20
66

Austria Type 12 *surcharged at foot as* Type 66, *in* black.

**1892.** (a) *Perf.* 9, 9½.

| 644d | 10 pi. on 1 gl., blue .. | | |
| 644e | 20 pi. on 2 gl., red .. | | |

(b) *Perf.* 10, 10½.

| 645 | 10 pi. on 1 gl., blue .. | 90 | 50 |
| 646 | 20 pi. on 2 gl., red .. | 1.25 | 1.00 |

(c) *Perf.* 11, 11½.

| 646a | 10 pi. on 1 gl., blue .. | 1.50 | 1.00 |
| 646b | 20 pi. on 2 gl., red (?).. | | |

**1896.** (a) *Perf.* 10½.

| 647 | 10 pi. on 1 gl., lilac .. | 62 | 36 |
| 648 | 20 pi. on 2 gl., green .. | 1.00 | 75 |

(b) *Perf.* 11½.

| 648a | 10 pi. on 1 gl., lilac .. | 1.25 | 75 |

**1903.** (c) *Perf.* 12½, 13.

| 648b | 20 pi. on 2 gl., dull green | 3.15 | |

**1900.** *New types surcharged as before.*
(a) *Perf.* 12½, 13½.

| 649 | 10 pa. on 5 h., green .. | 2 | 2 |
| 650 | 20 pa. on 10 h., rose .. | 4 | 2 |
| 651 | 1 pi. on 25 h., ultram. .. | 8 | 4 |
| 652 | 2 pi. on 50 h., pale blue | 12 | 12 |
| 652a | 5 pi. on 1 k., rose .. | 30 | 25 |
| 653 | 10 p. on 2 k., lavender . | 62 | 36 |
| 654 | 20 p. on 4 k., pale green | 1.25 | 50 |

(b) *Perf.* 10½.

| 655 | 1 pi. on 25 h., ultram. . | 8 | 6 |
| 656 | 2 pi. on 50 h., pale blue | | |

*With shiny bars. Perf.* 12½, 13.

| 657 | 10 pa. on 5 h., green .. | 2 | 2 |
| 658 | 1 pi. on 25 h., ultram. | — | 6 |
| 659 | 2 pi. on 50 h., pale blue | — | 12 |

## 5 ⌣ 5    10 — 10

## CENTIMES    CENTIMES
## 5 ⌣ 5    10 — 10
    67             68

**1903.** Types 14, 15, *and* 12 *surcharged as* Types 67 *to* 70, *in* black. *With shiny bars. Perf.* 13.

| 660 | 5 c. on 5 h., deep green | 2 | |
| 661 | 10 c. on 10 h., rose .. | 4 | |

No.     *Un.*   *Used.*

**FRANC**

69      70

| 662 | 25 c. on 25 h., ultramarine | 8 | |
| 663 | 50 c. on 50 h., pale blue .. | 16 | |
| 664 | 1 fr. on 1 kr., rose | 30 | |

*Austrian types with all figures of value removed surcharged as before, but at top and also at foot, in black. Perf. 12½, 13½.*

| 665 | 10 pa., dark green .. | 4 | |
| 666 | 20 pa., rose .. | 6 | 6 |
| 667 | 1 pi., ultramarine .. | 10 | |
| 668 | 2 pi., pale blue .. | 18 | |

UNPAID LETTER STAMPS.

**10 PARA**      **1 PIASTER**
101       102

**1902.** Austria Type 5a *surcharged, in* black, *as* Type 101 *or* 102.

| 801 | 10 pa. on 5 h., green.. | 2 |
| 802 | 20 pa. on 10 h. „ .. | 4 |
| 803 | 1 pi. on 20 h. „ .. | 6 |
| 804 | 2 pi. on 40 h. „ .. | 10 |
| 805 | 5 pi. on 100 h. „ .. | 30 |

**HUNGARY.**

1

**1871.** Type 1. *Lithographed. Perf.* 9½.

| 1 | 2 kr., yellow .. | .. | 3.75 | 2.50 |
| 2 | 2 kr., orange .. | .. | 1.85 | 2.50 |
| 3 | 3 kr., pale green | .. | 10.00 | 7.50 |
| 4 | 3 kr., deep „ | .. | | |
| 5 | 5 kr., dull rose.. | .. | 3.75 | 10 |
| 6 | 5 kr., rose .. | .. | 3.75 | 12 |
| 7 | 5 kr., red .. | .. | | |
| ? | 10 kr., pale blue.. | .. | 15.00 | 62 |
| | 10 kr., blue .. | .. | 15.00 | 62 |
| | 10 kr., deep blue | .. | — | 75 |

No.     *Un.*   *Used*

| 11 | 15 kr., bistre . | .. | 20.00 | 1.? |
| 12 | 15 kr., bistre-brown | .. | | |
| 13 | 25 kr., red-lilac .. | .. | 8.75 | 2 |
| 14 | 25 kr., deep lilac | .. | 10.00 | 3 |

All six values are met with imperforate.

**1871.** *Engraved. Perf.* 9½.

| 15 | 2 kr., orange .. | .. | 18 | |
| 16 | 2 kr., brownish orange | .. | 30 | 1 |
| 17 | 2 kr., yellow .. | .. | 5.00 | 6 |
| 18 | 3 kr., yellow-green | .. | 25 | 2 |
| 19 | 3 kr., blue-green | .. | 25 | |
| 20 | 5 kr., rose-red .. | .. | 25 | |
| 21 | 5 kr., carmine .. | .. | 18 | |
| 22 | 10 kr., blue | .. | 62 | |
| 23 | 10 kr., deep blue | .. | 1.00 | |
| 24 | 15 kr., brown .. | .. | 1.50 | 1 |
| 25 | 15 kr., deep brown | .. | 1.85 | 1 |
| 26 | 15 kr., chestnut .. | .. | — | 1.6 |
| 27 | 25 kr., grey-lilac .. | .. | 1.25 | |

All six values were reprinted in 1885 c the wmkd. paper of 1881, and are perf. 11½

2

**1874-76.** Type 2. *No wmk.*
*(a) Perf.* 12½ *to* 13½.

| 28 | 2 (kr.), mauve .. | .. | 25 |
| 29 | 2 (kr.), lilac .. | .. | 25 |
| 30 | 3 (kr.), yellow-green | .. | 50 |
| 31 | 3 (kr.), blue-green | .. | 30 |
| 32 | 5 (kr.), red .. | .. | 50 |
| 33 | 5 (kr.), carmine-rose | .. | 75 |
| 34 | 10 (kr.), blue | .. | 62 |
| 35 | 10 (kr.), bright blue | .. | 75 |
| 36 | 20 (kr.), bluish grey ('76) | | 7.50 |
| 37 | 20 (kr.), grey .. | .. | 8.75 |

*(b) Perf.* 11½ *to* 12.

| 38 | 2 (kr.), mauve .. | .. | 3.75 | 2 |
| 39 | 2 (kr.), rose-lilac | .. | — | 2 |
| 40 | 3 (kr.), yellow-green | .. | 3.15 | 2 |
| 41 | 3 (kr.), blue-green | .. | — | 2 |
| 42 | 5 (kr.), carmine-rose | .. | — | 2 |
| 43 | 10 (kr.), blue | .. | 2.50 | |
| 44 | 20 (kr.), bluish grey | .. | | |

*(c) Perf. compound of (a) and (b).*

| 44a | 2 (kr.), mauve .. | .. | | |
| 44b | 3 (kr.), green .. | .. | 1.25 | |
| 44c | 5 (kr.), red .. | .. | | |
| 44d | 10 (kr.), blue .. | .. | | |
| 44e | 20 (kr.), bluish grey .. | | — | 1.? |

The 2 kr., 5 kr., and 20 kr. are known i various other colours, and although pos marked specimens of these exist, they ca only be looked upon as proofs that hav passed the post.

| | | Un. | Used. |
|---|---|---|---|
| No. | | | |

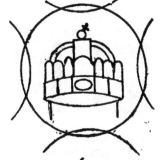

**3**

**1881.** Type 2. *Wmk.* Type 3.
(*a*) *Perf.* 11½ *to* 12.

| 45 | 2 (kr.), rose-lilac | .. | 4 | 2 |
| 46 | 2 (kr.), mauve .. | .. | 4 | 2 |
| 47 | 2 (kr.), slate .. | .. | 12 | 6 |
| 48 | 3 (kr.), yellow-green | .. | 8 | 2 |
| 49 | 3 (kr.), blue-green | .. | 4 | 2 |
| 50 | 5 (kr.), carmine-rose | .. | 12 | 2 |
| 51 | 10 (kr.), blue .. | .. | 8 | 2 |
| 52 | 10 (kr.), deep blue | .. | 6 | 2 |
| 53 | 20 (kr.), bluish grey | .. | 16 | 4 |
| 54 | 20 (kr.), grey .. | .. | 18 | 4 |

(*b*) *Perf.* 12½ *to* 13½.

| 55 | 2 (kr.), rose-lilac | .. | | |
| 56 | 2 (kr.), mauve .. | .. | | |
| 57 | 2 (kr.), slate .. | .. | | |
| 58 | 3 (kr.), yellow-green | .. | | |
| 59 | 3 (kr.), blue-green | .. | | |
| 60 | 5 (kr.), carmine-rose | .. | 50 | |
| 61 | 10 (kr.), blue .. | .. | 36 | |
| 62 | 20 (kr.), bluish grey | .. | — | 50 |

(*c*) *Perf. compound of* (*a*) *and* (*b*).
62*a* 10 (kr.), blue .. ..
62*b* 20 (kr.), bluish grey .. — 36

All the values of this issue are found printed from retouched plates. The retouching consists in the strengthening of the horizontal lines of the background in various parts of the stamp, chiefly at the top and bottom.

(1 kr.)   (1 fl.)

**4**   **5**

**1887-98.** Types 4, 5. *Numerals in* black *on the lower values, and in* red *on the* 1 fl. *and* 3 fl. *Perf.* 11½ *to* 12.

| | | Un. | Used. |
|---|---|---|---|
| **No.** | | | |

*The background is in the second colour.*

| 63 | 1 (kr.), black .. | .. | 2 | 2 |
| 64 | 1 (kr.), grey-black | .. | 2 | 2 |
| 65 | 2 (kr.), mauve .. | .. | 2 | 2 |
| 66 | 3 (kr.), green .. | .. | 2 | 2 |
| 67 | 5 (kr.), carmine | .. | 2 | 2 |
| 68 | 8 (kr.), orange & yellow | | 4 | 2 |
| 69 | 10 (kr.), blue .. | .. | 6 | |
| 70 | 12 (kr.), brown & green . | | 12 | 2 |
| 70*a* | 12 kr., brown & pale grn. | | 12 | 2 |
| 71 | 15 (kr.), rose and blue .. | | 12 | 2 |
| 72 | 20 (kr.), grey .. | .. | 16 | |
| 73 | 24 (kr.), purple and red . | | — | 2 |
| 74 | 30 (kr.), olive and brown | | 20 | 2 |
| 75 | 50 (kr.), oran.-red & oran. | | 30 | 2 |
| 76 | 1 fl., blue and silver | .. | 55 | 2 |
| 77 | 3 fl., violet-brn. & gold. | | 1.75 | 12 |

**6**

**1896.** *Same type. Wmk.* Type 6, *extending over four stamps. Perf.* 12.

| 78 | 1 (kr.), black .. | .. | 2 | 2 |
| 79 | 2 (kr.), mauve .. | .. | 2 | 2 |
| 80 | 3 (kr.), green .. | .. | 2 | 2 |
| 81 | 5 (kr.), rose .. | .. | 6 | 2 |
| 82 | 8 (kr.), orange .. | .. | 4 | 2 |
| 83 | 10 (kr.), blue .. | .. | 8 | 2 |
| 84 | 12 (kr.), brown and green | | | |
| 85 | 15 (kr.), rose and blue .. | | 10 | 2 |
| 86 | 20 (kr.), grey .. | .. | 12 | 2 |
| 87 | 24 (kr.), purple and red.. | | 16 | 2 |
| 88 | 30 (kr.), olive-grn. & brn. | | 16 | 2 |
| 89 | 50 (kr.), oran.-red & oran. | | — | 2 |

**7**   **8**

**1900-1.** *Values in* filler *and* korona, *in* black. *Perf.* 12. Type 7.

| 90 | 1 f., grey .. | .. | 2 | 2 |
| 90*a* | 1 f., dull lilac .. | .. | 2 | 2 |

|       |                       | *Un.* | *Used.* |
| ----- | --------------------- | ----- | ------- |
| **No.** |                     |       |         |
| 91    | 2 f., olive-yellow    | 2     | 2       |
| 92    | 3 f., orange          | 2     | 2       |
| 93    | 4 f., lilac           | 2     | 2       |
| 94    | 5 f., emerald         | 2     | 2       |
| 95    | 6 f., marone          | 2     | 2       |
| 95a   | 6 f., olive-yellow    | 2     | 2       |
| 95b   | 6 f., olive-green     | 2     |         |
| 96    | 10 f., rose           | 4     | 2       |
| 96a   | 20 f., brown          | 6     | 2       |
| 97    | 25 f., blue           | 8     | 2       |
| 98    | 30 f., brown          | 10    | 2       |
| 98a   | 35 f., red-lilac      | 12    | 2       |
| 99    | 50 f., lake           | 14    | 2       |
| 100   | 60 f., grey-green     | 16    | 2       |

### Type 8.

|     |                        | *Un.* | *Used.* |
| --- | ---------------------- | ----- | ------- |
| 101 | 1 kor., red-brown      | 30    | 2       |
| 102 | 2 ,, blue              | 55    | 8       |
| 103 | 3 ,, greenish blue     | 75    | 25      |
| 104 | 5 ,, claret            | 1.40  | 18      |

### NEWSPAPER STAMPS.

**11**  **12**

### 1871. · Type 11.
| 201 | (1 kr.), vermilion | 18 | 8 |
| --- | --- | --- | --- |

### 1872. Type 12.
| 202 | (1 kr.), red  | 8 | 2 |
| --- | --- | --- | --- |
| 203 | (1 kr.), rose | 2 | 2 |

This stamp was reprinted in 1885 on the wmkd. paper of 1881.

**13**  **14**

### 1874. Type 13.
| 204 | 1 (kr.), dull orange | 4 |
| --- | --- | --- |
| 205 | 1 (kr.), bright ,,   |   |
| 206 | 1 (kr.), yellow      |   |

### DEC., 1885. Wmk. Type 3.
| 207 | 1 (kr.), orange | 2 | 2 |
| --- | --- | --- | --- |
| 208 | 1 (kr.), yellow | 2 | 2 |

*Variety. Printed on both sides.*
| 208a | 1 (kr.), yellow | |
| --- | --- | --- |

### 1898. Same type. Wmk. Type 6.
| 9 | 1 (kr.), orange | |
| --- | --- | --- |

### 1900. Type 14. Imperf.
| 0 | (2 f.), orange | 2 | 2 |
| --- | --- | --- | --- |

---

**No.**

### JOURNAL TAX STAMPS.

**21**  **22**

### 1868. Types 21 and 22. Imperf.
| 251 | 1 kr., pale blue  | 4    |
| --- | --- | --- |
| 252 | 1 kr., blue       | 8    |
| 253 | 2 kr., brown      | 1.00 |
| 254 | 2 kr., red-brown  | 1.50 |

### 1890. Wmk. Type 3.
| 255 | 1 kr., blue  | 2 |
| --- | --- | --- |
| 256 | 2 kr., brown | 4 |

### 1899. Wmk. Type 6. Imperf.
| 257 | 1 kr., blue | |
| --- | --- | --- |

### UNPAID LETTER STAMPS.

**31**

### 1903. Type 31. Figures in centre: black.
| 301 | 1 f., green | |
| --- | --- | --- |
| 302 | 2 f., ,,    | |
| 303 | 5 f., ,,    | |
| 304 | 6 f., ,,    | |
| 305 | 10 f., ,,   | |
| 306 | 12 f., ,,   | |
| 307 | 20 f., ,,   | |
| 308 | 50 f., ,,   | |
| 309 | 100 f., ,,  | |

## BOSNIA AND HERZEGOVINA

**1**

### 1879. Type 1.
*(a) Perf. 12½, 13 (irregular).*
| 1 | 1 (nov.), lilac-grey    | 2.50 |
| --- | --- | --- |
| 2 | 1 ,, pale grey          | 18   |
| 4 | 1 ,, purple, p. 25 c.   | 3.75 |
| 5 | 2 ,, yellow (C)         | 8    |
| 6 | 2 ,, orange (C)         | 25   |
| 7 | 3 ,, blue-green         | 50   |

| No. | | | Un. | Used. |
|---|---|---|---|---|

A      B

C      D

| No. | | | | Un. | Used. |
|---|---|---|---|---|---|
| 8 | 3 (nov.), | yellow-green | .. | 62 | |
| 9 | 3 ,, | deep green | .. | 75 | |
| 10 | 5 ,, | rose-red | .. | 18 | 25 |
| 11 | 5 ,, | rose | .. .. | 25 | 12 |
| 12 | 5 ,, | dull vermilion | | 50 | 25 |
| 13 | 10 ,, | pale blue | .. | 1.85 | 25 |
| 14 | 10 ,, | blue | .. .. | — | 12 |
| 15 | 10 ,, | deep blue | .. | | |
| 16 | 15 ,, | bistre (A) | .. | 1.85 | 1.00 |
| 17 | 15 ,, | brown (,,) | .. | 1.25 | |
| 18 | 15 ,, | bistre (B) | .. | 90 | 18 |
| 19 | 15 ,, | brown (,,) | .. | 1.50 | 12 |
| 20 | 25 ,, | purple | .. | 2.10 | 12 |
| 21 | 25 ,, | aniline mauve | | 2.10 | 8 |

*(b) Perf. 11½, 12.*

| No. | | | | Un. | Used. |
|---|---|---|---|---|---|
| 22 | 1 (nov.), | dark grey | .. | 6 | |
| 22a | 1 ,, | pale grey | .. | 12 | |
| 23 | 1 ,, | lilac-grey | .. | 1.25 | |
| 24 | 2 ,, | yellow (C) | .. | 4 | 12 |
| 24a | 2 ,, | orange | .. | 1.00 | |
| 25 | 3 ,, | green | .. | 62 | |
| 26 | 3 ,, | blue-green | .. | 25 | |
| 27 | 5 ,, | rose-red | .. | 50 | 8 |
| 28 | 10 ,, | pale blue | .. | 18 | 4 |
| 29 | 10 ,, | blue | .. .. | — | 6 |
| 29a | 15 ,, | brown (A) | .. | | |
| 30 | 15 ,, | brown (B) | .. | — | 6 |
| 31 | 25 ,, | purple | .. | 1.85 | 8 |
| 31a | 25 ,, | red-lilac | .. | 90 | |
| 32 | 25 ,, | aniline mauve | | 62 | 12 |

**1891.** *Same type. (a) Perf. 10½.*

| No. | | | | Un. | Used. |
|---|---|---|---|---|---|
| 33 | ½ (nov.), | black | .. | 2 | 2 |
| 34 | 1 ,, | pale grey | .. | 25 | 2 |
| 35 | 1 ,, | dark grey | .. | 25 | 8 |
| 36 | 2 ,, | yellow (C) | .. | 25 | 4 |
| 37 | 2 ,, | orange (D) | .. | 36 | 4 |
| 38 | 3 ,, | pale green | .. | 25 | 4 |
| 39 | 3 ,, | green | .. .. | 25 | 4 |
| 40 | 3 ,, | dull green | .. | 36 | |
| 41 | 3 ,, | dark green | .. | 62 | 4 |
| 42 | 5 ,, | dull rose | .. | 6 | 2 |
| 42a | 5 ,, | deep ,, | .. | | |
| 42b | 5 ,, | red | .. .. | 1.85 | |
| 43 | 10 ,, | indigo | .. | 18 | 12 |
| 44 | 15 ,, | bistre-brown (B) | | 18 | 18 |

| No. | | | | Un. | Used. |
|---|---|---|---|---|---|
| 45 | 20 (nov.), | pale olive-green | | 36 | 4 |
| 46 | 20 ,, | sage-green | .. | 50 | 6 |
| 47 | 25 ,, | purple | | 50 | 8 |
| 48 | 25 ,, | mauve | .. | — | 12 |

*(b) Perf. 11½ (regular).*

| No. | | | | Un. | Used. |
|---|---|---|---|---|---|
| 49 | ½ (nov.), | black .. | .. | 8 | 4 |
| 50 | 1 ,, | grey .. | .. | 6 | 2 |
| 51 | 2 ,, | orange-yell. (C) | | 25 | 4 |
| 51a | 2 ,, | ,, ,, (D) | | — | 6 |
| 52 | 3 ,, | green.. | .. | — | 12 |
| 53 | 3 ,, | deep green | .. | 25 | 4 |
| 54 | 5 ,, | dull rose | .. | 18 | 4 |
| 56 | 10 ,, | blue .. | .. | 25 | 18 |
| 57 | 10 ,, | indigo | .. | 1.50 | 25 |
| 58 | 15 ,, | bistre (B) | .. | — | 50 |
| 59 | 20 ,, | pale olive-green | | — | 4 |
| 60 | 20 ,, | sage-green | .. | — | 12 |
| 61 | 25 ,, | purple | .. | 1.00 | 8 |
| 62 | 25 ,, | mauve | .. | 75 | |

*(c) Perf. 12½ (regular).*

| No. | | | | Un. | Used. |
|---|---|---|---|---|---|
| 63 | ½ (nov.), | black .. | .. | | |
| 64 | 1 ,, | pearl-grey | .. | 1.00 | |
| 65 | 2 ,, | orange-yell. (D) | | 90 | 4 |
| 66 | 3 ,, | blue-green | .. | 62 | 4 |
| 67 | 3 ,, | green .. | .. | 36 | 6 |
| 68 | 5 ,, | red | .. | 50 | 4 |
| 69 | 5 ,, | rose .. | .. | 12 | 12 |
| 70 | 10 ,, | blue .. | .. | — | 4 |
| 71 | 10 ,, | deep blue | .. | — | 6 |
| 72 | 15 ,, | bistre (B) | .. | 1.25 | 12 |
| 73 | 20 ,, | sage-green | .. | | |
| 74 | 25 ,, | mauve | .. | 3.75 | 12 |

*(d) Perf. 9½.*

| No. | | | | Un. | Used. |
|---|---|---|---|---|---|
| 74a | 5 (nov.), | red | .. | | |
| 75 | 10 ,, | blue | .. | — | 25 |

*(e) Compound perfs.*

| No. | | | Un. | Used. |
|---|---|---|---|---|
| 75a | ½ n. (11½ × 10½) | .. | | |
| 75b | 5 n. (12½ × 10½) | .. | | |
| 75c | 5 n. (10½ × 11½) | .. | — | 25 |
| 75d | 10 n. (11½ × 10½) | .. | | |

There are other varieties of perforation occasionally found. Previous to 1891 the perforation was irregular in spacing and also in alignment. The perforations from 1891 are much cleaner cut and more regular in every way, though varying considerably in gauge.

2          3

**1900.** *Type 2. Value in lower corners.*
*(a) Perf. 12½.*

| No. | | | | Un. | Used. |
|---|---|---|---|---|---|
| 76 | 1 (h.), | grey-black | .. | 2 | |
| 77 | 2 (h.), | pearl-grey | .. | | |

| No. | | Un. | Used. |
|---|---|---|---|
| 78 | 2 (h.), pale drab .. | 2 | |
| 79 | 3 (h.), orange-yellow .. | 2 | 4 |
| 80 | 5 (h.), blue-green .. | 2 | 2 |
| 81 | 5 (h.), sea-green .. | 2 | 2 |
| 82 | 6 (h.), brown .. .. | 36 | |
| 83 | 10 (h.), red .. .. | 4 | 2 |
| 84 | 20 (h.), rosine .. .. | 12 | 4 |
| 85 | 25 (h.), blue .. .. | 8 | 4 |
| 86 | 30 (h.), bistre .. .. | 10 | 12 |
| 87 | 40 (h.), orange .. .. | 12 | 8 |
| 88 | 50 (h.), mauve .. .. | 14 | 8 |

Type 3.  *Perf.* 12½.

| 89 | 1 k., carmine .. .. | 30 | 18 |
|---|---|---|---|
| 90 | 2 k., ultramarine .. | 60 | 45 |
| 90a | 5 k., slate-green .. | 1.45 | |

(*b*) *Perf.* 10½.

| 91 | 1 (h.), black .. .. | | |
|---|---|---|---|
| 92 | 2 (h.), grey .. .. | 2 | |
| 93 | 5 (h.), green .. .. | 12 | 12 |
| 94 | 6 (h.), brown .. .. | 4 | |
| 95 | 10 (h.), red .. .. | 12 | 12 |
| 96 | 20 (h.), rosine .. .. | 8 | 4 |
| 96a | 25 (h.), blue .. .. | 50 | 25 |
| 97 | 30 (h.), pale brown .. | 10 | 4 |

(*c*) *Perf.* 12½ × 10½.

| 98 | 3 (h.), yellow .. .. | | |
|---|---|---|---|
| 98a | 10 (h.), red .. .. | — | 25 |

### 1900.

Type 2.  Black *numerals.*

*Perf.* 12½.

| 99 | 20 (h.), rosine .. .. | 6 |
|---|---|---|
| 99a | 30 (h.), pale brown .. | 10 |
| 100 | 35 (h.), blue .. .. | 10 |
| 101 | 40 (h.), orange.. .. | 12 |

## BELGIUM.

Leopold I., King of the Belgians 1831–65.

1                2

### 1849–52.

Type 1.  *Wmk.* "*LL*" *in frame,*
Type 2.  *Imperf.*

| 1 | 10 c., grey-brown .. | 12.50 | 36 |
|---|---|---|---|
| 2 | 10 c., brown .. .. | 15.00 | 36 |
| 3 | 20 c., deep blue .. | 11.25 | 10 |
| 4 | 20 c., blue .. .. | — | 10 |
| | 20 c., milky blue .. .. | — | 25 |

Reprints of both values were made in
6 on unwatermarked paper and on laid
er, and again in 1898 in lighter colours
thin unwatermarked paper.

| No. | | Un. | Used |
|---|---|---|---|

3

### 1850.  Type 3.  *Wmk. as last. Imperf.*

| 6 | 10 c., brown .. .. | — | |
|---|---|---|---|
| 7 | 20 c., blue .. .. | — | |
| 8 | 40 c., carmine .. .. | — | 5 |
| 8a | 40 c., pale carmine .. | 30.00 | |

4

### 1851.  Type 3.  *Wmk. without frame.*
Type 4.  *Imperf.*

| 9 | 10 c., brown .. .. | 5.00 | |
|---|---|---|---|
| 10 | 20 c., blue .. .. | 4.00 | |
| 11 | 40 c., carmine .. .. | — | |
| 12 | 40 c., carmine-vermilion | — | |

Two distinct sets of the above three
issues may be made, on thick and thin
papers, and the 1851 set also exists on paper
showing ribbing.

### 1861.  Type 3.  *No wmk. Imperf.*

| 13 | 1 c., deep green .. | 50 |
|---|---|---|
| 14 | 10 c., grey-brown .. | 2.50 |
| 15 | 10 c., brown .. .. | 1.50 |
| 16 | 10 c., pale brown .. | 2.50 |
| 17 | 20 c., blue .. .. | 1.00 |
| 18 | 40 c., carmine-rose .. | 5.00 |
| 19 | 40 c., carmine-vermilion | 7.50 |

The 1 c. and 10 c. were reprinted
1898 upon thin paper; the former is a pale
yellowish green, the latter violet-brown.

### 1863.  Type 3.  *No wmk.*
(*a*) *Perf.* 12½.

| 20 | 1 c., deep green .. | 90 | 1. |
|---|---|---|---|
| 21 | 1 c., deep yell.-green .. | | |
| 22 | 1 c., bright yell.-green . | | |
| 23 | 10 c., brown .. .. | 1.85 | |
| 24 | 20 c., blue .. .. | 1.50 | |
| 25 | 40 c., carmine-rose .. | 3.15 | |

(*b*) *Perf.* 12½ × 13½.

| 26 | 1 c., deep yellow-green | 1.00 |
|---|---|---|
| 27 | 1 c., green .. .. | 75 |
| 28 | 1 c., yellow-green .. | 1.50 |
| 29 | 10 c., grey-brown .. | 1.25 |
| 30 | 10 c., pale grey-brown .. | 1.25 |
| 31 | 10 c., brown .. .. | 1.10 |
| 32 | 20 c., blue .. .. | 62 |
| 33 | 40 c., carmine-rose .. | 2.00 |

**No.** — Un. / Used.

### (c) Perf. 14½.

| No. | | Un. | Used. |
|---|---|---|---|
| 4 | 1 c., deep yellow-green | 2.50 | |
| 5 | 1 c., green .. | 90 | 30 |
| 6 | 1 c., yellow-green .. | 62 | 30 |
| 7 | 10 c., brown .. .. | 75 | 6 |
| 8 | 10 c., pale grey-brown.. | 1.50 | 10 |
| 9 | 20 c., blue .. .. | 1.25 | 4 |
| 0 | 40 c., carmine-rose .. | 3.75 | 12 |

**5**

**1865.** Type 5. *On highly-surfaced paper.*
*Perf.* 14.

| | | Un. | Used. |
|---|---|---|---|
| | 1 fr., lilac .. .. | 2.00 | 1.00 |

This stamp was printed and perforated London; all other Belgian stamps were ·inted in Brussels.

**6 7 8 9**

**1865.** Types 5 to 9.
(a) *Thin paper.* Perf. 14½ × 14.

| | Un. | Used. |
|---|---|---|
| 10 c., grey .. .. | 1.25 | 12 |
| 10 c., slate .. .. | 90 | 8 |
| 20 c., pale blue .. .. | 75 | 4 |
| 20 c., deep blue .. .. | 75 | 4 |
| 30 c., red-brown.. .. | 2.50 | 8 |
| 30 c., brown .. .. | 3.15 | 12 |
| 40 c., carmine .. .. | 2.50 | 12 |
| 1 fr.. lilac .. .. | 15.00 | 3.15 |
| 1 fr., violet .. .. | | |

(b) *Thick paper.* Perf. 15.

| | Un. | Used. |
|---|---|---|
| 10 c., grey .. .. | 90 | 2 |
| 10 c., slate .. .. | 62 | 2 |
| 20 c., pale blue .. .. | 2.50 | 2 |
| 20 c., blue .. .. | 1.85 | 2 |
| 20 c., deep blue .. .. | 1.85 | 8 |
| 20 c., pale ultramarine.. | 1.25 | 2 |
| 20 c., lilac-blue .. .. | 1.00 | 2 |

**No.**

| No. | | Un. | Used. |
|---|---|---|---|
| 58 | 30 c., brown .. .. | 2.10 | 8 |
| 59 | 30 c., pale brown .. | 1.50 | 8 |
| 60 | 30 c., yellow-brown .. | 2.50 | 12 |
| 61 | 40 c., carmine .. .. | 1.00 | 6 |
| 62 | 1 fr., violet .. .. | 5.00 | 1.25 |

Some of the above values have been found imperf. and used.
The 10 c., 30 c., 40 c., and 1 fr. were reprinted in 1898 on thin paper, imperf.

### King Leopold II., 1865.

**10**

**1866.** Type 10. (a) *Thin paper.*
*Perf.* 14½ × 14.

| No. | | Un. | Used. |
|---|---|---|---|
| 63 | 1 c., grey .. .. | 36 | 10 |
| 64 | 1 c., slate .. .. | 25 | 10 |
| 65 | 2 c., pale blue .. .. | 75 | 1.00 |
| 66 | 2 c., blue .. .. | 62 | 1.00 |
| 67 | 5 c., brown .. .. | 75 | 75 |
| 68 | 5 c., red-brown .. | 75 | 75 |

*Varieties, imperf.*

| No. | | Un. | Used. |
|---|---|---|---|
| 69 | 1 c., grey .. .. | 2.50 | |
| 70 | 1 c., slate .. .. | 1.25 | 2.50 |

(b) *Thick paper.* Perf. 15.

| No. | | Un. | Used. |
|---|---|---|---|
| 71 | 1 c., grey .. .. | 25 | 8 |
| 72 | 1 c., slate .. .. | 25 | 16 |
| 73 | 1 c., grey-black .. | 25 | 12 |
| 74 | 1 c., black .. .. | 25 | 8 |
| 75 | 2 c., blue .. .. | 1.50 | 1.25 |
| 76 | 2 c., pale blue .. .. | | |
| 77 | 2 c., pale ultramarine.. | 1.25 | 1.25 |
| 78 | 5 c., brown .. .. | 75 | 62 |
| 79 | 5 c., red-brown.. .. | 1.00 | 75 |

The 1 c. (imperf.) was reprinted in 1898 upon thinner paper than that of the issued stamp.

**11 12**

**1869-80.** Types 11 to 16. (a) *Perf.* 15.

| No. | | Un. | Used. |
|---|---|---|---|
| 80 | 1 c., deep green .. | 4 | 2 |
| 81 | 1 c., green .. .. | 4 | 2 |
| 82 | 1 c., yellow-green .. | 12 | 2 |
| 83 | 1 c., bright green .. | 2 | 2 |
| 84 | 1 c., grey-green .. | 90 | 50 |
| 85 | 2 c., deep blue .. | — | 12 |
| 86 | 2 c., pale blue .. | 50 | |
| 87 | 2 c., lilac-blue .. | 12 | 12 |

C

| No. | | Un. | Used. |
|---|---|---|---|

13

14

15

16

| No. | | Un. | Used. |
|---|---|---|---|
| 88 | 2 c., dull blue .. | 18 | 8 |
| 89 | 2 c., bright ultramarine | 4 | |
| 90 | 5 c., orange-buff .. | 18 | 4 |
| 91 | 5 c., buff .. .. | 4 | 4 |
| 92 | 5 c., orange-brown .. | — | 4 |
| 93 | 8 c., violet .. .. | 50 | 25 |
| 94 | 8 c., lilac .. .. | 50 | 30 |
| 95 | 10 c., deep green .. | 25 | 2 |
| 96 | 10 c., green .. .. | 18 | 2 |
| 97 | 10 c., pale green .. | 25 | 2 |
| 98 | 10 c., dull yellow-green | 25 | 2 |
| 99 | 10 c., bright yell.-green | 36 | 2 |
| 100 | 10 c., sage-green .. | 62 | 8 |
| 101 | 10 c., grey-green .. | 50 | 8 |
| 102 | 20 c., cobalt-blue .. | | |
| 103 | 20 c., lilac-blue.. .. | 1.00 | 2 |
| 104 | 20 c., ultramarine .. | 50 | 2 |
| 105 | 20 c., bright ultramarine | 1.85 | 12 |
| 106 | 20 c., deep dull blue .. | 1.00 | |
| 107 | 30 c., orange-buff .. | 62 | 6 |
| 108 | 30 c., buff .. .. | 62 | 4 |
| 109 | 40 c., pale carmine .. | 1.00 | 12 |
| 110 | 40 c., bright carmine .. | 1.25 | 8 |
| 111 | 40 c., deep flesh .. | 1.25 | 8 |
| 112 | 40 c., rosine .. .. | 1.50 | 6 |
| 113 | 40 c., scarlet .. | | |
| 114 | 1 fr., dull violet .. | 1.10 | |
| 115 | 1 fr., bright lilac .. | 62 | 8 |
| 116 | 1 fr., mauvine .. | — | 16 |

*Variety.*
"BELGIQUE" *for* "BELGIQUE."

| 116a | 1 c., grey-green .. | | |
|---|---|---|---|

(b) *Perf.* 14.

| 117 | 1 c., green .. .. | 36 | 4 |
|---|---|---|---|
| 118 | 1 c., grey-green .. | 8 | 4 |
| 119 | 2 c., dull blue .. .. | — | 4 |
| 120 | 2 c., bright ultramarine | 12 | 2 |
| 121 | 5 c., orange-brown .. | 10 | 2 |
| 122 | 5 c., bright orange .. | — | 2 |
| 123 | 10 c., green .. .. | — | 2 |
| 124 | 10 c., grey-green .. | 18 | 4 |

*Variety.*
"BELGIQUE" *for* "BELGIQUE."

| 124a | 1 c., grey-green | .. | |
|---|---|---|---|

17

18

19

**1875-81.** Types 17 *to* 19.
(a) *Perf.* 15.

| 125 | 25 c., olive-green .. | 90 | 2 |
|---|---|---|---|
| 126 | 25 c., olive-yellow .. | 62 | 2 |
| 127 | 25 c., ochre .. .. | 75 | |
| 128 | 50 c., grey-black .. | 1.25 | 12 |
| 129 | 50 c., slate .. .. | 1.25 | 4 |
| 130 | 50 c., purplish grey .. | 1.25 | 4 |
| 131 | 5 fr., yellow-brown .. | 6.25 | 5.00 |
| 132 | 5 fr., red-brown .. | 4.00 | 5.00 |

(b) *Perf.* 14.

| 133 | 25 c., olive-green .. | 75 | 6 |
|---|---|---|---|
| 134 | 25 c., olive-yellow .. | 75 | 4 |
| 135 | 25 c., ochre .. .. | | |

20

21

22

23

**1883.** Types 20 *to* 23. *Perf.* 14.

| 136 | 10 c., carmine .. .. | 10 | |
|---|---|---|---|
| 137 | 20 c., blue-grey .. .. | 18 | |
| 138 | 25 c., dull blue .. .. | 36 | |
| 139 | 50 c., violet .. .. | 75 | |

| No. | | Un. | Used. |
|---|---|---|---|

24

25

26

27

28

29

30

### 1884-91. Types 11, 24 to 30  Perf. 14.

| | | Un. | Used. |
|---|---|---|---|
| 140 | 1 c., olive-green .. | 4 | 2 |
| 141 | 1 c., grey .. | 2 | 4 |
| 142 | 1 c., iron-grey .. | 2 | 2 |
| 143 | 1 c., grey-black .. | 6 | 2 |
| 143a | 1 c., brown-black .. | 6 | |
| 144 | 2 c., chocolate .. | 2 | 2 |
| 145 | 5 c., blue-green .. | 4 | 2 |
| 146 | 5 c., pale blue-green .. | 12 | 2 |
| 147 | 10 c., carmine on grey .. | 1.85 | 36 |
| 148 | 10 c.    ,,    blue .. | 12 | 2 |
| 149 | 20 c., olive-green .. | 12 | 2 |
| 150 | 25 c., blue on rose | 8 | 2 |
| 151 | 25 c., blue on pale rose .. | 8 | 2 |
| 152 | 35 c., chocolate .. | 25 | 4 |
| 153 | 50 c., bistre on buff .. | 50 | 4 |
| 154 | 50 c., ochre .. .. | 25 | 2 |
| 155 | 1 fr., red-brn. on green | 75 | 6 |
| 156 | 2 fr., lilac on pale lilac | 75 | 8 |

In No. 168 the design is continued below the bottom line of the frame, which is not the case in No. 152.

| No. | | Un. | Used. |
|---|---|---|---|

#### Varieties.
##### (a) "BELGIGUE" for "BELGIQUE."

| 157 | 1 c., olive-green | .. | 4.75 | |
| 158 | 1 c., grey | .. | 3.75 | |

##### (b) "CENTIMF" for "CENTIME."

| 159 | 1 c., grey-black | .. | 36 | |

31

32

### 1893-98. Perf. 14.
Types 31 (1 c. to 5 c.) and 32 (other values).

| | | Un. | Used. |
|---|---|---|---|
| 160 | 1 c., grey .. | 2 | 2 |
| 161 | 1 c., grey-black .. | 2 | 2 |
| 162 | 2 c., yellow . | 2 | 2 |
| 163 | 2 c., brown . | 2 | 2 |
| 164 | 5 c., green . | 2 | 2 |
| 165 | 10 c., red-brown . | 4 | 2 |
| 166 | 20 c., olive-green . | 6 | 2 |
| 167 | 25 c., ultramarine .. | 3 | 2 |
| 168 | 35 c., chocolate .. | 18 | 2 |
| 169 | 35 c., lilac-brown .. | 25 | 2 |
| 169a | 35 c., purple-brown | 10 | |
| 170 | 50 c., bistre-brown | 36 | 6 |
| 171 | 50 c., grey .. .. | 14 | 4 |
| 173 | 1 fr., carmine on green | 45 | 4 |
| 174 | 2 fr., mauve .. .. | 1.50 | 5 |

Variety. No ball to figure "5" in left upper corner.

| 175 | 25 c., ultramarine | .. | | |

33

### 1894. Type 33.  For Antwerp Exhibition. Perf. 14.

| | | Un. | Used. |
|---|---|---|---|
| 176 | 5 c., green on deep rose | 4 | 2 |
| 177 | 5 c., green on pale rose | 2 | |
| 178 | 10 c., carmine on blue .. | 4 | 2 |
| 179 | 25 c., blue on deep rose | 8 | 4 |
| 180 | 25 c., blue on pale rose | 12 | |

| No. | | Un. | Used. |
|---|---|---|---|

13

14

15

16

| 88 | 2 c., dull blue .. | 18 | 8 |
| 89 | 2 c., bright ultramarine | 4 | |
| 90 | 5 c., orange-buff | 18 | 4 |
| 91 | 5 c., buff .. | 4 | 4 |
| 92 | 5 c., orange-brown .. | — | 4 |
| 93 | 8 c., violet .. | 50 | 25 |
| 94 | 8 c., lilac .. | 50 | 30 |
| 95 | 10 c., deep green | 25 | 2 |
| 96 | 10 c., green .. | 18 | 2 |
| 97 | 10 c., pale green | 25 | 2 |
| 98 | 10 c., dull yellow-green | 25 | 2 |
| 99 | 10 c., bright yell.-green | 36 | 2 |
| 100 | 10 c., sage-green | 62 | 8 |
| 101 | 10 c., grey-green | 50 | 8 |
| 102 | 20 c., cobalt-blue | | |
| 103 | 20 c., lilac-blue.. | 1.00 | 2 |
| 104 | 20 c., ultramarine | 50 | 2 |
| 105 | 20 c., bright ultramarine | 1.85 | 12 |
| 106 | 20 c., deep dull blue .. | 1.10 | |
| 107 | 30 c., orange-buff | 62 | 6 |
| 108 | 30 c., buff .. | 62 | 4 |
| 109 | 40 c., pale carmine | 1.00 | 12 |
| 110 | 40 c., bright carmine | 1.25 | 8 |
| 111 | 40 c., deep flesh | 1.25 | 8 |
| 112 | 40 c., rosine .. | 1.50 | 6 |
| 113 | 40 c., scarlet .. | | |
| 114 | 1 fr., dull violet | 1.10 | |
| 115 | 1 fr., bright lilac | 62 | 8 |
| 116 | 1 fr., mauvine | — | 16 |

*Variety.*

"BELGIQUE" *for* "BELGIQUE."

| 116a | 1 c., grey-green | .. | |

(*b*) *Perf.* 14.

| 117 | 1 c., green .. | 36 | 4 |
| 118 | 1 c., grey-green | 8 | 4 |
| 19 | 2 c., dull blue .. | — | 4 |
| 20 | 2 c., bright ultramarine | 12 | 2 |
| 21 | 5 c., orange-brown | 10 | 2 |
| 22 | 5 c., bright orange | — | 2 |
| 23 | 10 c., green .. | — | 2 |
| 24 | 10 c., grey-green | 18 | 4 |

| No. | | Un. | Use. |
|---|---|---|---|

*Variety.*

"BELGIQUE" *for* "BELGIQUE."

| 124a | 1 c., grey-green | .. |

17

18

19

**1875-81.** Types 17 *to* 19.

(*a*) *Perf.* 15.

| 125 | 25 c., olive-green | .. | 90 |
| 126 | 25 c., olive-yellow | .. | 62 |
| 127 | 25 c., ochre .. | .. | 75 |
| 128 | 50 c., grey-black | .. | 1.25 |
| 129 | 50 c., slate .. | .. | 1.25 |
| 130 | 50 c., purplish grey | .. | 1.25 |
| 131 | 5 fr., yellow-brown | .. | 6.25 |
| 132 | 5 fr., red-brown | .. | 4.00 |

(*b*) *Perf.* 14.

| 133 | 25 c., olive-green | .. | 75 |
| 134 | 25 c., olive-yellow | .. | 75 |
| 135 | 25 c., ochre .. | .. | |

20

21

22

23

**1883.** Types 20 *to* 23.  *Perf.* 14.

| 136 | 10 c., carmine .. | .. | 10 |
| 137 | 20 c., blue-grey .. | .. | 18 |
| 138 | 25 c., dull blue .. | .. | 36 |
| 139 | 50 c., violet .. | .. | 75 |

No.      *Un.*   *Used.*     No.      *Un.*   *Used.*

24

25

26

27

28

29

30

### 1884–91. Types 11, 24 *to* 30 *Perf.* 14.

| No. | | Un. | Used. |
|---|---|---|---|
| 140 | 1 c., olive-green .. | 4 | 2 |
| 141 | 1 c., grey .. .. | 2 | 4 |
| 142 | 1 c., iron-grey .. | . 2 | 2 |
| 43 | 1 c., grey-black .. | 6 | 2 |
| 43a | 1 c., brown-black .. | 6 | |
| 44 | 2 c., chocolate .. | 2 | 2 |
| 45 | 5 c., blue-green .. | 4 | 2 |
| 46 | 5 c., pale blue-green .. | 12 | 2 |
| 47 | 10 c., carmine on grey .. | 1.85 | 36 |
| 48 | 10 c.    ,,    blue .. | 12 | 2 |
| 49 | 20 c., olive-green .. | 12 | 2 |
| 50 | 25 c., blue on rose .. | 8 | 2 |
| 51 | 25 c., blue on pale rose .. | 8 | 2 |
| 52 | 35 c., chocolate .. | 25 | 4 |
| 53 | 50 c., bistre on buff .. | 50 | 4 |
| 54 | 50 c., ochre .. .. | 25 | 2 |
| 55 | 1 fr., red-brn. on green | 75 | 6 |
| 56 | 2 fr., lilac on pale lilac | 75 | 8 |

In No. 168 the design is continued below
ie bottom line of the frame, which is not
ie case in No. 152.

### *Varieties.*

(*a*) "BELGIUE" *for* "BELGIQUE."

| No. | | Un. | Used. |
|---|---|---|---|
| 157 | 1 c., olive-green .. | 4.35 | |
| 158 | 1 c., grey .. .. | 3.00 | |

(*b*) "CENTIMF" *for* "CENTIME."

| 159 | 1 c., grey-black .. | 36 | |
|---|---|---|---|

31

32

### 1893–98. *Perf.* 14.

Types 31 (1 c. *to* 5 c.) *and* 32 (*other values*).

| No. | | Un. | Used. |
|---|---|---|---|
| 160 | 1 c., grey .. .. | 2 | 2 |
| 161 | 1 c., grey-black .. | 2 | 2 |
| 162 | 2 c., yellow .. .. | 2 | 2 |
| 163 | 2 c., brown .. .. | 2 | 2 |
| 164 | 5 c., green .. .. | 2 | 2 |
| 165 | 10 c., red-brown .. | 4 | 2 |
| 166 | 20 c., olive-green .. | 6 | 2 |
| 167 | 25 c., ultramarine .. | 8 | 2 |
| 168 | 35 c., chocolate .. | 18 | 2 |
| 169 | 35 c., lilac-brown .. | 25 | 2 |
| 169a | 35 c., purple-brown .. | 10 | |
| 170 | 50 c., bistre-brown .. | 36 | 6 |
| 171 | 50 c., grey .. .. | 14 | 4 |
| 173 | 1 fr., carmine on green | 45 | 4 |
| 174 | 2 fr., mauve .. .. | 1.00 | 8 |

*Variety. No ball to figure* "5" *in left upper corner.*

| 175 | 25 c., ultramarine .. | | |
|---|---|---|---|

33

### 1894. Type 33. *For Antwerp Exhibition.* *Perf.* 14.

| No. | | Un. | Used. |
|---|---|---|---|
| 176 | 5 c., green on deep rose | 4 | 2 |
| 177 | 5 c., green on pale rose | 2 | |
| 178 | 10 c., carmine on blue .. | 4 | 2 |
| 179 | 25 c., blue on deep rose | 8 | 4 |
| 180 | 25 c., blue on pale rose | 12 | |

| No. | | Un. | Used. |
|---|---|---|---|

**34**      **35**

**1896.** Types 34 *and* 35. *For Brussels Exhibition of* 1897. *Perf.* 14.

| | | | Un. | Used |
|---|---|---|---|---|
| 181 | 5 c., deep lilac | .. | 2 | 2 |
| 182 | 10 c., terra-cotta | .. | 4 | 2 |
| 183 | 10 c., brown-lilac | .. | 4 | 4 |

**1900.** Type 32. *Perf.* 14.

| | | | | |
|---|---|---|---|---|
| 184 | 10 c., carmine | .. | 4 | 2 |
| 185 | 1 fr., orange | .. | 30 | 4 |
| 186 | 2 fr., lilac | .. | 60 | 10 |

## RED CROSS SOCIETY OF BELGIUM.

**41**

**1891.** Frank stamp. Type 41.

| | | | | |
|---|---|---|---|---|
| 251 | (No value), red, green, and black | .. | 18 | |

### UNPAID LETTER STAMPS.

**51**

**1870.** Type 51. *Perf.* 15.

| | | | Un. | Used |
|---|---|---|---|---|
| 101 | 10 c., green | .. | 6 | 4 |
| 102 | 20 c., ultramarine | .. | 8 | 4 |

*Variety. Half-stamps used for half value.*

| | | | | |
|---|---|---|---|---|
| 3 | Half of 10 c., green | .. | | |
| 3a | ,, 20 c., ultram. | .. | | |

---

| No. | | | Un. | Used. |
|---|---|---|---|---|

**52**

**1895.** Type 52. *Perf.* 14.

| | | | | |
|---|---|---|---|---|
| 304 | 5 c., green | .. | | 2 |
| 305 | 10 c., orange-brown | .. | | 8 |
| 306 | 20 c., bronze-green | .. | | 6 |
| 307 | 50 c., pale brown | .. | | 25 |
| 308 | 1 fr., carmine | .. | | 62 |

**1900.** *Same type and perf.*

| | | | | |
|---|---|---|---|---|
| 309 | 10 c., carmine | .. | .. | 4 |
| 310 | 50 c., grey | .. | .. | 16 |
| 311 | 1 fr., ochre | .. | .. | 30 |

### PARCEL POST STAMPS.

**71**

**1870-82.** Type 71. *Perf.* 14.

| | | | | |
|---|---|---|---|---|
| 401 | 10 c., claret | .. | .. | 75 |
| 402 | 20 c., blue | .. | .. | 50 |
| 403 | 25 c., green | .. | .. | 62 |
| 404 | 50 c., carmine | .. | .. | 1.50 |
| 405 | 80 c., orange-yellow | .. | .. | 2.50 |
| 406 | 1 fr., grey | .. | .. | 75 |

**72**

**1882-94.** Type 72. *Perf.* 15 × 14½.

| | | | |
|---|---|---|---|
| 407 | 10 c., cinnamon (1888) | .. | 30 |
| 408 | 10 c., pale brown | .. | — |
| 409 | 10 c., Venetian red | .. | 25 |
| 410 | 10 c., red-brown | .. | — |
| 411 | 15 c., slate (1894) | .. | 12 |
| 412 | 20 c., pale greenish blue ('86) | 1.00 | |
| 413 | 20 c., blue | .. | 50 |
| 414 | 20 c., ultramarine | .. | 25 |
| 415 | 25 c., yellow-green (1887) | | 36 |
| 416 | 50 c., carmine (1882) | .. | 90 |
| 417 | 50 c., rosine | .. | — |

| No. | | Un. | Used. |
|---|---|---|---|
| 418 | 50 c., flesh .. .. | — | 2 |
| 419 | 80 c., olive-yellow (1883) | 62 | 25 |
| 420 | 80 c., buff .. .. | 62 | 4 |
| 421 | 80 c., lemon .. .. | 62 | 4 |
| 422 | 1 fr., grey (1888) .. | — | 6 |
| 423 | 1 fr., drab .. .. | — | 25 |
| 424 | 1 fr., purple-brown .. | | |
| 425 | 2 fr., buff (1894) .. | 90 | 12 |

73

**1896-1902.** Type 73. *Numerals in* black
(*except the* 1 fr.). *Wmk. Belgian
Arms in the sheet.* Perf. 15 × 14½.

| 426 | 10 c., chestnut .. .. | 6 | 4 |
|---|---|---|---|
| 427 | 15 c., grey .. .. | 12 | 10 |
| 428 | 20 c., ultramarine .. | 12 | 4 |
| 429 | 25 c., green .. .. | 12 | 8 |
| 429a | 30 c., flesh (1902) .. | 18 | 12 |
| 429b | 40 c., blue-green (1902) | 25 | 16 |
| 430 | 50 c., carmine .. .. | 18 | 2 |
| 431 | 60 c., violet .. .. | 25 | 4 |
| 431a | 70 c., blue (1902) .. | — | 16 |
| 432 | 80 c., olive-yellow .. | 36 | 4 |
| 432a | 90 c., rosine (1902) .. | 50 | 18 |
| 433 | 1 fr., purple-brown .. | 50 | 4 |
| 434 | 2 fr., buff .. .. | — | 12 |

**1902.** Type 73. *No wmk.* Perf.
15½ × 14½. *Centre in second colour.*

| 435 | 10 c., brown and slate .. | 4 | 4 |
|---|---|---|---|
| 436 | 15 c., slate and purple .. | 6 | |
| 437 | 20 c., ultram. and brown | 8 | |
| 438 | 25 c., green & vermilion | 10 | |
| 439 | 30 c., orange and green. | 10 | |
| 440 | 40 c., blue-grn. & purple | 12 | |
| 441 | 50 c., dull pink & purple | 16 | 4 |
| 442 | 60 c., purple & vermilion | 18 | 4 |
| 443 | 70 c., blue ,, | 20 | 6 |
| 444 | 80 c., olive-yell. & purp. | 25 | 6 |
| 445 | 90 c., verm. and green .. | 30 | |

74

Type 74. *Centre and value in second
colour.*

| 446 | 1 fr., brn.-purp. & oran. | 30 | |
|---|---|---|---|

| No. | | Un. | Used. |
|---|---|---|---|
| 447 | 2 fr., bistre & blue-grn. | 62 | |
| 448 | 3 fr., black and ultram. | 90 | |

These stamps, although inscribed "CHE-
MINS DE FER" (Railways), are practically
Parcel Post stamps issued by the Govern-
ment.

## CONGO STATE.

Leopold II., Sovereign.

| 1 | 2 | 3 |

**1885.** Types 1 (5 c. *and* 5 f.), 2, *and* 3.
Perf. 15.

| 2 | 5 c., pale green .. | 6 | 18 |
|---|---|---|---|
| 3 | 10 c., carmine .. .. | 4 | |
| 4 | 10 c., pale carmine .. | 4 | 12 |
| 5 | 25 c., blue .. .. | 50 | 62 |
| 6 | 50 c., sage-green .. | 25 | 50 |
| 7 | 5 f., lilac .. .. | 3.75 | 3.75 |

4

**1887-92.** Type 4. Perf. 15.

| 8 | 5 c., green .. .. | 2 | 6 |
|---|---|---|---|
| 9 | 10 c., carmine .. .. | 4 | 8 |
| 10 | 25 c., blue .. .. | 8 | 12 |
| 11 | 50 c., chocolate .. .. | 36 | 12 |
| 12 | 50 c., grey (1892) .. | 36 | |
| 13 | 5 fr., lilac .. .. | 3.75 | 1.00 |
| 14 | 5 fr., grey (1892) .. | 1.35 | 1.00 |
| 15 | 10 fr., dull orange (1891) | 5.00 | 3.75 |

5

**1894.** Types 5 *to* 10. Perf. 12½ *to* 15.
*Central design in* black.

| 16 | 5 c., blue .. .. | 36 | 36 |
|---|---|---|---|

| No. | Un. | Used. |
|---|---|---|

6

7

8

9

10

| | | Un. | Used. |
|---|---|---|---|
| | 10 c., brown .. .. | 36 | 62 |
| | 25 c., orange .. .. | 10 | 10 |
| | 50 c., green .. .. | 18 | 8 |
| | 1 fr., lilac .. .. | 45 | 16 |
| | 5 fr., lake .. .. | 1.50 | 50 |

| No. | | Un. | Used |
|---|---|---|---|

**1895.** Types **5** *and* **6.**

*Perf.* 15. *Central design in* black.

| 22 | 5 c., red-brown | .. | 4 |
|---|---|---|---|
| 23 | 10 c., greenish blue | .. | 6 |

*Variety.*
*Centre inverted.*

| 24 | 10 c., greenish blue | .. | 12.50 |
|---|---|---|---|

11

12

**1896-98.**

Types **11** *and* **12.** *Central design in* bla⸱⸱

*Perf.* 12¼ *to* 15.

| 25 | 15 c., ochre | .. | .. | 6 |
|---|---|---|---|---|
| 26 | 40 c., green | .. | .. | 12 |

**1900-1.** *Centres in* black.

*Types and perf. as before.*

| 27 | 5 c., green | .. | .. | 2 |
|---|---|---|---|---|
| 28 | 10 c., carmine | .. | .. | 4 |
| 29 | 25 c., blue | .. | .. | 8 |
| 30 | 50 c., olive-green | .. | .. | 16 |
| 31 | 1 fr., lilac-rose .. | .. | 50 |
| 31a | 1 fr., rose | .. | .. | 32 |

PARCEL POST STAMPS.

COLIS POSTAUX

Fr. 3.50

13

**1887.**

Type 1 *or* 4 *surcharged, in* black.
*with* Type 13.

| 101 | 3 f. 50 c. on 5 f., lilac .. | |
|---|---|---|
| 102 | 3 f. 50 c. on 5 f. ,, .. | 3.75 |

| No. | | Un. | Used. |
|---|---|---|---|

*Surcharge inverted.*
103| 3 f. 50 c. on 5 f., lilac ..
104| 3 f. 50 c. on    ,,  ..

*Type 1 surcharged in blue.*
105| 3 f. 50 c. on 5 f., lilac ..

*Surcharge inverted.*
106| 3 f. 50 c. on 5 f., lilac ..

**14**

**1889-92.**
Type 4 *surcharged with* Type 14.
*(a) In blue.*
107| 3 f. 50 c. on 5 f., lilac ..

*Surcharge inverted.*
108| 3 f. 50 c. on 5 f., lilac ..

*(b) In black.*
109| 3 f. 50 c. on 5 f., lilac .. 1.85
110| 3 f. 50 c. on 5 f., grey .. 1.25 1.50

*Surcharge inverted.*
111| 3 f. 50 c. on 5 f., lilac .. — 7.50
112| 3 f. 50 c. on 5 f., grey ..

**15**

**16**

**1898.** Types **15** and **16.**
*Central design in* black.
*Perf.* 13½ *to* 15.
| 3 fr. 50 c., vermilion .. 1.00 | 90 |
| 10 fr., green .. .. 2.50 | 90 |

# BOLIVIA.

**1**

**1866.** Type 1. *Imperf.*

The stamps of 1866 and 1867 were used both for postal and fiscal purposes. The plate of the 5 c. was retouched or recut at least six times. There are 72 varieties on the plate. General varieties: (*a*) Vertical and diagonal lines on globe. (*b*) Diagonal lines only. (*c*) Diagonal and horizontal with faint traces of vertical lines. (*d*) Diagonal and horizontal lines. (*e*) Horizontal lines only. (*f*) No lines except the curved lines forming the shape of the globe.

| 1 | 5 c., yellow-green (*a*) .. | 5.00 | 3.75 |
|---|---|---|---|
| 2 | 5 c., grass-green (*a*) .. | 1.00 | |
| 3 | 5 c., green (*a*) .. | 8 | 25 |
| 4 | 5 c., blue-green (*a*) .. | 1.25 | 50 |
| 5 | 5 c., yellow-green (*b*) .. | | |
| 6 | 5 c., grass-green (*b*) .. | | |
| 7 | 5 c., green (*b*) .. | 12 | |
| 8 | 5 c., blue-green (*b*) .. | 1.25 | |
| 9 | 5 c., green (*c*) .. | | |
| 10 | 5 c., pale green (*d*) .. | 12 | |
| 11 | 5 c., deep ,, (*d*) .. | 12 | 4 |
| 12 | 5 c., pale green (*e*) .. | 8 | 50 |
| 13 | 5 c., deep ,, (*e*) .. | 8 | |
| 14 | 5 c., pale green (*f*) .. | 62 | 62 |
| 15 | 5 c., deep ,, (*f*) .. | 50 | |

In addition to the above, there are other varieties peculiar to certain stamps only on the plate, mostly consisting in the absence or presence of lines other than those usually to be found. Amongst these are varieties in which the letter "A" in "CENTAVOS," "CONTRATOS," or "BOLIVIA" has no bar. In the first two this is not uncommon, in the last it is rare.

**2**     **3**

The 10 c. and 100 c. have the value shown as Type **2**, the 50 c. as Type **3**.
| 16 | 10 c., brown .. .. | 7.50 | 6.25 |
| 17 | 10 c., deep brown .. | 8.75 | 1.85 |

| No. | | Un. | Used. |
|---|---|---|---|
| 18 | 10 c., black-brown | .. | |
| 19 | 10 c., grey-brown | .. | |
| 20 | 50 c., yellow .. | .. | 36 | 2.50 |
| 21 | 50 c., orange-yellow | .. | 62 | 2.50 |
| 22 | 50 c., lemon-yellow | .. | |
| 23 | 100 c., blue .. | .. | 36 | |
| 24 | 100 c., deep blue | .. | 62 | |

There is one plate only of each of these three values. That of the 10 c. has 78 varieties, those of the 50 c. and 100 c. have 30 varieties in each.

**1867.** *Same types. Colours changed. Imperf.*

| 25 | 5 c., lilac .. | .. | 3.75 | 3.75 |
|---|---|---|---|---|
| 26 | 5 c., grey-lilac | .. | 7.50 | 6.25 |
| 27 | 5 c., violet .. | .. | — | 6.25 |
| 28 | 50 c., pale blue.. | .. | — | 20.00 |
| 29 | 50 c., deep ,, .. | .. | — | 20.00 |
| 30 | 100 c., deep green | .. | — | 3.15 |
| 31 | 100 c., pale green | .. | 3.75 | 2.50 |

The 5 c. is from the plate in its last state. The 50 c. and 100 c. are on thinner paper than that of the first issue.

4

**1867.** Type 4. *Nine stars. Perf.* 12.

| 32 | 5 c., green | .. | .. | 25 | 30 |
|---|---|---|---|---|---|
| 33 | 10 c., red | .. | .. | 36 | 12 |
| 34 | 50 c., blue | .. | .. | 36 | |
| 35 | 100 c., orange | .. | .. | 90 | 2.00 |
| 36 | 500 c., black | .. | .. | 16.25 | 25.00 |

5  6

**1871.** Type 5. *Eleven stars. Perf.* 12.

| 37 | 5 c., green | .. | .. | 4 | 6 |
|---|---|---|---|---|---|
| 38 | 10 c., red | .. | .. | 30 | 30 |
| 39 | 50 c., blue | .. | .. | 62 | 75 |
| 40 | 100 c., orange | .. | .. | 25 | |
| 41 | 500 c., black | .. | .. | 37.50 | |

**1878.** Type 6. *Perf.* 12.

| 5 c., ultramarine | .. | .. | 75 | 10 |
|---|---|---|---|---|
| 10 c., orange | .. | .. | 50 | 4 |
| 20 c., green | .. | .. | 90 | 6 |
| 50 c., carmine | .. | .. | — | 36 |

| No. | | Un. | Used |
|---|---|---|---|

7

**1887.** Type 7. *Rouletted.*

| 46 | 1 c., carmine | .. | .. | 2 | |
|---|---|---|---|---|---|
| 47 | 2 c., violet | .. | .. | 2 | |
| 48 | 5 c., blue | .. | .. | 12 | |
| 49 | 10 c., orange | .. | .. | 18 | |

*End of* **1890.** *With 9 stars. Perf.* 12.

| 50 | 1 c., carmine | .. | .. | 2 | |
|---|---|---|---|---|---|
| 51 | 2 c., violet | .. | .. | 6 | |
| 52 | 5 c., blue | .. | .. | 8 | |
| 53 | 10 c., orange | .. | .. | — | |
| 54 | 20 c., green | .. | .. | 45 | |
| 55 | 50 c., red | .. | .. | 80 | |
| 56 | 100 c., yellow | .. | .. | 1.25 | |

**1893.** *Lithographed. Perf.* 11.

| 57 | 1 c. ( 9 stars), rose | .. | 4 | |
|---|---|---|---|---|
| 58 | 2 c. ( 9 ,, ), violet | .. | 6 | |
| 59 | 5 c. (11 ,, ), p. blue.. | | 8 | |
| 60 | 10 c. ( 9 ,, ), orange.. | | 18 | |
| 61 | 20 c. ( 9 ,, ), blue-grn. | | 50 | |

*Variety. Imperf.*

| 62 | 1 c., rose | .. | .. | 1.00 | |
|---|---|---|---|---|---|

8

**1894.** Type 8. *Thin paper. Perf.* 14 *to* 14½.

(Printed by Messrs. Bradbury, Wilkinson, and Co.)

| 63 | 1 c., ochre | .. | .. | 2 | |
|---|---|---|---|---|---|
| 64 | 2 c., orange - vermilion | | 2 | |
| 65 | 5 c., green | .. | .. | 4 | |
| 66 | 10 c., brown | .. | .. | 6 | |
| 67 | 20 c., blue | .. | .. | 25 | |
| 68 | 50 c., rose-lilac | .. | 50 | |
| 69 | 100 c., carmine-red | .. | 90 | |

Type 8. *Thick paper. Perf.* 13.

(Printed in Paris.)

| 63a | 1 c., yellow-ochre | .. | 6 | |
|---|---|---|---|---|
| 64a | 2 c., vermilion | .. | 8 | |

| No. | | | Un. | Used. |
|---|---|---|---|---|
| 65a | 5 c., green | .. .. | 8 | 8 |
| 66a | 10 c., brown | .. | 12 | 12 |
| 67a | 20 c., slate-blue | .. | 12 | 2 |
| 68a | 50 c., rose-lilac | .. | 12 | 10 |
| 69a | 100 c., lake | .. .. | 1.40 | |

*Error of colour.*

| 69b | 10 c., blue | .. | .. ˙ | |

This issue on thick paper was unauthorised, having been made to the order of an official of the Bolivian Government on his own responsibility. Eventually, the stamps having been put in circulation (by irregular and perhaps illegal means), they were recognised by the Government The true history of this issue is involved in great obscurity.

|  |  |
|---|---|
| (Frias.) | (Linares.) |
| 9 | 10 |

|  |  |
|---|---|
| (Murillo.) | (Monteagudo.) |
| 11 | 12 |

**1897.** Types 9 *to* 16. *Perf.* 12.

| 70 | 1 c., olive-green | .. | 4 | |
| 71 | 2 c., vermilion | .. | 4 | 4 |
| 72 | 5 c., blue-green | .. | 6 | 4 |
| 73 | 10 c., brown-purple | .. | 8 | 4 |

|  |  |
|---|---|
| (J. Ballivian.) | (Sucre.) |
| 13 | 14 |

|  |  |
|---|---|
| (Bolivar.) | 16 |
| 15 | |

| 74 | 20 c., rose and black | .. | 12 | 8 |
| 75 | 50 c., orange | .. .. | 30 | |
| 76 | 1 bol., blue | .. | 75 | 1.00 |
| 77 | 2 bol., red, yellow, green, and black | .. .. | 1.50 | |

17

**1899.**

*Stamps of* 1894 (*first set*) *surcharged with* Type 17, *in* violet.

| 78 | 1 c., ochre | .. | .. | 90 | |
| 79 | 2 c., vermilion | .. | .. | | |
| 80 | 5 c., green | .. | .. | 12 | 25 |
| 81 | 10 c., brown | .. | .. | 25 | 12 |
| 82 | 20 c., blue | .. | .. | 1.00 | |

These stamps were used in the northern part of Bolivia during the revolution only.

Illustration No. 17 is that of the forged overprint ; originals differ in the shape of the numerals.

|  |  | *Un.* | *Used.* |
|---|---|---|---|
| No. | | | |

18

**1899.** Type **18.** *Perf.* 11½, 12.

| 85 | 1 c., dull blue | .. | .. | 2 | 2 |
|---|---|---|---|---|---|
| 86 | 2 c., red | .. | .. | 2 | 2 |
| 87 | 5 c., deep green | | | 6 | 4 |
| 87a | 5 c., red (1901) | .. | | 6 | 6 |
| 88 | 10 c., orange | .. | | 10 | 6 |
| 89 | 20 c., rose | | | 18 | 8 |
| 90 | 50 c., bistre-brown | | | 50 | 36 |
| 91 | 1 bol., dull violet | | .. | 1.00 | 1.25 |

(Ballivian.)
19

(Camacho.)
20

(Campero.)
21

(Santa Cruz.)
23

24

**1901-3.** Types **19** *to* **24.** *Perf.* 11½, 12.

| 92 | 1 c., claret | .. | .. | 2 | |
|---|---|---|---|---|---|
| 93 | 2 c., green | .. | .. | 4 | 4 |
| 94 | 5 c., red | .. | .. | 8 | |
| 5 | 10 c., blue | .. | | | |
| 6 | 20 c., purple and black | | 18 | | |
| 7 | 2 bol., brown | .. | .. | 2.00 | |

---

|  |  | *Un.* | *Usel* |
|---|---|---|---|
| No. | | | |

**FISCALS USED FOR POSTAGE.**

51

**1871.** Type **51.** *Perf.* 12.

| 201 | 5 c., black | .. | .. | 2 | |
|---|---|---|---|---|---|
| 202 | 10 c., green | .. | .. | 8 | |
| 203 | 50 c., brown | .. | .. | 36 | |
| 204 | 100 c., red | .. | .. | 75 | |
| 205 | 500 c., blue | .. | .. | 2.50 | |

52

**1893.** Type **52.** *Perf.* 12.

| 205a | 1 c., blue | .. | .. | — | |
|---|---|---|---|---|---|
| 205b | 2 c., ,, | .. | .. | — | |
| 206 | 5 c., ,, | .. | .. | — | |
| 207 | 10 c., dark blue | .. | .. | — | |

53

*Surcharged with* Type **53,** *in red.*

| 208 | 5 c., blue (red) | .. | .. | 36 |
|---|---|---|---|---|

*Surcharge inverted.*

| 209 | 5 c., blue (red) | .. | .. | — |
|---|---|---|---|---|

# TIMBRE
54

*Surcharged with* Type **54,** *in the colou given in brackets.*

| 211 | 1 c., carm. (blue), No. 46 | 18 | |
|---|---|---|---|
| 212 | 1 c. ,, ( ,, ) ,, 50 | 7.50 | |
| 213 | 2 c., violet (red) ,, 47 | 25 | |
| 214 | 2 c. ,, ( ,, ) ,, 51 | | |

| No. | | Un. | Used. |
|---|---|---|---|

**55**

*Surcharged with* Type 55, *in* black.
215|*5 c., blue, No. 48 ..

NOTE.—The stamps formerly given in the Catalogue as "Interior Stamps" are now regarded by the best authorities as bogus.

## BRAZIL.

Dom Pedro II., Emperor of Brazil, 1831–89.

**1**

**1843.** Type 1. *Thick yellowish paper. Imperf.*

| | | Un. | Used. |
|---|---|---|---|
| 1 | 30 (reis), black .. .. | — | 2.50 |
| 2 | 60 ( ,, ) ,, .. .. | 5.00 | 1.00 |
| 3 | 90 ( ,, ) ,, .. .. | 15.00 | 11.25 |

*Thin greyish paper. Imperf.*

| 4 | 30 (reis), black .. .. | — | 2.50 |
|---|---|---|---|
| 5 | 60 ( ,, ) ,, .. .. | 4.50 | 1.25 |
| 6 | 90 ( ,, ) ,, .. .. | — | 10.00 |

**2**

**1844.** Type 2. *Yellowish paper. Imperf.*

| 7 | 10 (reis), black .. .. | 1.85 | 12 |
|---|---|---|---|
| 8 | 30 ,, ,, .. .. | 1.25 | 18 |
| 9 | 60 ,, ,, .. .. | 1.25 | 16 |
| 0 | 90 ,, ,, .. .. | 5.00 | 1.50 |
| 1 | 180 ,, ,, .. .. | — | 22.50 |
| 2 | 300 ,, ,, .. .. | — | 30.00 |
| 3 | 600 ,, ,, .. .. | — | 50.00 |

| No. | | Un. | Used. |
|---|---|---|---|

*Greyish paper. Imperf.*

| 14 | 10 (reis), black .. .. | 90 | 12 |
|---|---|---|---|
| 15 | 30 ( ,, ) ,, .. .. | 62 | 12 |
| 16 | 60 ( ,, ) ,, .. .. | 90 | 25 |
| 17 | 90 ( ,, ) ,, .. .. | 3.75 | 1.50 |
| 18 | 180 ( ,, ) ,, .. .. | — | 22.50 |
| 19 | 300 ( ,, ) ,, .. .. | — | 27.50 |
| 20 | 600 ( ,, ) ,, .. .. | — | 45.00 |

**3**      **4**

**1850.** Type 3.

*Yellowish paper. Imperf.*

| 21 | 10 (reis), black .. .. | 50 | 36 |
|---|---|---|---|
| 22 | 20 ( ,, ) ,, .. .. | 1.25 | 1.00 |
| 23 | 30 ( ,, ) ,, .. .. | 12 | 4 |
| 24 | 60 ( ,, ) ,, .. .. | 12 | 4 |
| 25 | 90 ( ,, ) ,, .. .. | 75 | 8 |
| 26 | 180 ( ,, ) ,, .. .. | 1.25 | 62 |
| 27 | 300 ( ,, ) ,, .. .. | 3.75 | 2.50 |
| 28 | 600 ( ,, ) ,, .. .. | 5.00 | 3.00 |

*Greyish paper. Imperf.*

| 29 | 10 (reis), black .. .. | 36 | 12 |
|---|---|---|---|
| 30 | 20 ( ,, ) ,, .. .. | 1.25 | 1.25 |
| 31 | 30 ( ,, ) ,, .. .. | 8 | 2 |
| 32 | 60 ( ,, ) ,, .. .. | 18 | 6 |
| 33 | 90 ( ,, ) ,, .. .. | 62 | 8 |
| 34 | 180 ( ,, ) ,, .. .. | 1.50 | 1.00 |
| 35 | 300 ( ,, ) ,, .. .. | 2.50 | 90 |
| 36 | 600 ( ,, ) ,, .. .. | 5.00 | 1.50 |

**1854–61.**

Types 3 and 4. *Greyish paper. Imperf.*

| 37 | 10 (reis), sky-blue .. | 18 | 8 |
|---|---|---|---|
| 38 | 10 ( ,, ), deep blue .. | 12 | 8 |
| 39 | 30 ( ,, ), ,, ,, .. | 90 | 90 |
| 40 | 30 ( ,, ), deep ultramar. | 25 | |
| 41 | 280 ( ,, ), vermilion-red. | 5.00 | 2.00 |
| 42 | 430 ( ,, ), deep yellow .. | 6.25 | 5.00 |

**1866.**

*Greyish paper. Perf. 13½.*

| 43 | 10 (reis), black .. .. | | |
|---|---|---|---|
| 44 | 20 ( ,, ) ,, . .. | 12.50 | 12.50 |
| 45 | 30 ( ,, ) ,, .. .. | | |
| 46 | 60 ( ,, ) ,, .. .. | 2.50 | 1.00 |
| 47 | 90 ( ,, ) ,, .. .. | 5.00 | 5.00 |
| 48 | 180 ( ,, ) ,, .. .. | 7.50 | |
| 49 | 300 ( ,, ) ,, .. .. | — | 7.50 |
| 50 | 600 ( ,, ) ,, .. .. | — | 8.75 |
| 51 | 10 ( ,, ), sky-blue .. | 3.00 | |
| 52 | 30 ( ,, ), deep blue .. | | |
| 53 | 280 ( ,, ), vermilion-red. | 15.00 | 15.00 |
| 54 | 430 ( ,, ), deep yellow .. | 17.50 | 17.50 |

No.

5

6

7

8

9

10

11

12

**1866.** Types **5** *to* **11.** *Perf.* **12.**

| No. | | | | Un. | Used |
|---|---|---|---|---|---|
| 55 | 10 reis, | vermilion-red | .. | 2 | 2 |
| 56 | 20 ,, | slate-purple | .. | 62 | 50 |
| 56a | 20 ,, | marone | .. | 62 | 18 |
| 57 | 20 ,, | rosy brown | .. | 4 | 2 |
| 58 | 50 ,, | blue | .. | 8 | 4 |
| 9 | 80 ,, | slate-purple | .. | 36 | 6 |
| 0 | 100 ,, | green | .. | 12 | 2 |
| | 200 ,, | black | .. | 25 | 4 |
| | 500 ,, | orange | .. | 62 | 12 |

No.                                   *Un.   Used*

*The same on blued paper.  Perf.* 12.

| 63 | 10 reis, | vermilion-red | .. | — | 6.25 |
|---|---|---|---|---|---|
| 64 | 20 ,, | rosy brown | .. | 1.25 | 1... |
| 65 | 50 ,, | blue | .. | 1.85 | . |
| 66 | 80 ,, | purple | .. | 3.75 | 1... |
| 67 | 100 ,, | green | .. | | |

**1876.** *The same, but rouletted.*

| 68 | 10 reis, | vermilion-red | .. | 90 | 5. |
|---|---|---|---|---|---|
| 69 | 20 ,, | rosy brown | .. | 50 | : |
| 70 | 50 ,, | blue | .. | 62 | |
| 71 | 80 ,, | slate-purple | .. | 1.25 | . |
| 72 | 100 ,, | green | .. | 25 | : |
| 73 | 200 ,, | black | .. | 50 | 4 |
| 74 | 500 ,, | orange | .. | 1.85 | .: |

*Variety.  Imperf.*

| 74a | 10 reis, | vermilion-red | .. | | |
|---|---|---|---|---|---|

**1878.** Type **12.** *Perf.* 12.

| 75 | 300 r., | green and orange | | 1.50 | :. |
|---|---|---|---|---|---|

13

14

15

16

17

18

**1878–80.** Types **13** *to* **22.** *Rouletted.*

| 77 | 10 reis, | vermilion-red | . | | 2 |
|---|---|---|---|---|---|
| 78 | 20 ,, | mauve | .. | | 4 |
| 79 | 50 ,, | blue | .. | | 8 |
| 80 | 80 ,, | lake-rose | .. | | 36 |
| 81 | 100 ,, | green | .. | | 25 |
| 82 | 200 ,, | black | .. | | 1.85 |

No. | Un. | Used.

No. | Un. | Used.

19

20

27

**1883.** Type **27.** *Perf.* 13 *to* 14.

| | | Un. | Used. |
|---|---|---|---|
| 97 | 100 r., lilac (lined ground) | 36 | 6 |
| 98 | 100 r. „ (solid „ ) | 2.50 | 62 |

21

22

28

29

| | | Un. | Used. |
|---|---|---|---|
| 83 | 260 reis, sepia .. .. | 1.85 | 1.25 |
| 84 | 300 „ bistre-brown.. | 62 | 4 |
| 85 | 700 „ brown-red .. | 2.50 | 1.85 |
| 86 | 1000 „ slate .. .. | 1.85 | 50 |

30

23

24

**1884-85.** Types **23** and **28 to 35.**
*Perf.* 12½ *to* 14.

| | | Un. | Used. |
|---|---|---|---|
| 99 | 10 r., orange-vermilion | 2 | 2 |
| 100 | 20 r., olive-green .. | 8 | 6 |
| 101 | 20 r., bottle-green .. | 2 | 2 |
| 102 | 100 r., lilac .. .. | 12 | 2 |
| 103 | 100 r. „ .. .. | 12 | 2 |

25

26

31

32

**1881-85.** Types **23 to 26.** *Perf.* 13 *to* 14.

| | | Un. | Used. |
|---|---|---|---|
| 87 | 10 r., grey-black .. | 2 | 4 |
| 88 | 50 r., blue (A) .. .. | 18 | 12 |
| 89 | 50 r. „ (B) .. .. | 8 | 4 |
| 90 | 100 r., olive-green (A) .. | 1.00 | 25 |
| 91 | 100 r. „ (B) | 75 | 12 |
| 92 | 100 r. „ (C) .. | 25 | 8 |
| 93 | 200 r., brown-rose (A) .. | 1.50 | 36 |
| 94 | 200 r. „ (B) .. | 75 | 8 |
| 95 | 200 r. „ (C) .. | 5.00 | 10 |
| 96 | 200 r., lilac-rose (C) .. | 62 | 4 |

33

34

Types A of all values have *smaller* heads than the other types. In the 100 r., Type B, there are *vertical* lines in the background, in Type C there are *horizontal* lines. In the 200 r., Type B, there are horizontal lines, which are absent in Type C. The heads in Types B and C also vary.

**1887-88.** *Perf.* 12½ *to* 14.

| | | Un. | Used. |
|---|---|---|---|
| 104 | 50 r., blue .. .. | 6 | 2 |
| 105 | 50 r., milky blue .. | 6 | 2 |
| 106 | 100 r., lilac .. .. | 25 | 2 |
| 107 | 300 r., dull blue .. | 36 | 8. |
| 108 | 500 r., olive-green .. | 50 | 4 |
| 109 | 700 r., violet .. .. | 50 | 25 |

| No. | | Un. | Used. |
|---|---|---|---|

35

| | | | |
|---|---|---|---|
| 110 | 1000 r., blue-grey .. | 2.50 | 18 |
| 111 | 1000 r., blue .. .. | 3.00 | 18 |

*Variety, imperf.*

| | | | |
|---|---|---|---|
| 112 | 100 r., lilac .. .. | 1.00 | 1.25 |

In this issue the 100 r. has the figures of value on *white*, instead of a netted background; the 1,000 r., *blue-grey*, is a clear impression, the 1,000 r., *blue*, is blurred like a lithograph.

## UNITED STATES OF BRAZIL.

36

**1890.** Type **36.** (*a*) *Perf.* 12½ *to* 14.

| | | | |
|---|---|---|---|
| 113 | 20 r., pale blue-green . | 4 | 2 |
| 114 | 20 r. ,, sea-green .. | 50 | 12 |
| 115 | 20 r., emerald-green .. | — | 50 |
| 116 | 50 r., olive-green .. | 4 | 4 |
| 117 | 50 r., bright green .. | 12 | 4 |
| 118 | 50 r., blue-green . .. | 36 | 6 |
| 119 | 50 r., bottle-green .. | 8 | |
| 120 | 50 r., pale sea-green .. | 12 | 6 |
| 121 | 100 r., mauve .. .. | 12 | 2 |
| 122 | 200 r., violet .. .. | 18 | 2 |
| 123 | 300 r., purple-blue .. | 36 | |
| 124 | 300 r., grey .. .. | 36 | 2 |
| 125 | 500 r., olive-buff .. | 1.00 | 8 |
| 126 | 500 r., slate-green .. | 36 | |
| 127 | 500 r., slate-grey .. | 36 | 36 |
| 128 | 700 r., bright brown .. | 36 | 18 |
| 129 | 1000 r., olive-yellow .. | 50 | 18 |

*Design redrawn.*

| | | | |
|---|---|---|---|
| 130 | 100 r., pale mauve .. | 8 | 2 |

(*b*) *Perf.* 11 *to* 11½.

| | | | |
|---|---|---|---|
| 131 | 20 r., pale blue-green . | 8 | 2 |
| 132 | 20 r., emerald-green .. | | |
| 133 | 50 r., olive-green .. | | |
| 134 | 50 r., pale sea-green .. | 25 | |
| 135 | 200 r., violet .. .. | — | 4 |
| '6 | 300 r., slate .. .. | 75 | 8 |
| r | 500 r., olive-buff .. | 75 | 25 |
| ⅼ | 700 r., pale brown .. | 36 | 50 |
| | 000 r., yellow-ochre .. | 90 | 8 |

| No. | | Un. | Used. |
|---|---|---|---|

*Design redrawn.*

| | | | |
|---|---|---|---|
| 140 | 100 r., pale mauve .. | | |

(*c*) *Perf. compound of* (*a*) *and* (*b*).

| | | | |
|---|---|---|---|
| 141 | 20 r., pale sea-green . | — | 1.00 |
| 142 | 20 r., emerald-green . | | |
| 142a | 50 r., pale sea-green . | | |
| 143 | 200 r., violet .. .. | 75 | 1. |
| 143a | 300 r., slate .. .. | | |
| 144 | 300 r., purple-blue .. | 1.00 | 1.0 |
| 144a | 500 r., olive-buff .. | | .7 |
| 144b | 1000 r., yellow-ochre .. | | |

*Design redrawn.*

| | | | |
|---|---|---|---|
| 145 | 100 r., pale mauve .. | — | 1. |

37

**1891.** Type **37.** (*a*) *Perf.* 12½ *to* 14.

| | | | |
|---|---|---|---|
| 146 | 100 r., blue & carmine .. | 6 | |
| 147 | 100 r., ultram. ,, | 6 | |

*Variety. Frame inverted.*

| | | | |
|---|---|---|---|
| 148 | 100 r., blue and carmine | — | 5.0 |
| 149 | 100 r., ultram. ,, | 2.50 | |

*Variety. Pair tête-bêche.*

| | | | |
|---|---|---|---|
| 150 | 100 r., blue and carmine | 5.00 | |

(*b*) *Perf.* 11, 11½.

| | | | |
|---|---|---|---|
| 151 | 100 r., blue and carmine | | |
| 152 | 100 r., ultram. ,, | 75 | |

*Variety. Frame inverted.*

| | | | |
|---|---|---|---|
| 152a | 100 r., blue and carmine | | |
| 152b | 100 r., ultram. ,, .. | 7.50 | |

*Variety. Pair tête-bêche.*

| | | | |
|---|---|---|---|
| 152c | 100 r., blue and carmine | 10.00 | |

(*c*) *Perf. compound of* (*a*) *and* (*b*).

| | | | |
|---|---|---|---|
| 153 | 100 r., blue and carmine | | |
| 154 | 100 r., ultram. ,, | | |

*Variety. Frame inverted.*

| | | | |
|---|---|---|---|
| 154a | 100 r., blue and carmine | | |

*Variety. Pair tête-bêche.*

| | | | |
|---|---|---|---|
| 154b | 100 r., blue and carmine | | |

In the first printing (which was in blue and carmine) there were two stamps inverted; in the attempt to correct these the *heads* only were altered, leaving the *frames* still inverted.

No.

38

**1893.** Type 38. *Same varieties of perf.*

| | | | | Un. | Used. |
|---|---|---|---|---|---|
| 155 | 100 reis, rose (*a*) | | .. | 4 | 2 |
| 156 | 100 ,, ,, (*b*) | | .. | 8 | 2 |
| 157 | 100 ,, ,, (*c*) | | .. | — | 36 |

39     40

41

**1894.** Types 39 (10 r. *to* 50 r.), 40 (100 r. *to* 700 r.), *and* 41 (1000 r. *and* 2000 r.). *Vignette and value in second colour.*

(*a*) *Perf.* 12½ *to* 14.

| | | Un. | Used. |
|---|---|---|---|
| 158 | 10 r., rose and blue .. | 4 | 4 |
| 159 | 20 r., orange-yellow . | | |
| 160 | 50 r., deep & pale blue | 18 | 12 |
| 161 | 100 r., rose and black . | — | 8 |
| 162 | 200 r., orange ,, .. | | |
| 163 | 300 r., green ,, .. | — | 1.25 |
| 163*a* | 500 r., blue and black. | | |
| 164 | 700 r., lilac ,, .. | — | 50 |
| 165 | 1000 r., green & mauve | | |

(*b*) *Perf.* 11, 11½.

| | | Un. | Used. |
|---|---|---|---|
| 166 | 10 r., rose and blue .. | 4 | 2 |
| 167 | 20 r., pale oran. ,, .. | 8 | 2 |
| 168 | 20 r., deep ,, ,, .. | 4 | 2 |
| 169 | 20 r., bt. yellow & blue . | 2 | |
| 170 | 50 r., deep and pale blue | 4 | |
| 171 | 50 r., blue .. .. | 4 | 2 |
| 172 | 100 r., rose and black.. | 6 | 4 |
| 173 | 200 r., orange ,, .. | 8 | 4 |
| 174 | 300 r., green ,, .. | 12 | 2 |
| 175 | 300 r., emerald .. | 12 | 2 |

No.

| | | Un. | Used. |
|---|---|---|---|
| 176 | 500 r., blue and black.. | 62 | 4 |
| 177 | 700 r., lilac ,, .. | 25 | 12 |
| 178 | 1000 r., deep green and mauve .. | 30 | 6 |
| 179 | 1000 r., pale green and mauve .. | 90 | 12 |
| 180 | 2000 r., grey and purple | 1.25 | 36 |

(*c*) *Perf. compound of .*(*a*) *and* (*b*).

| | | Un. | Used. |
|---|---|---|---|
| 181 | 10 r., rose and blue .. | | |
| 182 | 20 r., orange ,, .. | | |
| 182*a* | 50 r., deep & pale blue | | |
| 182*b* | 50 r., blue | | |
| 183 | 100 r., rose and black.. | — | 18 |
| 184 | 200 r., orange ,, .. | 18 | |
| 185 | 300 r., green ,, .. | — | 8 |
| 185*a* | 500 r., blue and black . | 75 | 75 |

*Thick paper.* (*a*) *Perf.* 12½ *to* 14.

| | | Un. | Used. |
|---|---|---|---|
| 185*a* | 50 r., deep and pale blue | | |
| 186 | 100 r., rose and black .. | — | 6 |
| 187 | 200 r., orange ,, .. | — | 62 |
| 188 | 500 r., blue ,, .. | — | 18 |

(*b*) *Perf.* 11, 11½.

| | | Un. | Used. |
|---|---|---|---|
| 189 | 10 r., rose and blue .. | 75 | 25 |
| 190 | 20 r., pale oran. ,, .. | 62 | 6 |
| 191 | 20 r., orange ,, .. | 36 | 6 |
| 191*a* | 50 r., deep & pale blue | | |
| 192 | 100 r., rose and black.. | — | 2 |
| 193 | 200 r., orange ,, .. | — | 18 |
| 194 | 500 r., blue ,, .. | 18 | 6 |
| 194*a* | 1000 r., green and mauve | | |
| 195 | 2000 r., grey and purple | 75 | 8 |

Except in the 10, 100, and 1,000 r. the word "REIS" is on both sides of the figures of value.

In the 100 r. the vignette only (and *not* the value) is in *black*.

**1897.** *Same type, but with* "REIS" *on both sides of figures of value.*

*Perf.* 11 × 11½.

| | | Un. | Used. |
|---|---|---|---|
| 196 | 10 r., rose and blue .. | 2 | 2 |
| 196*a* | 10 r., carmine .. | 2 | 2 |

**1899.** *Same types.*

(i.) *Perf.* 5½ *to* 7.

| | | Un. | Used. |
|---|---|---|---|
| 197 | 10 r., rose and blue .. | 25 | |
| 198 | 20 r., orange ,, .. | 18 | 20 |
| 199 | 20 r., bright yellow and blue .. .. | | |
| 200 | 50 r., blue .. .. | 12 | |
| 201 | 100 r., rose and black .. | 12 | 12 |
| 202 | 200 r., orange ,, .. | 36 | 20 |
| 203 | 300 r., emerald ,, .. | 18 | 8 |

(ii.) *Perf.* 8½ *to* 9½.

| | | Un. | Used. |
|---|---|---|---|
| 203*a* | 10 r., rose and blue.. | — | 18 |
| 203*b* | 20 r., orange ,, .. | — | 25 |
| 203*c* | 50 r., blue .. .. | | |

| No. | | Un. | Used. |
|---|---|---|---|
| 204 | 100 r., rose and black . | 62 | 12 |
| 205 | 200 r., orange ,, . | — | 4 |
| 206 | 300 r., emerald ,, . | — | 8 |
| 206a | 500 r., blue ,, . | | |
| 206b | 1000 r., green & mauve | 36 | 8 |

*Perf. compound of (b) and (ii.).*

| 206c | 20 r., orange & blue.. | | |
| 207 | 200 r., orange & black.. | — | 25 |

**1900.** Types **39** *and* **40.**
(a) *Perf.* 12½ *to* 14.

| 207a | 50 r., green .. .. | | |

(b) *Perf.* 11½.

| 208 | 50 r., green .. .. | 2 | 2 |
| 209 | 100 r., carmine .. | 4 | 2 |
| 210 | 200 r., blue .. .. | 6 | 2 |

*Re-engraved. Perf.* 11½.

| 211 | 100 r., carmine .. .. | | |
| 212 | 200 r., blue .. .. | 12 | 2 |

In the re-engraved 100 r. there is an extra frame outside the lined background of the head, which does not appear on the original type. In the 200 r. the converse is the case.

PROVISIONAL ISSUES.

**42**

**1898.** *Newspaper stamps surcharged.*
(a) Type **51** *surcharged as* Type **42.**

| 220 | 100, in *violet*, on 50 r., dull orange .. .. | 90 | |
| 221 | 200, in *black*, on 100 r., violet .. .. | 8 | 4 |
| 221a | 200, in *black*, on 100 r., mauve .. .. | 8 | 4 |
| 222 | 300, in *violet*, on 200 r., black.. .. .. | 12 | 8 |
| 223 | 500, in *black*, on 300 r., rose-red .. .. | 25 | 18 |
| 224 | 500, in *blue*, on 300 r., rose-red .. .. | 36 | 25 |
| 225 | 700, in *black*, on 500 r., blue-green .. .. | 25 | 25 |
| 226 | 700, in *green*, on 500 r., orange .. .. | 25 | 36 |
| 7 | 1000, in *green*, on 300 r., orange .. .. | 36 | 36 |
| | 1000, in *red*, on 700 r., ultramarine.. .. | 36 | 36 |

| No. | | Un. | Used. |
|---|---|---|---|
| 229 | 2000, in *green*, on 1000 r., orange .. .. | 75 | 75 |
| 230 | 2000, in *green*, on 1000 r., brown .. .. | 75 | |

*Error.*

| 230a | 700, in *green*, on 700 r., orange-yellow .. | | |

The figures of the date vary on the different values. There are two varieties of the 100 on 50 r.—one as above, the second being handstamped in a paler colour. The outline of the surcharge is rather blurred, and the figures of the date are taller and wider spaced.

*Handstamped surcharge.*

| 231 | 100, in *violet*, on 50 r., dull orange .. .. | 1.85 | |

Forgeries of this exist which differ in the shape of the figures.

**43**

(b) Type **51** *surcharged as* Type **43.**
(i.) *Perf.* 12½ *to* 14.

| 232 | 200, in *black*, on 100 r., mauve .. .. | | 8 |
| 232a | 200, in *black*, on 100 r., dull pink .. | | |
| 233 | 200, in *blue*, on 100 r., mauve .. .. | | 12 |

(ii.) *Perf.* 12½ *to* 14, *and* 11, 11½ *compound.*

| 234 | 200, in *blue*, on 100 r., mauve .. .. | 1.85 | |
| 234a | 200, in *black*, on 100 r., mauve .. .. | | |

**44**

(c) Type **53** *surcharged as* Type **44.**
(i.) *Perf.* 11, 11½.

| 235 | 20 r., in *black*, on 10 r., dull blue .. .. | 2 | |
| 235a | 20 r., in *black*, on 10 r., blue .. .. | 4 | |
| 236 | 50 r., in *blue*, on 20 r., emerald-green .. | | |
| 237 | 50 r., in *blue*, on 20 r., pale green .. .. | 4 | |
| 238 | 100 r., in *red*, on 50 r., yellow-green .. | 6 | |

| No. | | Un. | Used. |
|---|---|---|---|

**(ii.)** *Perf. 12½ to 14, compound with 11, 11½.*

| 239 | 20 r., in *black*, on 10 r., dull blue .. .. | 6 | |
| 239a | 50 r., in *blue*, on 20 r., emerald-green .. | | |
| 240 | 100 r., in *red*, on 50 r., yellow-green .. | 25 | |

**1899.**
*Postage stamps surcharged.*

## 1899

## 50 RÉIS

### 45

Type 36 *surcharged as* Type 45, *in magenta.*

**(a)** *Perf. 12½ to 14.*

| 241 | 50 r. on 20 r., green .. | 2 | |
| 242 | 500 r. on 300 r., purple-blue .. .. .. | 12 | 8 |
| 243 | 500 r. on 300 r., grey-blue | 12 | 6 |
| 244 | 700 r. on 500 r., olive-buff | — | 36 |
| 245 | 1000 r. on 700 r., brown | 36 | 25 |
| 246 | 1000 r. on 700 r., pale brn. | 30 | 18 |

**(b)** *Perf. 11, 11½.*

| 247 | 50 r. on 20 r., green .. | 4 | 8 |
| 248 | 100 r. on 50 r. ,, .. | 4 | 4 |
| 249 | 300 r. on 200 r., violet.. | 8 | 8 |
| 250 | 700 r. on 500 r., olive-buff | 25 | 25 |
| 251 | 1000 r. on 700 r., pale brn. | — | 12 |
| 252 | 2000 r. on 1000 r., olive-yell. | 75 | 25 |

46

47

**1900.** Types 46 *to* 49.
*Commemorative stamps. Perf.* 13.

| 253 | 100 r., red .. .. | 6 | |
| 254 | 200 r., blue and yellow.. | 12 | |

| .No. | | Un. | Used. |
|---|---|---|---|

48

49

| 255 | 500 r., blue .. .. | 25 | |
| 256 | 700 r., green .. .. | 25 | |

### NEWSPAPER STAMPS.

51

5a

**FEBRUARY, 1889. Type 51.** *Rouletted.*

| 401 | 10 r., orange-yellow .. | 8 | 10 |
| 402 | 20 r. ,, .. | 12 | 12 |
| 403 | 50 r. ,, .. | 12 | 12 |
| 404 | 100 r. ,, .. | 12 | 12 |
| 405 | 200 r. ,, .. | 18 | 12 |
| 406 | 300 r. ,, .. | 18 | 12 |
| 407 | 500 r. ,, .. | 30 | 25 |
| 408 | 700 r. ,, .. | 75 | |
| 409 | 1000 r. ,, .. | 1.25 | |

**MAY, 1889.** *The same type. Rouletted.*

| 410 | 10 r., slate-green .. | 2 | 2 |
| 411 | 20 r., grass-green .. | 2 | 2 |
| 412 | 50 r., dull orange .. | 2 | 2 |
| 413 | 100 r., violet .. .. | 6 | 6 |
| 414 | 200 r., black .. .. | 12 | 8 |
| 415 | 300 r., rose-red.. .. | 50 | 50 |
| 416 | 500 r., blue-green .. | 62 | 62 |
| 417 | 700 r., ultramarine .. | 1.85 | |
| 418 | 1000 r., brown .. .. | 1.00 | 1.00 |

**1890. Type 5a.** *(a) Perf.* 13, 13½.

| 419 | 10 r., blue .. .. | 4 | 2 |
| 420 | 10 r., ultramarine .. | | |
| 421 | 20 r., emerald-green.. | 8 | 4 |
| 421a | 20 r., deep sea-green | 8 | 4 |
| 422 | 100 r., mauve .. .. | 18 | 8 |
| 422a | 100 r., dull pink .. | | |

**(b)** *Perf.* 11, 11½.

| 423 | 10 r., blue .. .. | — | 25 |
| 424 | 20 r., emerald-green .. | | |
| 425 | 100 r., mauve .. .. | | |

| No. | | Un. | Used. |
|---|---|---|---|

**(c) Perf. compound of (a) and (b).**

| 425a | 20 r., emerald-green .. | | |
| 426 | 100 r., mauve .. .. | 6 | 6 |

In addition to the above varieties, two sets may be made on thin and thick papers.

**53**

**1890–94.** Type 53. (a) Perf. 12½ to 14.

| 427 | 10 r., ultramarine on buff | 2 | 2 |
| 428 | 10 r., blue .. | 4 | 6 |
| 429 | 10 r., ultramarine .. | 6 | 2 |
| 430 | 10 r., dull blue.. | 6 | 2 |
| 431 | 20 r., emerald-green .. | 12 | 2 |
| 431a | 20 r., bright green .. | 12 | 2 |

**(b) Perf. 11, 11½.**

| 432 | 10 r., ultramarine on buff | — | 2 |
| 433 | 10 r., blue .. .. | 8 | 8 |
| 434 | 10 r., ultramarine .. | | |
| 435 | 10 r., dull blue.. .. | 4 | 2 |
| 436 | 20 r., emerald-green .. | 4 | 2 |
| 436a | 50 r., yellow-green .. | | 12 |

**(c) Perf. compound of (a) and (b).**

| 437 | 10 r., ultramarine on buff | 62 | 12 |
| 438 | 10 r., blue .. .. | 25 | 25 |
| 439 | 10 r., ultramarine .. | | |
| 440 | 10 r., dull blue .. .. | 25 | 6 |
| 441 | 20 r., emerald-green .. | 25 | 2 |
| 442 | 50 r., yellow-green .. | 6 | 6 |

**UNPAID LETTER STAMPS.**

**71**

**1889.** Type 71. Rouletted.

| 501 | 10 reis, scarlet | .. | 2 | 2 |
| 502 | 20 ,, ,, | .. | 4 | 2 |
| 503 | 50 ,, ,, | .. | 8 | 4 |
| 504 | 100 ,, ,, | .. | 10 | 6 |
| 505 | 200 ,, ,, | .. | 25 | 12 |
| 506 | 300 ,, ,, | .. | 25 | 18 |
| 507 | 500 ,, ,, | .. | 36 | |
| | 700 ,, ,, | .. | 62 | 62 |
| | 1000 ,, ,, | .. | 90 | 90 |

| No. | | Un. | Used. |
|---|---|---|---|

**1890.** Rouletted.

| 510 | 10 r., orange | .. | 2 | 2 |
| 511 | 20 r., purple-blue | .. | 2 | 2 |
| 512 | 50 r., sage-green | .. | 6 | 4 |
| 513 | 200 r., magenta | .. | 10 | 6 |
| 514 | 300 r., blue-green | .. | 16 | 4 |
| 515 | 500 r., dark drab | .. | 36 | 36 |
| 516 | 700 r., violet | .. | 45 | 45 |
| 517 | 1000 r., deep purple | .. | 50 | 50 |

**72**

**1895–1901.** Type 72.

**(a) Perf. 12½ to 14.**

| 517a | 20 r., light green .. | 4 | |
| 217b | 50 r., yellow-green .. | | |
| 518 | 100 r., brick-red .. | 75 | 75 |
| 519 | 200 r., lilac .. .. | 1.25 | |

**(b) Perf. 11, 11½.**

| 519a | 10 r., deep blue .. | 2 | 2 |
| 519b | 50 r., yellow-green .. | 4 | |
| 520 | 100 r., brick-red .. | 8 | 2 |
| 521 | 200 r., violet .. .. | 12 | 4 |
| 522 | 200 r., lilac .. .. | 8 | 12 |
| 523 | 300 r., pale blue .. | — | 1 |

**(c) Perf. compound of (a) and (b).**

| 523a | 50 r., yellow-green .. | | |
| 524 | 100 r., brick-red .. | | |
| 525 | 300 r., blue .. .. | — | 1.25 |
| 526 | 2000 r., brown .. .. | 75 | |

Sets may be made without stop after "E" in the inscription at foot; the 2000 r. always has stop.

**WAR STAMPS.**

**81**

**1865–70.** Type 81.

Stamps used by soldiers and sailors in the campaign against Paraguay.

**(a) "EXERCITO" (Army).**

| 601 | (No value), blue | .. | |
| 602 | ,, green | .. | |
| 603 | ,, orange | .. | |
| 604 | ,, yellow | .. | |

| No. | | Un. | Used. |
|---|---|---|---|
| | (*b*) "ARMADA" (Navy). | | |
| 651 | (No value) .. .. | | |

The stamps being type-set there are several varieties of setting.

## BULGARIA.

Prince Alexander.

1 2

**1879.** Types 1 and 2 (1 fr.). *Laid paper. Wmk. wavy lines with a double dip forming a lozenge-shaped pattern. One or two rows of lozenges in the sheet have a letter in the middle. Perf.* 14½×15.

The background is in the second colour.

*Value expressed as* САНТИМ. *or* САНТ. (*centimes*), and ФРАНКЬ (*franc*).

| | | | |
|---|---|---|---|
| 1 | 5 c., black & orange .. | 16 | 25 |
| 1a | 5 c. ,, yellow .. | 50 | |
| 2 | 10 c. ,, green .. | 1.50 | 1.50 |
| 3 | 25 c. ,, purple .. | 75 | 36 |
| 4 | 50 c. ,, blue .. | 75 | 1.00 |
| 5 | 1 fr. ,, rose-red .. | 62 | 30 |

**1881.** Type 1. *Same wmk. and perf. Value expressed as* СТОТИНКИ, СТОТИН. *or* СТОТ. (*stotinki*), *and* ЛЕВЬ (*leva*).

| | | | |
|---|---|---|---|
| 6 | 3 st., dull carm. & grey | 6 | 8 |
| 7 | 5 st., black & yellow .. | 10 | 8 |
| 8 | 10 st. ,, green .. | 1.00 | 25 |
| 9 | 15 st., dull carm. & green | 1.00 | 25 |
| 10 | 25 st., black & purple .. | 3.00 | 1.25 |
| 11 | 30 st., blue and brown .. | 1.00 | 8 |

**1882.** *Same wmk. and perf.*

| | | | |
|---|---|---|---|
| 12 | 3 st., pale orange & yell. | 2 | 2 |
| 12a | 3 st., orange & yellow . | 2 | 2 |
| 13 | 5 st., grey-green & pale green .. .. | 8 | 2 |
| 13a | 5 st., deep & pale green | 2 | 2 |
| 14 | 10 st., carmine & pale rose | 4 | 4 |
| 14a | 10 st., scarlet ,, | 8 | 4 |
| 14b | 10 st., red ,, | 8 | 2 |
| 15 | 15 st., deep & pale purple | 6 | 2 |
| 15a | 15 st., lilac-mauve ,, | 8 | 2 |
| 16 | 25 st., blue & pale blue . | 10 | 2 |
| 17 | 30 st., deep violet & green | 18 | 4 |
| 17a | 30 st., purple ,, | 18 | 4 |
| 18 | 50 st., blue & rose .. | 30 | 6 |
| 18a | 50 st. ,, flesh .. | 25 | 6 |

| No. | | Un. | Used. |
|---|---|---|---|
| | *Error of colour.* | | |
| 19 | 5 st., rose & pale rose.. | | |

3 4 5 6

**1884–85.** *Issue of* 1882. (*a*) *Surcharged, in* black, *with* Types 3 *to* 6.

(i.) *Typographed.* (ii.) *Lithographed.*

| | | | |
|---|---|---|---|
| 20 | 3 on 10 stot. (i.) .. | 1.85 | 1.25 |
| 20a | 3 on 10 stot. (ii.) .. | | |
| 21 | 5 on 30 stot. .. .. | | |
| 22 | 50 on 1 fr. .. .. | 1.00 | 1.50 |

(*b*) *Surcharged in* carmine (C) *or* vermilion (V).

| | | | |
|---|---|---|---|
| 23 | 5 on 30 stot. .. .. | 1.00 | 1.00 |
| 24 | 15 on 25 stot. (C) .. | — | 1.25 |
| 24a | 15 on 25 stot. (V) .. | 75 | 50 |

A B

**1885.** Type 1. *Same wmk. and perf.*

| | | | |
|---|---|---|---|
| 25 | 1 st. (A), dull lilac and pale lilac .. .. | 2 | 4 |
| 26 | 2 st. (B), slate-green .. | 2 | 2 |

*a* *b*

**1886.** *Same wmk. and perf. Spelling altered.*

| | | | |
|---|---|---|---|
| 27 | 1 st. (*a*), dull lilac and pale lilac .. .. | 2 | 2 |
| 28 | 2 st. (*b*), slate-green .. | 2 | 2 |
| 29 | 1 leva, black and rose-red (1887) .. .. | 2.50 | 50 |

Prince Ferdinand.

7 8

**1889–90.**

Types 7 *and* 8 (1 l.). *No wmk. Perf.* 13.

| | | | |
|---|---|---|---|
| 30 | 1 st., bright lilac .. | 2 | 2 |
| 30a | 1 st., rosy lilac .. .. | 2 | 2 |

| No. | | Un. | Used. |
|---|---|---|---|
| 31 | 2 st., grey .. .. | 2 | 4 |
| 32 | 3 st., brown .. .. | 2 | 4 |
| 33 | 5 st., green .. .. | 4 | 2 |
| 33a | 5 st., pale green .. | 2 | 2 |
| 34 | 10 st., rose-red .. .. | 4 | 2 |
| 35 | 15 st., orange .. | 8 | 2 |
| 35a | 15 st., brown-orange .. | 12 | 2 |
| 35b | 15 st., yellow .. .. | 8 | 4 |
| 36 | 25 st., blue .. .. | — | 2 |
| 36a | 25 st., greenish blue .. | 8 | 2 |
| 37 | 30 st., dark brown .. | 10 | 2 |
| 38 | 50 st., blue-green .. | 16 | 4 |
| 39 | 1 leva, brick-red .. | 30 | 8 |

## 15

### 9

### 1892.

*Type 7 surcharged, in black, with Type 9.*

| | | | |
|---|---|---|---|
| 40 | 15 on 30 st., dark brown | 8 | 4 |

### 1893.

Type 7. *Perf.* 10½, 11, *and* 11½.

| | | | |
|---|---|---|---|
| 41 | 5 st., green .. .. | — | 25 |
| 42 | 10 st., rose-red .. .. | 12 | 4 |
| 43 | 15 st., orange .. .. | 12 | 2 |
| 44 | 25 st., pale blue .. | 12 | 2 |

*As last, but on very thin paper.*

| | | | |
|---|---|---|---|
| 42a | 10 st., rose-red .. .. | 8 | 4 |

## 01

### 10

### 1895.

*Surcharged, in* red, *with* Type 10.

| | | | |
|---|---|---|---|
| 45 | 11 \|01 on 2 st., slate-green | 2 | 2 |

*Variety. Surcharge inverted.*

| | | | |
|---|---|---|---|
| 46 | 11 \|01 on 2 st., slate-green | 62 | 50 |

### 1896.

Type 8. *No wmk. Perf.* 13.

| | | | |
|---|---|---|---|
| 47 | 2 leva, rose & pale rose | 90 | 75 |
| 48 | 3 ,, black and drab . | 1.25 | 1.25 |

### 11

### 1896.

*Prince Boris Commemoration stamp.*
Type 11. *Perf.* 13.

| | | | |
|---|---|---|---|
| 49 | 1 st., blue-green .. | 4 | 4 |
| 50 | 5 st., ultramarine .. | 6 | 4 |
| 50a | 5 st., dark blue .. | 6 | 4 |
| | 15 st., violet .. .. | 10 | 4 |
| | 15 st., red .. .. | 12 | 6 |

| No. | | Un. | Used. |
|---|---|---|---|

### 10
### —
### 12

### 1901.

*Surcharged as* Type 7, *in* black.

| | | | |
|---|---|---|---|
| 53 | 10 on 50 st., blue-green . | 6 | 8 |
| 54 | 5 on 3 st., brown .. | 4 | |

### 13

### 1901.

*Commemorative issue of the 25th Year of the War of Independence.*

Type 13. *Perf.* 13.

| | | | |
|---|---|---|---|
| 55 | 5 stot., carmine .. | 6 | 6 |
| 56 | 15 stot., green .. .. | 12 | 12 |

### 14      15

### 1902. Types 14 *and* 15. *Perf.* 12½.

Head and figures in upper corners in second colour given.

| | | | |
|---|---|---|---|
| 57 | 1 st., purple and black . | 2 | 2 |
| 58 | 2 st., slate-green & blue | 2 | 2 |
| 59 | 3 st., orange and black | 2 | |
| 60 | 5 st., emerald and brown | 2 | |
| 61 | 10 st., rose & deep brown | 4 | 2 |
| 62 | 15 st., lake and black .. | 6 | |
| 63 | 25 st., blue ,, .. | 8 | 2 |
| 64 | 30 st., grey-brown & blk. | 10 | 4 |
| 65 | 50 st., deep blue & brown | 16 | 16 |
| 66 | 1 l., pale-red and deep green .. .. | 30 | 25 |
| 67 | 2 l., red and black .. | 1.85 | |
| 68 | 2 l., carmine and black | 60 | |
| 69 | 3 l., grey & brown-lake | 80 | |

Un. Used.

No.

16

**1902.** Type 16. *Commemorative stamps.*
*Perf.* 11½.

| | | | |
|--|--|--|--|
| 70 | 5 st., carmine | .. .. | 4 |
| 71 | 10 st., green | .. .. | 4 |
| 72 | 15 st., blue | .. .. | 6 |

**1903.** Type 14 *surcharged with* Type 12,
*but without bar, in* black.

| | | |
|--|--|--|
| 73 | 10 on 15 st., lake & black | 6 |

### UNPAID LETTER STAMPS.

21

**1884.** Type 21. *No wmk.*
*Zigzag perf.* 5½ to 6½.

| | | | | |
|--|--|--|--|--|
| 101 | 5 stot., orange | .. | 62 | 12 |
| 102 | 25 stot., lake | .. | 62 | 25 |
| 102a | 25 ,, crimson-lake.. | | 50 | |
| 103 | 50 ,, blue | .. | 1.00 | 36 |
| 104 | 50 ,, deep blue | .. | 75 | 50 |

**1886.** *The same. Imperf.*

| | | | | |
|--|--|--|--|--|
| 105 | 5 stot., orange | .. | 8 | 12 |
| 105a | 5 ,, orange-verm. | . | 12 | |
| 106 | 25 ,, lake | .. | 18 | 10 |
| 107 | 50 ,, blue | .. | 36 | |
| 108 | 50 ,, deep blue | .. | 36 | 50 |

**1887.** *The same. Perf.* 11½.

| | | | | |
|--|--|--|--|--|
| 109 | 5 stot., orange | .. .. | 50 | 8 |
| 110 | 25 ,, lake | .. .. | 25 | 8 |
| 111 | 50 ,, blue | .. .. | 36 | 45 |
| 112 | 50 ,, deep blue | .. .. | 36 | 36 |

*The same. Perf.* 11½ × *zigzag.*

| | | | | |
|--|--|--|--|--|
| 112a | 25 stot., lake | .. .. | 2.50 | 2.50 |

Un. Used.

No.

22

**1893.** Type 22. Type 21 *re-engraved.*
*Larger lettering. Outlined figure of*
*value. Pelure paper. Perf.* 11½.

| | | | | |
|--|--|--|--|--|
| 113 | 5 stot., orange .. | .. | 50 | 6 |

    a            b

**1895.** Type 21 *redrawn.* (a) *Perf.* 10½.
*Thick paper.*

| | | | | |
|--|--|--|--|--|
| 114 | 5 stot., orange .. | .. | 4 | |
| 115 | 25 ,, dull lake | .. | — | 12 |

*Thin paper.*

| | | | | |
|--|--|--|--|--|
| 115a | 5 stot., orange | .. | 12 | |

(b) *Perf.* 11½.
*Thick paper.*

| | | | | |
|--|--|--|--|--|
| 115b | 5 stot., orange | .. | — | 25 |
| 115c | 25 ,, dull lake | .. | — | 12 |

*Thin paper.*

| | | | |
|--|--|--|--|
| 115d | 5 stot., orange | .. | |

In the original design (a) the lines of
the background are closer together than
in the redrawn design (b), and the semi-
circle of colour over the tablet containing
the figures of value is smaller. These are
the most noticeable points of difference.

**30**

23

**1895.** Type 21 *surcharged, in* red, *with*
Type 23.

| | | | | |
|--|--|--|--|--|
| 116 | 30 on 50 stot., No. 107.. | | 18 | 12 |
| 117 | 30 on 50 ,, ,, 108.. | | 25 | 25 |
| 118 | 30 on 50 ,, ,, 111.. | | 18 | 18 |
| 119 | 30 on 50 ,, ,, 112.. | | 18 | 18 |

| No. | Un. | Used. |
| --- | --- | --- |

**24**

**1896.** Type **24.** *Stamp smaller. Wmk. large Arms in the sheet. Perf.* 13.

| 120| 5 stot., orange .. | .. | 4 | |
| 121| 10 „ violet .. | .. | 4 | |
| 122| 30 „ blue-green | .. | 10 | 6 |
| 123| 30 „ emerald | .. | — | 12 |

**1901.** Type 14 *overprinted with a large* "T" *in a circle. Used provisionally at Rustchuk.*

| 124| 5 st., emerald & brown |
| 125| 10 st., rose & deep brown |
| 126| 30 st., grey-brn. & black |
| 127| 50 st., deep blue & brown |

**25**

**1902.** Type **25.** *Perf.* 11½.

| 128| 5 st., rose-red | .. | .. | 2 | 4 . |
| 129| 10 st., green | .. | .. | 4 | 4 . |
| 130| 30 st., marone | .. | .. | 10 | 4 |
| 131| 50 st., orange | .. | .. | 16 | |

## EASTERN ROUMELIA.

**1**          **2**

**1880(?).** Type **2.** *Various stamps of Turkey surcharged with Type* 1, *in* blue.
    (a) *Stamps of Jan.,* 1876.

| 1 | ½ pias., black and green | 36 | 36 |
| 2 | 2 „ „ red-brown | | |

    (b) *Stamps of April,* 1876.

| 3 | 10 par., black and lilac | |
| | 20 „ „ green | .. |
| | 1 pias. „ yellow | .. |

---

| No. | Un. | Used. |
| --- | --- | --- |

**3**

(c) Type **3.** *Stamps of Sept.,* 1876.

| 6 | 10 par., black and rose . | | |
| 6a | 1 pias. „ blue . | | |
| 7 | 20 par., plum and green | 50 | 6? |
| 8 | 2 pias., black and buff . | — | 3.co |
| 9 | 5 „ rose and blue.. | 12.50 | |

**4**

No. 6 *surcharged with* Type **4,** *in addition, in* blue.

| 10 | 10 par., black and rose . | 1.25 | 5? |

*Surcharged with* Type **4** *alone, in* blue.

| 11 | 10 par., black and rose . | 7.50 | |

Some authorities declare that this is only a proof or essay.

**5**

**1881.** Type **5.** *Perf.* 13½.

| 12 | 5 par., black and olive . | 12 | |
| 13 | 10 „ „ green | 8 | 1? |
| 14 | 20 „ „ rose . | 8 | 12 |
| 15 | 1 pias. „ blue . | 10 | 1c |
| 16 | 1 „ „ gy.-blue | 12 | |
| 17 | 5 „ red and blue .. | 4.50 | |

**1884.** *Perf.* 11½.

| 18 | 5 par., violet & lilac .. | 6 | 6 |
| 19 | 10 „ green & pale green | 6 | 25 |

20 p., rose, 1 p., blue, and 5 p., brown, were, it is believed, never issued.

No.

|  | | Un. | Used. |
|---|---|---|---|

*Perf.* 13½.

| 23 | 5 p., violet and lilac .. | 8 | |
| 24 | 10 p., green & pale green | | |

The stamps for Eastern Roumelia were superseded by those for South Bulgaria.

## SOUTH BULGARIA.

1    2

**22 SEPTEMBER, 1885.**

Type 1. *Stamps of Eastern Roumelia overprinted with* Type 2.

A. *Height of lion from end of claw on left leg to top of crown,* 14 mm.

(i.) Stamps of 1881.

(*a*) *In* blue.

| 1 | 5 par., black and olive . | |
| 2 | 10 ,, ,, green | |
| 3 | 20 ,, ,, rose . | |
| 4 | 1 pias. ,, blue . | 75 |

(*b*) *In* black.

| 4a| 1 pias., black and blue. | 25 | 50 |

(ii.) Stamps of 1884.

(*a*) *In* blue.

| 5 | 5 par., violet and lilac . | 8 | 18 |
| 6 | 10 ,, green & pale grn. | 6 | |
| 7 | 20 ,, rose & pale rose. | | |

(*b*) *In* black.

| 8 | 5 par., violet and lilac . | |
| 9 | 10 ,, green & pale grn. | 25 |
| 10 | 20 ,, rose & pale rose . | |

Many of the above are known with the overprint double or inverted.

B. *Height of lion,* 15 *to* 16 mm.

(i.) Stamps of 1881.

(*a*) *In* blue.

| 11 | 5 par., black and olive . | | |
| 12 | 20 ,, ,, rose.. | — | 1.25 |
| 13 | 1 pias. ,, blue . | 25 | |
| 14 | 5 ,, red and blue .. | | |

(*b*) *In* black.

| 15 | 20 par., black and rose . | — | 1.85 |
| 16 | 1 pias. ,, blue . | 25 | 36 |
| 17 | 5 ,, red and blue .. | 5.00 | |

(ii.) Stamps of 1885.

(*a*) *In* blue.

| 18 | 5 par., violet and lilac . | 1.25 |
| 19 | 10 ,, green & pale grn. | |
| 20 | 20 ,, rose & pale rose | 3.75 |

No.

|  | | Un. | Used. |
|---|---|---|---|

(*b*) *In* black.

| 21 | 5 par., violet and lilac . | 18 |
| 22 | 10 ,, green & pale grn. | 36 |
| 23 | 20 ,, rose & pale rose | 25 |

Many of the above are found with inverted or double overprint.

3

**24 SEPTEMBER, 1885.**

*The same issues overprinted with* Type 3.

(i.) Stamps of 1881.

(*a*) *In* blue.

| 24 | 1 pias., black and blue. | 1.00 |

(*b*) *In* black.

| 25 | 5 par., black and olive . | 7.50 | |
| 26 | 20 ,, ,, rose.. | 1.00 | 50 |
| 27 | 1 pias. ,, blue.. | 1.25 | 1.25 |
| 28 | 5 ,, red and blue .. | | |

(ii.) Stamps of 1885.

(*a*) *In* blue.

| 29 | 5 par., violet and lilac . | 3.15 |
| 30 | 10 ,, grn. & pale grn. | 3.75 |

(*b*) *In* black.

| 31 | 5 par., violet and lilac . | 8 | 12 |
| 32 | 10 ,, grn. & pale grn. | 16 | 18 |
| 33 | 20 ,, rose & pale rose | 25 | |

*With a different handstamp.*
*The second character in the word at the top is oval and not circular.*

(i.) Stamps of 1881.

(*a*) *In* blue.

| 34 | 5 pias., red and blue .. | |

(*b*) *In* black.

| 35 | 5 par., black and green | |
| 36 | 20 ,, ,, rose.. | |
| 37 | 1 pias. ,, blue.. | |
| 38 | 5 ,, red and blue .. | 7.50 |

(ii.) Stamps of 1885.

(*a*) *In* blue.

| 39 | 10 par., grn. & pale grn. | |
| 40 | 20 ,, rose & pale rose . | |

(*b*) *In* black.

| 41 | 5 par., violet and lilac . | 50 | 75 |
| 42 | 10 ,, grn. & pale grn. | 1.25 | |
| 43 | 20 ,, rose & pale rose | 5.00 | |

Many of the above are known with double or inverted overprint.

In 1886 the stamps of Bulgaria replaced those for South Bulgaria.

| No. | | Un. | Used. |
|---|---|---|---|

## CHILI.

The head on all stamps of Chili is that of Christopher Columbus.

**(Engraved and printed by Messrs. Perkins Bacon and Co.)**

1 JULY, **1853.** Type 1. Wmk. Type 2 *or* 3. *Imperf.*

| 1 | 5 c., brown-red on *blued* | | |
|---|---|---|---|
| 2 | 10 c., deep bright blue . | — | 1.25 |

The wmk. " 5 " is about 9 mm. high and 7 mm. wide, and has a sloping neck ; the " 10 " is about 8½ mm. high and 11 mm. wide, and the figures are narrow.

### (Printed in Chili.)

JUNE (?), **1854.** *Same type and wmk. Lithographed. Imperf.*

| 3 | 5 c., brown | .. | .. |
|---|---|---|---|
| 4 | 5 c., orange-brown | .. | |

AUG. *and* OCT., **1854.** *Same type and wmks., printed from the engraved plates.*

| 5 | 5 c., burnt sienna | .. | 1.85 |
|---|---|---|---|
| 6 | 5 c., pale reddish brown | — | 90 |
| 7 | 5 c., deep „ „ | — | 1.00 |
| 8 | 10 c., blue | .. | 90 |
| 9 | 10 c., sky-blue .. | .. | 62 |
| 10 | 10 c., deep blue .. | .. | — | 90 |

**4**

(Engraved and printed by Messrs. Perkins Bacon and Co. from a new plate.)

JAN., **1855.** Type 1. *Wmk.* Type 4. Blued *paper. Imperf.*

| 11 | 5 c., brownish red | .. | 12.50 | 18 |
|---|---|---|---|---|

The wmk. " 5 " is 10 to 10½ mm. high and 8 to 8½ mm. wide, and has an upright neck.

### (Printed in Chili.)

**1857-65.** Type 1. *Wmks.* Type 2 *or* 3.

| 12 | 5 c., dull reddish brown | | — | 62 |
|---|---|---|---|---|
| 13 | 5 c., orange | .. | — | 1.00 |
| 14 | 5 c., rose-red .. | .. | 2.50 | 6 |
| | 5 c., carmine-red | .. | — | 12 |
| | 10 c., dark blue .. | .. | 17.50 | 1.25 |

| No. | | Un. | Used. |
|---|---|---|---|

**5**  **6**  **7**

(Engraved and printed by Messrs. Perkins Bacon and Co.)

1 JAN., **1862.** Type 1. *Wmks.* Types 5, 6, *or* 7.

| 17 | 1 c., lemon-yell., p. 12 c. | 1.25 | 50 |
|---|---|---|---|
| 18 | 10 c., deep bright blue . | 2.10 | ε |
| 18a | 20 c., dark green | .. | 3.00 | 2.10 |

The wmk. " 10 " is about 9 mm. high and 12 mm. wide, and the middle parts of the figures are broader.

*Varieties.* (i.) Blued *paper.*

| 18b | 10 c., deep bright blue.. | — | 1.85 |
|---|---|---|---|

(ii.) *Error. Wmk.* " 20 " *instead of* " 10."

| 18c | 10 c., deep bright blue.. | | |
|---|---|---|---|

**8**

### (Printed in Chili.)

**1865.** Type 1. *Wmk.* Type 8.

| 18d | 5 c., rose-red .. | .. | 3.00 | 12 |
|---|---|---|---|---|
| 18e | 5 c., pale red .. | .. | 3.75 | ε |
| 18f | 5 c., carmine-red . | .. | — | 12 |

The wmk. " 5 " is about 12 mm. high and 7 mm. wide, and has a long upright neck.

*Variety. Printed on both sides.*

| 18g | 5 c., carmine-red | .. | |
|---|---|---|---|

The specimens of 5 c. found on ribbed paper without wmk., or on paper wmk. part of the Chilian Arms, are proofs.

**9**

**1867.** Type 9. *Perf.* 12.

| 19 | 1 c., orange-yellow | .. | 36 | 16 |
|---|---|---|---|---|
| 20 | 1 c., orange | .. | 18 | ε |
| 21 | 2 c., grey-black | .. | 12 | |
| 22 | 2 c., black | .. | 12 | ε |

| No. | | | | Un. | Used. |
|---|---|---|---|---|---|
| 23 | 5 c., pale red | .. | .. | — | 8 |
| 24 | 5 c., deep red | .. | .. | 25 | 2 |
| 25 | 10 c., blue | .. | .. | 25 | 4 |
| 26 | 10 c., deep blue | .. | | 25 | 4 |
| 27 | 20 c., green, p. 4 c. | | .. | 90 | 8 |

10

11

12

**1877-78.** Types 10 (1, 2, 10, *and* 20 c.), 11, *and* 12. *Rouletted.*

| No. | | | | Un. | Used. |
|---|---|---|---|---|---|
| 28 | 1 c., slate | .. | .. | 2 | 4 |
| 29 | 2 c., orange | .. | .. | 4 | 4 |
| 30 | 5 c., lake | .. | .. | 25 | 2 |
| 31 | 10 c., blue | .. | .. | 50 | 6 |
| 32 | 20 c., green | .. | .. | 1.00 | 8 |
| 33 | 50 c., lilac | .. | .. | 1.50 | 12 |
| 34 | 50 c., purple | .. | .. | 36 | 6 |

13

14

*a*

*b*

**1881-86.** Types 12 (10 *and* 20 c.), 13 (1 *and* 2 c.), *and* 14. *Rouletted.*

| No. | | | | Un. | Used. |
|---|---|---|---|---|---|
| 35 | 1 c., green (*a*) | .. | .. | 2 | 2 |
| 36 | 2 c., pale carmine (*b*) | .. | | 6 | 2 |
| 36*a* | 2 c., bright ,, (*b*) | .. | | — | 2 |
| 37 | 5 c., dull rose | .. | .. | 36 | 2 |
| 38 | 5 c., ultramarine ('83) | .. | | 8 | 2 |
| 39 | 10 c., yellow (1885) | .. | | 62 | 4 |
| 40 | 10 c., orange | .. | .. | 8 | 2 |
| 41 | 20 c., slate-grey (1886) | .. | | 18 | 2 |

No.

15

**1892-1900.** Types 12 *and* 15 (1 p.). *Rouletted.*

| No. | | | | Un. | Used. |
|---|---|---|---|---|---|
| 42 | 15 c., deep green | .. | | 12 | 4 |
| 43 | 25 c., red-brown | .. | | 18 | 4 |
| 43*a* | 30 c., rose-carmine | .. | | 50 | 12 |
| 44 | 1 p., black and brown | .. | | 50 | 18 |

*c*

*d*

**1894.** Type 13. *Re-engraved. Scrolls removed from each side of the base of figure. Rouletted.*

| No. | | | | Un. | Used. |
|---|---|---|---|---|---|
| 45 | 1 c., green (*c*) | .. | .. | 6 | 2 |
| 46 | 2 c., crimson-lake (*d*) | .. | | 6 | 2 |

16

**1900-1.** Type 16. *Rouletted.*

| No. | | | | Un. | Used. |
|---|---|---|---|---|---|
| 47 | 1 c., green | .. | .. | 4 | 2 |
| 48 | 2 c., lake | .. | .. | 12 | 2 |
| 49 | 5 c., blue | .. | .. | 16 | 4 |
| 50 | 10 c., violet | .. | .. | 50 | 6 |
| 50*a* | 20 c., grey | .. | .. | 50 | 25 |
| 51 | 30 c., orange-red | .. | | 25 | 12 |
| 52 | 50 c., red-brown | .. | | 50 | 12 |

17

**1900.**

*Surcharged with* Type 17, *in* black.

| No. | Type. | | | | Un. | Used. |
|---|---|---|---|---|---|---|
| 53 | 14 | 5 on 30 c., carmine | | | 8 | 4 |

|  |  | Un. | Used. |
|---|---|---|---|
| No. Type. | | | |

*Surcharge inverted.*
54 | 14 | 5 on 30 c., carmine   1.50

*Double surcharge.*
54a| 14 | 5 on 30 c., carmine

**1901.** Type 16. *Rouletted. Die recut.*
*Background all crossed lines.*

| 55 | 1 c., green | .. | .. | 4 | 4 |
|---|---|---|---|---|---|
| 56 | 2 c., lake | .. | .. | 6 | 4 |
| 57 | 5 c., blue | .. | .. | — | 4 |
| 58 | 10 c., violet | .. | .. | 12 | 12 |

18

**1901-2.** Type 18. *Perf.* 12.

| 59 | 1 c., green | .. | .. | 2 | 2 |
|---|---|---|---|---|---|
| 60 | 2 c., carmine | .. | .. | 2 | 2 |
| 61 | 5 c., blue | .. | .. | 12 | 2 |

*Head and figures of value in* black.

| 61a | 10 c., carmine and black | 8 | 2 |
|---|---|---|---|
| 62 | 30 c., violet   ,, | 25 | 12 |
| 63 | 50 c., red   ,, | 36 | 25 |

**1903.** *Surcharged " Diez Centavos,"*
*in* blue.
64 | 10 c. on 30 c. (No. 51) ..   18

**FISCALS USED FOR POSTAGE.**

21      22

**1880.** Type 21. *Perf.* 12.

| 101 | 1 c., red | .. | .. | 8 | 8 |
|---|---|---|---|---|---|
| 102 | 2 c., brown | .. | .. | — | 8 |
| 103 | 5 c., blue | .. | .. | — | 4 |
| 104 | 10 c., green | .. | .. | — | 8 |
| 105 | 20 c., orange | .. | .. | 50 | 1.25 |
| 106 | 1 p.   ,, | .. | .. | — | 62 |
| 107 | 2 p., green | .. | .. | — | 1.85 |
| 108 | 5 p., brown | .. | .. | | |
| 100 | 10 p., blue | .. | .. | — | 3.75 |

**1900.** Type 22.

| - | c., vermilion | .. | .. | 2 | |
|---|---|---|---|---|---|
| | c., blue | .. | .. | — | 12 |

|  | Un. | Used. |
|---|---|---|
| No. | | |

**TELEGRAPH STAMPS USED FOR POSTAGE.**
**1891.** *Perf.* 12.

| 151 | 2 c., yell.-brown, T.O 2 c. | — | 25 |
|---|---|---|---|
| 152 | 10 c., olive-green, T.O. 2 c. | — | 25 |
| 153 | 20 c., blue, T.O. 2 c. | .. | — | 25 |

**RETURN RECEIPT STAMP.**

41

**1894.** *Perf.*
161 | 41 | 5 c., chocolate   ..

**1898.** *Inscription altered.*
162 | 41 | 5 c., black ..   ..

**UNPAID LETTER STAMPS.**

51    52    53

**1888.** Type 51.
201 | 10 c., black   ..   ..

**1895.** Types 52 *and* 53 (10 c.). *Perf.* 13.

| 202 | 2 c., black on yellow | .. | — | 8 |
|---|---|---|---|---|
| 203 | 4 c. | ,, | ,, | — | 36 |
| 204 | 6 c. | ,, | ,, | .. | — | 50 |
| 205 | 8 c. | ,, | ,, | .. | — | 50 |
| 206 | 10 c. | ,, | ,, | .. | — | 6. |
| 207 | 16 c. | ,, | ,, | .. | — | 75 |
| 208 | 20 c. | ,, | ,, | .. | — | 1.00 |
| 209 | 30 c. | ,, | ,, | .. | — | 1.25 |
| 210 | 40 c. | ,, | ,, | .. | — | 5.00 |

54

**1895.** Type 54. *Perf.* 11.

| 211 | 1 c., rose on yellow | .. | 12 | 4 |
|---|---|---|---|---|
| 212 | 2 c. | ,, | ,, | .. | — | 4 |

| No. | | | | Un. | Used. |
|---|---|---|---|---|---|
| 213 | 4 c., rose on yellow | .. | | — | 8 |
| 214 | 6 c. | ,, | ,, | .. | — | 12 |
| 215 | 8 c. | ,, | ,, | .. | — | 12 |
| 216 | 10 c. | ,, | ,, | .. | — | 16 |
| 217 | 20 c. | ,, | ,, | .. | — | 25 |
| 218 | 40 c. | ,, | ,, | .. | — | 50 |
| 219 | 50 c. | ,, | ,, | .. | — | 90 |
| 220 | 60 c. | ,, | ,, | .. | — | 90 |
| 221 | 80 c. | ,, | ,, | .. | — | 1.50 |
| 222 | 1 p. | ,, | ,, | .. | 3.75 | 1.50 |

**1896.** *Same type. Perf.* 13½.

| 223 | 1 c., carmine on lemon | 25 | 8 |
|---|---|---|---|
| 224 | 2 c. | ,, | ,, | 8 | 4 |
| 225 | 4 c. | ,, | ,, | 12 | 8 |
| 226 | 6 c. | ,, | ,, | 36 | 16 |
| 227 | 8 c. | ,, | ,, | 45 | 18 |
| 228 | 10 c. | ,, | ,, | 20 | 16 |
| 229 | 20 c. | ,, | ,, | 90 | 75 |
| 230 | 40 c. | ,, | ,, | — | 7.50 |
| 231 | 50 c. | ,, | ,, | 15.00 | 7.50 |
| 232 | 60 c. | ,, | ,, | 15.00 | 7.50 |
| 233 | 80 c. | ,, | ,, | 15.00 | 7.50 |
| 234 | 100 c. | ,, | ,, | — | 10.00 |

55

**1898.** Type **55.** *Perf.* 13.

| 235 | 1 c., rose | .. | .. | 2 | |
|---|---|---|---|---|---|
| 236 | 2 c. | ,, | .. | .. | 4 | |
| 237 | 4 c. | ,, | .. | .. | 4 | 4 |
| 238 | 10 c. | ,, | .. | .. | 8 | |
| 239 | 20 c. | ,, | .. | .. | 16 | |

# CHINA.

IMPERIAL CUSTOMS POST.

I

**1878.** Type **1.** *No wmk. Perf.* 12½.
*(a) Thin paper.*

| 1 | 1 cand., yellow-green.. | 1.85 | 1.25 |
|---|---|---|---|
| 1a | 1 | ,, | green .. | .. | 1.25 | 1.25 |
| 2 | 3 | ,, | vermilion | .. | 50 | 50 |
| 3 | 5 | ,, | orange | .. | 90 | 36 |
| 3a | 5 | ,, | pale orange | .. | 1.00 | 36 |

*(b) Thicker paper.*

| 4 | 1 cand., green .. | .. | 50 | 62 |
|---|---|---|---|---|
| 5 | 1 | ,, | deep green | .. | 1.25 | 90 |
| 6 | 3 | ,, | brown-red | | 90 | 36 |
| 6a | 3 | ,, | vermilion | .. | 3.15 | 25 |
| 7 | 5 | ,, | yellow | .. | 75 | 36 |

2   3

**1886.**

Type **2.** *Wmk.* Type 3.

*Perf.* 12.

| 8 | 1 cand., deep green | .. | 8 | 4 |
|---|---|---|---|---|
| 9 | 1 | ,, | pale green | .. | 4 | 4 |
| 9a | 1 | ,, | green .. | .. | 8 | |
| 10 | 3 | ,, | mauve | .. | 12 | 4 |
| 10a | 3 | ,, | pale mauve | .. | 6 | 6 |
| 10b | 3 | ,, | deep mauve | .. | | |
| 10c | 5 | ,, | bistre-brown.. | 50 | |
| 11 | 5 | ,, | bistre .. | .. | 8 | 18 |
| 12 | 5 | ,, | olive-yellow | .. | 12 | 18 |

Nos. 8 and 9 have a yellow background.

4   5

6

**1895.**

Types **4** *to* **12.** *Same wmk. Perf.* 12.

| 13 | 1 c., orange-vermilion.. | 6 | 8 |
|---|---|---|---|
| 14 | 2 c., green | .. | .. | 10 | 12 |
| 15 | 3 c., orange-yellow | .. | 6 | 10 |

| No. | | *Un.* | *Used.* |
|---|---|---|---|

**7**

**8**      **9**

| 16 | 4 c., rose .. .. | 12 | 18 |
| 17 | 5 c., orange-yellow | 12 | 18 |
| 18 | 6 c., brown.. .. | 16 | 25 |

**10**

**11**

**12**

| 19 | 9 c., green .. .. | 18 | 18 |
| 20 | 12 c., orange .. .. | 50 | 62 |
| 21 | 24 c., rose-carmine .. | 90 | 50 |

*Variety. Tête-bêche.*

| 10 | 9 c., green (pair) .. | 7.50 | |

---

| No. | | *Un.* | *Used.* |
|---|---|---|---|

IMPERIAL POST.

壹洋暫
分銀作

**1**

**cent.**

**13**

**1897.**

*Issue of* 1895 *surcharged in* black.

(i.) *Small figures as* Type 13 (January).

*Surcharge* 17 *to* 17½ mm. *high.*

| 23 | ½ c. on 3 c., orange .. | 4 | 6 |
| 23a | ½ c. on 3 c., oran.-yellow | 4 | 6 |
| 23b | ½ c. on 3 c., ochre .. | 6 | |
| 24 | 1 c. on 1 c., vermilion.. | 8 | 8 |
| 25 | 2 c. on 2 c., green .. | 10 | 4 |
| 26 | 4 c. on 4 c., rose .. | 12 | 8 |
| 27 | 5 c. on 5 c., orange .. | 8 | 8 |
| 27a | 5 c. on 5 c., yellow .. | | |
| 28 | 8 c. on 6 c., brown .. | 8 | 12 |
| 29 | 8 c. on 6 c., red-brown. | 12 | 12 |
| 30 | 10 c. on 6 c., brown .. | 50 | 50 |
| 30a | 10 c. on 6 c., red-brown. | 50 | 50 |
| 31 | 10 c. on 9 c., green .. | 62 | 62 |
| 32 | 10 c. on 12 c., orange .. | 62 | 75 |
| 33 | 30 c. on 24 c., carmine.. | 1.10 | 50 |

*Error.* "2" *and fraction bar of* "½" *omitted.*

| 33a | 1 c. on 3 c., orange .. | | |

*Variety. Surcharge inverted.*

| 33b | 1 c. on 1 c., vermilion.. | | |

*Variety. Double surcharge.*

| 33c | ½ c. on 3 c., orange .. | | |
| 33d | 4 c. on 4 c., rose .. | | |
| 33e | 10 c. on 9 c., green .. | | |
| 33f | 2 c. on 2 c.    ,, | | |

壹洋暫      貳洋暫
分銀作      分銀作

**1**          **2**

**cent.**      **cents.**

**14**        **15**

(ii.) *Larger figures as* Types 14 *and* 15 (February).

(a) *Surcharge* 17 *to* 17½ mm. *high.*

| 34 | ½ c. on 3 c., yellow .. | 2 | |
| 34a | ½ c. on 3 c., orange .. | | |

| No. | | Un. | Used. |
|---|---|---|---|
| 35 | 1 c. on 1 c., vermilion.. | 4 | 4 |
| 36 | 2 c. on 2 c., yellow-grn. | 6 | 4 |
| 36a | 2 c. on 2 c., deep green | — | 12 |
| 37 | 4 c. on 4 c., rose .. | 10 | 10 |
| 38 | 5 c. on 5 c., orange | 90 | |
| 39 | 5 c. on 5 c., yellow .. | 18 | 18 |
| 40 | 8 c. on 6 c., brown | | |
| 41 | 8 c. on 6 c., red-brown. | 36 | 36 |
| 42 | 10 c. on 9 c., green .. | 36 | 36 |
| 42a | 10 c. on 9 c., emerald .. | 50 | |
| 43 | 10 c. on 12 c., orange-yell. | 50 | 12 |
| 44 | 30 c. on 24 c., carmine.. | 90 | 50 |

*Variety. "cen" for "cent."*

| 44a | ½ c. on 3 c., pale yellow | | |

*(b) Surcharge 16 to 16½ mm. high.*
*Figure of value closer to Chinese characters.*

| 45 | ½ c. on 3 c., orange-yell. | 2 | 12 |
|---|---|---|---|
| 46 | ½ c. on 3 c., pale yellow | 6 | 8 |
| 47 | 1 c. on 1 c., vermilion . | 4 | 6 |
| 48 | 2 c. on 2 c., green .. | 25 | 4 |
| 49 | 4 c. on 4 c., rose .. | 30 | 30 |
| 49a | 5 c. on 5 c., orange .. | — | 75 |
| 50 | 5 c. on 5 c., yellow .. | 62 | 12 |
| 51 | 8 c. on 6 c., brown .. | | |
| 52 | 10 c. on 9 c., green .. | 2.50 | 62 |
| 52a | 10 c. on 9 c., pale green .. | 3.75 | 90 |
| 53 | 10 c. on 12 c., orange .. | 1.85 | 62 |
| 53a | 10 c. on 12 c., brn.-orange | | 62 |
| 54 | 30 c. on 24 c., carmine.. | | |

*Varieties. Surcharge inverted.*

| 54a | ½ c. on 3 c., pale yellow | | |
|---|---|---|---|
| 54b | 2 c. on 2 c., green .. | | |
| 55 | 4 c. on 4 c., rose .. | 3.75 | |
| 56 | 10 c. on 9 c., green .. | 5.00 | |

*New plate with figures "2" in lower corners instead of "2."*

| 57 | 2 c. on 2 c., green .. | 18 | 12 |

*Issue of 1886 surcharged in black.*
i.) *Small figures as Type 13 (February).*
*Surcharge 17 mm. high.*

| ,8 | 1 c. on 1 c., green .. | 8 | 6 |
|---|---|---|---|
| ,9 | 1 c. on 1 c., pale green. | — | 50 |
| ,0 | 2 c. on 3 c., pale mauve | 12 | 8 |
| ,1 | 5 c. on 5 c., grey-bistre | 12 | 18 |

(ii.) *Large figures as Types 14 and 15 (May).*
(a) *Surcharge 16½ mm. high.*

| 2 | 1 c. on 1 c., green .. | 2.50 | 2.50 |

(b) *Surcharge 15½ mm. high.*

| 3 | 2 c. on 3 c., mauve .. | 2.50 | 2.50 |
|---|---|---|---|
| 4 | 5 c. on 5 c., olive-yellow | 2.50 | 2.50 |

No. Type.

大淸郵政
壹 當 分
**one cent.**
16

大淸郵政
暫 洋 作
貳 銀
分
**2 cents.**
17

*Revenue stamp surcharged in black.*

| No. | Type | | Un. | Used. |
|---|---|---|---|---|
| 65 | 16 | 1 c. on 3 c., red .. | 4 | 2 |
| 65a | ” | 1 c. on 3 c., red-brn. | 25 | |
| 66 | 17 | 2 c. on 3 c., red .. | 6 | 6 |

大淸郵政
暫 洋 作
貳 銀
分
**2 cents.**
18

大淸郵政
暫 洋 作
肆 銀
分
**4 cents**
18*

| 67 | 18 | 2 c. on 3 c., red .. | 4 | 4 |
|---|---|---|---|---|
| 68 | 18* | 4 c. on 3 c., „ | 12.50 | |
| 69 | 18 | 4 c. on 3 c., „ | 8 | 6 |

大淸郵政
當
壹
圓
**1 dollar**
19

| 70 | 19 | $1 on 3 c., red .. | 1.00 | 1.00 |
|---|---|---|---|---|
| 71 | - | $1 on 3 c. „ | | |
| 71a | 19 | $5 on 3 c. „ | | |

No. 71 differs from No. 70 in having the four Chinese characters at the top larger, as in Type 16. The $5 on 3 c. is known postmarked, and some copies were undoubtedly used for postal purposes.

*Surcharge inverted.*

| 71b | 17 | 2 c. on 3 c., red .. | 5.00 | 6.25 |
|---|---|---|---|---|
| 72 | 19 | $5 on 3 c. „ | | |

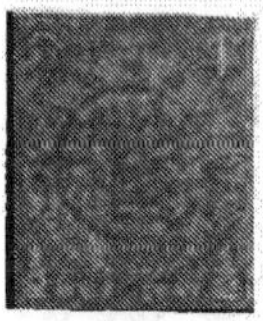

20

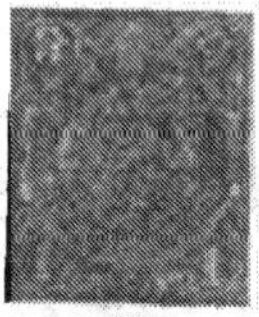

21

22

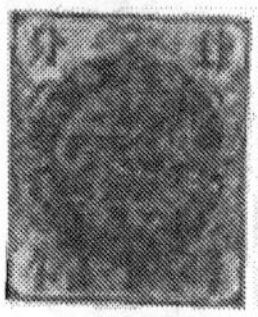

23

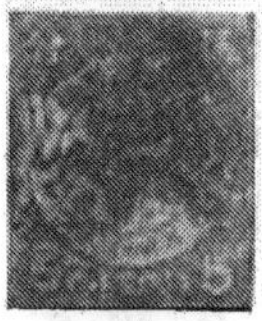

24

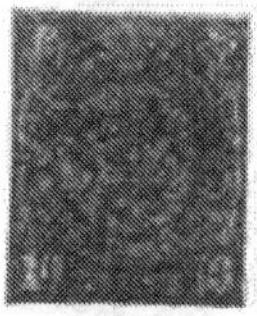

25

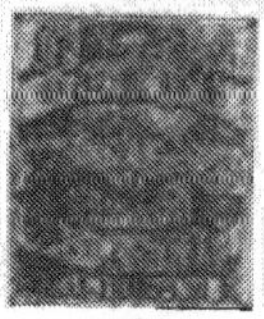

26

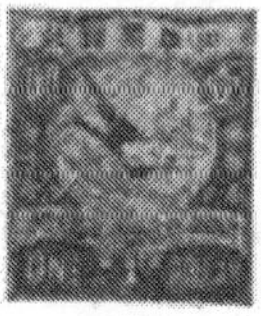

27

OCTOBER, **1897.**

*Japanese plates. "Imperial Chinese Post."* *Wmk.* Type 3. *Perf.* 11.

| No. | Type. | | Un. | Used. |
|---|---|---|---|---|
| 72a | 20 | ½ c., brown-purple . | 2 | |
| 72b | " | ½ c., lilac-rose .. | 6 | |
| 73 | " | ½ c., claret .. .. | 2 | 2 |
| 74 | 21 | 1 c., yellow .. | 2 | 2 |
| 75 | 22 | 2 c., deep orange .. | 2 | 2 |
| 76 | 23 | 4 c., brown.. .. | 8 | 2 |
| 76a | " | 4 c., bistre-brown .. | 16 | 4 |
| 76b | " | 4 c., deep brown .. | 12 | |
| 77 | 24 | 5 c., rose .. .. | 10 | 6 |
| 78 | 25 | 10 c., deep green .. | 12 | 4 |
| 78a | " | 10 c., green .. .. | 18 | |
| 79 | 26 | 20 c., brown-lake .. | 25 | 18 |
| 80 | " | 30 c., carmine .. | 50 | 36 |
| 81 | " | 50 c., yellow-green.. | 75 | 75 |
| 81a | " | 50 c., green .. .. | — | 1.25 |
| 82 | 27 | $1, carmine and rose | 1.85 | 1.85 |
| 83 | " | $2, orange & yellow | 5.00 | 5.00 |
| [illegible] | " | $5, yellow-green & rose .. ... | 12.50 | |

*Error, in colour of* 10 c.

| No. | Type. | | Un. | Used. |
|---|---|---|---|---|
| 85 | 26 | 50 c., deep green .. | 7.50 | |
| 85a | " | 50 c., green .. .. | | |

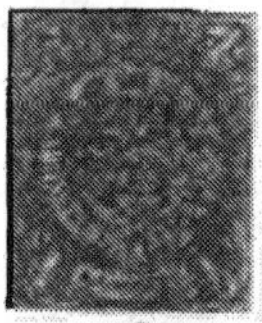

28

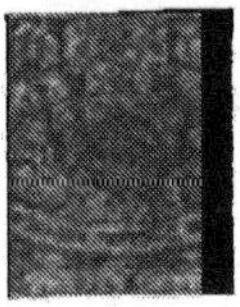

29

30

**1898.** *London plates. "Chinese Imperial Post." No wmk. Perf.* 14 *to* 15½.

| | | | | |
|---|---|---|---|---|
| 86 | 28 | ½ c., brown .. | 2 | [illegible] |
| 87 | " | 1 c., ochre-buff .. | 2 | [illegible] |
| 88 | " | 2 c., scarlet.. .. | 2 | |
| 89 | " | 4 c., yellow-brown.. | 4 | [illegible] |
| 90 | " | 5 c., salmon .. | 6 | [illegible] |
| 91 | " | 10 c., deep green .. | 8 | [illegible] |
| 92 | 29 | 20 c., brown-lake .. | 18 | [illegible] |
| 93 | " | 30 c., rose-red .. | 25 | [illegible] |
| 94 | " | 50 c., green .. .. | 36 | |
| 95 | 30 | $1, carm. & salmon | 75 | [illegible] |
| 96 | " | $2 " yellow | 1.50 | [illegible] |
| 97 | " | $5, green & salmon | 3.75 | [illegible] |

**1899.** Type 28. *Perf. as before.*

| | | | | |
|---|---|---|---|---|
| 99 | 28 | 5 c., red-orange .. | 4 | [illegible] |

**1903.** *Error of colour. Issued in Northern China.*

| | | | | |
|---|---|---|---|---|
| 100 | 28 | 5 c., orange-yellow. | 12 | [illegible] |

## COLOMBIA.

### (GRANADA CONFEDERATION.)

1

The stamps of the early issues were mostly cancelled in pen and ink, as cancelling handstamps were furnished to very

|  | | Un. | Used. |
|---|---|---|---|

No. .

few places. As these stamps are not known to have been used for fiscal purposes, pen-cancellation denotes postal use.

**1859.** Type 1. *Wove paper. Imperf.*

| 1 | 5 c., rosy lilac .. | .. | 3.15 | 3.15 |
|---|---|---|---|---|
| 2 | 5 c., grey-lilac .. | .; | 2.00 | 2.00 |
| 3 | 10 c., yellow | .. | 75 | 75 |
| 4 | 20 c., blue | .. | 5.00 | 5.00 |
| 4a | 20 c., pale blue .. | .. | — | 6.25 |

*Variety. Tête-bêche.*

| 5 | 10 c., yellow (pair) | | | |

*The same, on laid paper.*

| 6 | 5 c., rosy lilac .. | .. | 4.35 | 2.50 |

1

**1860.** Type 2. *Imperf.*

| 7 | 2½ c., green | .. | 2.50 | |
| 8 | 2½ c., yellow-green | .. | 1.00 | 1.25 |
| 9 | 5 c., violet | .. | — | 1.50 |
| 10 | 5 c., lilac | .. | — | 1.50 |
| 11 | 5 c., blue | .. | 1.25 | 1.25 |
| 12 | 10 c., brown-orange | .. | 3.75 | 2.50 |
| 13 | 10 c., bistre-brown | .. | 2.50 | 2.00 |
| 14 | 10 c., buff | .. | 1.85 | 1.25 |
| 15 | 20 c., blue | .. | 75 | 36 |
| 16 | 20 c., pale blue .. | .. | 36 | 36 |
| 17 | 1 p., carmine .. | .. | 50 | 1.25 |
| 18 | 1 p., rose on bluish | .. | 6.25 | |

The 10 c. is known in *green*, but is believed to be only a proof.

*Variety. Tête-bêche.*

| 19 | 5 c., lilac (pair) | |
| 20 | 5 c., blue ( „ ).. | .. |

*Error in the sheet of the 20 c.*

| 21 | 20 c.+5 c., blue (pair) .. |

*Error. " 50" for " 5" at top.*

| 21a | 5 c., lilac | .. | .. |

**(UNITED STATES OF NEW GRANADA.)**

3

**1861.** Type 3. *Imperf.*

| 22 | 2½ c., black | .. | .. | — | 12.50 |
| 23 | 5 c., orange-buff | .. | 8.75 | 5.00 |

|  | | Un. | Used. |
|---|---|---|---|

No.

| 24 | 5 c., mustard .. | .. | 6.25 | 5.00 |
| 24a | 5 c., pale yellow | .. | 7.50 | 5.00 |
| 25 | 10 c., blue | .. | 12.50 | 3.00 |
| 26 | 20 c., red.. | .. | 8.75 | 5.00 |
| 27 | 1 p., rose | .. | .. | — | 6.25 |

There are no varieties of the lower values, but there are as many varieties of the 1 peso as there are stamps on the sheet (? 54).

**(UNITED STATES OF COLOMBIA.)**

4

**1862.** Type 4. *Imperf.*

| 28 | 10 c., pale blue .. | .. | 10.00 | 5.00 |
| 29 | 10 c., blue | .. | 10.00 | |
| 30 | 20 c., red | .. | — | 25.00 |
| 31 | 50 c., blue-green | .. | — | 5.00 |
| 32 | 50 c., pale green | .. | — | 5.00 |
| 33 | 1 p., lilac | .. | 25.00 | 20.00 |
| 34 | 1 p., lilac on bluish | .. | — | 25.00 |

5

**1863.** Type 5. *Imperf.*

| 35 | 5 c., yellow | .. | 2.50 | 1.25 |
| 36 | 5 c., orange-buff | .. | 2.50 | 1.25 |
| 37 | 10 c., blue | .. | — | 50 |
| 38 | 20 c., red.. | .. | 6.25 | 1.25 |
| 38a | 50 c., green | .. | .. |

*Bluish paper.*

| 39 | 10 c., blue | .. | 2.00 | 1.25 |
| 40 | 50 c., green | .. | 4.50 | 4.50 |

*Error of colour.*

| 41 | 50 c., red .. | .. | .. |

The 50 c., red, was in the sheet of the 20 c.

There are several minor varieties of type of each value of this issue, some of which show portions of a Star before and after the value.

| No. | | Un. | Used. |
|---|---|---|---|

6

**1864.**  Type 6.  *Imperf.*

| | | | Un. | Used |
|---|---|---|---|---|
| 42 | 5 c., orange | .. | 90 | 62 |
| 43 | 5 c., yellow | .. | 1.00 | 62 |
| 44 | 10 c., pale blue | .. | 50 | 30 |
| 44a | 10 c., blue | .. | | |
| 45 | 10 c., deep blue | .. | 62 | 30 |
| 46 | 20 c., red .. | .. | 1.00 | 1.00 |
| 47 | 50 c., pale green | .. | 1.85 | 1.25 |
| 47a | 50 c., green | .. | 1.85 | 1.25 |
| 48 | 1 p., mauve | .. | 8.75 | 4.50 |

*Variety.*  *Tête-bêche.*

| 49 | 5 c., orange (pair) | .. | 10.00 | 2.50 |
|---|---|---|---|---|
| 50 | 5 c., yellow ( ,, ) | .. | | |

There are two varieties of each value of this issue.

7

7*

8

**1865.**  Types 7, 7*, and 8 (5 c., etc.).
*Imperf.*

| 51 | 1 c., rose, P.S. 8 c.. | .. | 12 | 8 |
|---|---|---|---|---|
| 52 | 2½ c., black on lilac | .. | 50 | 25 |
| 53 | 5 c., orange | .. | 62 | 25 |
| 54 | 5 c., orange-yellow | .. | 62 | 18 |
| 55 | 5 c., lemon | .. | 62 | 18 |
| 56 | 10 c., violet | .. | 50 | 12 |
| 57 | 10 c., mauve | .. | 36 | 8 |
| 57a | 10 c., lilac | .. | — | 12 |
| 58 | 20 c., deep blue .. | .. | 90 | 25 |

| No. | | | Un. | Used. |
|---|---|---|---|---|
| 59 | 20 c., pale blue .. | .. | 1.00 | 36 |
| 60 | 50 c., deep green | .. | 3.75 | 1.00 |
| 61 | 50 c., pale green | .. | 3.15 | 1.00 |
| 62 | 50 c., green | .. | 2.50 | 62 |
| 63 | 1 p., deep rose | .. | 2.50 | 50 |
| 63a | 1 p., pale rose .. | .. | 3.00 | |
| 64 | 1 p., vermilion .. | .. | 3.00 | 12 |
| 64a | 1 p., pale vermilion | .. | 3.00 | 12 |

*Variety on pelure paper.*

| 64b | 1 c., rose | .. | .. | 1.00 | 50 |
|---|---|---|---|---|---|

There are ten varieties of the 5, 10, 20, and 50 c., and six of the 1 peso.

9

10

11

12

13

14

15

**1867.**  Types 9 *to* 15.  *Imperf.*

| 65 | 5 c., orange | .. | .. | 1.00 | 12 |
|---|---|---|---|---|---|
| 66 | 10 c., lilac | .. | .. | 50 | 12 |
| 67 | 10 c., mauve | .. | .. | 1.85 | 50 |
| 68 | 20 c., blue | .. | .. | 90 | 37 |

|  | Un. | Used. |
|---|---|---|
| o. | | |
| 20 c., pale blue .. .. | 90 | 36 |
| 50 c., blue-green .. | 1.00 | 1.00 |
| 50 c., yellow-green .. | 1.00 | 1.00 |
| 1 p., vermilion .. .. | 1.50 | 12 |
| 1 p., carmine .. .. | 1.85 | 12 |
| 5 p., black on green .. | 7.50 | 2.50 |
| 10 p., black on vermilion | 10.00 | 1.50 |

There are some varieties of the "UN so" having the letters "U," "N," "S," "o" contracted. The highest two lues are on surface-coloured paper.

16       17

18       19

20

**1868–70.** Types **16** to **20.** *Imperf.*

|  | Un. | Used. |
|---|---|---|
| 5 c., dull orange-yellow | 1.00 | 36 |
| 10 c., violet .. .. | 18 | 4 |
| 10 c., mauve .. .. | 25 | 4 |
| 10 c., rosy lilac .. .. | 62 | 12 |
| 10 c., grey-lilac .. .. | 50 | 12 |
| 20 c., blue .. .. | 36 | 12 |
| 20 c., pale blue .. .. | 36 | 18 |
| 50 c., yellow-green .. | 1.50 | 6 |
| 1 p., rose-red .. .. | 1.25 | 12 |
| 1 p., vermilion .. .. | 1.50 | 12 |

here are two types of the 10 c. In the "B" of "COLOMBIA" is over the of "CENTAVOS," in (ii.) it is between "V" and the "o" (as in the illus-on).

*Variety. Tête-bêche (pairs).*

1 p., vermilion .. .. — 10.00

---

No.

|  | Un. | Used. |
|---|---|---|

21       22

**1870–77.**

Types **21, 22.** *Surface-coloured paper.*

| | | | | | |
|---|---|---|---|---|---|
| 85 | 5 p., blk. on grn. (Die I.) | | 5.00 | 75 |
| 86 | 5 p. | " | " ( " II.) | 3.75 | 1.50 |
| 87 | 10 p. | " | vermilion .. | 7.50 | 1.50 |

In Die I. the ornament on the left of "c" of "CINCO" impinges on the "c," in Die II. it only touches it.

22*

**1869–70.** Type **22*.** *Wove paper.*

| | | | | |
|---|---|---|---|---|
| 88 | 2½ c., black on violet .. | 18 | 18 |

*Laid paper.*

| | | | |
|---|---|---|---|
| 89 | 2½ c., black on violet .. | |

*Laid bâtonné paper.*

| | | |
|---|---|---|
| 89a | 2½ c., black on violet .. 18.75 |

There are two types of this stamp.

23       24

**1870–74.** Types **23** to **27.** *Wove paper.*

*Imperf.*

| | | | | |
|---|---|---|---|---|
| 90 | 1 c., green .. .. | 36 | |
| 91 | 1 c., olive-green .. | 18 | |
| 92 | 1 c., pale grey-green .. | 4 | |
| 93 | 1 c., carmine .. .. | 12 | 12 |
| 94 | 1 c., rose .. .. | 4 | 12 |
| 95 | 2 c., dark brown .. | 6 | 6 |
| 96 | 2 c., pale brown .. | 8 | 18 |
| 96a | 2 c., cinnamon .. | 6 | |

D

| No. | | | | Un. | Used. |
|---|---|---|---|---|---|

**25**

**26**    **27**

| 97 | 5 c., orange | .. | .. | 12 | 4 |
| 98 | 5 c., yellow | .. | .. | 36 | 4 |
| 99 | 10 c., mauve | .. | .. | 25 | 18 |
| 100 | 10 c., violet | .. | .. | 25 | 18 |
| 101 | 25 c., blk. on grey-blue | | 1.25 | | 62 |
| 101a | 25 c., ,, bright blue | .. | 1.25 | | |
| 102 | 25 c., green | .. | .. | 1.85 | 3.75 |
| 103 | 25 c., blue-green | .. | | 90 | |

There are two types of the 10 c. In (i.) the "o" and "s" of "CORREOS" are the same size, in (ii.) the "s" is larger than the "o."

*Varieties on laid paper.*

| 104 | 1 c., green | .. | .. | 50 |
| 104a | 1 c., olive-green | .. | |
| 105 | 1 c., rose | .. | .. |
| 105a | 5 c., yellow | .. | .. |
| 106 | 10 c., violet | .. | .. |
| 106a | 25 c., green | .. | .. |

**28**    **29**

**1876–84.** Types **28** *to* **30** *and* **19** (50 c.).
*Imperf.*

*(a) White wove paper.*

| 107 | 5 c., lilac | .. | .. | 50 | 8 |
| 108 | 5 c., mauve | .. | .. | 18 | 8 |
| 109 | 5 c., violet | .. | .. | 25 | 12 |
| 110 | 10 c., dark brown | .. | .. | 12 | 6 |
| 111 | 10 c., brown | .. | .. | 12 | 6 |
| 112 | 10 c., pale brown | .. | .. | 25 | 12 |
| 113 | 10 c., grey-brown | .. | .. | — | 25 |
| 114 | 10 c., cinnamon | .. | .. | — | 12 |
| 15 | 10 c., purple-brown | .. | | — | 50 |

| No. | | | | Un. | Use. |
|---|---|---|---|---|---|

**30**

| 116 | 20 c., pale greenish blue | | 62 | : |
| 117 | 20 c., blue | .. | .. | 36 | . |
| 118 | 20 c., deep blue | .. | .. | 30 | |
| 119 | 20 c., violet-blue | .. | | 3.00 | ! |
| 120 | 50 c., pale green | .. | | 1.25 | i. |
| 121 | 50 c., blue-green on greyish | .. | .. | 1.50 | |

*(b) Bluish paper.*

| 122 | 5 c., mauve | .. | .. | 62 |
| 123 | 10 c., brown | .. | .. | 50 |
| 124 | 20 c., pale blue | .. | .. | 50 |
| 125 | 50 c., dark green | .. | | 1.85 |
| 126 | 50 c., emerald | .. | | 1.85 | : |
| 127 | 1 p., vermilion | .. | | 1.85 | 1. |

*(c) Greenish paper.*

| 128 | 5 c., mauve | .. | .. | 90 |
| 129 | 10 c., brown | .. | .. | |
| 130 | 20 c., blue | .. | .. | 75 | ! |
| 131 | 50 c., green | .. | .. | 1.85 | |
| 132 | 1 p., vermilion | .. | .. | 2.50 | : ! |

*(d) White laid paper.*

| 133 | 5 c., pale lilac | .. | .. | 12 |
| 134 | 5 c., mauve | .. | .. | 25 |
| 135 | 10 c., grey-brown | .. | .. | 50 |
| 136 | 10 c., brown | .. | .. | .50 |
| 137 | 10 c., greenish blue | .. | — | : |
| 138 | 20 c., blue | .. | .. | 2.00 | 2 |
| 139 | 20 c., deep blue | .. | .. | 2.00 | |
| 140 | 50 c., green | .. | .. | | |
| 141 | 1 p., pale red | .. | .. | — | |

**1877.** Type **22.** *Die retouched.*

| 142 | 10 p., blk. on rose (Die I.) | 7.50 | : |
| 143 | 10 p., blk. on rose (Die II.) | 7.50 | : |

In Die II. the middle band of the s: has no shading, and the stars are disti: five-pointed. There is a line across left top corner, cutting through the c. of the design. This stamp has been printed.

*Provisionals used at Cali in the State of Cauca.*

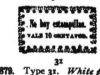

**31**

**1879.** Type **31.** *White paper.*

| 144 | 5 cent., black | .. | .. | |
| 145 | 10 ,, ,, | .. | .. | — | 1. |

*Un. Used.*

20 cent., black .. ..
,50 ,, ,, .. ..
1 peso ,, .. ..
un peso ,, .. ..

These stamps also exist on *blue* and *buff* ers. There are five types of each value.

32      33

34      35

36

**1881.** Types 32 *to* 36. *Imperf.*

1 c., blue-green .. 2
2 c., vermilion .. .. 2 8
2 c., rose-red .. .. — 8
5 c., blue .. 8
10 c., purple .. .. 12 12
20 c., black .. .. 25 36

*Variety. Printed both sides.*

1 5 c., blue .. ..
he stamps of this issue are found perf. ficially.

37

Type 37. Black *on coloured papers.*

1 c., green .. .. 2 4
2 c., rose .. .. 4
5 c., lilac .. .. 18 2
le stamps of this issue are found perf. ficially.

---

No. Type.      *Un. Used.*

38

**1883.** *The first issue of* 1881 *re-engraved.*

| No. | Type | | Un. | Used. |
|---|---|---|---|---|
| 159 | 32 | 1 c., green .. .. | 50 | 25 |
| 160 | 38 | 2 c., bright rose .. | 4 | 12 |
| 161 | 34 | 5 c., blue .. .. | 25 | 12 |
| 162 | ,, | 5 c., pale blue .. | 8 | 12 |
| 163 | ,, | 5 c., ultramarine .. | 12 | |
| 164 | 35 | 10 c., purple.. .. | 25 | 8 |

*Variety. Printed both sides.*

164a| 34 | 5 c., blue .. ..

The differences between these and the previous ones are as follows: The 1 c. has a *square* dot before "UNION," and the rays beneath the stars are partially or entirely erased; in the 5 c. the five pearls round the figure "5" in the upper left corner are unshaded; in the 10 c. the lettering is thicker, as well as all the white lines of the design, the figure "1" has a line of colour across the top, which in heavily-printed specimens makes the figure shorter than the "o," and there are no rays over the eagle.

This issue is found perf. unofficially.

39      40

**1883–86.** *Tinted papers.*

*(a) Perf.* 10½.

| No. | Type | | Un. | Used. |
|---|---|---|---|---|
| 165 | 39 | 1 c., yellow-green on green .. .. | 18 | 4 |
| 166 | ,, | 1 c., deep green on green .. .. | — | 2 |
| 167 | ,, | 1 c., blue-green on green .. ..· | 2 | 2 |
| 168 | ,, | 1 c., blue-green on bluish green .. | 2 | 2 |
| 169 | 40 | 5 c., blue on blue .. | 50 | 12 |
| 170 | ,, | 5 c., dull blue .. | 50 | 12 |
| 171 | ,, | 5 c., deep blue on azure .. .. | 62 | 4 |
| 172 | ,, | 50 c., brown on buff | 62 | 62 |
| 173 | ,, | 1 p., lake on bluish | 90 | 75 |
| 174 | ,, | 5 p., yellow-brown on yellow .. | 5.00 | 5.00 |
| 175 | ,, | 10 p., black on rose . | 7.50 | 6.25 |

| | | | *Un.* | *Used.* |
|---|---|---|---|---|
| No. | Type. | | | |

*(b)  Perf.* 13½.

| 176 | 40 | 2 c., red on rose .. | 4 | 8 |
| 177 | ,, | 2 c., deep red on rose | 4 | 8 |
| 178 | ,, | 2 c., red on buff .. | 5.00 | 5.00 |
| 179 | ,, | 10 c., orange on buff | 62 | 50 |
| 180 | ,, | 10 c.     ,,    yell. | 16 | 16 |
| 180a | ,, | 10 c., yellow on yell. pelure  .. | | |
| 181 | ,, | 20 c., mauve on lilac | 36 | |
| 182 | ,, | 20 c., purple on lilac | 36 | 8 |

*(c)  Perf.* 12.

| 182a | 40 | 50 c., brown on buff | | |
| 182b | 21 | 5 p., yellow-brown on yellow .. | 6.25 | |
| 182c | 22 | 10 p., black on rose | | |

*(d) Imperf.*

The following values are found :—1 c., green ; 2 c., rose on rose ; 5 c., blue on bluish, and also on azure ; 10 c., orange on buff ; 20 c., mauve on lilac ; 1 p., lake on bluish and also on pale lilac.

**1886.**  *Perf.* 10½.

| 183 | 21 | 5 p., orange-brown (Die III.)  .. | 4.00 | 5.00 |
| 184 | 22 | 10 p., black on lilac (Die II.) .. .. | 4.00 | 4.00 |

*Perf.* 12.

| 184a | 22 | 10 p., black on lilac (Die II.)  .. | 3.50 | |

*Both values are found imperf.*

**(REPUBLIC OF COLOMBIA.)**

41                     42

**1886-89.**  *Tinted papers.*

*(a)  Perf.* 10½.

| 185 | 41 | 1 c., yellow-green on bluish  .. | 2 | 2 |
| 186 | ,, | 1 c., blue-green on bluish .. .. | 2 | 2 |
| 187 | ,, | 1 c., myrtle-green.. | 8 | 4 |
| 188 | 42 | 5 c., blue on azure | 6 | 2 |
| 189 | ,, | 5 c., ultramarine ,, | 6 | 2 |
| 190 | 41 | 50 c., cinnamon on buff  .. .. | 50 | 25 |
| 191 | ,, | 1 p., lilac-rose .. | 2.50 | 25 |
| 192 | ,, | 1 p.  ,,  on bluish | 2.50 | 2.50 |
| 93 | ,, | 5 p., brown   ,, | 6.25 | 6.25 |
| 94 | ,, | 5 p., black .. .. | — | 4.50 |
| 15 | ,, | 10 p., black on rose | 3.75 | 1.25 |

| | | | *Un.* | *Used.* |
|---|---|---|---|---|
| No. | Type. | | | |

43                     44

45                     46

*(b)  Perf.* 13½.

| 196 | 43 | 2 c., red on rose .. | 4 | |
| 197 | ,, | 2 c.   ,,   yellow | 50 | |
| 198 | ,, | 2 c.   ,,   white | 50 | |
| 199 | 42 | 5 c., blue on azure | | |
| 200 | 44 | 10 c., orange  .. | 18 | |
| 200a | 45 | 20 c., violet  .. | | |
| 201 | ,, | 20 c., violet on lilac | 36 | |
| 202 | ,, | 20 c., deep violet on lilac  .. | 50 | |
| 203 | ,, | 20 c., violet on grn. | 1.00 | |

*(c)  Imperf.*

| 203a | 42 | 5 c., blue on azure | — | |
| 203b | 44 | 10 c., orange  .. | 1.25 | |
| 203c | 46 | 20 c., violet on lilac | | |
| 203d | 41 | 50 c., cinna. on buff | 1.25 | |

*Varieties on thinner paper.*

| 204 | 44 | 10 c., orange  .. | 50 | |
| 205 | ,, | 10 c., yellow  .. | 36 | |
| 206 | 45 | 20 c., violet on lilac . | 25 | |

"REPULICA" *corrected to* "REPUBLICA

| 206a | 46 | 20 c., violet on white | 2.50 | |
| 207 | ,, | 20 c.   ,,   lilac . | 18 | |
| 208 | ,, | 20 c.   ,,   green | 1.00 | |

50                     51

**1890-91.**  *Tinted papers. (a) Perf.*

| 209 | 50 | 1 c., gn. on pale gn. | 6 | |
| 210 | ,, | 1 c., deep gn.  ,, | 6 | |
| 211 | 51 | 2 c., rose-red on rose | 6 | |
| 212 | ,, | 2 c., rose-car.  ,, | 6 | |

| No. Type. | | Un. | Used. |
|---|---|---|---|

**52**

**53**

**54**

| 213 | 53 | 10 c., brn. on yellow | 8 | 8 |
| 214 | " | 10 c., red-bn.  " | 8 | 8 |
| 215 | 54 | 20 c., violet .. .. | 50 | 50 |

*(b) Perf.* 10½.

| 216 | 52 | 5 c., blue on blue .. | 4 | 2 |
| 217 | " | 5 c., dp. blue on blue | 4 | 2 |
| 218 | " | 5 c., dp. blue on azure | 6 | 2 |

*Variety. Imperf.*

| 219 | 52 | 5 c., blue on blue .. | 36 | 50 |
| 220 | " | 5 c., dp. blue on azure | 1.00 | |

**55**

**56**

**57**

**58**

**1892-97.** *Tinted papers.* (a) *Perf.* 13½.

| 221 | 50 | 1 c., red on yellow | 2 | 2 |
| 222 | 55 | 2 c., blue-green .. | 4 | 2 |
| 223 | " | 2 c., red on rose .. | 25 | 50 |
| 223a | 52 | 5 c., black on buff | | |
| 223b | 58 | 5 c., brown on pale brown .. .. | 8 | 2 |
| 223c | " | 5 c., brown on buff | | |
| 224 | 53 | 10 c., brown on rose | 10 | 2 |
| 224a | 56 | 20 c., brown on azure | 4 | 4 |
| 225 | 57 | 1 p., blue on green | 12 | 12 |
| 225a | 41 | 10 p., blue.. .. | 90 | |

| No. Type. | | Un. | Used. |
|---|---|---|---|

*(b) Perf.* 10½.

| 226 | 52 | 5 c., black on buff . | 6 | 2 |
| 227 | 56 | 20 c., brown on azure | 50 | 25 |
| 228 | 41 | 5 p., red on lilac-rose | 50 | 50 |
| 229 | " | 10 p., blue .. .. | 75 | 75 |

*Error of colour.*

| 229a | 56 | 20 c., brown on buff | | |

*(c) Perf.* 12.

| 229b | 50 | 1 c., red on yellow | 8 | 8 |
| 230 | 55 | 2 c., pale blue-green | 8 | 4 |
| 230a | 52 | 5 c., black on buff | 50 | 2 |
| 231 | 58 | 5 c., brown on buff | 4 | 2 |
| 231a | " | 5 c., red-brown on pale brown .. | | |
| 232 | 53 | 10 c., brown on rose | 25 | 6 |
| 233 | 56 | 20 c., brown on azure | 25 | 6 |
| 234 | 41 | 50 c., mauve on lilac | 36 | 12 |
| 235 | " | 50 c., violet  " | 8 | |
| 236 | 57 | 1 p., blue on green | — | 50 |

*(d) Perf. compound of* 13½ *and* 12.

| 236a | 52 | 1 c., red on yellow | — | 2 |
| 237 | 55 | 2 c., pale green .. | 12 | 4 |
| 238 | " | 2 c., dark green .. | — | 6 |
| 238a | 52 | 5 c., black on buff | — | 8 |
| 239 | 58 | 5 c., red-brown on buff .. .. | — | 6 |
| 240 | " | 5 c., deep brown on buff .. .. | — | 6 |
| 241 | " | 5 c., red-brown on pale brown .. | 6 | 2 |
| 241a | 53 | 10 c., brown on rose | — | 12 |
| 242 | 56 | 20 c., brn. on azure | 6 | 4 |
| 243 | " | 20 c., brn. on greenish blue .. .. | 25 | 25 |
| 243a | " | 20 c., brn. on white | | |
| 244 | 41 | 50 c., mauve on lilac | 1.00 | |

*(e) Perf.* 14 *to* 15½.

| 244a | 52 | 5 c., black on buff | — | 12 |
| 244b | 56 | 20 c., brn. on azure | | |

*(f) Perf. compound of* 10½ *and* 12.

| 244c | 52 | 5 c., black on buff. | — | 2 |

**59**

**60**

**1898-1901.** *Perf.* 13½.

| 245 | 59 | 1 c., red on yellow . | 2 | 2 |
| 246 | 60 | 5 c., brown on pale brown .. .. | 4 | 2 |

No. Type.

**61**

247| 61 |10 c., brown on rose .    6    2
249| ,, |50 c., blue on lilac ..    8    8

*Provisionals issued at Cartagena during the Civil War.*

**62          63**

**1899-1900.**
Types **62** and **63**.  *Overprinted with control mark in* blue *or* violet.  *Imperf.*
250 | 5 c., pale red on buff ..    18    18
25ca| 5 c., deep ,,    ,,    ..    50    18
251 |10 c., blue on buff    ..    25    25

*Pin-perf. by sewing machine about 12.*
252| 5 c., pale red on buff ..    —    1.25

*Overprinted with 7 parallel wavy lines, in* mauve.  *Pin-perf. about 6½.*
253| 5 c., marone on green    25    25
254|10 c., red on rose    ..    36    36

*Variety.  Tête bêche.*
254a| 5 c., marone on green

**64          65**

Types **64** and **65**.  *Pin-perf. 8 to 9.  Overprinted as last.*
The 1 c. and 2 c. are formed from the 5 c. and 10 c. by erasing the labels at the top and bottom, and replacing them with type-set inscriptions and a type-set frame round the stamp.  There are ten types of each value, nine being formed from the 5 c. (1) and one from the 10 c. (2).
| 64 | 1 c.,pale bn.on buff(1)    4
,,    | 1 c.    ,,    ,,    (2)   12    18
65 | 1 c., brown    ,,    (1)    6    12

---

No. Type.                              Un.  Used.
258| 65 | 1 c.,pale bn.on buff(2)    18
259| ,, | 2 c., black    ,,    (1)    12
260| ,, | 2 c.    ,,    ,,    (2)    62

*Stamp of Bolivar, 1891, overprinted as last.*
261| 1 c., black    ..    ..

**66**

**1900.**  Type **66**.  *Overprinted as last.  Imperf.*
262| 5 c., vermilion ..    ..    12

*Perf. 12.*
263| 5 c., vermilion ..    ..

**67          68**

**1901.**  *Pin-perf.*
*These stamps are overprinted with the letters "S" (repeated) in a frame, in violet.*
264| 67 | 1 c., black ..    ..    2
265| 68 | 2 c.    ,,    on red ..    2

**69          70**

**1902.**  *The 1 c. and 2 c. overprinted with a chain pattern in red, the 5 c. and 10 c. with a five-pointed star in magenta.  Pin-perf.*
266| 69 | 1 c., pale blue    ..    2
267| 70 | 2 c., bistre-brown ..    2

| | | Un. | Used. |
|---|---|---|---|

o. Type.

71            72

| 8 | 71 | 5 c., violet .. .. | 2 | 2 |
| 9 | 72 | 10 c., dark brown .. | 4 | |
| 0 | ,, | 10 c., pale brown .. | 4 | |

*Without star.*

| 1 | 71 | 5 c., violet .. .. | — | 62 |

*Overprint inverted.*

| 2 | 10 c., brown .. .. | 25 | 25 |

*Same type. Perf. 12.*

| 3 | 5 c., violet .. .. | 2 | 2 |
| 4 | 10 c., dark brown .. | 4 | 6 |

*The same with two stars.*

| 5 | 10 c., dark brown .. | |

*Imperf.*

| 5 | 5 c., violet .. .. | |

*Star in carmine-red. Perf. 12.*

| 1 | 10 c., pale brown .. | 4 | 4 |

73            74

75

*rprinted with 7 parallel wavy lines, in magenta. Pin-perf.*

| | 73 | 5 c., bistre-brown.. | 2 | 2 |
| | 74 | 10 c., black .. .. | 4 | 2 |
| | 75 | 20 c., magenta .. | 4 | 4 |

*The same, but wavy lines in mauve.*

| 2 | 73 | 5 c., bistre-brown . | — | 6 |
| | 74 | 10 c., black.. .. | — | 12 |
| | 75 | 20 c., magenta .. | — | 12 |

No. Type.    Un. Used.

76            77

78            79

80            81

82

**1902-03.** *Regular issues. Imperf.*

| 283 | 76 | 2 c., black on rose.. | 2 | 2 |
| 284 | 77 | 4 c., red on green.. | 2 | 4 |
| 285 | ,, | 4 c., blue on green. | 2 | |
| 286 | 78 | 5 c., green on green | 2 | 2 |
| 287 | ,, | 5 c., blue on blue . | 6 | 4 |
| 288 | 79 | 10 c., black on rose . | 2 | 4 |
| 289 | 80 | 20 c., bistre on buff . | 4 | 4 |
| 290 | ,, | 20 c., blue on buff .. | 4 | 8 |
| 291 | 81 | 50 c., blue-green on rose .. .. | 6 | 12 |
| 292 | ,, | 50 c., blue on rose .. | 12 | |
| 293 | 82 | 1 p., violet on buff . | 12 | |

| No. Type. | | | Un. | Used. |
|---|---|---|---|---|

*Pin-perf.*

| 294 | 79 | 10 c., black on rose. | 2 | 4 |
| 294a | 80 | 20 c., bistre on buff | | |
| | | (perf. 12) | .. | |

83

84

85

**1902. Types 83, 84, 85.** *Provisionals (issued at Barranquilla?)* (a) *Imperf.*

| 295 | 2 c., blue-green | .. | .. | 2 | 2 |
| 296 | 2 c., blue | .. | .. | 2 | 2 |
| 297 | 10 c., carmine | .. | .. | 2 | |
| 298 | 10 c., scarlet | .. | .. | 2 | 4 |
| 299 | 10 c., lilac-rose | .. | .. | 2 | 2 |
| 300 | 10 c., magenta | .. | .. | 2 | |
| 301 | 10 c., marone | .. | .. | 4 | |
| 302 | 20 c., violet | .. | .. | 8 | |
| 303 | 20 c., light blue | .. | .. | | |
| 304 | 20 c., dark blue | .. | .. | | |

*Variety. Printed both sides.*

| 305 | 10 c., scarlet | .. | .. | | |

(b) *Pin-perf.*

| 306 | 2 c., blue-green | .. | .. | | |
| 307 | 2 c., blue | .. | .. | | |
| 308 | 10 c., carmine | .. | .. | 4 | 8 |
| 309 | 10 c., scarlet | .. | .. | 2 | |
| 310 | 10 c., lilac-rose | .. | .. | 2 | |
| 311 | 10 c., magenta | .. | .. | 2 | |
| 312 | 10 c., marone | .. | .. | 2 | |
| 313 | 20 c., pale violet | .. | .. | 2 | 4 |
| 314 | 20 c., violet | .. | .. | 2 | 4 |
| 315 | 20 c., dark purple | .. | .. | | |
| ·16 | 20 c., blue | .. | .. | 6 | |

| No. | | | Un. | Use: |
|---|---|---|---|---|

(c) *Perf.* 12.

| 316a | 2 c., blue | .. | .. | 2 | |
| 317 | 20 c., mauve | .. | .. | 2 | |
| 318 | 20 c., dark purple | .. | 6 | |

86

Type **86.** *Perf.* 12.

| 319 | 1 c., green on pale yellow | 2 |
| 320 | 2 c., red on pale salmon | 2 |
| 321 | 5 c., blue on bluish | .. | 2 |
| 322 | 10 c., brown on pale yell. | 2 |
| 323 | 20 c., mauve on pale salm. | 4 |
| 324 | 50 c., red on greenish | .. | 6 |
| 325 | 1 p., black on bright yell. | 12 |
| 326 | 5 p., dark blue on azure | 62 |
| 327 | 10 p., brown on pale salm. | 1.25 |

87

88

89

**1903. Types 87 to 91.** *Imperf.*

| 328 | 5 c., blue | .. | .. | 2 |
| 329 | 5 c., deep blue | .. | .. | 2 |
| 330 | 50 c., green | .. | .. | 6 |
| 331 | 50 c., brown | .. | .. | 6 |
| 332 | 50 c., orange | .. | .. | 6 |
| 333 | 50 c., rosine | .. | .. | 6 |
| 334 | 50 c., vermilion | .. | .. | 6 |
| 335 | 1 p., brown | .. | .. | 8 |
| 336 | 1 p., pale brown | .. | .. | 8 |
| 337 | 1 p., rosine | .. | .. | 8 |
| 338 | 1 p., bright carmine | .. | 8 |
| 339 | 1 p., blue | .. | .. | 12 |
| 340 | 1 p., deep blue | .. | .. | 18 |

| No. | Un. | Used. |
|---|---|---|

**90**  **91**

| | | | Un. | Used. |
|---|---|---|---|---|
| .1 | 5 p., brown | .. .. | 50 | |
| .2 | 5 p., lilac-rose .. | .. | 50 | |
| .3 | 5 p., blue-green | .. | 50 | |
| .4 | 10 p., emerald-green | .. | 90 | |

The 1 peso, *blue* (both shades), is of the ıme design as the other varieties of that alue, but in a smaller size.

**92**  **93**

Types **92** *and* **93**. *Imperf.*

| 45 | 5 p., blue-green on blue | 50 |
|---|---|---|
| 46 | 10 p., green on pale yellow-green .. .. .. | 90 |

### LOCAL FOR THE CITY OF BOGOTA.

**91**  **92**

**1889.** Type **91**.

*Thin paper. Perf. 13½.*

| ,01 | ½ c., black | .. | .. | 2 |
|---|---|---|---|---|
| ,02 | ½ c. ,, (imperf.). | .. | 6½ |

*Thick paper. Perf. 13½.*

| ,02a | ½ c., black | .. | .. |
|---|---|---|---|

*Thick greenish paper. Perf. 13½.*

| 502b | ½ c., black | .. | .. |
|---|---|---|---|

**1896–99.**

Type **92** (Type **91** *re-engraved*).

| 503 | ½ c., black (perf. 12) | .. | 2 |
|---|---|---|---|
| 504 | ½ c. ,, ( ,, 13½) .. | | 2 |

**93**

**1903.** Type **93**. *Imperf.*

| 505 | 10 c., black on rose | .. | 2 |
|---|---|---|---|

### UNPAID LETTER STAMPS.

**A 1**  **A 2**  **A 3**

| No. | Type. | **1865.** *Imperf.* | | |
|---|---|---|---|---|
| 551 | A 1 | 25 c., black on blue. | 75 | 1.00 |
| 552 | A 2 | 50 c. ,, yellow | 50 | 75 |
| 553 | A 3 | 1 p. ,, rose. | 2.50 | 2.50 |

### TOO LATE STAMPS.

**B 1**  **B 2**

**1886–92.** *Perf. 10½.*

| 581 | B 1 | 2½ c., black on lilac . | 2 | 4 |
|---|---|---|---|---|
| 582 | B 2 | 2½ c., blue on salmon | 4 | 2 |

**B 3**

**1902.** Type **B 3**. *Imperf.*

| 583 | 5 c., violet on rose | .. | 2 |
|---|---|---|---|

| No. Type. | | | *Un.* | *Used.* |
|---|---|---|---|---|

REGISTRATION STAMPS.

C 1                    C 2

**1865.** *Imperf.*

| 601 | C 1 | 5 c., black .. | .. | 1.50 | 1.50 |
| 602 | C 2 | 5 c. ,, .. | .. | 1.25 | 1.25 |

C 3                    C 4

**1870.** *Vertical lines in centre.*

| 603 | C 3 | 5 c. (A), black | .. | 4 | 8 |
| 604 | C 4 | 5 c. (R) ,, | .. | 4 | |

**1877.** *Horizontal lines.*

| 605 | C 3 | 5 c. (A), black | .. | 18 | 50 |
| 606 | C 4 | 5 c. (R) ,, | .. | 18 | 25 |
| 607 | C 3 | 5 c. (A), blk. on bluish | 18 | 25 |
| 608 | C 4 | 5 c. (R) ,, ,, | 12 | 25 |

C 5                    C 6

**1881.**

| 609 | C 5 | 10 c., lilac (imperf.). | 62 | 1.00 |
| 10, | ,, | 10 c. ,, (pin-perf.) | | |

**1883.** *Perf.* 13½.

| C 6 | 10 c., red on orange | 12 |

---

C 7

**1889-92.** Type C 7. *Perf.* 13½.

| 612 | 10 c., red on bluish | .. | 12 |
| 613 | 10 c., red on yellowish .. | 12 |
| 614 | 10 c., brn. on pale brn. ('92) | — |

*Perf.* 12.

| 615 | 10 c., dark brown on buff | 2 |
| 616 | 10 c., yellow-brown ,, | 12 |

*Perf.* 13½.

| 617 | 10 c., yellow-brown on buff .. .. .. | — |

C 8

**1902.** Type C 8.

| 618 | 20 c., red on blue (imperf.) | 4 |
| 619 | 20 c., red on blue (perf.). | |

C 9

**1902.** Type C 9. *Laid paper. Perf.* :

| 620 | 10 c., purple | .. | .. | 2 |

**1903.** Type C 8. *Wove paper.* *Imp.*

| 621 | 20 c., blue on blue | .. | 4 |

RETURNED ACKNOWLEDGMENT STA\\'

C 21

**1894.** Type C 21. *Perf.* 13½.

| 651 | 5 c., vermilion on bluish | 12 |

| No. | | | | Un. | Used. |
|---|---|---|---|---|---|

*Perf.* 12.

| 652 | 5 c., vermilion on white | | 12 | |
|---|---|---|---|---|
| 653 | 5 c., scarlet | " | 25 | 12 |

C 22

**1902.** Type c 22. *Imperf.*

| 654 | 10 c., dark blue on pale blue | .. | .. | 2 | 4 |
|---|---|---|---|---|---|
| 655 | 10 c., blue on blue | | .. | 2 | |

## ANTIOQUIA.

1        2

3        4

No. Type.   **1868.** *Imperf.*

| 1 | 1 | 2½ cent., blue | .. | — | 50.00 |
|---|---|---|---|---|---|
| 2 | 2 | 5 " green | .. | — | 50.00 |
| 3 | 3 | 10 " lilac | .. | — | 100.00 |
| 4 | 4 | 1 peso, red.. | .. | 20.00 | 20.00 |

The 2½ c., 10 c., and 1 peso were re-printed in 1879 upon white to bluish paper, and at the same time a bogus variety of the 5 c. was made by altering the value on the die of the 2½ c. to 5 c. The reprints usually show diagonal lines or cuts across the design, the result of the cancellation of the dies from which the plates were made.

| No. Type. | | | | Un. | Used. |
|---|---|---|---|---|---|

5        6

7        8

**1869-71.** *Imperf.*

| 5 | 5 | 2½ c., pale blue | .. | 50 | 50 |
|---|---|---|---|---|---|
| 5a | " | 2½ c., blue .. | | 50 | |
| 6 | " | 2½ c., deep blue | .. | 50 | |
| 7 | 6 | 5 c., dark green | .. | 62 | |
| 7a | " | 5 c., green .. | .. | 62 | |
| 8 | 7 | 10 c., lilac .. | .. | 1.25 | 1.25 |
| 9 | " | 10 c., mauve | .. | 75 | 36 |
| 10 | " | 20 c., dark brown | .. | 36 | 25 |
| 10a | " | 20 c., pale brown | .. | 35 | |
| 11 | 8 | 1 p., carmine | .. | 2.50 | |
| 12 | " | 1 p., vermilion | .. | 2.50 | 2.50 |

9

*Variety.* With shaded figures "5" in corners.

| 13 | 9 | 5 c., blue-green | .. | 36 |
|---|---|---|---|---|

Reprints of Nos. 8, 11, and 13 were made in 1879 on bluish paper, the 1 peso being in dull rose and in carmine-rose. The 2½ c., 10 c., and 1 peso were reprinted in 1887 (?) on white paper, the 1 peso being in bright vermilion.

The error 10 c., in *blue* (No. 9), has also been reprinted from a new plate made from the defaced die. This was formerly catalogued, but there seems to be con-siderable doubt whether this error exists as a genuine original, as no trace of its existence can now be discovered.

No. Type.       *Un.   Used.*

No. Type.       *Un.   Used.*

10

11

12

13

14

15

16

17

18

19

20

21

22

### 1875-76. *Imperf.*

#### (a) *Wove paper.*

| No. | Type | | Un. | Used |
|---|---|---|---|---|
| 23 | 18 | 1 c., bk. on emerald | 12 | |
| 24 | " | 1 c., black on green | 4 | |
| 25 | " | 1 c., black ..   .. | 2 | |
| 26 | 19 | 2½ c., deep blue   .. | 4 | |
| 27 | 20 | 5 c., green ..   .. | 2.50 | 1 |
| 28 | 21 | 5 c.   "   ..   .. | 1.8₅ | 1 |
| 29 | " | 5 c., deep green   .. | — | 2 |
| 30 | 22 | 10 c., mauve     .. | 2.10 | 2. |

*Variety with pearl instead of cross the left of* "CORREOS."

| | | | |
|---|---|---|---|
| 30a | 21 | 5 c., green ..   .. | |
| 30b | " | 5 c., deep green .. | |

#### (b) *Laid paper.*

| | | | | |
|---|---|---|---|---|
| 31 | 18 | 1 c., black ..   .. | | |
| 32 | 20 | 5 c., deep green   .. | | |
| 33 | 21 | 5 c.   "     .. | — | 1 |
| 34 | 22 | 10 c., mauve     .. | — | 1. |

*Variety as before.*

| | | | |
|---|---|---|---|
| 34a | 21 | 5 c., deep green   .. | |

### 1873. *Imperf.*

| | | | Un. | Used |
|---|---|---|---|---|
| 14 | 10 | 1 c., yellow-green | 75 | 75 |
| 15 | " | 1 c., green ..   .. | 1.50 | |
| 16 | 11 | 5 c.   "   ..   .. | 1.00 | 1.00 |
| 17 | 12 | 10 c., mauve   .. | 1.50 | |
| 18 | 13 | 20 c., dark brown .. | 2.50 | |
| 18a | " | 20 c., yellow-brown | 75 | |
| 19 | 14 | 50 c., blue ..   .. | 25 | |
| 9a | " | 50 c., pale blue   .. | 25 | |
| - | 15 | 1 p., red ..   .. | 36 | 50 |
| | 16 | 2 p., blk. on yellow | 1.00 | 1.00 |
| | 17 | 5 p.   "   rose .. | 5.00 | 5.00 |

| No. Type. | | | Un. | Used. |
|---|---|---|---|---|

23

24

25

### 1879-81.  *Thin wove paper.*

| 35 | 23 | 2½ c., blue .. | .. | 12 | |
| 36 | 24 | 5 c., green .. | .. | — | 7.50 |
| 37 | 25 | 10 c., violet .. | .. | — | 30.00 |

26

27 *

### 1882-83.  *Imperf.*

#### (a) *Laid paper.*

| 38 | 23 | 2½ c., green | .. | — | 10.00 |
| 39 | 24 | 5 c.  ,, | .. | — | 75 |
| 40 | ,, | 5 c., violet .. | .. | | |
| 41 | 26 | 10 c., purple .. | .. | — | 2.00 |
| 42 | ,, | 10 c., bluish violet .. | | — | 3.75 |
| 43 | 27 | 20 c., brown .. | .. | 12 | |

#### (b) *Wove paper.*

| 44 | 23 | 2½ c., grey-green .. | | 6 | 6 |
| 44a | ,, | 2½ c., dp. grey-green | | 6 | |
| 45 | 24 | 5 c., deep green .. | | 16 | |
| 46 | ,, | 5 c., violet .. | .. | 25 | 25 |
| 47 | ,, | 5 c., blue .. | .. | — | 1.25 |
| 48 | 26 | 10 c., vermilion .. | | 25 | |
| 49 | 27 | 20 c., brown.. | .. | 18 | 25 |

#### *Variety. Tête-bêche.*

| 50 | 26 | 10 c., vermilion (*pair*) | 5.00 | |

| No. Type. | | | Un. | Used. |
|---|---|---|---|---|

28

29

30

### 1883-85.  *Imperf.*

#### (a) *Laid paper.*

| 51 | 18 | 1 c., mauve | .. | 50 | 50 |
| 52 | ,, | 1 c., blk. on pale gn. | | 12 | |
| 53 | 23 | 2½ c.  ,,  buff | .. | 2.50 | |
| 54 | 28 | 5 c., brown.. | .. | | |
| 55 | ,, | 5 c., yellow.. | .. | 8 | 8 |
| 56 | ,, | 5 c., green .. | .. | | |
| 57 | 29 | 10 c., blue-green | .. | 25 | |
| 58 | ,, | 10 c., lilac .. | .. | 25 | |
| 59 | 30 | 20 c., blue .. | .. | 18 | 18 |

#### (b) *Wove paper.*

| 60 | 18 | 1 c., blue-green | .. | 4 | |
| 61 | 28 | 5 c., brown.. | .. | 12 | |
| 62 | ,, | 5 c.  ,,  on buff | | | |
| 63 | ,, | 5 c., green.. | .. | 3.75 | 3.75 |
| 64 | 29 | 10 c., blue on azure . | | 18 | |
| 65 | ,, | 10 c., lilac .. | .. | | |

31

### 1886-87.  Type 31.  *Wove paper.*
#### *Imperf.*

| 66 | | 1 c., green on flesh | .. | 2 | |
| 67 | | 2½ c., black on orange .. | | 4 | 4 |
| 68 | | 5 c., blue on buff | .. | 12 | 12 |
| 69 | | 5 c., red on green | .. | 50 | 12 |
| 70 | | 10 c., rose-carm. on buff. | | 8 | 8 |
| 71 | | 20 c., purple on buff | .. | 10 | 10 |
| 72 | | 50 c., ochre on buff | .. | 25 | 25 |
| 74 | | 1 p., yellow on bluish grn. | | 36 | |
| 75 | | 2 p., green on lilac | .. | 62 | |

| No. | | | | Un. | Used. |
|---|---|---|---|---|---|

*Error on sheet of* 10 c.

| 75a | 50 c., red on buff | .. | 10.00 | |
|---|---|---|---|---|

*Variety. Centre of stamp erased, leaving frame only.*

| 76 | 10 c. (pair unsevered with variety) | .. | .. | |
|---|---|---|---|

### 1888. Type 31.
*Imperf.*

| 77 | 1 c., red on lilac | .. | 2 | |
|---|---|---|---|---|
| 78 | 2½ c., mauve on flesh | .. | 4 | 4 |
| 79 | 5 c., lake on buff | .. | 4 | 4 |
| 80 | 10 c., dark brown on grn. | | 10 | |

### Provisionals issued at Medellin.

32

33

34

35

### 1888.

| No. | Type. | *Imperf.* | | | |
|---|---|---|---|---|---|
| 81 | 32 | 2½ c., blk. on yellow | 2.50 | 2.50 |
| 82 | 33 | 2½ c., red on white.. | 1.25 | |
| 83 | 34 | 5 c., blk. on yellow | 1.00 | 1.00 |
| 84 | 35 | 5 c., red on orange. | 36 | |

There are two types of No. 81, ten of No. 82, and ten each of Nos. 83 and 84. The two types of No. 82 form the last row on the sheet which contains the ten types of No. 83.

36

37

### 1890.
*Perforated.*

| 36 | 2½ c., black on buff.. | 12 | |
|---|---|---|---|
| 37 | 5 c., „ yellow | 25 | 25 |

| No. Type. | | | Un. | Used. |
|---|---|---|---|---|

38

39

| 87 | 38 | 10 c., black on buff . | 50 | |
|---|---|---|---|---|
| 88 | „ | 10 c., „ rose . | 50 | |
| 89 | 39 | 20 c., „ yellow | 62 | |

There are ten types of each of the above. There are two settings of the 5 c.

40

41

42

43

44

45

### 1889-90. *Perf.* 13½.

| 90 | 40 | 1 c., blk. on rose.. | 2 | |
|---|---|---|---|---|
| 91 | „ | 2½ c., „ pale blue | 2 | |
| 92 | „ | 5 c., „ yellow | 4 | |
| 93 | 41 | 10 c., „ green . | 8 | |
| 94 | 42 | 20 c., blue .. .. | 18 | |
| 95 | 43 | 50 c., brown. .. | 25 | |
| 96 | „ | 50 c., green. .. | 1.00 | 1.c |
| 97 | 44 | 1 p., vermilion .. | 50 | |
| 98 | 45 | 2 p., blk. on magenta | 3.75 | 3 - |
| 99 | „ | 5 p., „ vermilion | — | 6. |

*Error of colour, on sheet of* 50 c.

| 100 | 42 | 20 c., brown,. | .. | |
|---|---|---|---|

|  | | | *Un.* | *Used.* |
|---|---|---|---|---|

No. Type.

*Varieties. Imperf.*

| 101 | 40 | 1 c., blk. on rose .. | | |
| 102 | ,, | 2½ c. ,, pale blue | 1.25 | |
| 103 | ,, | 5 c. ,, yellow .. | | |
| 104 | 45 | 2 p. ,, magenta | | |
| 105 | ,, | 5 p. ,, vermilion | | |

46          47

**1892-93.** *Perf.* 13½.

| 106 | 46 | 1 c., cinnamon on buff .. .. | 2 | |
| 107 | ,, | 1 c., blue .. .. | 2 | |
| 108 | ,, | 2½ c., violet on lilac . | 4 | |
| 109 | ,, | 2½ c., green .. | 4 | |
| 110 | ,, | 5 c., black .. .. | 8 | 8 |
| 111 | ,, | 5 c., red .. | 6 | 6 |
| 112 | 47 | 10 c., grey-brown .. | 6 | 6 |

*Error of colour.*

| 113 | 46 | 2½ c., black .. | | |

48

**1896.** Type 48. *Perf.* 14.

| 114 | 2 c., grey .. .. | 2 | 4 |
| 115 | 2½ c., Venetian red .. | 2 | 6 |
| 116 | 3 c., red .. .. | 2 | |
| 117 | 5 c., green .. .. | 2 | 4 |
| 118 | 10 c., violet .. | 4 | |
| 119 | 20 c., yellow-brown .. | 12 | 18 |
| 120 | 50 c., sepia .. | 25 | 36 |

*Colours changed.* *Perf.* 14.

| 121 | 2 c., lilac-rose .. .. | 2 | |
| 122 | 2½ c., blue .. .. | 2 | |
| 123 | 3 c., olive-green . .. | 2 | |
| 124 | 5 c., dull yellow . .. | 2 | 2 |
| 125 | 10 c., brown-lilac . .. | 4 | |
| 126 | 20 c., bright blue. .. | 12 | |
| 127 | 50 c., rose .. .. | 25 | |

*Same type and perf.*
In the following the centre is in black.

| 128 | 1 p., ultramarine .. | 1.00 | 1.00 |
| 129 | 1 p., rose .. .. | 1.00 | 1.00 |

|  | *Un.* | *Used.* |
|---|---|---|

No.

| 130 | 2 p., orange .. .. | | |
| 131 | 2 p., myrtle-green .. | | |
| 132 | 5 p., mauve .. .. | | |
| 133 | 5 p., violet .. .. | | |

49

**1899.** Type 49. *Perf.* 11.

| 134 | ½ c., slate-blue .. .. | 2 |
| 135 | 1 c. ,, .. .. | 2 |
| 136 | 2 c., grey-black . .. | 2 |
| 137 | 3 c., red .. .. | 4 |
| 138 | 4 c., sepia .. .. | 4 |
| 139 | 5 c., green .. .. | 4 |
| 140 | 10 c., red .. .. | 6 |
| 141 | 20 c., purple .. .. | 12 |
| 142 | 50 c., ochre .. .. | 30 |
| 143 | 1 p., greenish black .. | 62 |
| 144 | 2 p., slate-green . .. | 2.50 |

50          51

52

**1901-2.** PROVISIONALS.

No. Type. *Perf.* 12.

| 145 | 50 | 1 c., carmine .. | |
| 146 | 51 | 1 c., stone .. .. | 2 |
| 147 | ,, | 1 c., blue .. .. | 2 |
| 148 | 52 | 1 c., red .. .. | 2 |
| 149 | ,, | 1 c., blue .. .. | 2 |

The above stamps are type-set in blocks of four varieties.

No. Type.                     *Un. Used.*          No.

53              54

55              56

**1902.**  *Wove paper.   The* peso *values on laid paper.   Perf.* 12.

| 150 | 53 | 1 c., rose | .. | .. | 2 |
| 151 | ,, | 2 c., blue | .. | .. | 2 |
| 152 | ,, | 2 c., mauve | | .. | 2 |
| 153 | ,, | 3 c., green | .. | .. | 2 |
| 154 | ,, | 4 c., dull purple | .. | | 2 |
| 155 | ,, | 4 c., deep lilac | .. | | 2 |
| 156 | 54 | 5 c., rose-red | .. | .. | 2 |
| 157 | 55 | 10 c., rose-lilac | | .. | 4 |
| 158 | ,, | 20 c., green | .. | .. | 4 |
| 159 | ,, | 30 c., rose | .. | .. | 6 |
| 160 | ,, | 40 c., blue | .. | .. | 8 |
| 161 | ,, | 50 c., brown on yellow | | .. | 8 |
| 162 | 56 | 1 p., violet & black. | | | 12 |
| 163 | ,, | 2 p., rose       ,, | | | 25 |
| 164 | ,, | 5 p., grey-blue ,, | | | 62 |

*Error on sheet of* 2 c.

| 165 | 53 | 3 c., blue | .. | .. | 5.00 |

*Laid paper.*

| 166 | | 1 c., rose | .. | .. | 25 |

57              58

**1903.**  Types 57 *and* 58.  *Perf.* 12.

| 167 | 50 c., rose | .. | .. |
| 168 | 1 p., sepia | .. | .. |

No.                          *Un.  Used.*

L 1

**1903.**

Type L 1.  *Perf.* 12.

| 191 | 20 c., brown-red | .. | |
| 192 | 40 c., violet | .. | .. |

REGISTRATION STAMPS.

A 1

**1896.**

Type A 1.  *Perf.* 14.

| 201 | 2½ c., blue | .. | .. | 8 |
| 202 | 2½ c., rose | .. | .. | 8 |

A 2

A 3

**1899.**

No. Type.              *Perf.* 11.

| 203 | A 2 | 2½ c., blue | .. | .. | 4 |
| 204 | A 3 | 10 c., mauve | . | — | 12 |

| | Un. | Used. |
|---|---|---|
| No. | | |

**A 4**

**1902.** Type A 4.
*Perf.* 12.

205|10 c., violet on blue .. 4

TOO LATE STAMPS.

**A 11**

**1899.** Type A 11.
*Perf.* 11.

221|2½ c., green .. .. 2

**A 12**

**1901.** Type A 12.
*Laid paper. Perf.* 12.

122|2½ c., purple .. .. 62
Type-set. Four varieties.

AN., **1902.** *Similar to Type* A 12, 4 *fresh varieties. Wove paper. Perf.* 12.
22a|2½ c., lilac .. ..

**A 13**

**1902.** Type A 13. *Perf.* 12.
23|2½ c., violet .. .. 2

| | Un. | Used. |
|---|---|---|
| No. | | |

RETURNED ACKNOWLEDGMENT STAMPS.

**A 21**

**1902.** Type A 21. *Perf.* 12.
241| 5 c., black on rose .. 4

**1903.** *Same type and perf.*
242| 5 c., slate-green .. 4

## BOLIVAR.

**1**

No. Type. **1863–66.** *Imperf.*

| 1 | 1 | 10 c., green .. | .. | — | 30.00 |
| 2 | " | 10 c., rose .. | .. | 2.50 | 36 |
| 3 | " | 1 p., red .. | .. | 12 | |

There are two types of the 10 c.—one with 5, the other with 6 stars below the shield.

2          3

4          5

**1872.** *Imperf.*

| 4 | 2 | 5 c., blue .. | .. | 12 | |
| 5 | " | 5 c., deep blue | .. | 12 | |
| 6 | 3 | 10 c., pale mauve .. | | 36 | 36 |
| 7 | " | 10 c., deep mauve .. | | 36 | 36 |
| 8 | 4 | 20 c., green .. | .. | 5.00 | 3.75 |
| 9 | 5 | 80 c., vermilion | .. | 7.50 | 5.65 |

| No. Type. | | Un. | Used. |
|---|---|---|---|

6

7

**1874–77.** *Imperf.*

| 10 | 6 | 5 c., blue | .. | .. | — | 62 |
|---|---|---|---|---|---|---|
| 11 | 7 | 10 c., mauve | .. | .. | 25 | 25 |
| 12 | ,, | 10 c., lilac | .. | .. | 75 | 25 |

8

**1878.** *Imperf.*

| 13 | 8 | 5 c., blue | .. | .. | — | 1.25 |
|---|---|---|---|---|---|---|

9

10

11

12

**1879.** *Dated. Perf.* 12½.
(a) *Wove paper.*

| 14 | 9 | 5 c., blue | .. | .. | 12 | 10 |
|---|---|---|---|---|---|---|
| 15 | 10 | 10 c., mauve | .. | .. | 12 | 8 |
| 16 | 11 | 20 c., red | .. | .. | 25 | 12 |
| 17 | 12 | 40 c., brown | | .. | 36 | 36 |

*Error of colour.*

| 17a | 11 | 20 c., green | .. | .. | 25.00 | |
|---|---|---|---|---|---|---|

---

| No. Type. | | Un. | Used. |
|---|---|---|---|

13

14

(b) *Blue laid paper.*

| 18 | 9 | 5 c., blue | .. | .. | 18 |
|---|---|---|---|---|---|
| 19 | 10 | 10 c., mauve | | .. | 25 |
| 20 | 11 | 20 c., red | .. | .. | 45 |
| 21 | 12 | 40 c., brown.. | | .. | 75 |

**1880.** *Dated. Perf.* 12½.
(a) *Wove paper.*

| 22 | 9 | 5 c., blue | .. | .. | 2 |
|---|---|---|---|---|---|
| 23 | 10 | 10 c., mauve | | .. | 8 |
| 24 | 11 | 20 c., red | .. | .. | 18 |
| 25 | 12 | 40 c., brown.. | | .. | 25 |
| 26 | 13 | 80 c., green | .. | .. | 1.00 |
| 27 | 14 | 1 p., orange | | .. | 1.50 |

*Error of colour.*

| 27a | 11 | 20 c., green | .. | .. | 25.00 |
|---|---|---|---|---|---|

(b) *Blue laid paper.*

| 28 | 9 | 5 c., blue | .. | .. | 18 |
|---|---|---|---|---|---|
| 29 | 10 | 10 c., mauve | | .. | 50 |
| 30 | 11 | 20 c., red | .. | .. | 1.00 |
| 31 | 12 | 40 c., brown.. | | .. | 90 |
| 32 | 14 | 1 p., orange | | .. | 40.00 |

15

**1882.** *Head in second colour.*
(a) *Perf.* 12.

| 33 | 15 | 5 p., blue and carm. | 1.85 |
|---|---|---|---|
| 34 | ,, | 10 p., marone and blue | 2.50 |

(b) *Perf.* 16.

| 35 | 15 | 5 p., blue and carm. | 5.00 |
|---|---|---|---|
| 36 | ,, | 10 p., marone and blue | 3.75 |

|  | | | Un. | Used. |
|---|---|---|---|---|
| No. Type. | | | | |

16

17

18

19

20

21

### 1882. Dated.
#### (a) Perf. 12.

| 7 | 16 | 5 c., ultramarine .. | | |
| 8 | 17 | 10 c., lilac .. | — | 12 |
| 9 | 18 | 20 c., carmine .. | — | 8 |
| 0 | 19 | 40 c., brown.. | | |
| 1 | 20 | 80 c., green .. | | |
| 2 | 21 | 1 p., orange | 1.00 | 1.00 |

#### (b) Perf. 16×12.

| 3 | 16 | 5 c., ultramarine .. | 6 | 6 |
| 4 | 17 | 10 c., lilac .. | 6 | 6 |
| 5 | 18 | 20 c., carmine | 25 | 12 |
| 6 | 19 | 40 c., brown | 36 | 36 |
| 7 | 20 | 80 c., green | 1.60 | 1.60 |
| 8 | 21 | 1 p., orange | 1.50 | 1.50 |

### 1883. Dated.
#### (a) Perf. 12.

| 9 | 16 | 5 c., ultramarine .. | | |
| 0 | 17 | 10 c., lilac .. | — | 1.25 |
| 1 | 18 | 20 c., carmine | | |
| 2 | 19 | 40 c., brown.. | | |
| 3 | 20 | 80 c., green .. | 1.00 | 75 |
| 4 | 21 | 1 p., orange.. | 62 | 62 |

#### (b) Perf. 16×12.

| 55 | 16 | 5 c., ultramarine .. | 4 | 6 |
| 56 | 17 | 10 c., lilac .. | 16 | 4 |
| 57 | 18 | 20 c., carmine | 25 | 6 |
| 58 | 19 | 40 c., brown.. | 36 | 25 |
| 59 | 20 | 80 c., green .. | 62 | 50 |
| 60 | 21 | 1 p., orange | — | 62 |

### 1884. Dated.
#### (a) Perf. 12.

| 61 | 16 | 5 c., ultramarine .. | | |
| 62 | 17 | 10 c., lilac .. | | |
| 63 | 18 | 20 c., carmine | 25 | 25 |
| 64 | 19 | 40 c., brown.. | | |
| 65 | 20 | 80 c., green .. | 62 | |
| 66 | 21 | 1 p., orange | 90 | 90 |

#### (b) Perf. 16×12.

| 67 | 16 | 5 c., ultramarine .. | 8 | 8 |
| 68 | 17 | 10 c., lilac .. | 18 | 18 |
| 69 | 18 | 20 c., carmine | | |
| 70 | 19 | 40 c., brown.. | 30 | 30 |
| 71 | 20 | 80 c., green .. | 70 | 70 |
| 72 | 21 | 1 p., orange | 1.00 | 1.00 |

### 1885. Dated.
#### (a) Perf. 12.

| 73 | 16 | 5 c., ultramarine .. | 12 | 18 |
| 74 | 17 | 10 c., lilac .. | | |
| 75 | 18 | 20 c., carmine | | |
| 76 | 19 | 40 c., brown.. | | |
| 77 | 20 | 80 c., green .. | | |
| 78 | 21 | 1 p., orange | 90 | |

#### (b) Perf. 16×12.

| 79 | 16 | 5 c., ultramarine .. | 8 | 8 |
| 80 | 17 | 10 c., lilac .. | 8 | 4 |
| 81 | 18 | 20 c., carmine | 25 | 25 |
| 82 | 19 | 40 c., brown.. | 25 | 25 |
| 83 | 20 | 80 c., green .. | 62 | 62 |
| 84 | 21 | 1 p., orange | — | 1.85 |

22

### 1891. Perf. 14.

| 85 | 22 | 1 c., black .. | 2 | 4 |
| 86 | " | 5 c., orange | 12 | 8 |
| 87 | " | 10 c., red .. | 12 | 12 |
| 88 | " | 20 c., blue .. | 30 | 30 |
| 89 | " | 50 c., green .. | 70 | |
| 90 | " | 1 p., violet .. | 1.00 | |

No.                                    *Un.  Used.*

No.                                    *Un.  Used.*

23                                24

25                                26

**1903.**

Types 23 *to* 26.  *Laid paper.*  *Imperf.*

| No. | | Un. | Used |
|---|---|---|---|
| 91 | 50 c., green on rose .. | 4 | |
| 92 | 50 c., blue  ,,  .. | 4 | |
| · 93 | 50 c.  ,,  on bluish .. | 4 | |
| 94 | 1 p., vermil. on pale red | 8 | |
| 95 | 1 p., pale green on lavender  ..  .. | 8 | |
| 96 | 1 p., deep green on lavender  ..  .. | 8 | |
| 97 | 5 p., carm. on lavender | 36 | |
| 98 | 5 p., carmine on yellow | 36 | |
| 99 | 5 p.  ,,  brown | 36 | |
| 100 | 10 p., blue on greenish.. | 75 | |
| 101 | 10 p., purple on  ,,  .. | 75 | |

The sheets of the above are made up very irregularly with stamps sideways, etc.  Some values are said to exist pin-perf.

REGISTRATION STAMPS.

A 1

**1903.**

Type A 1.  *Laid paper.*  *Imperf.*

| | | |
|---|---|---|
| 1 | 20 c., brn.-orange on rose | 4 |
| 1 | 20 c.  ,,  buff .. | 4 |

---

TOO LATE STAMPS.

B 1

**1903,**  Type B 1.  *Laid paper.*  *Imperf.*

| | | |
|---|---|---|
| 251 | 20 c., purple on bluish.. | 4 |
| 252 | 20 c., carmine  ,,  .. | 4 |

RETURNED ACKNOWLEDGMENT STAMPS.

C 1

**1903.**  Type C 1.  *Laid paper.*  *Imperf.*

| | | |
|---|---|---|
| 301 | 20 c., orange on yellow . | 4 |
| 302 | 20 c., deep blue  ,,  .. | 4 |

## BOYACA.

1

**1899.**  Type 1.  *Perf.* 13½.

| | | |
|---|---|---|
| 1 | 5 c., blue-green  .. | |

**1902.**  *Same type.*  *Bluish paper.*

| | | |
|---|---|---|
| 2 | 5 c., blue-green (perf. 13½) | |
| 3 | 5 c., blue-green (imperf.) | |

2                                3

**1903.**  Types 2 *to* 7.  *Perf.* 12.

| | | |
|---|---|---|
| 4 | 10 c., grey-black  .. | 4 |
| 5 | 10 c., bluish grey  .. | 4 |
| 5a | 20 c., brown  ..  .. | 6 |

| | | | *Un.* | *Used.* |
|---|---|---|---|---|

No.

| | | |
|---|---|---|
| 2 | 3 | |

**1882–83.** *Handstamped.*

| 2 | 2 | 5 c., lilac-rose | .. | |
| 3 | 3 | (5 c.) | ,, | |

*Error. Fig. in lower left corner omitted.*

| 3a | 2 | 5 c., lilac-rose | .. | |

| | | | *Un.* | *Used.* |
|---|---|---|---|---|

4

| 4 | 4 | (5 c.), lilac-rose | — | 10.00 |

The monogram is "S.P.", for Salmon Posso, prefect of Atrato.

5

**1892.** *Imperf.*

| 5 | 5 | 5 c., red on rose | .. | |
| 6 | ,, | 10 c., gn. on pale gn. | | |

There is great doubt as to the authenticity of these last.

**CUCUTA.**

| 6 | 20 c., purple-brown | .. | 6 | 6 |
| 7 | 20 c., marone | .. .. | 6 | 6 |
| 7a | 20 c., rosy lake | .. | 6 | |
| 8 | 50 c., green | .. | 8 | 8 |
| 9 | 1 p., vermilion | .. .. | 12 | 12 |
| 9a | 5 p., black on rose | .. | 62 | |
| 9b | 10 p., ,, buff | .. | 1.10 | |

*Variety.* *Tête-bêche* (pair).

| 9c | 10 p., black on buff | .. | | |

*Imperf.*

| 10 | 10 c., grey-black | .. | 4 | 6 |
| 11 | 10 c., bluish grey | .. | | |
| 12 | 20 c., purple-brown | .. | 6 | |
| 12a | 20 c., marone | .. .. | 6 | 8 |
| 13 | 20 c., rosy lake | .. | 25 | 8 |
| 14 | 5 p., black on rose | .. | 62 | |
| 15 | 10 p., ,, buff | .. | 1.10 | |

*Variety.* *Tête-bêche* (pair).

| 16 | 10 p., black on buff | .. | | |

**CAUCA.**

1

**1879.**

No. Type. *Handstamped.*

| 1 | 1 | (5 c.), black | .. | |

**1900.** Type 1. Black *on coloured paper.*
*(a) Imperf.*

| 1 | 1 c., yellow (?) | .. | .. |
| 2 | 2 c., rose (?) | .. | .. |
| 3 | 5 c., green (?) | .. | .. |

| No. | | Un. | Used. |
|---|---|---|---|

(b) *Perf.* 11½ *vertically.* "Gobierno Provisorio" *at top. Value expressed by* "ctvo" *or* "cvos."

| 4 | 1 c., blue-green .. | .. | |
| 5 | 2 c., (?) .. | .. | |
| 6 | 5 c., deep pink .. | .. | — 5.00 |
| 7 | 10 c. ,, | .. | |
| 8 | 20 c., yellow .. | .. | |

(c) *Perf. as last.* "Gobierno Provisional" *at top. Value expressed by* "centavo" *or* "ctvos." *Both in italics. Surcharged* "Andez B. Fernandez" *up right side in* green (G.), *or* black (B.).

| 9 | 2 c., blue-green (G.) .. | | |
| 10 | 5 c., white (G.).. | .. 6.25 | 5.00 |
| 11 | 5 c. ,, (G.), ("ctvos." — | | 3.75 |
| | smaller) ., | .. | |
| 12 | 10 c., deep pink (B.) .. | | |
| 13 | 20 c., yellow (G.) | | |

## CUNDINAMARCA.

| | 1 | | 2 |

No. Type. **1870.** *Imperf. Wove paper.*

| 1 | 1 | 5 c., pale blue .. | 30 | 30 |
| 1a | ,, | 5 c., bright blue .. | 36 | |
| 2 | 2 | 10 c., scarlet .. | — | 50 |

The 5 c. has been reprinted. The reprints show traces of the diagonal lines or cuts made across the die at the time it was cancelled. The lines may be traced crossing the figure in the right upper corner, and across the "c" of "CINCO," etc.

| | 3 | | 4 |

**1877-82.** *Imperf.*

(a) *Wove paper.*

| 3 | 10 c., red .. | .. | 45 |
| 4 | 20 c., green .. | .. | 1.10 |

---

| No. Type. | | Un. | Used. |
|---|---|---|---|

| | 5 | | 6 |

| 5 | 5 | 50 c., pale mauve .. | 1.60 | 1.50 |
| 5a | ,, | 50 c., bright violet.. | 1.60 | |
| 6 | 6 | 1 p., dark brown .. | 5.00 | |
| 7 | ,, | 1 p., chestnut .. | 3.75 | |

(b) *Laid paper.*

| 8 | 3 | 10 c., salmon .. | .. | 18 | |
| 8a | ,, | 10 c., rose (thick paper) | | |
| 9 | 4 | 20 c., green .. | .. | — |

 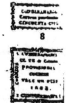

| | 7 | | 9 |

| | | | 8 |

**1883.** *Type-set. Imperf.*

| 10 | 7 | 10 c., black on yellow | 5.00 | |
| 11 | 8 | 50 c., ,, magenta | 2.10 | 2.50 |
| 12 | 9 | 1 p., ,, brown | — | |

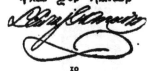

| | | 10 |

| 13 | 10 | 2 r., black on green. 10.00 |

There are four types of the 10 c., two each of the 50 c. and 1 p. The 1 and 2 reales are signed by the postmas:

**1884.** *Surcharged in black, with* "$." *in opposite corners. Wove paper.*

| 14 | 3 | 1 p. on 10 c., red .. |

No. Type. | Un. Used.

**II**

*a*     *b*

**1884.** *Imperf.*

| 15 | II | 5 c., blue (*a*) | .. | 25 |
| 16 | " | 5 c.    "   (*b*) | .. | 36 |

There are two types of this stamp, one (*a*) with a larger ball to the figures "5" than in the other (*b*).

*Variety. Tête-bêche* (pair).

| 16*a* | II | 5 c., blue (*a*) | .. |

**12**       **13**

**1885.** *Imperf.*

| 17 | 12 | 5 c., pale blue | .. | 12 |
| 17*a* | " | 5 c., deep blue | .. | 12 |
| 18 | 13 | 10 c., vermilion | .. | 36 |
| 19 | 13 | 10 c., verm. on lilac. | | 36 |
| 20 | " | 20 c., green .. | | 50 |
| 20*a* | " | 20 c., yellow-green . | | 2.50 |
| 21 | 12 | 50 c., violet .. | .. | 1.00 |
| 22 | 13 | 1 p., chestnut | .. | 1.75 |

The used stamps of this State are pen-cancelled only.

## GARZON.

| | |
|---|---|
| **R. DE C** GARZÓN, 1894 NO HAY Estampillas PAGÓ $ 0,01 | **R. DE C.** GARZÓN, 1894 No hay estampillas PAGO UN PESO |

**I**      **2**

**1894.** *Paper ruled with blue lines forming oblongs. Imperf.*

| 1 | I | 1 c., black .. | .. |
| 2 | 2 | 1 p.   "   .. | .. | 3.75 | 2.50 |

No. Type. | Un. Used.

**3**

| 3 | 3 | 1 c., black .. | .. |

## HONDA.

**I**

**1896.**

Colombia Type 55 *surcharged with* Type 1, *in* black.

| 1 | 1 | 1 c. on 2 c., green | .. | 1.85 | 75 |

There are forgeries of this surcharge in smaller type struck diagonally.

## PANAMA.

**I**      **2**

**1878.**

*Imperf.*

| 1 | I | 5 c., green .. | .. | 36 | |
| 2 | " | 5 c., blue-green | .. | 36 | |
| 3 | " | 5 c., dull green | .. | 12 | 8 |
| 4 | " | 10 c., blue .. | .. | — | 1.85 |
| 5 | " | 20 c., red .. | .. | 1.00 | |
| 6 | 2 | 50 c., yellow-ochre .. | | 1.60 | |

The 10 c., unused, usually found, is printed from a new plate, the distinguishing mark of which is a short stroke through the frame below the "TA" of "CENTAVOS." Some authorities consider it a reprint. All values exist perf. (unofficial).

No. Type.      *Un. Used.*     No. Type.      *Un. Used.*

**3**       **3***

**1887-88.** *Perf.* 13½.   Black *on colour.*

| | | | | |
|--|--|--|--|--|
| 7 | 3 | 1 c., green .. | 2 | 2 |
| 8 | 3* | 2 c., flesh .. | 12 | 6 |
| 9 | ,, | 2 c., pale rose .. | 2 | |
| 10 | ,, | 2 c., bright rose .. | 4 | |
| 11 | ,, | 5 c., blue .. | 2 | 2 |
| 12 | ,, | 5 c., greenish blue . | 18 | 2 |
| 13 | ,, | 10 c., yellow | 6 | 2 |
| 14 | ,, | 20 c., lilac .. | 12 | 12 |

*Error of colour.*

| | | | | |
|--|--|--|--|--|
| 15 | 3* | 10 c., lilac .. | | |

*Colour on thick white paper.*

| | | | | |
|--|--|--|--|--|
| 16 | 3* | 50 c., brown.. | 36 | 36 |

*Thin paper.*

| | | | | |
|--|--|--|--|--|
| 16a | 3* | 5 c., grey .. | 25 | |
| 17 | ,, | 50 c., brown | 75 | 75 |

These stamps are found imperf., and also imperf. horizontally or vertically.

**4**

**1892-96.** *Perf.* 12.

| | | | | |
|--|--|--|--|--|
| 18 | 4 | 1 c., green .. | 2 | 2 |
| 19 | ,, | 2 c., carmine | 2 | 2 |
| 20 | ,, | 5 c., blue .. | 6 | 2 |
| 21 | ,, | 10 c., orange | 12 | 2 |
| 22 | ,, | 20 c., violet .. | 25 | 8 |
| 23 | ,, | 50 c., bistre-brown.. | 50 | 36 |
| 24 | ,, | 1 p., lake .. | 1.25 | 1.25 |

HABILITADO.      HABILITADO.

**1894**         **1894**

**1**          **1**

CENTAVO.       CENTAVO.

**5**         **6**

**1894.** *Surcharged with* Types 5-10.

| | | | | |
|--|--|--|--|--|
| 5 | 5 | 1 c., in black, on 2 c. (No. 19) .. | 4 | 12 |
| 6 | 6 | 1 c., in black, on 2 c. (No 19) .. | 4 | |

HABILITADO      HABILITADO

**1894**         **1894**

**5**          **5**

CENTAVOS.       CENTAVOS.

**7**         **8**

HABILITADO.     HABILITADO.

**1894**         **1894**

**10**        **10**

CENTAVOS.      CENTAVOS.

**9**         **10**

| | | | | |
|--|--|--|--|--|
| 26 | 7 | 5 c., in red, on 20 c. (No. 14) .. | | 8 |
| 27 | 8 | 5 c., in red, on 20 c. (No. 14) .. | | 12 |
| 28 | 7 | 5 c., in green, on 20 c. (No. 14) .. | 5.00 | |
| 29 | 8 | 5 c., in green, on 20 c. (No. 14) .. | | |
| 30 | 9 | 10 c., in red, on 50 c. (No. 16) .. | | 36 |
| 30a | 10 | 10 c., in red, on 50 c. (No. 16) .. | | 1.25 |
| 31 | 9 | 10 c., in red, on 50 c. (No. 17) .. | | 12 |
| 31a | 10 | 10 c., in red, on 50 c. (No. 17) .. | | 36 |

*Varieties.* (a) *Surcharge inverted.*

| | | | |
|--|--|--|--|
| 32 | 5 | 1 c., in blk., on 2 c. | 1.25 |
| 32a | 6 | 1 c., in blk., on 2 c. | 1.25 |
| 33 | 7 | 5 c., in red, on 20 c. | 2.50 |
| 34 | 8 | 5 c. ,, on 20 c. | |
| 34a | 7 | 5 c., in grn., on 20 c. | |
| 35 | 9 | 10 c., in red, on 50 c. (No. 16) .. | |
| 35a | 10 | 10 c., in red, on 50 c. (No. 16) .. | |
| 36 | 9 | 10 c., in red, on 50 c. (No. 17) .. | 3.00 |
| 36a | 10 | 10 c., in red, on 50 c. (No. 17) .. | |

(b) *Surcharge sideways (reading up or down).*

| | | | |
|--|--|--|--|
| 37 | 7 | 5 c., in red, on 20 c. | |

(c) "CCNTAVO" *for* "CENTAVO."

| | | | | |
|--|--|--|--|--|
| 38 | 6 | 1 c., in black, on 2 c. | 1.25 | |
| 39 | 7 | 5 c., in red, on 20 c. | | |
| 39a | 8 | 5 c. ,, on 20 c. | 1.25 | 1 |
| 40 | 10 | 10 c. ,, on 50 c. (No. 16) .. | 1.85 | |
| 41 | ,, | 10 c., in red, on 50 c. (No. 17) .. | | |

*Un.   Used.*

**No. Type.**

(*d*) "CENTAVO" *for* "CENTAVO."
42 | 6 | 1 c., in black, on 2 c.   1.25

(*e*) "CENTAVO" *omitted.*
43 | 5 | 1 c., in black, on 2 c.
43*a*| 6 | 1 c.   ,,   on 2 c.

(*f*) *Date omitted.*
44 | 8 | 5 c., in red, on 20 c.
45 | 9 | 10 c.   ,,   on 50 c.
         (No. 16) ..   ..

(*g*) "1894" *and* "HABILITADO"
         *transposed.*
46 | 5 | 1 c., in black, on 2 c.
         (No. 19) ..   ..

(*h*) "HABILITAD."
47 | 5 | 1 c., in black, on 2 c.
         (No. 19) ..   ..
48 | 6 | 1 c., in black, on 2 c.
         (No. 19) ..   ..

There are two types of "1" in both 1 c.
and 10 c. There are also other minor
varieties of the surcharges.

REGISTERED LETTER STAMP.

**51**
**1888.** *Perf.*
101| 51 |10 c., black on drab.   25

**1897.** Type 4 *surcharged in* black.
(*a*) "AR COLON COLOMBIA."
102|10 c., orange   ..   ..

(*b*) "R COLON" *in a circle.*
103|10 c., orange   ..   ..

**1900.** Type 4 *surcharged* "R,"
*in a circle, in* black.
104|10 c., orange   ..   ..

**52**
Type 52.
105|10 c., black on pale green   8

**1901.** Type 52.
106|10 c., red   ..   ..

*Un.   Used.*

**No.**

**1902.** Type 52 *surcharged with figures*
       "20," *in* blue.
107|"20" on 10 c., red   ..   .

## RIO HACHA.

1

2

3

**1901.** *Type-set. Imperf.* Type 1.
1 | 5 c., black   ..   ..
2 | 5 c.   ,,   on yellow ..
3 |10 c., black   ..   ..
4 |10 c.   ,,   on blue-green

Type 2. "No" *and* "Vale."
5 | 5 c., black   ..   ..   —   2.00
6 | 5 c.   ,,   on yellow ..   —   3.00
7 |10 c., black   ..   ..   —   2.00
8 |10 c.   ,,   on blue-green   —   3.00

*Same type. Italic* "*P*" *in* "Postal."
9 | 5 c., black   ..   ..
10 | 5 c.   ,,   on yellow ..
11 |10 c.   ,,   ..   ..
12 |10 c.   ,,   on blue   ..

*Same type. Italic* "*t*" *in* "Agente."
13 |10 c., black on blue   ..

Type 3. "NO" *and* "Vale."
14 | 5 c., black   ..   ..   —   2.50
15 | 5 c.   ,,   on yellow ..   —   2.50
16 |10 c., black   ..   ..   —   2.00
17 |10 c.   ,,   on blue-green   —   4.00

Type 3. "NO" *and* "vale."
18 | 5 c., black   :.   ..
19 | 5 c.   ,,   on yellow ..
20 |10 c., black   ..   ..   —   7.50
21 |10 c.   ,,   on blue-green   .   ..

| No. Type. | Un. | Used. | No. Type. | Un. | Used. |
|---|---|---|---|---|---|

## SANTANDER.

**1884.** *Imperf.*

| 1 | 1 | 1 c., blue .. .. | 4 | 4 |
|---|---|---|---|---|
| 2 | ,, | 1 c., ultramarine .. | | |
| 3 | ,, | 5 c., vermilion, p, 6 c. | 8 | 6 |
| 4 | ,, | 10 c., violet, p, 18 c. | 18 | |

**1886.** *Imperf.*

| 5 | 2 | 1 c., blue .. .. | 8 | 18 |
|---|---|---|---|---|
| 6 | ,, | 1 c., sky-blue .. | 18 | |
| 7 | ,, | 1 c., ultramarine .. | | |
| 8 | 3 | 5 c., vermilion .. | 62 | 8 |
| 9 | ,, | 5 c., pale red .. | 6 | 12 |
| 10 | ,, | 10 c., purple.. .. | 12 | 8 |

*Variety. Stamp sideways.*

| 10a | 3 | 5 c. (block of 3) .. | 90 |
|---|---|---|---|
| 10b | 3 | 10 c. ( ,, ) .. | 1.25 |

*Error.* "CINCO" *instead of* "DIEZ."

| 11 | 3 | 5 c., purple.. .. | 8.75 |
|---|---|---|---|
| 12 | ,, | 5 c.+10 c. (pair) .. | 10.00 |

**1887.** *Imperf.*

| 13 | 4 | 1 c., blue .. .. | 12 | |
|---|---|---|---|---|
| 14 | ,, | 1 c., ultramarine .. | 4 | 6 |
| '5 | ,, | 5 c., vermilion .. | 8 | |
| 5 | ,, | 10 c., violet .. .. | | |

**1890.** *Thin paper. Perf.* 13½.

| 17 | 5 | 1 c., blue .. .. | 2 | |
|---|---|---|---|---|
| 18 | 6 | 5 c., vermilion .. | 25 | 25 |
| 19 | 7 | 10 c., violet .. .. | 18 | 25 |

**1895.** *Perf.* 13½.

| 20 | 8 | 5 c., red on buff .. | 8 | : |
|---|---|---|---|---|

**1895-96.** *Perf.* 13.

| 21 | 9 | 5 c., chocolate .. | 8 | 12 |
|---|---|---|---|---|
| 22 | ,, | 5 c., yellow-green.. | 8 | |

**1899.** *Perf.* 10.

| 24 | 10 | 1 c., black on green | 2 |
|---|---|---|---|
| 25 | 11 | 5 c. ,, rose . | 6 |
| 26 | 12 | 10 c., blue (perf. 13½) | 8 |

No. | *Un.* | *Used.*

No. Type. | *Un.* | *Used.*

# Provisional.

## Correos de Santander.

13

**1903.** *Oblong fiscal stamp overprinted with* Type 13, *in* black.

27|50 c., red .. .. .. 50

*Error.* "Corceos" *for* "Correos."

28|50 c., red .. .. ..

## TOLIMA.

1

**1870.** *Type-set. Imperf. Ten varieties arranged in 5 horizontal rows of 2 in a row.* Black *impression.*

No. Type. Plate I. *Azure* paper.

1 | 1 | 5 c., horizontally laid .. .. 20.00 20.00

Plate I. *reset. Azure* paper.

2 | 1 | 5 c., vertically laid — 6.25
3 | " | 5 c. ruled in blue ", " ..
4 | " | 5 c., quadrillé .. 12.50 7.50

Only Nos. 4, 8, and 10 on the plate are altered.

Plate II. *Azure and buff* papers.

5 | 1 | 5 c., blue wove .. 12.50 10.00
6 | " | 5 c. „ laid ..
7 | " | 5 c. „ quadrillé. 15.00 6.25
8 | " | 5 c., buff laid .. 20.00 10.00

All the types on this plate, except No. 1, differ from those on Plate I.

Plate II. *reset. White wove* paper.

9 | 1 | 5 c., plain paper .. 10.00 10.00
10 | " | 10 c. „ .. .. 7.50
11 | " | 5 c., ruled in blue ..
12 | " | 10 c. „ „

The last two rows of Plate II. were altered by changing the figure "5" to "10." There are therefore six types of the 5 c., and four of the 10 c.

So-called reprints of these stamps were made in 1886 upon blue and upon white papers, but as the original setting of the types had long before been broken up, these impressions are only official imitations.

2

3

4

5

**1871.** *Imperf.*

13 | 2 | 5 c., red-brown .. 6
14 | " | 5 c., dark brown .. 6
15 | 3 | 10 c., blue .. .. 3.75 3.75
16 | 4 | 50 c., deep green .. 3.75 3.75
17 | 5 | 1 p., rose-red .. 6.25 5.00

*Varieties.* "CINGO" *for* "CINCO."

18 | 2 | 5 c., dark brown .. 5.00

*Printed both sides.*

19 | 3 | 10 c., blue .. ..

*Laid paper.*

20 | 3 | 10 c., blue .. ..

The unused 10 c., 50 c., and 1 p. usually found are printed from new plates, made from the original dies after they had been defaced. These stamps can be recognised by the fine lines across the stamp, which are, of course, always *identical*.

Reprints of the 5 c. were also made at the same time, but the die of this value had been so effectually cancelled that it had to be entirely re-engraved. These reprints have a much larger star ornament at the top of the stamp.

6

7

**1879-80.** *Imperf.* (a) *White paper.*

21 | 6 | 5 c., purple-brown . 12
22 | " | 5 c., brown.. .. 12 12
23 | 7 | 10 c., blue .. .. 12 8

| No. Type. | | | *Un.* | *Used.* |
|---|---|---|---|---|

8

9

| 24 | 8 | 50 c., green .. | .. | 1.50 |
| 25 | " | 50 c., dark green | .. | |
| 26 | 9 | 1 p., vermilion | .. | 2.50 |

*(b) Greyish paper.*

| 27 | 6 | 5 c., brown.. | .. | 4 |
| 28 | 7 | 10 c., blue .. | .. | 4 |
| 29 | 8 | 50 c., green .. | .. | 18 |
| 30 | 9 | 1 p., vermilion | .. | 25 |

10

11

**1883-84.** *Imperf.*

| 31 | 6 | 5 c., orange | .. | 2 |
| 32 | 7 | 10 c., scarlet | .. | 6 |
| 33 | 10 | 20 c., violet .. | .. | 12 |
| 34 | 11 | 5 p., yellow.. | .. | |
| 34a | " | 5 p., orange-red | .. | 15.00 |

12

**1884.** Type 12. *Imp*

| 35 | 1 c., grey | .. | .. | |
| 36 | 2 c., lilac-rose | .. | | |
| 37 | 2½ c., dull orange | | | |
| 38 | 5 c., brown | .. | .. | |
| 38a | 5 c., purple-brown | .. | | |
| 39 | 10 c., blue | .. | .. | 50 |
| 40 | 10 c., slate-blue | .. | .. | 18 |
| 41 | 20 c., olive-yellow | .. | 1.10 | |
| 42 | 25 c., black | .. | .. | 1.10 |
| 43 | 50 c., blue-green | .. | .. | 75 |
| 43a | 50 c., emerald | .. | .. | 75 |
| 43b | 50 c., deep green | .. | .. | |

| No. | | | *Un.* | *Used.* |
|---|---|---|---|---|
| 44 | 1 p., vermilion .. | .. | 62 | |
| 45 | 2 p., violet | .. | .. | 2.50 |
| 46 | 5 p., orange | .. | .. | 5.00 |
| 47 | 10 p., rose | .. | .. | 7.50 |
| 48 | 10 p., slate | .. | .. | |

*Vertically laid paper.*

| 48a | 10 p., rose | .. | .. | |

*Variety. Value omitted.*

| 49 | (2 p.), violet | .. | .. | |

13

14

17    18

e    f

g    h

**1887.** *Same types, but with different labels of value. Lithographed. Perf.* 12.

| | | | | |
|---|---|---|---|---|
| 61 | 13 | 1 c., grey (a) .. | 2.50 | |
| 62 | 17 | 2 c., lilac-rose (e) .. | 2.50 | |
| 63 | 18 | 2½ c., flesh (f) .. | 6.25 | 2.50 |
| 64 | 13 | 5 c., brown (a) .. | 3.75 | 90 |
| 65 | 17 | 10 c., bright blue (f) | 75 | |
| 66 | " | 20 c., olive-yellow (f) | 1.25 | |
| 67 | " | 25 c., black (f) .. | 36 | |
| 68 | " | 50 c., green (f) .. | 62 | |
| 69 | 20 | 1 p., vermilion (g).. | 1.10 | |
| 70 | " | 2 p., violet (h) .. | 2.50 | 2.50 |
| 71 | " | 5 p., orange (h) .. | 7.50 | 6.25 |
| 72 | " | 10 p., rose (h) .. | 3.75 | 5.00 |

*Varieties. Têtes-bêches.*

| | | |
|---|---|---|
| 17 | 20 c., olive-yellow .. | .. |
| 20 | 2 p., violet .. | .. |

No. Type.

*Error on the sheet of* 5 c.
85 | 18 | 10 c., yellow-brown . 12.50

*Error on the sheet of* 5 p.
85a | 20 | 2 p., orange .. ..

*Error. Value label inverted.*
85b | 20 | 5 p., orange .. ..

*Variety. Tête-bêche.*
85c | 20 | 5 p., orange .. ..

22

**1888.** Type **22.** *Perf.* 10½.

| | | | | | |
|---|---|---|---|---|---|
| 86 | 5 c., vermilion .. | .. | 2 | 4 |
| 87 | 10 c., green .. | .. | 25 | 12 |
| 88 | 50 c., blue .. | .. | | |
| 89 | 1 p., brown .. | .. | 1.25 | 1.00 |

**1895.** *Same type. Perf.* 12.

| | | | |
|---|---|---|---|
| 90 | 1 c., blue on rose .. | 4 |
| 91 | 2 c., green on green .. | 4 |
| 92 | 20 c., blue on yellow .. | 25 |

**1900-2.** *Same type and perf.*

| | | | |
|---|---|---|---|
| 93 | 5 c., vermilion .. | .. |
| 94 | 10 c., green .. | .. |

*Perf.* 13½.

| | | | |
|---|---|---|---|
| 95 | 5 c., vermilion .. | .. |

### TUMACO.

Pagó $ 0.20
El Agente Postal
Manuel E. Jimenez.

**1901.** Type **1.** *Type-set. Imperf.*

| | | | | | | |
|---|---|---|---|---|---|---|
| 1 | 1 c., black | .. | .. | — | 2.50 |
| 2 | 2 c. " | .. | .. | — | 2.50 |
| 3 | 5 c. " | .. | .. | — | 2.10 |
| 4 | 10 c. " | .. | .. | — | 2.50 |
| 5 | 20 c. " | .. | .. | 2.50 | 2.50 |

*Perf.* 12.

| | | | | | |
|---|---|---|---|---|---|
| 6 | 1 c., black | .. | .. | 50 |
| 7 | 2 c. " | .. | .. | 25 |
| 8 | 2½ c. " | .. | .. | |
| 9 | 5 c. " | .. | .. | 25 |
| | 10 c. " | .. | .. | 50 |
| | 20 c. " | .. | .. | 1.25 |
| | 50 c. " | .. | .. | |
| | 1 p. " | .. | .. | |

**1903.** *Imperf.*
black on rose .. ..

| No. Type. | | | Un. | Used. |
|---|---|---|---|---|

8                                    9

| 24 | 8 | 50 c., green .. | .. | 1.50 |
| 25 | " | 50 c., dark green | .. | |
| 26 | 9 | 1 p., vermilion | .. | 2.50 |

*(b) Greyish paper.*

| 27 | 6 | 5 c., brown.. | .. | 4 |
| 28 | 7 | 10 c., blue .. | .. | 4 |
| 29 | 8 | 50 c., green .. | .. | 18 |
| 30 | 9 | 1 p., vermilion | .. | 25 |

10                                    11

**1883–84.** *Imperf.*

| 31 | 6 | 5 c., orange | .. | 2 |
| 32 | 7 | 10 c., scarlet | .. | 6 |
| 33 | 10 | 20 c., violet .. | .. | 12 |
| 34 | 11 | 5 p., yellow.. | .. | |
| 34a | " | 5 p., orange-red | .. | 15.00 |

12

**1884.** Type 12. *Imperf.*

| 35 | 1 c., grey | .. | .. | 4 |
| 36 | 2 c., lilac-rose .. | | .. | 6 |
| 37 | 2½ c., dull orange | | .. | 8 |
| 38 | 5 c., brown | .. | .. | 12 |
| 38a | 5 c., purple-brown | | .. | |
| 39 | 10 c., blue | .. | .. | 50 |
| 40 | 10 c., slate-blue .. | | .. | 18 |
| 41 | 20 c., olive-yellow | | . | 1.10 |
| 42 | 25 c., black | .. | .. | 1.10 | 1.10 |
| 43 | 50 c., blue-green | | .. | 75 |
| 43a | 50 c., emerald .. | | .. | 75 |
| 43b | 50 c., deep green | | .. | |

| No. | | | Un. | Used. |
|---|---|---|---|---|
| 44 | 1 p., vermilion .. | .. | 62 |
| 45 | 2 p., violet | .. | 2.50 |
| 46 | 5 p., orange | .. | 5.00 |
| 47 | 10 p., rose | .. | 7.50 |
| 48 | 10 p., slate | .. | |

*Vertically laid paper.*

| 48a | 10 p., rose | .. | .. |

*Variety. Value omitted.*

| 49 | (2 p.), violet | .. | .. |

13                                    14

15                                    16

a                                    b

c                                    d

**1886.** *Perf.* 10½.

No. Type.    *(a) Typographed.*

| 50 | 13 | 5 c., dark brown (a) | | 12 |
| 51 | " | 5 c., chestnut (a) .. | | 1.25 |
| 52 | 14 | 10 c., blue (b) | .. | 62 |
| 53 | 15 | 50 c., green (c) | .. | 18 |
| 54 | 16 | 1 p., vermilion (d).. | | 50 |

*(b) Lithographed. Bluish paper.*

| 55 | 13 | 5 c., dark brown .. | | |
| 56 | " | 5 c., dull brown .. | | |
| 57 | " | 5 c., red-brown .. | | |
| 58 | 14 | 10 c., indigo.. | .. | |
| 59 | 15 | 50 c., green .. | .. | 1.00 |
| 60 | 16 | 1 p., red .. | .. | 5.00 |

No. Type.  |  *Un.*  *Used.*

17

18

e

f

g

h

**1887.** *Same types, but with different labels of value. Lithographed. Perf. 12.*

| 61 | 13 | 1 c., grey (a) | .. | 2.50 | |
| 62 | 17 | 2 c., lilac-rose (e) | .. | 2.50 | |
| 63 | 18 | 2½ c., flesh (f) | .. | 6.25 | 2.50 |
| 64 | 13 | 5 c., brown (a) | .. | 3.75 | 90 |
| 65 | 17 | 10 c., bright blue (f) | | 75 | |
| 66 | " | 20 c., olive-yellow (f) | .. | 1.25 | |
| 67 | " | 25 c., black (f) | .. | 36 | |
| 68 | " | 50 c., green (f) | .. | 62 | |
| 69 | 20 | 1 p., vermilion(g) | .. | 1.10 | |
| 70 | " | 2 p., violet (h) | .. | 2.50 | 2.50 |
| 71 | " | 5 p., orange (h) | .. | 7.50 | 6.25 |
| 72 | " | 10 p., rose (h) | .. | 3.75 | 5.00 |

*Varieties. Têtes-bêches.*

| 73 | 17 | 20 c., olive-yellow | .. | |
| 74 | 20 | 2 p., violet | .. | .. |

19

20

*Same types. Imperf.*

| 75 | 13 | 1 c., grey | .. | | |
| 76 | 17 | 2 c., lilac-rose | .. | | |
| 77 | 18 | 2½ c., buff | .. | 12.50 | 12.50 |
| 78 | 19 | 5 c., brown | .. | 62 | 90 |
| 79 | " | 5 c., yellow-brown | . | 75 | 50 |
| 80 | 14 | 10 c., ultramarine | .. | 1.10 | |
| 80a | " | 10 c., blue | .. | — | 1.25 |
| 81 | " | 25 c., black | .. | | |
| 81a | 16 | 1 p., red | .. | — | 3.75 |
| 82 | 20 | 2 p., violet | .. | 5.00 | 5.00 |
| 83 | " | 5 p., orange | .. | 5.00 | 5.00 |
| 84 | " | 10 p., rose | .. | 15.00 | |

No. Type.  |  *Un.*  *Used.*

*Error on the sheet of 5 c.*

| 85 | 18 | 10 c., yellow-brown | . | 12.50 |

*Error on the sheet of 5 p.*

| 85a | 20 | 2 p., orange | | |

*Error. Value label inverted.*

| 85b | 20 | 5 p., orange | .. | |

*Variety. Tête-bêche.*

| 85c | 20 | 5 p., orange | .. | |

22

**1888.** Type **22.** *Perf.* 10½.

| 86 | 5 c., vermilion | .. | .. | 2 | 4 |
| 87 | 10 c., green | .. | .. | 25 | 12 |
| 88 | 50 c., blue | .. | .. | | |
| 89 | 1 p., brown | .. | .. | 1.25 | 1.00 |

**1895.** *Same type. Perf. 12.*

| 90 | 1 c., blue on rose | .. | 4 |
| 91 | 2 c., green on green | .. | 4 |
| 92 | 20 c., blue on yellow | .. | 25 |

**1900-2.** *Same type and perf.*

| 93 | 5 c., vermilion | .. | .. |
| 94 | 10 c., green | .. | .. |

*Perf.* 13½.

| 95 | 5 c., vermilion | .. | .. |

### TUMACO.

Pagó $ 0.20
El Agente Postal
*Manuel E. Jiménez*

1

**1901.** Type **1.** *Type-set. Imperf.*

| 1 | 1 c., black | .. | .. | — | 2.50 |
| 2 | 2 c., " | .. | .. | — | 2.50 |
| 3 | 5 c., " | .. | .. | — | 2.10 |
| 4 | 10 c., " | .. | .. | — | 2.50 |
| 5 | 20 c., " | .. | .. | 2.50 | 2.50 |

*Perf.* 12.

| 6 | 1 c., black | .. | .. | 50 |
| 7 | 2 c., " | .. | .. | 25 |
| 8 | 2½ c., " | .. | .. | |
| 9 | 5 c., " | .. | .. | 25 |
| 10 | 10 c., " | .. | .. | 50 |
| 11 | 20 c., " | .. | .. | 1.25 |
| 12 | 50 c., " | .. | .. | |
| 13 | 1 p., " | .. | .. | |

**1903.** *Imperf.*

| 14 | 20 c., black on rose | .. | |

*Un.   Used.*

No.

REGISTRATION STAMP.

R  Repùblica de Colombia
        Tumaco
        N°. . . . . . . . . .
DIEZ CENTAVOS

11

Type 11.  *Imperf.*
21 |10 c., black    ..    ..

## COREA.

1

2

3

4

5

**1885.**  (*a*) *Perf.* 8½.

| | | | | |
|---|---|---|---|---|
| 1 | 5 mon, rose | .. | .. | 50 |
| 2 | 10 ,, blue | .. | .. | 25 |

(*b*) *Perf.* 10.

| | | | | |
|---|---|---|---|---|
| 1a | 5 mon, rose | .. | .. | 75 |
| 2a | 10 ,, ,, | .. | .. | 10 |

(*c*) *Perf.* 11, 11½.

| | | | |
|---|---|---|---|
| 1b | 5 mon, rose | .. | 62 |

The 25 m., orange, 50 m., green, and
100 m., blue and pink (Types 3, 4, and 5),
were prepared for use, but were never
issued ; these can be supplied at 4 c. each.

*Un.   Used.*

No.

6

**1895.**  Type 6.  (*a*) *Perf.* 11½, 12.

| | | | | | |
|---|---|---|---|---|---|
| 3 | 5 p., yellow-green | ∴ | 25 | ∷ |
| 4 | 5 p., blue-green | .. | 4 | 4 |
| 5 | 10 p., deep blue .. | .. | 8 | |
| 6 | 25 p., lake | .. | 10 | |
| 7 | 50 p., violet | .. | 18 | |

**1896.**  (*b*) *Perf.* 12½, 13.

| | | | | |
|---|---|---|---|---|
| 8 | 5 p., yellow-green | .. | 36 | 4 |
| 9 | 10 p., deep blue .. | .. | | |
| 10 | 25 p., lake | .. | | |
| 11 | 50 p., violet | .. | 36 | ∴ |

(*c*) *Perf. compound of* (*a*) *and* (*b*).

| | | | |
|---|---|---|---|
| 12 | 50 p., violet | .. | .. |

7

**1900.**  Type 6 *surcharged with chara-
ters* Type 7 (*signifying Empire
Corea*), *at the ends of the upper a-
lower labels.*  (*a*) *Perf.* 11½, 12.

(i.) *Surcharged in* red.

| | | | |
|---|---|---|---|
| 13 | 5 p., blue-green | .. | 6 |
| 14 | 10 p., deep blue .. | .. | 12 |
| 15 | 25 p., lake | .. | 12 |
| 16 | 50 p., lilac | .. | — |

(ii.) *Surcharged in* black.

| | | | |
|---|---|---|---|
| 17 | 5 p., yellow-green | .. | — |
| 18 | 5 p., blue-green | .. | — |
| 19 | 10 p., deep blue .. | .. | — |
| 20 | 25 p., lake | .. | — |
| 21 | 50 p., violet | .. | — |

*Variety.  No surcharge at foot.*

| | | |
|---|---|---|
| 21a | 25 p., lake | .. |

(*b*) *Perf.* 12½, 13.
(i.) *Surcharged in* red.

| | | | | |
|---|---|---|---|---|
| 22 | 50 p., violet | .. | .. | 36 | ∴ |

**No.**      *Un.*   *Used.*      **No.**      *Un.*   *Used.*

*Variety. No surcharge at foot.*
23 | 50 p., violet .. ..

  (ii.) *Surcharged in* black.
24 | 5 p., green .. .. — 4
25 | 10 p., deep blue.. ..
26 | 25 p., lake .. ..
27 | 50 p., violet .. .. — 12

  (c) *Perf. compound of* (a) *and* (b).
    (i.) *Surcharged in* red.
28 | 50 p., violet . ..

    **8**         **9**

JANUARY, **1900.** Types **8** *and* **9.** *Perf.* 10.
29 | 2 cheun, blue .. .. 2
30 | 3 ,, red .. .. 4

    **10**       **11**

*The same surcharged with* Types **10** *and* **11** *respectively.*
31 | 2 ch., blue (brown-red) .
32 | 3 ch., red (black) ..

    **12**

Type **6** *surcharged with characters in* red, *and new value in* black, *as* Type **12.**
33 | 1 on 5 p., green (No. 3)
34 | 1 on 25 p., lake ( ,, 13) 25 18

  *Variety. Figure* "1" *omitted.*
35 | (1 on) 25 p., lake ..

    **13**       **14**
    **1900-1.**  (a) *Perf.* 10.
36 | 2 re, grey .. .. 2
37 | 1 cn., green .. .. 2

  **15**       **16**
  **17**       **18**
  **19**       **20**
  **21**       **22**
  **23**       **24**

38 | 4 cn., carmine .. .. 4
39 | 5 cn., pink .. .. 6 6
40 | 6 cn., deep blue .. 6

    (b) *Perf.* 11.
41 | 2 re, grey .. .. 2
41a | 1 cn., green .. .. 2
42 | 2 cn., blue .. .. 4
43 | 4 cn., carmine .. ..
44 | 6 cn., blue .. .. 12
45 | 10 cn., violet .. .. 10 10

|  | | **Un.** | **Used.** |
|---|---|---|---|
| **No.** | | | |
| 46 | 15 cn., grey-purple | .. | 12 |
| 47 | 20 cn., Venetian red | .. | 16 |
| 48 | 50 cn., green & pale rose | | 50 |
| 49 | 1 wn., black, red, & blue | | 1.00 |
| 50 | 2 wn., violet and green | | 1.85 |

25

**1902.** Type **25.** *Commemorative stamp.*
*Perf.* 11½.

| 52 | 3 ch., orange | .. | .. | 6 |
|---|---|---|---|---|

26

27

28

29

30

**1903.** Type **26** *surcharged with* Types
**26** *to* **30,** *in* black. *The* 25 p. *perf.*
11½, 12; *the* 50 p. *perf.* 12½, 13.

| 53 | **26** | 1 ch. on 25 p., lake | 8 | 4 |
|---|---|---|---|---|
| 54 | **27** | 1 ch. on 25 p. ,, | — | 12 |
| 55 | **28** | 2 ch. on 25 p. ,, | 10 | 10 |
| 56 | **29** | 3 ch. on 50 p., violet | 16 | 12 |
| 57 | **30** | 3 ch. on 50 p. ,, | — | 8 |

*Surcharge inverted.*

| 57*a* | **26** | 1 ch. on 25 p., lake | |
|---|---|---|---|
| 57*b* | **28** | 2 ch. ,, ,, | |
| 57*c* | **29** | 3 ch. on 50 p., violet | |

*Perf. compound.*

| 58 | **29** | 3 ch. on 50 p., violet | |
|---|---|---|---|

*Error.*

| 59 | **29** | 3 ch. on 25 p., lake | |
|---|---|---|---|

1 OCTOBER, **1903.** Type **31.** *Perf.* 13½ × 14.

| 60 | 2 rin, grey | .. | .. | 2 |
|---|---|---|---|---|
| 61 | 1 ch., brown-purple | .. | | 2 |
| 62 | 2 ,, green | .. | .. | 2 |
| 63 | 3 ,, orange | .. | .. | 4 |
| 64 | ,, rose | .. | — | 4 |

|  | | **Un.** | **Used** |
|---|---|---|---|
| **No.** | | | |

31

| 65 | 5 ch., cinnamon | .. | 6 |
|---|---|---|---|
| 66 | 6 ,, lilac | .. | .. |
| 67 | 10 ,, blue | .. | .. |
| 68 | 15 ,, red on yellow | .. | |
| 69 | 20 ,, brn.-purp. on yell. | | |
| 70 | 50 ,, red on green | .. | |
| 71 | 1 wn., lilac on pale lilac | | |
| 72 | 2 ,, purple on orange | | |

## COSTA RICA.

1

**1862.** Type **1.** *Imperf.*

| 1 | ½ real, blue | .. | .. | 10.00 |
|---|---|---|---|---|
| 2 | 2 reales, red | .. | .. | 3·75 |

**1863-64.** *Same type. Perf.* 12.

| 3 | ½ real, blue | .. | .. | 2 |
|---|---|---|---|---|
| 4 | ½ ,, deep blue | .. | .. | 6 |
| 5 | 2 reales, red | .. | .. | 4 |
| 6 | 4 ,, green | .. | .. | 16 |
| 7 | 1 peso, orange | .. | .. | 90 |

2

3

4

**1881-82.** Type **1** *surcharged as*
No. Type. Types **2, 3, 4,** *in* red.

| 8 | **2** | 1 c. on ½ r., blue | .. | 18 |
|---|---|---|---|---|
| 9 | **3** | 2 c. ,, ,, | .. | 6 |
| 10 | **4** | 1 c. ,, ,, | .. | 12 |
| 11 | **3** | 5 c. ,, ,, | .. | 6 |

| No. | | Un. | Used. | No. Type. | | Un. | Used. |

# 5 cts. U.P.U.

**6**

**1882.** *Surcharged as* Type **6.** *Perf.* 12.

| 12 | 5 c., in *red*, on ½ r., blue | 62 | 90 |
| 13 | 10 c., in *blk.*, on 2 r., red | 1.25 | |
| 14 | 20 c., in *red*, on 4 r., green | 3.75 | |

**7**

**1883.** Type **7.**
*Head of Gen. P. Fernandez.* *Perf.* 12.

| 15 | 1 c., green | .. | .. | 2 | 4 |
| 16 | 2 c., carmine | .. | .. | 2 | 4 |
| 17 | 5 c., purple | .. | .. | 6 | 4 |
| 18 | 10 c., orange | .. | .. | 18 | 18 |
| 19 | 40 c., blue | .. | .. | 25 | 12 |

**8**

**1887.** Type **8.**
*Head of President P. Soto.* *Perf.* 12.

| 20 | 5 c., purple | .. | .. | 12 | 4 |
| 21 | 10 c., orange | .. | .. | 18 | 12 |

**9**         **10**

**1889.** *Head of President Soto.*

| No. Type. | | *Perf.* 14 *or* 15. | | | |
| 22 | 9 | 1 c., sepia .. | .. | 2 | 2 |
| 23 | 10 | 2 c., greenish blue . | | 2 | 4 |

**11**         **12**

**13**         **14**

**15**         **16**

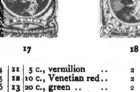

**17**         **18**

| 24 | 11 | 5 c., vermilion | .. | 2 | 2 |
| 25 | 12 | 10 c., Venetian red.. | | 2 | 2 |
| 26 | 13 | 20 c., green .. | .. | 2 | 4 |
| 27 | 14 | 50 c., rose-carmine.. | | 6 | 8 |
| 28 | 15 | 1 p., blue .. | .. | 18 | 18 |
| 28a | " | 1 p., pale blue | .. | 25 | 25 |
| 29 | 16 | 2 p., violet .. | .. | 36 | 50 |
| 30 | 17 | 5 p., olive-green | .. | 75 | 75 |
| 31 | 18 | 10 p., black .. | .. | 1.50 | 1.50 |

E

No. Type.                                    No. Type.

*Un.   Used.*                                *Un.   Used.*

40 | 27 | 5 p., blue on blue .. | 36 | 36
41 | 28 | 10 p., brown on buff. | 62 | 62

**1892.**

*Perf.* 14 *or* 15.

| 32 | 19 | 1 c., greenish blue . | 2 | 2 |
| 33 | 20 | 2 c., orange .. | 2 | 2 |
| 34 | 21 | 5 c., rosy lilac .. | 4 | 2 |
| 34a | ,, | 5 c., purple .. | — | 2 |
| 35 | 22 | 10 c., green .. | 8 | 2 |
| 36 | 23 | 20 c., scarlet.. .. | 18 | 2 |
| 7 | 24 | 50 c., ultramarine .. | 12 | 4 |
| 8 | 25 | 1 p., bronze-green on straw .. .. | 18 | |
| | 26 | 2 p., red on grey .. | 36 | |

**1901.** *Centres in first colour.*

*Perf.* 14, 15.

| | 42 | 29 | 1 cent., black & grn. | 2 |
| 2 | 43 | 30 | 2 ,, ,, verm. | 2 |
| 2 | 44 | 31 | 5 cent., black & pale blue .. .. | 4 |
| 12 | 46 | 33 | 20 cent., black & lake | 18 |
| 30 | 47 | 34 | 50 ,, blue & lilac | 36 |
| 4 | 45 | 32 | 10 cent., black and yellow-brown .. | 8 |

No. Type.          *Un. Used.*

35           36

37           38

| 48 | 35 | 1 col., black & olive | 1.00 | |
| 49 | 36 | 2 ,, ,, carm. | 1.85 | |
| 50 | 37 | 5 ,, ,, brn. | 4.50 | |
| 51 | 38 | 10 ,, brown-red and pale green | 9.00 | |

**1903.** *New types. Perf. as last.*

| 52 | 4 c., lilac and black | .. |
| 53 | 6 c., olive ,, | .. |
| 54 | 25 c., lilac and brown | .. |

**FISCALS USED FOR POSTAGE.**

51           52

**1881.** Type 51. *Perf. 12.*

| 101 | 1 c., carmine | .. | .. | 4 | 4 |
| 102 | 2 c., blue | .. | .. | 25 | 12 |

**1889.** Type 52. *Head of President Soto. Perf. 12.*

| 103 | 5 c., brown-red | .. | .. | 6 | 8 |
| 104 | 10 c., blue | .. | .. | 8 | |

## CORREOS
53

*The same surcharged, in black, with Type 53.*

| 105 | 51 | 1 c., dull carmine | 8 | 12 |
| 105a | ,, | 2 c., blue | .. | .. |
| 106 | 52 | 5 c., brown-red | 25 | 25 |

No. Type.          *Un. Used.*

U 1

**UNPAID LETTER STAMPS.**

**1903.** Type U 1. *Numerals in centre in black. Perf. 14.*

| 151 | 5 c., slate-blue | .. | .. |
| 152 | 10 c., orange-brown | .. | |
| 153 | 15 c., yellow-green | .. | |
| 154 | 20 c., carmine | .. | .. |
| 155 | 25 c., ultramarine | .. | |
| 156 | 30 c., dark brown | .. | |
| 157 | 40 c., bistre | .. | .. |
| 158 | 50 c., mauve | .. | .. |

**OFFICIAL STAMPS.**
A. *Stamps of 1883.*

## Oficial
O 1

**1883-85.** Type 7 *surcharged with* Type O 1, *13½ mm. long, in second colour given.*

| 201 | 1 c., green (red) | .. | 12 | |
| 202 | 1 c. ,, (black) | .. | 12 | |
| 203 | 2 c., carmine (blue) | .. | 36 | |
| 204 | 2 c. ,, (black) | .. | 25 | |
| 205 | 5 c., purple (red) | .. | 1.25 | 1.50 |
| 206 | 10 c., orange (green) | .. | 1.25 | |
| 207 | 40 c., blue (red) | .. | .. | 62 | |

## OFICIAL
O 2

**1886.** Type 7 *surcharged with* Type O 2, *13 mm. long.*

| 208 | 1 c., green (black) | .. | 6 |
| 209 | 2 c., carmine (black) | .. | 12 |
| 210 | 5 c., purple (red) | .. | 2.50 |
| 211 | 10 c., orange (black) | .. | 1.25 |

## OFICIAL
O 3

Type 7 *surcharged with* Type O 3, *15½ mm. long.*

| 212 | 1 c., green (black) | .. | 6 |
| 213 | 2 c., carmine (black) | .. | 18 |
| 214 | 5 c., purple (red) | .. | 1.50 |
| 215 | 10 c., orange (black) | .. | 1.50 |

## Oficial
O 4

Type 7 *surcharged with* Type O 4, *12 mm. long, in black.*

| 216 | 5 c., purple | .. | .. |
| 217 | 10 c., orange | .. | 3.75 |

| No. | | Un. | Used. |
|---|---|---|---|

# OFICIAL
## O 5

Type 7 *surcharged with* Type O 5,
15 mm. *long, in* black.

| 218 | 1 c., green | .. | .. | 6 |
|---|---|---|---|---|
| 219 | 2 c., carmine | .. | .. | 12 |
| 220 | 5 c., purple | .. | .. | |
| 221 | 10 c., orange | .. | .. | 36 |
| 222 | 40 c., blue | .. | .. | 12 |

### Errors. "OFICAL."

| 222a | 1 c., green | .. | .. | |
|---|---|---|---|---|
| 222b | 2 c., carmine | .. | .. | — | 3.15 |
| 222c | 5 c., purple | .. | .. | |
| 222d | 10 c., orange | .. | .. | |
| 222e | 40 c., blue | .. | .. | 1.25 |

There are two types of this surcharge,
in "Antique" and also in "Roman"
capitals.

B. Type 8. *Stamps of* 1887 *surcharged
with* Type O 5, *in* black.

| 224 | 5 c., purple | .. | .. | 50 | |
|---|---|---|---|---|---|
| 225 | 10 c., orange | .. | .. | 25 | 12 |

*Variety with double surcharge.*

| 225a | 10 c., orange | .. | .. | 1.50 |
|---|---|---|---|---|

*Variety. No stop after* "OFICIAL."

| 225b | 10 c., orange | .. | .. | 1.25 |
|---|---|---|---|---|

# OFICIAL
## O 6

C. *Stamps of* 1889, *perf.* 14 *or* 15,
*surcharged with* Type O 6, *in* black.
No. Type.

| 226 | 9 | 1 c., sepia .. | .. | 2 |
|---|---|---|---|---|
| 227 | 10 | 2 c., greenish blue .. | | 2 |
| 228 | 11 | 5 c., vermilion | .. | 4 |
| 229 | 12 | 10 c., lake .. | .. | 2 |
| 230 | 13 | 20 c., green .. | .. | 2 |
| 231 | 14 | 50 c., rose-carmine.. | | 4 |

# OFICIAL
## O 7

D. *Stamps of* 1892 *surcharged with*
Type O 7, *in* black.

| 232 | 19 | 1 c., greenish blue . | | 4 |
|---|---|---|---|---|
| 233 | 20 | 2 c., orange.. | .. | 4 |
| 234 | 21 | 5 c., lilac .. | .. | 4 |
| 235 | 22 | 10 c., green .. | .. | 62 |
| 236 | 23 | 20 c., scarlet | .. | 6 |
| 237 | 24 | 50 c., ultramarine .. | | 25 |

Type O 7 is slightly smaller than Type
O 6.

---

| No. | | Un. | Used. |
|---|---|---|---|

**1901-2.** Types 29 *to* 36 *surcharged with*
Type O 7, *in* black.

| 238 | 1 c., black and green .. | 2 |
|---|---|---|
| 239 | 2 c.,    „    vermilion | 4 |
| 240 | 5 c.,    „    pale blue | 6 |
| 241 | 10 c.    „    yellow-brn. | 16 |
| 242 | 20 c.    „    lake | 25 |
| 243 | 50 c., blue and lilac    .. | |
| 244 | 1 col., black and olive.. | |
| 245 | 2 "    "    carmine | |

Type 30 *surcharged* "PROVISORIO
OFICIAL," *in* green.

| 246 | 2 c., black and vermilion | |
|---|---|---|

*Error.* "PROVISOIO" *for* "PROVISORIO."

| 247 | 2 c., black and vermilion | |
|---|---|---|

*Error.* "PROVISIORO."

| 248 | 2 c., black and vermilion | |
|---|---|---|

**1903.** *New types of this date overprinted* "OFICIAL."

| 249 | 4 c., lilac and black .. | |
|---|---|---|
| 250 | 6 c., olive    „    .. | |
| 251 | 25 c., lilac and brown .. | |

FOR USE IN THE PROVINCE OF

## GUANACASTE.

A. *Stamps of* 1883.

# Guanacaste
## G 1

Type 7 *surcharged horizontally with*
Type G 1, 15¾ mm. *long.*

(*a*) *In* red.

| 301 | 1 c., green | .. | .. | 8 | 12 |
|---|---|---|---|---|---|
| 302 | 5 c., purple | .. | .. | 25 | 18 |
| 303 | 40 c., blue | .. | .. | 90 | |

(*b*) *In* black.

| 304 | 1 c., green | .. | .. | 8 | 12 |
|---|---|---|---|---|---|
| 305 | 2 c., carmine | .. | .. | 18 | 12 |
| 306 | 10 c., orange | .. | .. | 36 | |

(*c*) *Double surcharge, in* red *and* black.

| 307 | 1 c., green | .. | .. | |
|---|---|---|---|---|

*Error.* "Gnanacaste."

(*a*) *In* red.

| 301a | 1 c., green | .. | .. | |
|---|---|---|---|---|
| 302a | 5 c., purple | .. | .. | |
| 303a | 40 c., blue | .. | .. | |

(*b*) *In* black.

| 304a | 1 c., green | .. | .. | |
|---|---|---|---|---|
| 305a | 2 c., carmine .. | | .. | |
| 306a | 10 c., orange .. | | .. | |

| | | Un. | Used. |
|---|---|---|---|
| No. | | | |

## Guanacaste
### G 2

*Surcharged horizontally with* Type G 2,
17½ mm. *long.*
(a) *In* red.

| 308 | 5 c., purple | .. | .. | — | 1.25 |
|---|---|---|---|---|---|
| 308a | 40 c., blue | .. | .. | 2.50 | |

(b) *In* black.

| 309 | 1 c., green | .. | .. | 1.85 | |
|---|---|---|---|---|---|
| 310 | 2 c., carmine | .. | .. | 8 | |
| 311 | 5 c., purple | .. | .. | 25 | 25 |
| 312 | 10 c., orange | .. | .. | 50 | |
| 313 | 40 c., blue | .. | .. | 90 | |

## Guanacaste
### G 3

*Surcharged horizontally with* Type G 3,
18½ mm. *long.*
(a) *In* red.

| 314 | 1 c., green | .. | .. | 12 | 18 |
|---|---|---|---|---|---|
| 315 | 5 c., purple | .. | .. | 2.50 | 2.50 |
| 316 | 40 c., blue | .. | .. | 3.75 | 3.75 |

(b) *In* black.

| 317 | 2 c., carmine | .. | .. | 25 | |
|---|---|---|---|---|---|
| 318 | 10 c., orange | .. | .. | 75 | |

(c) *Double surcharge, in* red *and* black.

| 319 | 1 c., green | .. | .. | 5.00 | |
|---|---|---|---|---|---|

### G 4

*Surcharged vertically (reading* up *or* down) *with* Type G 4, 20 mm. *long,* in black.

| 321 | 1 c., green | .. | .. | | |
|---|---|---|---|---|---|
| 322 | 2 c., carmine | .. | .. | | |
| 323 | 5 c., purple | .. | .. | — | 2.50 |
| 324 | 10 c., orange | .. | .. | 25 | 36 |

*Surcharged vertically with* Type G 3,
in black.

| 325 | 1 c., green | .. | .. | | |
|---|---|---|---|---|---|
| 326 | 2 c., carmine | .. | .. | | |
| 327 | 5 c., purple | .. | .. | | |
| 328 | 10 c., orange | .. | .. | 62 | |

### G 5

*Surcharged vertically with* Type G 5,
15 mm. *long, in* black.

| 329 | 1 c., green | .. | .. | | |
|---|---|---|---|---|---|
| 330 | 2 c., carmine | .. | .. | | |
| 331 | 5 c., purple | .. | .. | — | 5.00 |
| 332 | 10 c.. orange | .. | .. | 36 | .50 |

### G 6

*Surcharged vertically with* Type G 6,
in black.

| 333 | 1 c., green | .. | .. | | |
|---|---|---|---|---|---|
| 334 | 2 c., carmine | .. | .. | | |
| 335 | 5 c., purple | .. | .. | — | 1.25 |
| 336 | 10 c., orange | .. | .. | 36 | |

### G 7

*Surcharged vertically with* Type G 7,
in black.

| 337 | 1 c., green | .. | .. | | |
|---|---|---|---|---|---|
| 338 | 2 c., carmine | .. | .. | | |
| 339 | 5 c., purple | .. | .. | | |
| 340 | 10 c., orange | .. | .. | 36 | 50 |

Types G 4, G 3 (vertical), G 5, G 6, and G 7 are on the same sheet.

| No. | | | Un. | Used. |
|---|---|---|---|---|

**GUANACASTE**

G 8

*Surcharged vertically with* Type G 8,
*in* black.

| | | Un. | Used. |
|---|---|---|---|
| 340a | 2 c., carmine .. | .. | |
| 341 | 5 c., purple .. | .. | |
| 341a | 10 c., orange .. | .. | |

Guanacaste
G 9

Guanacaste
G 10

Guanacaste
G 11

B. *Stamps of* 1887, *Type 7, surcharged
horizontally, in* black.

*With* G 9.

| 342 | 2 c., carmine .. | .. | 25 | |
| 343 | 10 c., orange .. | .. | 50 | |

*With* G 10.

| 344 | 5 c., purple .. | .. | 50 | 50 |

*With* G 11.

| 344a | 5 c., purple .. | .. | 62 | 50 |

Types G 10 and G 11 are on the same
sheet in alternate horizontal rows.

C. *Provisional of* 1889, No. 105a, *surcharged horizontally with* Type G 2,
*in* black.

| 344b | 2 c., blue .. | .. | |

D. *The same stamp surcharged
vertically, in* black.

No. Type.

| 344c | G 4 | 2 c., blue | |
| 344d | G 3 | 2 c., ,, | .. |
| 344e | G 5 | 2 c., ,, | .. |
| 344f | G 6 | 2 c., ,, | .. |
| 344g | G 7 | 2 c., ,, | .. |

No. Type.        Un.   Used.

E. *Stamps of* 1889, *perf.* 14 *and* 15.

**GUANACASTE**
G 12

*Surcharged horizontally with* Type G 12,
*in* black.

| 345 | 9 | 1 c., sepia .. | .. | 10.00 | 10.00 |
| 346 | 10 | 2 c., greenish blue . | 5.00 | 25 |
| 347 | 11 | 5 c., orange | .. | 3.75 | |
| 348 | 12 | 10 c., lake .. | .. | — | 50 |
| 349 | 13 | 20 c., green .. | .. | 12 | 16 |
| 350 | 14 | 50 c., rose-carmine.. | 12 | 18 |
| 351 | 15 | 1 p., blue .. | .. | 18 | |
| 352 | ,, | 1 p., ultramarine .. | 25 | 25 |
| 353 | 16 | 2 p., violet .. | .. | 18 | 25 |
| 354 | 17 | 5 p., olive-green .. | 1.00 | 1.25 |

*Error.* "GUAGACASTE."

| 354a | 1 p., blue .. | .. | 7.50 |
| 354b | 2 p., violet .. | .. | 10.00 |
| 354c | 3 p., olive green | .. | |

**GUANACASTE**
G 13

*Surcharged horizontally with* Type G 13,
*in* black.

| 355 | 9 | 1 c., sepia .. | .. | 2 | 6 |
| 356 | 10 | 2 c., greenish blue.. | 2 | 6 |
| 357 | 11 | 5 c., vermilion .. | 4 | 5 |
| 358 | 12 | 10 c., lake .. | .. | 6 | 8 |

*Variety.*

"GUANACASTE."

| 355a | 9 | 1 c., sepia.. | ... | 62 |
| 356a | 10 | 2 c., greenish blue | |
| 357a | 11 | 5 c., vermilion .. | |
| 358a | 12 | 10 c., lake .. | .. | |

F. *Postal Fiscals.*

Type 51 *surcharged horizontally with*
Type G 2, *in* black.

| 401 | 1 c., carmine .. | .. | 1.25 | |
| 402 | 2 c., blue .. | .. | 1.50 | 1.85 |

Type 51 *surcharged vertically,
in* black.

| 403 | G 4 | 1 c., carmine | .. |
| 404 | ,, | 2 c., blue .. | .. |
| 405 | G 3 | 1 c., carmine | .. |
| 406 | ,, | 2 c., blue .. | .. |
| 407 | G 5 | 1 c., carmine | .. |
| 408 | ,, | 2 c., blue .. | .. |
| 409 | G 6 | 1 c., carmine | .. |
| 410 | ,, | 2 c., blue .. | .. |
| 411 | G 7 | 1 c., carmine | .. |
| 412 | ,, | 2 c., blue .. | .. |

Type 51 *surcharged horizontally, in* black.

| 413 | G 9 | 10 c., blue .. | .. |

# CRETE.

Provisional Joint Administration by France, Great Britain, Italy, and Russia.

## I. BRITISH SPHERE OF ADMINISTRATION.

1　　　　　　　　2

**1898.**

*Local production.* Type 1.

*Imperf.*

| 1 | 20 parades, mauve | .. 10.00 | 7.50 |

Type 2. *Printed in Athens.*

*Perf.* 11½.

| 2 | 10 par., blue | .. | .. | 6 | 8 |
| 3 | 20 ,, green | .. | .. | 8 | 10 |

**1899.**

*Same type and perf.*

| 4 | 10 par., brown | .. | .. | 4 | |
| 5 | 20 ,, rose | .. | .. | 8 | |

*Variety. Imperf.*

| 6 | 10 par., brown | .. | .. 5.00 | |

## II. RUSSIAN SPHERE OF ADMINISTRATION.

3　　　　　　　　4

**1899.**

*With* violet *or* blue *control handstamped.*

No. Type.　　*Imperf.*

| 21 | 3 | 1 metallik, blue | .. | — | 75 |
| 22 | 4 | 1 ,, green | .. | — | 90 |
| 23 | ,, | 2 ,, rose | .. | | |
| 24 | ,, | 2 ,, green-blk. | — | | 50 |

5

Type 5. *Control mark of Russian double eagle in a circle,* in violet. *Perf.* 11½.

| 31 | 1 m., rose | .. | .. | 1.25 | 75 |
| 32 | 2 m. ,, | .. | .. | — | 1.00 |
| 33 | 1 gr. ,, | .. | .. | — | 1.25 |
| 34 | 1 m., blue | .. | .. | — | 75 |
| 35 | 2 m. ,, | .. | .. | — | 1.00 |
| 36 | 1 gr. ,, | .. | .. | — | 1.25 |
| 37 | 1 m., green | .. | .. | — | 75 |
| 38 | 2 m. ,, | .. | .. | — | 1.00 |
| 39 | 1 gr. ,, | .. | .. | — | 1.25 |
| 40 | 1 m., claret | .. | .. | — | 75 |
| 41 | 2 m. ,, | .. | .. | — | 1.00 |
| 42 | 1 gr. ,, | .. | .. | — | 1.25 |
| 43 | 1 m., orange | .. | .. | — | 90 |
| 44 | 2 m. ,, | .. | .. | — | 1.00 |
| 45 | 1 gr. ,, | .. | .. | — | 1.25 |
| 46 | 1 m., yellow | .. | .. | — | 75 |
| 47 | 2 m. ,, | .. | .. | — | 1.00 |
| 48 | 1 gr. ,, | .. | .. | — | 1.25 |
| 48a | 1 m., black | .. | .. | | |
| 48b | 2 m. ,, | .. | .. | | |
| 48c | 1 gr. ,, | .. | .. | | |

6

Type 6. *Stars at each side.*

*Same* control *mark and perf.*

| 49 | 1 m., rose | .. | .. | — | 10 |
| 50 | 2 m. ,, | .. | .. | — | 30 |
| 51 | 1 gr. ,, | .. | .. | — | 30 |
| 52 | 1 m., blue | .. | .. | — | 25 |
| 53 | 2 m. ,, | .. | .. | — | 50 |
| 54 | 1 gr. ,, | .. | .. | — | 75 |
| 55 | 1 m., green | .. | .. | — | 25 |
| 56 | 2 m. ,, | .. | .. | — | 18 |

| No. | | | | | Un. | Used. |
|---|---|---|---|---|---|---|
| 57 | 1 gr., green | .. | .. | — | | 50 |
| 58 | 1 m., claret | .. | .. | — | | 25 |
| 59 | 2 m. ,, | .. | .. | — | | 30 |
| 60 | 1 gr. ,, | .. | .. | — | | 50 |

Many of the above, Nos. 31 to 60, have been seen without the control mark.

### III. PERMANENT GOVERNMENT.

(Hermes.)  
7

(Hera.)  
8

(Prince George.)  
9

(Talos.)  
10

(Minos.)  
11

(St. George and the Dragon.)  
12

### ΠΡΟΣΩΡΙΝΟΝ

13

**1900.** *The four highest values overprinted with Type 13. Perf. 14.*

Printed by Messrs. Bradbury, Wilkinson, and Co.

| No. | Type. | | | | Un. | Used. |
|---|---|---|---|---|---|---|
| 71 | 7 | 1 l., red-brown | .. | | 2 | 2 |
| 72 | 8 | 5 l., green .. | .. | | 4 | 2 |
| 73 | 9 | 10 l., scarlet.. | .. | | 6 | 2 |
| 74 | 8 | 20 l., rose .. | .. | | 12 | 6 |

| | No. Type. | | | | Un. | Used. |
|---|---|---|---|---|---|---|

*(a) Overprint in vermilion.*

| 75 | 9 | 25 l., blue | .. | .. | 12 | 8 |
| 76 | 7 | 50 l., lilac | .. | .. | 36 | |
| 77 | 10 | 1 dr., dull violet | .. | | 75 | |
| 78 | 11 | 2 dr., brown | .. | | 1.50 | |
| 79 | 12 | 5 dr., green & black | | | 5.00 | |

*(b) Overprint in black.*

| 80 | 9 | 25 l., blue | .. | .. | 12 | 12 |
| 81 | 7 | 50 l., lilac | .. | .. | 25 | |
| 82 | 10 | 1 dr., dull violet | .. | | 50 | |
| 83 | 11 | 2 dr., brown | .. | | 1.25 | |
| 84 | 12 | 5 dr., green & black | | | 2.50 | |

*Variety. Overprint inverted.*

| 84a | 7 | 50 l., lilac | .. | .. | | |

*(c) Without overprint.*

| 85 | 9 | 25 l., blue | .. | .. | 8 | |
| 86 | 7 | 50 l., lilac | .. | .. | 16 | |
| 87 | 10 | 1 dr., dull violet | .. | | 30 | |
| 88 | 11 | 2 dr., brown | .. | | 62 | |
| 89 | 12 | 5 dr., green & black | | | 1.55 | |

**1901.** *Changes of colour. Perf. 14.*

| 90 | 7 | 1 l., bistre .. | .. | 12 | |
| 91 | 8 | 20 l., orange.. | .. | 6 | 4 |
| 93 | 7 | 50 l., ultramarine | .. | 16 | |

### ΠΡΟΣΩΡΙΝΟΝ

14

*Overprinted with Type 14, in grey-black.*

| 94 | 9 | 25 l., blue | .. | .. | — | 12 |

*Error. With first letter of overprint inverted.*

| 95 | 9 | 25 l., blue | .. | .. | | |

*Overprinted with Type 14, in deep black.*

| 96 | 9 | 25 l., blue | .. | .. | 10 | ? |

### UNPAID LETTER STAMPS.

21

22

**1900.** Type 21. *Perf.*

| 201 | 1 l., red .. | .. | .. | 2 |
| 202 | 5 l. ,, .. | .. | .. | 4 |
| 203 | 10 l. ,, .. | .. | .. | 4 |
| 204 | 20 l. ,, .. | .. | .. | 6 |
| 205 | 40 l. ,, .. | .. | .. | 12 |
| 206 | 50 l. ,, .. | .. | .. | 16 |
| 207 | 1 dr. ,, .. | .. | .. | 30 |
| 208 | 2 dr. ,, .. | .. | .. | 62 |

No.

*Surcharged with* Type 22,
*in* black.

209| 1 dr. on 1 dr., red .. 36

# DENMARK.

1      2

3

APRIL, **1851.** *Wmk. Crown.* Type 3.
No. Type.      *Imperf.*

| | | | | | Un. | Used. |
|---|---|---|---|---|---|---|
| 1 | 1 | 2 R.B.S., | blue | .. | 20.00 | 3.15 |
| 2 | 2 | 4 ,, | yellow-brn. | | 22.50 | 6 |
| 3 | ,, | 4 ,, | chestnut-brn. | — | | 10 |
| 4 | ,, | 4 ,, | dark brown | | 3.00 | 2 |

*Variety. Perf.* 12, *unofficially.*

5 | 2 | 4 R.B.S., dark brown — 2.50

In the 2 rigsbank skilling, *blue*, there are three varieties of the figure " 2," varying in the manner in which the downstroke and the tailpiece join.

Reprints of the 2 R.B.S. were made in 1886 on white wove, on yellowish wove, and on yellowish wove paper faced with buff wavy lines, all without wmk. A reprint of the 4 R.B.S. on the last-named variety of paper was made at the same time.

4

**1853–57.** Type 4. *Wmk. Crown. Dotted spandrels. Imperf.*

| | | | | | Un. | Used. |
|---|---|---|---|---|---|---|
| 6 | 2 sk., | blue | .. | .. | 25 | 8 |
| 7 | 4 ,, | chestnut | .. | | 2.50 | 2 |
| 8 | 4 ,, | pale chestnut | .. | | 2.50 | 2 |
| 9 | 8 ,, | green | .. | .. | 2.50 | 16 |
| 10 | 16 ,, | grey-lilac | .. | | 6.25 | 90 |
| 11 | 16 ,, | mauve | .. | .. | | |

No.

*Varieties.* (*a*) *Rouletted.*

| | | | | | Un. | Used. |
|---|---|---|---|---|---|---|
| 12 | 4 sk., | brown | .. | .. | | |
| 13 | 8 ,, | green | .. | .. | | |
| 14 | 16 ,, | mauve | .. | .. | 22.50 | 4.35 |

(*b*) *Perf.* 10 *to* 14, *unofficially.*

| | | | | | Un. | Used. |
|---|---|---|---|---|---|---|
| 15 | 2 sk., | blue | .. | .. | 1.25 | 3.75 |
| 16 | 4 ,, | brown | .. | .. | | |
| 17 | 8 ,, | green | .. | .. | | |
| 18 | 16 ,, | grey-lilac | .. | | | |

Reprints of the 2 sk. and 16 sk. were made in 1886 on yellowish unwmkd. wove paper, imperf.

5

**1858.** Type 5.
*Same wmk. Wavy lines in spandrels.
Imperf.*

| | | | | | Un. | Used. |
|---|---|---|---|---|---|---|
| 19 | 4 sk., | chestnut | .. | .. | 62 | 2 |
| 20 | 4 ,, | deep brown | .. | | 1.25 | 4 |
| 20a | 4 ,, | pale brown | .. | | 2.50 | 8 |
| 21 | 8 ,, | green | .. | .. | 4.35 | 30 |

*Varieties.* (*a*) *Rouletted.*

| | | | | | Un. | Used. |
|---|---|---|---|---|---|---|
| 22 | 4 sk., | chestnut | .. | .. | 75 | 6 |
| 23 | 4 ,, | deep brown | .. | | 90 | 2 |
| 24 | 8 ,, | green | .. | .. | | |

(*b*) *Perf.* 10 *to* 14, *unofficially.*

| | | | |
|---|---|---|---|
| 25 | 4 sk., | brown | .. .. |
| 26 | 8 ,, | green | .. .. |

Both values were reprinted in 1886 on white or yellowish unwmkd. wove paper, imperf.

6      7

**1864–68.** Type 6.
*Wmk. Crown,* Type 7. *Perf.* 12½ *to* 13.

| | | | | | Un. | Used. |
|---|---|---|---|---|---|---|
| 27 | 2 sk., | pale blue | .. | | 62 | 6 |
| 28 | 2 ,, | blue | .. | | 62 | 4 |
| 29 | 3 ,, | lilac-rose | .. | | 1.00 | 10 |
| 30 | 3 ,, | mauve | .. | | 90 | 12 |
| 31 | 4 ,, | pale red | .. | | 1.25 | 2 |
| 32 | 4 ,, | vermilion | .. | | 75 | 2 |
| 33 | 4 ,, | rose-red | .. | | 75 | 2 |
| 34 | 8 ,, | olive-bistre | .. | | 7.50 | 30 |
| 35 | 16 ,, | grey-green | .. | | 5.00 | 25 |
| 36 | 16 ,, | olive-green | .. | | 5.00 | 25 |

*Varieties. Imperf.*

| | | | |
|---|---|---|---|
| 37 | 2 sk., | blue | .. .. |
| 38 | 3 ,, | mauve | .. .. |

|  |  | Un. | Used. |
|---|---|---|---|
| **No.** |  |  |  |
| 39 | 4 sk., red    ..    .. |  |  |
| 40 | 8 ,,   olive-bistre |  |  |
| 41 | 16 ,,   olive-green    .. |  |  |

All five values were reprinted in 1886 on white unwmkd. wove paper, imperf.

**8**

**1870-71.**

Type 8. *Wmk.* Type 7. *Perf.* 14 × 13½.

*Centre in the first colour given.*

| 42 | 2 sk., dull blue & grey . | 36 | 2 |
|---|---|---|---|
| 43 | 2 ,,   blue    ,,    . | 12 | 2 |
| 44 | 2 ,,   deep blue ,,   . | 1.25 | 4 |
| 45 | 3 ,,   bright mauve and grey    .. | 1.00 | 12 |
| 46 | 3 sk., dull mauve & grey | 50 | 12 |
| 47 | 4 ,,   bright red    ,, | 75 | 2 |
| 48 | 4 ,,   dull rose-red and grey    ..    .. | 90 | 4 |
| 49 | 8 sk., yell.-brn. & grey | 1.00 | 4 |
| 50 | 8 ,,   dark brn.    ,, | — | 4 |
| 51 | 16 ,,   bright grn.    ,, | 3.75 | 18 |
| 52 | 16 ,,   pale grn.    ,, | 5.00 | 18 |

*Perf.* 12½.

| 52a | 2 sk., blue and grey    .. | 10.00 | 6.25 |
|---|---|---|---|
| 53 | 4 ,,   dull rose-red and grey    ..    .. | 3.00 | 62 |
| 54 | 48 sk., lilac & brown    .. | 8.75 | 2.50 |

*Varieties. Imperf.*

| 55 | 2 sk., blue and grey    .. |
|---|---|
| 56 | 3 ,,   mauve    ,,    .. |
| 57 | 4 ,,   red      ,,    .. |
| 58 | 8 ,,   brown    ,,    .. |
| 59 | 16 ,,   green    ,,    .. |
| 60 | 48 ,,   lilac & brown .. |

All the values of this issue were reprinted in 1886 on white unwmkd. wove paper, imperf.

**9**

**1875-79.**

Type 9. *Wmk. and perf. as before.*

*(a) Thin semi-transparent paper.*

| 61 | 3 öre, grey & grey-blue | 25 | 8 |
|---|---|---|---|
| 62 | 3 ,,   grey and blue    .. | 12 | 4 |

|  |  | Un. | Used. |
|---|---|---|---|
| **No.** |  |  |  |
| 63 | 4 öre, lilac-blue & grey | 12 | 8 |
| 64 | 4 ,,   sky-blue & slate | 36 | 4 |
| 65 | 4 ,,   blue and slate .. | 25 | 2 |
| 66 | 4 ,,   bright ultram. & drab    ..    .. | 2.50 | 2 |
| 67 | 5 ,,   blue and rose .. | 36 | 6 |
| 68 | 5 ,,     ,,    carmine | 50 | 6 |
| 69 | 8 ,,   rose & pale grey | 30 | 2 |
| 70 | 8 ,,   carmine and slate | 75 | 2 |
| 71 | 12 ,,   lilac and grey .. | 1.00 | 2 |
| 72 | 12 ,,   dull mauve & grey | — | 2 |
| 73 | 16 ,,   bn. and pale grey | 1.25 | 4 |
| 74 | 20 ,,   grey and rose .. | 1.25 | 2 |
| 75 | 20 ,,     ,,    carmine | 1.00 | 6 |
| 76 | 25 ,,   green and grey . | 62 | 6 |
| 77 | 50 ,,   dull violet & brn. | 2.50 | 18 |
| 78 | 50 ,,   dull purple and brown    ..    .. | 1.10 | 2 |
| 79 | 100 öre, orange - yellow and grey    ..    .. | 1.25 | 8 |

*Variety.*

*Loop of central "5" unfinished.*

| 80 | 5 öre, blue and rose .. | 2.50 |
|---|---|---|
| 81 | 5 ,,   blue & carmine.. | 2.50 |

*(b) Thick paper.*

| 82 | 3 öre, grey and blue .. | 6 | 2 |
|---|---|---|---|
| 83 | 3 ,,   grey & blue-grey | 12 | 2 |
| 84 | 4 ,,   blue and slate.. | 62 | 2 |
| 85 | 4 ,,   pale blue & slate | 30 | 2 |
| 86 | 8 ,,   rose-car. & slate | 25 | 2 |
| 87 | 12 ,,   dull mauve & slate | 25 | 2 |
| 88 | 12 ,,   purple and drab | 36 | 2 |
| 89 | 16 ,,   brown and slate | 25 | 2 |
| 90 | 25 ,,   green and grey . | 18 | 2 |
| 91 | 50 ,,   dull purple and brown    ..    .. | 36 | 4 |
| 92 | 50 öre, brown-purple & grey-brown ..    .. | 75 | 4 |
| 93 | 100 öre, orange - yellow and grey    ..    .. | 75 | - |

*Varieties. (a) Imperf.*

| 94 | 4 öre, blue and slate.. | — | 10.00 |
|---|---|---|---|
| 95 | 8 ,,   rose-carmine and slate ..    .. | | |
| 96 | 100 öre, orange - yellow and grey    ..    .. | | |

*(b) "D NMARK" for "DANMARK."*

| 97 | 3 öre, grey & grey-blue | 1.25 | 1.. |
|---|---|---|---|

*(c) "o " for "öre."*

| 97a | 8 öre, carmine and slate |
|---|---|

We only catalogue two sets of these stamps, but specialists may divide this issue into four or five sets, if due note is taken of the paper, gum, and impression.

**1896-99.** *Same type.* *Perf.* 12½.

| 98 | 3 öre, grey and blue . | 2 | . |
|---|---|---|---|
| 99 | 4 ,,   blue and slate . | 2 | 2 |

|     | Un. | Used. |
|-----|-----|-------|
| No. |     |       |
| 100 | 8 öre, carmine and slate | 4 | 2 |
| 101 | 12 ,, mauve and slate | 12 | 2 |
| 102 | 16 ,, brown and slate | 6 | 2 |
| 102a | 25 ,, green and grey | 10 | 4 |
| 103 | 50 ,, purple & brown | 18 | 6 |
| 104 | 100 ,, yellow and grey | 36 | 2 |

10

**Type 10.** *Wmk. and perf. as before.*

**1882.** *Small figures in the corners.*

| 105 | 5 öre, green | .. | .. | 50 | |
| 106 | 10 ,, rose | .. | .. | 4·35 | |
| 107 | 20 ,, dull blue | .. | 1·50 | | 2 |

*Larger figures in corners.*

| 108 | 5 öre, green | .. | .. | 12 | 2 |
| 109 | 10 ,, rose | .. | .. | 18 | 2 |
| 109a | 10 ,, rosine | .. | .. | 25 | 2 |
| 110 | 20 ,, pale blue | .. | .. | 18 | 2 |
| 110a | 20 ,, blue | .. | .. | 12 | 2 |

**1896–1902.** *Large figures. Perf. 12½.*

| 111 | 1 öre, orange | .. | .. | 2 | 2 |
| 112 | 5 ,, green | .. | .. | 2 | 2 |
| 113 | 10 ,, rose | .. | .. | 4 | 2 |
| 114 | 10 ,, rosine | .. | .. | 4 | 2 |
| 115 | 15 ,, lilac | .. | .. | 6 | 2 |
| 116 | 20 ,, blue | .. | .. | 8 | 2 |
| 117 | 20 ,, bright blue | .. | 8 | | 2 |
| 118 | 24 ,, brown | .. | .. | 8 | 4 |

*Varieties. Imperf.*

| 119 | 10 öre, rose | .. | .. | | |
| 120 | 20 ,, blue | .. | .. | | |

The paper of these stamps also varies
considerably.

OFFICIAL STAMPS.

51

**1871.** Type 51.

*Wmk. Crown.* (a) *Perf.* 14 × 13½.

| 201 | 2 sk., dull blue.. | .. | 36 | 12 |
| 202 | 2 sk., bright blue | .. | 90 | 12 |
| 203 | 2 sk., ultramarine | .. | 1·85 | 12 |
| 204 | 4 sk., rose-carmine | .. | 36 | 2 |
| 205 | 16 sk., green | .. | .. | 3·75 | 36 |

|     | Un. | Used. |
|-----|-----|-------|
| No. |     |       |

(b) *Perf.* 12½.

| 206 | 4 sk., rose-carmine | .. | 5·00 | 75 |
| 207 | 16 sk., green | .. | — | 50 |

(c) *Imperf.*

| 208 | 2 sk., dull blue | .. | .. | |
| 209 | 4 sk., rose-carmine | .. | .. | |
| 210 | 16 sk., green | .. | .. | |

The three values were reprinted in 1886
on white unwmkd. wove paper, imperf.

**1875.** *Same type and wmk.*
*Perf.* 14 × 13½.

| 211 | 3 öre, pale mauve | .. | 25 | 12 |
| 212 | 3 ,, mauve .. | .. | 4 | 4 |
| 213 | 3 ,, violet-mauve .. | | — | 2 |
| 214 | 4 ,, lilac-blue | .. | 25 | 8 |
| 215 | 4 ,, bright blue | .. | 4 | 2 |
| 216 | 4 ,, greenish blue .. | | 18 | 4 |
| 217 | 4 ,, ultramarine | .. | 25 | 6 |
| 217a | 4 ,, cobalt .. | .. | — | 2 |
| 218 | 8 ,, rose-carmine | .. | 4 | 2 |
| 219 | 32 ,, green .. | .. | 16 | 6 |
| 220 | 32 ,, deep green | .. | 18 | 6 |

**1899–1902.** *Same type and wmk.*
*Perf.* 12½.

| 221 | 1 öre, orange | .. | .. | 2 | 2 |
| 222 | 3 ,, reddish lilac | .. | 2 | |
| 223 | 4 ,, blue | .. | .. | 2 | 2 |
| 224 | 5 ,, green | .. | .. | 2 | |
| 225 | 8 ,, carmine .. | .. | 4 | 2 |
| 226 | 10 ,, ,, | .. | .. | 4 | |

## DANISH WEST INDIES.

1

Nov., **1855.**

**Type 1.** *Wmk. Crown* (Denmark
Type 3). *Imperf.*

(a) *With network of close* grey *wavy
lines, sometimes not showing. Deep
brown gum.*

| 1 | 3 cents, dull crimson-red | 5·00 | 4·00 |

(b) *Ordinary gum.*

| 2 | 3 cents, crimson (1860). | 12·50 | 3·00 |
| 3 | 3 ,, rose (1867) | .. | 1·85 | 50 |

OCT., **1871.** *Same wmk. Rouletted.*

| 4 | 3 cents, rose | .. | .. | |

**1872–73.** *Same wmk. Perf.* 12½.

| 5 | 3 cents, rose-carmine | .. | 2·50 | 2·50 |
| 6 | 4 ,, ultramarine | .. | 4·00 | 5·00 |

No.      *Un.*   *Used.*      No.      *Un.*   *Used.*

*Variety. Imperf.*

7 | 4 cents, ultramarine .. 12.50

**2**

**1873-79.** Type **2**. *Wmk. Crown*
(Denmark Type 7). *Perf.* 14 × 13½.
The centre in the first colour.

*(a) Thin semi-transparent paper.*

| | | | |
|---|---|---|---|
| 8 | 1 c., red-violet & green. | 12 | 6 |
| 8a | 1 c., mauve & yell.-grn. | 12 | 8 |
| 9 | 3 c., carm. & grey-blue | 62 | 6 |
| 9a | 3 c., carm. and blue .. | 1.50 | 12 |
| 10 | 4 c., blue and brown .. | 36 | 25 |
| 10a | 4 c., grey-blue & brown | 8 | 8 |
| 10b | 4 c., deep blue & brown | 1.25 | 12 |
| 11 | 5 c., grey and green .. | 25 | 8 |
| 11a | 7 c., yellow and lilac .. | 1.50 | 90 |
| 12 | 7 c., orange and lilac .. | 50 | 50 |
| 13 | 10 c., dark brown & grey-blue .. .. | 50 | 8 |
| 14 | 12 c., green and lilac .. | 62 | 50 |
| 15 | 12 c., green & red-lilac.. | 25 | 25 |
| 16 | 14 c., green and lilac .. | 8.75 | 8.75 |
| 17 | 50 c., deep mauve .. | 1.25 | 1.25 |

*(b) Thick paper.*

| | | | |
|---|---|---|---|
| 18 | 1 c., lilac-rose & green . | 8 | 4 |
| 18a | 1 c., claret & pale green | 25 | 4 |
| 19 | 3 c., rose & grey-blue.. | 36 | 18 |
| 20 | 3 c., rose and blue .. | 1.25 | 4 |
| 20a | 3 c., carm. and dull blue | 1.00 | 6 |
| 21 | 4 c., grey-blue & brown | | |
| 22 | 5 c., grey and green .. | 62 | 25 |
| 23 | 10 c., yellow-brown and grey .. .. .. | 75 | 16 |
| 24 | 10 c., dark brn. & indigo | 25 | 25 |
| 25 | 50 c., mauve .. .. | 5.00 | |
| 26 | 50 c., pale lilac .. .. | 1.50 | |

*Variety. Imperf.*

26a | 3 c., rose and blue ..

## I CENT

**3**

MAY, **1887.** *Surcharged with* Type **3**,
*in* black.

| | | | |
|---|---|---|---|
| 27 | 1 c. on 7 c., No. 11a .. | 75 | 1.00 |
| 27a | 1 c. ,, No. 12 .. | 75 | |

## 10 ·

## CENTS

## 1895

**4**

**1895.** *Surcharged with* Type **4**,
*in* black.

| | | | |
|---|---|---|---|
| 28 | 10 c. on 50 c., No. 25 .. | 36 | 36 |
| 28a | 10 c. ,, No. 26 .. | 25 | 36 |

**1898-1901.** *Same type and wmk.*
*Perf.* 12½.

| | | | |
|---|---|---|---|
| 29 | 1 c., mauve and green.. | 25 | 36 |
| 30 | 3 c., carmine and indigo | 62 | |
| 30a | 4 c., slate-blue & brown | 10 | 10 |
| 30b | 4 c., blue and pale brown | 8 | |
| 31 | 5 c., grey and green .. | 62 | 50 |
| 32 | 10 c., brown and grey .. | 18 | 18 |

**5**

**1900-3.** Type **5**. *Perf.* 12½.

| | | | |
|---|---|---|---|
| 33 | 1 c., green .. .. | 4 | 4 |
| 33a | 2 c., carmine .. .. | 4 | 2 |
| 34 | 5 c., blue .. .. | 12 | 12 |
| 34a | 8 c., brown .. .. | 12 | 12 |

## 8

## CENTS

## 1902.

**6**

JAN., **1902.** Type **2** *surcharged with date*
*and new value in* black, *as* Type **6**.

*(a) Perf.* 12½.

| | | | |
|---|---|---|---|
| 35 | 2 c. on 3 c. (No. 30).. | 12 | 15 |
| 36 | 8 c. on 10 c. ( ,, 32).. | 25 | 36 |

*Error. With date* "1901."

37 | 2 c. on 3 c. (No. 30) ..

*(b) Perf.* 14 × 13½ *(March).*

38 | 2 c. on 3 c. (No. 19) ..

No.

*Un. Used.*

**2**

**Cents**

**1902**

**7**

MAY, 1902. *Surcharged as* Type 7, *in* black. *Perf.* 12½.

| | | Un. | Used. |
|---|---|---|---|
| 39 | 2 c. on 3 c., carm. & blue | 6 | |
| 40 | 8 c. on 10 c., brn. ,, | 25 | 25 |

**UNPAID LETTER STAMPS.**

**11**

**1902.** Type 11. *Perf.* 11½.

| | | | |
|---|---|---|---|
| 101 | 1 c., blue | .. | .. |
| 102 | 4 c. ,, | .. | .. |
| 103 | 6 c. ,, | .. | .. |
| 104 | 10 c. ,, | .. | .. |

Set of 4, unused, $1.00.

**ICELAND.**

**1**

**1873.** Type 1. *Wmk. Crown* (Denmark Type 7). *Perf.* 12½.

| | | | Un. | Used. |
|---|---|---|---|---|
| 1 | 3 skill., grey | .. | 90 | 1.25 |
| 2 | 4 ,, carmine | .. | 3.75 | 2.50 |
| 3 | 16 ,, yellow | .. | 1.00 | 1.25 |

**1874.** *Perf.* 14 × 13½.

| | | | | |
|---|---|---|---|---|
| 4 | 2 skill., blue | .. | 2.50 | 3.15 |
| 5 | 4 ,, carmine | .. | 18 | 25 |
| 6 | 8 ,, brown | .. | 1.25 | 1.25 |
| 7 | 16 ,, yellow | .. | 3.75 | 3.75 |

*Imperf.*

| | | | | |
|---|---|---|---|---|
| 8 | 2 skill., blue | .. | 1.85 | |
| 8a | 3 c., grey | .. | | |
| 9 | 4 skill., carmine | .. | 2.50 | 3.75 |
| 10 | 8 ,, brown | .. | 1.85 | |
| 11 | 16 ,, yellow | .. | 1.85 | |

**1875.** *Same type and wmk.* (a) *Perf.* 12½.

| | | | | |
|---|---|---|---|---|
| 12 | 5 aur, blue | .. | 50 | 62 |

**1876.** (*b*) *Perf.* 14 × 13½.

| | | | | Un. | Used. |
|---|---|---|---|---|---|
| 13 | 5 aur, blue | .. | .. | 2.50 | 1.25 |
| 14 | 6 ,, dark drab | .. | 25 | 25 |
| 15 | 6 ,, pale slate | .. | 25 | 12 |
| 16 | 10 ,, rose | .. | 25 | 2 |
| 16a | 10 ,, carmine | .. | .. | 30 | 2 |
| 17 | 16 ,, yellow-brown | .. | 36 | 12 |
| 17a | 16 ,, brown | .. | 18 | 25 |
| 18 | 20 ,, purple | .. | 1.25 | 1.00 |
| 19 | 20 ,, pale mauve | .. | 2.50 | 1.25 |
| 20 | 40 ,, green | .. | 1.25 | 1.00 |

Imperf. specimens of all these exist.

A     2     B

**1882–92.** Types 1 and 2 (3 aur *with small figure as* A). *Same wmk. Perf.* 14 × 13½.

| | | | | Un. | Used. |
|---|---|---|---|---|---|
| 21 | 3 aur, yellow | .. | .. | 12 | 18 |
| 22 | 3 ,, yellow-ochre | .. | 10 | 4 |
| 23 | 5 ,, green | .. | 10 | 8 |
| 24 | 5 ,, deep green | .. | 12 | 10 |
| 25 | 20 ,, blue | .. | 25 | 8 |
| 26 | 20 ,, slate-blue | .. | 25 | 8 |
| 27 | 20 ,, ultramarine | .. | 1.00 | 12 |
| 28 | 40 ,, mauve | .. | 50 | 12 |
| 28a | 40 ,, pale violet | .. | 75 | 18 |
| 29 | 40 ,, lilac-rose | .. | 36 | 18 |
| 30 | 50 ,, carmine & blue | .. | 62 | 50 |
| 31 | 100 ,, lilac & brown | .. | 75 | 62 |

**3**    **4**    **5**    **6**

**1898.** Type 2 (No. 37) *surcharged in* blk. No. Type. *Perf.* 12½.

| | | | | Un. | Used. |
|---|---|---|---|---|---|
| 32 | 3 | 3 on 5 aur, green | .. | 3.75 | 3.75 |
| 33 | 4 | 3 on 5 ,, ,, | .. | — | 3.75 |

*Surcharged* "3," *in red, in addition.*

(i.) *Small word, and thin figure of* Type 6. *Perf.* 14 × 13½.

(ii.) *Small word and thick figure,* Type 5. *Perf.* 12½.

(iii.) *Large word and thin figure,* Type 6. *Perf.* 14 × 13½.

(iv.) *Large word and thin figure,* Type 6. *Perf.* 12½.

| | | | Un. | Used. |
|---|---|---|---|---|
| 34 | 3 on 5 aur, green (i.) | .. | | |
| 34a | 3 on 5 ,, ,, (ii.) | .. | — | 3.00 |
| 35 | 3 on 5 ,, ,, (iii.) | .. | — | 5.00 |
| 35a | 3 on 5 ,, ,, (iv.) | .. | | |

NOTE.—The first letter of the surcharges is not "p," but a Saxon letter called "thorn," the symbol for "th."

| No. | | | Un. | Used. |
|---|---|---|---|---|
| **1898–1902.** *Types and wmk. as before.* | | | | |
| *Perf.* 12½. | | | | |
| 36 | 3 aur, yellow .. .. | | 8 | 8 |
| 36a | 4 ,, grey and rose .. | | 18 | 25 |
| 37 | 5 ,, green .. .. | | 8 | 4 |
| 38 | 6 ,, grey .. .. | | 18 | 25 |
| 39 | 10 ,, carmine .. .. | | 25 | 12 |
| 39a | 16 ,, brown .. | | 90 | |
| 40 | 20 ,, ultramarine .. | | 50 | 8 |
| 41 | 25 ,, blue and yellow- | | | |
| | brown.. .. .. | | 75 | |
| 42 | 50 aur, carmine and blue | 1.50 | | |
| **1902.** Type 1 (*large figure as* B). *Wmk.* | | | | |
| *Crown. Perf.* 12½. | | | | |
| 43 | 3 aur, buff .. .. | | 16 | |

## Í GILDI

## '02—'03

### 7

*Stamps of* **1882–1902** *surcharged with*
Type 7, *in* carmine *on the* 5, 6, 20, *and*
25 aur, *in* black *on the other values.*
(i.) *Perf.* 12½.

| | | | Un. | Used. |
|---|---|---|---|---|
| 44 | 3 aur, yellow (A) .. | | 1.85 | |
| 45 | 3 ,, ,, (B) .. | | 25 | |
| 46 | 4 ,, grey and rose .. | | 50 | |
| 47 | 5 ,, green .. .. | | 18 | |
| 48 | 6 ,, grey .. .. | | 4 | |
| 49 | 10 ,, carmine .. .. | | 8 | |
| 50 | 16 ,, brown .. .. | | 90 | |
| 51 | 20 ,, ultramarine .. | | 12 | |
| 52 | 25 ,, blue and brown | | 16 | |
| 53 | 40 ,, lilac .. .. | | 25 | |
| 54 | 50 ,, carmine and blue | | 30 | |

*Varieties.*
(*a*) *Surcharge inverted.*

| | | | | |
|---|---|---|---|---|
| 55 | 3 aur, yellow (A) .. | | | |
| 56 | 3 ,, ,, (B) .. | | | |
| 57 | 4 ,, grey and rose .. | | | |
| 58 | 5 ,, green .. .. | 6.25 | | |
| 59 | 6 ,, grey .. .. | 3.15 | | |
| 60 | 10 ,, carmine .. .. | | | |
| 61 | 16 ,, brown .. .. | | | |
| 62 | 25 ,, blue and brown . | 3.15 | | |
| 63 | 40 ,, lilac .. .. | | | |

(*b*) *Surcharge double.*

| | | |
|---|---|---|
| 64 | 4 aur, grey and rose .. | |
| 65 | 6 ,, ,, .. | |
| 66 | 50 ,, carmine and blue | |

(*d*) *Error.* "GILDI" *for* "Í GILDI."

| | | |
|---|---|---|
| 67 | 3 aur, yellow (A) .. | |
| 68 | 3 ,, ,, (B) .. | |
| 69 | 4 ,, grey and rose .. | |
| 70 | 5 ,, green .. .. | |
| 71 | 16 ,, brown .. .. | |
| 72 | 50 ,, carmine and blue | |

(*g*) "02'" *for* "'02."

| | | |
|---|---|---|
| 73 | 3 aur, yellow (A) .. | |
| 74 | 3 ,, ,, (B) .. | |

| | | | Un. | Used. |
|---|---|---|---|---|
| 75 | 4 aur, grey and rose .. | | | |
| 76 | 5 ,, green .. .. | | | |
| 77 | 6 ,, grey .. .. | | | |
| 78 | 16 ,, brown .. .. | | | |
| 79 | 20 ,, ultramarine .. | | | |
| 80 | 50 ,, carmine and blue | | | |

(*j*) "'03–'03" *for* "'02–'03."

| | | |
|---|---|---|
| 81 | 3 aur, yellow (A) .. | |
| 82 | 4 ,, grey and rose .. | |
| 83 | 5 ,, green .. .. | |
| 84 | 6 ,, grey .. .. | |
| 85 | 16 ,, brown .. .. | |
| 86 | 20 ,, ultramarine .. | |
| 87 | 50 ,, carmine and blue | |

(*m*) *Error. Surcharge in* black.

| | | |
|---|---|---|
| 88 | 5 aur, green .. .. | |
| 89 | 20 ,, ultramarine .. | |

(*n*) *Variety.* "GILDI" *for* "Í GILDI."

| | | |
|---|---|---|
| 90 | 5 aur, green .. .. | |

(ii.) *Perf.* 14 × 13½.

| | | | |
|---|---|---|---|
| 91 | 3 aur, yellow (A) .. | 1.85 | |
| 92 | 5 ,, green .. .. | 3.75 | |
| 93 | 6 ,, grey .. .. | 3.75 | |
| 94 | 10 ,, carmine .. | | |
| 95 | 16 ,, brown .. .. | 3.15 | |
| 96 | 20 ,, ultramarine .. | 3.75 | |
| 97 | 40 ,, lilac .. .. | 1.25 | |
| 98 | 50 ,, carmine and blue | 1.85 | |
| 99 | 100 ,, lilac and brown | 2.10 | |

*Varieties.*
(*a*) *Surcharge inverted.*

| | | | |
|---|---|---|---|
| 100 | 40 aur, lilac .. .. | | |
| 101 | 50 ,, carmine & blue | | |
| 102 | 100 ,, lilac and brown | 7.50 | |

(*d*) *Error.* "GILDI" *for* "Í GILDI."

| | | |
|---|---|---|
| 103 | 100 aur., lilac and brown | |

(*e*) *As* (*d*) *inverted.*

| | | |
|---|---|---|
| 104 | 100 aur, lilac and brown | |

(*g*) "02'" *for* "'02."

| | | |
|---|---|---|
| 105 | 3 aur, yellow (A) .. | |
| 106 | 5 ,, green .. .. | |
| 107 | 100 ,, lilac and brown | |

(*h*) *As* (*g*) *inverted.*

| | | |
|---|---|---|
| 108 | 5 aur, green .. .. | |

(*j*) "'03–'03" *for* "'02–'03."

| | | |
|---|---|---|
| 109 | 40 aur, lilac .. .. | |
| 110 | 50 ,, carmine and blue | |

### 8

Type 8.   *Wmk. Crown. Perf.* 12½.
*Centre in first colour.*

| | | | | |
|---|---|---|---|---|
| 111 | 3 aur, orange .. .. | | 2 | |
| 112 | 4 ,, rose and grey .. | | 2 | 2 |

| No. | | Un. | Used. |
|---|---|---|---|
| 113 | 5 aur, green .. .. | 4 | |
| 114 | 6 ,, deep brown and | | |
| | grey-brown .. | 4 | |
| 115 | 10 ,, carmine .. .. | 4 | 4 |
| 116 | 16 ,, reddish brown .. | 6 | |
| 117 | 20 ,, blue .. .. | 8 | 8 |
| 118 | 25 ,, green and brown | 10 | |
| 119 | 40 ,, mauve .. .. | 16 | |
| 120 | 50 ,, slate and grey .. | 18 | |
| 121 | 1 krona, brown and dull | | |
| | blue .. .. .. | 36 | |

*Error in the sheet of* 20 aur. "PJONUSTA,"
*instead of* "FRIMERKI," *at right.*

| 122 | 20 aur, blue .. .. | 6.25 | |
|---|---|---|---|

### OFFICIAL STAMPS.

51      52

**1873.** Type 51. *Wmk. Crown.*
(*a*) *Perf.* 12½.

| 201 | 4 skill., green .. .. | 18 | 62 |
|---|---|---|---|

(*b*) *Perf.* 14×13½.

| 202 | 4 skill., green .. .. | — | 12.50 |
|---|---|---|---|
| 203 | 8 ,, lilac .. .. | 3.75 | 2.50 |

(*c*) *Imperf.*

| 204 | 4 skill., green .. .. | 2.50 | |
|---|---|---|---|
| 205 | 8 ,, lilac .. .. | 2.50 | |

**1876.** Type 52.
*Same wmk. Perf.* 14×13½.

| 206 | 10 aur, ultramarine .. | 50 | 8 |
|---|---|---|---|
| 207 | 10 ,, bright blue .. | 12 | |
| 208 | 16 ,, carmine .. .. | 25 | 25 |
| 209 | 20 ,, dark green .. | 75 | 12 |
| 210 | 20 ,, yellow-green .. | 25 | 8 |

**1878-95.** *Same type, wmk., and perf.*

| 211 | 3 aur, ochre (1882) .. | 18 | |
|---|---|---|---|
| 211a | 3 ,, yellow .. | 12 | 8 |
| 212 | 5 ,, dark brown (1878) | 8 | 8 |
| 213 | 5 ,, pale brown .. | 8 | 4 |
| 214 | 50 ,, rosy lilac (1895) | 62 | 50 |

The 5 aur is known imperforate.

**1898-1902.** *Same types and wmk.*
*Perf.* 12½.

| 215 | 3 aur, yellow .. .. | 18 | 12 |
|---|---|---|---|
| 216 | 4 ,, grey .. .. | 12 | |
| 217 | 10 ,, ultramarine .. | | |

**1902.** Type 52 *surcharged with* Type 7,
*in black.*
(i.) *Perf.* 12½.

| 218 | 3 aur, yellow .. .. | 25 | |
|---|---|---|---|
| 219 | 4 ,, grey .. .. | 25 | |
| 220 | 5 ,, brown .. .. | 4 | |
| 221 | 10 ,, deep blue .. | 8 | |
| 222 | 20 ,, green .. .. | 18 | |

| No. | | Un. | Used. |
|---|---|---|---|
| | (*a*) *Surcharge inverted.* | | |
| 223 | 3 aur, yellow .. .. | 2.50 | |
| 224 | 4 ,, grey .. .. | 2.50 | |
| 225 | 10 ,, deep blue .. | 2.25 | |
| | (*d*) *Errors.* "GILDI" *for* "I GILDI." | | |
| 226 | 3 aur, yellow .. .. | | |
| 227 | 4 ,, grey .. .. | | |
| 228 | 10 ,, deep blue .. | | |
| | (*e*) *As* (*d*) *inverted.* | | |
| 229 | 4 aur, grey .. .. | | |
| | (*g*) "o2" *for* "'o2." | | |
| 230 | 5 aur, brown .. .. | | |
| 231 | 10 ,, deep blue .. | | |
| | (*j*) "'o3-'o3" *for* "'o2-'o3." | | |
| 232 | 10 aur, deep blue .. | | |
| | (ii.) *Perf.* 14×13½. | | |
| 233 | 3 aur, yellow .. .. | 75 | |
| 234 | 5 ,, brown .. .. | 50 | |
| 235 | 10 ,, ultramarine .. | 2.10 | |
| 236 | 10 ,, deep blue .. | | |
| 237 | 16 ,, carmine .. .. | 75 | |
| 238 | 20 ,, green .. .. | 12 | |
| 239 | 50 ,, rosy lilac .. | 30 | |
| | (*a*) *Surcharge inverted.* | | |
| 240 | 5 aur, brown .. .. | 1.85 | |
| 241 | 16 ,, carmine .. .. | | |
| | (*b*) *Surcharge double.* | | |
| 242 | 16 aur, carmine .. .. | | |
| 243 | 50 ,, rosy lilac .. | | |
| | (*c*) *Double surcharge, one inverted.* | | |
| 244 | 16 aur, carmine .. .. | | |
| | (*d*) *Error.* "GILDI" *for* "I GILDI." | | |
| 245 | 10 aur, deep blue .. | | |
| 246 | 16 ,, carmine .. .. | | |
| 247 | 50 ,, rosy lilac .. | | |
| | (*g*) "o2" *for* "'o2." | | |
| 248 | 5 aur, brown .. .. | | |
| 249 | 10 ,, ultramarine .. | | |
| | (*j*) "'o3-'o3" *for* "'o2-'o3." | | |
| 250 | 5 aur, brown .. .. | | |
| 251 | 10 ,, ultramarine .. | | |
| 252 | 20 ,, green .. .. | | |

53

Type 53. *Centre in* sepia. *Wmk. Crown.*
*Perf.* 12½.

| 253 | 3 aur, buff .. .. | 2 | |
|---|---|---|---|
| 254 | 4 ,, dark green .. | 2 | |
| 255 | 5 ,, chestnut .. .. | 4 | |
| 256 | 10 ,, blue .. .. | 4 | |
| 257 | 16 ,, carmine .. .. | 6 | |
| 258 | 20 ,, green .. .. | 8 | |
| 259 | 50 ,, mauve .. .. | 18 | |

|  | *Un.* | *Used.* |
|---|---|---|

No.

## DOMINICAN REPUBLIC.

1

2

**1862.** Type 1. *Wove paper. Imperf.*

1 | ½ rl., black on rose .. 7.50
2 | 1 rl. ,, green .. 50.00

There are twelve varieties of type for each value.

**1865.** Type 2. *Laid paper.*

3 | ½ rl., blk. on pale green 15.00
4 | 1 rl. ,, ,, yellow

There are twelve varieties of type of the ½ rl., but only, it is believed, ten varieties of the 1 rl.

3

**1866.**

Type 3. Black *impression. Laid paper.*

5 | ½ rl., on buff .. .. 5.00 6.25
6 | "UN" rl., on pale green 3.75 2.50
7 | "Un" rl. ,, ,,

*Wmk. Lozenge pattern.*

8 | "Un" rl., on pale green

*Wove paper.*

9 | "Un" rl., on pale green 7.50 5.00

**1867.** *Wove paper.*

10 | ½ rl., on rose .. .. 3.75 5.00
11 | ½ rl., on pale rose .. 3.75 5.00
12 | "Un" rl., on pale blue 2.50 2.50
13 | "Un" rl., on grey-blue 2.50 2.50

*Error.* "Unreal" *one word.*

14 | "Un" rl., on blue ..

*Without inscription at top or bottom.*

15 | (1 rl.), on blue .. ..

*Pelure paper.*

16 | ½ rl., on flesh .. .. 1.50
17 | "Un" rl., on lavender. 3.15 3.75

The space between the words " Medio real " varies.

|  | *Un.* | *Used.* |
|---|---|---|

No.

**1868.** *Pelure paper.*

19 | ½ rl., on lavender ..
20 | ½ rl., on grey .. .. 4.50 4.50
21 | "UN " rl., on flesh .. 4.35 4.35

The space between the words " Medio real " varies.

**1869.** *Pelure paper.*

23 | ½ rl., on greenish yellow
24 | "UN " rl., on magenta

**1870.** *Wove paper.*

25 | ½ rl., on magenta .. 40.00
26 | "UN " rl., on green .. 1.85 2.50

**1871.** *Inscription at top and bottom, in black.*

27 | ½ rl., blue on rose .. 3.00 2.50

*Without inscription at top or bottom.*

28 | ½ rl., blue on rose ..

**1873-74.** *Wove paper.* Black *impression.*

29 | ½ rl., on yellow.. .. 1.50 1 50
30 | ½ rl., on buff ..
31 | "UN " rl., on lilac ('74) 2.50 2.50

*No inscription at top or bottom.*

32 | (½ rl.) on yellow ..
33 | (1 rl.) on lilac .. ..

4

**1879.** Type 4. *Perf.* 13.

34 | ½ r., violet on white .. 12 25
35 | ½ r. ,, lilac .. 12 25
36 | 1 r., carmine on white . 12 25
37 | 1 r. ,, salmon.. 12 25

5

**1880.** Type 5. *Wove paper. Rouletted.*

38 | 1 c., blue-green .. 4
39 | 1 c., dull green .. 8
40 | 2 c., red .. .. 12
41 | 2 c., orange-red .. 6 8
42 | 5 c., blue .. .. 12
43 | 10 c., pink .. .. 18 12
44 | 20 c., bistre .. .. 36
45 | 20 c., yellow-bistre .. 50

|  | Un. | Used. |
|---|---|---|

Io.
| 5 |25 c., mauve .. .. | 25 | 12 |
| 7 |50 c., orange .. .. | 1.00 | 30 |
| 3 | 75 c., blue .. .. | 2.50 | 36 |
| ) | 75 c., ultramarine .. | 1.00 | 36 |
| ) | 1 p., gold .. .. | 1.50 | 50 |

*Variety.* "CEN‾AVO." *This is* No. 11
*on the right-hand pane of* 25.
| . | 1 c., blue-green .. | 1.85 | 2.50 |
| ! | 1 c., dull green .. | 2.50 |  |

*Laid paper.*
| , | 1 c., dull green |  |  |
|  | 1 p., gold .. .. | 10.00 | 10.00 |

*Variety.* "CEN‾AVO."
| | 1 c., dull green.. .. |  |  |

**1881.**
*aper covered with rose-coloured network.*
| | 1 c., blue-green .. | 12 | 18 |
| | 1 c., dull green .. | 4 | 6 |
| | 2 c., red .. .. | 6 | 6 |
| | 2 c., orange-red .. |  |  |
| | 5 c., blue .. .. | 16 | 8 |
| | 10 c., pink .. | 25 | 6 |
| | 20 c., yellow-bistre .. | 36 | 8 |
| | 25 c., mauve .. | 50 | 16 |
| | 50 c., orange .. .. | 1.00 | 25 |
| | 75 c., ultramarine .. | 1.00 | 30 |
| | 1 p., gold .. | 1.25 | 62 |

*Variety.* "CEN‾AVO."
| | 1 c., blue-green .. |  |  |
| | 1 c., dull green .. | 2.50 |  |

## 5

## éntimos.
6

## 1

## franco.
8

## 1

## franco
. 7

## 1

## Franco.
9

**1883.** Type 5 *surcharged in* black.
. Type. A. ISSUE OF 1880.
| 6 | 5 c. on 1 c., dull grn. | 8 |  |
| ,, | 10 c. on 2 c., red | 50 |  |
| ,, | 25 c. on 5 c., blue .. | 1.00 | 12 |
| ,, | 50 c. on 10 c., pink .. | 2.50 | 1.00 |
| 7 | 1 f. on 20 c., bistre. | 3.75 |  |
| ,, | 1 f. on 20 c., yellow-bistre .. .. | 6.25 |  |
| 8 | 1 f. on 20 c., bistre. | 1.25 |  |
| ,, | 1 f. on 20 c., yellow-bistre .. .. | 1.50 |  |
| 9 | 1 f. on 20 c., bistre. | 1.50 |  |

No. Type.

## 1
## franco,
## 25
## céntimos.
10

|  |  | Un. | Used. |
|---|---|---|---|
| 78 | 9 | 1 f. on 20 c., yellow-bistre .. .. 1.25 |  |
| 79 | 10 | 1 f. 25 c. on 25 c., mauve .. 90 |  |
| 80 | ,, | 2 f. 50 c. on 50 c., orange .. .. 1.25 |  |
| 81 | ,, | 3 f. 75 c. on 75 c., blue .. .. 1.40 |  |

*Variety on laid paper.*
| 81a | 10 | 3 f. 75 c., ultram. .. 7.50 |

*Variety.* "CEN‾AVO."
| 82 | 6 | 5 c. on 1 c., dull grn. 1.85 |

The "5" of Type 6 should show a curved top.

*Surcharge inverted.*
| 82a | 5 c. on 1 c., dull green | — | 15.00 |
| 82b | 10 c. on 2 c., red .. |  |  |
| 82c | 25 c. on 5 c., blue .. | 22.50 |  |
| 82d | 50 c. on 10 c., pink | — | 5.00 |
| 82e | 1 f. on 20 c., bistre .. |  |  |
| 82f | 1 f. on 20 c., yell.-bistre |  |  |
| 82g | 1 f. 25 c. on 25 c., mauve | — | 22.50 |
| 82h | 2 f. 50 c. on 50 c., orange | — | 15.00 |
| 82i | 3 f. 75 c. on 75 c., blue.. | — | 15.00 |

The 1 f. on 20 c. is Type 7 only.

*Errors. Surcharge on wrong values.*
| 83 | 5 c. on 2 c., red .. | 25.00 |  |
| 84 | 5 c. on 5 c., blue .. |  |  |
| 84a | 10 c. on 5 c. ,, .. |  |  |
| 84b | 25 c. on 1 c., dull green . |  |  |
| 84c | 25 c. on 2 c., red .. |  |  |
| 85 | 50 c. on 5 c., blue .. | — | 25.00 |

*Minor varieties.*
(a) *Accent over* "i" *of* "centimos."
| 85a | 5 c. on 1 c., dull green | 75 |  |
| 85b | 10 c. on 2 c., red | — | 3.00 |
| 85c | 10 c. on 5 c., blue .. |  |  |
| 85d | 25 c. on 1 c., dull green |  |  |
| 85e | 25 c. on 5 c., blue .. | 10.00 | 7.50 |
| 85f | 50 c. on 10 c., pink .. |  |  |

(b) *Same as last, but inverted.*
The same surcharges.

(c) *Figure* "5" *with straight top,*
*as shown in* Type 6.
| 85g | 5 c. on 1 c., dull green | 36 |  |
| 85h | 25 c. on 5 c., blue .. | — | 7.50 |
| 85k | 50 c. on 10 c., pink .. |  |  |

|  | Un. | Used. |
|---|---|---|

**No.**

*(d) Figure "1" with straight serif, as shown in Type 9.*

| 85l | 10 c. on 2 c., red .. | 1.25 |  |
| 85m | 1 f. on 20 c., bistre (7) | 5.00 |  |
| 85n | 1 f. " (8) | — | 2.50 |
| 85o | 1 f. " " (9) |  |  |
| 85p | 1 f. 25 c. on 25 c., mauve |  |  |

It is probable the varieties (c) and (d) exist inverted.

5

5

**céntimos** **céntimos.**
12         13

5

**francos**
14

**No. Type.** *Tall, thin figures of value.*

| 86 | 12 | 5 c. on 1 c., dull gn. | 1.25 | 50 |
| 87 | 13 | 5 c. on 1 c. " | 50 | 50 |
| 88 | " | 10 c. on 2 c., red .. | 18 | 25 |
| 89 | 13 | 25 c. on 5 c., blue.. | 62 | 25 |
| 90 | " | 50 c. on 10 c., pink. | 5.00 | 1.00 |
| 91 | 14 | 5 f. on 1 p., gold.. | 30.00 |  |

*Variety. "CEN-AVO."*

| 92 | 12 | 5 c. on 1 c., dull gn. |
| 93 | 13 | 5 c. on 1 c. " |

*Surcharge inverted.*

| 93a | 5 c. on 1 c., dull green (12) |  |  |
| 93b | 25 c. on 5 c., blue .. | — | 20.00 |
| 93c | 50 c. on 10 c., pink .. |  |  |

*Errors. (i.) Surcharge on wrong values.*

| 94 | 13 | 5 c. on 5 c., blue .. |  |  |
| 95 | " | 10 c. on 1 c., dull grn. | 5.00 |  |
| 96 | " | 10 c. on 5 c., blue .. |  |  |
| 97 | " | 25 c. on 1 c., dull grn. | 15.00 | 15.00 |
| 98 | " | 25 c. on 2 c., red .. |  |  |
| 98a | " | 50 c. on 10 c., pink .. |  |  |

The variety "CEN-AVO" is found with Nos. 95 and 97.

*(ii.) "1" for "10."*

| 99 | 13 | 1 on 2 c., red .. |

*(iii.) Figures omitted.*

| 100 | 13 | (10)c. on 2 c., red.. | 18.75 |
| 100a | " | (25)c. on 5 c., blue. |  |

*(iv.) With surcharge on a set-off at back of stamp.*

| 101 | 13 | 25 c. on 5 c., blue .. |

---

**No. Type.** Un. Un.

5

**francos.**
15

### B. ISSUE OF 1881 WITH NETWORK

| 102 | 6 | 5 c. on 1 c., blue-grn. | 25 |
| 103 | " | 5 c. on 1 c., dull green | 18 |
| 104 | " | 10 c. on 2 c., red .. | 3.15 |
| 105 | " | 25 c. on 5 c., blue .. | 1.00 |
| 106 | " | 50 c. on 10 c., pink .. | 5.00 |
| 107 | 7 | 1 f. on 20 c., yellow-bistre .. .. | 1.25 |
| 108 | 8 | 1 f. on 20 c., yellow-bistre .. | 90 |
| 109 | 9 | 1 f. on 20 c., yellow-bistre .. | 1.25 |
| 110 | 10 | 1 f. 25 c. on 25 c., mauve .. .. | 5.00 |
| 111 | " | 2 f. 50 c. on 50 c., orange .. .. | 5.00 |
| 112 | " | 3 f. 75 c. on 75 c., ultramarine .. | 5.00 |
| 113 | 15 | 5 f. on 1 p., gold .. | 7.50 |

*Variety. "CEN-AVO."*

| 114 | 5 c. on 1 c., blue-green | 2.50 |
| 115 | 5 c. on 1 c., dull green. | — |

*Surcharge inverted.*

| 115b | 5 c. on 1 c., blue-green |  |
| 115c | 5 c. on 1 c., dull green |  |
| 115d | 50 c. on 10 c., pink .. | 12.50 |
| 115e | 1 f. 25 c. on 25 c., mauve |  |
| 115f | 2 f. 50 c. on 50 c., orange | 20.00 |
| 115g | 5 f. on 1 p., gold |  |

*Errors. Surcharge on wrong va..*

| 116 | 5 c. on 2 c., red .. | — |
| 116a | 5 c. on 5 c., blue .. |  |
| 117 | 25 c. on 1 c., dull green |  |
| 117a | 25 c. on 2 c., red .. |  |
| 118 | 25 c. on 10 c., pink .. |  |
| 119 | 50 c. on 5 c., blue .. |  |

*Minor varieties.*

*(a) Accent over "i" of centim.*

| 119a | 5 c. on 1 c., blue-green | 1.25 |
| 119b | 5 c. on 1 c., dull green | 1.85 |
| 119c | 10 c. on 2 c., red .. | 7.50 |
| 119d | 25 c. on 5 c., blue .. | — |
| 119e | 50 c. on 10 c., pink .. | — |

*(b) Same as last, but inverted. The same surcharges.*

*(c) Figure "5" with straight top. Type 16.*

| 119f | 5 c. on 1 c., blue-green |  |
| 119g | 5 c. on 1 c., dull green | 1.00 |
| 119h | 25 c. on 5 c., blue .. | 3.75 |
| 119i | 50 c. on 10 c., pink .. |  |

o.

') *Figure "1" with straight serif, as in Type 9.*

|  |  | Un. | Used. |
|---|---|---|---|
| 9j | 10 c. on 2 c., red .. | 3.75 | |
| 9k | 1 f. on 20 c., bistre (7) | 3.75 | |
| 9l | 1 f. on 20 c. ,, (8) | 1.85 | |
| 9m | 1 f. on 20 c. ,, (9) | 2.50 | |
| 9n | 1 f. 25 c. on 25 c., mauve | | |

It is probable that the varieties (c) and ) exist inverted.

o. *Type. Tall, thin figures of value.*

|  |  |  | Un. | Used. |
|---|---|---|---|---|
| 0 | 12 | 5 c. on 1 c., blue-grn. | 2.50 | 50 |
| 1 | ,, | 5 c. on 1 c., dull grn. | 4.35 | 50 |
| 2 | 13 | 5 c. on 1 c., blue-grn. | — | 2.50 |
| 3 | ,, | 5 c. on 1 c., dull grn. | | |
| 4 | ,, | 10 c. on 2 c., red .. | 8 | 8 |
| 5 | ,, | 25 c. on 5 c., blue .. | — | 7.50 |
| 6 | ,, | 50 c. on 10 c., pink .. | 1.85 | 50 |
| 7 | 14 | 5 f. on 1 p., gold .. | 10.00 | 10.00 |

*Variety.* "CEN—AVO."

|  |  |  | Un. | Used. |
|---|---|---|---|---|
| 8 | 12 | 5 c. on 1 c., blue-grn. | 12.50 | |
| 9 | ,, | 5 c. on 1 c., dull grn. | — | 2.50 |
| 0 | 13 | 5 c. on 1 c., blue-grn. | | |
| 1 | ,, | 5 c. on 1 c., dull grn. | | |

*Surcharge inverted.*

| 1a | 5 c. on 1 c., blue-green | |
|---|---|---|
| 1b | 5 c. on 1 c., dull green | 5.00 |
| 1c | 10 c. on 2 c., red .. | 15.00 |

*Errors. Surcharge on wrong value.*

| 1d | 10 c. on 1 c., dull grn. | 20.00 | 20.00 |
|---|---|---|---|

*Variety.* "CEN—AVO."

| 1e | 10 c. on 1 c., dull green |
|---|---|

*Surcharged on back.*

| 1f | 25 c. on 5 c., blue .. |
|---|---|

*Minor varieties.*

(a) *Accent over "i" of* "centimos."

| 1g | 5 c. on 1 c., dull green |
|---|---|

(b) *Same as last, but inverted.*

| 1h | 5 c. on 1 c. dull green |
|---|---|

18     19

## 1885-91.

*Numerals in lower corners. Perf. 12.*

|  |  |  |  | Un. | Used. |
|---|---|---|---|---|---|
| 2 | 18 | 1 c., green .. | .. | 4 | 4 |
| 3 | ,, | 2 c., scarlet | .. | 4 | 4 |
| 4 | ,, | 5 c., blue .. | .. | 8 | 8 |
| 5 | 19 | 10 c., orange | .. | 12 | 6 |
| 6 | ,, | 20 c., brown.. | .. | 18 | |

No. Type.          Un. Used.

20          21

| No. | Type |  | Un. | Used. |
|---|---|---|---|---|
| 137 | 20 | 50 c., purple ('91) .. | 1.00 | |
| 138 | 18 | 1 p., carmine ('91).. | 2.10 | |
| 139 | ,, | 2 p., brown ('91) .. | 3.50 | |

## 1895. *Numerals in the four corners.*

*Perf. 12½×14.*

| No. | Type |  |  | Un. | Used. |
|---|---|---|---|---|---|
| 140 | 21 | 1 c., green .. | .. | 6 | 6 |
| 141 | ,, | 2 c., scarlet | .. | 6 | 6 |
| 142 | ,, | 5 c., blue .. | .. | 6 | |
| 143 | 22 | 10 c., orange | .. | 12 | |

22          23

24

25          26

## 1899. *Types 23 to 30. Perf. 11½.*

| No. |  |  | Un. | Used. |
|---|---|---|---|---|
| 144 | 1 c., brown-purple | .. | 25 | |
| 145 | 2 c., rosine .. | .. | 6 | 4 |
| 146 | 5 c., blue .. | .. | 10 | 4 |
| 147 | 10 c., orange | .. | 20 | |

_Un._   _Used._

No.

27

28

29                    30

| 148 | 20 c., brown | .. | .. | 50 |
| 149 | 50 c., yellow-green | .. | 75 |
| 150 | 1 p., black on azure | .. | 1.85 |
| 151 | 2 p., yell.-brn. on cream | 3.75 |

_Varieties, tête-bêche._

147a | 10 c., orange | .. | ..
149a | 50 c., yellow-green | ..

**1900.** Type **23.** _Perf._ 11½.

| 152 | 1 c., green | .. | .. | 2 | 4 |

31

**1900.** Type **31.** _Perf._ 14.

| 153 | ½ c., blue | .. | .. | 2 |
| 154 | ½ c., rose | .. | .. | 4 |
| 155 | 1 c., olive-green | .. | 4 | 4 |
| 156 | 2 c., deep green | .. | 4 | 4 |
| 157 | 5 c., red-brown.. | .. | 8 | 6 |

_Errors._

"ATLANTICO" _and_ "MAR CARIBE"
_transposed._

157a | 5 c., red-brown | .. | 7.50 | 7.50

"HAITI" _on right instead of left._

157b | 2 c., deep green | .. | 10.00 | 10.00

---

No.                    _Perf._ 12.                    _Un._   _U._

| 158 | 10 c., orange | .. | .. | 16 |
| 159 | 20 c., purple | .. | .. | 30 |
| 160 | 50 c., black | .. | .. | 75 |
| 161 | 1 p., brown | .. | .. | 1.40 |

_Variety, tête-bêche._

161a | 10 c., orange | .. | ..

_Error of colour._

161b | 20 c., carmine | .. | .. | 10.00

"CINCO" _instead of_ "CINCUENTA
at foot._

161c | 50 c., black | .. | .. | 11.25

No. Type.                    _Imperf._

| 162 | 25 | ½ c., black | .. | .. |
| 163 | 29 | ½ c.   " | .. | .. |

_Perf._ 11½.

| 164 | 25 | ½ c., black | .. | .. | 75 |
| 165 | 29 | ½ c.   " | .. | .. | 75 |

32

**1901.** Type **32.** _Centre in_ lilac.   _P._

| 166 | ½ c., carmine | .. | .. | 2 |
| 167 | 1 c., olive-green | .. | 2 |
| 168 | 2 c., dark green | .. | 4 |
| 169 | 5 c., orange-brown | .. | 5 |
| 170 | 10 c., orange | .. | .. | 16 |
| 171 | 20 c., marone | .. | .. | 30 |
| 172 | 50 c., black | .. | .. | 62 |
| 173 | 1 p., dark brown | .. | 1.25 |

33        .        34

35                    35

**1902.** "SERIE COMMEMORAT:."
_Centre in_ black.   _Perf._ 14.

| 174 | 33 | 1 c., deep green | .. | 2 |
| 175 | 34 | 2 c., red | .. | .. |
| 176 |  " | 5 c., blue | .. | .. | 10 |
| 177 | 35 | 10 c., orange | .. | 20 |

| No. | Type. | | Un. | Used. |
|---|---|---|---|---|
| 178 | **36** | 12 c., mauve .. | | 25 |
| 179 | **37** | 20 c., bright rose .. | | 32 |
| 180 | **38** | 50 c., brown | .. | 90 |

Set of 7, unused, $1.50.

37       38

*Errors. Centre inverted.*

| 181 | **33** | 1 c., deep green | .. | 5.00 |
|---|---|---|---|---|
| 182 | **34** | 2 c., red | .. | 7.50 |
| 183 | " | 5 c., blue .. | .. | 8.75 |
| 184 | **36** | 12 c., mauve | .. | 8.75 |
| 185 | **37** | 20 c., rose .. | .. | 8.75 |
| 186 | **38** | 50 c., brown.. | .. | 8.75 |

All the values of this issue are stated to exist *imperforate*.

## UNPAID LETTER STAMPS.

71

**1901.** Type **71.** *Perf.* 14.

| 301 | 2 (c.), sepia | .. | .. | — | 4 |
|---|---|---|---|---|---|
| 302 | 4 (c.) " | .. | .. | — | 8 |
| 303 | 5 (c.) " | .. | .. | — | 12 |
| 304 | 10 (c.) " | .. | .. | — | 25 |

## OFFICIAL STAMPS.

81

**1902.** Type **81.** *Centre in* black.
*Perf.* 12.

| 501 | 2 c., scarlet | .. | .. | 4 |
|---|---|---|---|---|
| 502 | 5 c., dark blue .. | .. | 10 |
| 503 | 10 c., yellow-green | .. | 18 |
| 504 | 20 c., yellow | .. | .. | 36 |

# ECUADOR.

1

**1865–72.** Type 1.
*Quadrillé paper.*

| | | Un. | Used. |
|---|---|---|---|
| 1 | 1 rl., yellow .. .. | 90 | 90 |

*Wove paper.*

| 2 | ½ rl., grey-blue.. | .. | 12 | 12 |
|---|---|---|---|---|
| 3 | ½ rl., blue .. | .. | 6 | 4 |
| 4 | ½ rl., bright blue | .. | 4 | 6 |
| 5 | 1 rl., dull green | .. | 36 | 25 |
| 6 | 1 rl., yellow-buff | .. | 8 | 18 |
| 6a | 1 rl., yellow-ochre | .. | 8 | 18 |
| 7 | 1 rl., olive-yellow | .. | 8 | 18 |
| 8 | 1 rl., orange-buff | .. | — | 25 |

*Laid paper.*

| 9 | 1 rl., yellow .. .. | 2.50 | |
|---|---|---|---|

*Bluish paper.*

| 10 | 1 rl., dull yellow ('72) .. | 1.85 | 1.00 |
|---|---|---|---|

Nos. 1, 3, 5, 6, and 10 have been reprinted. The colour of No. 1 is too glossy. The ½ r. measures 19½ × 23½ mm. instead of 19 × 22½ mm., and the reprints of Nos. 5, 6, and 10 measure 20 × 24 mm. instead of 19 × 23 mm. All the reprints are without gum.

2

**1866.** Type 2.
*Imperf.*

| 11 | 4 rls., red .. .. | 1.50 | 1.85 |
|---|---|---|---|
| 12 | 4 rls., red-brown | .. | |

*Variety.*
*Printed on both sides.*

| 12a | 4 rls., red-brown .. | 2.00 | |
|---|---|---|

This stamp has been reprinted in *vermilion*.

There are several varieties of this stamp, the most marked point of difference being the shape of the circle or oval containing the Arms.

| No. Type. | | | *Un.* | *Used.* |
|---|---|---|---|---|

3            4

5

**1872.** *Perf.* 11. *Two varieties of the ½ real.*

(*a*) *No stop after* " MEDIO."
(*b*) *Stop after* " MEDIO."

| 13 | 3 | ½ rl., blue (*a*) | .. | | |
| 14 | " | ½ rl., blue (*b*) | .. | 4 | 6 |
| 15 | 4 | 1 rl., orange | .. | 12 | 4 |
| 16 | 5 | 1 p., rose | .. | 50 | |
| 17 | " | 1 p., carmine | .. | 25 | 45 |

The 1 rl. and the 1 peso are also often found with a large irregular perforation, gauging from 6 to 11. These are false and unofficial perfs., and copies are not sold by us.

6            7

8            9

**1881.** Types 6 *to* 11.
*Perf.* 12.

| 18 | 1 c., brown | .. | .. | 2 | 2 |
| 19 | 2 c., lake | .. | .. | 2 | 2 |
| 20 | 5 c., blue | .. | .. | 4 | 2 |
| 1 | 10 c., orange | .. | .. | 2 | 2 |

| No. | | | *Un.* | *Use:* |
|---|---|---|---|---|

10            11

| 22 | 20 c., slate | .. | .. | 2 |
| 23 | 50 c., green | .. | .. | 4 |

# DIEZ

## CENTAVOS

12

**1883.** *Surcharged with* Type 12, *in* bl.
| 24 | 10 c. on 50 c., green | .. | 1.85 | 1 |

13            14

15            16

**1887.** Types 13 *to* 16. *Perf.* 12.

| 25 | 1 c., green | .. | .. | 2 |
| 26 | 2 c., red | .. | .. | 2 |
| 27 | 5 c., blue | .. | .. | 4 |
| 28 | 80 c., olive-green | .. | 8 |

17

**1892.** Type 17.
*Values in* centavos *and* sucres. *Per* ..

| 29 | 1 c., orange | — | .. | 2 |
| 30 | 2 c., brown | — | .. | 2 |

| No. | | | Un. | Used. |
|---|---|---|---|---|
| 31 | 5 c., vermilion .. | .. | 2 | 2 |
| 32 | 10 c., green .. | .. | 4 | |
| 33 | 20 c., chestnut-brown .. | | 4 | 8 |
| 34 | 50 c., marone .. | .. | 4 | 6 |
| 35 | 1 s., deep blue .. | .. | 8 | 12 |
| 36 | 5 s., violet .. | .. | 12 | 25 |

18   19

20

**1893-94.** Type 14 *surcharged in* black.

| 37 | 18 | 5 c. on 1 s., deep blue | 25 | 16 |
|---|---|---|---|---|
| 38 | ,, | 5 c. on 5 s., violet .. | 12 | 12 |
| 39 | 19 | 5 c. on 1 s., deep blue | 12 | 10 |
| 40 | ,, | 5 c. on 5 s., violet .. | — | 1.25 |
| 41 | 20 | 5 c, on 50 c., marone | 10 | 10 |
| 42 | ,, | 5 c. on 1 s., deep blue | 10 | 10 |
| 43 | ,, | 5 c. on 5 s., violet .. | — | 12 |

*Variety. Surcharge inverted.*

| 45 | 20 | 5 c. on 50 c., marone | | |

21

**1894.** Type 21. *Dated* 1894.
*Perf.* 12.

| 46 | 1 c., pale blue .. | .. | 2 | 2 |
|---|---|---|---|---|
| 47 | 2 c., yellow-brown | .. | 2 | 2 |
| 48 | 5 c., green .. | .. | 4 | 2 |
| 49 | 10 c., vermilion .. | .. | 6 | 4 |
| 50 | 20 c., black | .. | 8 | 8 |
| 51 | 50 c., orange | .. | 8 | 10 |
| 52 | 1 s., carmine | .. | 12 | 16 |
| 53 | 5 s., dark blue .. | .. | 16 | 25 |

| No. | | | Un. | Used. |
|---|---|---|---|---|
| | *Variety. Perf.* 14. | | | |
| 53a | 5 c., green .. | .. | — | 25 |

**1895.** *Same type, dated* 1895.
*Perf.* 12.

| 54 | 1 c., blue .. | .. | 2 | |
|---|---|---|---|---|
| 55 | 2 c., yellow-brown | .. | 2 | |
| 56 | 5 c., blue-green | .. | 6 | 8 |
| 57 | 10 c., pale red .. | | 6 | |
| 58 | 20 c., black | .. | 8 | |
| 59 | 50 c., pale orange | .. | 10 | 25 |
| 60 | 1 s., carmine .. | .. | 12 | |
| 61 | 5 s., indigo .. | .. | 16 | |

22   23

**1895.** *Jubilee issue.*

| No. | Type. | *Perf.* 11½. | | |
|---|---|---|---|---|
| 62 | 22 | 1 c., carmine | .. | 4 | 10 |
| 63 | 23 | 2 c., blue | .. | 4 | 4 |
| 64 | 22 | 5 c., green .. | .. | 4 | 8 |
| 65 | 23 | 10 c., ochre .. | .. | 6 | 16 |
| 66 | 22 | 20 c., vermilion | .. | 8 | 8 |
| 67 | 23 | 50 c., purple | .. | 12 | 12 |
| 68 | 22 | 1 s., orange | .. | 12 | 16 |

24   25

26   27

**1896.** *Wmk. Cap of Liberty.*
*Perf.* 11½.

| 69 | 24 | 1 c., dark green .. | 4 | |
|---|---|---|---|---|
| 70 | 25 | 2 c., vermilion .. | 4 | |
| 71 | 26 | 5 c., ultramarine .. | 4 | |
| 72 | 27 | 10 c., brown.. | .. | 6 | 4 |

| No. Type. | | | *Un.* | *Used.* |
|---|---|---|---|---|

28            28*

30            31

| 73 | 28 | 20 c., orange .. | 8 | 12 |
| 74 | 28* | 50 c., dark blue .. | 8 | 12 |
| 75 | 30 | 1 s., yellow-brown . | 8 | 12 |
| 76 | 31 | 5 s., violet .. .. | 12 | 50 |

*CINCO CENTAVOS*

32

*Types of 1896 surcharged with Type 25 or 11.*

| 77 | 25 | 5 c., in *black*, on 20 c. | 45 | |
| 78 | 11 | 10 c., in *magenta*, on 50 c. .. .. | 30 | 50 |

33   1897.   34

*Issues of 1894 to 1896 surcharged in black.*
(a) *With* Type 33.
*Issue of* 1894.

| 79 | 1 c., pale blue .. | 12 | 12 |
| 80 | 2 c., yellow-brown .. | 12 | 8 |
| 81 | 5 c., green .. .. | 12 | 8 |
| 82 | 10 c., vermilion .. | — | 18 |
| 83 | 20 c., black .. .. | 36 | 12 |
| 84 | 50 c., orange .. .. | 1.00 | 12 |
| 85 | 1 s., carmine .. .. | 1.25 | 36 |
| 86 | 5 s., dark blue .. | | |

*Varieties. Inverted surcharge.*

| 87 | 2 c., yellow-brown .. | — | 25 |
| 88 | 5 c., green .. .. | — | 1.25 |

| No. | | *Un.* | *Used.* |
|---|---|---|---|

| 88a | 10 c., vermilion .. .. | — | 1.5 |
| 89 | 20 c., black .. .. | — | |
| 90 | 50 c., orange .. .. | 1.25 | |
| 91 | 1 s., carmine .. .. | | |
| 92 | 5 s., dark blue .. | | |

*Issue of* 1895.

| 93 | 1 c., blue .. .. | 12 | |
| 94 | 2 c., yellow-brown .. | 8 | |
| 95 | 5 c., blue-green .. | 36 | |
| 96 | 10 c., pale red .. .. | 25 | |
| 97 | 20 c., black .. .. | 2.50 | |
| 98 | 50 c., orange .. .. | — | |
| 99 | 1 s., carmine .. .. | 2.50 | |
| 100 | 5 s., dark blue .. | 2.50 | |

*Varieties. Inverted surcharge.*

| 100a | 10 c., vermilion .. | 50 | |
| 100b | 20 c., black .. .. | 1.25 | |
| 101 | 1 s., carmine .. | — | |

*Issue of* 1896.

| 102 | 2 c., vermilion .. .. | | |

(b) *With* Type 34. *Issue of* 1894.

| 103 | 1 c., blue .. .. | 8 | |
| 104 | 2 c., yellow-brown .. | 8 | |
| 105 | 5 c., green .. .. | 8 | |
| 106 | 10 c., vermilion .. .. | 36 | |
| 107 | 20 c., black .. .. | 1.25 | |
| 108 | 50 c., orange .. .. | 1.85 | |
| 109 | 1 s., carmine .. .. | 1.85 | |
| 110 | 5 s., dark blue .. .. | | |

*Variety. Inverted surcharge.*

| 111 | 5 s., dark blue .. .. | | |

*Issue of* 1895.

| 112 | 1 c., blue .. .. | 12 | |
| 113 | 2 c., yellow-brown .. | 12 | |
| 114 | 5 c., blue-green .. | 36 | |
| 115 | 10 c., pale red .. .. | | |
| 116 | 20 c., black .. .. | 1.50 | |
| 117 | 50 c., pale orange .. | 25 | |
| 118 | 1 s., carmine .. .. | 1.25 | |
| 119 | 5 s., dark blue .. .. | 2.50 | |

*Issue of* 1896.

| 119a | 1 c., green .. .. | | |
| 120 | 2 c., vermilion .. | | |
| 121 | 5 c., blue .. .. | | |
| 121a | 20 c., orange .. | | |

Types 33 and 34 are found reading downwards and upwards, from left right.

*1897 X 1895*

35

*Issue of* 1895, Type 21, *surcharged u* : Type 35, *in black.*

| 122 | 1 c., blue .. .. | | |
| 123 | 2 c., yellow-brown .. | | |

| No. | | | Un. | Used. |
|---|---|---|---|---|
| 124 | 5 c., green | .. | .. | |
| 125 | 10 c., vermilion | .. | .. | |
| 126 | 20 c., black | .. | .. | |
| 127 | 50 c., orange | .. | .. | |
| 128 | 1 s., carmine | .. | .. | 1.85 |
| 129 | 5 s., deep blue | .. | .. | 3.00 |

**1897.** *Jubilee issue.* Types **22** and **23** *surcharged in* black.

*(a) With Type* **33.**

| 130 | 1 c., carmine | .. | .. | 6 | 12 |
|---|---|---|---|---|---|
| 131 | 2 c., blue.. | | .. | | |
| 132 | 5 c., green | .. | .. | | |
| 133 | 10 c., ochre | | .. | | |

*(b) With Type* **34.**

| 134 | 1 c., carmine | .. | | 8 | |
|---|---|---|---|---|---|
| 135 | 2 c., blue | .. | .. | 12 | 18 |
| 135a | 5 c., green | | | | |
| 136 | 10 c., ochre | .. | .. | 12 | 25 |
| 136a | 20 c., vermilion | | .. | | |
| 136b | 50 c., purple | .. | .. | | |
| 136c | 1 s., orange | .. | .. | | |

**36**

*(c) With Type* **36.**

| 137 | 1 c., carmine | .. | .. | 8 | 12 |
|---|---|---|---|---|---|
| 138 | 2 c., blue | .. | .. | 8 | 25 |
| 139 | 5 c., green | .. | .. | 8 | 36 |
| 140 | 10 c., ochre | .. | .. | 12 | |

The 20 c., 50 c., and 1 sucre with *black* surcharge, and all seven values with the surcharge in *blue*, are reprints.

**37**

**1897.** Type **37.** *Perf.* 15, 16.

| 41 | 1 c., green | .. | .. | 6 | 2 |
|---|---|---|---|---|---|
| 42 | 2 c., orange | .. | .. | 8 | 2 |
| 43 | 5 c., lake | .. | .. | — | 2 |
| 44 | 10 c., brown | .. | .. | — | 4 |
| 45 | 20 c., yellow | .. | .. | — | 10 |
| 46 | 50 c., ultramarine | .. | | | |
| 47 | 1 s., bistre | .. | .. | | |
| 48 | 5 s., lilac | .. | .. | | |

**38** **39**

**1899.**

Type **37** *surcharged with* Types **38, 39,** *in* black.

| 149 | 38 | 1 c. on 2 c., orange | 4 | 4 |
|---|---|---|---|---|
| 150 | 39 | 5 c. on 10 c., brown | 8 | |

**40** **41**

**42** **43**

**44** **45**

**1899.** *Vignette in* black.

Types **41** *to* **47.** *Perf.* 15, 16.

| 151 | 1 c., dull blue | .. | .. | 2 | 4 |
|---|---|---|---|---|---|
| 152 | 2 c., brown-lilac | | .. | 2 | 2 |
| 153 | 5 c., carmine | .. | .. | 4 | 2 |
| 154 | 10 c., dull violet | .. | | 8 | 4 |
| 155 | 20 c., green | .. | .. | 12 | 8 |
| 156 | 50 c., rose | .. | .. | 30 | 36 |

| No. | *Un.* | *Used.* |
|---|---|---|

| No. | *Un.* | *Un.* |
|---|---|---|

46             47

| 157 | 1 s., ochre | .. | .. | 75 | |
| 158 | 5 s., lilac | .. | .. | 3.15 | |

*The 1 s. of 1896 surcharged " DIEZ
CENTAVOS" in two lines.*

| 159 | 10 c., in *black*, on 1 s., yellow-brown | .. | |
| 160 | 10 c., in *black* and *blue*, on 1 s., yellow-brown | |

**1901.** *Colours changed.
Centre in black.*

| 161 | 1 c., carmine | .. | .. | 2 | 2 |
| 162 | 2 c., green | .. | .. | 2 | 2 |
| 163 | 5 c., purple | .. | .. | 4 | 2 |
| 164 | 10 c., indigo | .. | .. | 6 | 4 |
| 165 | 20 c., slate | .. | .. | 10 | 12 |
| 166 | 50 c., pale blue | .. | .. | 25 | 25 |
| 167 | 1 s., brown | .. | .. | 50 | |

48

**1902.** *Stamps of 1899-1901 overprinted
"C. Benj. R." as Type 48.*
*(a) In blue.*

| 168 | 1 c., carmine | .. | .. | |
| 169 | 2 c., green | .. | .. | 6 |
| 170 | 5 c., purple | .. | .. | |

*(b) In black.*

| 171 | 1 c., carmine | .. | .. | 4 |
| 172 | 2 c., green | .. | .. | |
| 173 | 5 c., purple | .. | .. | |
| 174 | 10 c., indigo | .. | .. | — | 1.25 |
| 175 | 20 c., slate | .. | .. | |
| 176 | 50 c., pale blue | .. | .. | |
| 177 | 1 s., brown | .. | .. | |
| 178 | 5 s., lilac | .. | .. | |

In addition to the above there exist
many others, as " RIOS," " DE" (in various
types), "PUE," etc., and also with printers'
fancy ornaments *in* red, black, violet,

blue, etc. These surcharges were app
to stocks in hand in the various pro\.
(after a fire at Guayaquil which destr :
a large quantity of stamps), to prevent
use of any stamps which might have '..
stolen during the fire. The over;
given above is the signature of C.
Rosales, Governor of the province
Guayaquil.

## POSTAL FISCALS.

F I

I. Type F 1. *Perf.* 12.
*(a) Plain label without date.*

| 301 | 1 c., ultramarine | .. | 90 |
| 302 | 2 c., bistre | .. | .. | 1.00 |
| 303 | 50 c., green | .. | .. | 1.00 |

*(b) 1881 1882 engraved in label.*

| 304 | 1 c., ultramarine | .. | 1.25 |
| 305 | 2 c., bistre | .. | .. | 1.25 |
| 306 | 5 c., vermilion | .. | .. | 1.25 |
| 307 | 10 c., orange | .. | .. | 1.25 |
| 308 | 20 c., violet | .. | .. | 1.50 |

**1884 1885**      **1884. 188**

A           B

Type F 1. *Dated* **1884 1885**, *in* bla.
*(a) Thick figures* (A).

| 309 | 1 c., blue | .. | .. | 12 |
| 310 | 2 c., bistre | .. | .. | |
| 311 | 5 c., vermilion | .. | .. | 6 |
| 312 | 10 c., orange | .. | .. | — |
| 313 | 20 c., violet | .. | .. | — |
| 314 | 50 c., green | .. | .. | — |
| 315 | 1 p., brown | .. | .. | — |

*(b) Thinner and larger figures* (I

| 316 | 1 c., blue | .. | .. | 13 |
| 317 | 2 c., bistre | .. | .. | — |
| 318 | 5 c., vermilion | .. | .. | 12 |
| 319 | 10 c., orange | .. | .. | |
| 320 | 20 c., violet | .. | .. | — |
| 321 | 50 c., green | .. | .. | |
| 322 | 1 p., brown | .. | .. | |

| | | | Un. | Used. |
|---|---|---|---|---|
No.

F 2

*Dated* **1886 1887**, *in* black. Type F 2.

| 323 | 1 c., blue | .. | .. | — | 12 |
| 324 | 2 c., bistre | .. | .. | 36 | 12 |
| 325 | 5 c., vermilion .. | .. | — | 8 |
| 326 | 10 c., orange | .. | .. | — | 12 |
| 327 | 20 c., violet | .. | .. | — | 12 |
| 328 | 50 c., green | .. | .. | 50 | 12 |
| 329 | 1 p., brown | .. | .. | | |

*Dated* 1881 1882 *in the engraving, but surcharged* **1886 1887** *diagonally, in* black.

| 329a | 1 c., ultramarine | .. | — | 12 |
| 329b | 2 c., bistre | .. | — | 12 |
| 329c | 5 c., vermilion | .. | — | 12 |
| 330 | 10 c., orange | .. | — | 12 |
| 331 | 20 c., violet | .. | — | 8 |
| 332 | 50 c., green | .. | 18 | 12 |
| 333 | 1 p., brown | .. | — | 12 |

*Variety. Surcharged horizontally on lower label.*

| 334 | 50 c., green | .. | .. | — | 12 |

*Dated* **1887 1888** *in the engraving.*

| 135 | 1 c., slate | .. | .. | 12 | 6 |
| 136 | 2 c., lake | .. | .. | 12 | 6 |
| 137 | 4 c., brown | .. | .. | — | 8 |
| 138 | 10 c., orange | .. | .. | — | 6 |
| 139 | 1 s., green | .. | .. | — | 6 |
| 140 | 5 s., dark blue .. | .. | — | 12 |
| 141 | 10 s., vermilion .. | .. | — | 18 |

*Stamps of the last set surcharged*

**1889 1890** *across stamp, in* black.

| 142 | 1 c., slate | .. | .. | 50 | 8 |
| 143 | 2 c., lake | .. | .. | 50 | 8 |
| 144 | 4 c., brown | .. | .. | 50 | 8 |
| 145 | 10 c., orange | .. | .. | 62 | 6 |
| 146 | 1 s., green | .. | .. | 36 | 8 |
| 147 | 5 s., dark blue .. | .. | 25 | 18 |
| 148 | 10 s., vermilion .. | .. | 1.60 | 30 |

*Dated* **1891 1892** *in the engraving.*

| 149 | 1 c., slate-green | .. | 25 | 12 |
| 150 | 2 c., lake | .. | .. | 25 | 8 |
| 151 | 4 c., brown | .. | .. | — | 12 |
| 152 | 10 c., orange | .. | .. | — | 12 |
| 153 | 1 s., green | .. | .. | — | 8 |
| 154 | 5 s., blue | .. | .. | — | 25 |
| 155 | 10 s., vermilion .. | .. | — | 25 |

| | | | Un. | Used. |
|---|---|---|---|---|
No.

*Stamps of the set dated* 1887–88
*surcharged*

**1891. 1892.**

*in* black.

| 356 | 1 c., slate-green | .. | — | 12 |
| 357 | 2 c., lake | .. | .. | — | 12 |
| 358 | 4 c., brown | .. | .. | — | 12 |
| 359 | 10 c., orange | .. | .. | — | 12 |
| 360 | 1 s., green | .. | .. | — | 12 |
| 361 | 5 s., blue | .. | .. | — | 25 |
| 362 | 10 s., vermilion .. | .. | — | 25 |

*Dated* **1893 1894** *in the engraving.*

| 363 | 1 c., vermilion .. | .. | — | 8 |
| 364 | 2 c., blue | .. | .. | — | 6 |
| 365 | 4 c., green | .. | .. | — | 8 |
| 366 | 10 c., orange | .. | .. | — | 8 |
| 367 | 1 s., brown | .. | .. | — | 12 |
| 368 | 5 s., dull red | .. | .. | — | 25 |
| 369 | 10 s., greenish black | .. | — | 36 |

*Dated* 1887 1888 *in the engraving.*
(*a*)

*Surcharged* **1893 y 1894** *in* black.

| 370 | 1 c., slate-green | .. | — | 8 |
| 371 | 2 c., lake | .. | .. | — | 12 |
| 372 | 4 c., brown | .. | .. | — | 50 |
| 373 | 10 c., orange | .. | .. | — | 12 |
| 374 | 1 s., green | .. | .. | — | 25 |
| 375 | 5 s., blue | .. | .. | — | 36 |
| 376 | 10 s., vermilion .. | .. | — | 36 |

(*b*)

*Surcharged* **1893 y 1894.** *in* black.

| 377 | 1 c., slate-green | .. | — | 12 |
| 378 | 4 c., brown | .. | .. | — | 18 |
| 379 | 1 s., green | .. | .. | — | 25 |
| 380 | 5 s., blue | .. | .. | — | 50 |

*Dated* 1891–92 *in the engraving.*
*Surcharged as above.*

| 380a | 1 c., slate-green | .. | — | 12 |

F 3

*Dated* 1895–96. Type F 3.

| 381 | 1 c., deep blue .. | .. | — | 12 |
| 382 | 2 c., orange | .. | .. | — | 12 |

|  |  | Un. | Used. |
|---|---|---|---|
| **No.** |  |  |  |
| 383 | 4 c., brown .. .. | — | 12 |
| 384 | 10 c., slate .. .. | — | 12 |
| 385 | 1 s., red .. .. .. | — | 12 |
| 386 | 5 s., mauve .. .. | — | 25 |
| 387 | 10 s., green .. .. | — | 30 |

**1897-98.**

*(a) Stamps of* **1887-88** *(date engraved) surcharged with* Type **33.**

| 388 | 1 c., slate-green .. .. | — | 12 |
|---|---|---|---|
| 389 | 2 c., lake .. .. | — | 12 |
| 390 | 4 c., brown .. .. | — | 12 |
| 391 | 10 c., orange .. .. | — | 12 |
| 392 | 1 s., green .. .. | — | 12 |
| 393 | 5 s., blue .. .. | — | 18 |
| 394 | 10 s., vermilion .. | — | 25 |

*(b) Stamp of* 1891-92 *(date engraved) surcharged with* Type **33,** *in* black.

| 395 | 1 c., slate-green .. .. | — | 12 |
|---|---|---|---|

*(c) Stamps of* 1893-94 *(date engraved) surcharged with* Type **33,** *in* black.

| 396 | 1 c., vermilion .. .. | — | 12 |
|---|---|---|---|
| 397 | 2 c., blue .. .. | — | 12 |
| 398 | 4 c., green .. .. | — | 12 |
| 399 | 10 c., orange .. .. | — | 12 |
| 400 | 1 s., brown .. .. | — | 12 |
| 401 | 5 s., dull red .. .. | — | 18 |
| 402 | 10 s., greenish black .. | — | 25 |

*(d) As last, but surcharged with* Type **34,** *in* black.

| 403 | 1 c., vermilion .. .. | 12 | 12 |
|---|---|---|---|
| 404 | 2 c., blue .. .. | 18 | 12 |
| 405 | 4 c., green .. .. | — | 12 |
| 406 | 10 c., orange .. .. | — | 12 |
| 407 | 1 s., brown .. .. | — | 12 |
| 408 | 5 s., dull red .. .. | — | 18 |
| 409 | 10 s., greenish black .. | — | 25 |

# 1896
## CORREOS
## 5CTŞ

F 4

**1896.** *Surcharged as* Type F **4,** *in* black.
*(a) On stamps of* 1887-88.

| 451 | 5 c. on 10 c., orange .. | 25 | 25 |
|---|---|---|---|
| 452 | 10 c. on 4 c., brown .. | 36 | 36 |

*Varieties. Inverted surcharge.*

| 453 | 5 c. on 10 c., orange .. | 2.50 | 2.50 |
|---|---|---|---|
| 454 | 10 c. on 4 c., brown .. | 2.50 | 2.50 |

|  |  | Un. | Us. |
|---|---|---|---|
| **No.** |  |  |  |

*(b) On stamps of* 1891-92.

| 455 | 10 c. on 4 c., brown .. — | :: |
|---|---|---|

*Variety. Surcharge inverted.*

| 456 | 10 c. on 4 c., brown .. 6.25 | 5. |
|---|---|---|

*(c) On stamps of* 1893-94.

| 457 | 1 c. on 1 c., vermilion.. | 16 | : |
|---|---|---|---|
| 458 | 2 c. on 2 c., blue .. | 18 |  |
| 459 | 5 c. on 10 c., orange .. | — | : |

*Varieties. Surcharge inverted.*

| 460 | 1 c. on 1 c., vermilion.. | — | 3 |
|---|---|---|---|
| 461 | 2 c. on 2 c., blue .. | — | 3 |
| 462 | 5 c. on 10 c., orange .. | — | 3 |

F 5

**1898.** Type F **5.** *Dated* **1897-1898.**

| 476 | 1 c., in black, on 5 c., pale blue .. .. | — |
|---|---|---|
| 477 | 2 c., carmine .. .. | — |
| 478 | 4 c., in magenta, on 20 c., deep blue .. .. | — |
| 479 | 10 c., grey .. .. | ː |
| 480 | 50 c., lilac .. .. |  |
| 481 | 1 s., orange .. .. | — |

# CINCO
## CENTAVOS
F 6

**1900.** Type F **5.** *Perf.* **14,** 13
*Dated* 1899-1900.
*Surcharged as* Type F **6,** *vertical.*
*in* black.

| 482 | 5 c. on 1 c., green .. |  |
|---|---|---|
| 483 | 5 c. on 2 c., brown .. |  |
| 484 | 5 c. on 4 c., orange .. | 6 |
| 485 | 10 c. on 5 c. on 50 c., lilac |  |

*Surcharged similarly to the lower ː of* Type T **5,** *in* black.

| 485a | 10 c. on 50 c., lilac |  |
|---|---|---|

Type F **5.**

| 486 | 1 c., green .. .. | — | ː |
|---|---|---|---|
| 487 | 2 c., brown .. .. | — |  |
| 488 | 10 c., blue .. .. | — |  |

|  | Un. | Used. |
|---|---|---|

0.

F 7

03. Type F 5, *dated* 1901-1902, *surcharged with* Type F 7, *vertically, in* black.

| 9. | 1 c. on 25 c., orange | .. | 6 | |
|---|---|---|---|---|

ELEGRAPH STAMPS USED FOR POSTAGE.

**TELEGRAFOS**

T 1

893. Type 17 *surcharged with* Type T 1.

(*a*) *In* red.

| 1 | 1 c., slate | .. | .. | 4 | 6 |
|---|---|---|---|---|---|
| 2 | 10 c., blue | .. | .. | 4 | 4 |

(*b*) *In* black.

| 3 | 2 c., green | .. | .. | 4 | 6 |
|---|---|---|---|---|---|
| 4 | 5 c., yellow | .. | .. | 4 | 6 |
| 5 | 20 c., sepia | .. | .. | 4 | 6 |
| 6 | 50 c., green | .. | .. | 6 | 25 |
| 7 | 1 s., bistre | .. | .. | 6 | 25 |
| 8 | 5 s., carmine | .. | .. | 12 | |

**TELEGRAFOS**

T 2

*Surcharged with* T 2, *in* black.

| 9 | 10 c., green | .. | .. | 18 | 8 |
|---|---|---|---|---|---|

T 3

1893. Type T 3. *Perf.* 11½.

| 0 | 10 c., yellow | .. | .. | 12 | 18 |
|---|---|---|---|---|---|
| 1 | 20 c., vermilion | .. | .. | 12 | 12 |
| 2 | 40 c., blue | .. | .. | 18 | 25 |

1894. *Telegraph stamps similar to* Type 21. *Perf.* 11½.

| 3 | 10 c., green | .. | .. | — | 2 |
|---|---|---|---|---|---|
| 4 | 20 c., red | .. | .. | — | 2 |
| 5 | 40 c., brown | .. | .. | — | 2.50 |

No. 508 *surcharged with* Type 20, *in* black.

| 6 | 5 c. on 5 s., carmine | .. | 25 | |
|---|---|---|---|---|

|  | Un. | Used. |
|---|---|---|

No.

1897-98. *Telegraphs of* 1894 *surcharged in* black.

(*a*) *With* Type 33.

| 517 | 10 c., green | .. | .. | 62 | 90 |
|---|---|---|---|---|---|
| 518 | 20 c., vermilion | .. | .. | 50 | 25 |
| 519 | 40 c., brown | .. | .. | | |

(*b*) *With* Type 34.

| 520 | 10 c., green | .. | .. | — | 36 |
|---|---|---|---|---|---|
| 521 | 20 c., vermilion | .. | .. | — | 6 |
| 522 | 40 c., brown | .. | .. | — | 2.50 |

(*c*) *With* Type 35.

| 523 | 20 c., vermilion | .. | .. | — | 12 |
|---|---|---|---|---|---|
| 524 | 40 c., brown | .. | .. | — | 2.50 |

T 4

T 5

*Telegraphs of* 1894 *surcharged with*
No. Type. Type T 4 *or* T 5, *in* black.

| 525 | T 4 | 10 c. on 20 c., verm. | 62 | 12 |
|---|---|---|---|---|
| 526 | T 5 | 10 c. ,, ,, | 62 | 1.00 |

STAMPS CUT FROM LETTER CARDS USED FOR POSTAGE.

| 551 | 5 c., blue on rose | .. | — | 25 |
|---|---|---|---|---|
| 552 | 10 c., vermilion on blue | . | — | 25 |

STAMPS CUT FROM WRAPPERS USED FOR POSTAGE.

| 553 | 1 c., orange on blue | .. | | |
|---|---|---|---|---|
| 554 | 2 c., brown on blue | .. | | |

UNPAID LETTER STAMPS.

U 1

1896. Type U 1. *Wmk. Cap of Liberty. Perf.* 11½.

| 601 | 1 c., blue-green | .. | 4 |
|---|---|---|---|
| 602 | 2 c. ,, | .. | 4 |
| 603 | 5 c. ,, | .. | 6 |
| 604 | 10 c. ,, | .. | 6 |
| 605 | 20 c. ,, | .. | 8 |
| 606 | 50 c. ,, | .. | 8 |
| 607 | 100 c. ,, | .. | 8 |

| No. | | | | *Un.* | *Used.* |
|---|---|---|---|---|---|

**OFFICIAL STAMPS.**

# OFICIAL

**O 1**

**1886.**

Types 6-11 *surcharged with* Type O 1.
(*a*) *In* black.

| 701 | 1 c., brown | .. | .. | 25 | 12 |
|---|---|---|---|---|---|
| 702 | 2 c., lake | .. | .. | 25 | 18 |
| 703 | 5 c., ultramarine | .. | .. | 50 | 50 |
| 704 | 10 c., orange | .. | .. | 1.00 | 18 |
| 705 | 20 c., purple | .. | .. | — | 18 |
| 706 | 50 c., green | .. | .. | | |

(*b*) *In* red.

| 707 | 1 c., brown | .. | .. | | |
|---|---|---|---|---|---|
| 708 | 2 c., lake | .. | .. | | |
| 709 | 5 c., ultramarine | .. | .. | | |
| 710 | 10 c., orange | .. | .. | | |
| 711 | 20 c., purple | .. | .. | | |
| 712 | 50 c., green | .. | .. | | |

**1887.** Types 12-16 *similarly surcharged.*
(*a*) *In* black.

| 713 | 1 c., green | .. | .. | | |
|---|---|---|---|---|---|
| 714 | 2 c., red .. | .. | .. | — | 25 |
| 715 | 5 c., blue | .. | .. | 25 | 12 |
| 716 | 80 c., olive-green | .. | 36 | 50 |

(*b*) *In* red.

| 717 | 1 c., green | .. | .. | | |
|---|---|---|---|---|---|
| 718 | 5 c., blue | .. | .. | | |

This surcharge is found horizontal, vertical, and diagonal, and each way inverted.

**FRANQUEO OFICIAL**

**O 2**

**1892.** Type 17 *surcharged with* Type O 2, *in* red.

| 719 | 1 c., ultramarine | .. | 2 | |
|---|---|---|---|---|
| 720 | 2 c., | ,, | .. | 2 | |
| 721 | 5 c., . | ,, | .. | 2 | |
| 722 | 10 c., | ,, | .. | 4 | 12 |
| 723 | 20 c. | ,, | .. | 4 | 12 |
| 724 | 50 c. | ,, | .. | 4 | 12 |
| 725 | 1 s. | ,, | .. | 12 | 25 |

**1894.** Issue of 1894, Type 20, *similarly surcharged.*

| 726 | 1 c., grey | .. | .. | 2 | 4 |
|---|---|---|---|---|---|
| 727 | 2 c., | ,, | . | .. | 2 | 4 |
| 728 | 5 c. | ,, | .. | .. | 6 | 8 |
| 729 | 10 c. | ,, | .. | .. | 6 | 12 |
| 730 | 20 c. | ,, | .. | .. | 8 | 25 |
| 731 | 50 c. | ,, | .. | .. | 8 | 25 |
| 732 | 1 s. | ,, | .. | .. | 12 | 50 |

**1895.** Issue of 1895, Type 21, *similarly surcharged.*

| 733 | 1 c., grey | .. | .. | 4 | |
|---|---|---|---|---|---|
| 734 | 2 c., | ,, | .. | .. | 4 | |
| 735 | 5 c. | ,, | .. | .. | 6 | 25 |
| 736 | 10 c. | ,, | .. | .. | 6 | 25 |

| No. | | | | *Un.* | *U* |
|---|---|---|---|---|---|
| 737 | 20 c., grey | .. | .. | 8 | |
| 738 | 50 c. | ,, | .. | .. | 8 | |
| 739 | 1 s. | ,, | .. | .. | 12 | |

**FRANQUEO OFICIAL**

**O 3**

**1896.** Types 26-31 *surcharged with* Type O 3, *in* red.

| 740 | 1 c., olive-bistre | .. | 4 | |
|---|---|---|---|---|
| 741 | 2 c. | ,, | .. | .. | 4 |
| 742 | 5 c. | ,, | .. | .. | 6 |
| 743 | 10 c. | ,, | .. | .. | 6 |
| 744 | 20 c. | ,, | .. | .. | 6 |
| 745 | 50 c. | ,, | .. | .. | 8 |
| 746 | 1 s. | ,, | .. | .. | 8 |
| 747 | 5 s. | ,, | .. | .. | 8 |

Various Official stamps were used ordinary postage in 1896.

# OFICIAL

**1894 y 1895.**

**O 4**

**1894-95.** *Postal fiscals of* 1891-9:
Type F 1, *surcharged with* Type O 4.

| 748 | 1 c., slate (*red* sur.) | .. | 18 |
|---|---|---|---|
| 749 | 2 c., lake (blk. ,, ) | .. | 25 |

**1897.** *Official issues of* 1894 *and* (Type 21) *with additional sur.* of 1897-1898, *in* black.
(*a*) *With* Type 33.
*Issue of* 1894.

| 750 | 1 c., grey | .. | .. | 62 |
|---|---|---|---|---|
| 751 | 2 c. | ,, | .. | .. | 62 |
| 752 | 5 c. | ,, | .. | .. | 62 |
| 753 | 10 c. | ,, | .. | .. | 1.25 |
| 754 | 20 c. | ,, | .. | .. | 1.25 |
| 755 | 50 c. | ,, | .. | .. | 1.85 |
| 756 | 1 s. | ,, | .. | .. | |

*Variety. Surcharge inverted.*

| 757 | 20 c., grey | .. | .. | — |
|---|---|---|---|---|

*Issue of* 1895.

| 758 | 1 c., grey | .. | .. | 62 |
|---|---|---|---|---|
| 759 | 2 c. | ,, | .. | .. | |
| 760 | 5 c. | ,, | .. | .. | 1.00 |
| 761 | 10 c. | ,, | .. | .. | 18 |
| 762 | 20 c. | ,, | .. | .. | 1.25 |
| 763 | 50 c. | ,, | .. | .. | 1.85 |
| 764 | 1 s. | ,, | .. | .. | — |

(*b*) *With* Type 34.
*Issue of* 1894.

| 765 | 1 c., grey | .. | .. | 1.85 |
|---|---|---|---|---|
| 766 | 2 c. | ,, | .. | .. | |
| 767 | 5 c. | ,, | .. | .. | |
| 768 | 10 c. | ,, | .. | .. | |
| 769 | 20 c. | ,, | .. | .. | 1.25 |
| 770 | 50 c. | ,, | .. | .. | |
| 771 | 1 s. | ,, | .. | .. | |

| No. | | | Un. | Used. |
|---|---|---|---|---|
| | *Issue of* 1895. | | | |
| 72 | 1 c., grey | .. .. | 1.00 | 1.00 |
| 73 | 2 c. ,, | .. .. | | |
| 74 | 5 c. ,, | .. .. | — | 50 |
| 75 | 10 c. ,, | .. .. | 1.85 | 45 |
| 76 | 20 c. ,, | .. .. | | |
| 77 | 50 c. ,, | .. .. | | |
| 78 | 1 s. | .. .. | | |

*(c) With* Type 35.
*Issue of* 1894.

| | | | | |
|---|---|---|---|---|
| 78a | 1 c., grey | .. .. | | |
| 78b | 2 c. ,, | .. .. | | |
| 78c | 5 c. ,, | .. .. | | |
| 78d | 10 c. ,, | .. .. | | |
| 78e | 20 c. ,, | .. .. | | |
| 78f | 50 c. ,, | .. .. | 3.75 | |
| 78g | 1 s. ,, | .. .. | | |

*Issue of* 1895.

| | | | | |
|---|---|---|---|---|
| 79 | 1 c., grey | .. .. | 12 | |
| 80 | 2 c. ,, | .. .. | 12 | |
| 81 | 5 c. ,, | .. .. | 12 | 12 |
| 82 | 10 c. ,, | .. .. | | |
| 83 | 20 c. ,, | .. .. | | |
| 84 | 50 c. ,, | .. .. | 1.85 | |
| 85 | 1 s. ,, | .. .. | | |

o 5

**898.** *Fiscal stamps,* Type F 4, *surcharged as* Type o 5.

| | | | | |
|---|---|---|---|---|
| 86 | 5 c., in *green,* on 50 c., lilac | .. .. | 6 | 8 |
| 87 | 5 c., in *black,* on 50 c., lilac | .. .. | 6 | 12 |
| 88 | 5 c., in *red,* on 50 c., lilac | .. .. | 6 | |
| 89 | 10 c., in *black,* on 20 s., orange | .. .. | 25 | |
| 90 | 20 c., in *red,* on 50 s., green | .. .. | 36 | |
| 91 | 20 c., in *black,* on 50 s., green .. | .. .. | 36 | |

**899.** *Same type surcharged in four lines.*

| | | | | |
|---|---|---|---|---|
| 92 | 1 c., in *black,* on 5 c., blue .. | .. .. | | |
| 93 | 2 c., in *red,* on 5 c., blue | | | |
| 94 | 4 c. ,, on 20 c. ., | | | |

| No. | | | Un. | Used. |
|---|---|---|---|---|

o 6

**1899.** *Types of regular issue surcharged with* Type o 6, *in* black.
*Vignettes in* black.

| | | | | |
|---|---|---|---|---|
| 796 | 2 c., orange | .. .. | 6 | |
| 798 | 10 c. ,, | .. .. | 12 | |
| 799 | 20 c. ,, | .. .. | 18 | |
| 800 | 50 c. ,, | .. .. | 25 | |

OFFICIAL TELEGRAPH STAMPS USED
FOR POSTAGE.

O T 1

**1897.** *Fiscal stamps,* Type F 1, *dated* 1887 1888 *in the engraving, surcharged vertically with* Type O T 1.

| | | | | |
|---|---|---|---|---|
| 901 | 10 c. on 1 c., slate-green (red surcharge) | .. | 1.85 | |
| 902 | 20 c. on 2 c., lake (blue surcharge) | .. .. | 1.75 | |

O T 2

*Surcharged with* Type O T 2, *in* black.

| | | | | |
|---|---|---|---|---|
| 903 | 1 c., slate-green | .. | 50 | |
| 904 | 2 c., lake | .. .. | 50 | |

No. Type.                     *Un.  Used.*  | No.                          *Un.  U*

**EGYPT.**

*Errors.*

*With overprint of* 10 piastres.

8 | 5 pias., rose    ..    ..

*With overprint of* 5 piastres.

9 | 10 pias., slate-blue    ..

*Variety, tête-bêche.*

9a| 10 pias., slate-blue    ..

*Varieties. Imperf.*
*Same types and wmk.*

| 10 | 5 paras, grey .. | .. |      |
|----|------------------|----|------|
| 11 | 10  ,,  brown.. | .. | 3.75 |
| 12 | 20  ,,  blue .. | .. | 3.15 |
| 13 | 1 pias., red-lilac | .. |    |
| 14 | 2  ,,  yellow .. | .. | 2.50 |
| 15 | 5  ,,  rose  .. | .. |      |
| 16 | 10  ,,  slate-blue | .. |   |

**1866.** *Wmk.* Type **8**, *except the* 1 piastre,
*which has no wmk.* *Perf.* 12½.

*Various designs overprinted, in* black, *as*
Type **9.** *The lowest group of charac-*
*ters indicates the value.*

| 1 | 1 | 5 paras, grey | .. | 50 | 50 |
|---|---|---------------|----|----|----|
| 2 | 2 | 10  ,,  brown | .. | 2.00 | 2.00 |
| 3 | 3 | 20  ,,  blue | .. | 2.00 | 2.00 |
| 4 | 4 | 1 pias., red-lilac | .. | 50 | 18 |
| 5 | 5 | 2  ,,  yellow | .. | 1.50 | 1.50 |
| 6 | 6 | 5  ,,  rose | .. | 7.50 |   |
| 7 | 7 | 10  ,,  slate-blue | .. | 7.50 | 7.50 |

**1867.** *Wmk.* Type **12.**

No. Type.      *Perf.* 15×12½.

| 17 | 10 | 5 par., oran.-yellow | | 50 |
|----|----|----------------------|--|-----|
| 18 | ,, | 10  ,,  violet | .. | 50 |
| 19 | ,, | 10  ,,  mauve | .. | 62 |
| 20 | ,, | 10  ,,  dull mauve . | | 30 |
| 21 | ,, | 20  ,,  blue-green.. | | 50 |
| 22 | ,, | 20  ,,  green | .. | 62 |
| 23 | 11 | 1 pias., rose-red | .. | 12 |
| 24 | ,, | 1  ,,  rose | .. | 12 |
| 25 | ,, | 2  ,,  blue | .. | 75 |
| 26 | ,, | 5  ,,  brown | .. | 3.75 |

There are four types of each valu-
this issue.

| No. | | Un. | Used. |
|-----|--|-----|-------|

**13**

**1872–75.** Type **13.** *Wmk.* Type **12.**
*Perf.* 12½, 13½, *and compound.*

| No. | | | | Un. | Used. |
|-----|--|--|--|-----|-------|
| 27 | 5 par., | brown .. | .. | 18 | 18 |
| 28 | 10 ,, | red-lilac | .. | 8 | 8 |
| 29 | 10 ,, | grey-lilac | .. | 36 | 6 |
| 30 | 20 ,, | blue .. | .. | 8 | 6 |
| 31 | 20 ,, | blue-grey | .. | 8 | 4 |
| 32 | 1 pias., | bright red | .. | 8 | 2 |
| 33 | 1 ,, | rose-red | .. | 30 | 4 |
| 34 | 2 ,, | yellow .. | .. | 18 | 6 |
| 35 | 2½ ,, | dull purple | .. | 25 | 18 |
| 35a | 2½ ,, | purple .. | .. | 25 | |
| 36 | 5 ,, | green .. | .. | 50 | 50 |

*Varieties.* Tête-bêche (*pairs*).

| 36a | 5 par., brown .. | .. | | |
|-----|-----------------|----|--|--|
| 36b | 10 ,, grey-lilac | .. | 10.00 | 10.00 |
| 36c | 1 pias., bright red | .. | 6.25 | |
| 36d | 2 ,, yellow.. | .. | 20.00 | |
| 36e | 2½ ,, purple.. | .. | | |
| 36f | 5 ,, green .. | .. | | |

*Error.*
*Middle section of design inverted.*

| 37 | 5 paras, brown.. | .. | 4 | 2 |
|----|-----------------|----|---|---|

*Tête-bêche variety of error.*

| 38 | 5 paras, brown (pair) .. | 25 | |
|----|------------------------|----|--|

**14**

**1879.**
Type **13** *surcharged, in* black, *as* Type **14.**

| 39 | 5 paras on 2½ pias. | .. | 10 | 12 |
|----|---------------------|----|----|----|
| 40 | 10 ,, 2½ ,, | .. | 18 | 12 |

*Surcharge inverted.*

| 41 | 5 paras on 2½ pias. | .. | 4.35 | |
|----|---------------------|----|------|--|
| 42 | 10 ,, 2½ ,, | .. | 5.00 | 5.00 |

*Varieties.* Tête-bêche.

| 42a | 5 paras on 2½ pias. | .. | | |
|-----|---------------------|----|--|--|
| 42b | 10 ,, 2½ ,, | .. | | |

| No. Type. | | Un. | Used. |
|-----------|--|-----|-------|

**15**          **16**

**17**          **18**

**19**          **20**

**1879.** *Same wmk. Perf.* 14.

| 43 | 15 | 5 paras, | pale brown | 4 | 2 |
|----|----|----------|-----------|---|---|
| 43a | ,, | 5 ,, | brown .. | 2 | 2 |
| 44 | 16 | 10 ,, | lilac-rose .. | 50 | 18 |
| 45 | ,, | 10 ,, | lilac .. | 8 | 8 |
| 46 | ,, | 10 ,, | blue-grey . | 4 | 2 |
| 47 | 17 | 20 ,, | blue .. | 8 | 2 |
| 48 | 18 | 1 pias., | rose .. | 12 | 2 |
| 49 | 19 | 2 ,, | orange .. | 50 | 2 |
| 50 | 20 | 5 ,, | green .. | 1.25 | 12 |

**21**

**1884.** *Surcharged, in* black, *with* Type **21.**

| 51 | 20 | 20 paras on 5 pias. | 6 | 8 |
|----|----|---------------------|---|---|

*Surcharge inverted.*

| 52 | 20 | 20 paras on 5 pias. | 75 | |
|----|----|---------------------|----|--|

**1884.** *Same wmk. and perf.*

| 53 | 16 | 10 paras, green .. | 2 | 2 |
|----|----|--------------------|---|---|
| 54 | 17 | 20 ,, rose .. | 8 | 2 |
| 55 | 18 | 1 pias., ultramarine | 8 | 2 |
| 56 | ,, | 1 ,, pale ,, | 8 | 2 |
| 57 | 20 | 5 ,, slate .. | 50 | 2 |

F

| No. Type. | | *Un.* | *Used.* |
|---|---|---|---|

22

23

24

#### 1888-93.  *Same wmk. and perf.*

| 58 | 15 | 1 mil., brown | .. | 2 | 2 |
|---|---|---|---|---|---|
| 59 | ,, | 1 ,, pale brown | .. | 2 | 2 |
| 60 | 16 | 2 ,, green | .. | 2 | 2 |
| 61 | 22 | 3 ,, marone | .. | 6 | 2 |
| 62 | ,, | 3 ,, orange | .. | 2 | 2 |
| 63 | 23 | 5 ,, rose-carmine | | 4 | 2 |
| 64 | 19 | 2 pias., oran.-brown | | 18 | 2 |
| 65 | 24 | 10 ,, violet | .. | 62 | 6 |

#### 1902.  *Same types on chalk-surfaced paper.  Same wmk. and perf.*

| 66 | 15 | 1 mil., brown | .. | 2 | 2 |
|---|---|---|---|---|---|
| 67 | 16 | 2 ,, green | .. | 2 | 2 |
| 68 | 22 | 3 ,, orange | .. | 2 | 2 |
| 69 | 23 | 5 ,, rose-carmine | | 4 | 2 |
| 70 | 18 | 1 pias., blue | .. | 8 | 2 |
| 71 | 19 | 2 ,, orange-brown | | 16 | |
| 72 | 24 | 10 ,, violet | .. | 75 | |

#### UNPAID LETTER STAMPS.

51

#### 1884.  Type 51.  Wmk. Type 12.  Perf. 10½.

| 201 | 10 paras, red | .. | .. | 12 | 12 |
|---|---|---|---|---|---|
| 202 | 20 ,, ,, | .. | .. | 75 | 18 |
| 203 | 1 pias. ,, | .. | .. | 1.25 | 8 |
| 204 | 2 ,, ,, | .. | .. | 1.25 | 8 |
| 205 | 5 ,, ,, | .. | .. | 1.00 | |

#### 1886.  No wmk.  Perf. 10½

| 206 | 10 paras, rose-red | .. | 50 | 8 |
|---|---|---|---|---|
| 207 | 20 ,, ,, | .. | 18 | 12 |
| 208 | 1 pias. ,, | .. | 18 | 4 |
| 209 | 2 ,, red .. | .. | 18 | 2 |
| 209a | 5 ,, ,, .. | .. | | |

| No. | | *Un.* | *Used.* |
|---|---|---|---|

52

#### 1888.

*Types 51 and 52.  No wmk.  Perf.* 11½.

| 210 | 2 mil., green | .. | .. | 6 | 2 |
|---|---|---|---|---|---|
| 211 | 5 ,, rose-carmine | .. | 6 | 2 |
| 212 | 1 pias., blue | .. | .. | 36 | 12 |
| 213 | 2 ,, orange.. | .. | 2.50 | 50 |
| 214 | 5 ,, grey | .. | .. | 5.00 | |

53

#### 1889.  Type 53.  Wmk. Type 12.  Perf. 14.

| 215 | 2 mil., green | .. | .. | 2 | . |
|---|---|---|---|---|---|
| 216 | 4 ,, marone | .. | .. | 4 | |
| 217 | 1 pias., ultramarine | .. | 8 | . |
| 218 | 2 ,, orange.. | .. | 12 | . |

54

#### 1898.  Type 53 *surcharged with* Type 54 *in* black.

| 219 | 3 m. on 2 pias., orange. | |
|---|---|

#### OFFICIAL STAMP.

61

#### 1892.  Type 61.  Wmk. Type 12.  *Perf.* 14.

| 251 | (No value), chestnut .. | 8 |
|---|---|---|

| No. | | *Un.* | *Used.* |
|---|---|---|---|

## FRANCE.
### REPUBLIC.

(Ceres.)

**1**

**1849-50.** Type 1. *Imperf.*

| | | | *Un.* | *Used.* |
|---|---|---|---|---|
| 1 | 10 c., yell.-bistre on yell. | | 3.00 | 1.00 |
| 2 | 10 c., deep  ,,   ,, | | 1.85 | 1.00 |
| 3 | 15 c., deep green on grn. | | — | 2.50 |
| 4 | 15 c., yell.-grn.  ,, | | — | 2.50 |
| 5 | 20 c., black  ..   .. | | 50 | 8 |
| 6 | 20 c.  ,,  on toned  .. | | 62 | 8 |
| 8 | 25 c., dull blue on toned | | 12.50 | 6 |
| 9 | 25 c., deep blue ..   .. | | 15.00 | 6 |
| 10 | 25 c., pale blue .. | | — | 6 |
| 11 | 40 c., orange  ..   .. | | 6.25 | 1.00 |
| 12 | 40 c., orange-vermilion . | | 10.00 | 1.25 |
| 13 | 1 fr., bright orange-red | | | |
| 14 | 1 fr., orange-brown  .. | | | |
| 15 | 1 fr., carmine-brown .. | | — | 1.85 |
| 16 | 1 fr., deep ,,   ,,  .. | | 25.00 | 1.50 |
| 17 | 1 fr., carmine ..   .. | | 20.00 | 1.50 |
| 18 | 1 fr., carmine-rose  .. | | — | 1.85 |

*Variety. Wider figure* "**4.**"

| | | | | |
|---|---|---|---|---|
| 19 | 40 c., orange  ..   .. | | | |

This variety exists in the figure of value, and occurs twice in the bottom row only of each sheet. One of these stamps has the wide "4" on both sides, the other on one side only.

*Varieties. Tête-bêche.*

| | | | | |
|---|---|---|---|---|
| 20 | 10 c., yellow-bistre  .. | | | |
| 21 | 15 c., green  ..   .. | | | |
| 22 | 20 c., black  ..   .. | | 30.00 | 20.00 |
| 23 | 25 c., deep blue ..  .. | | | |
| 24 | 1 fr., orange-red  .. | | | |
| 25 | 1 fr., carmine  .. | | | |

The 20 c. was printed in *blue*, surcharged in *red* "25 c—," for provisional use, but this was not issued ; and the best authorities maintain that the 20 c., *blue*, was likewise never issued.

All six values were reprinted in 1862, including the 20 c., blue. The shades of the reprints differ from those of the originals. The reprints have white instead of brownish or toned gum. They do not exist *tête-bêche*. The 1 fr. in the orange shades was never reprinted.

The 25 c. on 20 c. has also been reprinted, but the surcharge differs from the original.

### PRESIDENCY.

(Louis Napoléon, President.)

**2**

**1852.** Type 2. *Imperf.*

| | | | *Un.* | *Used.* |
|---|---|---|---|---|
| 26 | 10 c., yellow-bistre  .. | | — | 1.85 |
| 27 | 10 c., deep  ,,   .. | | — | 1.85 |
| 28 | 25 c., blue  ..   .. | | 11.25 | 8 |
| 29 | 25 c., deep blue ..   .. | | 7.50 | 8 |

These two values were reprinted in 1862, the 10 c. in a shade of bistre different from those of the originals, and the 25 c. in a bright or sky blue.

The letter "B" below the bust is the initial of the engraver, M. Barre.

### EMPIRE.

(Napoléon III., Emperor of the French.)

**3**

**1853-60.** Type 3. *Imperf.*

| | | | *Un.* | *Used.* |
|---|---|---|---|---|
| 30 | 1 c., deep bronze-green on blue  ..   .. | | 75 | 8 |
| 31 | 1 c., pale bronze-green on blue  ..   .. | | 50 | 8 |
| 32 | 1 c., olive-green on blue | | 50 | 8 |
| 33 | 5 c., deep green  ,, | | 5.00 | 25 |
| 34 | 5 c., green on greenish. | | 3.00 | 8 |
| 35 | 5 c., yellow-grn.  ,,  . | | 2.50 | 8 |
| 36 | 10 c., olive-bistre  .. | | 2.00 | 4 |
| 37 | 10 c., bistre  ..   .. | | 2.00 | 4 |
| 38 | 10 c., bistre-brown  .. | | 2.00 | 8 |
| 39 | 10 c., yellow-buff  .. | | 3.75 | 6 |
| 40 | 10 c., ochre  ..   .. | | 12.50 | 8 |
| 41 | 10 c., brown-ochre  .. | | 2.50 | 4 |
| 42 | 20 c., pale blue on pale bluish ..   ..   .. | | 1.25 | 2 |
| 43 | 20 c., bright blue on pale bluish ..   ..   .. | | 1.25 | 2 |

|  | | *Un.* | *Used.* |
|---|---|---|---|
| No. | | | |
| 44 | 20 c., deep blue on pale bluish .. .. .. | 2.50 | 2 |
| 45 | 20 c., violet-blue  ,, | 3.15 | 2 |
| 46 | 20 c., blue on green .. | — | 1.25 |
| 47 | 20 c., blue on azure .. | — | 50 |
| 48 | 25 c., dull blue .. .. | 6.25 | 1.00 |
| 49 | 25 c., deep  ,, .. .. | 7.50 | 1.00 |
| 50 | 40 c., orange-vermilion . | 5.00 | 6 |
| 51 | 40 c., deep vermilion .. | 6.25 | 6 |
| 52 | 40 c., orange on yellow .. | | |
| 53 | 80 c., carmine-orange .. | 15.00 | 25 |
| 54 | 80 c., carmine .. .. | 12.50 | |
| 55 | 80 c., carmine-rose .. | — | 12 |
| 56 | 80 c., rose .. .. | 8.75 | 12 |
| 57 | 80 c., rose on pale rose .. | 7.50 | 12 |
| 58 | 1 fr., dull carmine .. | 7.50 | 4.50 |
| 59 | 1 fr., deep  ,, .. | 8.75 | 5.00 |

*Varieties. . Tête-bêche.*

| 60 | 20 c., blue  · .. .. | | |
| 61 | 80 c., rose .. .. | | |
| 62 | 1 fr., dull carmine .. | | |

Reprints of the 25 c. and 1 fr. were made in 1862, the 25 c. in bright or sky blue, and the 1 fr. in carmine, but in a different shade from the originals; this value is known *tête-bêche.*

**1861.** *Variety. Perf. 7 (unofficial).*

| 63 | 1 c., bronze-green .. | 5.00 | 3.75 |
| 64 | 1 c., olive-green  ● .. | — | 3.75 |
| 65 | 5 c., green .. .. | — | 3.75 |
| 66 | 10 c., bistre .. .. | — | 1.25 |
| 67 | 20 c., pale blue .. | | |
| 68 | 20 c., blue .. .. | 5.00 | 50 |
| 69 | 20 c., deep blue .. .. | | |
| 70 | 40 c., orange .. .. | — | 1.25 |
| 71 | 80 c., rose .. .. | — | 1.85 |

This is an unofficial perforation, applied by Messrs. Susse to stamps used by them. These stamps are also known rouletted, and some of the values pinperf., etc.

**1862.** *Same type. Perf. 14 × 13½.*

| 72 | 1 c., bronze-green .. | 4 | 4 |
| 73 | 1 c., olive-green .. | 4 | 4 |
| 74 | 5 c., yell.-grn. on grnish. | 18 | 2 |
| 75 | 5 c., green on greenish . | 18 | 2 |
| 76 | 5 c., green on bluish .. | 50 | 12 |
| 77 | 10 c., pale bistre .. | 1.00 | 2 |
| 78 | 10 c., bistre .. .. | 1.00 | 2 |
| 79 | 20 c., blue .. .. | 25 | 2 |
| 80 | 20 c., deep blue .. .. | 25 | 2 |
| 80*a* | 20 c., pale blue .. .. | 50 | 4 |
| 80*b* | 20 c., blue on bluish .. | 1.25 | 2 |
| 81 | 40 c., pale orange .. | 1.50 | 2 |
| 82 | 40 c., orange .. .. | 1.60 | 2 |
| 83 | 80 c., rose .. .. | 1.50 | 4 |
| 84 | 80 c., rose-carmine .. | — | 4 |

*Varieties. Tête-bêche (pairs).*

| 85 | 20 c., blue .. .. | 30.00 | 10.00 |
| | 80 c., rose .. .. | | |

| | | *Un.* | *Used.* |
|---|---|---|---|
| No. | | | |

**4**

**1862–70.** *Perf. 14 × 13½.*
Type 4.

| 87 | 1 c., bronze-green .. | 4 | 4 |
| 88 | 1 c., olive-green .. | 4 | 4 |
| 89 | 2 c., red-brown .. | 4 | 4 |
| 90 | 2 c., pale  ,, .. | 4 | 4 |
| 91 | 2 c., chocolate .. .. | 25 | 18 |
| 92 | 4 c., pale grey .. .. | 25 | 8 |
| 93 | 4 c., grey .. .. | 25 | 8 |
| 94 | 4 c., lilac-grey .. .. | — | 8 |

**5**

Type 5.

| 95 | 10 c., bistre .. .. | 50 | 2 |
| 96 | 10 c., pale bistre .. | 25 | 2 |
| 97 | 20 c., blue .. .. | 36 | 2 |
| 98 | 20 c., deep blue .. .. | 25 | 2 |
| 99 | 30 c., brown .. .. | 1.25 | 4 |
| 100 | 30 c., dark brown .. | 1.10 | 4 |
| 101 | 30 c., grey-brown .. | 1.50 | 4 |
| 102 | 40 c., orange .. .. | 1.85 | 2 |
| 103 | 40 c., orange-vermilion . | 3.00 | 2 |
| 104 | 80 c., pale rose .. .. | 1.50 | 4 |
| 105 | 80 c., rose .. .. | 1.50 | 4 |

*Variety. Tête-bêche.*

| 106 | 4 c., grey | | |

All the above values were obtained imperforate by favour, and in this state were allowed to pay postage. We can supply these to collectors.

**6**

Type 6.
(*a*) " 5 " *and* " F " 3½ mm. *high.*
(*b*)  ,,  ,,  ,, 4  ,,  ,,

| 107 | 5 fr., grey-lilac (*a*) .. | 7.50 | 1.25 |
| 108 | 5 fr.  ,,  (*b*) .. | 12.50 | 1.60 |

This stamp is known without " 5 " or " F.

Un. Used.

No.

## 10

The 10 c., bistre, Type 5, surcharged "10," as above, was prepared for provisional use in 1871, but was never issued. These can be supplied at 50 c. each.

REPUBLIC.

(Ceres.)　　(Ceres.)
7　　　　8

13 NOV., 1870.

*Lithographed at Bordeaux.*

Type 7 *for the* 1, 2, *and* 4 c., Type 8 *for the other values. Four types of the* 20 c. I. *With wide space between inner circle and outer frame at top; inscription in smaller letters, shading of dots on neck.* II. *Thicker lettering, shading of horizontal lines on neck.* III. *Taller lettering, lines on neck, and fuller shading under the eye.* IV. *Similar to* III., *but with point of bust* 1 mm. *from the pearled circle. Imperf.*

| 110 | 1 c., bronze-grn. on grn. | 8 | 12 |
|---|---|---|---|
| 111 | 1 c., olive-green ,, | 8 | 12 |
| 112 | 1 c., deep olive-green on green .. .. | 8 | 12 |
| 114 | 2 c., brown-red on yellowish .. .. | | |
| 115 | 2 c., brick-red.. .. | 6.25 | 1.00 |
| 116 | 2 c., brown-red on toned | 90 | 75 |
| 117 | 4 c., pale grey .. | 62 | 1.00 |
| 118 | 4 c., grey .. .. | 50 | 90 |
| 119 | 4 c., pale lilac-grey .. | — | 90 |
| 120 | 5 c., yellow-green .. | 62 | 16 |
| 121 | 5 c., deep ,, .. | 75 | 16 |
| 122 | 10 c., bistre .. .. | 2.50 | 12 |
| 123 | 10 c., bistre-buff .. | 2.50 | 12 |
| 124 | 10 c., bistre-brown .. | 2.50 | 12 |
| 125 | 10 c., ochre .. .. | 4.35 | 12 |
| 126 | 20 c., sky-blue (I.) . | — | 1.50 |
| 127 | 20 c., blue (I.) . | — | 1.25 |
| 128 | 20 c., deep blue (I.) . | — | 2.50 |
| 129 | 20 c. ,, (II.). | 2.50 | 6 |
| 130 | 20 c., bright blue (II.). | 3.00 | 6 |
| 131 | 20 c., deep ,, (III.). | 7.50 | 8 |
| 132 | 20 c., blue (III.). | 7.50 | 8 |
| 132a | 20 c., lilac-blue (III.). | | |
| 133 | 20 c., deep ,, (IV.). | 3.00 | 4 |
| 134 | 20 c., blue (IV.). | 2.50 | 4 |

| 135 | 20 c., lilac-blue (IV.) . | — | 25 |
|---|---|---|---|
| 136 | 30 c., pale brown .. | 50 | 45 |
| 137 | 30 c., brown .. .. | 50 | 45 |
| 138 | 40 c., scarlet-vermilion. | 15.00 | 2.00 |
| 139 | 40 c., orange-vermilion. | 6.00 | 25 |
| 140 | 40 c., orange .. .. | 75 | 30 |
| 141 | 40 c., orange-yellow .. | — | 1.25 |
| 142 | 80 c., pale rose .. | 62 | 55 |
| 143 | 80 c., bright rose .. | 62 | 55 |
| 144 | 80 c., dull carmine .. | — | 1.85 |
| 145 | 80 c., dull rose .. | 2.00 | |

All the values of this issue are known rouletted, pin-perforated, etc., and prices for these varieties can be quoted on application.

DEC., 1870. *Lithographed at Tours.*

| 145a | 2 c., Venetian red on toned .. .. | 10.00 |
|---|---|---|

**1870-73.** Type 7 *for the* 1, 2, 4, *and* 5 c., Type 8 *for the other values. Printed from the plates in Paris.*

*Perf.* 14×13½.

| 146 | 1 c., bronze-green .. | 4 | 2 |
|---|---|---|---|
| 147 | 1 c., olive-green .. | 4 | 2 |
| 148 | 2 c., pale red-brown .. | 6 | 2 |
| 149 | 2 c., red-brown .. | 12 | 2 |
| 150 | 4 c., grey .. .. | 16 | 6 |
| 151 | 4 c., pale grey .. | 16 | 6 |
| 152 | 5 c., blue-green .. | 18 | 2 |
| 153 | 5 c., yellow-green .. | 12 | 2 |
| 154 | 5 c., pale green on green | 36 | 8 |
| 155 | 5 c., green on blue .. | 36 | 8 |
| 156 | 10 c., bistre .. .. | 36 | 12 |
| 157 | 10 c., bistre-brown .. | 50 | 12 |
| 157a | 10 c., bistre on rose .. | 36 | 2 |
| 158 | 15 c., bistre .. .. | 1.25 | 2 |
| 159 | 15 c., pale bistre .. | 50 | 2 |
| 160 | 20 c., blue .. .. | 75 | 2 |
| 161 | 20 c., pale blue .. | 30 | 2 |
| 162 | 20 c., bright ,, .. | 30 | 4 |
| 163 | 25 c., blue .. .. | 50 | 2 |
| 164 | 25 c., bright blue .. | 36 | 2 |
| 165 | 25 c., pale ,, .. | 62 | 6 |
| 166 | 40 c., pale orange .. | 2.50 | 2 |
| 167 | 40 c., orange .. .. | 36 | 2 |
| 168 | 40 c., deep orange .. | 62 | 2 |

*Variety. Wider figure "4."*

| 171 | 40 c., orange .. .. | 2.50 |
|---|---|---|

(See note after No. 19.)

*Varieties. Tête-bêche (pairs).*

| 172 | 10 c., bistre .. .. |
|---|---|
| 173 | 10 c. ,, on rose .. |
| 174 | 15 c. ,, .. .. |
| 175 | 20 c., blue .. .. 25.00 |
| 176 | 25 c. ,, .. .. |

9

**1872-75.** *Type 9.* *Larger figures of value. Perf. 14×13½.*

| No. | | Un. | Used. |
|---|---|---|---|
| 177 | 10 c., bistre on rose .. 1.00 | | 2 |
| 178 | 10 c., „ pale rose | 50 | 2 |
| 179 | 15 c., pale bistre .. 1.25 | | 2 |
| 180 | 30 c., brown .. .. 1.00 | | 2 |
| 181 | 30 c., deep brown .. 1.25 | | 2 |
| 182 | 80 c., rose .. .. 1.25 | | 4 |
| 183 | 80 c., rose-carmine .. 1.00 | | 4 |

*Error on sheet of* 10 c.

| 184 | 15 c., bistre on rose .. 60.00 | | |

(Peace and Commerce.)

**10**

**1876.** Type 10. *Tinted paper. Perf. 14×13½.*
*Two varieties.*

a　　　　　　b

(a) Letter "N" of "INV" under "B" of "REPUBLIQUE."

| No. | | Un. | Used. |
|---|---|---|---|
| 185 | 1 c., green .. .. 50 | | 10 |
| 186 | 2 c., „ .. .. 2.50 | | 25 |
| 187 | 4 c., „ .. .. 10 | | 10 |
| 188 | 5 c., „ .. .. 1.85 | | 2 |
| 189 | 10 c., „ .. .. 50 | | 4 |
| 190 | 15 c., pale grey-lilac .. 1.85 | | 2 |
| 191 | 15 c., grey-lilac .. .. — | | 2 |
| 192 | 20 c., brown on pale yell. 50 | | 2 |
| 193 | 25 c., ultramarine .. 15.00 | | 36 |
| 194 | 30 c., cinnamon .. .. 1.00 | | 2 |
| 195 | 40 c., red on pale yellow 3.00 | | 4 |
| 196 | 75 c., carmine .. 1.00 | | 2 |
| 197 | 1 fr., olive-green .. 1.85 | | 2 |

The 20 c., *blue,* is a stamp prepared for use, but never issued. It was reprinted in 1887 in *dark blue* (imperf.). It is found with a forged perforation. This reprint always variety (b).

(b) Letter "N" of "INV" under "U" of "REPUBLIQUE."

| No. | | Un. | Used. |
|---|---|---|---|
| 198 | 2 c., green .. .. | 6 | 2 |
| 199 | 5 c., deep green .. | 6 | 2 |
| 200 | 5 c., deep yellow-green | 6 | 2 |
| 201 | 5 c., green .. .. | 4 | 2 |
| 202 | 5 c., blue-green .. | 4 | 2 |
| 203 | 5 c., pale green .. | 6 | 2 |
| 204 | 10 c., green .. .. | 62 | 18 |
| 205 | 15 c., grey-lilac .. .. | 30 | 2 |
| 206 | 15 c., slate-lilac .. .. | 30 | 2 |
| 207 | 25 c., ultramarine .. | 36 | 2 |
| 208 | 25 c., blue .. .. | 62 | 2 |
| 209 | 30 c., cinnamon .. .. | 25 | 2 |
| 210 | 30 c., yellow-brown .. | 30 | 2 |
| 211 | 75 c., rose .. .. | — | 6 |
| 212 | 1 fr., pale yellow-green | 50 | 6 |
| 213 | 1 fr., olive-green .. | 30 | 2 |
| 214 | 1 fr., deep olive-green . | 30 | 2 |
| 215 | 1 fr., grey-green .. | 30 | 2 |

The two varieties of type differ in the shapes of the numerals, as well as in the point above described. A pair of the 25 c., blue, has been seen with the two types joined together.

**1877-97.**
Type 10. *Perf.* 14×13½.
*Varieties (b) only.*

| No. | | Un. | Used. |
|---|---|---|---|
| 216 | 1 c., black on grey-blue | 4 | 2 |
| 217 | 1 c., „ grey .. | 4 | 2 |
| 218 | 1 c., „ azure .. | 2 | 2 |
| 219 | 1 c., „ Prussian blue .. .. | | |
| 220 | 2 c., deep red-brown on yellow .. | 2 | 2 |
| 221 | 2 c., pale red-brown on yellow .. .. | 2 | |
| 222 | 3 c., ochre on yellow.. | 18 | 6 |
| 223 | 3 c., drab .. .. | 4 | |
| 223a | 3 c., grey .. .. | 4 | |
| 224 | 4 c., purple-brn on grey | 8 | |
| 225 | 4 c., brown-lilac „ | — | 4 |
| 226 | 4 c., plum on grey-blue | 4 | 2 |
| 227 | 10 c., black on grey-lilac | 8 | |
| 228 | 10 c., „ reddish lilac .. .. | 4 | |
| 229 | 15 c., blue on toned | 12 | |
| 230 | 15 c., „ bluish .. | 25 | |
| 231 | 15 c., deep blue on bluish | 25 | |
| 232 | 20 c., red on yellow-green | 12 | |
| 233 | 20 c., red on deep green | 36 | |
| 234 | 25 c., black on deep red . | 1.25 | |
| 235 | 25 c., bistre on yellow . | 36 | 4 |
| 236 | 25 c., yellow on saffron | 30 | |
| 237 | 25 c., bistre-brown on pale yellow .. .. | 50 | |
| 238 | 25 c., black on rose .. | 8 | 2 |
| 239 | 25 c., „ pale rose .. | 8 | |
| 240 | 35 c., dark brn. on yell.. | 1.00 | 4 |
| 241 | 40 c., pale red „ | 16 | |

| No. | | Un. | Used. |
|---|---|---|---|
| 242 | 40 c., red on yellow .. | 18 | 2 |
| 243 | 50 c., pale rose.. | 36 | 2 |
| 244 | 50 c., deep ,, .. .. | 25 | 2 |
| 245 | 50 c., carmine .. .. | 25 | 2 |
| 246 | 75 c., brn. on pale oran. | 1.00 | 12 |
| 247 | 75 c., brn. on deep oran. | 36 | 6 |
| 248 | 75 c., dull brn. ., | 50 | 6 |
| 249 | 5 fr., lilac on pale lilac | 3.75 | 62 |
| 250 | 5 fr., bright lilac ,, | 3.75 | 12 |
| 251 | 5 fr., pale mauve ,, | 1.60 | 25 |
| 252 | 5 fr., bright mauve ,, | 1.85 | 25 |

The 15 c. in *ochre* is only a proof.

**1892.**

*Same type and perf. Quadrillé paper.*

| | | | |
|---|---|---|---|
| 253 | 15 c., pale blue .. .. | 25 | 2 |
| 254 | 15 c., deep ,, .. .. | 6 | 2 |
| 255 | 15 c., ultramarine-blue.. | 6 | 2 |

**1898-1900.**

*Same type and perf. Plain paper.*

| | | | |
|---|---|---|---|
| 256 | 5 c., bright yell.-grn. (a) | 4 | 2 |
| 257 | 5 c. ,, (b) | 2 | 2 |
| 258 | 10 c., black on reddish lilac (a) .. .. | 6 | |
| 259 | 50 c., carmine (a) | 1.25 | |
| 260 | 50 c., carmine-rose (a) .. | 25 | 2 |
| 261 | 2 f., brn. on pale blue (a) | 62 | 12 |

**11**      **12**

**1900.**

*New types. Perf.* 14 × 13½.

Type **11.**

| | | | |
|---|---|---|---|
| 262 | 1 c., grey .. .. | 2 | 2 |
| 263 | 2 c., claret .. .. | 2 | 2 |
| 264 | 3 c., orange-red .. | 2 | 2 |
| 265 | 4 c., brown .. .. | 2 | 2 |
| 266 | 5 c., green .. .. | 2 | 2 |

Type **12.** *First issue.*

*Figures of value inserted at a second printing.*

| | | | |
|---|---|---|---|
| 267 | 10 c., carmine .. .. | 12 | |
| 268 | 20 c., brown-purple .. | 8 | 4 |
| 269 | 25 c., blue .. .. | 12 | 2 |
| 270 | 30 c., lilac .. .. | 12 | 4 |

*The entire stamp printed at one time.*

| | | | |
|---|---|---|---|
| 271 | 10 c., carmine .. .. | 4 | 2 |
| 272 | 15 c., orange .. .. | 6 | 2 |
| 273 | 25 c., blue .. .. | 8 | 2 |

| No. | | Un. | Used. |
|---|---|---|---|

**13**

Type 13.

| | | | |
|---|---|---|---|
| 274 | 40 c., red and pale blue . | 12 | 4 |
| 275 | 50 c., cinnamon and lav. | 14 | 2 |
| 276 | 1 fr., lake and yell.-grn. | 26 | 4 |
| 277 | 2 fr., slate and dull yell. | 55 | 10 |
| 278 | 5 fr., deep blue and buff | 1.30 | 18 |

**14**

**1902.** Type 14. Perf. 14 × 13½.

| | | | |
|---|---|---|---|
| 279 | 10 c., carmine .. .. | 4 | 2 |
| 280 | 15 c., pale red .. .. | 6 | 2 |
| 281 | 20 c., brown-purple .. | 8 | 2 |
| 282 | 25 c., blue .. .. | 10 | 2 |
| 283 | 30 c., lilac .. .. | 12 | 2 |

**15**

**1903.** Type 15. Perf. 14 × 13½.

| | | | |
|---|---|---|---|
| 284 | 10 c., rose-carmine .. | 4 | 2 |
| 285 | 15 c., slate-green .. | 4 | 2 |
| 286 | 20 c., brown-purple .. | 6 | 2 |
| 287 | 25 c., blue .. .. | 8 | 2 |
| 288 | 30 c., lilac .. .. | 10 | 2 |

MILITARY FRANK STAMP.

# F. M.

**21**

**1901.** No. 272 *overprinted with* Type 21, *in* black.

(F. M. = *Franchise Militaire.*)

| | | | |
|---|---|---|---|
| 351 | 15 c., orange .. .. | 36 | |

*Variety. Overprint inverted.*

| | | | |
|---|---|---|---|
| 352 | 15 c., orange .. .. | | |

| | Un. | Used. |
|---|---|---|
| No. | | |

**1903.**  Type 14 *similarly overprinted.*
353|15 c., pale red .. .. 50

JOURNAL STAMPS.

51

*1868.*  Type 51.  *Imperf.*

| 401 | 2 c., mauve | .. | .. 1.85 | 75 |
|---|---|---|---|---|
| 402 | 2 c., blue | .. | .. 3.15 | 2.50 |
| 403 | 2 c., rose | .. | .. 22.50 | |

*The same. Perf.* 12½.

| 404 | 2 c., mauve | .. | .. — | 6 |
|---|---|---|---|---|
| 405 | 2 c., blue | .. | 50 | 25 |
| 406 | 2 c., rose | .. | .. 1.00 | 62 |
| 407 | 5 c., mauve | .. | .. 6.25 | 6.25 |

These stamps represented a fiscal and
postal charge combined. The 5 c. were for
the Department of the Seine and Oise, and
the 2 c. for all the other Departments. The
5 c., *mauve*, imperf., and in *blue* and *rose*,
perf., are only proofs, and were not issued.

UNPAID LETTER STAMPS.

52

**1859.** Type 52.  *Lithographed. Imperf.*
601|10 c., black .. .. — 3.00

**1859-63.**  *Typographed.*

| 602 | 10 c., black | .. | 8 | 6 |
|---|---|---|---|---|
| 603 | 15 c. | ,, (1863) | .. 12 | 8 |

**1870-71.**  *Lithographed.*
604|15 c., black .. .. 1.00

In the typographed 15 c. the space
between the head and body of the "5" is
about ⅓ mm.; in the lithographed the
curves are nearly touching. The accent
over "a" in the typographed slants considerably; in the lithographed it is nearly
horizontal.

**1871-78.**  *Typographed.*

| 605 | 25 c., black (1871) | .. | — | 12 |
|---|---|---|---|---|
| 606 | 30 c. | ,, (1878) | .. 75 | 18 |
| 607 | 40 c., blue (1871) | .. | 2.50 | 4.35 |
| 8 | 40 c., ultramarine | . | .. 10.00 | |

| | Un. | Used. |
|---|---|---|
| No. | | |

| 609 | 60 c., ochre (1871) | .. | 3.75 | |
|---|---|---|---|---|
| 610 | 60 c., blue (1878) | .. | — | 25 |
| 611 | 60 c., pale blue | .. | 25 | 25 |

The 20 c., *black*, is a stamp that was
prepared for use, but not issued. Many
of the values are found rouletted or perforated.

53

**1881-90.**  Type 53.  *Perf.* 14 × 13½.

| 612 | 1 c., black | .. | .. | 2 | 2 |
|---|---|---|---|---|---|
| 613 | 2 c. | ,, | .. | .. | 4 | |
| 614 | 3 c. | ,, | .. | .. | 4 | |
| 615 | 4 c. | ,, | .. | .. | 4 | 4 |
| 616 | 5 c. | ,, | .. | .. | 6 | 4 |
| 617 | 10 c. | ,, | .. | .. | 8 | 4 |
| 618 | 15 c. | ,, | .. | .. | 12 | 2 |
| 619 | 20 c. | ,, | .. | .. | 12 | 12 |
| 620 | 30 c. | ,, (1881) | .. | 16 | 2 |
| 621 | 40 c. | ,, | .. | .. | 25 | 1. |
| 622 | 50 c. | ,, (1890) | .. | 36 | 6 |
| 623 | 60 c. | ,, | .. | .. | 25 | 12 |
| 624 | 1 fr. | ,, | .. | .. | 55 | 55 |
| 625 | 2 fr. | ,, | .. | .. | 62 | 75 |
| 626 | 5 fr. | ,, | .. | .. | 2.00 | 2.5 |

**1884-90.**

| 627 | 1 fr., reddish brown | .. | 50 | 10 |
|---|---|---|---|---|
| 628 | 2 fr. | ,, ,, | .. | 1.00 | 75 |
| 629 | 5 fr. | ,, ,, | .. | 1.85 | 1.5 |

**1894.**  *Colours changed.*

| 630 | 5 c., pale blue | .. | .. | 2 | 2 |
|---|---|---|---|---|---|
| 631 | 10 c., pale brown | .. | 4 | |
| 632 | 15 c., pale green | .. | 12 | |
| 633 | 30 c., carmine | .. | .. | 25 | 2 |
| 634 | 30 c., vermilion | .. | .. | — | 6 |
| 635 | 50 c., lilac | .. | .. | 25 | 4 |
| 636 | 1 fr., rose | .. | .. | 50 | |

## STAMPS SURCHARGED FOR USE IN FRENCH CONSULAR OFFICES ABROAD.

### CHINA.

Chine

1

**1894-1901.**  *Stamps of France,* Type 10.
*Perf.* 14 × 13½.  *Overprinted with*
Type 1, *in* vermilion (V), *or* carmine
(C), *or* black (Bk).  *All values* Var
(b) *except when otherwise stated.*

| A 1 | 5 c., deep grn on grn. (V) | 25 | |
|---|---|---|---|
| A 2 | 5 c. | ,, | (C) | 6 | |

| No. | | Un. | Used. |
|---|---|---|---|
| A 3 | 5 c., bright yellow-grn. | | |
| | (a)(C) | 2 | 2 |
| A 4 | 5 c. „ (b) (") | 2 | 2 |
| A 5 | 10 c., blk. on lilac (b) (V) | 25 | |
| A 6 | 10 c. „ (a)(C) | 4 | |
| A 7 | 10 c. „ (b) (") | 4 | 4 |
| A 8 | 15 c., blue .. (V) | 36 | |
| A 9 | 15 c. „ .. (C) | 6 | 8 |
| A 10 | 20 c., red on green (Bk) | 8 | |
| A 11 | 25 c., black on rose (V) | 12 | 2 |
| A 12 | 25 c. „ (C) | 10 | 2 |
| A 13 | 30 c., cinnamon (Bk) | 12 | |
| A 14 | 40 c., pale red on yellow | | |
| | (Bk) | 16 | |
| A 15 | 40 c., deep „ ( „ ) | 16 | |
| A 16 | 50 c., carmine .. (C) | 1.50 | |
| A 17 | 50 c., pale carmine (Bk) | 25 | 18 |
| A 18 | 50 c., deep „ ( „ ) | 20 | 12 |
| A 18a | 50 c., carmine (a) ( „ ) | 62 | 36 |
| A 19 | 75 c., brn. on orange (V) | — | 2.50 |
| A 20 | 75 c. „ (C) | 2.50 | |
| A 21 | 1 fr., olive-green (Bk) | 62 | |
| A 21a | 1 fr., grey-green ( „ ) | 36 | 25 |
| A 22 | 2 fr., brown on azure | | |
| | (a) (Bk) | 62 | |
| A 23 | 5 fr., lilac .. (C) | 12.50 | |
| A 24 | 5 fr. „ .. (Bk) | 1.60 | |
| A 25 | 5 fr., mauve .. ( „ ) | — | 1.85 |

**Chine 25**

**Chine 16Cents**

2  3

**1900.** *Surcharged as Type 2, in black.*

A 26 | 25 on 1 fr., olive-green.. | 5.00 | 5.00

**1901.** *Stamps of 1894–1900 surcharged as Type 3, in red.*

| A 27 | 2 cents on 25 c., black on rose .. .. | | |
| A 28 | 4 cents on 25 c., black on rose .. .. | | |
| A 29 | 6 cents on 25 c., black on rose .. .. | | |
| A 30 | 16 cents on 25 c., black on rose .. | 2.50 | 2.50 |

## CHINE

仙 六

4

**1902.** *Stamps of Indo-China, Type 4, surcharged with the word "CHINE," and with the value in Chinese, in black (as Type 4).*

| A 31 | 1 c. black on azure .. | 2 |
| A 32 | 2 c., brown on buff .. | 2 |

| No. | | Un. | Used. |
|---|---|---|---|
| A 33 | 4 c., purple-brown on grey .. .. | | 4 |
| A 34 | 5 c., pale green .. | | 6 |
| A 35 | 10 c., rose-red .. .. | | 6 |
| A 36 | 15 c., grey .. | | 8 |
| A 37 | 20 c., red on green .. | | 12 |
| A 38 | 25 c., black on rose .. | | 12 |
| A 39 | 30 c., cinnamon on drab | | 18 |
| A 40 | 40 c., red on yellow .. | | 50 |
| A 41 | 50 c., carmine on rose.. | | 50 |
| A 42 | 75 c., brown on orange. | | 55 |
| A 43 | 1 fr., olive-grn. on toned | | 62 |
| A 44 | 5 fr., lilac on pale lilac . | | 3.15 |

The above set was in use in the offices at Canton, Hoi-Hao, Mongtzé, Tchonking, and Packhoi for a short time pending separate issues for each of these offices.

5  6

7

Types 5, 6, and 7 (*designs of France, 1900-2, altered*).

| A 45 | 1 c., grey .. .. | |
| A 46 | 2 c., claret .. .. | |
| A 47 | 3 c., orange-red .. | |
| A 48 | 4 c., brown .. .. | |
| A 49 | 5 c., green .. .. | 2 |
| A 50 | 10 (c.), carmine.. .. | 4 |
| A 51 | 15 „ pale red .. | 6 |
| A 52 | 20 „ brown-purple .. | 6 |
| A 53 | 25 „ blue .. .. | 8 |
| A 54 | 30 „ lilac .. .. | 10 |
| A 55 | 40 „ red and pale blue | 12 |
| A 56 | 50 „ brn. & lavender . | 14 |
| A 57 | 1 fr., lake & yellow-grn. | 26 |
| A 58 | 2 fr., slate & deep buff | 55 |
| A 59 | 5 fr., deep blue and buff | 1.30 |

The above set is in use at those offices not furnished with special issues.

No.                                    No.

| | | |
|---|---|---|
| A 219 | 4 c., pur.-brn. on grey | |
| A 220 | 5 c., bright yell.-grn. | |
| A 221 | 10 c., rose-red .. .. | |
| A 222 | 15 c., grey .. .. | |
| A 223 | 20 c., red on green .. | |
| A 224 | 25 c., blue .. .. | |
| A 225 | 30 c., cinnamon on drab | |
| A 226 | 40 c., red on yellow .. | |
| A 227 | 50 c., carmine on rose . | |
| A 228 | 75 c., brown on orange | |
| A 229 | 1 fr., olive-grn. on toned | |
| A 230 | 5 fr., lilac on pale lilac | |

*Provisional issued at* SMALLCAPS SHANGHAI.

# 5
### 8

Type 6 *surcharged with* Type **8**, *in* black.

| | | |
|---|---|---|
| A 71 | 5 on 15 c., pale red .. | |

#### UNPAID LETTER STAMPS.

**1901.** *Unpaid Letter stamps of France of 1894 overprinted with* Type 1.

| | | | |
|---|---|---|---|
| A 101 | 5 c., pale blue (C).. | 4 | 2 |
| A 102 | 10 c.,  ,,  brown (C).. | 6 | 4 |
| A 103 | 15 c.,  ,,  green (C).. | 8 | 4 |
| A 104 | 30 c., rose (Bk) .. | — | 8 |
| A 105 | 50 c., lilac (Bk) .. | 18 | 12 |

*Varieties.* (*a*) *Double surcharge.*

| | | |
|---|---|---|
| A 106 | 5 c., pale blue .. | 2.50 |
| A 107 | 30 c., rose .. | 2.50 |

(*b*) *Triple surcharge.*

| | | |
|---|---|---|
| A 108 | 50 c., lilac .. | 3.00 |

No. A 13 *overprinted* "A percevoir," *in* red.

| | | |
|---|---|---|
| A 109 | 30 c., cinnamon .. | |

#### CANTON.

# CANTON
# 州廣
### 11

**1901.** *Stamps of Indo China,* Type **4**, *surcharged with* Type **11**, *in* carmine. *The Chinese characters represent* "Canton."

| | | |
|---|---|---|
| A 201 | 1 c., black on azure .. | 2 |
| A 202 | 1 c., grey-black .. | 2 |
| A 203 | 2 c., brown on buff .. | 2 |
| A 204 | 4 c., pur.-brn. on grey | 4 |
| A 205 | 5 c., bright yell.-green | 4 |
| A 206 | 10 c., black on lilac .. | 6 |
| A 207 | 15 c., blue on *quadrillé* | 16 |
| A 208 | 15 c., grey .. .. | 8 |
| A 209 | 20 c., red on green .. | 18 |
| A 210 | 25 c., black on rose .. | 12 |
| A 211 | 30 c., cinnamon on drab | 25 |
| A 212 | 40 c., red on yellow . | 30 |
| A 213 | 50 c., carmine on rose . | 36 |
| A 214 | 75 c., black on orange | 50 |
| A 215 | 1 fr., olive-grn. on toned | 55 |
| A 216 | 5 fr., lilac on pale lilac | 3.75 |

*Surcharged similarly to above (but Chinese characters represent value),* in black.

| | | |
|---|---|---|
| A 217 | 1 c., black on azure .. | |
| 218 | 2 c., brown on buff .. | |

#### HOI-HAO.

**1902.** *Stamps of Indo China,* Type **4** *surcharged similarly to* Type **11** (*the Chinese characters represent* "Hoi-Hao"), *in* carmine.

| | | | |
|---|---|---|---|
| A 301 | 1 c., black on azure.. | .2 | |
| A 302 | 2 c., brown on buff . | 4 | |
| A 303 | 4 c., pur.-brn. on grey | 4 | |
| A 304 | 5 c., pale green .. | 6 | 6 |
| A 305 | 10 c., black on lilac .. | 12 | |
| A 306 | 15 c., blue on *quadrillé* | | |
| A 307 | 15 c., grey .. .. | 12 | |
| A 308 | 20 c., red on green .. | 62 | |
| A 309 | 25 c., black on rose .. | 25 | |
| A 310 | 30 c., cinnamon on drab | 62 | |
| A 311 | 40 c., red on yellow .. | 90 | |
| A 312 | 50 c., carmine on rose | 1.25 | |
| A 313 | 75 c., black on orange | 1.85 | |
| A 314 | 1 fr., olive-green on toned .. .. | | |
| A 315 | 5 fr., lilac on pale lilac | | |

*Surcharged similarly to above (but Chinese characters represent value),* in black.

| | | |
|---|---|---|
| A 316 | 1 c., black on azure.. | |
| A 317 | 2 c., brown on buff .. | |
| A 318 | 4 c., pur.-brn. on grey | |
| A 319 | 5 c., pale green .. | |
| A 320 | 10 c., rose-red .. .. | |
| A 321 | 15 c., grey .. .. | |
| A 322 | 20 c., red on green .. | |
| A 323 | 25 c., blue .. .. | |
| A 324 | 30 c., cinnamon on drab | |
| A 325 | 40 c., red on yellow .. | |
| A 326 | 50 c., carmine on rose . | |
| A 327 | 75 c., brown on orange | |
| A 328 | 1 fr., olive-grn. on toned | |
| A 329 | 5 fr., lilac on pale lilac | |

#### LONG-TCHÉOU.

**1903.** *Stamps of Indo China,* Type **4** *surcharged* "LONG-TCHÉOU" *and value in Chinese, as* Type **15** (Packhoi), *in* black.

| | | |
|---|---|---|
| A 351 | 1 c., black on azure .. | |
| A 352 | 2 c., brown on buff .. | |
| A 353 | 4 c., pur.-brn. on grey | |
| A 354 | 5 c., bright yell.-grn. | |
| A 355 | 10 c., carmine .. .. | |
| A 356 | 15 c., grey .. .. | |

| No. | | Un. | Used. |
|---|---|---|---|
| A 357 | 20 c., red on green .. | | |
| A 358 | 25 c., blue .. .. | | |
| A 359 | 30 c., cinnamon on drab | | |
| A 360 | 40 c., red on yellow .. | | |
| A 361 | 50 c., carmine on rose . | | |
| A 362 | 75 c., black on orange | | |
| A 363 | 1 fr., olive-grn. on toned | | |
| A 364 | 5 fr., lilac on pale lilac | | |

The above stamps have not been issued, the office now being temporarily closed.

### MONGTZÉ.

**1903.** *Stamps of Indo China*, Type 4, *overprinted* "MONGTZÉ" *and value in Chinese, similar to* Type 15 (Packhoi), *in* black.

| A 401 | 1 c., black on azure.. |
|---|---|
| A 402 | 2 c., brown on buff .. |
| A 403 | 4 c. pur.-brn. on grey |
| A 404 | 5 c., pale green |
| A 405 | 10 c., rose-red.. |
| A 406 | 15 c., grey .. .. |
| A 407 | 20 c., red on green .. |
| A 408 | 25 c., blue .. .. |
| A 409 | 30 c., cinnamon on drab |
| A 410 | 40 c., red on yellow .. |
| A 411 | 50 c., carmine on rose. |
| A 412 | 75 c., brown on orange |
| A 413 | 1 fr., olive-grn. on toned |
| A 414 | 5 fr., lilac on pale lilac |

### PACKHOI.

**PACKHOI**

仙 二

15

**APRIL, 1903.** *Stamps of Indo China,* Type 4, *surcharged* "PACKHOI" *and value in Chinese, as* Type 15, *in* black.

| A 451 | 1 c., black on azure .. | 10 |
|---|---|---|
| A 452 | 2 c., brown on buff .. | 10 |
| A 453 | 4 c., purple-brn. on grey | 10 |
| A 454 | 5 c., pale green .. | 12 |
| A 455 | 10 c., rose-red .. | 12 |
| A 456 | 15 c., grey .. .. | 12 |
| A 457 | 20 c., red on green .. | 25 |
| A 458 | 25 c., blue .. .. | 25 |
| A 459 | 30 c., cinnamon on drab | 25 |
| A 460 | 40 c., red on yellow .. | 36 |
| A 461 | 50 c., carmine on rose | 50 |
| A 462 | 75 c., brown on orange | 90 |
| A 463 | 1 fr., olive-grn. on toned | 1.25 |
| A 464 | 5 fr., lilac on pale lilac | |

### TCHONGKING.

**1903.** *Stamps of Indo China*, Type 4, *surcharged* "TCHONGKING" *and value in Chinese, in* black.

| A 501 | 1 c., black on azure .. |
|---|---|
| A 502 | 2 c., brown on buff .. |
| A 503 | 4 c., purple-brn. on grey |

| No. | | Un. | Used. |
|---|---|---|---|
| A 504 | 5 c., pale green .. | | |
| A 505 | 10 c., rose-red .. | | |
| A 506 | 15 c., grey .. .. | | |
| A 507 | 20 c., red on green .. | | |
| A 508 | 25 c., black on rose .. | | |
| A 509 | 30 c., cinnamon on drab | | |
| A 510 | 40 c., red on yellow .. | | |
| A 511 | 50 c., carmine on rose.. | | |
| A 512 | 75 c., brown on orange | | |
| A 513 | 1 fr., olive-grn. on toned | | |
| A 514 | 5 fr., lilac on pale lilac | | |

### YUNNAN-SEN.

**1903.** *Stamps of Indo China*, Type 4, *overprinted* "YUNNAN-SEN" *and value in Chinese, similar to* Type 15, *in* black.

| A 601 | 1 c., black on azure .. |
|---|---|
| A 602 | 2 c., brown on buff .. |
| A 603 | 4 c., purple-brn. on grey |
| A 604 | 5 c., pale green .. |
| A 605 | 10 c., rose .. .. |
| A 606 | 15 c., grey .. .. |
| A 607 | 20 c., red on green .. |
| A 608 | 25 c., blue .. .. |
| A 609 | 30 c., cinnamon on drab |
| A 610 | 40 c., red on yellow .. |
| A 611 | 50 c., carmine on rose.. |
| A 612 | 75 c., brown on orange |
| A 613 | 1 fr., olive-grn. on toned |
| A 614 | 5 fr., lilac on pale lilac |

### CRETE.

1

2

3

**1902.** Types 1, 2, and 3.

| C 1 | 1 c., grey .. .. | 2 |
|---|---|---|
| C 2 | 2 c., claret .. .. | 2 |
| C 3 | 3 c., orange-red .. | 2 |
| C 4 | 4 c., brown .. .. | 2 |
| C 5 | 5 c., green .. .. | 2 |
| C 6 | 10 (c.), carmine .. | 4 |

| No. | | Un. | Used. |
|---|---|---|---|
| C 7 | 15 (c.), pale red .. | 6 | |
| C 8 | 20 ,, brown-purple.. | 6 | |
| C 8a | 25 ,, blue .. .. | | |
| C 9 | 30 ,, lilac .. .. | 10 | |
| C 10 | 40 ,, red & pale blue | 12 | |
| C 11 | 50 ,, brn. & lavender | 18 | |
| C 12 | 1 fr., lake & yell.-grn. | 36 | |
| C 13 | 2 fr., slate & deep buff | 62 | |
| C 14 | 5 fr., deep blue & buff | 1.60 | |

## | PIASTRE |

**4**

## 2 PIASTRES

**5**

**1903.** Types **2** and **3.** *Surcharged with values in Turkish currency, as Types* **4** *and* **5,** *in* black.

| | | | |
|---|---|---|---|
| C 15 | 1 pias. on 25 (c.) .. | 8 | |
| C 16 | 2 ,, 50 ,, .. | 14 | |
| C 17 | 4 ,, 1 fr. .. | 26 | |
| C 18 | 8 ,, 2 fr. .. | 55 | |
| C 19 | 20 ,, 5 fr. .. | 1.30 | |

## EGYPT.

### 1. ALEXANDRIA.

## ALEXANDRIE

**1**

**1899.** *Stamps of France,* Type 10. *Overprinted with* Type 1, *in* carmine (C), blue (B), *or* black (Bk). *All stamps Var.* (b) *unless otherwise described.*

| | | Un. | Used. |
|---|---|---|---|
| E 1 | 1 c., black on blue (C) | 2 | 4 |
| E 2 | 2 c., red-bn. on buff (B) | 2 | 4 |
| E 3 | 3 c., drab .. (B) | 2 | |
| E 4 | 4 c., bn.-lilac on gry.(,,) | 4 | |
| E 5 | 5 c., bright yellow-grn. | | |
| | (a) (C) | 4 | 4 |
| E 5a | 5 c. ,, (b) (,,) | | |
| E 6 | 10 c., blk. on lilac (a)(C) | 6 | |
| E 7 | 10 c. ,, ,, (b) (,,) | 6 | |
| E 8 | 15 c., blue .. (,,) | 8 | |
| E 9 | 20 c., red on green (Bk) | 10 | 12 |
| E 10 | 25 c., black on rose (C) | 10 | 10 |
| E 11 | 30 c., cinnamon (Bk) | 12 | 12 |
| E 12 | 40 c., red on yellow (,,) | 16 | 16 |
| E 13 | 50 c., carmine (a) (Bk) | 18 | |
| E 14 | 50 c., carmine (b) (,,) | 18 | |
| E 15 | 1 fr., olive-green (,,) | 36 | |
| E 16 | 2 fr., brown on azure | | |
| | (a) (Bk) | 75 | |
| E 17 | 5 fr., deep lilac (,,) | 1.60 | 1.60 |

*Errors.*

(i.) *Overprint inverted.*

| E 18 | 25 c., black on rose .. | 3.15 | |
|---|---|---|---|

(ii.) *Double overprint.*

| E 19 | 1 c., black on blue (C) | 6.25 | |
|---|---|---|---|

(iii.) *Overprinted twice, once inverted.*

| ·20 | 25 c., black on rose .. | | |
|---|---|---|---|

**2**　　　　**3**

**4**

**1902.** Types **2, 3,** and **4.**

| No. | | Un. | Used. |
|---|---|---|---|
| E 21 | 1 c., grey .. .. | 2 | |
| E 22 | 2 c., claret .. .. | 2 | |
| E 23 | 3 c., orange-red .. | 2 | |
| E 24 | 4 c., brown .. | 2 | |
| E 25 | 5 c., green .. .. | 2 | |
| E 26 | 10 (c.), carmine .. | 4 | |
| E 27 | 15 ,, pale red .. | 6 | |
| E 28 | 20 ,, brown-purple.. | 6 | |
| E 29 | 25 ,, blue .. .. | 8 | |
| E 30 | 30 ,, lilac .. .. | 10 | |
| E 31 | 40 ,, red & pale blue | 12 | |
| E 32 | 50 ,, brn. & lavender | 14 | |
| E 33 | 1 fr., lake & yell.-grn. | 26 | |
| E 34 | 2 fr., slate & deep buff | 55 | |
| E 35 | 5 fr., deep blue & buff | 1.30 | |

### 2. PORT SAID.

## PORT-SAID

**21**

**1899-1900.**

*Overprinted with* Type **21.**
*Otherwise as for Alexandria.*

| | | Un. | Used. |
|---|---|---|---|
| E 101 | 1 c., black on blue (C) | 2 | |
| E 102 | 2 c., red-bn. on buff (B) | 2 | |
| E 103 | 3 c., drab .. (,,) | 2 | |
| E 104 | 4 c., bn.-lilac on gry.(,,) | 2 | |
| E 105 | 5 c., bright yell.-green | | |
| | (a)(C) | 2 | |
| E 106 | 5 c., bright yellow-green (b) (C) | | |
| E 107 | 10 c., blk. on lilac (a)(,,) | 6 | 6 |
| E 108 | 10 c. ,, ,, (b) (,,) | | |
| E 109 | 15 c., pale blue (,,) | 8 | |
| E 110 | 15 c., deep ,, (,,) | 6 | |
| E 111 | 20 c., red on green (Bk) | 10 | |
| E 112 | 25 c., black on rose (C) | 10 | 10 |

| No. | | | Un. | Used. |
|---|---|---|---|---|
| E 113 | 30 c., cinnamon | (Bk) | 12 | |
| E 114 | 40 c., red on yellow | ( ,, ) | 18 | |
| E 115 | 50 c., carmine (a) | ( ,, | | |
| E 116 | 50 c. ,, (b) | ( ,, ) | 20 | 25 |
| E 117 | 1 fr., olive-green | ( ,, ) | 36 | 36 |
| E 118 | 2 fr., brown on azure | | | |
| | (a) (Bk) | | 80 | 90 |
| E 119 | 5 fr., deep lilac | ( ,, ) | 1.75 | |

*Errors.*

(i.) *Overprint inverted.*

E 120|30 c., cinnamon (Bk)..

(ii.) *Double overprint.*

C 121|50 c., carmine (B) ..

*Surcharged with value also in red.*
(i.) *In figures and words.*
(ii.) *In words only.*

| E 122 | 25 c. on 10 c., black on lilac (i.) .. .. | — | 6.25 |
|---|---|---|---|
| E 123 | 25 c. on 10 c., black on lilac (ii.) .. .. | — | 4.35 |

22          23

24

1902. Types 22, 23, *and* 24.

| E 124 | 1 c., grey | .. | .. | 2 |
|---|---|---|---|---|
| E 125 | 2 c., claret | .. | .. | 2 |
| E 126 | 3 c., orange-red | .. | .. | 2 |
| E 127 | 4 c., brown | .. | .. | 2 |
| E 128 | 5 c., green | .. | .. | 2 |
| E 129 | 10 (c.), carmine | | .. | 4 |
| E 130 | 15 ,, pale red | | .. | 6 |
| E 131 | 20 ,, brown-purple | | .. | 6 |
| E 132 | 25 ,, blue | .. | .. | 8 |
| E 133 | 30 ,, lilac | .. | .. | 10 |
| E 134 | 40 ,, red & pale blue | | | 12 |
| E 135 | 50 ,, brn. & lavender | | | 14 |
| E 136 | 1 fr., lake & yell.-grn. | | | 26 |
| E 137 | 2 fr., slate & deep buff | | | 55 |
| E 138 | 5 fr., deep blue & buff | | | 1.30 |

No.

**MADAGASCAR.**

**POSTE FRANÇAISE**

**Madagascar**

1

FEBRUARY, 1895. *Stamps of France,*
Type 10. *Perf.* 14×13½. *Overprinted
with* Type 1, *in* vermilion (V), *or*
black (Bk).

| | | | Un. | Used. |
|---|---|---|---|---|
| M 1 | 5 c., deep green | (V) | 6 | 6 |
| M 2 | 10 c., black on lilac | ( ,, ) | 8 | |
| M 3 | 15 c., blue | ( ,, ) | 18 | 18 |
| M 4 | 25 c., black on rose | ( ,, ) | 25 | 12 |
| M 5 | 40 c., red on yellow | (Bk) | | |
| M 6 | 50 c., carmine | ( ,, ) | 36 | 25 |
| M 7 | 75 c., brn. on orange | (V) | 50 | 50 |
| M 8 | 1 fr., olive-green | (Bk) | 62 | 62 |
| M 9 | 5 fr., lilac | ( ,, ) | 1.85 | 1.85 |

2

MARCH, 1896.
*Surcharged as* Type 2, *in* black.

| M 10 | 5 c. on 1 c., black on azure .. .. | — | 8.75 |
|---|---|---|---|
| M 11 | 15 c. on 2 c., red-brown | — | 7.50 |
| M 12 | 25 c. on 3 c., grey .. | — | 8.75 |
| M 13 | 25 c. on 4 c., claret on azure .. .. | | |
| M 14 | 25 c. on 40 c., red .. | — | 10.00 |

(See also MADAGASCAR under
FRENCH COLONIES.)

**MAJUNGA (MADAGASCAR).**

28 FEBRUARY, 1895. *Stamps of France,*
Type 10. *Perf.* 14×13½. *Surcharged vertically, handstamped in*
black.

M 21|15 on 25 c., black on rose
M 22|15 on 1 fr., olive-green on
toned.. .. ..

*Manuscript surcharge, in* red.

M 23|0.15 on 25 c., blk. on rose
M 24|0.15 on 1 fr., olive-green
on toned .. ..

No. 1 exists with at least two different
sizes of surcharge.

| No. | *Un.* | *Used.* |
|---|---|---|

## MOROCCO.

## 5          1

## CENTIMOS   PESETA

1            2

1 JAN., **1891-1900**. *French stamps*, Type 10.
*Perf.* 14×13½. *Overprinted as* Types 1
*and* 2, *in* vermilion (V), carmine (C),
*or* black (Bk). *All stamps Var.* (*b*)
*unless otherwise described.*

| | | | | |
|---|---|---|---|---|
| M 101 | 5 c., deep green | (C) | 4 | 4 |
| M 102 | 5 c. | „ (V) | — | 2 |
| M 103 | 5 c., bright yell.-green | | | |
| | | (*a*)(C) | 2 | 2 |
| M 104 | 5 c. | „ (*b*)(„) | 4 | 4 |
| M 105 | 10 c., black on lilac | | | |
| | | (*a*)(C) | 4 | 2 |
| M 106 | 10 c. | „ (*b*)(C) | 4 | 2 |
| M 107 | 10 c. | „ (*b*)(V) | — | 25 |
| M 108 | 20 c., red on deep | | | |
| | green | .. (Bk) | 6 | 8 |
| M 109 | 20 c., red on green (Bk) | | 12 | 8 |
| M 110 | 25 c., black on rose (V) | | | |
| M 111 | 25 c. | „ (C) | 8 | 2 |
| M 112 | 50 c., rose | (*b*)(Bk) | 25 | 25 |
| M 113 | 50 c., carmine (*a*) ( „ ) | | | |
| M 114 | 50 c., pale carm.(*b*)( „ ) | | 18 | |
| M 115 | 50 c., rose „ ( „ ) | | | |
| M 116 | 50 c. „ „ (*b*)( „ ) | | | |
| M 117 | 1 pes., olive-grn. ( „ ) | | 30 | |
| M 118 | 2 pes., brown on azure | | 62 | |

**1899.** *Error. Surcharged on wrong
value.*

| | | | |
|---|---|---|---|
| M 119 | 10c. on 25 c., blk. on rose | | |
| | | (C) | 7.50 |

*Error. Double surcharge.*

| | | | |
|---|---|---|---|
| M 120 | 25 c., blk. on rose (C). | | 3.15 |

## T I M B R E

## [surcharge image]

## TIMBRE

3

**⟶93.** *"Unpaid" French stamps*, Type 53.
*Perf.* 14×13½. *Surcharged with*
Type 3, *in* red.

| | | | | |
|---|---|---|---|---|
| 1 | 5 c., black | .. | .. | |
| 2 | 10 c. „ | .. | .. | 7.50 | 3.75 |

| No. | *Un.* | *Used.* |
|---|---|---|

4            5

6

## 20 CENTIMOS

7

**1902.** Types **4, 5,** *and* **6** *surcharged in
Spanish currency* (*on* 5 c. *in* red, *other
values* black), *on* Type **5**, *as* Type **7**.

| | | | |
|---|---|---|---|
| M 123 | 5 c., green | .. | 2 |
| M 124 | 10 c., carmine | .. | 4 |
| M 125 | 15 c., pale red.. | | |
| M 126 | 20 c., brown-purple | .. | 4 |
| M 127 | 25 c., blue | .. | 8 |
| M 128 | 30 c., lilac | .. | |
| M 129 | 50 c., brown & lavender | | 14 |
| M 130 | 1 p., lake and green.. | | 26 |
| M 131 | 2 p., slate & deep buff | | 55 |
| M 132 | 5 p., deep blue & buff | | |

### UNPAID LETTER STAMPS.

**1896.** *"Unpaid" French stamps*, Type **53**.
*Perf.* 14×13½. *Overprinted as* Types
**1** *and* **2**, *in* vermilion (V), carmine (C),
*or* black (Bk).

| | | | | |
|---|---|---|---|---|
| M 181 | 5 c., blue | .. | (V) | 4 |
| M 182 | 5 c. „ | .. | (C) | 2 |
| M 183 | 10 c., brown | .. | (V) | 25 |
| M 184 | 10 c. „ | .. | (C) | 4 |
| M 185 | 10 c., dark brown | („) | 4 | 4 |
| M 186 | 30 c., rose | .. | (Bk) | 10 |
| M 187 | 50 c., lilac | ( „ ) | 30 | |
| M 188 | 50 c., dull mauve ( „ ) | | 16 | 12 |
| M 189 | 1 pes., brown | (C) | 1.85 | 1.85 |

### TURKISH EMPIRE.

#### LEVANT.

## 1 PIASTRE 1

1

**1885-1902.** *Stamps of France*, Type **10.**
*Perf.* 14×13½. *Surcharged as* Type **1.**
*in* vermilion (V), carmine (C), black
(Bk), *or* blue (B).

| | | | | |
|---|---|---|---|---|
| T 1 | 1 pias. on 25 c., yellow- | | | |
| | ochre | .. | (Bk) | 12 | 12 |

| No. | | Un. | Used. |
|---|---|---|---|
| T2 | 2 pias. on 50 c., rose (Bk) | 18 | 6 |
| T3 | 2 ,, 50 c., car. ( ,, ) | 18 | 6 |
| T4 | 3 ,, 75 c. ,, ( ,, ) | 25 | 25 |
| T5 | 4 ,, 1 fr., olive-grn. (Bk) | 30 | 8 |
| T6 | 8 ,, 2 fr., brown on azure .. (Bk) | 62 | 62 |
| T7 | 20 pias. on 5 fr., mve. ( ,, ) | 2.50 | 2.50 |
| T8 | 20 ,, 5 fr., lilac ( ,, ) | 1.50 | 1.25 |
| T9 | 1 ,, 25 c., bk. on rose (V) | | |
| T10 | 1 ,, 25 c. ,, (C) | 8 | 2 |
| T11 | 2 ,, 50 c., carmine (a) (Bk) | | |

*Variety. Surcharge inverted.*

| T12 | 1 pias. on 25 c., black on rose .. (V) | | |

**2**      **3**

**4**

**1902.** Types **2, 3,** *and* **4.**

| T13 | 1 c., grey .. .. | 2 | 2 |
|---|---|---|---|
| T14 | 2 c., claret .. .. | 2 | 2 |
| T15 | 3 c., orange-red .. | 2 | 2 |
| T16 | 4 c., brown .. .. | 2 | 2 |
| T17 | 5 c., green .. .. | 2 | |
| T18 | 10 (c.), carmine .. .. | 4 | |
| T19 | 15 ,, pale red .. .. | 6 | |
| T20 | 20 ,, brown-purple .. | 6 | |
| T21 | 30 ,, lilac .. .. | 10 | |
| T22 | 40 ,, red and pale blue | 12 | |

**2**

**1 PIASTRE 1**     **PIASTRES**

**5**         **6**

*Same types surcharged as Types 5 and 6.*

| T23 | 1 pias. on 25, blue .. | 8 | 8 |
|---|---|---|---|
| T24 | 2 ,, on 50, brown and lavender .. .. | 14 | 14 |
| T25 | 4 pias. on 1 fr., lake and yellow-green .. | 26 | |
| T26 | 8 pias. on 2 fr., violet and deep buff .. | 55 | |

| No. | | Un. | Used. |
|---|---|---|---|
| T27 | 20 pias. on 5 fr., deep blue and buff .. | 1.30 | |

**CAVALLE.**

**Cavalle**       **2 Piastres 2**

**11**         **12**

**1893.** *Contemporary stamps of France surcharged with Type 11, and the four higher values as Type 12 as well.*

| T51 | 5 c., blue-green (C) | 4 | |
|---|---|---|---|
| T52 | 5 c. ,, (V) | | |
| T53 | 5 c., yell.-green (a)(C) | 2 | |
| T53a | 5 c. ,, (,,)(V) | | |
| T54 | 5 c. ,, (b)(C) | | |
| T54a | 5 c. ,, (,,)(V) | | |
| T55 | 10 c., blk. on lilac (a)(B) | | |
| T56 | 10 c., blk. on lilac (b)(,,) | 6 | |
| T57 | 15 c., blue .. (V) | 8 | |
| T58 | 15 c. ,, (C) | 12 | |
| T59 | 1 pias. on 25 c., bk. on rose .. (B) | 12 | 12 |
| T60 | 2 pias. on 50 c., pale rose .. (B) | 25 | |
| T61 | 2 pias. on 50 c., rose (,,) | 20 | |
| T62 | 2 ,, 50 c., car. (,,) | 50 | |
| T63 | 4 ,, 1 fr., olive-green .. (V) | 45 | |
| T64 | 4 pias. on 1 fr., olive-green - (C) | 36 | |
| T65 | 4 pias. on 1 fr., grey-green .. (C) | | |
| T66 | 8 pias on 2 fr., brown on azure .. (Bk.) | 55 | |

**13**      **14**

**1902.** Types **13** *and* **14.**

| T67 | 5 c., green .. .. | 2 | |
|---|---|---|---|
| T68 | 10 (c.), carmine .. .. | 4 | |
| T69 | 15 ,, pale red .. .. | 6 | |
| T70 | 30 c., lilac .. .. | | |

**15**

Types **14** *and* **15** *surcharged as* Types **5** *and* **6** *respectively, in* black.

| T71 | 1 pias. on 25, blue .. | 8 | |

| No. | | Un. | Used. |
|---|---|---|---|
| T72 | 2 pias. on 50, brown and lavender .. .. | 14 | |
| T73 | 4 pias. on 1 fr., lake and yellow-green .. | 26 | |
| T74 | 8 pias. on 2 fr., violet and deep buff .. | 55 | |
| T75 | 20 pias. on 5 fr., deep blue and buff .. | | |

### DEDEAGH.

**Bédéagh**

**21**

**1893.** *Contemporary stamps of France surcharged with* Type **21**, *and the four higher values as* Type **12** *as well.*

| | | | Un. |
|---|---|---|---|
| T101 | 5 c., green .. | (V) | 6 |
| T102 | 5 c., deep green | (C) | |
| T103 | 5 c., green .. | (,,) | 12 |
| T104 | 5 c., yell.-green(a)(,,) | | 2 |
| T104a | 5 c. ,, | (,,)(V) | |
| T104b | 5 c. ,, | (b)(,,) | |
| T105 | 10 c., black on lilac (a)(B) | | 6 |
| T106 | 10 c., black on lilac (b)(B) | | 4 |
| T107 | 15 c., blue .. | (V) | 8 |
| T108 | 15 c. ,, .. | (C) | 8 |
| T109 | 1 pias. on 25 c., black on rose | (B) | 12 |
| T110 | 2 pias. on 50 c., rose | (B) | 25 |
| T111 | 2 ,, 50 c., carmine. .. | (B) | |
| T111a | 2 pias. on 50 c., carmine. ..(b)(B) | | |
| T112 | 4 pias. on 1 fr., olive-green | (C) | 30 |
| T113 | 4 pias. on 50 c. | (V) | |
| T114 | 8 ,, 2 fr., brown on azure .. | (Bk) | 75 |

**22**             **23**

**1902.** Types **22** *and* **23**.

| | | | |
|---|---|---|---|
| 115 | 5 c., green .. | .. | 2 |
| 16 | 10 (c.), carmine | .. | 4 |
| 17 | 15 ,, pale red | .. | 6 |
| 18 | 30 c., lilac .. | .. | |

**24**

Types **23** *and* **24** *surcharged as* Types **5** *and* **6** *respectively, in* black.

| | | | Un. |
|---|---|---|---|
| T119 | 1 pias. on 25, blue .. | | 8 |
| T120 | 2 ,, on 50, brown and lavender .. | | 14 |
| T121 | 4 pias. on 1 fr., lake and yellow-green . | | 26 |
| T122 | 8 pias. on 2 fr., violet and deep buff .. | | 55 |
| T123 | 20 pias. on 5 fr., deep blue and buff .. | | |

### PORT LAGOS.

**Port-Lagos**

**31**

**1893.** *Contemporary stamps of France surcharged with* Type **31**, *and the three higher values as* Type **12** *as well.*

| | | | Un. |
|---|---|---|---|
| T151 | 5 c., deep green | (C) | 62 |
| T152 | 5 c. ,, | (V) | |
| T153 | 10 c., blk. on lilac(a)(B) | | |
| T154 | 10 c. ,, (b)(,,) | | 50 |
| T155 | 15 c., blue .. | (C) | 62 |
| T156 | 15 c. ,, .. | (V) | |
| T157 | 1 pias. on 25 c., black on rose .. | (B) | 50 |
| T158 | 2 pias. on 50 c., rose(,,) | | |
| T159 | 2 ,, 50 c., carm.(,,) | | 1.50 |
| T160 | 4 ,, 1 fr., olive-green .. | (C) | 2.50 |
| T161 | 4 pias. on 1 fr., olive-green .. | (V) | |

### VATHY.

**Vathy**

**41**

**1893–1900.** *Contemporary stamps of France surcharged with* Type **41**, *and the five higher values as* Type **12** *as well.*

| | | | Un. |
|---|---|---|---|
| T201 | 5 c., deep green | (C) | 50 |
| T202 | 5 c. ,, | (V) | |
| T203 | 5 c., bright yellow-green .. | (a)(C) | 2 |
| T204 | 5 c., bright yellow-green .. | (b)(C) | 6 |
| T204a | 5 c., bright yellow-green .. | (b)(V) | |

| No. | | Un. | Used. |
|---|---|---|---|
| T 205 | 10 c., blk. on lilac (a)(B) | 8 | |
| T 206 | 10 c., blk. on lilac (b)(B) | 6 | |
| T 207 | 15 c., blue .. (C) | 10 | |
| T 208 | 15 c. ,, .. (V) | | |
| T 209 | 1 pias. on 25 c., black on rose .. (B) | 12 | |
| T 210 | 1 pias. on 25 c., black on flesh .. (B) | 12 | |
| T 211 | 2 pias. on 50 c., rose (B) | 25 | |
| T 212 | 2 pias. on 50 c., carmine .. (B) | | |
| T 213 | 4 pias. on 1 fr., olive-green .. (C) | 36 | |
| T 214 | 4 pias. on 1 fr., olive-green .. (V) | | |
| T 215 | 8 pias. on 2 fr., brown on azure .. (Bk) | 62 | |
| T 216 | 20 pias. on 5 fr., lilac (Bk) | 1.75 | |

### ZANZIBAR.

ZANZIBAR

2½ ANNAS

**1/2 ANNA**

**25**

1          2

**1894.** *French stamps,* Type 10.
*Perf.* 14 × 13½. *Surcharged as* Type 1.

| | | Un. | Used. |
|---|---|---|---|
| Z 1 | ½ a. on 5 c., deep grn. (V) | 36 | |
| Z 2 | ½ a. on 5 c. ,, (C) | 6 | 6 |
| Z 3 | 1 a. on 10 c., blk. on lilac (B) | 25 | 25 |
| Z 4 | 2½ a. on 25 c. ,, rose (B) | 12 | 12 |
| Z 5 | 5 a. on 50 c., rose (,,) | 62 | |
| Z 6 | 5 a. on 50 c., carmine (,,) | 62 | 62 |
| Z 7 | 10 a. on 1 fr., olive-grn.(C) | 1.00 | |

**1894.** *Surcharged as* Type 2, *with value in Indian currency and corresponding value in French currency over original value.*

| | | Un. | Used. |
|---|---|---|---|
| Z 8 | ½ a. & 5 on 1 c., blk. on azure .. .. (V) | 3.00 | |
| Z 9 | 1 a. & 10 on 3 c., grey (,,) | 3.15 | |
| Z 10 | 2½ a. & 25 on 4 c., purple-brown on grey (Bk) | 3.75 | |
| Z 11 | 5 a. & 50 on 20 c., red on green .. (Bk) | 3.75 | |
| Z 12 | 10 a. & 1 fr. on 40 c., red (Bk) | | |

There are several types of the large figures and of the "1 Fr."

**1896.** *Surcharged as* Type 1.

| | | Un. | Used. |
|---|---|---|---|
| Z 13 | 1½ a. on 15 c., blue (V) | 62 | |
| Z 14 | 2 a. on 20 c., red on green .. (Bk) | 36 | 50 |

| No. | | Un. | Used. |
|---|---|---|---|
| Z 15 | 3 a. on 30 c., cinnamon (Bk) | 50 | 50 |
| Z 16 | 4 a. on 40 c., red ( ,, ) | 50 | |
| Z 17 | 7½ a. on 75 c., brown on orange .. (Bk) | 15.00 | |
| Z 18 | 50 a. on 5 fr., lilac ( ,, ) | | |

*Error.* "ANNAS" *instead of* "ANNA."

| | | Un. | Used. |
|---|---|---|---|
| Z 19 | 1½ a. on 15 c., blue (V) | 4.35 | |

**1/2**

**ANNA**

**ZANZIBAR**

3

**1897-1902.** *Surcharged with name and value, as* Type 3.

| | | Un. | Used. |
|---|---|---|---|
| Z 20 | ½ a. on 5 c., green (V) | 36 | |
| Z 21 | ½ a. on 5 c., deep grn. (C) | 12 | 25 |
| Z 22 | ½ a. on 5 c., bright yellow-green (a)(C) | 2 | 4 |
| Z 23 | ½ a. on 5 c., bright yellow-green (b)(C) | 4 | |
| Z 24 | 1 a. on 10 c., black on lilac (a)(B) | 6 | 6 |
| Z 25 | 1 a. on 10 c., blk. on lilac (b)(B) | 4 | |
| Z 26 | 1½ a. on 15 c., blue (V) | 16 | |
| Z 27 | 1½ a. on 15 c. ,, (C) | 6 | |
| Z 28 | 2 a. on 20 c., red on green .. (Bk) | 8 | 8 |
| Z 29 | 2½ a. on 25 c., blk. on rose (B) | 8 | 8 |
| Z 30 | 3 a. on 30 c., cinnamon (Bk) | 10 | 12 |
| Z 31 | 4 a. on 40 c., red on yellow .. (Bk) | 12 | 16 |
| Z 32 | 5 a. on 50 c., carm. (a)(B) | 18 | 18 |
| Z 33 | 5 a. on 50 c. ,, (b)(B) | 16 | |
| Z 34 | 7½ a. on 75 c., brown on orange .. (Bk) | | |
| Z 35 | 10 a. on 1 fr., olive-green (V) | 50 | |
| Z 36 | 10 a. on 1 fr. ,, (C) | 30 | 30 |
| Z 37 | 20 a. on 2 fr., brown on azure .. (a)(Bk) | 62 | 62 |
| Z 38 | 50 a. on 5 fr., mauve (Bk) | 1.60 | 1.60 |
| Z 39 | 50 a. on 5 fr., lilac (Bk) | 1.60 | 1.60 |

*Variety.* "ZANZIBAR" *double.*

| | | Un. | Used. |
|---|---|---|---|
| Z 40 | 2 a. on 20 c., red on grn. (Bk) | 1.85 | |

*Error.* "ZANZIBAS."

| | | Un. | Used. |
|---|---|---|---|
| Z 41 | 20 a. on 2 f., brn. on azure | | |

There are two printings of the above, in the first of which the word "ZANZIBAR" was added to stamps of the 1894 issue, and in the other the whole surcharge was made at one printing.

| No. | | *Un.* | *Used.* |
|---|---|---|---|

**4**

**1897.** *Stamps of 1894 and 1896 further surcharged with new figures of value (for both annas and centimes), and with "ZANZIBAR" as in Type 4, vertically downwards on the right side of the stamp—all in black.*

| z 42 | 2½ & 25 on ½ a. (z 1) | — | 5.00 |
|---|---|---|---|
| z 43 | 2½ & 25 on 1 a. (z 3) | — | 30.00 |
| z 44 | 2½ & 25 on 1½ a. (z 13) | — | 17.50 |
| z 45 | 5 & 50 on 3 a. (z 15) | — | 12.50 |
| z 46 | 5 & 50 on 4 a. (z 16) | — | 27.50 |

**1897.** *Printed on margins of sheets and the horizontal spaces between vertical panes of the regular issues, as Type 4, in black.*

| z 47 | 2½ a. & 25 c., on green and white (from 5 c.) | — | 25.00 |
|---|---|---|---|
| z 48 | 2½ a. & 25 c., on lilac and white (from 10 c.) | | |
| z 49 | 2½ a. & 25 c., on blue and white (from 15 c.) | | |
| z 50 | 5 a. & 50 c., on buff and white (from 30 c.) | | |
| z 51 | 5 a. & 50 c., on straw and white (from 40 c.) | | |
| z 52 | 5 a. and 50 c., on white | | |

In both of the above sets there are three types of the figures "2½" corresponding to those found on the contemporary stamps for the British Protectorate of Zanzibar (see Part I.).

**5**          **6**

**1902.** Types **5** *surcharged with Type 8, in red,* **6** *surcharged as Type 9, in black, and* **7** *surcharged as Type 10, in black.*

| z 53 | ½ a. on 5 c., green | .. | 2 |
|---|---|---|---|
| z 54 | 1 a. on 10, carmine | .. | 4 |
| 55 | 1½ a. on 15, pale red | .. | 6 |

---

| No. | | *Un.* | *Used.* |
|---|---|---|---|

**7**

**1/2**          **5**

**ANNA**  **1 1/2 ANNA**  **ANNAS**

**8**       **9**         **10**

| z 56 | 2 a. on 20, brown-purple | 6 | |
|---|---|---|---|
| z 57 | 2½ a. on 25, blue | 8 | |
| z 58 | 3 a. on 30, lilac | 10 | |
| z 59 | 4 a. on 40, red & pale blue | 12 | |
| z 60 | 5 a. on 50, brn. & laven. | 14 | |
| z 61 | 10 a. on 1 fr., lake and yellow-green | 26 | |
| z 62 | 20 a. on 2 fr., slate and deep buff | 55 | |
| z 63 | 50 a. on 5 fr., deep blue and buff | 1.30 | |

*Error on sheet of 3 a.*

| z 64 | 5 a. on 30, lilac | .. | |
|---|---|---|---|

**UNPAID LETTER STAMPS.**

**1897.** *Current "UNPAID" French stamps. Perf. 14×13½. Surcharged as Type 3.*

| z 101 | ½ a. on 5 c., blue | .. | 1.00 | : |
|---|---|---|---|---|
| z 102 | 1 a. on 10 c., brown | .. | 1.50 | |
| z 103 | 1½ a. on 15 c., green | .. | 1.50 | |
| z 104 | 3 a. on 30 c., carmine | 1.85 | 1 | |
| z 105 | 5 a. on 50 c., lilac | .. | 2.50 | 1 |

*Error. Surcharged with wrong value.*

| z 106 | 2½ a. on 50 c., lilac | .. | |
|---|---|---|---|

*Error. Surcharge inverted.*

| z 107 | 1 a. on 10 c., brown | .. | |
|---|---|---|---|

# FRENCH COLONIES.

## I. GENERAL ISSUES.

A. *Eagle.*

**1859-62.** Type A. *Tinted paper. Imperf.*

| 1 | 1 c., bronze-green | .. | 10 | : |
|---|---|---|---|---|
| 2 | 5 c., yellow-green | .. | 16 | 3 |
| 3 | 10 c., bistre | .. | 8 | 4 |
| 4 | 10 c., bistre-brown | .. | 12 | 4 |
| 5 | 20 c., pale blue | .. | 1.85 | |

|  | No. | | | Un. | Used. |
|---|---|---|---|---|---|
|  | 6 | 20 c., blue .. .. | 18 | | |
|  | 7 | 20 c., deep blue.. .. | 18 | 6 | |
|  | 8 | 40 c., orange .. | 18 | | |
|  | 9 | 40 c., pale orange .. | 18 | 8 | |
|  | 10 | 80 c., carmine .. .. | 36 | 50 | |
|  | 11 | 80 c., deep carmine .. | 50 | 50 | |

*Variety. Stamp turned sideways with top to the left.*

| 12 | 10 c., bistre (pair) .. | 3.15 | 3.75 |
|---|---|---|---|
| 13 | 10 c., bistre-brown (pair) | | |

This issue is also found pin-perf. (unofficial).

All six values were reprinted (in sheets of 4 by 4) in 1887; these have no gum.

B. *Empire.*     c. *Laureated.*

| No. | Type. | **1871.** *Tinted paper. Imperf.* | | |
|---|---|---|---|---|
| 14 | B | 5 c., green (Jan. 1872) .. .. | 3.75 | 3.75 |
| 15 | C | 1 c., bronze-green.. | 75 | |

D. *Laureated.*

### JULY, 1870.

| 16 | D | 30 c., bistre-brown.. | 50 | 50 |
|---|---|---|---|---|
| 17 | ,, | 30 c., dark brown .. | 75 | 75 |
| 18 | ,, | 80 c., rose-carmine.. | 5.00 | 1.50 |

Nos. 14 to 17 are also found pin-perf. (unofficial).

The 1 c. and 30 c. were reprinted in 1887, but are without gum.

E. *Ceres.*

F. *Ceres.*    FRANCE Type 8.

### 1871-76. *Imperf.*

| 19 | E | 1 c., bronze-green on azure .. .. | 25 | 8 |
|---|---|---|---|---|
| 20 | ,, | 2 c., brown on buff.. | 6.25 | 7.50 |
| 21 | ,, | 4 c., grey .. .. | 20.00 | 11.25 |

| No. | Type. | | Un. | Used. |
|---|---|---|---|---|
| 22 | E | 5 c., green on bluish | 12 | 8 |
| 23 | ,, | 5 c., green on pale green' .. .. | 12 | 4 |
| 24 | F | 10 c., bistre .. .. | 3.75 | 90 |
| 25 | ,, | 15 c. ,, .. | 2.00 | 12 |
| 26 | ,, | 20 c., blue .. .. | 3.00 | 1.00 |
| 27 | ,, | 25 c. ,, .. .. | 30 | 18 |
| 28 | ,, | 40 c., orange(Type I.) | 2.50 | 25 |
| 29 | ,, | 40 c., pale ,, ( ,, ) | 1.00 | 25 |
| 30 | ,, | 40 c., oran.(Type II.)* | | |

\* See note after France, No. 19.

*Variety. Tête-bêche.*

| 30a | 10 c., bistre .. .. | | |
|---|---|---|---|
| 30b | 15 c. ,, .. .. | | |
| 30c | 20 c., blue .. .. | | |
| 30d | 25 c. ,, .. .. | | |

The 10, 20, and 25 c. were reprinted in 1887, but are without gum. The 10 c. is *yellow,* and the two other values *blue* or *dark blue.*

### 1872-77. *Ceres (large figures).*

FRANCE Type 9. *Imperf.*

| 31 | 10 c., brown on rose .. | 90 | 10 |
|---|---|---|---|
| 32 | 15 c., bistre .. .. | 2.00 | 2.00 |
| 33 | 30 c., drab .. .. | 1.00 | 50 |
| 34 | 30 c., grey-brown .. | 1.00 | 36 |
| 35 | 80 c., pale rose.. .. | 3.00 | 75 |
| 35a | 80 c., deep rose .. | 5.00 | 62 |

Nos. 19 to 35 are also found pin-perf. (unofficial).

H. *Peace and Commerce.*

**1876.** *Tinted papers.* Type H. *Imperf.*

(*a*) Letter N *of* INV *under* B *of* REPUBLIQUE.
(*b*)    ,,    U    ,,
(*See illustrations above France, No. 185.*)

| 36 | 1 c., green (*a*) .. .. | 50 | |
|---|---|---|---|
| 37 | 2 c. ,, (*b*) .. .. | 25 | 25 |
| 38 | 4 c. ,, (*a*) .. .. | 25 | 18 |
| 39 | 5 c. ,, (*b*) .. .. | 36 | 4 |
| 40 | 5 c., deep green on pale green (*b*) .. .. | 75 | 4 |
| 41 | 10 c., green (*b*) .. .. | 2.00 | 12 |
| 42 | 15 c., grey (*b*) .. .. | 5.00 | 4.00 |
| 43 | 20 c., brown (*b*) .. .. | 62 | 6 |
| 44 | 25 c., ultramarine (*b*) .. | 62 | 25 |
| 45 | 25 c., blue (*b*) .. .. | — | 1.25 |
| 46 | 30 c., cinnamon (*a*) .. | 62 | 62 |
| 47 | 35 c., black on yellow (*b*) | 2.50 | 2.00 |
| 48 | 35 c. ,, orange (*b*) | 62 | 62 |
| 49 | 40 c., red (*a*) .. .. | 30 | 30 |
| 50 | 75 c., rose-carmine (*a*) .. | 1.25 | 1.10 |

| No. | | Un. | Used. |
|---|---|---|---|
| 51 | 75 c., carmine (a) .. | 2.00 | 1.60 |
| 52 | 1 fr., olive-green (a) .. | 50 | 45 |

The above are also found pin-perf. (unofficial).

The 20 c., *blue*, was prepared but never issued.

Reprints of all values were made in 1887, but are without gum; they are all variety (b), and differ in shade from the originals.

### 1878-80. Type H.
#### All values (b). *Imperf.*

| No. | | Un. | Used. |
|---|---|---|---|
| 53 | 1 c., black on azure .. | 25 | 25 |
| 54 | 2 c., brown on buff .. | 36 | |
| 55 | 4 c., purple-brown on grey .. .. .. | 62 | 62 |
| 56 | 10 c., black on lilac .. | 1.25 | 75 |
| 57 | 15 c., blue on pale blue.. | 62 | 30 |
| 58 | 20 c., red on green .. | 1.25 | 16 |
| 59 | 25 c., black on red .. | 10.00 | 10.00 |
| 60 | 25 c., ochre on yellow .. | 2.50 | 1.00 |

All the above were reprinted in 1887, but are without gum, and the shades differ from the issued stamps. The 3 c., ochre; 3 c., grey; 25 c., black on rose; and 5 fr., lilac—four stamps that were never issued for colonial use—are sometimes put forward as colonial stamps; they are, however, simply stamps of France imperforate.

J. *Commerce.*

MAY, 1881. Type J. *Perf.* 14×13½.

| No. | | Un. | Used. |
|---|---|---|---|
| 61 | 1 c., black on azure .. | 2 | 2 |
| 62 | 2 c., brown on buff .. | 8 | 4 |
| 63 | 2 c., deep brown on buff | — | 2 |
| 64 | 4 c., purp.-brn. on grey | 8 | 8 |
| 65 | 4 c., pale purple-brown on grey .. | 4 | 4 |
| 66 | 5 c., green on green .. | 4 | 2 |
| 67 | 5 c., ,, pale grn. | 4 | 2 |
| 68 | 10 c., black on lilac .. | 6 | 2 |
| 69 | 10 c., ,, pale grey | 12 | 2 |
| 70 | 15 c., blue on pale blue . | 6 | 2 |
| 71 | 15 c., deep blue on pale blue | 6 | 2 |
| 72 | 20 c., red on green .. | 12 | 4 |
| 73 | 20 c., ,, deep green. | 25 | 4 |
| 74 | 25 c., ochre on yellow .. | 12 | 6 |
| 75 | 25 c., black on rose .. | 10 | 2 |
| 76 | 30 c., cinnamon on drab | 25 | 25 |
| 77 | 35 c., black on orange .. | 50 | 30 |
| 78 | 35 c., ,, yellow .. | 1.25 | 1.25 |
| '9 | 40 c., red on yellow .. | 36 | 25 |
| 'o | 40 c., ,, buff .. | 36 | 25 |
| * | 75 c., rose-carmine on rose | 50 | 50 |
| | 1 fr., olive-grn. on toned | 50 | 12 |

| No. | | Un. | Used. |
|---|---|---|---|

### UNPAID LETTER STAMPS.

U

### 1884-85. Type U. *Imperf.*

| No. | | Un. | Used. |
|---|---|---|---|
| 501 | 1 c., black .. .. | 6 | 6 |
| 502 | 2 c., ,, .. .. | 6 | |
| 503 | 3 c., ,, .. .. | 6 | |
| 504 | 4 c., ,, .. .. | 6 | |
| 505 | 5 c., ,, .. .. | 6 | |
| 506 | 10 c., ,, .. .. | 8 | 12 |
| 507 | 15 c., ,, .. .. | 8 | |
| 508 | 20 c., ,, .. .. | 10 | |
| 509 | 30 c., ,, .. .. | 12 | |
| 510 | 40 c., ,, .. .. | 25 | |
| 511 | 60 c., ,, .. .. | 36 | 36 |
| 512 | 1 franc, brown .. .. | 62 | |
| 513 | 2 francs ,, .. .. | 55 | |
| 514 | 5 ,, ,, .. .. | 2.00 | |

### 1894. *Imperf.*

| No. | | Un. | Used. |
|---|---|---|---|
| 515 | 5 c., pale blue .. .. | 4 | 4 |
| 516 | 10 c., grey-brown .. | 6 | |
| 517 | 15 c., pale green .. | 8 | |
| 518 | 30 c., carmine .. .. | 16 | |
| 519 | 50 c., lilac .. .. | 25 | |
| 520 | 60 c., brown on buff .. | 25 | |
| 521 | 1 fr., rose .. .. | 50 | |

### II. SPECIAL ISSUES.

In the issue for Sultanat d'Anjouan and other "tablet" issues of the same type the name is in *red* on the 1 c., 5 c., 15 c., 25 c., 75 c., and 1 fr., and in *blue* on the 2 c., 4 c., 10 c., 20 c., 30 c., 40 c., 50 c., and 5 frs.

## ANJOUAN (SULTANAT D').

1

### 1892. Type 1. *Perf.* 14×13½.

| No. | | Un. |
|---|---|---|
| 1 | 1 c., black on azure .. | 2 |
| 2 | 2 c., brown on buff .. | 2 |
| 3 | 4 c., purple-brn. on grey | 2 |
| 4 | 5 c., green on pale green | 2 |
| 5 | 10 c., black on lilac .. | 4 |
| 6 | 15 c., blue .. .. | 6 |
| 7 | 20 c., red on green .. | 8 |
| 8 | 25 c., black on rose .. | 8 |
| 9 | 30 c., cinnamon on drab. | 10 |

| No. | | Un. | Used. |
|---|---|---|---|
| 10 | 40 c., red on yellow .. | 12 | |
| 11 | 50 c., carmine on rose .. | 16 | |
| 12 | 75 c., brown on orange.. | 25 | |
| 13 | 1 fr., olive-gn. on toned | 30 | |

Complete set of 13, unused, $1.10.

In the above set, as well as in those of the same type that follow, the 15 c., blue, is on paper with a *quadrillé* pattern.

**1900.** *Same type and perf. Colours changed.*

| 14 | 10 c., rose-red .. .. | 4 |
|---|---|---|
| 15 | 15 c., grey .. .. | 6 |
| 16 | 25 c., blue .. .. | 8 |
| 17 | 50 c., brown on azure .. | 16 |

In this set, as well as in those simultaneously issued for other colonies, the name is in *blue* on the 10 c., and in *red* on the 15 c., 25 c., and 50 c.

## ANNAM AND TONQUIN.

A&T 1

A & T 5

1 2

**1888.** Commerce Type. *Perf.* 14×13½. *Surcharged in black as* Types 1 *and* 2.

| 1 | 1 on 2 c., brown .. | 36 | 36 |
|---|---|---|---|
| 2 | 1 on 4 c., purple-brown. | 25 | 30 |
| 3 | 5 on 10 c., blk. on lilac | 36 | 36 |

A&T 1

A&T 5

3 4

*Surcharged as* Types 3 *and* 4.

| 4 | 1 on 2 c., brown .. | 30 | 50 |
|---|---|---|---|
| 5 | 1 on 4 c., purple-brown | 36 | |
| 6 | 5 on 10 c., blk. on lilac | 25 | 36 |

*Similar surcharge, but with hyphen "-" in place of "&."*

| 7 | 1 on 2 c., brown | | |
|---|---|---|---|
| 8 | 1 on 4 c., purple-brown | | |
| 9 | 5 on 10 c., blk. on lilac | 1.50 | |

There are three distinct types of the figure "1," and several minor varieties of the letters "A" and "T."

This colony is now included in INDO CHINA.

| No. | | Un. | Used. |
|---|---|---|---|

## BENIN.

BENIN

1

**1892-93.** Commerce Type. *Perf.* 14×13½. *Surcharged with* Type 1.

*(a) In* black.

| 1 | 1 c., black on azure .. | 4.35 | |
|---|---|---|---|
| 2 | 2 c., brown on buff .. | 4.35 | |
| 3 | 4 c., purple-brn. on grey | 5.00 | |
| 4 | 5 c., green on pale green | 30 | |
| 5 | 10 c., black on lilac .. | 1.00 | |
| 6 | 15 c., blue on pale blue.. | 50 | |
| 7 | 20 c., red on green .. | 2.50 | |
| 8 | 25 c., black on rose .. | 1.25 | |
| 9 | 30 c., cinnamon on drab. | 1.85 | |
| 10 | 35 c., black on orange .. | 5.00 | |
| 11 | 40 c., red on buff .. | 4.35 | |
| 12 | 75 c., rose-carmine on rose | 5.00 | |
| 13 | 1 fr., olive-grn. on toned | 5.00 | |

*(b) In* blue.

| 14 | 5 c., green on pale green | |
|---|---|---|
| 14a | 15 c., blue on pale blue | |
| 14b | 25 c., black on rose .. | |

*(c) In* red.

| 15 | 15 c., blue on pale blue . | 2.50 |
|---|---|---|

There is a variety of the surcharge on all values with accent over "E" of "BENIN." The surcharge is also found diagonal, and inverted on all values.

O1

2

**1892.** *With name, as above, in* black, *and surcharged in addition as* Type 2.

*(a) In* red.

| 16 | O1 on 5 c., green .. | 3.00 | |
|---|---|---|---|
| 17 | 40 on 15 c., blue .. | 3.75 | |
| 18 | 75 on 15 c. ,, .. | | |

*(b) In* black.

| 19 | 75 on 15 c., blue .. | 20.00 |
|---|---|---|

3

**1893.** Type 3. *Perf.* 14×13½.

| 20 | 1 c., black on azure .. | 8 | 8 |
|---|---|---|---|
| 21 | 2 c., brown on buff .. | 8 | 8 |
| 22 | 4 c., purple-bn. on grey | 6 | |
| 23 | 5 c., green on pale green | 4 | |

| No. | | Un. | Used. |
|---|---|---|---|
| 24 | 10 c., black on lilac .. | | |
| 25 | 15 c., blue .. .. | 6 | |
| 26 | 20 c., red on green .. | 8 | |
| 27 | 25 c., black on rose .. | 25 | |
| 28 | 30 c., cinnamon on drab | 12 | 16 |
| 29 | 40 c., red on yellow .. | 16 | |
| 30 | 50 c., carm. on rose .. | 25 | |
| 31 | 75 c., ,, orange .. | 1.10 | 1.10 |
| 32 | 1 fr., olive-gn. on toned | 1.10 | 1.10 |

4

**1894.** Type 4. *Perf.* 14×13½.

| 33 | 1 c., black on azure .. | 2 | |
|---|---|---|---|
| 34 | 2 c., brown on buff .. | 2 | |
| 35 | 4 c., purple-bn. on grey | 2 | |
| 36 | 5 c., green on pale green | 4 | 4 |
| 37 | 10 c., black on lilac .. | 6 | 8 |
| 38 | 15 c., blue .. .. | 6 | 6 |
| 39 | 20 c., red on green .. | 10 | 12 |
| 40 | 25 c., black on rose .. | 10 | 10 |
| 41 | 30 c., cinnamon on drab.. | 12 | |
| 42 | 40 c., red on yellow .. | 16 | 25 |
| 43 | 50 c., carmine on rose.. | 18 | |
| 44 | 75 c., brown on orange.. | 25 | |
| 45 | 1 fr., olive-gn. on tinted | 30 | 30 |

UNPAID LETTER STAMPS.

**1894.** *Colonial* Type U. *Imperf.*
*Surcharged with* Type 1, *in* black.

| 201 | 5 c., black .. .. .. | 1.85 | 1.85 |
|---|---|---|---|
| 202 | 10 c., ,, .. .. | 1.50 | |
| 203 | 20 c., ,, .. .. | 1.50 | |
| 204 | 30 c., ,, .. .. | 1.85 | |

The surcharge is horizontal on the 5 c.,
vertically upwards on the 10 c. and 30 c.,
and vertically downwards on the 20 c.

### COCHIN CHINA.

**5**
1

**5**
**C. CH.**
2

**5**
3

**1886.** Commerce Type. *Perf.* 14×13½.

λ. Type. *Surcharged in* black.

| 1 | 5 on 25 c., ochre on yellow .. .. | 1.50 | 1.00 |
|---|---|---|---|
| 2 | 5 on 2 c., brn. on buff | 12 | |

| No. Type. | | Un. | Used. |
|---|---|---|---|
| 3 | 2 | 5 on 25 c., ochre on yellow .. .. | 25 | 25 |
| 4 | ,, | 5 on 25 c., blk. on rose | | |
| 5 | 3 | 5 on 25 c., ,, | 12 | 25 |

*Double surcharge.*

| 6 | 2 | 5 on 25 c., blk. on rose | | |
|---|---|---|---|
| 7 | 2-3 | 5 on 25 c., ,, ,, .. | | |

*Similar to last, but* Type 2 *twice.*

| 8 | 2-3 | 5 on 25 c., blk. on rose |
|---|---|---|

*Surcharged* "COCHIN-CHINA," *in* red,
*and* Type 2, *in* black.

| 9 | 2 | 5 on 2 c., brn. on buff |
|---|---|---|

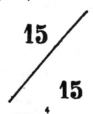

4

In 1888 the 30 c., cinnamon, was surcharged with Type 4, so that it could be
severed diagonally and each half used for
15 c., but a consignment of the 15 c.
blue, arrived before they were put in
issue. Specimens have been postmarked
by favour. The half-stamp can be supplied
unused or postmarked for 25 c., or entire,
50 c. Unpaid Letter stamps with a diagonal
surcharge "COCHIN-CHINE" were never
issued.

This colony is now included in INDO
CHINA.

### COMORO ISLANDS.

(*See* GRAND COMORO.)

### DAHOMEY AND DEPENDENCIES.

1

**1899.**

Type 1. *Perf.* 14×13½.

| 1 | 25 c., black on rose .. | 8 |
|---|---|---|

No.                                    Un.   Used.

### 1900-1.

*Same type and perf.*

| | | | Un. | Used. |
|---|---|---|---|---|
| 2 | 1 c., black on azure | .. | | 2 |
| 3 | 10 c., rose-red | .. | .. | 4 |
| 4 | 15 c., grey | .. | .. | 6 |
| 5 | 25 c., blue | .. | .. | 8 |
| 6 | 50 c., brown on azure | .. | | 16 |

## DIEGO SUAREZ.

**1**

### 1890.

Commerce Type.   *Perf.* 14 × 13½.

*Surcharged with* Type 1, *in* violet.

| | | | Un. | Used. |
|---|---|---|---|---|
| 1 | 15 on 1 c., black on azure | 2.50 | 1.00 |
| 2 | 15 on 5 c., green.. | .. | — | 1.25 |
| 3 | 15 on 10 c., blk. on lilac. | — | 1.50 |
| 4 | 15 on 20 c., red on green | 2.00 | |
| 5 | 15 on 25 c., black on rose | 1.25 | 50 |

This surcharge varies in position, but is always more or less sideways.

**2**

**3**

**4**

**5**

No. Type.   **1890.**  *Imperf.*

| | | | | | Un. | Used. |
|---|---|---|---|---|---|---|
| 6 | 2 | 1 c., black | .. | .. | 1.50 | 1.00 |
| 7 | 3 | 5 c. ,, | .. | .. | 1.50 | |
| 8 | 4 | 15 c. ,, | .. | .. | 1.00 | 50 |
| 9 | 5 | 25 c. ,, | .. | .. | 75 | 75 |

Very good forgeries of these four stamps exist, and are sold at cheap prices.

No.                                    Un.   Used.

**6**

**1891.**   Type 6.   *Imperf.*

| | | | Un. | Used. |
|---|---|---|---|---|
| 10 | 5 centimes, black | .. | | |

**7**

**1891.**   Commerce Type.   *Perf.* 14 × 13½.
*Surcharged with* Type 7.

| | | | Un. | Used. |
|---|---|---|---|---|
| 11 | 5 c., in *red*, on 10 c., black on lilac | .. | 1.50 | 1.50 |
| 12 | 5 c., in *black*, on 20 c., red on green .. | .. | | |

*Surcharge inverted.*

| | | | | |
|---|---|---|---|---|
| 12a | 5 c., in *black*, on 20 c., red on green .. | .. | | |

**8**

**1892.**   *Surcharged with* Type 8.
(a) *In* red.

| | | | Un. | Used. |
|---|---|---|---|---|
| 13 | 1 c., black on azure | .. | 62 | 62 |
| 14 | 30 c., cinnamon .. | .. | — | 9.00 |
| 15 | 1 fr., olive-green | .. | 1.25 | 1.25 |

*Surcharge inverted.*

| | | | |
|---|---|---|---|
| 15a | 30 c., cinnamon | .. | |

(b) *In* black.

| | | | Un. | Used. |
|---|---|---|---|---|
| 16 | 2 c., brown on buff | .. | 50 | |
| 17 | 4 c., purple-bn. on grey | 62 | |
| 18 | 5 c., green on pale green | 50 | |
| 19 | 10 c., black on rose | 50 | |
| 20 | 15 c., blue | .. | 50 | 50 |
| 21 | 20 c., red on green | 50 | |
| 22 | 25 c., black on rose | .. | 45 | 36 |
| 22a | 30 c., cinnamon .. | | |
| 23 | 35 c., black on orange .. | — | 6.25 |
| 24 | 75 c., carmine on rose .. | 1.25 | 1.25 |

*Variety.   Surcharge inverted.*

| | | |
|---|---|---|
| 24a | 5 c., green on pale green | |
| 24b | 35 c., black on orange .. | |

| No. | | Un. | Used. |
|---|---|---|---|

9

**1892.** Type 9.  *Perf.* 14×13½.

| 25 | 1 c., black on azure .. | 4 | 2 |
| 26 | 2 c., brown on buff .. | 4 | 2 |
| 27 | 4 c., purple-brn. on grey | 6 | 4 |
| 28 | 5 c., green on pale green | 2 | 2 |
| 29 | 10 c., black on lilac .. | 4 | |
| 30 | 15 c., blue .. .. | | 6 |
| 31 | 20 c., red on green .. | 25 | |
| 32 | 25 c., black on rose .. | 10 | 6 |
| 33 | 30 c., cinnamon on drab . | 25 | |
| 34 | 40 c., red on yellow .. | 25 | |
| 35 | 50 c., carmine on rose .. | 36 | |
| 36 | 75 c., brown on orange.. | 75 | |
| 37 | 1 fr., olive-grn. on toned | 1.00 | |

In 1894 the series for "Diego Suarez et Dependances" was replaced by three series, for "Diego Suarez," "Nossi Bé," and "Ste. Marie de Madagascar."

10

**1894.** Type 10.  *Perf.* 14×13½.

| 38 | 1 c., black on azure .. | 2 | |
| 39 | 2 c., brown .. .. | 2 | |
| 40 | 4 c., pur.-brown on grey | 2 | |
| 41 | 5 c., green on pale green | 2 | |
| 42 | 10 c., black on lilac .. | 4 | |
| 43 | 15 c., blue .. .. | 6 | |
| 44 | 20 c., red on green .. | 6 | 6 |
| 45 | 25 c., blk. on rose .. | 8 | 8 |
| 46 | 30 c., cinnamon .. .. | 10 | |
| 47 | 40 c., red on yellow .. | 12 | 12 |
| 48 | 50 c., carmine on rose .. | 16 | 16 |
| 49 | 75 c., brown on orange .. | 25 | |
| 50 | 1 fr., olive-grn. on toned | 30 | |

UNPAID LETTER STAMPS.

51                                52

**No. Type.    1891.** *Imperf.*

| 'o1 | 51 | 5 c., violet .. .. | 2.50 | |
| 12 | 52 | 50 c., black on buff . | 2.50 | 2.00 |

| No. | | | Un. | Used |
|---|---|---|---|---|

**1892.** *Colonial* Type U. *Surcharged with* Type 8, *in* black. *Imperf.*

| 103 | 1 c., black .. .. | 1.25 | 1.00 |
| 104 | 2 c., ,, .. .. | 1.25 | |
| 105 | 3 c., ,, .. .. | 1.25 | |
| 106 | 4 c., ,, .. .. | 1.25 | 1.25 |
| 107 | 5 c., ,, .. .. | 1.00 | 1.00 |
| 108 | 10 c., ,, .. .. | 30 | |
| 109 | 15 c., ,, .. .. | 30 | 5 |
| 110 | 20 c., ,, .. .. | — | 1.25 |
| 111 | 30 c., ,, .. .. | 1.25 | 1.00 |
| 112 | 60 c., ,, .. .. | | |
| 113 | 1 fr., brown .. .. | | |

These stamps are now all obsolete, the new series for MADAGASCAR AND DEPENDENCIES being used here.

**DJIBOUTI.**

1                                2

**1894.** *Obock* Type 5.  *Perf.* 14×13½. No. Type. *Surcharged in* black.

| 1 | 1 | 5 c., green .. .. | 25 | 50 |
| 2 | 2 | 5 c., ,, .. .. | | 3.75 |

As No. 2 was issued for use in both Obock and Djibouti, the word "Obock" was not obliterated.

3

**1894.** *The same surcharged with* Types 3 *and* 4. *Name in* blue, *and value in* black.

3 | 3 | 25 on 2 c., brn. on buff  1.50

*Error.* "25" *omitted.*

3a | 3 | (25) on 2 c., brn. on buff  6.25

4

*Name in* red, *and value in* blue.

4 | 4 | 50 on 1 c., blk. on azure  1.50

No. Type. | Un. | Used.

*Error.* " 5 " *for* " 50."
4a | 4 | 5 on 1 c., blk. on azure

|

8

# DJIBOUTI
5

**1894.** *Obock* Type 7 *surcharged in* blue.

5 | 5 | 1 fr. on 5 fr., rose .. | 3.15
6 | " | 5 fr., rose .. | .. | 7.50

In the last stamp, the figure "I" of the surcharge is omitted, as this would cancel the original value.

6

9

18 | 8 | 1 fr., olive-gn. & blk. | 62 | 75
19 | " | 2 fr., grey & rose .. | 1.00
20 | 9 | 5 fr., rose & blue .. | 2.50

7

**1894-1902.** *Quadrillé paper. Imperf.*
*The central design is in the second colour.*

7 | 6 | 1 c., black & claret | 4 | 12
8 | " | 2 c., claret & black. | 4 |
9 | " | 4 c., brown & blue . | 8 | 12
10 | " | 5 c., blue-gn. & red | 4 | 12
10a | " | 5 c., yellow-green.. | 25 |
11 | " | 10 c., brown & green | 18 |
12 | 7 | 15 c., lilac & green.. | 25 |
13 | " | 25 c., blue & rose .. | 16 |
14 | " | 30 c., olive-brn. & rose | 30 | 50
15 | " | 40 c., yellow & blue. | 25 |
16 | " | 50 c., blue & carmine | 30 |
17 | " | 75 c., mauve & orange | 45 | 50

*Variety. Thick card paper.*

17a | 6 | 4 c., brown and blue | 5.00

10

21 | 10 | 25 fr., rose and blue . | 8.75
22 | " | 50 fr., blue and rose . | 15.00

The apparent perforation in the illustrations is part of the engraving.

11

**1899.**

Type 6 *surcharged with* Type 11, *in* black.

23 | 0.40 on 4 c., brn. and blue | — | 62

| No. Type. | | | *Un.* | *Used.* |
|---|---|---|---|---|

# 0.05
**12**

25 JAN., **1902.** *Stamps of 1894–1900 surcharged as* Type **12**, *in* blue (*in* black *on* No. 27).

| 24 | 7 | 0.05 on 75 c., mauve and orange .. | 45 | |
| 25 | 8 | 0,10 on 1 fr., olive-green and black .. | 50 | |
| 26 | ,, | 0.40 on 2 fr., grey-brown and rose .. | 5.00 | |
| 27 | 9 | 0,75 on 5 fr., rose and blue .. .. | 7.50 | 7.50 |

*Error.*

| 28 | | 0·05 on 75 c., mauve and orange .. .. | | |

*Variety. Without point.*

| 28*a* | | 0 10 on 1 fr., olive-green and black .. .. | | |

*Surcharge inverted.*

| 28*b* | | 0 10 on 1 fr., olive-green and black .. | | |

*Stamp of Obock*, Type **8**, *surcharged with* Type **12**, *in* blue.

| 28*c* | | 0·05 on 75 c., mauve and orange .. .. .. | | |

# 5

# CENTIMES
**13**

*Stamps of Obock surcharged as* Type **13**, *in* black.

| 29 | | 5 c. on 25 fr., brn. & blue | 1.50 | 1.25 |
| 30 | | 10 c. on 50 fr., lake & grn. | 1.50 | 1.50 |

*Error. "01" for* 10.

| 30*a* | | 01 c. on 50 fr., lake and green .. .. .. | | 10.00 |

# 5 centimes
**14**

*tmp of* 1894, Type **7**, *surcharged with* Type **14**, *in* black.

| | | 5 c. on 40 c., yell. & blue | 18 | 25 |

| No. Type. | | | *Un.* | *Used.* |
|---|---|---|---|---|

# 10
**CENTIMES**
**DJIBOUTI**
**15**

# 10
**CENTIMES**
**DJIBOUTI**
**16**

# 10
**CENTIMES**
**DJIBOUTI**
**17**

*Stamps of Obock surcharged in* red (R) *or* black (B).

| 32 | 15 | 10 c. on 25 c., black and blue (R) .. | 25 | |
| 33 | 16 | 10 c. on 2 fr., lilac and orange (B) .. | 1.00 | 1.00 |
| 34 | 17 | 10 c. on 10 fr., red and mauve (B) .. | 1.00 | 1.00 |

*Error. "*DJIBOUTI*" inverted.*

| 35 | 16 | 10 c. on 2 fr., lilac and orange .. | 7.50 | |

*Error. Surcharge inverted.*

| 35*a* | | 10 c. on 25 c., black and blue (R) .. .. | | |

JULY, **1902.** *Stamp of Obock surcharged in* black.

| 36 | | 5 c. on 30 c., bistre & grn. | 25 | |

*Stamp of Djibouti surcharged as* Type **14**, *in* black.

| 37 | | 10 c. on 50 c., blue & carm. | 36 | |

*Error. Surcharge inverted.*

| 38 | | 10 c. on 50 c., blue and carmine .. .. | 3.75 | |

(For later issues see FRENCH SOMALI COAST.)

No.     *Un. Used.*

No.     *Un. Used.*

## FRENCH CONGO.

### Congo Français

# 5 c.

1

**1891.** Commerce Type. *Perf.* 14×13½.
*Surcharged as* Type **1**, *with stop after*
"c."

#### (a) *In* black.

| | | | |
|---|---|---|---|
| 1 | 5 c. on 1 c., blk on azure | 1.25 | 1.25 |
| 2 | 5 c. on 15 c., blue .. | 1.50 | 1.50 |
| 3 | 5 c. on 25 c., bk. on rose | 1.85 | 1.25 |

#### (b) *In* red.

| | | | |
|---|---|---|---|
| 4 | 5 c. on 1 c., bk. on azure | — | 40.00 |

**1892.**
*Similar to last, but name thus* "COngo."
*Surcharged in* black.

| | | | |
|---|---|---|---|
| 5 | 5 c. on 20 c., red on gn. | — | 5.25 |
| 6 | 5 c. on 25 c., blk. on rose | — | 2.00 |
| 7 | 10 c. on 25 c.  ,, | 2.50 | 1.00 |
| 8 | 10 c. on 40 c., red on yell. | — | 6.00 |
| 9 | 15 c. on 25 c., blk. on rose | 1.25 | 90 |

*Surcharge inverted.*

| | | | |
|---|---|---|---|
| 10 | 10 c. on 25 c., blk. on rose | 3.75 | 3.00 |

*Varieties. Surcharge sideways.*

#### (a) *Reading upwards.*

| | | | |
|---|---|---|---|
| 11 | 5 c. on 25 c., blk. on rose | — | 1.00 |
| 12 | 15 c. on 25 c.  ,, | — | 1.10 |

#### (b) *Reading downwards.*

| | | | |
|---|---|---|---|
| 12a | 5 c. on 25 c., blk. on rose | | |
| 12b | 15 c. on 25 c.  ,, | 1.60 | |

### 5 c.

2

**1892.** *Surcharged as* Type **2**, *no stop
after* "c", *in* black.

| | | | |
|---|---|---|---|
| 13 | 5 c. on 25 c., blk. on rose | 1.50 | |
| 14 | 10 c. on 25 c.  ,, | — | 2.00 |
| 15 | 15 c. on 25 c.  ,, | — | 1.25 |

*Same surcharge reading upwards.*

| | | | |
|---|---|---|---|
| 16 | 5 c. on 25 c., blk. on rose | 2.00 | |
| 17 | 10 c. on 25 c.  ,, | 1.75 | 1.50 |

### 5 c.

3

20 Nov., **1892.** *Colonial* Type **u.**
*Imperf. Surcharged as* Type **3.**

#### (a) *In* red.

| | | | |
|---|---|---|---|
| 18 | 5 c. on 5 c., black .. | 1.50 | |
| 19 | 5 c. on 20 c.  ,, .. | 1.50 | 1.50 |
| 20 | 5 c. on 30 c.  ,, .. | 1.50 | 1.50 |

*Surcharge inverted (upwards).*

| | | | |
|---|---|---|---|
| 20a | 5 c. on 5 c., black .. | 3.00 | |
| 21 | 5 c. on 20 c.  ,, | — | 3.00 |
| 21a | 5 c. on 30 c.  ,, | | |

#### (b) *In* black (*downwards*).

| | | | |
|---|---|---|---|
| 22 | 10 c. on 1 fr., brown .. | 3.15 | 2.50 |

*Surcharge inverted (upwards).*

| | | | |
|---|---|---|---|
| 23 | 10 c. on 1 fr., brown .. | 2.00 | 1.25 |

*Surcharge horizontal.*

| | | | |
|---|---|---|---|
| 23a | 10 c. on 1 fr., brown .. | | |

4

**1892.** Type **4.** *Perf.* 14×13½.

| | | | |
|---|---|---|---|
| 24 | 1 c., black on azure .. | 2 | 4 |
| 25 | 2 c., brown on buff .. | 2 | |
| 26 | 4 c., purple-brn. on grey | 2 | |
| 27 | 5 c., green on pale green | 2 | |
| 28 | 10 c., black on lilac .. | 4 | |
| 29 | 15 c., blue .. .. | 8 | |
| 30 | 20 c., red on green .. | | |
| 31 | 25 c., black on rose .. | 12 | |
| 32 | 30 c., cinnamon on drab . | 10 | |
| 33 | 40 c., red on yellow .. | 12 | |
| 34 | 50 c., carmine on rose .. | 16 | |
| 35 | 75 c., brown on orange . | 25 | |
| 36 | 1 fr., olive-grn. on toned | 30 | 25 |

*Name in* black *and also in* blue.

| | | | |
|---|---|---|---|
| 36a | 4 c., purple-brn. on grey | 2.50 | |

*Name twice in* blue.

| | | | |
|---|---|---|---|
| 36b | 10 c., black on lilac .. | 2.50 | 2.50 |

| | | Un. | Used. |
|---|---|---|---|

No.

**1900.** Type 4 *surcharged* "Valeur" *and figure of value below.*

(a) *In* black.

| | | | |
|---|---|---|---|
| 36c | 5 on 20 c., red on green | | |
| 36d | 15 on 30 c., cinnamon .. | | |

(b) *In* blue.

| | | | |
|---|---|---|---|
| 36e | 15 on 30 c., cinnamon .. | | |

**1900.** *Same type and perf. Colours changed.*

| 37 | 10 c., rose-red .. .. | 4 |
|---|---|---|
| 38 | 15 c., grey .. .. | 6 |
| 39 | 25 c., blue .. .. | 8 |
| 40 | 50 c., brown on azure .. | 16 |

These stamps are stated to have been issued in error, the new set given below having previously appeared.

| 5 | | 6 |
|---|---|---|

**1900.** *Perf.* 11.

Type **5.** *Wmk.* Type **6.**

| 41 | 1 (c.), purple and grey . | 2 |
|---|---|---|
| 42 | 2 (c.), brown & yellow . | 2 |
| 43 | 4 (c.), vermilion & grey | 2 |
| 44 | 5 (c.), grn. & grey-green | 2 |
| 45 | 10 (c.), red and pale red . | 4 |
| 46 | 15 (c.), violet & olive-grn. | 6 |

| 7 | | 8 |
|---|---|---|

Type **7.** *Wmk.* Type **8.**

| 47 | 20 (c.), green & pale red | 6 |
|---|---|---|
| 48 | 25 (c.), blue & pale blue. | 8 |
| 49 | 30 (c.), carmine & yellow | 10 |
| 50 | 40 (c.), chestnut & green | 12 |
| 51 | 50 (c.), violet and lilac .. | 16 |
| 52 | 75 (c.), claret and orange | 25 |

---

| | | Un. | Used. |
|---|---|---|---|

No.

| 9 | | 10 |
|---|---|---|

Type **9.** *Wmk.* Type **10.**

| 53 | 1 f., drab & slate-green | 30 |
|---|---|---|
| 54 | 2 f., carm. & grey-brn. | 62 |
| 55 | 5 f., orange and black . | 1.40 |

*Error. Printed in colours of* 10 c.

| 56 | 2 c., red and pale red .. | 7.50 |
|---|---|---|

*Imperf.*

| 57 | 2 c., brown and yellow | 3.15 |
|---|---|---|
| 58 | 40 c., chestnut and green | 3.75 |
| 59 | 2 fr., carm. & grey-brn. | 4.35 |

**1903.** *Stamps of* 1900 *surcharged in* black.

| 60 | 5 on 30 (c.), carmine and yellow .. .. | |
|---|---|---|
| 61 | 10 on 2 fr., carmine and grey-brown .. .. | |

## FRENCH GUIANA.

Types G. Ceres (large figures), *and* H. Peace and Commerce, *imperf.*, *and* J, Commerce, *perf.* 14×13½.

Dec 1.886.
CUY FRANÇ.
**0 05**

1

**1886.** *Surcharged with* Type 1, *in* black.

| No. | Type. | | | |
|---|---|---|---|---|
| 1 | H | 005 on 2 c., green .. | — | 6.55 |
| 2 | J | 005 on 2 c., brown .. | 6.25 | 6.55 |

*Variety.* (a) *With* "f" *after first* "0 as in* Type **2.**

| 3 | H | of 05 on 2 c., green.. | 3.75 |
|---|---|---|---|
| 4 | J | of 05 on 2 c., brown . | 6.25 |

(b) "GUY. FRANC." *as in* Type 3.

| 4a | H | 005 on 2 c., green .. | |
|---|---|---|---|

There is usually an accent on the "e" of "Déc," and stops after "Déc." and "GUY."

| No. Type. | Un. | Used. |
|---|---|---|

**AV 20 20**

**GUY. FRANC**

**0ᶠ 20**

**2**

**1887.** *Surcharged as Type 2, in black.*

| 5 | H | 0·05 on 2 c., green .. | | |
|---|---|---|---|---|
| 6 | " | 0·20 on 35 c., black on orange .. | 2.50 | 2.50 |
| 7 | " | of 0·5 on 2 c., green.. | 1.85 | |
| 7a | " | of 20 on 35 c., black on orange .. | 5.00 | |
| 8 | G | 0·25 on 30 c., drab .. | 1.25 | |

On Nos. 7, 7a, and 8 the inverted V in the surcharge has been corrected.

**DÉC. 1887.**

**GUY. FRANC**

**5ˢ**

**3**

Dec., 1887.
*Surcharged with Type 3, in black.*

| 9 | G | 5 c. on 30 c., drab . | 1.25 |
|---|---|---|---|
| 10 | H | 5 c. on 30 c., cinnam. | |

**Fevrier 1888**

**GUY. FRAN.**

**5**

**4**

**Fevrier 1888.**

**GUY. FRANC**

**10**

**5**

**1888.**
*Surcharged as Types 4 and 5, in black.*

| 11 | G | 5 on 30 c., drab .. | 1.25 | |
|---|---|---|---|---|
| 12 | H | 10 on 75 c., rose-car. | | |
| 13 | " | 10 on 75 c., deep car. | 1.85 | 2.10 |

The figure "5" in the first surcharge is only 4 mm. high.

**GUYANE**

**6**

8 Feb., 1892.
*Surcharged with Type 6, in black.*

| 14 | G | 30 c., drab .. .. | 90 | |
|---|---|---|---|---|
| 15 | H | 2 c., green .. .. | 7.50 | |
| 16 | " | 35 c., blk. on orange | 15.00 | 15.00 |

| No. Type. | Un. | Used. |
|---|---|---|

| 17 | H | 40 c., red on yellow . | 90 | 1.00 |
|---|---|---|---|---|
| 18 | " | 75 c., deep carmine . | 1.25 | 1.50 |
| 19 | " | 1 fr., olive-green on toned .. .. | 1.25 | |
| 20 | J | 1 c., black on azure | 10 | |
| 21 | " | 2 c., brown on buff. | 15 | |
| 22 | " | 4 c., purple-bn. on gy. | 36 | |
| 23 | " | 5 c., gn. on pale gn. | 12 | |
| 24 | " | 10 c., black on lilac . | 18 | |
| 25 | " | 15 c., blue .. .. | 25 | |
| 26 | " | 20 c., red on green .. | 30 | |
| 27 | " | 25 c., black on rose . | 25 | 25 |
| 28 | " | 30 c., cinnamon on drb. | 50 | 62 |
| 29 | " | 35 c., black on orange | 1.00 | |
| 30 | " | 40 c., red on yellow . | | |
| 31 | " | 75 c., carmine .. | 1.10 | |
| 32 | " | 1 fr., olive-green on toned .. .. | 1.25 | |

*Surcharge inverted.*

| 33 | H | 75 c., rose-carmine . | |
|---|---|---|---|
| 34 | " | 1 fr., olive-green on toned .. .. | |
| 35 | J | 10 c., black on lilac . | |
| 36 | " | 40 c., red on yellow . | |

Most of these stamps exist either with or without stop after "GUYANE."

**GUYANE DEC 92**

**0·05**

**7**

**1892.** *Surcharged with Type 7, in black.*

| 37 | J | 0·05 on 15 c., blue .. | |
|---|---|---|---|
| 37a | " | of 0·5 on 15 c. " .. | 50 |

**8**

**1892–1900.** *Type 8. Perf. 14 × 13½.*

| 38 | 1 c., black on azure .. | 2 |
|---|---|---|
| 39 | 2 c., brown on buff .. | 2 |
| 40 | 4 c., purple-bn. on grey | 2 |
| 41 | 5 c., green on pale green | 2 |
| 42 | 5 c., bright yellow-green | |
| 43 | 10 c., black on lilac .. | 4 |
| 44 | 15 c., blue .. .. | 6 |
| 45 | 20 c., red on green .. | 6 |
| 46 | 25 c., black on rose .. | 8 |
| 47 | 30 c., cinnamon on drab | 10 |
| 48 | 40 c., red on yellow .. | 12 |
| 49 | 50 c., carmine on rose .. | 16 |
| 50 | 75 c., brown on orange .. | 25 |
| 51 | 1 fr., olive-gn. on toned | 30 |

| No. | | | Un. | Used. |
|---|---|---|---|---|
| | *Name double.* | | | |
| 51*a* | 4 c., purple-brn. on grey | | 1.85 | |

**1900-2.** *Same type and perf.*
*Colours changed.*

| | | | | |
|---|---|---|---|---|
| 52 | 10 c., rose-red | .. | .. | 4 |
| 53 | 15 c., grey | .. | .. | 6 |
| 54 | 25 c., blue | .. | .. | 8 |
| 55 | 50 c., brown on azure | .. | | 16 |
| 56 | 2 fr., violet on lilac | .. | | 55 |

## FRENCH GUINEA.

**1892.** Type 1. *Perf.* 14 × 13½.

| | | | |
|---|---|---|---|
| 1 | 1 c., black on azure | .. | 2 |
| 2 | 2 c., brown on buff | .. | 2 |
| 3 | 4 c., purple-brn. on grey | | 2 |
| 4 | 5 c., green on pale green | | 2 |
| 5 | 10 c., black on lilac | .. | 4 |
| 6 | 15 c., blue | .. | 6 |
| 7 | 20 c., red on green | .. | 6 |
| 8 | 25 c., black on rose | .. | 8 |
| 9 | 30 c., cinnamon on drab | | 10 |
| 10 | 40 c., red on yellow | .. | 12 |
| 11 | 50 c., carmine on rose | .. | 16 |
| 12 | 75 c., brown on orange | .. | 25 |
| 13 | 1 fr., olive-gn. on toned | | 30 |

**1900.** *Same type and perf.*
*Colours changed.*

| | | | |
|---|---|---|---|
| 14 | 10 c., rose-red | .. | 4 |
| 15 | 15 c., grey | .. | 6 |
| 16 | 25 c., blue | .. | 8 |
| 17 | 50 c., brown on azure | .. | 16 |

## FRENCH SOMALI COAST.

**1902.** Type 1. *Perf.* 11. *Centre in second colour.*

| | | | |
|---|---|---|---|
| 1 | 1 (c.), lilac and orange | | 2 |
| 2 | 2 „ bistre-brn. & grn. | | 2 |
| 3 | 4 „ blue and carmine | | 2 |
| 4 | 5 „ blue - green and yellow-green . | | 2 |
| 5 | 10 „ carmine & oran. | | 4 |
| 6 | 15 „ orange and blue | | 6 |

| No. | | Un. | Used. |
|---|---|---|---|

Type 2.

| | | | |
|---|---|---|---|
| 7 | 20 (c.), purple and green | | 6 |
| 8 | 25 „ blue and pale blue | | 8 |
| 9 | 30 „ red and black | .. | 10 |
| 10 | 40 „ brn.-yell. & blue | | 12 |
| 11 | 40 „ orange and blue . | | 12 |
| 12 | 50 „ green and pale red | | 16 |
| 13 | 75 „ orange and lilac . | | 20 |

Type 3.

| | | | |
|---|---|---|---|
| 14 | 1 fr., orange-red & lilac | | 26 |
| 15 | 2 „ green & carmine | | 55 |
| 16 | 5 „ orange and blue . | | 1.30 |

*Error.* (i.) *Colours reversed.*

| | | |
|---|---|---|
| 17 | 1 c., orange and lilac .. | |
| 18 | 2 c., grn. & bistre-brn. | |
| 19 | 5 c., yellow-green and blue-green | .. .. |
| 20 | 20 c., green and purple.. | |

(ii.) *Centre inverted.*

| | | |
|---|---|---|
| 21 | 4 c., blue and carmine . | |
| 22 | 20 c., purple and green . | |
| 23 | 25 c., blue and pale blue | |
| 24 | 30 c., red and black | .. |

**1903.** *Same types, wmks., and perf. centres in black.*

| | | | |
|---|---|---|---|
| 25 | 1 (c.), lilac | .. | .. |
| 26 | 2 (c.), brown | .. | .. |
| 27 | 4 (c.), carmine | .. | .. |
| 28 | 5 (c.), green | .. | .. |

| No. | | Un. | Used. |
|---|---|---|---|
| 29 | 10 (c.), carmine .. | .. | |
| 30 | 15 (c.), orange .. | .. | |
| 31 | 20 (c.), purple .. | .. | |
| 32 | 25 (c.), blue .. | .. | |
| 33 | 30 (c.), carmine .. | .. | |
| 34 | 40 (c.), orange .. | .. | |
| 35 | 50 (c.), green .. | .. | |
| 36 | 75 (c.), orange .. | .. | |
| 37 | 1 fr. ,, .. | .. | |
| 38 | 2 fr., green .. | .. | |
| 39 | 5 fr., orange .. | .. | |

## FRENCH SOUDAN.

1

**1894.** Type H, Peace and Commerce.
*Imperf.*
*Surcharged as* Type 1, *in* black.

1 |0.15 c. on 75, rose-carm.

Type J, Commerce. *Perf.* 14×13½.
*Surcharged as* Type 1, *in* black.

2 |0.15 on 75 c., carmine ..
3 |0.25 on 1 fr., olive-green

The line in the middle of the surcharge was put in by hand. It is very doubtful whether No. 1 exists genuine.

2

**1894.** Type 2. *Perf.* 14×13½.

| 4 | 1 c., black on azure .. | 2 |
|---|---|---|
| 5 | 2 c., brown on buff .. | 2 |
| 6 | 4 c., purple-brn. on grey | 2 |
| 7 | 5 c., green on pale green | 2 |
| 8 | 10 c., black on lilac .. | 4 |
| 9 | 15 c., blue .. | 6 |
| 10 | 20 c., red on green .. | 6 |
| 11 | 25 c., black on rose .. | 8 |
| 12 | 30 c., cinnamon on drab . | 10 |
| 13 | 40 c., red on yellow .. | 12 |
| 14 | 50 c., carmine on rose .. | 16 |
| 15 | 75 c., brown on orange .. | 25 |
| 16 | 1 fr., olive-gn. on toned | 30 |

| No. | | Un. | Used. |
|---|---|---|---|

**1900.** *Same type and perf.*
*Colours changed.*

| 17 | 10 c., rose-red .. | .. | 4 |
|---|---|---|---|
| 18 | 15 c., grey .. | .. | 6 |
| 19 | 25 c., blue .. | .. | 8 |
| 20 | 50 c., brown on azure .. | | 16 |

This set is stated to have been issued in error.

## GABOON.

1                2

3

**1886.** Commerce Type. *Perf.* 14×13½.
No. Type. *Surcharged in* black.

| 1 | 1 | 5 on 20 c., red on gn. | 7.50 |
|---|---|---|---|
| 2 | 2 | 10 on 20 c. ,, ,, | 6.25 |
| 3 | 3 | 25 on 20 c. ,, ,, | 1.00 |
| 4 | ,, | 50 on 15 c., blue .. | 15.00 |
| 5 | ,, | 75 on 15 c. ,, | 15.00 |

Varieties may be found differing in the number of dots round "GAB."; in some only 12 dots appear, and in others as many as 56 dots have been counted.

4

**1888–89.** *Surcharged, in* black, *as* Type 4.

| 6 | 15 on 10 c., black on lilac | | |
|---|---|---|---|
| 7 | 15 on 1 fr., olive-green .. | 10.00 | 7.50 |
| 8 | 25 on 5 c., green | .. | 3.75 |
| 9 | 25 on 10 c., black on lilac | — | 12.50 |
| 10 | 25 on 75 c., carmine .. | — | 10.00 |

Reprints of the above surcharges have been made of all five varieties. On the originals the surcharge is in intense black,

No.          *Un. Used.*

and the figure "5" higher than the "1" or "2," while on the reprints the two figures are in line, and the surcharge is less intense in colour. The reprints also exist with official obliterations.

# GABON

5

**1889.** *Colonial* Type v. *Surcharged as* Type **5**, *in* black. *Imperf.*

| | | | | |
|---|---|---|---|---|
| 11 | 15 on 5 c., black | .. | 3.00 | 3.00 |
| 12 | 15 on 30 c. ,, | .. | | |
| 13 | 25 on 20 c. ,, | .. | 1.85 | 2.10 |

6

No. Type. **1889.** *Imperf.*

| | | | | |
|---|---|---|---|---|
| 14 | 6 | 15 c., black on pink . | 7.50 | |
| 15 | ,, | 25 c., black on green | 4.35 | |

This now forms part of French Congo.

## GRAND COMORO.

1

**1897.** Type 1. *Perf.* 14 × 13½.

| | | |
|---|---|---|
| 1 | 1 c., black on azure .. | 2 |
| 2 | 2 c., brown on buff .. | 2 |
| 3 | 4 c., purple-brn. on grey | 2 |
| 4 | 5 c., green on pale green | 2 |
| 5 | 10 c., black on lilac .. | 4 |
| 6 | 15 c., blue .. .. | 6 |
| 7 | 20 c., red on green .. | 6 |
| 8 | 25 c., black on rose .. | 8 |
| 9 | 30 c., cinnamon on drab. | 10 |
| 10 | 40 c., red on yellow .. | 12 |
| 11 | 50 c., carmine on rose .. | 16 |
| 12 | 75 c., brown on orange.. | 25 |
| 13 | 1 fr., olive-grn. on toned | 30 |

No.          *Un. Used.*

**1900.** *Same type and perf).*
*Colours changed.*

| | | | | |
|---|---|---|---|---|
| 14 | 10 c., rose-red | .. | .. | 4 |
| 15 | 15 c., grey | .. | .. | 6 |
| 16 | 25 c., blue | .. | .. | 8 |
| 17 | 50 c., brown on azure | .. | | 16 |

## QUADELOUPE.

1                      2

3

**1884-85.** Peace and Commerce Type.
*Imperf.*

Surcharged as Types 1, 2, *and* 3, *in* black.
No. Type.

| | | | | | |
|---|---|---|---|---|---|
| 1 | 1 | 20 on 30 c., dull brn. | 36 | | |
| 2 | 2 | 20 on 30 c. ,, | 10.00 | | |
| 3 | 1 | 25 on 35 c., bk. on or. | 30 | 50 | |
| 4 | 2 | 25 on 35 c. ,, | 5.00 | | |
| 5 | 3 | 25 on 35 c. ,, | 3.75 | 4.00 | |

*Figures "20". double.*

| | | |
|---|---|---|
| 5a | 1 | 20 on 30 c., dull brown |

4

**1889.** Commerce Type. *Perf.* 14 × 13½.
*Surcharged as* Type **4**, *in* black.

| | | | | |
|---|---|---|---|---|
| 6 | 3 c. on 20 c., red on green | 6 | | |
| 7 | 15 c. on 20 c. ,, ,, | 16 | 16 | |
| 8 | 25 c. on 20 c. ,, ,, | 20 | | |

No. Type. *Un. Used.*

5        6

**1889.** *Surcharged as* Types **5** *and* **6**, *in* black.

| | | | Un. | Used. |
|---|---|---|---|---|
| 9 | 5 | 5 c. on 1 c., black on azure .. .. | 8 | |
| 10 | 6 | 5 c. on 1 c., black on azure .. .. | 6 | 6 |
| 11 | 5 | 10 c. on 40 c., red on yellow .. .. | 36 | |
| 12 | 6 | 10 c. on 40 c., red on yellow .. .. | 30 | |
| 13 | 5 | 15 c. on 20 c., red on gn. | 25 | |
| 14 | 6 | 15 c. on 20 c.    ,, | 36 | |
| 15 | 5 | 25 c. on 30 c., cinnamon | 30 | |
| 16 | 6 | 25 c. on 30 c.    ,, | 36 | |

*Surcharge inverted.*

| | | | | |
|---|---|---|---|---|
| 16a | 5 | 5 c. on 1 c., black on azure .. | | |

There are many other varieties of this surcharge, with both the corner ornaments of the above types in the same frame, parts of the frame mis-set, etc. The setting of each value consists of 25 varieties.

## 5 C.
## G P E
7.

**1890-91.** *Surcharged with* Type **7**, *in* black.

| | | Un. | Used. |
|---|---|---|---|
| 17 | 5 c. on 10 c., blk. on lilac | 6 | 8 |
| 18 | 5 c. on 1 fr., olive-green | 12 | |

## GUBDELOUPE
8

**1891.** Types G, Ceres (large figures), *imperf., and* J, Commerce, *perf.* 14×13½. *Surcharged with* Type **8**, *in* black.

| | | | Un. | Used. |
|---|---|---|---|---|
| 19 | G | 30 c., drab .. .. | 2.00 | |
| 20 | ,, | 80 c., carmine .. | 6.25 | |
| 21 | J | 1 c., black on azure | 4 | 6 |
| 22 | ,, | 2 c., brown on buff | 4 | 6 |
| 23 | ,, | 4 c., purple-brown on grey .. .. | 12 | |
| 24 | ,, | 5 c., green on pale green .. .. | 4 | 4 |

No. Type. *Un. Used.*

| | | | Un. | Used. |
|---|---|---|---|---|
| 25 | J | 10 c., black on lilac . | 8 | |
| 26 | ,, | 15 c., blue .. .. | 12 | 4 |
| 27 | ,, | 20 c., red on green.. | 25 | |
| 28 | ,, | 25 c., black on rose . | 25 | 4 |
| 29 | ,, | 30 c., cinnamon on drab | 50 | |
| 30 | ,, | 35 c., blk. on orange | 50 | |
| 31 | ,, | 40 c., red on yellow . | 50 | |
| 32 | ,, | 75 c., carm. on rose . | 1.10 | |
| 33 | ,, | 1 fr., olive-green on toned .. .. | 1.00 | |

*Variety. Double surcharge.*

| | | | | |
|---|---|---|---|---|
| 33a | J | 2 c., brown on buff | | |
| 33b | ,, | 5 c., green on pale green .. .. | 5.00 | |
| 33c | ,, | 25 c., black on rose . | | |
| 34 | ,, | 30 c., cinnamon on drab .. .. | 5.65 | |

*Surcharge inverted.*

| | | | | |
|---|---|---|---|---|
| 34a | J | 5 c., green on pale green .. .. | 5.00 | |
| 34b | ,, | 25 c., black on rose . | 5.65 | |

*Errors.*

(1) "GNADELOUPE."

| | | | | |
|---|---|---|---|---|
| 35 | G | 30 c., drab .. .. | | |
| 36 | ,, | 80 c., carmine .. | | |
| 37 | J | 1 c., black on azure | 25 | |
| 38 | ,, | 2 c., brown on buff | 36 | |
| 39 | ,, | 4 c., purple-brown on grey .. .. | | |
| 40 | ,, | 5 c., green on pale green .. .. | 50 | |
| 41 | ,, | 10 c., black on lilac . | | |
| 42 | ,, | 15 c., blue .. .. | | |
| 43 | ,, | 20 c., red on green.. | | |
| 44 | ,, | 25 c., black on rose . | | |
| 45 | ,, | 30 c., cinnamon on drab | | |
| 46 | ,, | 35 c., blk. on orange | | |
| 47 | ,, | 40 c., red on yellow . | | |
| 48 | ,, | 75 c., carmine on rose | | |
| 49 | ,, | 1 fr., olive-green on toned .. .. | | |

(2) "GUADELOUEP."

| | | | | |
|---|---|---|---|---|
| 50 | G | 30 c., drab .. .. | | |
| 51 | ,, | 80 c., carmine .. | | |
| 52 | J | 1 c., black on azure | | |
| 53 | ,, | 2 c., brown on buff | | |
| 54 | ,, | 4 c., purple-brown on grey .. .. | | 62 |
| 55 | ,, | 5 c., green on pale green .. .. | | |
| 56 | ,, | 10 c., black on lilac . | | |
| 57 | ,, | 15 c., blue .. .. | | |
| 58 | ,, | 20 c., red on green.. | | |
| 59 | ,, | 25 c., black on rose . | | |
| 60 | ,, | 30 c., cinnamon on drab | | |
| 61 | ,, | 35 c., blk. on orange | | |
| 62 | ,, | 40 c., red on yellow . | | |
| 63 | ,, | 75 c., carm. on rose | | |
| 64 | ,, | 1 fr., olive-green on toned .. .. | | |

G

| No. | Type. | | Un. | Used. |
|---|---|---|---|---|
| | | **(3) "GUADELONPE."** | | |
| 65 | G | 30 c., brown.. .. | | ' |
| 66 | " | 80 c., carmine | | |
| 67 | J | 1 c., black on azure | | |
| 68 | " | 2 c., brown on buff. | 90 | 90 |
| 69 | " | 4 c., purple-brown on grey .. .. | | 62 |
| 70 | " | 5 c., gn. on pale gn. | 75 | |
| 71 | " | 10 c., black on lilac . | 1.00 | |
| 72 | " | 15 c., blue .. .. | 1.50 | |
| 73 | " | 20 c., red on green .. | 1.85 | |
| 74 | " | 25 c., black on rose.. | | |
| 75 | " | 30 c., cinnamon on drab .. .. | | |
| 76 | G | 35 c., black on orange | | |
| 77 | " | 40 c., red on yellow . | | |
| 78 | " | 75 c., carmine on rose | | |
| 79 | " | 1 fr., olive-green on toned .. .. | | |
| | | **(4) "GUADBLOUPE."** | | |
| 80 | G | 30 c., drab .. .. | | |
| 81 | " | 80 c., carmine .. | | |
| 82 | J | 1 c., black on azure | 1.00 | |
| 83 | " | 2 c., brown on buff. | 1.00 | |
| 84 | " | 4 c., purple-brown on grey .. .. | 1.25 | |
| 85 | " | 5 c., gn. on pale gn. | 1.10 | |
| 86 | " | 10 c., black on lilac . | | |
| 87 | " | 15 c., blue .. .. | | |
| 88 | " | 20 c., red on green.. | | |
| 89 | " | 25 c., black on rose.. | | |
| 90 | " | 30 c., cinnamon on drab .. .. | | |
| 91 | " | 35 c., black on orange | | |
| 92 | " | 40 c., red on yellow . | | |
| 93 | " | 75 c., carmine on rose | | |
| 94 | " | 1 fr., olive-green on toned .. .. | | |
| | | **(5) "UADELOUPE."** | | |
| 94a | J | 10 c., black on lilac | | |
| | | **(6) Surcharge inverted.** | | |
| 94b | J | 5 c., gn. on pale gn. | | |
| 94c | " | 25 c., black on rose | | |

Probably varieties 1 to 4 above have
existed on the 5 c. and 25 c., inverted.

9

| | **1892.** Type 9. *Perf.* 14×13½. | | | |
|---|---|---|---|---|
| 95 | 1 c., black on azure .. | 2 | 2 | |
| 96 | 2 c., brown on buff .. | 2 | 4 | |
| 97 | 4 c., purple-brn. on grey | 2 | 4 | |
| 98 | 5 c., grn. on pale green | 4 | 2 | |
| 79 | 10 c., black on lilac .. | 6 | | |

| No. | | Un. | Used. |
|---|---|---|---|
| 100 | 15 c., blue .. .. | 10 | |
| 101 | 20 c., red on green .. | 6 | |
| 102 | 25 c., black on rose ' .. | 8 | |
| 103 | 30 c., cinnamon on drab. | 10 | |
| 104 | 40 c., red on yellow .. | 12 | |
| 105 | 50 c., carmine on rose .. | 16 | |
| 106 | 75 c., brown on orange . | 25 | |
| 107 | 1 fr., olive-grn. on toned | 30 | |

**1900-1.**
*Same type and perf. Colours changed.*

| | | | |
|---|---|---|---|
| 108 | 5 c., bright yellow-green | 2 | |
| 109 | 10 c., rose-red .. .. | 4 | |
| 110 | 15 c., grey .. .. | 6 | |
| 111 | 25 c., blue .. .. | 8 | |
| 112 | 50 c., brown on azure .. | 16 | |

G & D
1 fr.
10

G & D
15
11

G & D
1 fr.
12

Get D
10
13

Get D
10
14

Get D
10
15

Get D
1 0
16

Get D
40
17

Get D
4 0
18

**1903.** PROVISIONALS.
*Varieties of letters.*
(a) "G," "D," and ampersand
Roman, as Type 10.
(b) As (a), but sans-serif ampersand.
(c) As (b), but narrower "G."
(d) As Type 11.
(e) As (d), but sans-serif ampersand.
(f) As Type 12.
(g) As (f), but error "C" for "G."
(h) As (f), but Roman ampersand.
Numerals as in Type 11.

| | | | |
|---|---|---|---|
| 113 | 5 on 30 c., cinnamon (a) | 50 | |
| 114 | 5 on 30 c. ,, (b) | 18 | |

| No. | | Un. | Used. |
|---|---|---|---|
| 115 | 5 on 30 c., cinnamon (c) | | |
| 116 | 5 on 30 c. ,, (d) | 50 | . |
| 117 | 5 on 30 c. ,, (e) | 50 | |
| 118 | 5 on 30 c. ,, (f) | 12 | |
| 119 | 5 on 30 c. ,, (g) | | |
| 120 | 5 on 30 c. ,, (h) | 25 | |
| 121 | 15 on 50 c., carmine (a) | | |
| 122 | 15 on 50 c. ,, (b) | 25 | |
| 123 | 15 on 50 c. ,, (c) | | |
| 124 | 15 on 50 c. ,, (d) | | |
| 125 | 15 on 50 c. ,, (e) | 75 | |
| 126 | 15 on 50 c. ,, (f) | 18 | |
| 127 | 15 on 50 c. ,, (g) | | |
| 128 | 15 on 50 c. ,, (h) | 36 | |

*The same varieties of lettering as above
in combination with—*
  (i.) *Figure "1" as in* Type 10.
  (ii.) *Figure "1" as in* Type 12.

1 fr. on 75 c., black on orange.

| 129 | 1 fr., (a) and (i.) | .. | |
| 130 | 1 fr., (a) and (i.) inverted | .. | |
| 131 | 1 fr., (b) and (i.) | .. | 1.00 |
| 132 | 1 fr., (b) and (i.) inverted | .. | |
| 133 | 1 fr., (c) and (i.) | .. | |
| 134 | 1 fr., (d) and (i.) | .. | |
| 135 | 1 fr., (d) and (i.) inverted | .. | |
| 136 | 1 fr., (e) and (i.) | .. | |
| 137 | 1 fr., (f) and (i.) | .. | 62 |
| 138 | 1 fr., (f) and (i.) inverted | .. | |
| 139 | 1 fr., (f) and (i.) inverted and lines transposed | .. | |
| 139a | 1 fr., (g) and (i.) | .. | |
| 140 | 1 fr., (h) and (i.) | .. | 1.25 |
| 141 | 1 fr., (h) and (i.) inverted | .. | |
| 142 | 1 fr., (f) and (ii.) | .. | |
| 143 | 1 fr., (h) and (ii.) inverted | . | .. |

*Lettering as in* Types **13** *to* **18**.
  (i.) *Numerals as in* Type 13.
  (ii.) *Numerals as in* Type 13, *but "1" inverted.*
  (iii.) *Numerals as in* Type 14.
  (iv.) ,, ,, ,, 15.
  (v.) *Numerals as in* Type 15, *but error "C" for "G."*
  (vi.) *Numerals as in* Type 16.
  (vii.) *Numerals as in* Type 16, *but error "C" for "G."*

| 144 | 10 on 40 c., red on buff (i.) | 18 | |
| 145 | 10 on 40 c. ,, (ii.) | | |
| 146 | 10 on 40 c. ,, (iii.) | 36 | |
| 147 | 10 on 40 c. ,, (iv.) | 25 | |
| 148 | 10 on 40 c. ,, (v.) | | |
| 149 | 10 on 40 c. ,, (vi.) | | |
| 150 | 10 on 40 c. ,, (vii.) | | |

| No. | | Un. | Used. |
|---|---|---|---|
| | (i.) *Numerals as in* Type 17. | | |
| | (ii.) *Numerals as in* Type 17, *but error "C" for "G."* | | |
| | (iii.) *Numerals as in* Type 18. | | |
| | (iv.) *Numerals as in* Type 18, *but error "C" for "G."* | | |
| 151 | 40 on 1 fr., green on toned (i.) | .. | 36 |
| 152 | 40 on 1 fr., green on toned (ii.) | .. | .. |
| 153 | 40 on 1 fr., green on toned (iii.) | .. | 1.85 |
| 154 | 40 on 1 fr., green on toned (iv.) | .. | .. |

## UNPAID LETTER STAMPS.

51    52    53

### 1877-79.

No. Type. *Type-set. Imperf.*

| 301 | 52 | 15 c., black on blue | 75 | 1.00 |
| 302 | 51 | 25 c. ,, white | — | 16.25 |
| 303 | 52 | 30 c. ,, ,, | 75 | 1.00 |
| 304 | 53 | 40 c., black on white | 16.25 | |
| 305 | ,, | 40 c. ,, blue | | |

The sheet consists of 20 varieties (5 rows of 4).

So-called reprints of the 25 c. and 40 c. were made in 1884, but inasmuch as the type was entirely reset and there are only 8 varieties (2 rows of 4), these can only be considered imitations. They are on whiter and thinner paper than the originals.

54

### 1884.

Type 54. *Type-set. Imperf.*

| 306 | 5 c., black on toned | .. | 50 | |
| 307 | 5 c. ,, white | .. | 25 | |
| 308 | 10 c. ,, blue | .. | 36 | |
| 309 | 15 c. ,, lilac | .. | 50 | |
| 310 | 20 c. ,, rose | .. | 75 | 1.00 |
| 311 | 30 c. ,, yellow | . | 62 | |
| 311a | 30 c. ,, oran.-yell. | | | |
| 312 | 35 c. ,, drab | .. | 62 | 62 |
| 313 | 50 c. ,, green | .. | 62 | 62 |
| 314 | 50 c. ,, yell.-grn. | | 62 | |

|  | Un. | Used. |
|---|---|---|

No.
*Variety.* "UADELOUPE."
315 |35 c., black on drab .. 2.50 2.50
Many other minor varieties occur in
the type and setting of this issue.

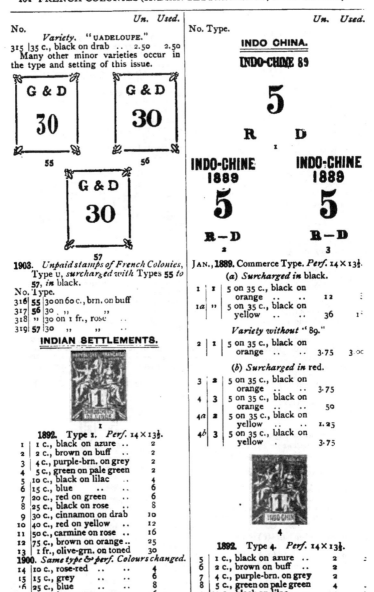

55      56

57

**1903.** *Unpaid stamps of French Colonies,*
*Type v, surcharged with Types 55 to*
*57, in* black.

No. Type.
316| 55 |30 on 60 c., brn. on buff
317| 56 |30 . „ „
318| „ |30 on 1 fr., rose ..
319| 57 |30 „ „ ..

## INDIAN SETTLEMENTS.

1

**1892. Type 1.** *Perf.* 14 × 13½.
1 | 1 c., black on azure ..   2
2 | 2 c., brown on buff ..   2
3 | 4 c., purple-brn. on grey   2
4 | 5 c., green on pale green   2
5 | 10 c., black on lilac ..   4
6 | 15 c., blue .. ..   6
7 | 20 c., red on green ..   6
8 | 25 c., black on rose ..   8
9 | 30 c., cinnamon on drab   10
10 | 40 c., red on yellow ..   12
11 | 50 c., carmine on rose ..   16
12 | 75 c., brown on orange ..   25
13 | 1 fr., olive-grn. on toned   30
**1900.** *Same type & perf. Colours changed.*
14 |10 c., rose-red .. ..   4
15 |15 c., grey .. ..   6
16 |25 c., blue .. ..   8
  |50 c., brown on azure ..   16

|  | Un. | Used. |
|---|---|---|

No. Type.

## INDO CHINA.

INDO-CHINE 89

5

R      D
1

INDO-CHINE    INDO-CHINE
1889        1889
5           5
R – D      R – D
2           3

JAN., **1889.** Commerce Type. *Perf.* 14 × 13½.
    (*a*) *Surcharged in* black.
1 | 1 | 5 on 35 c., black on
       orange .. ..   12
1*a*| „ | 5 on 35 c., black on
       yellow .. ..   36
    *Variety without* "89."
2 | 1 | 5 on 35 c., black on
       orange .. ..   3·75   3·00
    (*b*) *Surcharged in* red.
3 | 2 | 5 on 35 c., black on
       orange .. ..   3·75
4 | 3 | 5 on 35 c., black on
       orange .. ..   50
4*a*| 2 | 5 on 35 c., black on
       yellow .. ..   1.25
4*b*| 3 | 5 on 35 c., black on
       yellow .   3·75

4

**1892. Type 4.** *Perf.* 14 × 13½.
5 | 1 c., black on azure ..   2
6 | 2 c., brown on buff ..   2
7 | 4 c., purple-brn. on grey   2
8 | 5 c., green on pale green   4
9 |10 c., black on lilac ..   4

| No. | | | Un. | Used. |
|---|---|---|---|---|
| 10 | 15 c., blue .. .. | | 10 | 2 |
| 11 | 20 c., red on green .. | | 6 | 8 |
| 12 | 25 c., black on rose .. | | 8 | 2 |
| 13 | 30 c., cinnamon on drab. | | 10 | |
| 14 | 40 c., red on yellow .. | | 12 | 16 |
| 15 | 50 c., carmine on rose .. | | 16 | 8 |
| 16 | 75 c., brown on orange . | | 25 | 12 |
| 17 | 1 fr., olive-gn. on toned | | 30 | 8 |
| 18 | 5 fr., lilac on pale lilac ('96) | | 1.50 | 50 |

*Error, with name inverted.*

18a|75 c., black on orange ..

*Error. Name omitted.*

18b|25 c., black on rose ..

**1899–1901.** *Same type and perf.*
*Colours changed.*

| 19 | 5 c., pale green .. | | 2 | 2 |
|---|---|---|---|---|
| 19a | 5 c., bright yellow-green | | 2 | 2 |
| 20 | 10 c., rose-red .. .. | | 4 | |
| 21 | 15 c., grey .. .. | | 6 | |
| 22 | 25 c., blue .. .. | | 8 | |
| 23 | 50 c., brown on azure .. | | 16 | |

## 15
5

**1903.** Type 4 *surcharged with* Type 5,
*in* black.

24 |15 on 25 c., blue ..

INDO-CHINE

TIMBRE

COLIS-POSTAUX
11

The 10 c., black on lilac, overprinted
with Type 11, in *red*, is a fiscal stamp
used on parcels. Price, *unused* or *used*, 25 c.

### IVORY COAST.

1

**1892.** Type 1. *Perf.* 14 × 13½.
1 | 1 c., black on azure .. | 2
2 | 2 c., brown on buff .. | 2

| No. | | | Un. | Used. |
|---|---|---|---|---|
| 3 | 4 c., purple-brn. on grey | | 2 | |
| 4 | 5 c., green on pale green | | 2 | 2 |
| 4a | 5 c., deep green on green | | 4 | 4 |
| 5 | 10 c., black on lilac . | | 4 | |
| 6 | 15 c., blue .. .. | | 6 | 10 |
| 7 | 20 c., red on green .. | | 6 | |
| 8 | 25 c., black on rose .. | | 8 | 4 |
| 9 | 30 c., cinnamon on drab. | | 10 | |
| 10 | 40 c., red on yellow .. | | 12 | |
| 11 | 50 c., carmine on rose .. | | 16 | 18 |
| 12 | 75 c., brown on orange . | | 25 | 25 |
| 13 | 1 fr., olive-gn. on toned | | 30 | 12 |

**1900.** *Same type and perf.*
*Colours changed.*

| 14 | 10 c., rose-red .. .. | | 4 |
|---|---|---|---|
| 15 | 15 c., grey .. .. | | 6 |
| 16 | 25 c., blue .. .. | | 8 |
| 17 | 50 c., brown on azure .. | | 16 |

In 1903 appeared the 50 c. and 1 fr. of
Unpaid stamps of French Colonies overprinted "Côte d'Ivoire—Colis Postaux,"
and also the 5 c., 10 c., 15 c., and 60 c. of
the same set similarly overprinted, and
with the new values of 50 c., 1 fr., or 4 fr.
surcharged in various types. We have yet
to learn that these are true postage stamps
for parcels, and not fiscal stamps affixed
to parcels liable to import duties.

### MADAGASCAR.

## 05   25
1      2

Commerce Type. *Perf.* 14 × 13½.
**1889.** *Surcharged in* black.

No. Type.
| 1 | 1 | 05 on 10 c., bk. on lilac | 2.50 | 2.00 |
|---|---|---|---|---|
| 2 | " | 05 on 25 c., bk. on rose | 2.00 | 1.50 |
| 3 | 2 | 25 on 40 c., red on yell. | 1.50 | 1.50 |

No. 1 may also be found with the surcharge vertical, up or down.

*Error.*

3a| 2 |25 on 10 c., black on lilac

## 05   5   15
3     4    5

APRIL, **1891.** Black *surcharge.*
| 4 | 3 | 05 on 40 c., red on yell. | 75 | 75 |
|---|---|---|---|---|
| 5 | 4 | 50 on 10 c., bk. on lilac | 1.00 | 90 |
| 6 | " | 5 on 25 c. ,, rose | 1.25 | 75 |
| 7 | 5 | 15 on 25 c. ,, ,, | 1.00 | 1.00 |

In No. 6 the surcharge is placed
diagonally.

| No. Type. | | | *Un.* | *Used.* |
|---|---|---|---|---|

*Variety.   Surcharge sideways.*

| 8 | **5** | 15 on 25 c., bk. on rose | 2.50 | |

6

**1891.**   Type **6.**   *Type-set.   Imperf.*

| 9 | 5 c., black on green | .. | 62 | 50 |
| 10 | 10 c.,   ,,   blue | .. | 62 | |
| 11 | 15 c., blue on   ,, | .. | 1.25 | 50 |
| 12 | 25 c., brown on buff | .. | 36 | 25 |
| 13 | 1 fr., blk. on yellow | .. | 3.00 | 1.85 |
| 14 | 5 fr., lilac on lilac (*value in* black) | .. | 15.00 | 11.25 |

On the 1 fr. and 5 fr. there is also an orange-red pattern.

## MADAGASCAR & DEPENDENCIES.

1

**1896-99.**   Type **1.**   *Perf.* 14 × 13½.

| 1 | 1 c., black on azure | .. | 2 | |
| 2 | 2 c., brown on buff | .. | 2 | |
| 3 | 4 c., pur.-brn. on grey | .. | 2 | |
| 4 | 5 c., green on pale green | | 4 | |
| 4ª | 5 c., deep green on green | | 6 | 4 |
| 5 | 10 c., black on lilac | .. | 4 | 6 |
| 6 | 15 c., blue | .. | 6 | 6 |
| 7 | 20 c., red on green | .. | 6 | |
| 8 | 25 c., black on rose | .. | 8 | 4 |
| 9 | 30 c., cinnamon on drab | | 10 | |
| 10 | 40 c., red on yellow | .. | 12 | |
| 11 | 50 c., carmine on rose | .. | 18 | 18 |
| 12 | 75 c., brown on orange | .. | 25 | |
| 13 | 1 fr., olive-grn. on toned (in *red*) | .. | 30 | |
| 14 | 1 fr., olive-grn. on toned (in *blue*) | .. | 62 | |
| 15 | 5 fr., lilac on lilac (in *blue*) | 1.50 | |

**1900-02.**   *Same type and perf.*
*Colours changed.*

| ··ª | 5 c., bright yellow-grn. | | 2 | 2 |
| | 10 c., rose-red | .. | 4 | |
| | 15 c., grey | .. | 6 | |
| | 25 c., blue | .. | 8 | |
| | 50 c., brown on azure | .. | 16 | |

| | | *Un.* | *Used.* |
|---|---|---|---|

No.

| | | 2 | 3 |

**1902.**   Type **1** *surcharged as* Type **2** *or* **3**, *in* black.

| 20 | 05 on 50 c., carmine on rose | .. | .. | .. | 12 | 12 |
| 21 | 10 on 5 fr., lilac on lilac | 1.00 | |
| 22 | 15 on 1 fr., olive-green on toned | .. | .. | .. | 25 | 30 |

*Surcharge inverted.*

| 23 | 05 on 50 c., carm. on rose | 3.15 | |
| 24 | 10 on 5 fr., lilac on lilac. | 4.35 | |
| 25 | 15 on 1 fr., olive-green on toned | .. | .. | .. | 3.15 | |

| | | 4 | 5 |

*Stamps of* 1896-99 *surcharged in* black.

*(a) As* Type **4,** *with narrow* "o."

| 26 | 0,01 on 2 c., brown on buff | 6 | |
| 27 | 0,05 on 30 c., cinn. on drab | 8 | |
| 28 | 0,10 on 50 c., carm. on rose | 10 | 12 |
| 29 | 0,15 on 75 c., brn. on oran. | 16 | 13 |
| 30 | 0,15 on 1 fr., olive-green on toned | .. | .. | 12 | |

*Surcharge inverted.*

| 31 | 0,01 on 2 c., brown on buff | |
| 32 | 0,05 on 30 c., cinn. on drab | |
| 33 | 0,10 on 50 c., carm. on rose | |
| 34 | 0,15 on 75 c., brn. on oran. | |
| 35 | 0,15 on 1 fr., olive-green on toned | .. | .. | |

*Error.*   "00,1" *for* "0,01."

| 36 | 00,1 on 2 c., brn. on buff | |

*The same inverted.*

| 36a | 00,1 on 2 c., brn. on buff | |

*Error.*   "00,5" *for* "0,05."

| 37 | 00,5 on 30 c., cinn. on drab | 2.50 |

*The same, inverted.*

| 38 | 00,5 on 30 c., cinn. on drab | |

*(b) As* Type **5,** *with wide* "o."

| 39 | 0,01 on 2 c., brown on buff | 4 |
| 40 | 0,05 on 30 c., cinn. on drab | 12 |
| 41 | 0,10 on 50 c., carm. on rose | 12 |

*Surcharge inverted.*

| 42 | 0,01 on 2 c., brown on buff | |
| 43 | 0,05 on 30 c., cinn. on drab | 1.50 |
| 44 | 0,10 on 50 c., carm. on rose | 1.50 |

| No. | | | Un. | Used. |
|---|---|---|---|---|

*Stamp of Diego Suarez, Type 10, similarly surcharged.*

45 | 0,05 on 30 c., cinnamon (Type 4) .. ..
46 | 0,05 on 30 c., cinnamon (Type 5) .. ..
47 | 00,5 on 30 c., cinnamon (*Error*) .. ..

**1902.** No. 15 *surcharged as* Type 4, *in* black.

48 | 0·10 on 5 fr., lilac ` ..

*Stamp of Diego Suarez similarly surcharged.*

49 | 0·10 on 50 c., carmine (4)
50 | 0·10 on 50 c. ,, (5)·

UNPAID LETTER STAMPS.

**Madagascar**

**et**

**DEPENDANCES**

2

**1897.** Type v. *Imperf. Overprinted with* Type 2, *in* red *on* 5 c., 10 c., 40 c., *and* 1 fr. ; *in* blue *on* 20 c., 30 c., *and* 50 c.

101 | 5 c., blue .. .. 50
102 | 10 c., brown .. .. 36
103 | 20 c., yellow .. .. 25
104 | 30 c., rose .. .. 30
105 | 40 c., lilac .. .. 50
106 | 50 c., violet .. .. 50
107 | 1 fr., green .. .. 75

**MARTINIQUE.**

**MARTINIQUE**

**5**

1

Commerce Type. *Perf.* 14×13½.
**1886-87.** *Surcharged in* black.

No. Type.
1 | 1 | 5 on 20 c., red on gn. 50
2 | ,, | 05 on 20 c. ,, 8
3 | ,, | 15 on 20 c. ,, 50
4 | ,, | 015 on 20 c. ,, 45
5 | — | 5 c. on 20 c. ,,

No. Type. | | | Un. | Used.
---|---|---|---|---

**MQE** | **MQE**
**1 8** | **1 8 c**
3 | 4

**1887.** *Surcharged in* black.

6 | 3 | 15 c. on 20 c., red on gn. 50
7 | 4 | 15 c. on 20 c. ,, 1.50
Type 3 should show a "c" after the "15."

*Surcharge inverted.*

7a | 3 | 15 c. on 20 c. red on grn.

**MARTINIQUE**

**01ᶜ·**

5

**1888-90.** *Surcharged as* Types 1 *and* 5, *in* black.

8 | 5 | 01 c. on 2 c., bn. on buff 6
9 | ,, | 01 c. on 4 c., purple-bn. 18
10 | 1 | 01 on 20 c., red on gn. 8
11 | 5 | 05 c. on 4 c., purple-bn.
12 | ,, | 05 c. on 10 c., bk. on lilac 16 | 25
13 | ,, | 05 c. on 20 c., red on gn. 18 | 18
14 | ,, | 05 c. on 30 c., cinnamon 36
15 | ,, | 05 c. on 35 c., bk. on or. 50
16 | ,, | 05 c. on 35 c., bk. on yel. 36 | 45
17 | ,, | 05 c. on 40 c., red on yell. 25 | 30
18 | ,, | 15 c. on 4 c., purple-bn.
19 | ,, | 15 c. on 20 c., red on gn. 36 | 50
20 | ,, | 15 c. on 25 c., bk. on rose 16 | 16
21 | ,, | 15 c. on 75 c., carmine 1.50

*Variety. Surcharge inverted.*

21a | — | 05 c. on 35 c., black on yellow ..
22 | 5 | 15 c. on 25 c., black on rose .. ..

**TIMBRE-POSTE**

**05ᶜ·**

**MARTINIQUE**

6

**1891.** *Colonial* Type v. *Imperf.* *Surcharged as* Type 6.
(*a*) *In* black.

23 | 05 c. on 5 c., black .. 50 | 50
24 | 05 c. on 15 c. ,, .. 16
25 | 15 c. on 20 c. ,, .. 25
26 | 15 c. on 30 c. ,, .. 30

|  | | *Un.* | *Used.* |
|---|---|---|---|
| **No.** | | | |

*Error.* "PCSTE" *for* "POSTE."

| 27 | 05 c. on 15 c., black .. | | |

*Error.* "POSUE" *for* "POSTE."

| 28 | 15 c. on 20 c., black .. | | |

(*b*) *In* red.

| 29 | 05 c. on 10 c., black .. | 16 | 18 |
| 30 | 05 c. on 15 c.  ,,  .. | 18 | |
| 31 | 15 c. on 20 c.  ,,  .. | 36 | 36 |

*Error.* "TIM RE" *for* "TIMBRE."

| 32 | 05 c. on 15 c., black .. | 2.50 | |

*Variety. Surcharge inverted.*

| 33 | 15 c. on 20 c., black .. | — | 10.00 |
| 33*a* | 15 c. on 30 c.  ,, | | |

**TIMBRE-POSTE**

# 01ᶜ·

**MARTINIQUE**

**7**

**1891-92.** Commerce Type. *Perf.* 14×13½.
No. Type. *Surcharged in* black.

| 34 | 7 | 01 c. on 2 c., bn. on buff | 12 | 12 |

**1892**

**MARTINIQUE**

# 15ᶜ·

**8**

# 15ᶜ·

**MARTINIQUE**

**9**

| 35 | 8 | 05 c. on 25 c., bk. on rose | 50 | |
| 36 | ,, | 15 c. on 25 c., bk.  ,, | 36 | 36 |
| 37 | 9 | 05 c. on 25 c., bk.  ,, | 25 | |
| 38 | ,, | 15 c. on 25 c., bk.  ,, | 25 | |

*Errors.* (*a*) "1882" *for* "1892."

| 39 | 9 | 05 c. on 25 c., bk. on rose | 3.15 | |
| 40 | ,, | 15 c. on 25 c., bk.  ,, | | |

(*b*) "95" *for* "05."

| 41 | 9 | 95 c. on 25 c., black on rose .. | 10.00 | |

**10**

**1892.** Type 10. *Perf.* 14×13½.

| 1 | 1 c., black on azure .. | 2 | 2 |
| 3 | 2 c., brown on buff .. | 2 | 2 |

|  | | *Un.* | *Used.* |
|---|---|---|---|
| **No.** | | | |

| 44 | 4 c., purp.-brn. on grey | 2 | |
| 45 | 5 c., grn. on pale green | 2 | 2 |
| 46 | 10 c., black on lilac .. | 6 | 6 |
| 47 | 15 c., blue  .. | 10 | 6 |
| 48 | 20 c., red on green .. | 6 | |
| 49 | 25 c., black on rose .. | 8 | 8 |
| 50 | 30 c., cinnamon on drab | 10 | |
| 51 | 40 c., red on yellow .. | 12 | |
| 52 | 50 c., carmine on rose .. | 16 | |
| 53 | 75 c., brown on orange.. | 25 | |
| 54 | 1 fr., olive-grn. on toned | 30 | 25 |

*Errors.* (i.) *Name in* blue.

| 55 | 1 c., black on azure .. | | |

(ii.) *Name in* red.

| 55*a* | 10 c., black on lilac .. | | |

**1899-1903.** *Same type and perf.
Colours changed.*

| 56 | 5 c., yellow-green .. | 2 | |
| 57 | 10 c., rose-red .. .. | 4 | |
| 58 | 15 c., grey .. .. | 6 | |
| 59 | 25 c., blue .. .. | 8 | |
| 60 | 50 c., brown on azure .. | 16 | |
| 61 | 5 fr., lilac on pale lilac . | | |

**UNPAID LETTER STAMPS.**

**MARTINIQUE**

**51**

**1887.** Colonial Type v. *Imperf.
Surcharged with* Type 51, *in* red.

| 501 | 1 c., black .. .. | 25 | |
| 502 | 2 c.  ,, .. .. | 25 | |
| 503 | 3 c.  ,, .. .. | 25 | |
| 504 | 4 c.  ,, .. .. | 25 | |
| 505 | 5 c.  ,, .. .. | 12 | |
| 505*a* | 10 c.  ,, .. .. | | |
| 506 | 15 c.  ,, .. .. | 62 | |
| 507 | 20 c.  ,, .. .. | 25 | |
| 508 | 30 c.  ,, .. .. | 50 | |
| 509 | 40 c.  ,, .. .. | 50 | |
| 510 | 60 c.  ,, .. .. | | |
| 511 | 1 fr., brown .. .. | | |
| 512 | 2 fr.  ,, .. .. | | |
| 513 | 5 fr.  ,, .. .. | | |

The surcharge exists reading from upper
left to lower right corner, from lower
left to upper right corner, and both these
inverted.

The 60 c. exists surcharged "5 fr.—
Colis Postaux." See note after "Ivory
Coast."

| No. | | | Un. | Used. |
|---|---|---|---|---|

## MAYOTTE.

I

**1892–99. Type 1.** *Perf.* 14×13½.

| | | | | |
|---|---|---|---|---|
| 1 | 1 c., black on azure .. | 2 | | |
| 2 | 2 c., brown on buff .. | 2 | | |
| 3 | 4 c., purple-bn. on grey | 2 | | |
| 4 | 5 c., green on pale green | 4 | | |
| 5 | 10 c., black on lilac .. | 6 | | |
| 6 | 15 c., blue .. .. | 6 | | |
| 7 | 20 c., red on green .. | 6 | | |
| 8 | 25 c., black on rose .. | 8 | 8 | |
| 9 | 30 c., cinnamon on drab. | 10 | | |
| 10 | 40 c., red on yellow .. | 12 | | |
| 11 | 50 c., carmine on rose .. | 16 | | |
| 12 | 75 c., brown on orange . | 25 | | |
| 13 | 1 fr., olive-gn. on toned | 30 | | |
| 14 | 5 fr., lilac and lilac (in *blue*) | 1.50 | | |

**1899–1900.** *Same type and perf. Colours changed.*

| | | | |
|---|---|---|---|
| 15 | 5 c., bright yellow-green | | |
| 16 | 10 c., rose-red .. .. | 4 | |
| 17 | 15 c., grey .. .. | 6 | |
| 18 | 25 c., blue .. .. | 8 | |
| 19 | 50 c., brown on azure .. | 16 | |

## NEW CALEDONIA.

I

**1860. Type 1.** *Imperf.*

| | | | |
|---|---|---|---|
| 1 | 10 c., grey-black .. | 6.25 | |

### N C E 05

2

**Peace and Commerce Type.** *Imperf.*
**1881–82. Surcharged as Type 2, in black.**

| | | | | |
|---|---|---|---|---|
| 2 | 5 on 40 c., red on yellow | 1.85 | | |
| 3 | 05 on 40 c. ,, ,, | 18 | 18 | |

| No. | | | Un. | Used. |
|---|---|---|---|---|
| 4 | 25 on 35 c., blk. on yellow | | 3.15 | 3.15 |
| 5 | 25 on 35 c. ,, orange | | — | 4.35 |
| 6 | 25 on 75 c., rose-carmine | | 2.50 | 2.50 |

*Varieties. Surcharge inverted.*

| | | | |
|---|---|---|---|
| 7 | 5 on 40 c., red on yellow | | |
| 8 | 25 on 35 c., blk. on ,, | 7.50 | 6.25 |
| 9 | 25 on 75 c., rose-carmine | | |

### N C E 5

3

**1884. Surcharged with Type 3, in black.**

| | | | |
|---|---|---|---|
| 10 | 5 on 40 c., red on yellow | 18 | 25 |
| 11 | 5 on 75 c., rose-carmine | 36 | 50 |
| 12 | 5 on 75 c., deep carmine | 36 | |

*Varieties. Surcharge inverted.*

| | | | |
|---|---|---|---|
| 13 | 5 on 40 c., red on yellow | 25 | 25 |
| 14 | 5 on 75 c., rose-carmine | 36 | 36 |
| 15 | 5 on 75 c., deep carmine | 36 | 36 |

### N.C.E. 5c    N.C.E. 5c.

4          5

**1886. Surcharged with Type 4, in black.**

| | | | |
|---|---|---|---|
| 16 | 5 c. on 1 fr., olive-green on toned .. .. | | |

**Commerce Type.** *Perf.* 14×13½.
No. Type. *Surcharged in black.*

| | | | | |
|---|---|---|---|---|
| 17 | 4 | 5 c. on 1 fr., olive-gn. on toned .. .. | 12 | |
| 18 | 5 | 5 c. on 1 fr., olive-gn. on toned .. .. | 18 | 25 |

*Varieties.*
*Surcharge inverted.*

| | | | | |
|---|---|---|---|---|
| 19 | 4 | 5 c. on 1 fr., olive-green on toned .. | 25 | |
| 20 | 5 | 5 c. on 1 fr., olive-green on toned .. | 3.40 | |

*Double surcharge.*

| | | | |
|---|---|---|---|
| 20a | 4 | 5 c. on 1 fr., olive-green on toned .. | |

No. Type.                                    *Un.    Used.*

*Double surcharge. One inverted.*

21 | 5 | 5 c. on 1 fr., olive-
              green on toned ..

*Double surcharge, both inverted.*

21*a* | 4 | 5 c. on 1 fr., olive-
                green on toned ..

**8**

Peace and Commerce Type H, *imperf.*,
and Commerce Type J, *perf.* 14 × 13½.
**1892.** *Surcharged, in* black, *with* Type **8.**

| | | | | Un. | Used. |
|---|---|---|---|---|---|
| 31*b* | H | 2 c., red-brown .. | | | |
| 32 | ,, | 4 c., purple-brown . | | | |
| 33 | ,, | 20 c., red on green .. | 3.75 | | |
| 34 | ,, | 35 c., black on orange | 75 | | |
| 35 | ,, | 40 c., red on buff .. | 10.00 | | |
| 35*a* | ,, | 75 c., carmine .. | | | |
| 36 | ,, | 1 fr., olive-green on toned .. .. | 3.00 | | |
| 37 | J | 1 c., black on azure. | — | 8.75 | |
| 38 | ,, | 2 c., brown on buff. | 8.75 | | |
| 39 | ,, | 4 c., purple-brown. | — | 11.25 | |
| 40 | ,, | 5 c., gn. on pale gn. | 25 | | |
| 41 | ,, | 10 c., black on lilac . | 62 | | |
| 42 | ,, | 15 c., blue .. .. | 25 | | |
| 43 | ,, | 20 c., red on green .. | 62 | | |
| 44 | ,, | 25 c., ochre on yellow | 50 | 50 | |
| 45 | ,, | 25 c., black on rose.. | — | 50 | |
| 46 | ,, | 30 c., cinnamon on drab | 62 | | |
| 47 | ,, | 35 c., black on orange | | | |
| 48 | ,, | 40 c., red on yellow . | 8.75 | | |
| 49 | ,, | 75 c., carmine on rose | — | 1.85 | |
| 50 | ,, | 1 fr., olive-green on toned .. .. | 1.50 | | |

*Surcharge inverted.*

50*a* | J | 25 c., ochre on yell.

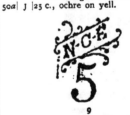

**9**

**1892-93.** *Surcharged as* Type **9.**
   (*a*) *In* black.

| | | | Un. | Used. |
|---|---|---|---|---|
| 51 | J | 5 on 20 c., red on grn. | 50 | |
| 52 | ,, | 5 on 75 c., carmine. | 25 | ... |
| 53 | H | 10 on 1 fr., olive-grn. | | |
| 53*a* | J | 10 on 1 fr., olive-grn. | 18 | 1. |

*Varieties. Surcharge inverted.*

| 54 | J | 5 on 20 c., red on grn. | 1.85 | |
| 55 | ,, | 5 on 75 c., carmine. | 2.50 | |
| 55*a* | ,, | 10 on 1 fr., olive-grn. | | |

*Double inverted.*

56 | J | 5 on 20 c., red on grn.

---

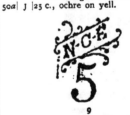

**6**                    **7**

Peace and Commerce Type. *Imperf.*
**1891-92.** *Surcharged in* black.

22 | 6 | 10 c. on 40 c., red on
                 yellow .. .. | 62

*Surcharge inverted.*

23 | 6 | 10 c. on 40 c. .. | 75

*Double surcharge, one inverted.*

23*a* | 6 | 10 c. on 40 c., red on
                    yellow .. ..

Commerce Type. *Perf.* 14 × 13½.
*Surcharged in* black.

24 | 6 | 10 c. on 40 c., red on
                 yellow .. .. | 16
25 | 7 | 10 c. on 30 c., cinnamon | 12 | 36

*Varieties.*
(*a*) *Surcharge inverted.*

26 | 6 | 10 c. on 40 c., red on
                 yellow .. .. | 16
27 | 7 | 10 c. on 30 c., cinnamon | 18

(*b*) *Double surcharge.*

28 | 7 | 10 c. on 30 c., cinnamon | 2.50 | 2.50

(*c*) *Double surcharge inverted.*

29 | 7 | 10 c. on 30 c., cinnamon | 2.50

(*d*) "10" *a second time diagonally,
           both inverted.*

30 | 7 | 10 c. on 30 c., cinnamon | 2.50

(*e*) *Double surcharge, one inverted.*

31 | 6 | 10 c. on 40 c., red on
                 yellow .. .. | 1.85
1*a* | 7 | 10 c. on 30 c., cinnam.

There are several varieties of these surcharges, especially of Type 6, which has
:ts of the frame mis-set.

| No. Type. | (b) In blue. | Un. | Used. |
|---|---|---|---|
| 57 | J | 5 on 75 c., carmine. | 18 | 18 |
| 58 | ,, | 10 on 1 fr., olive-grn. | 25 | 25 |

*Varieties. Surcharge inverted.*

| 59 | J | 5 on 75 c., carmine. | 2.50 |
| 60 | ,, | 10 on 1 fr., olive-grn. | 3.75 |

**10**

### 1892. Type 10. *Perf.* 14×13½.

| 61 | 1 c., black on azure | .. | 2 |
| 62 | 2 c., brown on buff | .. | 2 |
| 62a | 2 c., purple-brn. on buff | 2 | 4 |
| 63 | 4 c., purp.-brn. on grey | .. | 2 |
| 64 | 5 c., grn. on pale green | 4 | 2 |
| 65 | 10 c., black on lilac | 4 | 6 |
| 66 | 15 c., blue | .. .. | — | 6 |
| 67 | 20 c., red on green | .. | 6 | 8 |
| 68 | 25 c., black on rose | .. | 8 | 4 |
| 69 | 30 c., cinnamon on drab | 10 |
| 70 | 40 c., red on yellow | .. | 12 |
| 71 | 50 c., carmine on rose | .. | 16 | 25 |
| 72 | 75 c., brown on orange.. | 25 |
| 73 | 1 fr., olive-grn. on toned | 30 |

## N.C.E.

**11**

### 1900. Type 10 *surcharged with* Type 9 or 11, *in* black.

| 74 | 5 on 4 c., claret | .. | 6 |
| 75 | 15 on 30 c., cinnamon | .. | 12 |

*Varieties. Double surcharge.*

| 75a | 5 on 4 c., claret | .. | 3.15 |

*Surcharge inverted.*

| 76 | 5 on 4 c., claret | .. | — | 3.15 |
| 77 | 15 on 30 c., cinnamon | .. | — | 5.00 |

Type 10. *Colours changed.*

| 78 | 5 c., bright yell.-green | 2 | 2 |
| 79 | 10 c., rose-red | .. .. | 4 |
| 80 | 15 c., grey | .. .. | 6 |
| 81 | 25 c., blue | .. .. | 8 |
| 82 | 50 c., brown on azure | .. | 16 |

### 1901. Type 10 *surch. as* Type 9, *in* black.

| 83 | 5 c. on 2 c., brn. on buff | 6 |

*Surcharged as* Type 11, *in* black.

| 84 | 15 c. on 75 c., brn. on oran. | 25 |
| 85 | 15 c. on 1 fr., olive-green | 25 |

| No. | | Un. | Used. |
|---|---|---|---|

*Surcharge inverted.*

| 86 | 15 c. on 75 c., brn. on oran. | 10.00 |

*Double surcharge.*

| 87 | 15 c. on 75 c., brn. on oran. |

## N C E    N.-C.E.

**12**    **13**

### 1902. Type 10 *surcharged with* Type 12 or 13, *in* black.

| 88 | 5 on 30 c., cinnamon | .. | 12 |
| 89 | 15 on 40 c., red on buff.. | 12 |

*Surcharge inverted.*

| 90 | 5 on 30 c., cinnamon | .. | 1.50 |
| 91 | 15 on 40 c., red on buff.. | 1.50 |

**14**

### 1903. Type 10 *overprinted with* Type 14, *in* carmine (C.), blue (Bl.), gold (G.), *or* black (B.).

| 92 | 1 c., black on azure (Bl.) |
| 93 | 2 c., purp.-brn. on buff(,,) |
| 94 | 4 c.,  ,,  grey(,,) |
| 95 | 5 c., grn. on pale grn.(C.) |
| 96 | 5 c., bright yell.-grn. (,,) |
| 97 | 10 c., black on lilac  (,,) |
| 98 | 10 c.  ,,  ,,  (G.) |
| 99 | 15 c., grey  ..  (C.) |
| 100 | 20 c., red on green (Bl.) | 12 |
| 101 | 25 c., black on rose  (,,) | 12 |
| 102 | 30 c., cinnamon  (C.) | 16 |
| 103 | 40 c., red on yellow (Bl.) | 18 |
| 104 | 50 c., carmine on rose(,,) | 25 |
| 105 | 75 c., brn. on orange (B.) |
| 106 | 1 fr., olive-green on toned (Bl.) | .. |

Set of 8 lowest values, unused, 36 c.

*As last, but with new value added with-in the inscription, in* blue, upright *or* sideways (S.).

| 107 | 1 on 2 c. (S.) | .. | .. |
| 108 | 2 on 4 c. (,,) | .. | .. |
| 109 | 4 on 5 c., green (S.) | .. |
| 110 | 4 on 5 c., yellow-green. |
| 111 | 10 on 15 c. (S.) | .. | .. |
| 112 | 15 on 20 c. (,,) | .. | .. |
| 113 | 20 on 25 c. | .. | .. |

Set of 7, unused, $1.10.

| | | | Un. | Used. |
|---|---|---|---|---|
| **No.** | | | | |

UNPAID LETTER STAMPS.

**1903.** *Unpaid Letter stamps of French Colonies, Type* U, *overprinted with Type* 14.

| | | | | |
|---|---|---|---|---|
| 301 | 5 c., pale blue .. | .. | | |
| 302 | 10 c., grey-brown | .. | | |
| 303 | 15 c., pale green | .. | | |
| 304 | 30 c., carmine .. | .. | | |
| 305 | 50 c., violet .. | .. | | |
| 306 | 60 c., brown on buff | .. | | |
| 307 | 1 fr., rose .. | .. | | |

### · NOSSI-BÉ.

$$\textbf{25 C.} \qquad \textbf{25}$$

|  1  |  2  |
|---|---|

**1889.**   Peace and Commerce Type.
*Imperf.*

No. Type. *Surcharged in* blue.

| | | | |
|---|---|---|---|
| 1 | 1 | 25 c. on 40 c., red on buff | |
| 2 | 2 | 25 on 40 c.    ,, | |

*Perf.* 14×13½.

| | | | |
|---|---|---|---|
| 2a | 2 | 25 on 40 c., red on buff | |

Commerce Type.   *Perf.* 14×13½.

*With similar surcharge to* Type 1, *in* blue.

| | | | |
|---|---|---|---|
| 3 | 5 c. on 10 c., blk. on lilac | 17.50 | 15.00 |
| 4 | 5 c. on 20 c., red on green | 20.00 | 18.75 |

*Similar, but with larger "* 5,*" as in* Type 2.

| | | | |
|---|---|---|---|
| 5 | 5 c. on 20 c., red on grn. | 15.00 | 15.00 |

*With large figures as in* Type 2, *in* blue.

| | | | |
|---|---|---|---|
| 6 | 5 c. on 10 c., blk. on lilac | 15.00 | 15.00 |
| 7 | 15 on 20 c., red on green . | 13.75 | 13.75 |
| 9 | 25 c. on 30 c., cinnamon . | 11.25 | 11.25 |

Reprints have been made of all five varieties. The originals have the surcharge in pale or dull blue, the same colour that was used for the postmark, while in the reprint the colour is ultramarine. The obliteration on the reprints is also ultramarine.

$$\textbf{N S B} \qquad \textbf{N S B}$$
$$\textbf{0 25} \qquad \textbf{25 C}$$

|  3  |  4  |
|---|---|

**90.**   *Same type. Surcharged in* black.

| | | | |
|---|---|---|---|
| | 3 | 0 25 on 20 c., red on green .. .. | 6.25   6.25 |

| | | | Un. | Used. |
|---|---|---|---|---|
| No. | Type. | | | |
| 12 | 3 | 0 25 on 75 c., carmine on rose .. .. | 7.50 | 7.50 |
| 13 | ,, | 0 25 on 1 fr., olive-green .. .. | 7.50 | 10.00 |
| 15 | 4 | 25 c. on 20 c., red on green .. .. | 7.50 | |

5

| | | | | |
|---|---|---|---|---|
| 16 | 5 | 25 on 20 c., red on grn. | 7.50 | 7.50 |
| 18 | 4 | 25 c. on 75 c., carmine on rose .. .. | 8.75 | |
| 19 | 5 | 25 on 75 c., carmine on rose .. .. | 8.75 | 7.50 |
| 20 | 4 | 25 c. on 1 fr., olive-green .. .. | 7.50 | |
| 21 | 5 | 25 on 1 fr., olive-green | — | 7.50 |

No. 13 has no ornament over the figures; No. 16 is in similar figures to Type 1, but with frame like Type 5; and No. 21 is similar to Type 5 without frame.

|  6  |  7  |
|---|---|

**1893.**   *Same type and perf. Surcharged.*

*(a) In* vermilion.

| | | | | |
|---|---|---|---|---|
| 23 | 6 | 10 c., black on lilac . | 1.00 | |

*(b) In* carmine, *reading up from right to left.*

| | | | | |
|---|---|---|---|---|
| 24 | 6 | 10 c., black on lilac . | 1.00 | 1.00 |

*In* carmine, *reading up from left to right.*

| | | | | |
|---|---|---|---|---|
| 25 | 6 | 10 c., black on lilac . | 1.00 | 1.00 |

*(c) In* black.

| | | | | |
|---|---|---|---|---|
| 27 | 6 | 15 c., blue .. .. | 1.00 | 75 |
| 28 | ,, | 20 c., red on green .. | 1.25 | 1.00 |

*(d) In* blue.

| | | | | |
|---|---|---|---|---|
| 29 | 7 | 20 c., red on green .. | 1.85 | 1.25 |

| | *Un.* | *Used.* |
|---|---|---|

No.

**Nossi Bé**

**25**

8

**1893.** *Same type and perf. Surcharged as* Type 8, *in* black.

| | | | *Un.* | *Used.* |
|---|---|---|---|---|
| 30 | 25 on 20 c., red on green | | 1.00 | 1.00 |
| 31 | 50 on 10 c., black on lilac | | 1.25 | |
| 32 | 75 on 15 c., blue | .. | 2.50 | |
| 33 | 1 fr. on 5 c., green | .. | 2.50 | |

*Surcharge inverted.*

| 34 | 50 on 10 c., black on lilac | — | 11.25 |
|---|---|---|---|
| 35 | 1 fr. on 5 c., green | .. | — | 10.00 |

9

**1894.** Type 9. *Perf.* 14 × 13½.

| 36 | 1 c., black on azure | .. | 2 | |
|---|---|---|---|---|
| 37 | 2 c., brown on buff | .. | 2 | |
| 38 | 4 c., purple-brn. on grey | | 2 | 4 |
| 39 | 5 c., green on pale green | | 2 | |
| 40 | 10 c., black on lilac | .. | 4 | 8 |
| 41 | 15 c., blue | .. | 6 | |
| 42 | 20 c., red on green | .. | 6 | 8 |
| 43 | 25 c., black on rose | .. | 8 | 8 |
| 44 | 30 c., cinnamon on drab. | | 10 | 12 |
| 45 | 40 c., red on yellow | .. | 12 | 16 |
| 46 | 50 c., carmine on rose | .. | 16 | |
| 47 | 75 c., brown on orange | .. | 25 | |
| 48 | 1 fr., olive-gn. on toned | | 30 | |

**UNPAID LETTER STAMPS.**

**Nossi-Bé**
**chiffre-taxe**
**0.30**
**A PERCEVOIR**

51

**1891-92.** Commerce Type. *Perf.* 14 × 13½. No. Type. *Surcharged in* black.

| 101 | 51 | 0.20 on 1 c., black on azure | .. | .. | 8.75 | 8.75 |
|---|---|---|---|---|---|---|

No. Type.

**Nossi-Bé**
**chiffre-taxe**
**0.35**
**A PERCEVOIR**

52

**Nossi-Bé**
**chiffre-taxe**
**1F**
**A PERCEVOIR**

53

| 102 | 51 | 0.30 on 2 c., brown on buff | .. | .. | 7.50 | 7.50 |
|---|---|---|---|---|---|---|
| 103 | 52 | 0.35 on 4 c., purple-brown on grey | .. | 6.25 | 7.50 |
| 104 | " | 0.35 on 20 c., red on green | .. | 7.50 | 7.50 |
| 105 | 51 | 0.50 on 30 c., cinnamon on drab | .. | 5.00 | 5.00 |
| 106 | 53 | 1 fr. on 35 c., black on orange | .. | 6.25 | 6.25 |

*Surcharge inverted.*

| 106a | 51 | 0.20 on 1 c., black on azure | .. |
|---|---|---|---|
| 106b | 51 | 0.30 on 2 c., brown on buff | .. |
| 106c | 52 | 0.35 on 4 c., purple-brown on grey | |

**Nossi-Bé**
**5 C.**
**A PERCEVOIR**

54

**Nossi-Bé**
**5 C.**
**A PERCEVOIR**

55

| 107 | 54 | 5 c. on 20 c., red on green | .. | .. | 3.00 | 2.50 |
|---|---|---|---|---|---|---|
| 108 | 55 | 5 c. on 20 c., red on green | .. | .. | 3.00 | |
| 109 | " | 0.10 on 5 c., green | 1.50 | 62 |
| 110 | 54 | 10 c. on 15 c., blue | 3.00 | |
| 111 | 55 | 10 c. on 15 c. " | 3.00 | |
| 112 | " | 0.15 on 20 c., red on green | .. | 1.00 | 1.00 |
| 113 | 54 | 15 c. on 10 c., black on lilac | .. | 3.00 | |
| 114 | 55 | 15 c. on 10 c., black on lilac | .. | 3.00 | 2.50 |
| 115 | 54 | 25 c. on 5 c., green | 3.00 | |
| 116 | 55 | 25 c. on 5 c. " | 3.00 | 3.00 |
| 117 | " | 0.25 on 75 c., carmine | 7.50 | 7.50 |
| 118 | " | 0.25 on 20 c., red on green (error) | .. | |

All the stamps of Nossi-Bé are now obsolete, the new series for MADAGASCAR AND DEPENDENCIES being used there.

| No. | | Un. | Used. |
|---|---|---|---|

## OBOCK.

**1**

Commerce Type.  *Perf.* 14×13½.

1 FEB., **1892.**

*Surcharged with* Type 1,
*in* black.

| | | | |
|---|---|---|---|
| 1 | 1 c., black on azure .. | 50 | |
| 2 | 2 c., brown on buff .. | 36 | |
| 3 | 4 c., purple-bn. on grey | 7.50 | |
| 4 | 5 c., green on pale green | 25 | |
| 5 | 10 c., black on lilac .. | 50 | |
| 6 | 15 c., blue .. .. | 50 | |
| 7 | 25 c., black on rose .. | 50 | |
| 8 | 35 c., ,, orange .. | 1.50 | |
| 9 | 40 c., red on buff .. | 1.50 | |
| 10 | 75 c., carmine on rose .. | 1.50 | |
| 11 | 1 fr., olive-grn. on toned | 1.85 | |

The surcharge on the 4 c. has been reprinted. In this reprint the letters "O" of "OBOCK" are 4 mm. instead of 3½ mm. in height.

## OBOCK

**2**

*Surcharged with* Type 2,
*in* black.

| | | | |
|---|---|---|---|
| 12 | 4 c., purple-brn. on grey | 12 | |
| 13 | 5 c., green on pale green | 12 | |
| 14 | 10 c., black on lilac .. | 16 | 25 |
| 15 | 15 c., blue .. .. | 25 | |
| 16 | 20 c., red on green .. | 50 | |
| 17 | 25 c., black on rose .. | 35 | |
| 18 | 40 c., red on buff .. | 62 | |
| 19 | 75 c., carmine on rose .. | 1.00 | |
| 20 | 1 fr., olive-grn. on toned | 1.00 | 1.25 |

The 1, 2, 30, and 35 c. with this surcharge are only proofs, and were never issued.

Some values are found with double surcharge.

**3**          **4**

*Surcharged with* Type 2, *in* black, *and with value.*

(*a*) *As* Type 3, *in* red.

| | | | |
|---|---|---|---|
| 1 on 25 c., black on rose | 8 | | |
| 2 on 10 c. ,, lilac | 90 | | |
| 2 on 15 c., blue .. | 12 | 18 | |

---

| No. | | Un. | Used |
|---|---|---|---|
| 24 | 5 on 25 c., black on rose | 12 | |
| 25 | 20 on 10 c. ,, lilac | 1.10 | |
| 26 | 30 on 10 c. ,, ,, | 1.25 | |
| 27 | 35 on 25 c. ,, rose | 1.50 | |
| 28 | 75 on 1 fr., olive-green on toned .. .. .. | 1.50 | |

*Surcharge inverted.*

| | | | |
|---|---|---|---|
| 28*a* | 1 on 25 c., black on rose | | |
| 28*b* | 20 on 10 c. ,, lilac | | |
| 28*c* | 75 on 1 fr., olive-green on toned .. .. | | |

*Surcharge double.*

| | | | |
|---|---|---|---|
| 28*d* | "22" on 10 c., black on lilac .. .. | | |
| 28*e* | "22" on 15 c., blue .. | | |

*Errors.*

| | | | |
|---|---|---|---|
| 28*f* | "3" on 25 c., black on rose .. .. | | |
| 28*g* | "7" on 1 fr., olive-green on toned .. .. | | |

(*b*) *As* Type 3, *in* black.

| | | | |
|---|---|---|---|
| 29 | 4 on 15 c., blue.. .. | 12 | |
| 30 | 4 on 25 c., black on rose | 25 | 36 |

*Surcharge inverted.*

| | | | |
|---|---|---|---|
| 30*a* | 4 on 15 c., blue.. .. | | |
| 30*b* | 4 on 25 c., black on rose | | |

*Surcharge double.*

| | | | |
|---|---|---|---|
| 30*c* | "44" on 25 c., black on rose .. .. .. | | |

(*c*) *As* Type 3, *in* blue.

| | | | |
|---|---|---|---|
| 30*d* | 2 on 15 c., blue .. | | |

(*d*) *With* Type 4, *in* blue.

| | | | |
|---|---|---|---|
| 31 | 5 fr. on 1 fr., olive-green on toned .. .. | 6.25 | |

"F" *inverted.*

| | | | |
|---|---|---|---|
| 31*a* | 5 fr. on 1 fr., olive-green on toned .. .. | | |

**5**

**1892.** Type 5.  *Perf.* 14×13½.

| | | | |
|---|---|---|---|
| 32 | 1 c., black on azure .. | 4 | 4 |
| 33 | 2 c., brown on buff .. | 10 | 4 |
| 34 | 4 c., purple-brn. on grey | 8 | 4 |
| 35 | 5 c., green on pale green | 4 | |
| 36 | 10 c., black on lilac .. | 25 | |

| No. | | Un. | Used. | No. | | Un. | Used. |
|---|---|---|---|---|---|---|---|
| 37 | 15 c., blue .. .. | 10 | 12 | 49 | 4 c., pur.-brn. and oran. | 8 | |
| 38 | 20 c., red on green .. | 50 | | 50 | 5 c., blue-grn. and brn. | 4 | |
| 39 | 25 c., black on rose .. | 12 | 16 | 51 | 10 c., black and green.. | 8 | |
| 40 | 30 c., cinnamon on drab. | 25 | | 52 | 15 c., ultramarine & rose | 8 | 12 |
| 41 | 40 c., red on yellow .. | 25 | | 53 | 20 c., orange and purple | 12 | |
| 42 | 50 c., carmine on rose .. | 25 | | 54 | 25 c., black and blue .. | 12 | |
| 43 | 75 c., brown on orange.. | 30 | | 55 | 30 c., bistre and green .. | 16 | |
| 44 | 1 fr., olive-grn. on toned | 36 | | 56 | 40 c., red and blue-green | 18 | |
| | | | | 57 | 50 c., rose and blue .. | 50 | |
| | | | | 58 | 75 c., lilac and orange .. | 36 | |
| | | | | 59 | 1 fr., olive-grn. & purp. | | |

*Variety. Name printed twice.*

| 44a | 75 c., brown on orange . | 2.50 |
|---|---|---|

6

9

*Type 9. Quadrillé paper. Imperf.*

*Vignette in second colour.*

| 60 | 2 fr., lilac and orange.. | 1.25 |
|---|---|---|
| 61 | 5 fr., blue and rose .. | 2.50 |
| 62 | 10 fr., red and mauve .. | 5.00 |
| 63 | 25 fr., brown and blue .. | 10.00 |
| 64 | 50 fr., lake and green .. | 18.75 |

7

**1893.** *Quadrillé paper. Imperf.*

| 45 | 6 | 2 fr., slate-green .. | 1.85 | 2.50 |
|---|---|---|---|---|
| 46 | 7 | 5 fr., rose .. | | |

The apparent perforation in the illustrations is part of the engraved design, and the same is the case in the next issue.

8

**1893-94.** Type **8.** *Quadrillé paper. Imperf.*

*The value, the oriental inscriptions in the upper corners, and the tablet below containing the name and date, are in the second colour.*

| 47 | 1 c., black and rose .. | 4 |
|---|---|---|
| 48 | 2 c., purp.-brn. and grn. | 6 |

## UNPAID LETTER STAMPS.

**1892.** Colonial Type (v). *Imperf.*

*Surcharged, in black, with Types 1 and 2.*

| No. | Type. | | | | |
|---|---|---|---|---|---|
| 201 | 1 | 5 c., black .. | .. | | |
| 202 | " | 10 c. " | .. | .. | 2.00 |
| 203 | " | 30 c. " | .. | .. | 2.00 |
| 204 | " | 60 c. " | .. | .. | 5.00 |
| 205 | 2 | 1 c. " | .. | .. | 50 |
| 206 | " | 2 c. " | .. | .. | 50 |
| 207 | " | 3 c. " | .. | .. | 50 |
| 208 | " | 4 c. " | .. | .. | 50 |
| 209 | " | 5 c. " | .. | .. | 25 |
| 210 | " | 10 c. " | .. | .. | 25 |
| 211 | " | 15 c. " | .. | .. | 50 |
| 212 | " | 20 c. " | .. | .. | 36 |
| 213 | " | 30 c. " | .. | .. | 36 |
| 214 | " | 40 c. " | .. | .. | 62 |
| 215 | " | 60 c. " | .. | .. | 75 |
| 216 | " | 1 fr., brown | .. | .. | 1.00 |
| 217 | " | 2 fr. " | .. | .. | 1.50 |
| 218 | " | 5 fr. " | .. | .. | 3.00 |

Some of the values are found with double and inverted surcharges of Type 2.

The surcharge on the 5 c., No. 201, has been reprinted. On the original the surcharge is 12½ mm. wide by 3¾ high. On the reprint it is 12×3½ mm.

No. *Un. Used.*

## OCEANIC SETTLEMENTS.

1

**1892.**

Type 1. *Perf.* 14×13½.

| | | | | |
|---|---|---|---|---|
| 1 | 1 c., black on azure .. | 2 | | |
| 2 | 2 c., brown on buff .. | 2 | | |
| 3 | 4 c., purp.-brn. on grey | 2 | | |
| 4 | 5 c., green on pale grn. | 2 | 2 | |
| 5 | 10 c., black on lilac .. | 4 | 6 | |
| 6 | 15 c., blue .. .. | 6 | | |
| 7 | 20 c., red on green .. | 6 | 8 | |
| 8 | 25 c., black on rose .. | 8 | | |
| 9 | 30 c., cinnamon on drab | 10 | | |
| 10 | 40 c., red on yellow .. | 12 | 16 | |
| 11 | 50 c., carmine on rose .. | 16 | | |
| 12 | 75 c., brown on orange.. | 25 | | |
| 13 | 1 fr., olive-grn. on toned | 30 | | |

**1900.**

*Colours changed.*

| | | | |
|---|---|---|---|
| 14 | 5 c., bright yellow-grn. | | |
| 15 | 10 c., rose-red .. .. | 4 | |
| 16 | 15 c., grey .. .. | 6 | |
| 17 | 25 c., blue .. .. | 8 | |
| 18 | 50 c., brown on azure .. | 16 | |

## REUNION.

1      2

**1852.**

No. Type. *Bluish paper. Imperf.*

| | | | |
|---|---|---|---|
| 1 | 1 | 15 c., black .. .. | |
| 2 | 2 | 30 c. ,, .. | |

There are four varieties of type of each value.

These stamps have been reprinted five times. The originals are framed by two in lines and one thick line, whereas all reprints have only two lines, one thin, one thick.

---

No. Type. *Un. Used.*

**5c.** **25c.**
**R** **R**
3      4

**1885.** Types 3, 4, *and* 5 *surcharged, in* black, *on*

(a) Eagle Type. *Imperf.*

| | | | | |
|---|---|---|---|---|
| 3 | 3 | 5 c. on 40 c., orange | 1.85 | |
| 4 | 4 | 25 c. on 40 c. ,, | 36 | |

*Surcharge inverted.*

| | | | |
|---|---|---|---|
| 5 | 3 | 5 c. on 40 c., orange | |
| 6 | 4 | 25 c. on 40 c. ,, | |

*Double surcharge.*

| | | | |
|---|---|---|---|
| 6a | 4 | 25 c. on 40 c., orange | |

(b) Laureated Type. *Imperf.*

| | | | | |
|---|---|---|---|---|
| 7 | 3 | 5 c. on 30 c., bistre-brn. | 25 | 25 |
| 8 | ,, | 5 c. on 30 c., drab.. | 18 | 12 |

*Surcharge inverted.*

| | | | |
|---|---|---|---|
| 8a | 3 | 5 c. on 30 c., bistre-brown .. | |

*Double surcharge.*

| | | | |
|---|---|---|---|
| 8b | 3 | 5 c. on 30 c., bistre-brown .. | |

*Figure "5" inverted.*

| | | | |
|---|---|---|---|
| 9 | 3 | 5 c. on 30 c., drab.. | |

(c) Ceres Type. *Imperf.*

| | | | | |
|---|---|---|---|---|
| 10 | 3 | 5 c. on 40 c., orange | 50 | 36 |
| 11 | ,, | 5 c. on 40 c., pale oran. | 50 | 36 |

*Surcharge inverted.*

| | | | |
|---|---|---|---|
| 12 | 3 | 5 c. on 40 c., pale oran. | 7.50 |

*Double surcharge.*

| | | | |
|---|---|---|---|
| 12a | 3 | 5 c. on 40 c., pale oran. | |

**20c.**
**R**
5

(d) Peace and Commerce Type. *Imperf.*

| | | | | |
|---|---|---|---|---|
| 13 | 3 | 5 c. on 30 c., dull brn. | 18 | 18 |
| 14 | ,, | 5 c. on 40 c., red on buff | 62 | |
| 15 | 5 | 10 c. on 40 c., red on buff .. .. | 18 | 25 |
| 16 | ,, | 20 c. on 30 c., dull brn. | 50 | |

*Surcharge inverted.*

| | | | |
|---|---|---|---|
| 16a | 3 | 5 c. on 30 c., dull brn. | |
| 17 | ,, | 5 c. on 40 c., red on buff .. .. | |
| 17a | ,, | 10 c. on 40 c., red on buff .. .. | |

*Double surcharge.*

| | | | |
|---|---|---|---|
| 17b | 3 | 5 c. on 40 c., red on buff .. .. | |
| 17c | ,, | 5 c. on 30 c., dull brn. | |
| 17d | ,, | 10 c. on 40 c., red on buff .. .. | |

Many of the above surcharges on the 40 c. doubtless exist with wide figure

| No. Type. | Un. | Used. |
|---|---|---|

"4," but no list has yet been compiled, and therefore in the absence of fuller knowledge they are not given.

6

**1891.** Ceres Type (F), *the same with* large figures (G), *and* Peace and Commerce Type (H), *imperf., and* Commerce Type (J), *perf.* 14×13½. *Surcharged with* Type 6, *in black.*

| 18 | F | 40 c., orange | .. | | |
|---|---|---|---|---|---|
| 19 | G | 80 c., carmine | | 75 | 1.00 |
| 20 | H | 30 c., dull brown | .. | 62 | |
| 21 | " | 40 c., red on buff | .. | 36 | 36 |
| 22 | " | 75 c., deep carmine . | 3.00 | | |
| 23 | " | 1 fr., olive-green on | | | |
| | | toned | .. | 90 | 90 |
| 24 | J | 1 c., black on azure | | 4 | 8 |
| 25 | " | 2 c., brown on buff. | | 6 | 8 |
| 26 | " | 4 c., purple-brn. on | | | |
| | | grey | .. | 10 | 10 |
| 27 | " | 5 c., gn. on pale gn. | | 6 | 4 |
| 28 | " | 10 c., black on lilac . | | 6 | 6 |
| 29 | " | 15 c., blue | .. | 10 | 4 |
| 30 | " | 20 c., red on green.. | | 30 | 30 |
| 31 | " | 25 c., black on rose . | | 18 | 12 |
| 32 | " | 35 c., black on yellow | | 50 | |
| 33 | " | 35 c.  ,,  orange | | 62 | |
| 34 | " | 40 c., red on buff | .. | 75 | |
| 35 | " | 75 c., carmine on rose | 2.50 | | |
| 36 | " | 1 fr., olive-green on | | | |
| | | toned | .. | 2.50 | |

The 2, 5, 10, and 15 c. are known with the surcharge inverted.

The errors of this issue are very numerous. Apart from those errors due to a failure of the printing of letters, or parts of letters, the following bona fide errors of spelling are known:—BUNION, REUNIONR, RIUNION, RÚNION, REUNOIN, ERUNION, RUENION, REUNIO, RƷUNION, and PEUNION.

02<sup>c</sup>

02c

7

**1891.** No. 30 *surcharged with value in addition, in black.*

| 37 | 7 | 02 c. on 20 c. | .. | 4 | |
|---|---|---|---|---|---|
| 38 | " | 15 c. on 20 c. | .. | 10 | 12 |

The errors of spelling found on the above two stamps are:—PEUNION, RUNION, RIUNION. The "c" is found in varying positions after the numerals.

| No. Type. | Un. | Used. |
|---|---|---|

| 39 | 8 | 2 on 20 c. | .. | .. | 8 | |
|---|---|---|---|---|---|---|
| 40 | 9 | 1 on 20 c. | .. | .. | 4 | 8 |
| 41 | 10 | 2 on 20 c. | .. | .. | 4 | 8 |

No. 39 is known with RUENION, and Nos. 40 and 41 with RUENION, REUNOIN, and PEUNION.

11

**1892.** Type 11. *Perf.* 14×13½.

| 42 | 1 c., black on azure | .. | 2 | 2 |
|---|---|---|---|---|
| 43 | 2 c., brown on buff | .. | 2 | 2 |
| 44 | 4 c., purple-bn. on grey | | 2 | 2 |
| 45 | 5 c., green on pale green | | 4 | 2 |
| 46 | 10 c., black on lilac | .. | 4 | 2 |
| 47 | 15 c., blue | .. | 18 | 2 |
| 48 | 20 c., red on green | | 6 | 8 |
| 49 | 25 c., black on rose | | 8 | 2 |
| 50 | 30 c., cinnamon on drab. | | 10 | |
| 51 | 40 c., red on yellow | .. | 12 | 16 |
| 52 | 50 c., carmine on rose | .. | 16 | |
| 53 | 75 c., brown on orange.. | | 25 | |
| 54 | 1 fr., olive-gn. on toned | | 30 | |

*Error. Name in red and blue.*

| 55 | 50 c., carmine on rose .. | | |
|---|---|---|---|

*Error. Name twice printed.*

| 55a | 25 c., black on rose | .. | 5.00 |
|---|---|---|---|
| 55b | 75 c., brown on orange . | | 3.00 |

2 c.

12

**1893.** Commerce Type. *Perf.* 14×13½. *Surcharged in black.*

| 56 | 12 | 2 c. on 20 c., red on | | | |
|---|---|---|---|---|---|
| | | green | .. | .. | 4 |

2 c.  2 c.

13  14

| 57 | 13 | 2 c. on 20 c. | .. | 6 |
|---|---|---|---|---|
| 58 | 14 | 2 c. on 20 c. | .. | 50 |

Type 13 is also found without stop after "c."

| No. | | Un. | Used. |
|---|---|---|---|

**1900.**  *Type and perf. of 1892.*
*Colours changed.*

| 59 | 5 c., bright yellow-green | 2 |
| 60 | 10 c., rose-red .. | 4 |
| 61 | 15 c., grey .. | 6 |
| 61a | 15 c., pale grey .. | 6 |
| 62 | 25 c., blue .. | 8 |
| 63 | 50 c., brown on azure .. | 16 |

# 5 c.

**—**

**15**

30 SEPT., **1901.**
Type **11** *surcharged as* Type **15,** *in* black.

| 64 | 5 c. on 40 c., red on yell. | 8 |
| 65 | 5 c. on 50 c., carm. on rose | 8 |
| 66 | 15 c. on 75 c., brn. on oran. | 12 |
| 67 | 15 c. on 1 fr., olive-green | 12 |

*Smaller figure " 1."*

| 68 | 15 c. on 75 c., brn. on oran. | 16 |
| 69 | 15 c. on 1 fr., olive-green | 16 |

*Variety.  Bar omitted.*

| 69a | 15 c. on 75 c., brown on orange .. |
| 69b | 15 c. on 1 fr., olive-green |

*Surcharge inverted.*

| 70 | 5 c. on 40 c., red on yell. | 1.25 |
| 71 | 5 c. on 50 c., carmine .. | 2.10 |
| 72 | 15 c. on 75 c., brn. on oran. | 1.50 |
| 73 | 15 c. on 1 fr., olive-green | 1.85 |

*Smaller figure " 1."*

| 74 | 15 c. on 75 c., brn. on oran. | 2.50 |
| 75 | 15 c. on 1 fr., olive-green | 1.85 |

*Variety.  Bar omitted.*

| 76 | 15 c. on 75 c., brown on orange .. |
| 77 | 15 c., on 1 fr., olive-green |

UNPAID LETTER STAMPS.

**51**

**1889.**  Type **51.**  *Toned paper.*
*Imperf.*

| 201 | 5 c., black | .. | .. | 36 |
| 202 | 10 c., ,, | .. | .. | 36 |
| 203 | 20 c., ,, | .. | .. | 36 |
| 204 | 30 c., ,, | .. | .. | 50 |

| No. | | Un. | Used. |
|---|---|---|---|

**1892.**  *Thin, bluish white paper.*

| 205 | 5 c., black | .. | .. | — | 50 |
| 206 | 10 c., ,, | .. | .. | 36 | |
| 207 | 15 c., ,, | .. | .. | 36 | 36 |
| 208 | 30 c., ,, | .. | .. | | |

## STE. MARIE DE MADAGASCAR.

**1**

**1894.**  Type **1.**  *Perf.* 14 × 13½.

| 1 | 1 c., black on azure .. | 2 |
| 2 | 2 c., brown on buff .. | 2 |
| 3 | 4 c., purple-brown on grey | .. | 2 |
| 4 | 5 c., green on pale green | 2 |
| 5 | 10 c., black on lilac .. | 4 |
| 6 | 15 c., blue .. | 6 |
| 7 | 20 c., red on green .. | 6 |
| 8 | 25 c., black on rose .. | 8 |
| 9 | 30 c., cinnamon on drab. | 10 |
| 10 | 40 c., red on yellow .. | 12 |
| 11 | 50 c., carmine on rose .. | 16 |
| 12 | 75 c., brown on orange.. | 25 |
| 13 | 1 fr., olive-green on toned | .. | .. | 30 |

These stamps are now obsolete, the new series for MADAGASCAR AND DEPEN-DENCIES being used here.

## ST. PIERRE AND MIQUELON.

**1**

JAN. *to* MARCH, **1885.**
Peace and Commerce Type (H).  *Imperf.*
*Surcharged in* black.
Type **2** *is similar to* Type **4.**
No. Type.

| 1 | 1 | 25 on 1 fr., olive-grn. |
| 2 | 2 | 25 on 1 fr. ,, |

*Varieties.*

(a) *Surcharge sideways reading upwards.*

| 3 | 1 | 25 on 1 fr., olive-grn. |
| 4 | 2 | 25 on 1 fr. ,, |

| | | | Un. | Used. |
|---|---|---|---|---|

No. Type.

*(b) Surcharge sideways reading downwards.*

| 5 | 1 | 25 on 1 fr., olive-grn. | | |
| 6 | 2 | 25 on 1 fr. ,, | | |

*Surcharge inverted.*

| 6a | 1 | 05 on 1 fr., olive-grn. | | |
| 6b | 2 | 25 on 1 fr. ,, | | |

S P M    S P M

3         4

Commerce Type (J). *Perf.* 14×13½.
*Surcharged in* black.

| 7 | 3 | 5 on 2 c., brn. on buff | | |
| 8 | 4 | 5 on 4 c., purple on lilac .. .. | 2.50 | 2.50 |

*Surcharge inverted.*

| 9 | 3 | 5 on 2 c., brn. on buff | | |
| 10 | 4 | 5 on 4 c., purple on lilac .. | | |

5         6

JULY, 1885.
Peace and Commerce Type (H). *Imperf.*
*Surcharged in* black.

| 11 | 5 | 05 on 40 c., red on buff | — | 25 |
| 12 | ,, | 10 on 40 c. ,, ,, | | 25 |
| 13 | 6 | 10 on 40 c. ,, ,, | | 2.50 |
| 14 | 5 | 15 on 40 c. ,, ,, | | 25 |
| 15 | 6 | 15 on 40 c. ,, ,, | | 50 |

*Surcharge inverted.*

| 16 | 5 | 10 on 40 c., red on buff | | |
| 16a | ,, | 15 on 40 c. ,, | | |

S P M

7

DEC., 1885. *Same types surcharged, in black, with Type 7.*

| 17 | H | 05 on 35 c., black on yellow .. .. | 1.00 | 50 |

---

| | | | Un. | Used. |
|---|---|---|---|---|

No. Type.

| 17a | H | 05 on 35 c., black on orange .. .. | 1.00 | |
| 18 | ,, | 05 on 75 c., deep carmine .. .. | 3.00 | |
| 19 | ,, | 05 on 75 c., rose-carmine .. .. | | |
| 20 | ,, | 05 on 1 fr., olive-grn. | 45 | 36 |
| 21 | J | 05 on 20 c., red on grn. | 62 | 30 |

PD / 15

8

1886. *Struck on plain paper. Imperf.*

| 22 | 8 | 5 (c.), black .. | — | .5.00 |
| 23 | ,, | 10 (c.) ,, .. | — | 6.25 |
| 24 | ,, | 15 (c.) ,, .. | — | 5.00 |

It seems doubtful whether these are anything more than marks applied to letters the postage on which was paid in cash.

15 c.    15 c.

S P M    S P M

9         10

1891. Commerce Type. *Perf.* 14×13½.
*Surcharged in* black.

| 25 | 9 | 15 c. on 30 c., cinnam. | 50 | 50 |
| 26 | ,, | 15 c. on 35 c., black on orange .. | 6.25 | 6.25 |
| 27 | 10 | 15 c. on 35 c., black on orange .. | | |
| 28 | 9 | 15 c. on 40 c., red on buff .. | 50 | 50 |

*Varieties. Surcharge inverted.*

| 28a | 9 | 15 c. on 30 c., cinnam. | | |
| 29 | ,, | 15 c. on 35 c., black on orange .. | | |
| 30 | 10 | 15 c. on 35 c., black on orange .. | — | 12.50 |
| 30a | 9 | 15 c. on 40 c., red on buff .. | | |

ST. PIERRE M 00

11

1891-92. *Same type surcharged with Type 11. (a) In* black.

| 31 | 1 c., black on azure .. | 10 | |
| 32 | 2 c., brown on buff .. | 12 | |

| No. | | Un. | Used. |
|---|---|---|---|
| 33 | 4 c., purple-brown on grey .. .. .. | 16 | |
| 34 | 5 c., green on pale green | 12 | |
| 35 | 10 c., black on lilac .. | 1.50 | |
| 36 | 15 c., blue .. .. | 18 | |
| 37 | 20 c., red on green .. | 62 | |
| 38 | 25 c., black on rose .. | 36 | 36 |
| 39 | 30 c., cinnamon on drab. | 75 | 90 |
| 40 | 35 c., black on orange .. | 6.25 | |
| 41 | 40 c., red on buff .. | 1.00 | 1.00 |
| 42 | 75 c., carmine on rose .. | 1.50 | 1.00 |
| 43 | 1 fr., olive-green on toned .. .. .. | 1.50 | |

*Variety. Imperf.*
43a| 1 fr., olive-grn. on toned

*Surcharge inverted.*

| 44 | 1 c., black on azure .. | 25 | |
| 45 | 2 c., brown on buff .. | 25 | |
| 46 | 4 c., purple-brown on grey .. .. .. | 1.25 | |
| 47 | 5 c., green on pale green | | |
| 48 | 10 c., black on lilac .. | 7.50 | |
| 53 | 35 c., black on orange .. | | |
| 55 | 75 c., carmine on rose .. | | |
| 56 | 1 fr., olive-green on toned .. .. .. | | |

*(b) In red.*

| 57 | 1 c., black on azure .. | 8 | |
| 58 | 2 c., brown on buff .. | 18 | |
| 59 | 4 c., purple-brown on grey .. .. | 36 | |
| 60 | 10 c., black on lilac .. | 36 | 36 |

*Surcharge inverted.*

| 61 | 1 c., black on azure .. | 50 | |
| 62 | 2 c., brown on buff .. | 50 | |
| 63 | 4 c., purple-brown on grey .. .. .. | — | 1.25 |
| 64 | 10 c., black on lilac .. | 50 | 50 |

12

*Same type surcharged, in black, as*
Type 12.

| 65 | 1 c. on 5 c., green on pale green .. .. | 8 | |
| 66 | 1 c. on 10 c., blk. on lilac | 8 | |
| 67 | 1 c. on 25 c., blk. on rose | 4 | |
| 68 | 2 c. on 10 c., blk. on lilac | 10 | |
| 69 | 2 c. on 15 c., blue .. | 16 | |
| 70 | 2 c. on 25 c., blk. on rose | 6 | |
| 71 | 4 c. on 20 c., red on gn. | 12 | |

| No. | | Un. | Used. |
|---|---|---|---|
| 72 | 4 c. on 25 c., blk. on rose | 6 | |
| 73 | 4 c. on 30 c., cinnamon. | 18 | |
| 74 | 4 c. on 40 c., red on buff | 50 | |

13

**1892.** *Surcharged, in black, with Type 11 and a double-lined shaded figure, as Type 13.*

| 75 | 1 on 5 c., gn. on pale gn. | 4 |
| 76 | 2 on 5 c. ,, ,, | 4 |
| 77 | 4 on 5 c. ,, ,, | 6 |

14

*With a thick figure as Type 14.*

| 78 | 1 on 25 c., black on rose | 4 |
| 79 | 2 on 25 c. ,, ,, | 4 |
| 80 | 4 on 25 c. ,, ,, | 4 |

15

Colonial Type (u). *Imperf. Surcharge with* Type 15. *(a) In* red.

| 81 | 10 c., black | .. | .. | 50 |
| 82 | 20 c. ,, | .. | .. | 50 |
| 83 | 30 c. ,, | .. | .. | 50 |
| 84 | 40 c. ,, | .. | .. | 50 |
| 85 | 60 c. ,, | .. | .. | 90 |

| No. | | | Un. | Used. |
|---|---|---|---|---|

**(b) In black.**

| 86 | 1 fr., brown | .. | .. | 1.25 |
| 87 | 2 fr., ,, | .. | .. | 1.60 |
| 88 | 5 fr., ,, | .. | .. | 6.25 |

**16**

**1892.** Type 16. *Perf.* 14×13½.

| 89 | 1 c., black on azure | .. | 2 | 2 |
| 90 | 2 c., brown on buff | .. | 2 | 2 |
| 91 | 4 c., purple-bn. on grey | 2 | 2 |
| 92 | 5 c., green on pale green | 2 | |
| 93 | 10 c., black on lilac | .. | 4 | 6 |
| 94 | 15 c., blue | .. | .. | 6 | |
| 95 | 20 c., red on green | .. | 6 | |
| 96 | 25 c., black on rose | .. | 8 | 8 |
| 97 | 30 c., cinnamon on drab. | 10 | |
| 98 | 40 c., red on yellow | .. | 12 | 12 |
| 99 | 50 c., carmine on rose .. | 16 | |
| 100 | 75 c., brown on orange.. | 25 | 25 |
| 101 | 1 fr., olive-grn. on toned | 30 | 30 |

**1900.** *Same type and perf.*
*Colours changed.*

| 102 | 10 c., rose-red | .. | .. | 4 |
| 103 | 15 c., grey | .. | .. | 6 |
| 104 | 25 c., blue | .. | .. | 8 |
| 105 | 50 c., brown on azure .. | 16 |

**UNPAID LETTER STAMPS.**
**1892.** Colonial Type (U). *Imperf.*
*Surcharged with Type 11.*
**(a) In red.**

| 301 | 5 c., black | .. | .. | 75 |
| 302 | 10 c., ,, | .. | .. | 36 |
| 303 | 15 c., ,, | .. | .. | 36 |
| 304 | 20 c., ,, | .. | .. | 36 |
| 305 | 30 c., ,, | .. | .. | 36 |
| 306 | 40 c., ,, | .. | .. | 50 |
| 307 | 60 c., ,, | .. | .. | 75 | 75 |

**(b) In black.**

| 308 | 1 fr., brown | .. | .. | 1.25 | 1.50 |
| 309 | 2 fr., ,, | .. | .. | 1.85 |

**SENEGAL**

**1887.** Commerce Type. *Perf.* 14×13½.
*Surcharged in black.*

| No. | Type. | | | Un. | Used. |
|---|---|---|---|---|---|
| 1 | 1 | 5 on 20 c., red on grn. | 1.00 | |
| 2 | 2 | 5 ,, ,, ,, | 1.00 | 1.00 |
| 3 | 3 | 5 on 20 c., red on grn. | 5.00 | |
| 4 | 4 | 5 ,, ,, ,, | 3.75 | |
| 5 | 5 | 5 ,, ,, ,, | 3.75 | |
| 6 | 1 | 5 on 30 c., cinnamon | 4.35 | |
| 7 | 2 | 5 ,, ,, | 3.75 | 5.00 |
| 9 | 4 | 5 ,, ,, | | |
| 11 | 6 | 10 on 4 c., purple-brown on grey .. | — | 50 |
| 12 | 7 | 10 on 4 c. | .. | .. | 1.85 | 50 |
| 13 | 8 | 10 on 4 c. | .. | .. | 1.60 | |
| 14 | 9 | 10 on 4 c. | .. | .. | 1.85 | 62 |
| 15 | 6 | 10 on 20 c., red on grn. | | |
| 16 | 7 | 10 ,, ,, ,, | — | 7.50 |
| 17 | 8 | 10 ,, ,, ,, | — | 7.50 |
| 18 | 9 | 10 ,, ,, ,, | — | 7.50 |
| 19 | 10 | 10 on 20 c., red on grn. | | |
| 20 | 11 | 10 ,, ,, ,, | | |
| 21 | 12 | 10 ,, ,, ,, | | |
| 22 | 13 | 10 ,, ,, ,, | | |
| 23 | 14 | 15 on 20 c., red on grn. | 1.25 | 62 |
| 24 | 15 | 15 ,, ,, ,, | 2.50 | |
| 25 | 16 | 15 ,, ,, ,, | 2.50 | |
| 26 | 17 | 15 ,, ,, ,, | 1.25 | 50 |
| 27 | 18 | 15 on 20 c., red on grn. | 1.25 | 50 |
| 28 | 19 | 15 ,, ,, ,, | 1.50 | 75 |
| 29 | 20 | 15 ,, ,, ,, | 1.25 | 75 |
| 30 | 21 | 15 ,, ,, ,, | — | 1.50 |
| 31 | 22 | 15 ,, ,, ,, | 1.50 | 1.25 |
| 31a | 22a | 15 ,, ,, ,, | — | 2.50 |
| 31b | 22b | 15 ,, ,, ,, | | |

| No. | | | *Un.* | *Used.* |
|---|---|---|---|---|

**23**                **24**

**1892.**  *Same type and perf.  Surcharged.*
          *(a) In* black.

| 32 | **23** | 75 on 15 c., blue .. | 1.25 | 1.25 |
| 33 | **24** | 1 F on 5 c., green .. | 1.25 | 1.25 |

          *(b) In* red.

| 34 | **23** | 75 on 15 c., blue .. | — | 50.00 |
| 35 | **24** | 1 F on 5 c., green .. | — | 30.00 |

**25**

**1892.**  Type **25.**  *Perf.* 14 × 13½.

| 36 | 1 c., black on azure .. | 2 | 2 |
| 37 | 2 c., brown on buff .. | 2 | 2 |
| 38 | 4 c., purple-brn. on grey | 2 | |
| 39 | 5 c., green on pale green | 2 | 2 |
| 40 | 10 c., black on lilac .. | 6 | 6 |
| 41 | 15 c., blue      .. | 6 | 4 |
| 42 | 20 c., red on green .. | 6 | 6 |
| 43 | 25 c., black on rose .. | 8 | 4 |
| 44 | 30 c., cinnamon on drab | 10 | 10 |
| 45 | 40 c., red on yellow .. | 12 | |
| 46 | 50 c., carmine on rose .. | 16 | |
| 47 | 75 c., brown on orange . | 25 | 25 |
| 48 | 1 fr., olive-grn. on toned | 30 | |

**1899-1900.**  *Same type and perf.*
            *Colours changed.*

| 49 | 5 c., bright yellow-green | 2 | 2 |
| 50 | 10 c., rose-red .. .. | 4 | |
| 51 | 15 c., grey .. .. | 6 | |
| 52 | 25 c., blue .. .. | 8 | |
| 53 | 50 c., brown on azure .. | 16 | |

**5**                **10**

**26**                **27**

Oct., **1903.**  Type **25** *surcharged with*
          Types **26** *or* **27**, *in* black.

| 1 | 5 on 40 c., red on yellow |

| No. | | | *Un.* | *Used.* |
|---|---|---|---|---|
| 55 | 10 on 50 c., carm. on rose | | |
| 56 | 10 on 75 c., brn. on oran. | | |
| 57 | 10 on 1 fr., olive-green on toned .. .. | | |

## SENEGAMBIA AND NIGER.

**1**

**1903.**  Type **1.**  *Perf.* 14 × 13½.

| 1 | 1 c., black on azure .. | |
| 2 | 2 c., purp.-brn. on buff | |
| 3 | 4 c.,  „       grey | |
| 4 | 5 c., yellow-green .. | |
| 5 | 10 c., rose-red .. .. | |
| 6 | 15 c., grey .. .. | |
| 7 | 20 c., red on green .. | |
| 8 | 25 c., blue .. .. | |
| 9 | 30 c., cinnamon on drab | |
| 10 | 40 c., red on yellow .. | |
| 11 | 50 c., brown on azure .. | |
| 12 | 75 c.,  „       orange .. | |
| 13 | 1 fr., olive-grn. on toned | |

## TAHITI.

**1**

**1882.**  Peace and Commerce Type.
          *Imperf.*
*Surcharged with* Type **1**, *in* black.

| 1 | 25 c. on 35 c., blk. on oran. |

**TAHITI**
**5c**

**2**

**1884.**  Commerce Type.  *Perf.* 14 × 13½.
          *Surcharged in* black.

No. Type.  *(a) Horizontally.*

| 2 | **2** | 5 c. on 20 c., red on gn. |

_Un. Used._

No. Type.

3

4

| | | | | |
|---|---|---|---|---|
| 3 | 3 | 10 c. on 20 c., red on gn. | | |
| 4 | 4 | 25 c. on 1 fr., olive-gn. | | |

*(b) Inverted.*

| | | | | |
|---|---|---|---|---|
| 5 | 2 | 5 c. on 20 c., red on gn. | 10.00 | |
| 6 | 3 | 10 c. on 20 c. „ | | |
| 7 | 4 | 25 c. on 1 fr., olive-gn. | — | 25.00 |

*(c) Vertically, reading upwards.*

| | | | | |
|---|---|---|---|---|
| 8 | 2 | 5 c. on 20 c., red on gn. | 10.00 | |
| 9 | 3 | 10 c. on 20 c. „ | | |
| 10 | 4 | 25 c. on 1 fr., olive-gn. | | |

*(d) Vertically, reading downwards.*

| | | | | |
|---|---|---|---|---|
| 11 | 2 | 5 c. on 20 c., red on gn. | | |
| 12 | 3 | 10 c. on 20 c. | | |
| 13 | 4 | 25 c. on 1 fr., olive-gn. „ | | |

5

1 JULY, 1893. *Same type surcharged, in black, with* Type 5.

| | | | | |
|---|---|---|---|---|
| 14 | 1 c., black on azure | .. | | |
| 15 | 2 c., brown | .. | | |
| 16 | 4 c., purple-bn. on grey | | | |
| 17 | 5 c., green on pale green | 25 | | |
| 18 | 10 c., black on lilac | .. | 50 | |
| 19 | 15 c., blue | .. | 36 | 36 |
| 20 | 20 c., red on green | .. | 1.00 | 1.00 |
| 21 | 25 c., black on rose | .. | 36 | 36 |
| 22 | 35 c., black on orange | .. | | |
| 23 | 75 c., carmine on rose | .. | 90 | 90 |
| 24 | 1 fr., olive-gn. on toned | 2.00 | | |

This surcharge is also found reading downwards diagonally from left to right.

### 1893

### TAHITI

6

27 AUG., 1893. *Surcharged, in black, with* Type 6.

| | | | |
|---|---|---|---|
| 25 | 1 c., black on azure | .. | |
| 26 | 2 c., brown | .. | .. |

_Un. Used._

No.

| | | | | |
|---|---|---|---|---|
| 27 | 4 c., purple-brn. on grey | | | |
| 28 | 5 c., green on pale green | | | |
| 29 | 10 c., black on lilac | .. | | |
| 30 | 15 c., blue | .. | 45 | 45 |
| 31 | 20 c., red on green | .. | 62 | |
| 32 | 25 c., ochre | .. | | |
| 33 | 25 c., black on rose | .. | 50 | 50 |
| 34 | 35 c., black on orange | .. | | |
| 35 | 75 c., carmine on rose | .. | 75 | 75 |
| 36 | 1 fr., olive-grn. on toned | 1.25 | 1.25 | |

*Variety. Surcharge inverted.*

| | | | | |
|---|---|---|---|---|
| 37 | 10 c., black on lilac | .. | | |
| 38 | 15 c., blue | .. | | |
| 39 | 75 c., carmine on rose | .. | 3.75 | |

### TAHITI   TAHITI

### 10   10

**centimes**  CENTIMES

7    8

1903. *Stamps of* "OCEANIC SETTLE-MENTS" (Etablissements de l'Oceanie) *surcharged with* Type **7** *or* **8**; "centimes" *as* Type **7** *on the* 15 c., *as* Type **8** *on the other values; in black on the* 15 c. *and* 40 c., *in carmine on* 25 c.

*(a)* "10" *as* Type 7.

| | | | |
|---|---|---|---|
| 40 | 10 c. on 15 c., blue | .. | 12 |
| 41 | 10 c. on 25 c., blk. on rose | | 12 |
| 42 | 10 c. on 40 c., red on yell. | | |

*(b)* "10" *as* Type 8.

| | | | |
|---|---|---|---|
| 43 | 10 c. on 15 c., blue | .. | 62 |
| 44 | 10 c. on 25 c., blk. on rose | | 62 |
| 45 | 10 c. on 40 c., red on yell. | | |

*Surcharge inverted.*

| | | |
|---|---|---|
| 46 | 10 c. on 40 c. *(a)* | .. |
| 47 | 10 c. „ *(b)* | .. |

#### UNPAID LETTER STAMPS.

1893. Colonial Type (U). *Imperf.*

*Surcharged in* black.

*(a) With* Type 5.

| | | | |
|---|---|---|---|
| 201 | 1 c., black | .. | .. |
| 202 | 2 c. „ | .. | .. |
| 203 | 3 c. „ | .. | .. |
| 204 | 4 c. „ | .. | .. |
| 205 | 5 c. „ | .. | .. |
| 206 | 10 c. „ | .. | .. |
| 207 | 15 c. „ | .. | .. |
| 208 | 20 c. „ | .. | .. |
| 209 | 30 c. „ | .. | .. |
| 210 | 40 c. „ | .. | .. |
| 211 | 60 c. „ | .. | .. |
| 212 | 1 fr., brown | .. | .. |
| 213 | 2 fr. „ | .. | .. |

| No. | | | Un. | Used. |
|---|---|---|---|---|
| | **(b) With Type 6.** | | | |
| 214 | 1 c., black | .. | .. | |
| 215 | 2 c., ,, | .. | .. | |
| 216 | 3 c., ,, | .. | .. | |
| 217 | 4 c., ,, | .. | .. | |
| 218 | 5 c., ,, | .. | 3.00 | 3.00 |
| 219 | 10 c., ,, | .. | 3.00 | 3.00 |
| 220 | 15 c., ,, | .. | 3.75 | 3.00 |
| 221 | 20 c., ,, | .. | 2.00 | 1.60 |
| 222 | 30 c., ,, | .. | 3.75 | 3.00 |
| 223 | 40 c., ,, | .. | 4.35 | 4.35 |
| 224 | 60 c., ,, | .. | 3.75 | |
| 225 | 1 fr., brown | .. | 5.00 | 5.00 |
| 226 | 2 fr., ,, | .. | 5.65 | 5.65 |

The series for OCEANIC SETTLEMENTS is now used here.

## TUNIS.

1

### JULY, 1888.
#### Type 1.   *Perf.* 14 × 13½.

| | | | | |
|---|---|---|---|---|
| 1 | 1 c., black on azure | .. | 2 | |
| 2 | 2 c., brown-pink on buff | | 2 | |
| 2a | 2 c., brown on yellow | .. | | |
| 3 | 5 c., green on pale green | | 6 | 8 |
| 4 | 15 c., blue on pale blue . | | 25 | 18 |
| 5 | 25 c., black on rose | .. | 25 | 18 |
| 6 | 40.c., red on yellow | .. | 25 | 36 |
| 7 | 75 c., rose on pale rose.. | | 30 | |
| 8 | 5 fr., lilac on lilac | .. | 3.00 | 3.00 |

All the values were reprinted in 1893 with white instead of greyish gum. The shades are different from those of the issued stamps, being for the most part brighter.

2

### OCTOBER, 1888.
#### Type 2.   *Perf.* 14 × 13½.

| | | | | |
|---|---|---|---|---|
| 9 | 1 c., black on azure | .. | 2 | 2 |
| 10 | 1 c.,  ,,  grey-blue | | 2 | 2 |
| 1 | 2 c., brown-pink on buff | | 2 | 2 |
| 2 | 2 c., purple-brown  ,, | | 2 | 2 |
| 1 | 5 c., green on pale green | | 2 | 2 |

| No. | | | Un. | Used. |
|---|---|---|---|---|
| 14 | 15 c., blue on pale blue . | | 8 | 4 |
| 15 | 25 c., black on rose | .. | 10 | 2 |
| 16 | 40 c., red on yellow | .. | 12 | 6 |
| 17 | 75 c., rose on pale rose.. | | 1.00 | 1.00 |
| 18 | 1 fr., olive-gn. on toned | | 30 | 36 |
| 19 | 5 fr., lilac on lilac | .. | 1.50 | 62 |

#### Type 2. **1893-99.**   *Perf.* 14 × 13½.

| | | | | |
|---|---|---|---|---|
| 19a | 5 c., yellow-green | .. | 2 | 2 |
| 20 | 10 c., black on lilac | .. | 6 | 2 |
| 21 | 15 c., blue on *quadrillé*. | | 10 | 4 |
| 22 | 20 c., red on green | .. | 6 | 4 |
| 23 | 75 c., brown on orange . | | 25 | 25 |
| 24 | 1 fr., pale green | .. | 30 | 15 |

#### 1901-2.   *Same type and perf.*

| | | | |
|---|---|---|---|
| 25 | 10 c., carmine | .. | 4 |
| 26 | 15 c., grey | .. | 6 |
| 27 | 25 c., blue | .. | 8 |
| 28 | 35 c., brown | .. | 10 |
| 29 | 2 fr., violet | .. | 55 |

## 25

3

**1902.**   *Surcharged with* Type 3, *in* red.

| | | | |
|---|---|---|---|
| 30 | 25 on 15 c., blue on *quad.* | 18 | 2 |

### UNPAID LETTER STAMPS.

51

**1888.**   Type 1 *perforated with a* "T *as* Type 51, *small holes.*

| | | |
|---|---|---|
| 101 | 1 c., black on azure | .. |
| 102 | 2 c., brown-pink on buff | |
| 103 | 5 c., green on pale green | |
| 104 | 15 c., blue on pale blue . | |
| 105 | 25 c., black on rose | .. |
| 106 | 40 c., red on yellow | .. |
| 107 | 75 c., rose on pale rose.. | |
| 108 | 5 fr., lilac on lilac | .. |

*Varieties.   The* "T" *inverted.*

| | | |
|---|---|---|
| 109 | 1 c., black on azure | .. |
| 110 | 2 c., brown-pink on buff | |
| 111 | 5 c., green on pale green | |
| 112 | 15 c., blue on pale blue . | |
| 113 | 25 c., black on rose | .. |
| 114 | 40 c., red on yellow | .. |
| 115 | 75 c., rose on pale rose.. | |
| 116 | 5 fr., lilac on lilac | .. |

| No. | | | Un. | Used. |
|---|---|---|---|---|

**52**

**1888.** Type 1 *perforated with a "T" as Type 52, large holes.*

| 117 | 1 c., black on azure .. | 12 | |
|---|---|---|---|
| 118 | 2 c., brown-pink on buff | 12 | |
| 119 | 5 c., green on pale green | 25 | |
| 120 | 15 c., blue on pale blue . | 50 | |
| 121 | 25 c., black on rose | 62 | |
| 122 | 40 c., red on yellow .. | — | 1.00 |
| 123 | 75 c., rose on pale rose . | 1.50 | |
| 124 | 5 fr., lilac on lilac .. | | |

*Varieties. The "T" inverted.*

| 125 | 1 c., black on azure .. | 8 | |
|---|---|---|---|
| 126 | 2 c., brown-pink on buff | 12 | |
| 127 | 5 c., green on pale green | | |
| 128 | 15 c., blue on pale blue . | | |
| 129 | 25 c., black on rose .. | 50 | |
| 130 | 40 c., red on yellow .. | 1.25 | |
| 131 | 75 c., rose on pale rose . | 1.50 | |
| 132 | 5 fr., lilac on lilac .. | | |

**1888-98.** Type 2 *perforated as Type 52.*

| 133 | 1 c., black on azure .. | 6 | |
|---|---|---|---|
| 134 | 1 c. ,, grey-blue | | |
| 135 | 2 c., brown-pink on buff | 50 | |
| 136 | 2 c., purple-brown ,, | 8 | |
| 137 | 5 c., green on pale green | 12 | 12 |
| 138 | 10 c., black on lilac .. | 25 | |
| 139 | 15 c., blue on pale blue. | 25 | |
| 140 | 15 c. ,, on *quadrillé* | | |
| 140a | 20 c., red on green .. | | |
| 141 | 25 c., black on rose .. | 25 | |
| 142 | 40 c., red on yellow .. | | |
| 143 | 75 c., rose on pale rose. | | |
| 144 | 75 c., brown on orange | | |
| 145 | 1 fr., olive-green on toned.. .. .. | 90 | |
| 146 | 5 fr., lilac on lilac .. | 2.50 | |

*Varieties. The "T" inverted.*

| 147 | 1 c., black on azure .. | 6 | |
|---|---|---|---|
| 148 | 1 c. ,, grey-blue | | |
| 149 | 2 c., brn.-pink on buff | 12 | |
| 150 | 2 c., purp.-brown ,, | 12 | |
| 151 | 5 c., grn. on pale green | 18 | 6 |
| 152 | 10 c., black on lilac .. | 12 | 6 |
| 153 | 15 c., blue on pale blue | 25 | 25 |
| 153a | 20 c., red on green .. | 25 | |
| 154 | 25 c., black on rose .. | 25 | 25 |
| 155 | 40 c., red on yellow .. | 36 | |
| 156 | 75 c., rose on pale rose | | |
| 156a | 75 c., brown on orange | | |
| 157 | 1 fr., olive-green on toned .. .. | 1.50 | |
| 158 | 5 fr., lilac on lilac .. | 2.50 | |

| No. | | | Un. | Used. |
|---|---|---|---|---|

**1901.** *Perforated as* Type 52.

| 159 | 10 c., carmine .. .. | 25 | |
|---|---|---|---|
| 160 | 15 c., grey .. .. | 25 | |
| 161 | 25 c., blue .. .. | 50 | |

*Varieties. The "T" inverted.*

| 161a | 10 c., carmine .. .. | | |
|---|---|---|---|
| 161b | 15 c., grey .. .. | | |
| 161c | 25 c., blue .. .. | | |

**53**

**1901-3.** Type 53. *Perf.* 14 × 13½.

| 162 | 1 c., black .. .. | 10 | 2 |
|---|---|---|---|
| 163 | 2 c., orange .. .. | 12 | 2 |
| 164 | 5 c., blue .. .. | 12 | 4. |
| 165 | 10 c., brown .. .. | 16 | 6 |
| 166 | 20 c., blue-green .. | 25 | 25 |
| 167 | 30 c., carmine .. .. | 25 | 18 |
| 168 | 50 c., lake .. .. | 36 | 25 |
| 169 | 1 fr., olive .. .. | 50 | |
| 170 | 2 fr., red on green .. | | |
| 171 | 5 fr., black on yellow.. | | |

# GERMANY.
## BADEN.

**1**

**1851.** Type 1. Black *impression.*

| 1 | 1 kr., on buff .. .. | 15.00 | 90 |
|---|---|---|---|
| 2 | 3 ,, yellow .. | — | 2 |
| 3 | 3 ,, orange .. | 15.00 | 6 |
| 4 | 6 ,, yellow-green .. | — | 12 |
| 5 | 6 ,, blue-grn. .. .. | — | 12 |
| 6 | 9 ,, lilac-rose .. | 1.50 | 4 |

*Error of colour.*

| 7 | 9 kr., on green .. .. | | |
|---|---|---|---|

**1854-58.** *Same type and impression.*

| 8 | 1 kr., on white.. .. | 3.75 | 6 |
|---|---|---|---|
| 9 | 3 ,, green.. .. | 6.25 | 2 |
| 10 | 3 ,, blue (1858) .. | 15.00 | 10 |
| 11 | 6 ,, orange .. | 12.50 | 4 |

The above, unused, with original gum, are worth considerably more than the prices quoted.

Reprints of all the above stamps except

|  |  | *Un.* | *Used.* |
|---|---|---|---|
| No. |  |  |  |

the 9 kr. were made in 1867. The paper used is thicker for all values except the 6 kr., orange, and the gum is white and smooth. The shades of the reprints differ from those of the originals.

2

**1860-62.** Type **2.** *Coloured impression. Perf.* 13½.

| 12 | 1 kr., grey-black | .. | 1.85 | 12 |
| 13 | 1 ,, black .. | .. | 3.15 | 12 |
| 14 | 3 ,, dull blue.. | .. | 10.00 | 12 |
| 15 | 3 ,, ultramarine | .. | 1.25 | 8 |
| 16 | 3 ,, deep ,, | .. | 1.50 | 25 |
| 17 | 6 ,, orange .. | .. | 2.25 | 25 |
| 18 | 6 ,, orange-yellow | .. | 2.00 | 25 |
| 19 | 9 ,, rose | .. | 1.85 | 75 |

**1862.** *Same type. Perf.* 10.

| 20 | 1 kr., grey-black | .. | 90 | 18 |
| 21 | 1 ,, black .. | .. | 75 | 18 |
| 22 | 6 ,, blue .. | .. | 1.25 | 36 |
| 23 | 6 ,, deep blue | .. | 1.25 | 36 |
| 24 | 9 ,, brown .. | .. | 1.25 | 30 |
| 25 | 9 ,, bistre .. | .. | 1.85 | 75 |

3

**1862.** Type 3. *Perf.* 13½.

| 26 | 3 kr., rose | .. | 25.00 | 90 |

**1862-64.** *Same type. Perf.* 10.

| 27 | 1 kr., black | .. | 50 | 6 |
| 28 | 3 ,, pale rose.. | .. | 1.00 | 2 |
| 29 | 3 ,, deep ,, .. | .. | 1.00 | 2 |
| 30 | 6 ,, ultramarine | .. | 4 | 8 |
| 30a | 6 ,, blue .. | .. | — | 8 |
| 31 | 6 ,, Prussian blue | .. | 12.50 | 16 |
| 32 | 9 ,, bistre .. | .. | 2.50 | 12 |
| 33 | 9 ,, pale brown | .. | 6 | 10 |
| 34 | 9 ,, brown .. | .. | 6 | 10 |
| 35 | 9 ,, dark brown | .. | 3.00 |  |
| 36 | 18 ,, green .. | .. | 4.50 | 1.85 |
| -- | 18 ,, deep green | .. | — | 2.50 |
| ¦ | 30 ,, orange .. | .. | 16 | 3.75 |

|  |  | *Un.* | *Used.* |
|---|---|---|---|
| No. |  |  |  |

4

**1868.** Type 4. *Perf.* 10.

| 39 | 1 kr., pale green | .. | 2 | ? |
| 40 | 1 ,, green .. | .. | 2 | ? |
| 41 | 3 ,, rose .. | .. | 2 | ? |
| 42 | 3 ,, deep rose | .. | 25 | 4 |
| 43 | 7 ,, pale blue | .. | 12 | 1? |
| 44 | 7 ,, blue .. | .. | 6 | 1. |
| 45 | 7 ,, deep blue | .. | 6 | 1? |

RURAL POST STAMPS.

5

**1862.** Type 5. *Perf.* 10.

| 51 | 1 kr., black on yellow . | 2 | 1.2? |
| 52 | 3 ,, ,, ,, . | 2 | 3. |
| 53 | 12 ,, ,, ,, . | 8 |  |

Separate issues for Baden ceased in 18?? when the Grand Duchy was incorporate in the postal administration of the German Empire.

**BAVARIA.**

1                    2

**1849.** Type 1. *Imperf.*

| 1 | 1 kr., black .. | .. | 5.00 | 3.? |
| 2 | 1 ,, grey-black | .. | 3.75 | 3. |

*Variety. Tête-bêche.*

2a| 1 kr., grey-black ..

This stamp is known with a silk threa in the paper, but was not issued in th? state.

**1849.** *Similar to Type 2, but the laie? at top, bottom, and sides cut the circ? A silk thread in the paper.*

| 3 | 3 kr., greenish blue .. | 50 |
| 4 | 3 ,, blue .. | .. | 1.25 |

| No. | | | | Un. | Used. |
|---|---|---|---|---|---|
| 5 | 3 kr., | deep blue | .. | 4.35 | 2 |
| 6 | 3 ,, | grey-blue | .. | 62 | 2 |
| 7 | 6 ,, | brown .. | .. | — | 75 |

**1850-58.** *Type 2. Same paper as last.*

| | | | | | |
|---|---|---|---|---|---|
| 8 | 1 kr., | rose | | 36 | 6 |
| 9 | 6 ,, | cinnamon | .. | | 4 |
| 10 | 6 ,, | bistre-brown | .. | 90 | 6 |
| 11 | 6 ,, | brown | .. | 62 | 2 |
| 12 | 6 ,, | bright brown | .. | 50 | 2 |
| 13 | 6 ,, | chestnut .. | .. | 25 | 2 |
| 14 | 6 ,, | dark brown | .. | | |
| 15 | 9 ,, | pale blue-green .. | | — | 12 |
| 16 | 9 ,, | ,, yell.-green .. | | 2.50 | 4 |
| 17 | 9 ,, | deep ,, | | 62 | 4 |
| 18 | 12 ,, | red (1858) | .. | 1.25 | 1.00 |
| 19 | 18 ,, | orange-yell. (1854) | | 1.25 | 1.00 |

**1862.** *Same type. Colours changed.*

| | | | | | |
|---|---|---|---|---|---|
| 20 | 1 kr., | yellow | .. | 25 | 4 |
| 21 | 1 ,, | orange-yellow | .. | 1.00 | 4 |
| 22 | 3 ,, | rose | .. | 1.00 | 4 |
| 23 | 3 ,, | carmine .. | .. | 36 | 2 |
| 24 | 3 ,, | crimson .. | .. | 50 | 2 |
| 25 | 6 ,, | blue | .. | 50 | 4 |
| 26 | 6 ,, | deep blue | .. | 1.00 | 2 |
| 27 | 6 ,, | ultramarine | .. | 12.50 | 50 |
| 28 | 9 ,, | pale bistre | .. | 1.00 | 6 |
| 29 | 9 ,, | bistre-brown | .. | 1.25 | 6 |
| 30 | 12 ,, | yellow-green | .. | 1.25 | 62 |
| 31 | 12 ,, | green | .. | — | 62 |
| 32 | 18 ,, | brick-red .. | .. | 3.00 | 1.85 |
| 33 | 18 ,, | bright red | .. | 2.50 | 62 |

3

**1867-68.** Type 3. *With silk thread.*
*Imperf.*

| | | | | | |
|---|---|---|---|---|---|
| 34 | 1 kr., | yellow-green | .. | 62 | 4 |
| 35 | 1 ,, | green .. | .. | 75 | 4 |
| 36 | 1 ,, | blue-green | .. | 62 | 4 |
| 37 | 3 ,, | rose .. | .. | 75 | 2 |
| 38 | 3 ,, | rose-carmine | .. | 1.25 | 2 |
| 39 | 6 ,, | pale blue | .. | 3.00 | 12 |
| 40 | 6 ,, | blue .. | .. | 3.75 | 18 |
| 41 | 6 ,, | pale bistre | .. | 3.00 | 30 |
| 42 | 6 ,, | dark bistre | .. | 3.75 | 30 |
| 43 | 7 ,, | blue .. | .. | 3.75 | 12 |
| 44 | 7 ,, | deep blue | .. | — | 8 |
| 45 | 7 ,, | Prussian blue | .. | — | 25 |
| 46 | 9 ,, | pale bistre | .. | 3.00 | 62 |
| 47 | 9 ,, | yellow-bistre | .. | 3.75 | .62 |
| 48 | 12 ,, | red-lilac .. | .. | 5.00 | 90 |
| 49 | 12 ,, | pale purple | .. | 3.75 | 1.00 |
| 50 | 18 ,, | brick-red .. | .. | 3.00 | 90 |

| No. | | | | Un. | Used. |
|---|---|---|---|---|---|

**1870-73.** *Same type. Wmk. Lozenges.*
*Perf.* 11½.

| | | | | | |
|---|---|---|---|---|---|
| 51 | 1 kr., | pale green | .. | 8 | 2 |
| 52 | 1 ,, | deep ,, | .. | — | 6 |
| 53 | 3 ,, | rose | .. | 36 | 2 |
| 54 | 3 ,, | rose-carmine | .. | 36 | 2 |
| 55 | 6 ,, | bistre | .. | 12 | 8 |
| 56 | 7 ,, | pale blue .. | .. | 8 | 2 |
| 57 | 7 ,, | blue | .. | 12 | 2 |
| 58 | 7 ,, | Prussian blue | .. | 18 | |
| 59 | 9 ,, | pale brown | .. | 4 | 2 |
| 60 | 10 ,, | ochre | .. | 4 | 2 |
| 62 | 12 ,, | red-lilac .. | .. | 5.00 | 6.25 |
| 63 | 18 ,, | pale red .. | .. | 25 | 8 |
| 64 | 18 ,, | red | .. | — | 12 |

NOTE.—In the first issues of the above set, the lozenge is nearly square and the diagonal is 14 mm. long ; in the later it is diamond-shaped and the longer diagonal is 17 mm. in length ; the 9 kr. and 10 kr. are only found with the second.

4

**1874.** Type 4. *Wmk. Lozenges. Imperf.*

| | | | | | |
|---|---|---|---|---|---|
| 65 | 1 mark, | mauve | .. | 15.00 | 1.00 |

**1875.** *Same type and wmk. Perf.* 11½.

| | | | | | |
|---|---|---|---|---|---|
| 66 | 1 mark, | mauve | .. | 5.00 | 6 |

4a

**1875.** Type 3. *Wmk. horizontal wavy lines, wide apart,* Type 4a. *Perf.* 11½.

| | | | | | |
|---|---|---|---|---|---|
| 67 | 1 kr., | green | .. | 2 | 18 |
| 68 | 1 ,, | pale green | .. | 2 | 18 |
| 69 | 3 ,, | rose | .. | 2 | 4 |
| 70 | 3 ,, | deep rose | .. | 4 | 4 |
| 71 | 7 ,, | blue .. | .. | 2 | 36 |
| 72 | 7 ,, | ultramarine | .. | 2 | 36 |
| 73 | 10 ,, | ochre | .. | 4 | 18 |
| 74 | 18 ,, | brick-red .. | .. | 4 | 18 |

| No. | | | | Un. | Used. |
|---|---|---|---|---|---|

**5**

**1876–79.** Types 5 *and* 4. *Currency changed.*
*Wmk. horizontal wavy lines, wide*
*apart. Perf.* 11½.

| 75 | 3 pf., yellow-green | .. | 18 | 2 |
|---|---|---|---|---|
| 76 | 3 ,, pale green | .. | 18 | 2 |
| 77 | 5 ,, pale blue-green.. | 36 | 4 |
| 78 | 5 ,, deep ,, | .. | 50 | 4 |
| 79 | 5 ,, sage-green | .. | 5.00 | |
| 80 | 5 ,, mauve | .. | 3.00 | 4 |
| 81 | 10 ,, rose | .. | 50 | 2 |
| 82 | 10 ,, carmine | .. | 62 | 2 |
| 83 | 20 ,, Prussian blue | .. | — | 2 |
| 84 | 20 ,, blue | .. | 1.00 | 2 |
| 85 | 25 ,, bistre-brown | .. | 2.00 | 6 |
| 86 | 50 ,, vermilion | .. | 2.00 | 2 |
| 87 | 50 ,, grey-brown | .. | 6.25 | 6 |
| 88 | 1 mk., pale mauve | .. | 25.00 | 18 |
| 89 | 2 ,, orange .. | .. | 75 | 4 |

**6**

**1881.** *Same types. Wmk. close perpen-*
*dicular wavy lines,* Type 6. *Perf.* 11½.

| 90 | 3 pf., yellow-green | .. | 8 | 2 |
|---|---|---|---|---|
| 91 | 5 ,, mauve .. | | 75 | 2 |
| 92 | 5 ,, lilac-rose | | 36 | 2 |
| 93 | 10 ,, carmine .. | | 16 | 2 |
| 94 | 10 ,, aniline red | | 25 | 2 |
| 95 | 20 ,, ultramarine | | 25 | 2 |
| 96 | 25 ,, bistre-brown | | 1.50 | 2 |
| 97 | 50 ,, grey-brown | | 2.50 | 2 |
| 98 | 50 ,, brown | | 2.50 | 2 |
| 99 | 1 mk., lilac-rose | | 32 | 2 |
| 99a | 1 ,, mauve .. | | | |
| 100 | 2 ,, orange-yellow . | 62 | 4 |

**7**

**1888–1900.** Type 5. *Wmk. close horizontal*
*wavy lines,* Type 7. *Toned paper.*
*Perf.* 14½.

| 2a | 2 pf., grey | .. | .. | 2 | 2 |
|---|---|---|---|---|---|

| No. | | | | Un. | Used. |
|---|---|---|---|---|---|
| 101 | 3 pf., yellow-green | .. | 6 | 2 |
| 101a | 3 ,, brown .. | | 2 | 2 |
| 102 | 3 ,, grey-brown | .. | 2 | |
| 103 | 5 ,, mauve .. | .. | 12 | 4 |
| 104 | 5 ,, pale lilac-rose | .. | 8 | 4 |
| 105 | 5 ,, deep green | .. | 4 | 2 |
| 105a | 5 ,, deep blue-green . | 4 | 2 |
| 106 | 10 ,, rose .. | .. | 4 | 2 |
| 107 | 10 ,, carmine .. | .. | 4 | 2 |
| 108 | 20 ,, blue .. | .. | 8 | 2 |
| 109 | 20 ,, ultramarine | .. | 8 | 2 |
| 110 | 25 ,, bistre-brown | .. | 62 | 2 |
| 111 | 25 ,, orange .. | .. | 8 | |
| 112 | 50 ,, grey-brown | .. | 1.25 | 2 |
| 113 | 50 ,, dark ,, | .. | 1.50 | 2 |
| 114 | 50 ,, marone .. | .. | 16 | 2 |
| 115 | 50 ,, deep marone .. | 16 | 2 |

**1900–1.** *As last, but very white paper.*

| 116 | 2 pf., grey | .. | 2 | |
|---|---|---|---|---|
| 117 | 3 ,, dark brown | .. | 2 | |
| 118 | 5 ,, deep green | .. | 2 | |
| 119 | 10 ,, carmine | .. | 4 | |
| 120 | 20 ,, bright ultram. .. | 8 | |
| 120a | 25 ,, orange .. | .. | 8 | |
| 121 | 30 ,, olive-green | .. | 10 | 2 |
| 122 | 40 ,, yellow-ochre | .. | 14 | 2 |
| 122a | 50 ,, marone .. | .. | 16 | |
| 123 | 80 ,, lilac .. | .. | 30 | 4 |
| 123a | 1 mk., lilac-rose | .. | 32 | |

Type 4. *Wmk. perpendicular wavy line.*
*Perf.* 11½.

| 123b | 5 pf., deep green | .. | | |
|---|---|---|---|---|
| 124 | 3 m., olive-brown | .. | 1.00 | 10 |
| 125 | 5 m., pale green | .. | 1.60 | 1.50 |

**UNPAID LETTER STAMPS.**

**51**

**1862.** Type 51. *Silk thread. Imperf.*
| 301| 3 kr., black | .. | .. | 1.00 | 1. |

*Variety.* "Empfange."
| 302| 3 kr., black | .. | .. | — | 1.50 |

**1870.** *Same type. Wmk. Lozenges.*
*Perf.* 11½.
| 303| 1 kr., black | .. | .. | 4 | 1. |
| 304| 3 ,, ,, | .. | .. | 8 | 1.2 |

**52**

**1876.** Type 5 *surcharged with* Type 52
*in carmine. Wmk. horizontal wavy*
*lines, wide apart.*
| 305| 3 pf., grey | .. | .. | 12 | |

| No. | | | Un. | Used. |
|---|---|---|---|---|
| 306 | 3 pf., greenish grey | .. | 12 | |
| 307 | 5 ,, grey | .. | 8 | |
| 308 | 5 ,, greenish grey | .. | 10 | 8 |
| 309 | 10 ,, grey | .. .. | 10 | 4 |
| 310 | 10 ,, greenish grey | .. | 8 | 2 |

**1883-87.** *The same. Wmk. close perpendicular wavy lines. Perf. 11½.*

| 311 | 3 pf., grey | .. .. | 50 | 75 |
|---|---|---|---|---|
| 312 | 5 ,, ,, | .. .. | 36 | |
| 313 | 10 ,, ,, | .. .. | 18 | 18 |

*Errors.*
(i.) *"empfanper."* (ii.) *"zahlhar."*

| 313a | 10 pf., grey (i.).. | .. | | |
|---|---|---|---|---|
| 313b | 10 ,, ,, (ii.).. | | | |

**1888-95.** *Wmk. close horizontal wavy lines. Perf. 14½.*

| 314 | 2 pf., greenish grey | .. | 4 | 6 |
|---|---|---|---|---|
| 315 | 3 ,, ,, ,, | .. | 4 | 2 |
| 316 | 5 ,, ,, ,, | .. | 4 | 4 |
| 317 | 10 ,, ,, ,, | .. | 6 | 2 |

**4 SEPT., 1895.** *Surcharged in red on each corner.*

| 317a | 2 on 3 pf. (No. 315) .. | | | |
|---|---|---|---|---|

The so-called Return Letter stamps formerly catalogued are not postage stamps in any sense, but simply labels applied by the Post Office officials for their own convenience.

The Kingdom of Bavaria still retains its own postal administration, independent of that of the German Empire.

## BERGEDORF.

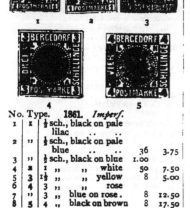

1    2    3

4      5

No. Type. **1861.** *Imperf.*

| 1 | 1 | ½ sch., black on pale lilac | .. | | |
|---|---|---|---|---|---|
| 2 | ,, | ¼ sch., black on pale blue | .. .. | 36 | 3.75 |
| 3 | ,, | ½ sch., black on blue | 1.00 | | |
| 4 | 2 | 1 ,, ,, white | 50 | 7.50 | |
| 5 | 3 | 1½ ,, ,, yellow | 8 | 5.00 | |
| 6 | 4 | 3 ,, ,, rose | | | |
| 7 | ,, | 3 ,, blue on rose . | 8 | 12.50 | |
| 8 | 5 | 4 ,, black on brown | 8 | 17.50 | |

| No. Type. | | | Un. | Used. |
|---|---|---|---|---|

*Varieties.* *Tête-bêche.*

| 9 | 2 | 1 sch., blk. on white | 3.75 | |
|---|---|---|---|---|
| 10 | 3 | 1½ ,, ,, yellow | 2.00 | |

It is doubtful whether Nos. 1 and 6 were ever issued.

These stamps have been several times reprinted. The 1½ SCHILLINGE, with final "E," is believed to be an essay. The ½ sch., black on lilac, and the 3 sch., black on rose, were reprinted in 1867. The impression of the first is less sharp, and the "H" of "SCHILLING" has either no crossbar, or it is hardly visible. The tint of the paper is also slightly different. The reprint of the 3 sch. is on thin instead of thick paper, and there are two dots on the centre of the letter "s" of "POSTMARKE." The other stamps were reprinted in 1872 and 1887; the 4 sch. also in 1874, and the 1 sch. and 3 sch. again in 1888. All the reprints of the 1½ sch. have "SCHILLINGE" with final "E." The impressions of all the values are less sharp, and the shades of the papers vary from those of the original stamps.

In 1867, the free city of Hamburg having acquired complete jurisdiction over Bergedorf, the stamps of the former were used there.

## BREMEN.

1

**1855.** *Laid paper:—(a) Horizontal. (b) Vertical. Imperf.*

| 1 | 1 | 3 gr., blk. on blue (a) | 5.00 | 5.00 |
|---|---|---|---|---|
| 2 | ,, | 3 ,, ,, ,, (b) | 5.00 | 5.65 |

2

3

**1856-61.** *Wove paper. Imperf.*

| 3 | 2 | 5 gr., blk. on rose.. | 2.50 | 5.00 |
|---|---|---|---|---|
| 4 | ,, | 7 ,, ,, yel.('60) | 3.00 | 10.00 |
| 5 | 3 | 5 sgr., deep gn. ('61) | 6.25 | 4.00 |
| 6 | ,, | 5 ,, moss-green.. | 3.75 | 4.00 |

|     |       |                        | *Un.* | *Used.* |
| --- | ----- | ---------------------- | ----- | ------- |
| No. | Type. |                        |       |         |

*On thick paper.*

| 7 | **3** | 5 sgr., bright green | 1.10 |

I.    II.    III.

There are three types of the 3 grote, shown above in the variations of the central ornament at the foot of the stamp below the "EM" of "BREMEN," and two of the 5 grote, and all three types of the former value are found with and without a broken line under the words "STADT POST AMT." This applies to the subsequent issues also.

4        5

**1861–63.** *Laid paper for the* 3 gr., *wove for the other values. Percés en scie* 15.

| 8  | **4** | 2 gr., orange (1863)          | 7.50  |       |
| 9  | ,,    | 2 ,, orange-red ..            | 10.00 |       |
| 10 | **1** | 3 gr., black on blue *(a)* (1862).. | — | 12.50 |
| 11 | ,,    | 3 gr., black on blue *(b)* (1862) | 10.00 | |
| 12 | **2** | 5 gr., black on rose (1862) .. | 3.75 | 3.00 |
| 13 | **5** | 10 gr., black (1861).. | 10.00 | 10.00 |
| 14 | ,,    | 10 ,, grey-black .. | 10.00 | 10.00 |
| 15 | **3** | 5 sgr., pale yellow-green (1862) .. | 12.50 | 3.50 |
| 16 | ,,    | 5 sgr., yell.-gn.(1862) | 10.00 | 3.15 |

**1867.** *Perf.* 13.

| 17 | **4** | 2 gr., orange       | 3.00  | 5.00  |
| 18 | ,,    | 2 ,, bwnish. oran.  | 10.00 |       |
| 19 | **1** | 3 ,, blk. on blue *(a)* | 2.50 | 7.50 |
| 20 | **2** | 5 ,, ,, pale rose   | 2.50  | 3.75  |
| 21 | ,,    | 7 ,, blk. on yellow | 2.50  |       |
| 22 | **5** | 10 ,, black..       | 4.00  | 15.00 |
| 23 | ,,    | 10 ,, grey-black .. | 4.00  |       |
| 24 | **3** | 5 sgr., yellow-green | 12.50 | 5.00  |
| 25 | ,,    | 5 ,, green          | 3.75  |       |

The 3 types of the 3 gr., unsevered, $15.00.

Nos. 22 and 23 are sometimes found with the outer single-lined frame, as on Nos. 13 and 14.

Bremen ceased to issue stamps on joining the North German Confederation, Jan., 68.

|     | *Un.* | *Used* |
| --- | ----- | ------ |
| No. |       |        |

## BRUNSWICK.

1

**1852.** *Type* 1. *No wmk. Imperf.*

| 1 | 1 sgr., rose     | .. | .. | — | 3.75 |
| 2 | 2 ,, blue        | .. | .. | — | 2.10 |
| 3 | 3 ,, vermilion   | .. | .. | — | 2.60 |

These stamps are often met with washed, but are *very rare* in *fine unused* condition.

**1853–56.** *Type* 1. Black *impression. Wmk. Posthorn. Imperf.*

| 4  | ½ ggr., on brown      | .. | 12.50 | 1.6 |
| 5  | ½ ,, white            | .. | 3.00  | 3.5 |
| 6  | 1 sgr., on brown-buff | .. | 15.00 | 50 |
| 7  | 1 ,, buff ..          | .. | 15.00 | 5 |
| 8  | 2 ,, blue ..          | .. | 2.50  |   |
| 9  | 2 ,, deep blue        | .. | 2.50  | 3 |
| 10 | 3 ,, pale rose        | .. | 30.00 | 6 |
| 11 | 3 ,, rose ..          | .. | —     | 5 |

2

**1857.** *Type* 2. *Same wmk. Imperf.*

| 12 | ¼ ggr., black on brown | 36 | 5 |
| 13 | ¼ ,, ,, pale ,,        |    |   |

The ¼ ggr., brown on white, although prepared for use, was never put in circulation (price 2 c.).

**1861–63.** *Type* 1. *Same wmk. Imperf.*

| 15 | ½ sgr., on yellow-grn. ('63) | 12   | 6 |
| 16 | ½ ,, blue-green ('63)        |      |   |
| 17 | 1 ,, yellow ('61) ..         | 3.75 | 36 |

**1862–64.** *Same type and wmk.* *(a) Imperf.* (1862).

| 18 | 3 sgr., rose        | .. | .. | — | 1.2 |
| 19 | 3 ,, deep rose      | .. | 10.00 | 1.0 |

*(b) Rouletted* 12 (1864).

| 20  | 1 sgr., yellow      | .. | 6.25 | 1.2 |
| 20a | 1 ,, black on yellow | .. |     |     |
| 21  | 3 ,, rose           | .. | ..  |     |

*(c) Percés en arc* 16½ *to* 17½ (1864).

| 22 | ½ ggr., black on white . | 10.00 | 10. c |
| 23 | ½ sgr. ,, yellow-green .. | |    |
| 24 | 1 sgr., black on yellow . | |    |
| 25 | 1 ,, yellow on white .   | 6.25 | 1.5 |
| 26 | 2 ,, black on blue ..    | 10.00 | 4.5 |
| 27 | 3 ,, rose on white ..    | 25.00 | 3 |

No.  Un. Used.

**3**

**1865.** Type 3.

*No wmk. Percés en arc* 16½ *to* 17½.

| 28 | ½ gr., black | .. | .. | 12 | 1.25 |
|---|---|---|---|---|---|
| 29 | 1 ,, red | .. | .. | 2 | 12 |
| 30 | 1 ,, rose-red | .. | | 2 | 12 |
| 31 | 1 ,, rose | .. | .. | — | 12 |
| 32 | 2 ,, blue | .. | .. | 8 | 36 |
| 33 | 2 ,, ultramarine | .. | | | |
| 34 | 3 ,, bistre | .. | | 2 | 62 |
| 35 | 3 ,, bistre-brown | .. | | 2 | 62 |

All four values are found imperforate. Pairs of 1 gr. can be supplied at $2.50 each.

Brunswick ceased to issue stamps on joining the North German Confederation, 1 Jan., 1868.

## HAMBURG.

N.B.—The large remainders of these stamps are all without gum. The stamps as issued, with the old *brown* gum, are so much scarcer than these remainders, that we think it better to quote prices for both, giving collectors the opportunity of ordering those which they prefer.

**1**

**1859.** Type 1. *Wmk. wavy lines.*
*Imperf.*

| | | | Unused. With gum. | Unused. No gum. | Used. |
|---|---|---|---|---|---|
| 1 | ½ sch., black | .. | 2.50 | 1.00 | 3.75 |
| 2 | 1 ,, brown | .. | 2.50 | 1.25 | 1.10 |
| 3 | 2 ,, red | .. | 3.00 | 2.00 | 1.25 |
| 4 | 3 ,, Prus. blue | | 2.50 | 2.00 | 2.00 |
| 5 | 4 ,, yell.-green | | 1.25 | — | 7.50 |
| 6 | 4 ,, green | .. | 1.25 | — | 7.50 |
| 7 | 7 ,, orange | .. | 2.50 | 1.85 | 75 |
| 8 | 7 ,, oran.-yell. | | 2.50 | 1.85 | 75 |
| 9 | 9 ,, yellow | .. | 3.75 | | |
| 10 | 9 ,, pale yellow | | | | |

No.  Unused. With gum.  Unused. No gum.  Used.

**2**

**3**

**1864.** Types 2 *and* 3. *Wmk. wavy lines.*
*Imperf.*

| 11 | 1½ sch., dull mauve | — | 25 | |
|---|---|---|---|---|
| 12 | 1½ ,, red-lilac | .. | 1.25 | |
| 13 | 1½ ,, purple | .. | — | — | 75 |
| 14 | 1½ ,, lilac | | 5.00 | — | 1.00 |
| 15 | 1½ ,, grey | | 1.35 | — | 1.00 |
| 16 | 1½ ,, greenish grey | | 5.65 | — | 1.00 |
| 17 | 1½ ,, blue | .. | 21.25 | — | 20.00 |
| 18 | 2½ ,, blue-green | | 3.75 | — | 1.25 |

**1864-65.** *Same types. Wmk. wavy lines.*
*Perf.* 13½.

| 19 | ½ sch., black | .. | 16 | 12 | 18 |
|---|---|---|---|---|---|
| 20 | 1 ,, brown | | 36 | 25 | 25 |
| 21 | 1½ ,, red-lilac | .. | 1.25 | | |
| 22 | 1½ ,, purple | .. | 1.50 | 1.25 | 12 |
| 23 | 1½ ,, violet | .. | 1.25 | — | 12 |
| 24 | 1½ ,, grey-lilac | . | 1.00 | — | 25 |
| 25 | 2 ,, red | .. | 36 | 30 | 36 |
| 26 | 2½ ,, green | | 1.00 | — | 36 |
| 27 | 2½ ,, yell.-green | | | | |
| 28 | 2½ ,, pale green | | 2.50 | | |
| 29 | 3 ,, Prus. blue | | 4.00 | 3.00 | 2.00 |
| 30 | 3 ,, ultramarine | | 1.25 | 62 | 75 |
| 31 | 3 ,, deep ultram. | | — | -. | 75 |
| 32 | 4 ,, bright grn. | | 25 | 18 | 36 |
| 33 | 4 ,, dull green | | 25 | 18 | 36 |
| 34 | 7 ,, orange | .. | 7.50 | — | 3.75 |
| 35 | 7 ,, oran.-yell.) | | — | 7.50 | 3.75 |
| 56 | 7 ,, mauve ('65) | | 25 | 18 | 36 |
| 37 | 7 ,, magenta | .. | — | — | 36 |
| 38 | 9 ,, yellow | .. | 1.25 | 12 | 7.50 |
| 39 | 9 ,, pale yellow | | 36 | — | 7.50 |

*Varieties. Imperf.*

| 41 | 3 sch., ultram. | 1.00 | |
|---|---|---|---|
| 42 | 7 ,, mauve | .. | |

The 1½ sch. and 2½ sch. were privately reprinted about 1872 and later, on white wove *unwatermarked* paper, both imperf. and perf. roughly 13½, and also clean-cut 11½. The 1½ sch. is found in *reddish lilac* (imperf. only), *lilac, brownish lilac, greyish lilac,* and *reddish brown* (perf. only); the 2½ sch. in *deep green, yellow-green,* and *pale yellow-green.*

| No. | Unused. With gum. | Used. No gum. |
| --- | --- | --- |

**4**

**1866.** Type 4. *No wmk. Rouletted* 10.

| | | | | | |
| --- | --- | --- | --- | --- | --- |
| 43 | 1½ sch., mauve | .. | 30 | — | 50 |
| 44 | 1½ ,, violet | | 50 | — | 50 |
| 45 | 1½ ,, rose | .. | 8 | — | 1.00 |

The 1½ sch. is octagonal, having the corners removed.

Reprints of both values were made about 1872 and in later years, on white wove unwatermarked paper, and are found rouletted 8½ or 10. The reprint of the 1½ sch. is from a retouched die, and differs from the original stamp in having the circle, in the centre of the four rosettes which separate the inscription, filled in with colour, and there is no line in the upper part of "G" of "SCHILLING." The 1½ sch. was reprinted from the envelope die, and has a longer line in the upper part of the "G" of "SCHILLING." The paper is thicker, and the impression does not show through as it does in the originals. The reprints are often found with forged postmarks.

**1867.** Type 1. *Wmk. wavy lines. Perf.* 13½.

| | | | | | |
| --- | --- | --- | --- | --- | --- |
| 46 | 2½ sch., dull green. | 62 | 8 | 75 |
| 47 | 2½ ,, green .. | — | 8 | 75 |
| 48 | 2½ ,, dark green | 2.50 | | |

*Varieties. Imperf.*

| | | |
| --- | --- | --- |
| 49 | 2½ sch., dull green | |
| 50 | 2½ ,, dark ,, | |

Hamburg ceased to issue stamps on joining the North German Confederation, 1 Jan., 1868.

## HANOVER.

**1**

**1850.** Type 1. *Wmk. a rectangle. Imperf.*

| | | | | |
| --- | --- | --- | --- | --- |
| 1 | 1 ggr., blk. on grey-blue | — | 62 |

This stamp was reprinted on unwatermarked paper in 1864, without gum. The colour of the paper is grey.

| No. | | Un. | Use. |
| --- | --- | --- | --- |

**2**

**3**

**1851-55.** Types 1 *and* 2. *Wmk.* Type 3. Black *impression. Imperf.*

| | | | | | |
| --- | --- | --- | --- | --- | --- |
| 2 | 1 ggr. on grey-green | .. | 1.25 | |
| 3 | $\frac{1}{10}$ th. on salmon | .. | 4.00 | 5 |
| 4 | $\frac{1}{10}$ ,, crimson | .. | 3.50 | |
| 5 | $\frac{1}{10}$ ,, blue .. | .. | 3.50 | 5 |
| 6 | $\frac{1}{10}$ ,, orange | .. | 6.25 | |
| 7 | $\frac{1}{10}$ ,, orange-yellow | — | | 5. |

The $\frac{1}{10}$ th. was reprinted on unwatermarked paper in 1889, with white gum, and this reprint is found *tête-bêche.*

**4**

**1853.** Type 4. *White paper. Same wmk. Imperf.*

| | | | | |
| --- | --- | --- | --- | --- |
| 8 | 3 pf., pale rose .. | .. | 5.00 | 2. |

**1856.** Type 2. *No wmk. Fine coloured network.*

| | | | | |
| --- | --- | --- | --- | --- |
| 9 | $\frac{1}{10}$ th., blk. & yellow | .. | 5.00 | |
| 10 | $\frac{1}{10}$ ,, ,, orange | .. | 5.00 | 1.00 |

The other values found with the fine network are essays.

**1856.** *No wmk. Coloured network of larger meshes.*

| No. | Type. | | | Un. | Use. |
| --- | --- | --- | --- | --- | --- |
| 11 | 4 | 3 pf., pale rose & gry. | 12.50 | 4. |
| 12 | ,, | 3 ,, ,, blk. | 7.50 | 2. |
| 14 | 2 | 1 ggr., black & grn. | 1.50 | |
| 15 | ,, | $\frac{1}{10}$ th., black & rose . | 5.00 | 1 |
| 16 | ,, | $\frac{1}{10}$ ,, ,, blue . | 3.15 | |
| 17 | ,, | $\frac{1}{10}$ ,, ,, orange | — | |

All five values were reprinted in 1864 on white wove unwatermarked paper, with yellowish white gum. The network in the reprints only extends over blocks of four stamps, whereas on the originals it extends over the entire sheet. The $\frac{1}{10}$ th. was again reprinted in 1889, on similar paper, and with white gum. In this reprint the network was applied stamp by stamp. These reprints are found *tête-bêche.*

| No. Type. | | | | Un. | Used. |
|---|---|---|---|---|---|

| | | | | 5 | 6 |
|---|---|---|---|---|---|

**1859-63.** *No wmk. Rose gum.*

| 18 | 4 | 3 pf., dull rose | .. | 75 | 75 |
|---|---|---|---|---|---|
| 19 | " | 3 ,, bright rose | .. | 75 | 75 |
| 20 | " | 3 ,, deep ,, | .. | 90 | 75 |
| 21 | " | 3 ,, yell.-grn. ('63) | 3.75 | 5.00 |
| 22 | 5 | ½ gr., black (1850) | .. | 10.00 | 6.25 |
| 23 | 6 | 1 ,, claret | .. | 7.50 | |
| 24 | " | 1 ,, carmine | .. | 2.50 | 12 |
| 25 | " | 1 ,, rose | .. | 1.00 | 4 |
| 26 | " | 1 ,, pale rose | .. | 1.50 | 4 |
| 27 | " | 2 ,, Prussian blue | 3.00 | 25 |
| 28 | " | 2 ,, ultramarine | .. | 2.50 | 25 |
| 29 | " | 3 ,, orange-yellow | 2.00 | 75 |
| 30 | " | 3 ,, yellow | .. | 3.75 | 75 |
| 31 | " | 3 ,, brown (1861) | 6.25 | 36 |
| 32 | " | 3 ,, dark ,, ,, | 7.50 | 50 |
| 33 | " | 10 ,, olive-green | .. | 10.00 | 12.50 |

The 3 pf. was reprinted in 1889 on yellowish white wove unwatermarked paper, with brownish gum applied in stripes. The reprint is from a retouched die, and the ends of the scroll at the right and left sides of the stamp point downwards, whereas on the originals they bend slightly towards the side borders of the stamp. The 3 gr. was reprinted in yellow and in brown in 1891, with white gum.

**1863.** Type 7. *No wmk.*
*White gum.*

| 34 | ½ gr., black | .. | .. | 3.75 | 1.85 |
|---|---|---|---|---|---|

This stamp was reprinted in 1883 on yellowish white wove paper, with yellowish white gum, and is found *tête-bêche*.

**1864.** *Same types. No wmk.*
*Percés en arc 16.*
*(a) Rose gum.*

| 35 | 3 pf., green | .. | .. | 2.50 | 1.25 |
|---|---|---|---|---|---|
| 36 | ½ gr., black | .. | .. | 8.00 | 5.00 |

*(b) Yellow or white gum.*

| 37 | 3 pf., green | .. | .. | 1.25 | 75 |
|---|---|---|---|---|---|
| 38 | 3 ,, deep green | .. | — | 75 |
| 39 | ½ gr., black | .. | .. | 7.50 | 5.00 |

Type 6.
*(a) Rose gum.*

| 40 | 1 gr., rose | .. | .. | 2.00 | 8 |
|---|---|---|---|---|---|
| 41 | 3 ,, brown | .. | .. | 6.25 | |

| No. | | | | Un. | Used. |
|---|---|---|---|---|---|

*(b) Yellow or white gum.*

| 42 | 1 gr., rose | .. | .. | 1.00 | 6 |
|---|---|---|---|---|---|
| 43 | 1 ,, pale rose.. | ... | 1.25 | 6 |
| 44 | 2 ,, deep ultramarine | 3.00 | 75 |
| 45 | 2 ,, ultramarine | .. | 2.50 | 50 |
| 46 | 2 ,, pale ultramarine | . | 2.00 | 50 |
| 47 | 3 ,, brown | .. | .. | 2.50 | 62 |
| 48 | 3 ,, dark brown | .. | 3.75 | 62 |

The 3 gr. was reprinted in 1891 with white gum, and *percés en arc* 13½.

Hanover ceased to have a separate issue in 1866, when it became a province of Prussia.

## LUBECK.

| | | | 1 | | 2 |
|---|---|---|---|---|---|

**1859.** Type 1. *Wmk.* Type 2. *Imperf.*

| | | | | Unused. With No gum. | Used. gum. |
|---|---|---|---|---|---|
| 1 | ½ sch., purple | .. | — | 7.50 | 7.50 |
| 2 | 1 ,, orange | .. | 8.75 | 5.00 | 5.00 |
| 3 | 2 ,, brown | .. | 75 | 12 | 2.00 |
| 4 | 2½ ,, rose-red | .. | 1.25 | 75 | 6.25 |
| 5 | 2½ ,, rose | .. | 1.25 | 75 | 6.25 |
| 6 | 4 ,, deep green | 62 | 8 | 2.50 |
| 7 | 4 ,, yell.-green | — | 18 | |

*Error.* "ZWEI EIN HALB" *on* 2 *sch.*

| 8 | 2 (2½) sch., brown | — | 15.00 | 25.00 |
|---|---|---|---|---|

Uncut sheet of 100 stamps, 98 being 2 sch. and two errors 2½ sch., price $80.00 (*no gum*).

**1862.** *No wmk. Imperf.*

| 9 | ½ sch., dull lilac.. | 75 | 18 | 5.00 |
|---|---|---|---|---|
| 10 | 1 ,, orang.-yell. | 1.50 | 50 | 5.00 |

All five values were reprinted in 1871 on thin, white wove unwatermarked paper, with smooth white gum, and in shades different from those of the originals.

3

**1863.** Type 3. *No wmk. Rouletted* 11½.

| 11 | ½ sch., green | .. | .. | 62 | 1.00 |
|---|---|---|---|---|---|
| 12 | ½ ,, yellow-green | .. | 62 | 1.00 |

H

*Un.   Used.*

No.
13 | 1 sch., orange-vermilion 1.85 1.50
14 | 2 ,, rose-red .. 36 75
15 | 2 ,, rose .. 36 75
16 | 2½ ,, ultramarine .. 1.00 3.75
17 | 4 ,, bistre .. .. 1.00 1.25

All five values were reprinted in 1871. The reprints show no embossing, and are imperforate.

4

**1864.** Type 4. *No wmk. Imperf.*
18 | 1½ sch., chestnut-brown. 75 1.10
19 | 1½ ,, pale brown .. 1.25 1.10
20 | 1½ ,, dark ,, .. 1.50 75

5.

**1865.** Type 5. *No wmk. Rouletted 11½.*
21 | 1½ sch., red-lilac .. 25 75

This stamp was reprinted in 1871, but the reprint shows no embossing, and is imperforate.

**1867.** Type 3. *No wmk. Rouletted 10.*
22 | 1 sch., orange .. .. 2.00

Lübeck ceased to have a separate issue on joining the North German Confederation, 1 Jan., 1868.

## MECKLENBURG-SCHWERIN.

1    2

No. Type. **1856.** *Imperf.*
1 | 1 | ¼ sch., red .. .. 4.50 1.50
2 | 2 | 3 ,, yellow .. 2.00 50
3 | ,, | 3 ,, orange-yellow 1.50 50
4 | ,, | 5 ,, blue .. .. 3.75 2.50

*Un.   Used.*

No. Type.
**1864.** *Rouletted 11½.*
5 | 1 | ¼ sch., red .. .. 60.00 25.00
Type 1 has a dotted ground, Type 3 plain ground.

3

**1864.** *Rouletted 11½.*
6 | 3 | ¼ sch., red .. .. 62 50
7 | 2 | 5 ,, bistre .. 3.00 3.00
8 | ,, | 5 ,, ,, on thick
paper .. 3.75 3.75

**1865.** Type 2. *Rouletted 11½. Two varieties, one with the roulette at a greater distance from the frame of the stamp than in the other. (a) The stamp is 23 mm. square. (b) The stamp is 24 mm. square.*
9 | 3 sch., oran.-yellow (a) 7.50 1.50
10 | 3 ,, ,, (b) 90

**1866-67.** Type 2. *Rouletted 11½.*
11 | 2 sch., mauve .. .. 5.00 3.75
12 | 2 ,, grey-lilac ('67).. 2.50 15.00
13 | 2 ,, bluish ,, ( ,, )..

Mecklenburg-Schwerin ceased to have a separate issue of stamps on joining the North German Confederation, 1 Jan., 1868.

## MECKLENBURG-STRELITZ.

1    2

**1864.** *Rouletted 11½.*
1 | 1 | ¼ sgr., orange .. 5.00
2 | ,, | ¼ ,, orange-red.. 1.50 20.00
3 | ,, | ¼ ,, pale green .. 90
4 | ,, | ¼ ,, dark ,, .. 1.25
5 | ,, | 1 ,, purple .. — 25.00
6 | ,, | 1 ,, mauve .. 3.00
7 | 2 | 1 ,, rose .. .. 1.50 5.00
8 | ,, | 1 ,, rose-carmine 1.50
9 | ,, | 2 ,, pale ultram. 36 6.25
10 | ,, | 2 ,, bright ,, 36 6.25
11 | ,, | 3 ,, bistre .. 25 10.00

Mecklenburg-Strelitz ceased to have a separate issue of stamps on joining the North German Confederation, 1 Jan., 1868.

| No. | | Un. | Used. |
|---|---|---|---|

**OLDENBURG.**

1

**1852.** Type 1. Black *impression. Imperf.*
*Three varieties of the* 1/30 *thaler.*
(a) *The letter "A" of "THALER" has no horizontal stroke at the top.*
(b) *Similar to (a), but the letter "H" of "THALER" touches the indentation of the shield.*
(c) *The letter "A" of "THALER" has a horizontal stroke along the top, and the left side scroll is further away from the outer frame line. Varieties (b) and (c) are found on the same sheet.*

*Three varieties of the* 1/15 *thaler.*
(a) *The letter "H" of "THALER" is well above the indentation of the shield.*
(b) *The letter "H" of "THALER" almost touches the indentation of the shield.*
(c) *Similar to (b), but the mantle is fully shaded beneath the arms.*

| 1 | 1/30 th., on pale blue (a) .. | — | 3.75 |
|---|---|---|---|
| 2 | 1/30 ,, blue (a) | | |
| 3 | 1/30 ,, dull blue (b) .. | 5.00 | 25 |
| 4 | 1/30 ,, bright blue (b). | — | 25 |
| 5 | 1/30 ,, dull ,, (c). | 7.50 | 25 |
| 6 | 1/30 ,, bright ,, (c). | — | 25 |
| 7 | 1/15 ,, rose (a) | .. | |
| 8 | 1/15 ,, ,, (b) | .. 50.00 | 95 |
| 9 | 1/15 ,, pale rose (b) | — | 95 |
| 10 | 1/15 ,, rose (c) | .. — | 1.85 |
| 11 | 1/15 ,, yellow .. | — | 1.25 |
| 12 | 1/15 ,, pale yellow .. | — | 1.25 |

**1855.** *Same type. Imperf.*

| 13 | 1/3 sgr., on green | .. 12.50 | 10.00 |
|---|---|---|---|

2

**1859.** Type 2. Black *impression. Imperf.*

| 14 | 1/3 gr., on green .. | .. 30.00 | 35.00 |
|---|---|---|---|
| 15 | 1 ,, blue .. | .. 7.50 | 62 |
| 16 | 1 ,, grey-blue .. | — | 62 |
| 17 | 1 ,, bright blue .. | | |
| 18 | 2 ,, rose .. | .. 40.00 | 11.25 |
| 19 | 2 ,, pale rose .. | — | 11.25 |
| 20 | 3 ,, yellow .. | .. 30.00 | 7.50 |

**1861.** *Same type. Coloured impression.*
*Imperf.*

| 21 | 1/3 gr., orange-yellow .. | 6.25 | 20.00 |
|---|---|---|---|
| 22 | 1/3 ,, moss-green .. | 15.00 | 18.75 |
| 23 | 1/3 ,, green .. | 10.00 | 11.25 |
| 24 | 1/3 ,, pale bluish green | 10.00 | 11.25 |
| 25 | 1/3 ,, chestnut-brown .. | 10.00 | 11.25 |
| 26 | 1/3 ,, brown .. | .. 15.00 | 9.50 |
| 27 | 1 ,, bright blue | .. 10.00 | 2.10 |
| 28 | 1 ,, deep ,, | .. 10.00 | 2.50 |
| 29 | 1 ,, pale ,, | .. 7.50 | 2.10 |
| 30 | 1 ,, dull ,, | .. — | 3.75 |
| 31 | 2 ,, red .. | .. 15.00 | 7.50 |
| 32 | 2 ,, rose-red .. | .. 15.00 | 7.50 |
| 33 | 3 ,, pale yellow | .. 18.75 | 7.00 |
| 34 | 3 ,, deep ,, | .. 18.75 | 7.50 |

*Errors caused by defective transfers.*

| 35 | 1/3 gr. (OLDEIBURG) | .. 37.50 | 37.50 |
|---|---|---|---|
| 36 | 1/3 ,, (Dritto) .. | .. — | 20.00 |
| 37 | 1/3 ,, (Drittd) .. | .. 22.50 | 20.00 |
| 38 | 3 ,, (OLDEIBURG) | .. — | 25.00 |

Several other variations are found in the lettering and in the frame of these two values. The 1 gr. is known with a pointed numeral "1" at the right side, and this value and the 3 gr. have been found printed on both sides.

3

**1862.** Type 3. *Rouletted 11½.*

| 39 | 1/3 gr., pale green | .. 1.50 | 2.50 |
|---|---|---|---|
| 40 | 1/3 ,, yellow-green | .. 1.50 | 2.50 |
| 41 | 1/3 ,, orange .. | .. 3.75 | 2.50 |
| 42 | 1/3 ,, orange-red | .. 3.75 | 2.50 |
| 43 | 1 ,, rose-red .. | .. 3.75 | 18 |
| 44 | 1 ,, rose-carmine | .. 5.00 | 25 |
| 45 | 2 ,, Prussian blue .. | 7.50 | 75 |
| 46 | 2 ,, ultramarine | .. — | 75 |
| 47 | 3 ,, bistre .. | .. 5.00 | 1.00 |
| 48 | 3 ,, bistre-brown .. | — | 1.00 |

**1867.** *Rouletted 10.*

| 49 | 1/3 gr., pale green | .. 45 | |
|---|---|---|---|
| 50 | 1/3 ,, orange | .. 36 | |
| 51 | 1 ,, rose-carmine | .. 16 | 2.50 |
| 52 | 2 ,, ultramarine | .. 30 | |
| 53 | 3 ,, bistre .. | .. 75 | |

Oldenburg ceased to have a separate issue of stamps on joining the North German Confederation, 1 Jan., 1868.

| No. | | | | Un. | Used. |
|---|---|---|---|---|---|

**PRUSSIA.**

1

**1850-56.** Type 1. *Wmk. Type 2.*
*Imperf.  Background of crossed lines.*

| 1 | 4 pf., yellow-green ('56) | 1.85 | 50 |
|---|---|---|---|
| 2 | 4 ,, dark yell.-gn.('56) | — | 50 |
| 3 | 6 ,, orange .. .. | 1.10 | 12 |
| 4 | 6 ,, vermilion .. | 1.10 | 12 |
| 5 | 1 sgr., black on rose .. | 3.75 | 4 |
| 6 | 2 ,, ,, blue .. | 4.35 | 4 |
| 7 | 3 ,, ,, orange | 5.00 | 4 |
| 8 | 3 ,, ,, buff .. | 10.00 | 12 |

The shape of the watermark varies considerably in different specimens.  All five values were reprinted in 1864 on unwatermarked paper, and a second time in 1873 on paper with a similar watermark to that of the originals.  The reprints in both sets vary in shade from the originals.

**1857.** *Same type.  No wmk.  Imperf.*
*Solid background.*

| 9 | 1 sgr., rose .. .. | 22.50 | 6 |
|---|---|---|---|
| 10 | 2 ,, pale blue .. | 30.00 | 50 |
| 11 | 2 ,, dark ,, .. .. | — | 62 |
| 12 | 3 ,, yellow .. .. | 10.00 | 12 |
| 13 | 3 ,, orange .. .. | 7.50 | 16 |

The so-called reprints of these stamps are nothing better than official imitations. Two printings were made, in 1864 and in 1873.  The letters of "FREIMARKE," of the words of value, and the numerals differ in type from the originals, and there is only one period in place of two after the word "SILBERGR."

**1858-60.** Type of 1850.  *No wmk.*
*Imperf.*

| 14 | 4 pf., yellow-green .. | 1.50 | 45 |
|---|---|---|---|
| 15 | 4 ,, green .. .. | 1.50 | 45 |
| 16 | 6 ,, pale vermil. ('60). | 5.00 | 1.00 |
| 17 | 6 ,, dark ,, ( ,, ). | 5.00 | 1.00 |
| 18 | 1 sgr., pale rose .. | 2.10 | 2 |
| 19 | 1 ,, carmine-rose .. | 2.50 | 2 |
| 20 | 2 ,, pale blue .. | 3.75 | 6 |
| 21 | 2 ,, indigo-blue .. | 3.75 | 6 |
| 22 | 3 ,, pale orange-yell. | 2.50 | 6 |
| 23 | 3 ,, dark ,, | 2.50 | 6 |

| No. | | | | Un. | Used. |
|---|---|---|---|---|---|

| 3 | | | 4 | | |
|---|---|---|---|---|---|

**1861-65.**  Types 3 *and* 4.  *Rouletted* 11½.

| 24 | 3 pf., mauve (1865) .. | 25 | 25 |
|---|---|---|---|
| 25 | 3 ,, reddish lilac(1865) | 25 | 25 |
| 26 | 4 ,, green .. | 16 | 6 |
| 27 | 4 ,, pale green .. | 16 | 6 |
| 28 | 6 ,, orange .. .. | 16 | 6 |
| 29 | 6 ,, orange-red .. | 16 | 6 |
| 30 | 1 sgr., rose .. .. | 10 | |
| 31 | 1 ,, dull rose .. | 10 | |
| 32 | 1 ,, carmine .. .. | — | 2 |
| 33 | 2 ,, Prussian blue .. | 15.00 | 1.50 |
| 34 | 2 ,, pale ultramarine | 8 | 2 |
| 35 | 2 ,, dark ,, .. | 25 | 2 |
| 36 | 3 ,, bistre-yellow .. | 8 | 2 |
| 37 | 3 ,, bistre-brown .. | — | |

All six values are found imperforate, but in this state must be looked upon as proofs, although postmarked specimens are known.  The stamps with an inscription at the back are essays.

| 5 | | 6 | |
|---|---|---|---|

**1866.** Type 5.  *On gold-beater's skin.*
No. Type.　　　*Rouletted* 10.

| 38 | 5 | 10 sgr., rose .. | 45 | 90 |
|---|---|---|---|---|
| 39 | 6 | 30 ,, blue .. .. | 75 | 2.50 |

These two stamps were not sold to the public, but were applied in the Post Office to heavy packets requiring them.

7

**1867.**  Type 7.  *Rouletted* 16.

| 40 | 1 kr., green .. .. | 50 | 75 |
|---|---|---|---|
| 41 | 1 ,, yellow-green .. | 50 | 75 |

| No. | | | Un. | Used. |
|---|---|---|---|---|
| 42 | 2 kr., orange | .. .. | 1.25 | 1.50 |
| 43 | 3 ,, rose | .. .. | 25 | 18 |
| 44 | 3 ,, carmine-rose | .. | 36 | 18 |
| 45 | 6 ,, ultramarine | .. | 25 | 30 |
| 46 | 9 ,, bistre | .. | 25 | 30 |

This set of stamps in *kreuzer* currency was issued for use in the States served by the Thurn and Taxis office, Prussia having taken over the management of those Post Offices from July 1st, 1867. The remarks attached to Nos. 24 to 37 apply equally to Nos. 40 to 46.

Prussia ceased to have a separate issue on the formation of the North German Confederation, 1 Jan., 1868.

## SAXONY.

1

### 1850. Type 1. *Imperf.*

| 1 | 3 pf., pale red | .. | — | 30.00 |
|---|---|---|---|---|
| 2 | 3 ,, brick-red | .. | — | 30.00 |
| 3 | 3 ,, brownish red | .. | | |

2

3

### 1851. Type 2. *Imperf.*

| 4 | 3 pf., yellow-green | .. | 3.15 | 62 |
|---|---|---|---|---|
| 5 | 3 ,, blue-green | .. | 2.50 | 62 |

### Type 3. Black *impression.*

| 6 | ½ ngr., on grey-white | .. | 3.75 | 8 |
|---|---|---|---|---|
| 7 | ½ ,, blue-grey | .. | 3.75 | 8 |
| 8 | 1 ,, pale rose | .. | 5.00 | 6 |
| 9 | 1 ,, deep ,, | .. | 5.00 | 6 |
| 10 | 2 ,, pale blue | .. | 6.25 | 62 |
| 11 | 2 ,, blue .. | .. | 6.25 | 62 |
| 12 | 2 ,, dark blue | .. | 17.50 | 36 |
| 13 | 3 ,, yellow | .. | 10.00 | 12 |

### Error of paper.

| 14 | ½ ngr., on pale blue | .. | | |

The numerals on some of the values vary in shape.

4

### 1856. Type 4. *Imperf.*

| 15 | ½ ngr., on grey-white | .. | 25 | 2 |
|---|---|---|---|---|
| 16 | ½ ,, blue-grey | .. | 25 | 2 |
| 17 | 1 ,, pale rose | .. | — | 2 |
| 18 | 1 ,, deep ,, | .. | 50 | 2 |
| 19 | 2 ,, blue .. | .. | 75 | 8 |
| 20 | 2 ,, dark blue | .. | 75 | |
| 21 | 2 ,, greenish blue | . | 12 | |
| 22 | 3 ,, yellow | .. | 1.25 | 4 |
| 23 | 3 ,, pale yellow | .. | 1.25 | ¼ |

### Coloured impression.

| 24 | 5 ngr., pale rose-red | .. | 3.00 | 62 |
|---|---|---|---|---|
| 25 | 5 ,, deep ,, | .. | 3.00 | 62 |
| 26 | 5 ,, brown-red | .. | 12.50 | 62 |
| 27 | 5 ,, vermilion | .. | 3.75 | |
| 28 | 10 ,, blue .. | .. | 8.75 | 3.15 |
| 29 | 10 ,, dark blue | .. | 8.75 | 3.15 |

As in the previous issue, the numerals on some of the values vary in shape. The 5 and 10 ngr. may be found on thick and on thinner semi-transparent paper.

5

6

### 1863. Type 5. *Perf.* 13.

| 30 | 3 pf., yellow-green | .. | 2 | 12 |
|---|---|---|---|---|
| 31 | 3 ,, blue-green | .. | 2 | 12 |
| 31a | ½ ngr., deep yellow | .. | 5.00 | 2 |
| 31b | ½ ,, orange-yellow | .. | 1.00 | 2 |
| 32 | ½ ,, orange .. | .. | 2 | 2 |
| 33 | ½ ,, orange-vermilion | | 50 | 2 |

### Type 6.

| 34 | 1 ngr., pale rose | .. | 2 | 2 |
|---|---|---|---|---|
| 35 | 1 ,, deep ,, | .. | 2 | 2 |
| 36 | 1 ,, lilac-rose | .. | — | 4 |
| 37 | 2 ,, Prussian blue | .. | 75 | 4 |
| 38 | 2 ,, blue .. | .. | 2 | 4 |
| 39 | 2 ,, ultramarine | .. | 2 | 4 |
| 40 | 3 ,, chestnut-brown | . | 4 | 6 |
| 41 | 3 ,, dark brown | .. | 6 | 6 |
| 42 | 5 ,, dull lilac | .. | 50 | |
| 43 | 5 ,, slate .. | .. | 1.25 | |
| 44 | 5 ,, dull purple | .. | 90 | 62 |

| No. | | | Un. | Used. |
|---|---|---|---|---|
| 45 | 5 ngr., | blue-grey .. | 90 | 62 |
| 46 | 5 ,, | pale grey .. | 62 | 62 |

Saxony ceased to have a separate issue on joining the North German Confederation, 1 Jan., 1868.

## SCHLESWIG-HOLSTEIN.

1

2

**1850.** Type 1. *Imperf. Arms in centre embossed.*

| | | | Un. | Used. |
|---|---|---|---|---|
| 1 | 1 sch., | Prussian blue .. | 15.00 | |
| 2 | 1 ,, | blue .. .. | 6.00 | 15.00 |
| 3 | 1 ,, | dull blue .. | 6.50 | |
| 4 | 2 ,, | pale rose .. | 11.25 | |
| 5 | 2 ,, | deep ,, .. | 12.50 | |

**1865.** Type 2. *Rouletted* 11½.

| | | | Un. | Used. |
|---|---|---|---|---|
| 6 | ½ sch., | rose .. .. | 1.00 | |
| 7 | 1¼ ,, | green .. .. | 62 | 12 |
| 8 | 1⅓ ,, | lilac-mauve .. | 1.50 | 2.00 |
| 9 | 2 ,, | ultramarine .. | 1.85 | 2.50 |
| 10 | 4 ,, | bistre .. .. | 1.85 | 10.00 |

The 1¼ sch. is found imperforate, and was apparently issued in this condition, as pairs are known used.

## SCHLESWIG.

3

**1864.** Type 3. *Rouletted* 11½.

| | | | Un. | Used. |
|---|---|---|---|---|
| 21 | 1¼ sch., | green .. .. | 75 | |
| 22 | 4 ,, | rose .. .. | 1.00 | 2.50 |
| 23 | 4 ,, | carmine .. | 1.00 | 2.50 |

**1865.** *Rouletted* 11½.

| | | | Un. | Used. |
|---|---|---|---|---|
| 24 | ½ sch., | pale yellow-green | 75 | 1.00 |
| 25 | 1¼ ,, | reddish lilac .. | 1.00 | 10 |
| 26 | 1¼ ,, | grey-lilac .. | — | 50 |
| 27 | 1⅓ ,, | rose .. .. | 90 | 75 |
| 28 | 2 ,, | ultramarine .. | 75 | 62 |
| 29 | 4 ,, | bistre .. .. | 90 | 75 |

**1867.** *Rouletted* 10.

| | | | Un. | Used. |
|---|---|---|---|---|
| | 1¼ sch., | reddish lilac .. | 1.00 | 16 |
| | 1¼ ,, | lilac .. .. | 1.00 | 16 |
| | 1¼ ,, | grey .. .. | 15.00 | 50 |

## HOLSTEIN.

4

**1864.** Type 4. *Imperf.*

A. *Small lettering in frame,* "SCHILLING" *large.*

| No. | | | Un. | Used. |
|---|---|---|---|---|
| 51 | 1¼ sch., | pale blue .. | 2.50 | 1.25 |
| 52 | 1¼ ,, | blue .. .. | 2.50 | 1.25 |
| 53 | 1¼ ,, | ,, (roul. 9½) .. | | |

B. *Larger lettering in frame,* "SCHILLING" *small, wavy lines in spandrels wider apart.*

| | | | Un. | Used. |
|---|---|---|---|---|
| 54 | 1¼ sch., | blue .. .. | 15.00 | 7.50 |

C. *Larger and thicker lettering still,* "SCHILLING" *small, and no dots over the two letters* "I."

| | | | Un. | Used. |
|---|---|---|---|---|
| 55 | 1¼ sch., | blue .. .. | 1.25 | 75 |
| 56 | 1¼ ,, | pale blue .. | 1.25 | |

*Varieties. Rouletted* 9½.

| | | | Un. | Used. |
|---|---|---|---|---|
| 57 | 1¼ sch., | blue .. .. | | |
| 58 | 1¼ ,, | pale blue .. | | |

The other varieties of these stamps, given by M. Moens, have since been proved to be forgeries.

5

**1864.** Type 5. *Rouletted* 8.

| | | | Un. | Used. |
|---|---|---|---|---|
| 59 | 1¼ sch., | pale blue .. | 1.00 | [illegible] |
| 60 | 1¼ ,, | dark ,, .. | 1.00 | |

Types 4, A, B, and C, are printed upon white paper with a grey network, while Type 5 is on paper with a rose network.

6

7

**1865.** *Rouletted* 8.

| No. | Type. | | | Un. | Used. |
|---|---|---|---|---|---|
| 61 | 6 | ½ sch., | pale green .. | 1.85 | [illegible] |
| 62 | ,, | 1¼ ,, | ,, lilac .. | 2.10 | 2.50 |
| 63 | 7 | 1⅓ ,, | carmine-rose | 1.00 | 90 |
| 64 | 6 | 2 ,, | pale blue .. | 75 | 1.00 |
| 65 | 7 | 4 ,, | bistre .. | 75 | 90 |

8

**1866.** Type 8. *Rouletted* 8.

| No. | | | Un. | Used. |
|---|---|---|---|---|
| 66 | 1½ sch., | reddish lilac .. | 2.50 | |
| 67 | 2 ,, | pale blue .. | 1.85 | 2.10 |

*The same. Rouletted* 7.

| No. | | | Un. | Used. |
|---|---|---|---|---|
| 68 | 1½ sch., | reddish lilac .. | | |
| 69 | 2 ,, | pale blue .. | | |

The Duchies of Schleswig and of Holstein were annexed to Prussia in 1866, but all separate issues were superseded on 1 Jan., 1868, by those of the North German Confederation.

## THURN AND TAXIS.

(The postal monopoly, possessed and managed by the Counts of "Thurn and Taxis"—a princely house of Austria—extended throughout those States and parts of Germany, now forming part of the German Empire, which did not possess a postal administration of their own, or separate issues of stamps.)

### NORTHERN DISTRICT.

1

**1852-58.** Type 1. Black *impression*.

*Imperf.*

| No. | | | Un. | Used. |
|---|---|---|---|---|
| 1 | ¼ sgr., | on red-bn. (1854) | 6.25 | 25 |
| 2 | ⅓ ,, | flesh ('58) .. | 1.10 | 90 |
| 3 | ½ ,, | pale green .. | 17.50 | 12 |
| 4 | ½ ,, | pale bluish gn. | 15.00 | 12 |
| 5 | 1 ,, | deep blue .. | — | 36 |
| 6 | 1 ,, | blue (1853) .. | 15.00 | 8 |
| 7 | 1 ,, | grey-blue ('58) | 17.50 | 12 |
| 8 | 2 ,, | rose .. .. | 17.50 | 10 |
| 9 | 2 ,, | pale rose .. | — | 10 |
| 10 | 3 ,, | yellow .. | 10.00 | 8 |
| 11 | 3 ,, | yellow-buff .. | — | 8 |

Fine copies, with full gum, can be supplied in most cases, but at higher prices, and the same applies to Nos. 53–59.

2

**1859-60.**

Type 1. *Coloured impression.*

*Imperf.*

| No. | | | Un. | Used. |
|---|---|---|---|---|
| 12 | ¼ sgr., | light red (1860) . | 1.50 | 25 |
| 13 | ½ ,, | blue-green .. | 5.00 | 25 |
| 14 | 1 ,, | pale blue .. | 8.75 | 12 |
| 15 | 2 ,, | rose (1860) .. | 1.50 | |
| 16 | 2 ,, | pale rose (1860).. | 1.50 | |
| 17 | 3 ,, | brn.-red ( ,, ).. | 3.75 | 16 |

Type 2.

| No. | | | Un. | Used. |
|---|---|---|---|---|
| 18 | 5 sgr., | red-lilac .. | 6 | 50 |
| 19 | 10 ,, | orange .. .. | 12 | 5.00 |

The last two values are known rouletted, and also perforated, but both these additions are of a purely private nature.

**1862-64.**

Type 1. *Imperf.*

| No. | | | Un. | Used. |
|---|---|---|---|---|
| 20 | ¼ sgr., | black (1864) .. | 36 | 50 |
| 21 | ⅓ ,, | yellow-green ('63) | 36 | 50 |
| 22 | ⅓ ,, | blue-green ( ,, ) | 36 | 50 |
| 23 | ½ ,, | orange ( ,, ) | 1.50 | 12 |
| 24 | ½ ,, | orange-yell. ( ,, ) | 1.50 | 12 |
| 25 | 1 ,, | pale rose ('62) | 2.00 | 12 |
| 26 | 1 ,, | deep ,, ( ,, ) | 1.85 | 12 |
| 27 | 2 ,, | pale blue ('64) | 75 | 36 |
| 28 | 2 ,, | deep ,, ( ,, ) | 90 | |
| 29 | 3 ,, | bistre (1863) .. | 36 | 18 |
| 30 | 3 ,, | yellow-brown .. | 25 | 18 |

**1865.**

Type 1. *Rouletted* 16.

| No. | | | Un. | Used. |
|---|---|---|---|---|
| 31 | ¼ sgr., | black .. .. | 12 | 1.50 |
| 32 | ⅓ ,, | green .. .. | 10 | 1.00 |
| 33 | ½ ,, | orange-yellow .. | 25 | 25 |
| 34 | 1 ,, | rose .. .. | 75 | 16 |
| 35 | 2 ,, | blue .. .. | 4 | 30 |
| 36 | 3 ,, | bistre .. .. | 8 | 12 |
| 37 | 3 ,, | bistre-brown .. | — | 12 |

**1867.**

Type 1. *Rouletted* 16, *in colour.*

| No. | | | Un. | Used. |
|---|---|---|---|---|
| 38 | ¼ sgr., | black .. .. | 4 | 5.00 |
| 39 | ⅓ ,, | pale green .. | 8 | 3.00 |
| 40 | ⅓ ,, | green .. .. | 8 | 3.00 |
| 41 | ½ ,, | orange-yellow .. | 6 | 75 |
| 42 | 1 ,, | rose .. .. | 4 | 25 |
| 43 | 2 ,, | blue .. .. | 4 | 3.15 |
| 44 | 3 ,, | yellow-brown .. | 8 | 1.25 |

|  | *Un.* | *Used.* |
|---|---|---|
| No. | | |

## SOUTHERN DISTRICT.

**3**

**1852-58.**

Type 3.  Black *impression.*
*Imperf.*

| 51 | 1 kr., on pale green '.. | 1.85 | 4 |
| 52 | 1  ,,   ,,  bluish gn. | 3.00 | 4 |
| 53 | 3  ,,    deep blue | 20.00 | 12 |
| 54 | 3  ,,    blue (1853) | 15.00 | |
| 55 | 3  ,,    grey-blue(1858) | 12.50 | 6 |
| 56 | 6  ,,    rose | 15.00 | 6 |
| 57 | 6  ,,    pale rose | 15.00 | 6 |
| 58 | 9  ,,    yellow | 10.00 | 4 |
| 59 | 9  ,,    yellow-buff | — | 6 |

**4**

**1859.**

Type 3.  *Coloured impression.*
*Imperf.*

| 60 | 1 kr., blue-green | 1.60 | 4 |
| 61 | 1  ,,   green | 1.60 | 4 |
| 62 | 3  ,,   pale blue.. | 15.00 | 6 |
| 63 | 6  ,,   rose | 10.00 | 18 |
| 64 | 9  ,,   orange-yellow | 20.00 | 18 |
| 65 | 9  ,,   yellow | — | 18 |

Type 4.

| 66 | 15 kr., red-lilac | 6 | 36 |
| 67 | 30  ,,  orange | 8 | 2.00 |

The same remarks apply to Nos. 66 and 67 as we made upon Nos. 18 and 19.

The 3 kr., *yellow-green,* formerly catalogued as an "error," is now looked upon as a proof.

**1862.**

Type 3.  *Imperf.*

| 68 | 3 kr., pale rose .. | 1.25 | 4 |
| 69 | 3  ,,  deep ,, .. | — | 4 |
| 0 | 6  ,,  pale blue.. | 36 | 10 |
| 1 | 6  ,,  deep ,, .. | 25 | 10 |
| · | 9  ,,  bistre | 25 | 6 |
| | 9  ,,  brown | 25 | 6 |

|  | *Un.* | *Used.* |
|---|---|---|
| No. | | |

**1865.**  Type 3.  *Rouletted* 16.

| 74 | 1 kr., pale green | .. | 36 | |
| 75 | 3  ,,   rose | .. | 18 | 12 |
| 76 | 6  ,,   blue | .. | 2 | 12 |
| 77 | 9  ,,   bistre | .. | 4 | 18 |
| 78 | 9  ,,   bistre-brown | .. | 6 | 18 |

**1867.**  Type 3.  *Rouletted* 16, *in colour.*

| 79 | 1 kr., green | .. | 2 | 12 |
| 80 | 1  ,,   pale green | .. | 2 | 12 |
| 81 | 3  ,,   rose | .. | 2 | 18 |
| 82 | 6  ,,   blue | .. | 4 | 50 |
| 83 | 9  ,,   yellow-bistre | .. | 10 | 62 |
| 84 | 9  ,,   yellow-ochre | .. | 12 | 62 |

*Variety, rouletted plain, and also in colour.*

| 85 | 3 kr., bright rose, *pair.* | 1.25 |

Separate issues ceased on the 1st July, 1867, when the above postal monopoly was ceded to Prussia.  At that time Prussia had only an issue in silbergröschen; the 1867 issue of Prussia was therefore created for use in the South District, formerly served by the "Thurn and Taxis" administration.

## WURTEMBERG.

**1**

**1851-52.**  Type 1.  Black *impression.*
*Imperf.*

| 1 | 1 kr., on light buff | .. | 10.00 | 30 |
| 2 | 1  ,,   buff | .. | — | 30 |
| 3 | 3  ,,   yellow | .. | 3.75 | 2 |
| 4 | 3  ,,   orange-yellow | | — | 8 |
| 5 | 6  ,,   yellow-green | | 20.00 | 5 |
| 6 | 6  ,,   blue-green | .. | 22.50 | 5 |
| 7 | 9  ,,   pale rose | .. | 45.00 | 8 |
| 8 | 9  ,,   rose | .. | — | 8 |
| 9 | 18  ,,  dull purple ('52) | 10.00 | 5.00 |

The word "Wurttemberg" varies in length, measuring 18, 18½, or 19 mm. The so-called reprints of this issue are nothing better than official imitations. They were made in 1864, and they have the letter "W" of "Wurttemberg" 1½ mm. from the left side-line of the label, instead of 1 mm. as in the originals.

No. | | *Un.* | *Used.*

2

DEC., **1856.** Type **2.** *With orange silk thread. Imperf.*

| | | | | *Un.* | *Used.* |
|---|---|---|---|---|---|
| 10 | 1 kr., | pale brown | .. | 15.00 | 62 |
| 11 | 1 „ | deep „ | .. | — | 62 |
| 12 | 3 „ | orange .. | .. | — | 4 |
| 13 | 3 „ | orange-yellow | .. | 17.50 | 4 |
| 14 | 6 „ | pale yellow-green | — | | 36 |
| 15 | 6 „ | green .. | .. | — | 30 |
| 16 | 6 „ | deep green | .. | — | 75 |
| 17 | 9 „ | rose .. | .. | 30.00 | 36 |
| 18 | 9 „ | carmine .. | .. | — | 75 |
| 19 | 18 „ | blue .. | .. | — | 8.75 |
| 20 | 18 „ | pale blue .. | .. | — | 8.75 |

All five values were reprinted in 1864 with a *red* silk thread, and the 6 kr. also with a *yellow* silk thread. On the sheets of reprints the stamps are 1¾ mm. apart, instead of ¾ mm. as in the originals.

**1858-60.** *Without silk thread.*
(a) *Imperf.*

| | | | | | |
|---|---|---|---|---|---|
| 21 | 1 kr., | brown | .. | 7.00 | 50 |
| 22 | 1 „ | deep brown | .. | 7.50 | 50 |
| 23 | 3 „ | orange .. | .. | — | 4 |
| 24 | 3 „ | orange-yellow | .. | 20.00 | 4 |
| 25 | 6 „ | pale green | .. | — | 50 |
| 26 | 6 „ | deep „ | .. | — | 62 |
| 27 | 9 „ | rose .. | .. | — | 36 |
| 28 | 9 „ | carmine .. | .. | 37.50 | 30 |
| 29 | 18 „ | blue .. | .. | — | 6.25 |
| 30 | 18 „ | dark blue | .. | 20.00 | 6.25 |

(b) *Perf.* 13½.

| | | | | | |
|---|---|---|---|---|---|
| 31 | 1 kr., | brown .. | .. | — | 75 |
| 32 | 3 „ | orange .. | .. | 25.00 | 4 |
| 33 | 3 „ | orange-yellow | .. | — | 6 |
| 34 | 6 „ | green .. | .. | — | 36 |
| 35 | 6 „ | deep green | .. | — | 36 |
| 36 | 9 „ | carmine .. | .. | 30.00 | 1.00 |

This issue, like the last, was reprinted in 1864 (imperf.), but the reprints have a space of 2 mm. between the stamps, whereas the originals have only 1½ mm.

**1861.** *Thin paper. Perf.* 13½.

| | | | | | |
|---|---|---|---|---|---|
| 37 | 1 kr., | brown .. | .. | 6.25 | 62 |
| 38 | 1 „ | deep brown | .. | 6.25 | 50 |
| 39 | 1 „ | black-brown | .. | 7.50 | 50 |
| 40 | 3 „ | orange-yellow | .. | 1.85 | 4 |
| 41 | 6 „ | green .. | .. | 3.75 | 25 |
| 42 | 9 „ | carmine .. | .. | 12.50 | 62 |
| 43 | 9 „ | lilac-rose .. | .. | 10.00 | 1.00 |
| 44 | 18 „ | blue .. | .. | 8.75 | 7.50 |

All five values are found imperforate, but it is doubtful if the stamps in this condition were issued for use.

No. | | *Un.* | *Used.*

**1862.** *The same. Perf.* 10.

| | | | | | |
|---|---|---|---|---|---|
| 45 | 1 kr., | black-brown | .. | 7.50 | 1.10 |
| 46 | 3 „ | orange-yellow | .. | 5.65 | 6 |
| 47 | 6 „ | green .. | .. | 10.00 | 50 |
| 48 | 9 „ | lilac-rose.. | .. | 25.00 | 3.00 |

**1863-64.** *Perf.* 10.

| | | | | | |
|---|---|---|---|---|---|
| 49 | 1 kr., | yellow-green | .. | 75 | 4 |
| 50 | 1 „ | green .. | .. | 1.10 | 6 |
| 51 | 1 „ | blue-green | .. | 1.25 | 8 |
| 52 | 3 „ | carmine .. | .. | 1.00 | 2 |
| 53 | 3 „ | deep rose | .. | 1.00 | 2 |
| 54 | 6 „ | blue (1864) | .. | 2.50 | 36 |
| 55 | 6 „ | deep blue ('64) | .. | 2.50 | 36 |
| 56 | 9 „ | yellow-brown | .. | 4.50 | 25 |
| 57 | 9 „ | chestnut .. | .. | 5.00 | 25 |
| 58 | 9 „ | black-brown | .. | 10.00 | 1.00 |
| 59 | 18 „ | orange (1864) | .. | 7.50 | 2.00 |

**1865-68.** *Rouletted* 10.

| | | | | | |
|---|---|---|---|---|---|
| 60 | 1 kr., | yellow-green | .. | 62 | 4 |
| 61 | 1 „ | pale „ | .. | — | 4 |
| 62 | 3 „ | pale rose.. | .. | 1.00 | 2 |
| 63 | 3 „ | rose .. | .. | 1.00 | 2 |
| 64 | 6 „ | blue .. | .. | 5.00 | 25 |
| 65 | 6 „ | deep blue | .. | 5.00 | 25 |
| 66 | 7 „ | slate-blue ('68) | .. | 8.75 | 1.60 |
| 67 | 7 „ | indigo .. | .. | — | 1.60 |
| 68 | 9 „ | brown (1867) | .. | 7.50 | 1.00 |
| 69 | 9 „ | chestnut .. | .. | 7.50 | 75 |
| 70 | 9 „ | bistre (1867) | .. | — | 62 |
| 71 | 18 „ | orange (1868) | .. | 20.00 | 7.50 |

3

**1869-73.** Type **3.** *Rouletted* 10.

| | | | | | |
|---|---|---|---|---|---|
| 72 | 1 kr., | green .. | .. | 25 | 4 |
| 73 | 1 „ | yellow-green | .. | 36 | 2 |
| 74 | 2 „ | orange .. | .. | 1.00 | 62 |
| 75 | 2 „ | deep orange | .. | 1.10 | 50 |
| 76 | 3 „ | pale rose | .. | 30 | 2 |
| 77 | 3 „ | deep „ .. | .. | 50 | 2 |
| 78 | 7 „ | blue .. | .. | 1.10 | 8 |
| 79 | 7 „ | deep blue | .. | 1.00 | 8 |
| 80 | 9 „ | bistre (1873) | .. | 62 | 12 |
| 81 | 14 „ | dull yellow | .. | 5.00 | 62 |
| 82 | 14 „ | orange-yellow | .. | 1.50 | 45 |
| 83 | 14 „ | orange .. | .. | 1.50 | 36 |

The 14 kr. is found *imperf.*, but is not known used. (*Price unused*, $3.15.)

**1873.** Type **2.** *Imperf.*

| | | | | | |
|---|---|---|---|---|---|
| 84 | 70 kr., | purple .. | .. | 18.75 | 15.00 |
| 85 | 70 „ | red-lilac .. | .. | 15.00 | 15.00 |

| No. | *Un.* | *Used.* |
|---|---|---|

**1874.** Type 3. *Perf.* 11½×11.

| 86 | 1 kr., yellow-green | .. | 36 | 12 |
| 87 | 1 ,, green | .. | 36 | 12 |

Other values of this type are sometimes seen perforated, but these are fraudulent productions.

4

**1875-79.** Type 4. *Perf.* 11½×11.

| 88 | 3 pf., pale blue-green | .. | — | 2 |
| 89 | 3 ,, green | .. | 12 | 2 |
| 90 | 5 ,, violet | .. | — | 2 |
| 91 | 5 ,, pale violet | .. | 12 | 2 |
| 92 | 10 ,, pale rose | .. | 8 | 2 |
| 93 | 10 ,, carmine | .. | 6 | 2 |
| 94 | 20 ,, Prussian blue | .. | 2.10 | 6 |
| 95 | 20 ,, ultramarine | .. | 6 | 2 |
| 96 | 20 ,, pale ,, | .. | 18 | 2 |
| 97 | 25 ,, pale brown | .. | 90 | 2 |
| 98 | 25 ,, chestnut-brown | .. | 62 | 8 |
| 99 | 50 ,, grey | .. | 3.00 | 6 |
| 100 | 50 ,, grey-green ('78) | .. | 1.00 | 2 |
| 101 | 50 ,, sage-green ('78) | .. | — | 2 |
| 102 | 2 mk., yellow | .. | 30.00 | 3.50 |
| 103 | 2 ,, vermilion on oran. (1879) | .. | 31.25 | 2.00 |

Two sets of most of the above values may be formed, one with yellow and the other with white gum.

5

**1881-83.** Type 5. *Perf.* 11½×11.
*Numeral in centre in* black.

| 104 | 2 mk., orange-yellow | .. | 3.75 | 8 |
| 105 | 2 ,, orange | .. | 1.00 | 12 |
| 106 | 5 ,, pale blue | .. | 2.50 | 1.85 |

The 2 marks, No. 105, is known *imperf.* A sheet was accidentally issued in this condition.

**1890-93.** Type 4. *Perf.* 11½×11.

| 107 | 2 pf., slate-grey ('93) | .. | 2 | 2 |
| 108 | 3 ,, brown | .. | — | 2 |
| —9 | 3 ,, deep brown | .. | 2 | 2 |
| | 5 ,, yellow-green | .. | 12 | 2 |
| | 5 ,, green | .. | 4 | 2 |
| | 5 ,, blue-green | .. | | |

| No. | *Un.* | *Used.* |
|---|---|---|

| 113 | 25 pf., orange-yellow | .. | 12 | 2 |
| 114 | 25 ,, deep orange | .. | 12 | 2 |
| 115 | 50 ,, pale red-brown | .. | 1.00 | 8 |
| 116 | 50 ,, reddish purple | .. | 16 | .. |

**1900.** Type 5. *Numeral in centre in* black.

| 117 | 30 pf., orange | .. | .. | 10 | 2 |
| 118 | 40 ,, carmine | .. | .. | 14 | 4 |

### MUNICIPAL SERVICE STAMPS.

51

**1875-97.** Type 51. *Perf.* 11½×11.

| 201 | 3 pf., brown (1897) | .. | 6 | 4 |
| 202 | 5 ,, lavender | .. | | |
| 203 | 5 ,, violet | .. | — | 4 |
| 204 | 5 ,, mauve | .. | — | 2 |
| 205 | 5 ,, yellow-green | .. | — | 2 |
| 206 | 5 ,, green | .. | — | 2 |
| 207 | 5 ,, deep blue-green | .. | 8 | 2 |
| 208 | 10 ,, rose | .. | 12 | 4 |
| 209 | 10 ,, carmine | .. | 36 | 2 |

*Variety. Imperf.*

| 210 | 5 pf., violet | .. | .. | — | 5.00 |

**1900.** *Same type and perf.*

| 211 | 2 pf., slate | .. | .. | 8 | 4 |
| 212 | 25 ,, orange | .. | .. | 62 | 6 |

### OFFICIAL STAMPS.

61

**1881-82.** Type 61. *Perf.* 11½×11.

| 301 | 3 pf., pale yellow-green | .. | 25 | 4 |
| 302 | 3 ,, ,, blue-green | .. | 25 | 4 |
| 303 | 5 ,, violet | .. | — | 2 |
| 304 | 5 ,, red-lilac | .. | 8 | 2 |
| 305 | 5 ,, purple | .. | — | 2 |
| 306 | 10 ,, pale rose | .. | 6 | 2 |
| 307 | 10 ,, rose | .. | 8 | 2 |
| 308 | 20 ,, ultramarine | .. | 8 | 2 |
| 309 | 20 ,, pale ,, | .. | 12 | 2 |
| 310 | 25 ,, chestnut-brown | .. | 30 | 6 |
| 311 | 25 ,, brown | .. | 25 | 4 |
| 312 | 50 ,, grey-green | .. | 25 | 2 |
| 313 | 1 mk., yellow (1882) | .. | 1.10 | 1.00 |

**1890-1900.** *Perf.* 11½×11.

| 313a | 2 pf., grey | .. | .. | — | 2 |
| 314 | 3 ,, brown | .. | .. | 4 | 2 |
| 315 | 5 ,, green | .. | .. | — | 2 |

| No. | | | Un. | Used. |
|---|---|---|---|---|
| 316 | 5 pf., deep green | .. | 4 | 2 |
| 317 | 25 ,, orange .. | .. | — | 2 |
| 318 | 25 ,, deep orange | .. | 12 | 2 |
| 319 | 50 ,, red-brown | .. | | 2 |
| 320 | 50 ,, deep marone | .. | 50 | 16 |
| 321 | 1 mark, violet.. | .. | 45 | 12 |

**1903.** *Same type and perf.*

| | | | Un. | Used. |
|---|---|---|---|---|
| 322 | 30 pf., black and orange | — | 8 |
| 323 | 40 ,, ,, carmine | — | 12 |

The Kingdom of Wurtemberg ceased to have separate stamps on 1 April, 1902, the stamps of the German Empire superseding them. Official stamps are still used.

## NORTH GERMAN CONFEDERATION.

1          2

**1868.** Type **1** *for the* "groschen" *values.*
Type **2** *for the* "kreuzer" *values.*
*Rouletted 8½ to 10, and 11 to 12½.*

| 1 | ½ gr., lilac | .. | .. | 36 | 8 |
|---|---|---|---|---|---|
| 2 | ⅓ ,, red-lilac .. | .. | 36 | 8 |
| 3 | ⅓ ,, green | .. | .. | 30 | 4 |
| 4 | ⅓ ,, pale green | .. | 30 | 4 |
| 5 | ⅓ ,, orange | .. | .. | 1.00 | 2 |
| 6 | 1 ,, rose | .. | .. | 75 | 2 |
| 7 | 1 ,, carmine-rose | .. | — | 2 |
| 8 | 2 ,, dark blue | .. | 2.50 | 2 |
| 9 | 2 ,, ultramarine | .. | 1.50 | 2 |
| 10 | 5 ,, bistre | .. | .. | 2.50 | 4 |
| 11 | 1 kr., pale green | .. | 1.00 | 25 |
| 12 | 1 ,, dark ,, | .. | 1.00 | 25 |
| 13 | 2 ,, orange | .. | .. | 1.50 | 25 |
| 14 | 3 ,, rose | .. | .. | 1.85 | 4 |
| 15 | 3 ,, carmine-rose | .. | 1.85 | 4 |
| 16 | 7 ,, dark blue | .. | 4.35 | 18 |
| 17 | 7 ,, ultramarine | .. | 4.35 | 18 |
| 18 | 18 ,, bistre | .. | .. | 30 | 36 |

All the above are known imperforate ; but stamps in this condition were not issued for use, although some specimens were passed through the post.

**1869.** *Same types. Perf.* 14 × 14½.

| 19 | ½ gr., lilac | .. | .. | 12 | 12 |
|---|---|---|---|---|---|
| 20 | ⅓ ,, red-violet | .. | 1.25 | 12 |
| 21 | ⅓ ,, green | .. | .. | 12 | 4 |
| 22 | ⅓ ,, yellow-green | .. | 4 | 4 |
| 23 | ⅓ ,, orange | .. | .. | 4 | 2 |
| 24 | ⅓ ,, orange-vermilion | .. | 2 | 4 |
| 25 | 1 ,, rose | .. | .. | 2 | 2 |
| 26 | 1 ,, rose-carmine | .. | 4 | 2 |
| 27 | 2 ,, ultramarine | .. | 4 | 2 |
| 28 | 2 ,, pale ,, | .. | .. | 2 | 2 |
| 29 | 5 ,, bistre | .. | .. | 6 | 6 |

| 30 | 1 kr., green | .. | .. | 8 | 10 |
|---|---|---|---|---|---|
| 31 | 1 ,, yellow-green | .. | 8 | 10 |
| 32 | 2 ,, orange | .. | .. | 30 | 62 |
| 33 | 3 ,, rose | .. | .. | 6 | 2 |
| 34 | 3 ,, rose-carmine | .. | 6 | 2 |
| 35 | 7 ,, ultramarine | .. | 8 | 8 |
| 36 | 7 ,, pale ,, | .. | 8 | 8 |
| 37 | 18 ,, bistre | .. | .. | 1.25 | 3.75 |

3          4

No. Type. **1869.** *Perf.* 14½ × 14.

| 38 | 3 | 10 gr., grey | .. | .. | 1.85 | 2.50 |
|---|---|---|---|---|---|---|
| 39 | 4 | 30 ,, light blue | .. | 1.50 | 1.25 |

These two stamps were not sold to the public, but were affixed in the Post Office to packets requiring them.

### OFFICIAL STAMPS.

5

**1870.** Type **5.** *Perf.* 14½ × 14.
*Network in* pale red-brown.

| 51 | ½ gr., black | .. | .. | 25 | 50 |
|---|---|---|---|---|---|
| 52 | ⅓ ,, ,, | .. | .. | 8 | 25 |
| 53 | ⅓ ,, ,, | .. | .. | 4 | 6 |
| 54 | 1 ,, ,, | .. | .. | 4 | 4 |
| 55 | 2 ,, ,, | .. | .. | 6 | 8 |

*Network in* grey.

| 56 | 1 kr., black | .. | .. | 25 | 3.15 |
|---|---|---|---|---|---|
| 57 | 2 ,, ,, | .. | .. | 36 | 5.00 |
| 58 | 3 ,, ,, | .. | .. | 12 | 62 |
| 59 | 7 ,, ,, | .. | .. | 25 | 3.75 |

### LOCAL FOR HAMBURG.

6

**1868.** Type **6.** *Rouletted* 8½ *to* 10, *and* 11 *to* 12½.

| 81 | (½ sch.), purple-brown.. | 75 | 50 |
|---|---|---|---|

**1869.** *Same type. Perf.* 14 × 14½.

| 82 | (½ sch.), purple-brown.. | 4 | 4 |
|---|---|---|---|
| 83 | ,, red-violet | .. | 2 | 8 |

The issues for North German Confederation were superseded by those for the German Empire.

|     |     |     | *Un.* | *Used.* |
|-----|-----|-----|-------|---------|

No.

**1874.** Type 3. *Perf.* 11½ × 11.

| No. |     |     | Un. | Used. |
|-----|-----|-----|-----|-------|
| 86 | 1 kr., yellow-green | .. | 36 | 12 |
| 87 | 1 „ green | .. .. | 36 | 12 |

Other values of this type are sometimes seen perforated, but these are fraudulent productions.

4

**1875-79.** Type 4. *Perf.* 11½ × 11.

| 88 | 3 pf., pale blue-green | .. | — | 2 |
|----|------------------------|-----|------|---|
| 89 | 3 „ green | .. .. | 12 | 2 |
| 90 | 5 „ violet | .. | — | 2 |
| 91 | 5 „ pale violet | .. | 12 | 2 |
| 92 | 10 „ pale rose | .. | 8 | 2 |
| 93 | 10 „ carmine | .. | 6 | 2 |
| 94 | 20 „ Prussian blue | .. | 2.10 | 6 |
| 95 | 20 „ ultramarine | .. | 6 | 2 |
| 96 | 20 „ pale „ | .. | 18 | 2 |
| 97 | 25 „ pale brown | .. | 90 | 2 |
| 98 | 25 „ chestnut-brown | .. | 62 | 8 |
| 99 | 50 „ grey | .. .. | 3.00 | 6 |
| 100 | 50 „ grey-green ('78) | .. | 1.00 | 2 |
| 101 | 50 „ sage-green ('78) | .. | — | 2 |
| 102 | 2 mk., yellow | .. .. | 30.00 | 3.50 |
| 103 | 2 „ vermilion on oran. (1879) | .. .. | 31.25 | 2.00 |

Two sets of most of the above values may be formed, one with yellow and the other with white gum.

5

**1881-83.** Type 5. *Perf.* 11½ × 11.
*Numeral in centre in* black.

| 104 | 2 mk., orange-yellow | .. | 3.75 | 8 |
|-----|----------------------|-----|------|---|
| 105 | 2 „ orange | .. | 1.00 | 12 |
| 106 | 5 „ pale blue | .. | 2.50 | 1.85 |

The 2 marks, No. 105, is known *imperf.* A sheet was accidentally issued in this condition.

**1890-93.** Type 4. *Perf.* 11½ × 11.

| 107 | 2 pf., slate-grey ('93) | .. | 2 | 2 |
|-----|-------------------------|-----|---|---|
| 108 | 3 „ brown | .. | — | 2 |
| 109 | 3 „ deep brown | .. | 2 | 2 |
| 110 | 5 „ yellow-green | .. | 12 | 2 |
| 1 | 5 „ green | .. | 4 | 2 |
| | 5 „ blue-green | .. | | |

| 113 | 25 pf., orange-yellow | .. | 12 | 2 |
|-----|-----------------------|-----|------|---|
| 114 | 25 „ deep orange | .. | 12 | 2 |
| 115 | 50 „ pale red-brown | .. | 1.00 | 8 |
| 116 | 50 „ reddish purple | .. | 16 | 2 |

**1900.** Type 5. *Numeral in centre in* black.

| 117 | 30 pf., orange | .. .. | 10 | 2 |
|-----|----------------|-------|----|---|
| 118 | 40 „ carmine | .. .. | 14 | 4 |

MUNICIPAL SERVICE STAMPS.

51

**1875-97.** Type 51. *Perf.* 11½ × 11.

| 201 | 3 pf., brown (1897) | .. | 6 | 4 |
|-----|---------------------|-----|----|---|
| 202 | 5 „ lavender | .. | | |
| 203 | 5 „ violet | .. .. | — | 4 |
| 204 | 5 „ mauve | .. | — | 2 |
| 205 | 5 „ yellow-green | .. | — | 2 |
| 206 | 5 „ green | .. .. | — | 2 |
| 207 | 5 „ deep blue-green | .. | 8 | 2 |
| 208 | 10 „ rose | .. | 12 | 4 |
| 209 | 10 „ carmine | .. .. | 36 | 2 |

*Variety. Imperf.*

| 210 | 5 pf., violet | .. .. | — | 5.00 |
|-----|---------------|-------|---|------|

**1900.** *Same type and perf.*

| 211 | 2 pf., slate | .. .. | 8 | 4 |
|-----|--------------|-------|---|---|
| 212 | 25 „ orange | .. .. | 62 | 6 |

OFFICIAL STAMPS.

61

**1881-82.** Type 61. *Perf.* 11½ × 11.

| 301 | 3 pf., pale yellow-green | .. | 25 | 4 |
|-----|--------------------------|-----|----|---|
| 302 | 3 „ „ blue-green | .. | 25 | 4 |
| 303 | 5 „ violet | .. .. | — | 2 |
| 304 | 5 „ red-lilac | .. .. | 8 | 2 |
| 305 | 5 „ purple | .. .. | — | 2 |
| 306 | 10 „ pale rose | .. .. | 6 | 2 |
| 307 | 10 „ rose | .. | 8 | 2 |
| 308 | 20 „ ultramarine | .. | 8 | 2 |
| 309 | 20 „ pale „ | .. | 12 | 2 |
| 310 | 25 „ chestnut-brown | .. | 30 | 6 |
| 311 | 25 „ brown | .. | 25 | 4 |
| 312 | 50 „ grey-green | .. | 25 | 2 |
| 313 | 1 mk., yellow (1882) | .. | 1.10 | 1.00 |

**1890-1900.** *Perf.* 11½ × 11.

| 313a | 2 pf., grey | .. .. | — | 2 |
|------|-------------|-------|---|---|
| 314 | 3 „ brown | .. .. | 4 | 2 |
| 315 | 5 „ green | .. .. | — | 2 |

| No. | | | Un. | Used. |
|---|---|---|---|---|
| 316 | 5 pf., deep green | .. | 4 | 2 |
| 317 | 25 ,, orange .. | .. | — | 2 |
| 318 | 25 ,, deep orange | .. | 12 | 2 |
| 319 | 50 ,, red-brown | .. | | |
| 320 | 50 ,, deep marone | .. | 50 | 16 |
| 321 | 1 mark, violet.. | .. | 45 | 12 |

**1903.** *Same type and perf.*

| | | | |
|---|---|---|---|
| 322 | 30 pf., black and orange | — | 8 |
| 323 | 40 ,, ,, carmine | — | 12 |

The Kingdom of Wurtemberg ceased to have separate stamps on 1 April, 1902, the stamps of the German Empire superseding them. Official stamps are still used.

## NORTH GERMAN CONFEDERATION.

1

2

**1868.** Type 1 *for the* "groschen" *values.* Type 2 *for the* "kreuzer" *values. Rouletted* 8½ *to* 10, *and* 11 *to* 12½.

| | | | | |
|---|---|---|---|---|
| 1 | ¼ gr., lilac | .. .. | 36 | 8 |
| 2 | ¼ ,, red-lilac .. | .. | 36 | 8 |
| 3 | ⅓ ,, green | .. .. | 30 | 4 |
| 4 | ⅓ ,, pale green | .. | 30 | 4 |
| 5 | ½ ,, orange .. | .. | 1.00 | 2 |
| 6 | 1 ,, rose | .. .. | 75 | 2 |
| 7 | 1 ,, carmine-rose | .. | — | 2 |
| 8 | 2 ,, dark blue | .. | 2.50 | 2 |
| 9 | 2 ,, ultramarine | .. | 1.50 | 2 |
| 10 | 5 ,, bistre | .. .. | 2.50 | 4 |
| 11 | 1 kr., pale green | .. | 1.00 | 25 |
| 12 | 1 ,, dark ,, | .. | 1.00 | 25 |
| 13 | 2 ,, orange .. | .. | 1.50 | 25 |
| 14 | 3 ,, rose | .. .. | 1.85 | 4 |
| 15 | 3 ,, carmine-rose | .. | 1.85 | 4 |
| 16 | 7 ,, dark blue | .. | 4.35 | 18 |
| 17 | 7 ,, ultramarine | .. | 4.35 | 18 |
| 18 | 18 ,, bistre | .. .. | 30 | 36 |

All the above are known imperforate; but stamps in this condition were not issued for use, although some specimens were passed through the post.

**1869.** *Same types. Perf.* 14 × 14½.

| | | | | |
|---|---|---|---|---|
| 19 | ¼ gr., lilac | .. .. | 12 | 12 |
| 20 | ¼ ,, red-violet | .. | 1.25 | 12 |
| 21 | ⅓ ,, green | .. .. | 12 | 4 |
| 22 | ⅓ ,, yellow-green | .. | 4 | 4 |
| 23 | ½ ,, orange .. | .. | 4 | 2 |
| 24 | ½ ,, orange-vermilion | | 2 | 2 |
| 25 | 1 ,, rose | .. .. | 2 | 2 |
| 26 | 1 ,, rose-carmine | .. | 4 | 2 |
| 27 | 2 ,, ultramarine | .. | 4 | 2 |
| 28 | 2 ,, pale ,, | .. | 2 | 2 |
| 29 | 5 ,, bistre | .. .. | 6 | 6 |

| No. | | | Un. | Used. |
|---|---|---|---|---|
| 30 | 1 kr., green | .. .. | 8 | 10 |
| 31 | 1 ,, yellow-green | .. | 8 | 10 |
| 32 | 2 ,, orange .. | .. | 30 | 62 |
| 33 | 3 ,, rose | .. .. | 6 | 2 |
| 34 | 3 ,, rose-carmine | .. | 6 | 2 |
| 35 | 7 ,, ultramarine | .. | 8 | 8 |
| 36 | 7 ,, pale ,, | .. | 8 | 8 |
| 37 | 18 ,, bistre | .. .. | 1.25 | 3.75 |

3

4

No. Type. **1869.** *Perf.* 14½ × 14.

| | | | | | |
|---|---|---|---|---|---|
| 38 | 3 | 10 gr., grey | .. .. | 1.85 | 2.50 |
| 39 | 4 | 30 ,, light blue | .. | 1.50 | 1.25 |

These two stamps were not sold to the public, but were affixed in the Post Office to packets requiring them.

### OFFICIAL STAMPS.

5

**1870.** Type 5. *Perf.* 14½ × 14.
*Network in* pale red-brown.

| | | | | |
|---|---|---|---|---|
| 51 | ¼ gr., black | .. .. | 25 | 50 |
| 52 | ⅓ ,, ,, | .. .. | 8 | 25 |
| 53 | ½ ,, ,, | .. .. | 4 | 6 |
| 54 | 1 ,, ,, | .. .. | 4 | 4 |
| 55 | 2 ,, ,, | .. .. | 6 | 8 |

*Network in* grey.

| | | | | |
|---|---|---|---|---|
| 56 | 1 kr., black | .. .. | 25 | 3.15 |
| 57 | 2 ,, ,, | .. .. | 36 | 5.00 |
| 58 | 3 ,, ,, | .. .. | 12 | 62 |
| 59 | 7 ,, ,, | .. .. | 25 | 3.75 |

### LOCAL FOR HAMBURG.

6

**1868.** Type 6. *Rouletted* 8½ *to* 10, *and* 11 *to* 12½.

| | | | |
|---|---|---|---|
| 81 | (½ sch.), purple-brown.. | 75 | 50 |

**1869.** *Same type. Perf.* 14 × 14½.

| | | | |
|---|---|---|---|
| 82 | (½ sch.), purple-brown.. | 4 | 4 |
| 83 | ,, red-violet .. | 2 | 8 |

The issues for North German Confederation were superseded by those for the German Empire.

| | | Un. | Used. |
|---|---|---|---|
| No. | | | |

## GERMAN ARMY OF
## OCCUPATION.

COMMONLY CALLED

## ALSACE AND LORRAINE.

These stamps were used in those parts of France occupied by the German Army in the war of 1870–71, and afterwards provisionally in the annexed provinces of Alsace and Lorraine, until superseded by the issues for the German Empire.

1 •

**1870.** Type 1.  *Perf.* 13½ × 14½.

A. *With points of the net upwards.*

| | | | | Un. | Used. |
|---|---|---|---|---|---|
| 1 | 1 c., olive-green | .. | | 18 | 1.25 |
| 2 | 1 c., sage-green | | | 18 | 1.25 |
| 3 | 2 c., chestnut-brown | .. | | 1.00 | 1.25 |
| 4 | 2 c., dark brown | | | 1.25 | 1.25 |
| 5 | 4 c., grey | .. | | 75 | 75 |
| 6 | 5 c., pale yellow-green . | | | 1.00 | 18 |
| 7 | 5 c., dark | ,, | | 25 | 12 |
| 8 | 10 c., light brown | .. | | 1.00 | 8 |
| 9 | 10 c., bistre | .. | | 18 | 18 |
| 10 | 10 c., bistre-brown | .. | | 50 | 4 |
| 11 | 20 c., pale ultramarine.. | | | 62 | 25 |
| 12 | 20 c., dark | ,, | | — | 25 |
| 13 | 25 c., dark brown | .. | | 62 | 50 |

B. *With points of the net downwards.*

| | | | | | |
|---|---|---|---|---|---|
| 14 | 1 c., olive-green | .. | | | |
| 15 | 1 c., sage-green | .. | | 12.50 | |
| 16 | 2 c., chestnut-brown | .. | | 2.00 | 7.50 |
| 17 | 4 c., grey | .. | | 1.50 | 2.00 |
| 18 | 5 c., pale yellow-green. | — | | | 8.75 |
| 19 | 10 c., light brown | .. | | 2.50 | 18 |
| 20 | 10 c., bistre-brown | .. | | 2.00 | 18 |
| 21 | 20 c., ultramarine | .. | | 12.50 | 3.00 |
| 22 | 25 c., brown | .. | | 15.00 | 5.00 |

*Variety.* Blue *net with points* downwards, *and also* yellow *nets with points* upwards.

| | | |
|---|---|---|
| 23 | 20 c., ultramarine | .. |

There are numbers of varieties to be found in these stamps, varying in the relative positions of different parts of the inscription, and the word "POSTES" also varies in length. An official imitation of all the values was made in 1885. In the imitations the "P" of "POSTES" is only 2½ mm. from the left border, whereas in the originals the distance is 3 to 3½ mm. Almost all the imitations have the points f the network downwards.

---

| | | Un. | Used. |
|---|---|---|---|
| No. | | | |

## GERMAN EMPIRE.

1

1 JAN., **1872.**  Type 1.  *Small shield.*
*Perf.* 13½ × 14½.

| | | | | Un. | Used. |
|---|---|---|---|---|---|
| 1 | ⅓ gr., pale violet | .. | | 50 | 12 |
| 2 | ⅓ ,, mauve | .. | | 36 | 12 |
| 3 | ⅓ ,, pale yellow-green | | | 75 | 2 |
| 4 | ⅓ ,, dark ,, | | | 90 | 2 |
| 5 | ⅓ ,, orange-vermilion | | | 75 | 4 |
| 6 | ½ ,, orange-yellow | .. | | 1.85 | 6 |
| 7 | 1 ,, rose | .. | ... | 62 | 2 |
| 8 | 1 ,, carmine | .. | | 1.00 | 2 |
| 9 | 2 ,, blue | .. | | 1.50 | 2 |
| 10 | 2 ,, ultramarine | .. | | 1.25 | 2 |
| 11 | 5 ,, bistre | .. | | 90 | 4 |
| 12 | 1 kr., pale yellow-green | | | 50 | 6 |
| 13 | 1 ,, yellow-green | .. | | 62 | 4 |
| 14 | 2 ,, orange-vermilion. | | | 36 | 25 |
| 15 | 2 ,, orange-yellow | .. | | 4 | 16 |
| 16 | 3 ,, rose-carmine | .. | | 1.25 | 2 |
| 17 | 7 ,, blue | .. | | 2.50 | 6 |
| 18 | 7 ,, ultramarine | .. | | 3.00 | 6 |
| 19 | 18 ,, bistre | .. | | 62 | 30 |

Many of the values have been seen with the embossed eagle inverted, but these varieties are fraudulent. The 2 and 5 gr. are known imperf.

2      3

FEB., **1872.**  *Lettered* "DEUTSCHE REICHS-
No. Type.    POST."  *Perf.* 14½ × 13½.

| | | | | Un. | Used. |
|---|---|---|---|---|---|
| 20 | 2 | 10 gr., grey, P.S. 6 c. | | 4 | 2.00 |
| 21 | 3 | 30 ,, blue .. | .. | 6 | 3.00 |

1 JULY, **1873.**  Type 1.  *Large shield.*
*Perf.* 13½ × 14½.

| | | | | Un. | Used. |
|---|---|---|---|---|---|
| 22 | ⅓ gr., mauve | .. | .. | 4 | 4 |
| 23 | ⅓ ,, violet | .. | .. | 4 | 4 |
| 24 | ⅓ ,, yellow-green | .. | | 2 | 2 |
| 25 | ⅓ ,, blue-green | .. | | 4 | 2 |
| 26 | ½ ,, orange-yellow | .. | | 6 | 2 |
| 27 | ½ ,, orange | .. | .. | 4 | 2 |
| 28 | 1 ,, rose | .. | .. | 2 | 2 |
| 29 | 1 ,, carmine | .. | .. | 2 | 2 |

| No. | | | | Un. | Used. |
|---|---|---|---|---|---|
| 30 | 2 gr., | ultramarine | .. | 4 | 2 |
| 31 | 2 ,, | blue | .. | 4 | 2 |
| 32 | 2½ ,, | chestnut-brown.. | | 3.75 | 4 |
| 34 | 5 ,, | bistre | .. | 6 | 4 |
| 35 | 1 kr., | pale yellow-green | | 2 | 2 |
| 36 | 1 ,, | yellow-green | .. | 4 | 2 |
| 37 | 1 ,, | blue-green | | — | 2 |
| 38 | 2 ,, | orange-yellow | .. | 1.25 | 2.50 |
| 39 | 3 ,, | rose | .. | 2 | 2 |
| 40 | 3 ,, | carmine .. | | 2 | 2 |
| 41 | 7 ,, | ultramarine | .. | 4 | 4 |
| 42 | 7 ,, | blue | .. | 4 | 4 |
| 43 | 9 ,, | chestnut-brown.. | | 30 | 12 |
| 44 | 9 ,, | brown | .. | 62 | 25 |
| 46 | 18 ,, | bistre | .. | 8 | 1.25 |

The ½, 1, and 5 gr. are known imperf.

5

1 FEB., 1874.

Type 1 *with figures in centre.*

Type 5.

| 46a | 2½ gr., | pale reddish brn. | 6 | 4 |
|---|---|---|---|---|
| 46b | 9 kr., | reddish brown .. | 8 | 12 |

The varieties with inverted eagle are forgeries.

6         7

**1875-77.**

Types 6, 7, *and* 8. "PFENNIGE" *with final* "E." *Perf.* 13½ × 14½.

| 47 | 3 pf., | pale green | .. | 6 | 2 |
|---|---|---|---|---|---|
| 48 | 3 ,, | dark ,, | .. | 6 | 2 |
| 49 | 5 ,, | lilac-mauve | .. | 18 | 2 |
| 50 | 5 ,, | violet | .. | 18 | 2 |
| 51 | 10 ,, | rose | .. | 12 | 2 |
| 52 | 10 ,, | carmine .. | | 12 | 2 |
| 53 | 20 ,, | ultramarine | | 50 | 2 |
| 54 | 25 ,, | chocolate.. | | 1.25 | 2 |
| 55 | 25 ,, | bistre-brown | .. | 1.25 | 2 |
| 56 | 50 ,, | grey | .. | 2.50 | 2 |
| 57 | 50 ,, | dark grey | .. | 3.00 | 2 |
| 58 | 50 ,, | grey-green (1877) | | — | 2 |
| 59 | 50 ,, | olive-green (1877) | | — | 3 |

8

**1875-82.** Type 8. *Perf.* 14½ × 13½.

| 60 | 2 mks., | purple .. | .. | 10.00 | 25 |
|---|---|---|---|---|---|
| 61 | 2 ,, | lilac-rose | .. | 3.75 | 4 |
| 62 | 2 ,, | dull mauve | .. | 75 | 2 |

**1880.**

Types 6 *and* 7, *but* "PFENNIG" *without final* "E." *Perf.* 13½ × 14½.

| 63 | 3 pf., | green | .. | 4 | 2 |
|---|---|---|---|---|---|
| 64 | 3 ,, | yellow-green | .. | 4 | 2 |
| 65 | 5 ,, | lilac-mauve | .. | 12 | 2 |
| 66 | 5 ,, | violet | .. | 4 | 2 |
| 67 | 10 ,, | rose | .. | 12 | 2 |
| 68 | 10 ,, | carmine-rose | .. | 12 | 2 |
| 69 | 20 ,, | pale ultramarine . | | 18 | 2 |
| 70 | 20 ,, | dark ,, | .. | 12 | 2 |
| 71 | 20 ,, | dull blue .. | .. | — | 2 |
| 72 | 25 ,, | red-brown | .. | 36 | 2 |
| 73 | 25 ,, | chocolate.. | .. | 12 | 2 |
| 74 | 50 ,, | grey-green | .. | 50 | 2 |
| 75 | 50 ,, | olive-green | .. | 30 | 2 |
| 76 | 50 ,, | myrtle-green | .. | 36 | 4 |

All the values of this issue are found printed in aniline as well as in ordinary colours.

9         10

**1889.**

Types 9 *and* 10. *Perf.* 13½ × 14½.

| 77 | 3 pf., | grey-brown | .. | 2 | 2 |
|---|---|---|---|---|---|
| 78 | 3 ,, | bistre-brown | .. | 2 | 2 |
| 79 | 5 ,, | yellow-green | .. | 2 | 2 |
| 80 | 5 ,, | bluish ,, | .. | 2 | 2 |
| 81 | 10 ,, | rose | .. | 4 | 2 |
| 82 | 10 ,, | rose-carmine | .. | 4 | 2 |
| 83 | 20 ,, | ultramarine | .. | 25 | 2 |
| 84 | 20 ,, | dark ,, | | 6 | 2 |
| 85 | 20 ,, | Prussian blue | .. | | 2 |
| 86 | 25 ,, | orange-yellow | .. | 10 | 2 |
| 87 | 50 ,, | lake-brown | .. | 1.50 | 2 |
| 88 | 50 ,, | chocolate.. | .. | 14 | 2 |

The 3 pf., 25 pf., and 50 pf. are found imperf., but are not believed to have been issued.

| No. | | Un. | Used. |
|---|---|---|---|

**1900.**

Type 9. *Perf.* 13½ × 14½.

| 89 | 2 pf., grey | .. | .. | 2 | 2 |
|---|---|---|---|---|---|

**11**

**1900.**

Type 11. *Inscribed* " REICHSPOST."

*Perf.* 14.

| 89a | 2 pf., grey | .. | .. | 2 | 2 |
|---|---|---|---|---|---|
| 90 | 3 ,, brown | .. | .. | 2 | 2 |
| 91 | 5 ,, green | .. | .. | 2 | 2 |
| 92 | 10 ,, carmine | .. | .. | 4 | 2 |
| 93 | 20 ,, ultramarine | .. | 8 | 2 |
| 94 | 25 ,, blk. & oran. on yel. | — | 2 |
| 95 | 30 ,, ,, buff | 12 | 2 |
| 96 | 40 ,, black & carmine | 12 | 2 |
| 97 | 50 ,, blk. & lilac on buff | 16 | 2 |
| 98 | 80 ,, blk. & car. on rose | 25 | 4 |

**12**

**13**

**14**

Types 12 *to* 15.

| m., carmine | .. | .. | 30 | 2 |
|---|---|---|---|---|
| n., blue | .. | .. | 60 | 12 |
| n., violet-black | .. | 1.10 | 60 |

| No. | | Un. | Used. |
|---|---|---|---|

**15**

| 102 | 5 m., black & lake | .. | |
|---|---|---|---|

**16**

*Variety.* Type 16. Type 15 *redrawn.*

| 103 | 5 m., black and lake | .. | |
|---|---|---|---|

**17**

**1902.** Type 17. *Inscribed* " DEUTSCHES REICH." *The* 1, 3, *and* 5 m. *differ from the types of* 1900 *only in the altered inscription. Perf.* 14.

| 104 | 2 pf., grey | .. | .. | 2 | 2 |
|---|---|---|---|---|---|
| 105 | 3 ,, brown | .. | .. | 2 | 2 |
| 106 | 5 ,, green | .. | .. | 2 | 2 |
| 107 | 10 ,, carmine | .. | .. | 4 | 2 |
| 108 | 20 ,, ultramarine | .. | 8 | 2 |
| 109 | 25 ,, blk. & oran. on yel. | 10 | 2 |
| 110 | 30 ,, ,, ,, buff | 12 | 2 |
| 111 | 40 ,, black and carmine | 14 | 2 |
| 112 | 50 ,, blk. & lilac on buff | 16 | 2 |
| 113 | 80 ,, blk. & car. on rose | 25 | 2 |
| 114 | 1 m., carmine | .. | .. | 30 | 4 |

**18**

| 115 | 2 m., blue (Type 18) | .. | 75 | 36 |
|---|---|---|---|---|

| No. | | *Un.* | *Used.* |
|---|---|---|---|

**19**

| 116 | 2 m., blue (Type 19) .. | 62 | 6 |
|---|---|---|---|
| 117 | 3 m., violet-black .. | 95 | 10 |
| 118 | 5 m., black and lake .. | 1.55 | 36 |

*Error.* "DEUTCHES" *for* "DEUTCHES."

| 119 | 3 pf., brown .. .. | 36 | 50 |
|---|---|---|---|

OFFICIAL STAMPS.
Kingdom of Prussia.

**O. 1**

**1903. Type O. 1.**

| 201 | 2 (pf.), grey .. .. | — | 4 |
|---|---|---|---|
| 202 | 3 ,, brown .. .. | — | 8 |
| 203 | 5 ,, green .. .. | — | 2 |
| 204 | 10 ,, carmine .. .. | — | 2 |
| 205 | 20 ,, ultramarine .. | — | 4 |
| 206 | 25 ,, black & orange on yellow .. | — | 6 |
| 207 | 30 ,, black & orange on buff .. | | |
| 208 | 40 ,, black & carmine | — | 6 |
| 209 | 50 ,, black and lilac on buff .. | — | 8 |

There are 30 different States and Administrations which possess the privilege of having their postal correspondence franked. Hitherto this has been carried out without stamps. The Administration of the Kingdom of Prussia is, however, the only one which has issued a set of stamps (*see M. J.*, Sept., 1903, p. 49).

## STAMPS SURCHARGED FOR USE IN GERMAN POST OFFICES ABROAD.

NOTE.—Varieties of the German Empire stamps surcharged for use in Post Offices Abroad or in Colonial Possessions, are known with the surcharges double, inverted, etc. These were never issued for use, or even retailed in Berlin to collectors or dealers, but are from waste sheets of the printers, which should have been destroyed, but were retained, and afterwards leaked out into the hands of certain dealers.

### CHINA.

**21**

**1897.**

*Stamps of the German Empire,* Types 9 and 10, *overprinted with* Type 21, *in black.*

| C 1 | 3 pf., brown .. .. | 2 | |
|---|---|---|---|
| C 2 | 5 ,, green .. .. | 4 | |
| C 3 | 10 ,, carmine .. .. | 6 | 6 |
| C 4 | 20 ,, ultramarine .. | 8 | 8 |
| C 5 | 20 ,, Prussian blue .. | | |
| C 6 | 25 ,, orange .. .. | 12 | |
| C 7 | 50 ,, lake-brown .. | | |
| C 8 | 50 ,, chocolate .. | 25 | 18 |

Sets may be made with the overprint inclined at two different slopes.

**22**

**7 JUNE, 1900.**

*Issued at Foochow. No.* C 3 *surcharged* "5 pf." *as Type* 22, *in black.*

| C 9 | 5 pf. on 10 pf., carmine | 10.00 | 5.00 |
|---|---|---|---|

**1900.**

*Stamps of the German Empire,* Type 11, *surcharged as* Type 21, *in black.*

*Local print.*

| C 10 | 3 pf., brown .. .. | 5.00 | |
|---|---|---|---|
| C 11 | 5 ,, green .. .. | 5.00 | |
| C 12 | 10 ,, carmine .. | 6.25 | |
| C 13 | 20 ,, blue .. .. | | |
| C 14 | 30 ,, black & orange on buff .. .. | 15.00 | |
| C 14a | 40 pf., black and carm. | | |
| C 15 | 50 ,, ,, lilac on buff .. .. | | |
| C 16 | 80 pf., black and carm. on rose .. .. | | |

The surcharge is known inverted on the 5, 10, 20, 30, and 80 pf.

| No. | | | Un. | Used. |
|---|---|---|---|---|
| | **1900.** | | | |

*Stamps of the German Empire*, Types 11 to 14, *overprinted with* Type 21, *horizontally, in* black.

| | | | Un. | Used. |
|---|---|---|---|---|
| C 17 | 3 pf., brown .. .. | | 2 | |
| C 18 | 5 ,, green .. .. | | 2 | 2 |
| C 19 | 10 ,, carmine .. | | 4 | 4 |
| C 20 | 20 ,, ultramarine ... | | 8 | 8 |
| C 21 | 25 ,, black & orange on yellow .. | | 10 | 10 |
| C 22 | 30 pf., black & orange on buff | | 12 | 12 |
| C 23 | 40 pf., black and carm. | | 14 | |
| C 24 | 50 ,, ,, lilac on buff .. | | 16 | |
| C 25 | 80 pf., black and carm. on rose .. .. | | 30 | |
| C 26 | 1 m., carmine | | 32 | |
| C 27 | 2 m., blue .. .. | | 65 | |
| C 28 | 3 m., violet-black .. | | 1.00 | |
| C 29 | 5 m., black and lake.. | | 1.60 | |

### MOROCCO.

**31**

**1899.**

*Stamps of the German Empire*, Types 9 and 10, *surcharged as* Type 31, *in* black.

| | | Un. | Used. |
|---|---|---|---|
| M 1 | 3 c. on 3 pf., brown .. | 2 | 2 |
| M 2 | 5 c. on 5 ,, green .. | 2 | 2 |
| M 3 | 10 c. on 10 ,, carmine . | 4 | 4 |
| M 4 | 25 c. on 20 ,, ultra. .. | 8 | |
| M 5 | 30 c. on 25 ,, orange.. | 12 | |
| M 6 | 60 c. on 50 ,, red-brown | 18 | |

**32**

**1900.**

*Stamps of the German Empire*, Types 11 to 15, *surcharged in* black or red (R.), *as* Type 32.

| | | Un. | Used. |
|---|---|---|---|
| M 7 | 3 c. on 3 pf., brown .. | 2 | |
| M 8 | 5 c. on 5 ,, green .. | 2 | 2 |
| M 9 | 10 c. on 10 ,, carmine. | 4 | 4 |
| M 10 | 25 c. on 20 ,, ultra. .. | 8 | 8 |
| M 11 | 30 c. on 25 ,, black & orange on yellow .. | 10 | |
| M 12 | 35 c. on 30 pf., black & orange on buff .. | 12 | |
| | 50 c. on 40 pf., black and carmine .. | 16 | |

| No. | | | Un. | Used. |
|---|---|---|---|---|
| M 14 | 60 c. on 50 pf., black and lilac on buff .. | | 18 | |
| M 15 | 1 p. on 80 pf., black and carmine on rose | | 30 | |

**33**

**34**

| No. | Type. | | Un. | Used. |
|---|---|---|---|---|
| M 16 | 33 | 1 p. 25 c. on 1 m., carmine .. | 32 | |
| M 17 | ,, | 2 p. 50 c. on 2 m., blue .. .. | 62 | |
| M 18 | 34 | 3 p. 75 c. on 3 m., violet (R.) .. | 95 | |
| M 19 | 33 | 6 p. 25 c. on 5 m., black and lake . | 1.55 | |

### TURKISH EMPIRE.

**51**

**52**

**53**

**54**

**55**

**56**

**1884.**

*Stamps of the German Empire*, Types 6 and 7, *surcharged in* black.

| | | | Un. | Used. |
|---|---|---|---|---|
| T 1 | 51 | 10 para on 5 pf., lilac-mauve .. .. | 18 | 25 |
| T 2 | ,, | 20 para on 10 pf., rose | 12 | |
| T 3 | 52 | 1 pias. on 20 pf., ultramarine .. | 12 | 4 |
| T 4 | 53 | 1¼ pias. on 25 pf., red-brown .. | 90 | |
| T 5 | 54 | 1¼ pias. on 25 pf., red-brown .. .. | 1.00 | 1.10 |
| T 6 | 55 | 2½ pias. on 50 pf., olive-green .. | 1.25 | 1.25 |

| No. | Type. | | Un. | Used. |
|---|---|---|---|---|
| T 7 | 55 | 2½ pias. on 50 pf., myrtle-green .. | 1.85 | 1.25 |
| T 8 | 56 | 2½ pias. on 50 pf., olive-green .. | 1.00 | |

No. T 8 may also be distinguished from T 7 by the shiny ink, the other surcharge being in a dead black.

*Surcharged in blue.*

| T 9 | 52 | 1 pias. on 20 pf., ultramarine .. | 5.00 | 1.50 |

10 PARA 10
57

1 PIASTER 1
58

1¼ PIASTER 1¼
59

2½ PIASTER 2½
60

**1889.**
Types 9 *and* 10 *surcharged in* black.

| T 10 | 57 | 10 para on 5 pf., yel.-green .. .. | 2 | |
| T 11 | " | 10 para on 5 pf., blue-green .. .. | 2 | 2 |
| T 12 | 51 | 20 para on 10 pf., rose | 4 | 4 |
| T 13 | 58 | 1 pias. on 20 pf., ultramarine .. | 8 | 4 |
| T 14 | " | 1 pias. on 20 pf., dull blue .. .. | 25 | 12 |
| T 15 | 59 | 1¼ pias. on 25 pf., orange-yellow .. | 16 | 16 |
| T 16 | 60 | 2½ pias. on 50 pf., lake-brown .. | 5.00 | 50 |
| T 17 | " | 2½ pias. on 50 pf., chocolate .. | 18 | 12 |

10 PARA 10
61

4 PIASTER 4
62

2½ Piaster 2½
63

5 PIASTER 5
64

**1900.**
*Stamps of the German Empire*, Types 11 to 15, *surcharged in* black *or* red (R.).

| T 18 | 61 | 10 pa. on 5 pf., grn. | 2 | 2 |
| T 19 | " | 20 pa. on 10 pf., carm. | 4 | 2 |
| T 20 | 62 | 1 pia. on 20 pf., ultramarine .. | 18 | 8 |
| T 21 | 63 | 1½ pia. on 25 pf., blk. & orange on yell. | 10 | 8 |
| T 22 | " | 1½ pia. on 30 pf., blk. & orange on buff | 12 | 10 |

| No. | Type. | | Un. | Used. |
|---|---|---|---|---|
| T 23 | 62 | 2 pia. on 40 pf., blk. on carmine .. | 16 | 12 |
| T 24 | 63 | 2½ pia. on 50 pf., blk. & lilac on buff .. | 18 | 18 |
| T 25 | 62 | 4 pia. on 80 pf., blk. & carm. on rose | 30 | 30 |
| T 26 | 64 | 5 pia. on 1 m., carm. | 90 | 90 |
| T 27 | " | 10 pia. on 2 m., blue | 62 | 62 |

15 PIASTER 15
65

15 PIASTER 15

| T 28 | 65 | 15 pia. on 3 m., vio. (R) | 95 | 95 |
| T 29 | 64 | 25 " 5 m., blk. and lake.. .. | 1.85 | |

1 PIASTER 1
66

5 PIASTER 5
67

**1903.** Types 62 *and* 64 *altered, letter* "A" *with a horizontal serif at top, as* Types 66 *and* 67.

| T 30 | 66 | 1 pias. on 20 (pf.), ultramarine .. | 8 | 6 |
| T 31 | 67 | 5 pias. on 1 mark, dull lake .. | 32 | |
| T 32 | " | 25 pias. on 5 m., blk. and lake.. .. | | |

## GERMAN COLONIES.
### CAMEROONS.

Kamerun
C 1

**1897.** Types 9 *and* 10 *of the German Empire overprinted with* Type C 1, *in* black.

| 1 | 3 pf., grey-brown .. | 4 | |
| 2 | 3 " slate-brown .. | 25 | |
| 3 | 3 " brown .. .. | — | 12 |
| 4 | 3 " yellow-brown .. | 4 | 6 |

| No. | | Un. | Used. |
|---|---|---|---|
| 5 | 5 pf., green | 6 | |
| 6 | 10 " carmine | 10 | 10 |
| 7 | 20 " Prussian blue | | |
| 8 | 20 " ultramarine | 10 | 12 |
| 9 | 25 " orange | 30 | 30 |
| 10 | 50 " red-brown | 62 | |
| 11 | 50 " marone | | |

C 2    C 3

See note after China, C 8.

**1900.** Types C 2 (pfennig *values*) *and* C 3 (mark *values*) *inscribed* "KAMERUN." *Perf.* 14.

| No. | | Un. | Used. |
|---|---|---|---|
| 13 | 3 pf., brown | 2 | |
| 14 | 5 " green | 2 | |
| 15 | 10 " carmine | 4 | 4 |
| 16 | 20 " ultramarine | 8 | |
| 17 | 25 " blk. & red on yell. | 10 | |
| 18 | 30 " " oran. on buff | 12 | |
| 19 | 40 " " carmine | 14 | |
| 20 | 50 " blk. & vio. on buff | 16 | |
| 21 | 80 " " carm. on rose | 30 | |
| 22 | 1 m., carmine | 32 | |
| 23 | 2 m., blue | 65 | |
| 24 | 3 m., violet | 1.00 | |
| 25 | 5 m., carmine and black | 1.60 | |

## CAROLINE ISLANDS.

C 11

**1899.** Types 9 *and* 10 *overprinted with* Type C 11, *in* black.

| No. | | Un. | Used. |
|---|---|---|---|
| 1 | 3 pf., brown | 12 | |
| 2 | 5 " green | 25 | |
| 3 | 10 " carmine | 18 | |
| 4 | 20 " ultramarine | 18 | |
| 5 | 25 " orange | 25 | |
| 6 | 50 " red-brown | 36 | |

**1900.** Types C 2 *and* C 3, *but inscribed* "KAROLINEN."

| No. | | Un. | Used. |
|---|---|---|---|
| 7 | 3 pf., brown | 2 | |
| 8 | 5 " green | 2 | |
| 9 | 10 " carmine | 4 | |
| 10 | 20 " ultramarine | 8 | |
| 11 | 25 " blk. & red on yell. | 10 | |
| 12 | 30 " " oran. on buff | 12 | |
| 13 | 40 " " carmine | 14 | |

| No. | | Un. | Used. |
|---|---|---|---|
| 14 | 50 pf., blk. & violet on buff | 16 | |
| 15 | 80 " " carm. on rose | 30 | |
| 16 | 1 m., carmine | 32 | |
| 17 | 2 " blue | 65 | |
| 18 | 3 " violet | 1.00 | |
| 19 | 5 " carmine and black | 1.60 | |

## GERMAN EAST AFRICA.

### 2 PESA 2

E 1

**1893.**

Types 9 *and* 10 *surcharged as* Type E 1, *in* black.

(i.) *Surcharge measures* 16½ mm.

(ii.) 17½ mm.

| No. | | Un. | Used. |
|---|---|---|---|
| 1 | 2 p. on 3 pf., brown | 25 | |
| 2 | 3 p. on 5 " green | 25 | |
| 3 | 5 p. on 10 " rose | — | 1? |
| 4 | 5 p. on 10 " carm. | 18 | 18 |
| 5 | 10 p. on 20 " Pruss. blue | | |
| 6 | 10 p. on 20 " ultram. | 25 | 1? |
| 7 | 25 p. on 50 " pale red-brown (i.) | 50 | 30 |
| 8 | 25 p. on 50 pf., red-bn.(ii.) | 36 | 2? |

2 Deutsch-Ostafrika Pesa

E 2

**1896.**

*Surcharged as* Type E 2, *in* black.

| No. | | Un. | Used. |
|---|---|---|---|
| 9 | 2 p. on 3 pf., brown | 4 | |
| 10 | 3 p. on 5 " green | 4 | 6 |
| 11 | 5 p. on 10 " rose | 6 | 6 |
| 12 | 10 p. on 20 " Pruss. blue | | |
| 13 | 10 p. on 20 " ultram. | 8 | 8 |
| 14 | 25 p. on 50 " lake-bn. | 25 | 2? |

**1900.**

Types C 2 *and* C 3, *but inscribed* "DEUTSCH-OSTAFRICA."

| No. | | Un. | Used. |
|---|---|---|---|
| 15 | 2 pesa, brown | 2 | 4 |
| 16 | 3 " green | 2 | |
| 17 | 5 " carmine | 4 | 4 |
| 18 | 10 " ultramarine | 6 | |
| 19 | 15 " blk. & oran. on buff | 10 | |
| 20 | 20 " " carmine | 12 | |
| 21 | 25 " " violet | 16 | |
| 22 | 40 " " carm. on rose | 25 | |
| 23 | 1 rupie, claret | 45 | |
| 24 | 2 rupien, green | 90 | |
| 25 | 3 " blue-blk. & red | 1.25 | |

| | | *Un.* | *Used.* |
|---|---|---|---|
| No. | | | |

## GERMAN NEW GUINEA.

N I

### 1897.

*Types* 9 *and* 10 *overprinted with* Type N 1,
*in* black.

| 1 | 3 pf., yellow-brown | .. | 8 | 8 |
|---|---|---|---|---|
| 2 | 3 ,, dark brown | .. | 4 | 6 |
| 3 | 5 ,, green | .. | 4 | 6 |
| 4 | 10 ,, carmine .. | .. | 8 | 8 |
| 5 | 20 ,, ultramarine | .. | 12 | 12 |
| 6 | 25 ,, orange | .. | 25 | 30 |
| 7 | 50 ,, red-brown | .. | 36 | 36 |

N 2

N 3

### 1900.

Types N 2 *and* N 3.

| 9 | 3 pf., brown | .. | .. | 2 | 2 |
|---|---|---|---|---|---|
| 10 | 5 ,, green | .. | .. | 2 | 2 |
| 11 | 10 ,, carmine .. | .. | 4 | 2 |
| 12 | 20 ,, ultramarine | .. | 8 | 4 |
| 13 | 25 ,, blk. & red on yell. | 10 | 6 |
| 14 | 30 ,, ,, oran.on buff | 12 | 10 |
| 15 | 40 ,, ,, carmine .. | 14 | 12 |
| 16 | 50 ,, ,, vio. on buff | 16 | 16 |
| 17 | 80 ,, ,, carm.on rose | 30 | 25 |
| 18 | 1 m., carmine .. | .. | 32 | 32 |
| 19 | 2 ,, blue | .. | .. | 65 | 65 |
| 20 | violet | .. | .. | 1.00 | 1.00 |
| | carmine and black | 1.60 | 1.50 |

| | | *Un.* | *Used.* |
|---|---|---|---|
| No. | | | |

## GERMAN SOUTH-WEST AFRICA.

S I

### 1897.

*Types* 9 *and* 10 *overprinted with*
Type S 1, *in* black.

| 1 | 3 pf., brown | .. | .. | 8 | 12 |
|---|---|---|---|---|---|
| 2 | 5 ,, green | .. | .. | 8 | 12 |
| 3 | 10 ,, carmine .. | .. | 75 | 75 |
| 4 | 20 ,, ultramarine | .. | 25 | 18 |

The 25 and 50 pf. were prepared for issue,
but not sent to the colony. Price $3.75
each.

S 2

### 1898. *Same types overprinted with*
Type S 2.

| 7 | 3 pf., brown | .. | .. | 4 | 6 |
|---|---|---|---|---|---|
| 8 | 5 ,, green | .. | .. | 6 | 8 |
| 9 | 10 ,, carmine .. | .. | 10 | 12 |
| 10 | 20 ,, ultramarine | .. | 36 | |
| 11 | 25 ,, orange | .. | | |
| 12 | 50 ,, red-brown | .. | 36 | 36 |

### 1900. Types C 2 *and* C 3 *inscribed*
"DEUTSCH-SUDWESTAFRIKA."

| 14 | 3 pf., brown | .. | .. | 2 |
|---|---|---|---|---|
| 15 | 5 ,, green | .. | .. | 2 |
| 16 | 10 ,, carmine .. | .. | 4 |
| 17 | 20 ,, ultramarine | .. | 8 |
| 18 | 25 ,, blk. & red on yell. | 10 |
| 19 | 30 ,, ,, oran. on buff | 12 |
| 20 | 40 ,, ,, carmine .. | 14 |
| 21 | 50 ,, ,, vio. on buff | 16 |
| 22 | 80 ,, ,, carm.on rose | 30 |
| 23 | 1 m., carmine .. | .. | 32 |
| 24 | 2 ,, blue | .. | .. | 65 |
| 25 | 3 ,, violet | .. | .. | 1.00 |
| 26 | 5 ,, carmine and black | 1.60 |

| No. Type. | | *Un.* | *Used.* |
|---|---|---|---|

**KIAUTOHOU.**

5 Pfg.    5 Pfg.

1    2

5 Pfg.    5 Pfg.

3    4

5 Pfg.    5 Pfg.

5    6

MAY, **1900.** *Issued at Tsingtsau. Stamp of China*, No. C 3, *surcharged in black.*

| 1 | 1 | 5 Pfg. on 10 pf., carm. | — | 2.50 |
|---|---|---|---|---|
| 2 | 2 | 5 Pfg. on 10 pf. | ,, | 1.25 | |
| 3 | 3 | 5 Pfg. on 10 pf. | ,, | 2.50 | 2.50 |
| 4 | 4 | 5 Pfg. on 10 pf. | ,, | 1.85 | 1.50 |
| 5 | 5 | 5 Pfg. on 10 pf. | ,, | | |
| 6 | 6 | 5 Pfg. on 10 pf. | ,, | | |

JULY, **1900.** *Similar to Type* 1, *but* " Pf." *only.*

| 7 | 1 | 5 pf. on 10 pf., carm. | | |
|---|---|---|---|---|

*Additional surcharge of* " **5 Pf.** "

| 7a | 3 | 5 pf. on 10 pf., carm. | | |
|---|---|---|---|---|

**1900.** Types C 2 *and* C 3 *inscribed* " KIAUTCHOU."

| 51 | 3 pf., brown | .. | .. | 2 | |
|---|---|---|---|---|---|
| 52 | 5 ,, green | .. | .. | 2 | |
| 53 | 10 ,, carmine .. | | .. | 4 | |
| 54 | 20 ,, ultramarine | | .. | 8 | 8 |
| 55 | 25 ,, blk. & red on yell. | | | 10 | |
| 56 | 30 ,, ,, oran. on buff | | | 12 | |
| 57 | 40 ,, ,, carm. on rose | | | 14 | |
| 58 | 50 ,, ,, vio. on buff | | | 16 | |
| 59 | 80 ,, ,, carm. on rose | | | 30 | |
| 60 | 1 m., carmine .. | | .. | 32 | |
| 61 | 2 ,, blue | | .. | 65 | |
| 62 | 3 ,, violet-black | | .. | 1.00 | |
| 63 | 5 ,, carmine and black | | | 1.60 | |

**MARIANNE ISLANDS.**

M 1

**1900.** Types 9 *and* 10 *overprinted with* Type M 1, *in black.*

| | 3 pf., brown | .. | .. | 36 |
|---|---|---|---|---|
| | 5 ,, green | .. | .. | 50 |
| | ,, carmine | .. | . | 30 |

| No. | | *Un.* | *Used.* |
|---|---|---|---|
| 4 | 20 pf., ultramarine | .. | 30 |
| 5 | 25 ,, orange | .. | .. | 75 |
| 6 | 50 ,, red-brown | .. | 75 |

See note after China, C 8.

**1900.** Types C 2 *and* C 3 *inscribed* " MARIANEN."

| 7 | 3 pf., brown | .. | .. | 2 |
|---|---|---|---|---|
| 8 | 5 ,, green | .. | .. | 2 |
| 9 | 10 ,, carmine .. | | .. | 4 |
| 10 | 20 ,, ultramarine | | .. | 8 |
| 11 | 25 ,, blk. & red on yell. | | | 10 |
| 12 | 30 ,, ,, oran. on buff | | | 12 |
| 13 | 40 ,, ,, carmine .. | | | 14 |
| 14 | 50 ,, ,, vio. on buff | | | 16 |
| 15 | 80 ,, ,, carm. on rose | | | 30 |
| 16 | 1 m., carmine .. | | .. | 32 |
| 17 | 2 m., blue | | .. | 65 |
| 18 | 3 m., violet | .. | .. | 1.00 |
| 19 | 5 m., carmine and black | | | 1.60 |

**MARSHALL ISLANDS.**

*Marschall-inseln*

M 11

**1897.** Types 9 *and* 10 *overprinted with* Type M 11, *in black.*

| 1 | 3 pf., brown | .. | .. | 1.85 | |
|---|---|---|---|---|---|
| 2 | 5 ,, green | .. | .. | 1.85 | |
| 3 | 10 ,, carmine .. | | .. | 50 | 50 |
| 4 | 20 ,, ultramarine | | .. | 50 | 50 |

The 25 and 50 pf. were prepared for use, but not sent to the colony. Price $1.50 each.

*Marshall-Inseln*

M 12

**1899.** *As last, but overprinted with* Type M 12 (*letter* " C " *omitted*).

| 7 | 3 pf., brown | .. | .. | 12 |
|---|---|---|---|---|
| 8 | 5 ,, green | .. | .. | 12 |
| 9 | 10 ,, carmine .. | | .. | 36 |
| 10 | 20 ,, ultramarine | | .. | 36 |
| 11 | 25 ,, orange | .. | .. | 25 |
| 12 | 50 ,, red-brown | .. | 30 |

**1900.** Types N 2 *and* N 3, *but inscribed* " MARSHALL-INSELN."

| 13 | 3 pf., brown | .. | .. | 2 |
|---|---|---|---|---|
| 14 | 5 ,, green | .. | .. | 2 |

| No. | | Un. | Used. |
|---|---|---|---|
| 15 | 10 pf., carmine .. .. | 4 | |
| 16 | 20 ,, ultramarine .. | 8 | |
| 17 | 25 ,, blk. & red on yell. | 10 | |
| 18 | 30 ,, ,, oran. on buff | 12 | |
| 19 | 40 ,, ,, carmine .. | 14 | |
| 20 | 50 ,, ,, vio. on buff | 16 | |
| 21 | 80 ,, ,, carm.on rose | 30 | |
| 22 | 1 m., carmine .. .. | 32 | |
| 23 | 2 m., blue .. .. | 65 | |
| 24 | 3 m., violet .. .. | 1.00 | |
| 25 | 5 m., carmine and black | 1.60 | |

## SAMOA.

S 1

**1900.** Types **9** and **10** overprinted with
Type S 1, in black.

| | | | |
|---|---|---|---|
| 1 | 3 pf., brown .. .. | 12 | 12 |
| 2 | 5 ,, green .. .. | 12 | 25 |
| 3 | 10 ,, carmine .. .. | 12 | 16 |
| 4 | 20 ,, ultramarine .. | 18 | 18 |
| 5 | 25 ,, orange .. .. | 25 | 30 |
| 6 | 50 ,, red-brown .. | 36 | 36 |

**1900.** Types C **2** and C **3**, but inscribed
"SAMOA."

| | | | |
|---|---|---|---|
| 7 | 3 pf., brown .. .. | 2 | 2 |
| 8 | 5 ,, green .. .. | 2 | 4 |
| 9 | 10 ,, carmine .. .. | 4 | 4 |
| 10 | 20 ,, ultramarine .. | 8 | 6 |
| 11 | 25 ,, blk. & red on yell. | 10 | |
| 12 | 30 ,, ,, oran. on buff | 12 | |
| 13 | 40 ,, ,, carmine .. | 14 | 18 |
| 14 | 50 ,, ,, vio. on buff | 16 | |
| 15 | 80 ,, ,, carm.on rose | 30 | |
| 16 | 1 m., carmine .. .. | 32 | |
| 17 | 2 m., blue .. .. | 65 | |
| 18 | 3 m., violet .. .. | 1.00 | |
| 19 | 5 m., carm. and black.. | 1.60 | |

## TOGO.

T 1

**1897.** Types **9** and **10** overprinted with
Type T 1, in black.

| | | | |
|---|---|---|---|
| 1 | 3 pf., brown .. .. | — | 8 |
| 2 | 3 ,, yellow-brown .. | 6 | |
| 3 | 3 ,, dark brown .. | 6 | |
| 4 | 5 ,, green .. .. | 6 | 6 |

| No. | | Un. | Used. |
|---|---|---|---|
| 5 | 10 pf., carmine .. .. | 10 | 8 |
| 6 | 20 ,, ultramarine .. | 12 | 12 |
| 7 | 25 ,, orange .. .. | 30 | |
| 8 | 50 ,, red-brown .. | 55 | |

**1900.** Types C **2** and C **3**, but inscribed
"TOGO."

| | | | |
|---|---|---|---|
| 9 | 3 pf., brown .. .. | 2 | |
| 10 | 5 ,, green .. .. | 2 | |
| 11 | 10 ,, carmine .. .. | 4 | |
| 12 | 20 ,, ultramarine .. | 8 | |
| 13 | 25 ,, blk. & red on yell. | 10 | |
| 14 | 30 ,, ,, oran. on buff | 12 | |
| 15 | 40 ,, ,, carmine .. | 14 | |
| 16 | 50 ,, ,, vio. on buff | 16 | |
| 17 | 80 ,, ,, carm. on rose | 30 | |
| 18 | 1 m., carmine .. .. | 32 | |
| 19 | 2 m., blue .. .. | 65 | |
| 20 | 3 m., violet .. .. | 1.00 | |
| 21 | 5 m., carmine & black | 1.60 | |

## GREECE.

1

*Paris print.*

**1861.** Type **1**. *Paris print.*
(i.) *Without figures at back.*

| | | | Un. | Used. |
|---|---|---|---|---|
| 1 | 1 l., deep chocolate on | | | |
| | cream .. .. | | 2.50 | 2.50 |
| 1a | 1 l., red-brown .. .. | | 6.25 | 3.15 |
| 2 | 2 l., olive-yellow on straw | | 50 | 62 |
| 3 | 2 l., brown-buff on buff | | 50 | 62 |
| 4 | 5 l., emerald on greenish | | 2.50 | 75 |
| 5 | 20 l., blue on bluish .. | | 1.25 | 50 |
| 6 | 40 l., violet on pale blue | | 90 | 90 |
| 7 | 80 l., rose-carm. on cream | | 3.15 | 1.25 |

The prices of the 15, 20, and 40 l.,
*unused*, are for specimens without gum.

|   |   | Un. | Used. |
|---|---|---|---|
| No. | | | |

**(ii.) With large figures, 8 mm. high, at back.**

| 7a|10 l., orange on bluish.. | 8.75 | 1.85 |

The Paris-printed stamps have the shading on the cheek and neck of Mercury made up of fine lines and dots. In those printed in Athens the lines are unbroken and thicker.

*Athens print.*

### 1861–62.
*First Athens print.*
**(i.) Without figures at back.**

| 8 | 1 l., deep chocolate on cream | .. | .. | 7.50 | |
| 9 | 2 l., yellow-brown on straw | .. | .. | | 62 |
| 10 | 10 l., yellow-ochre on greenish blue | .. | | | |
| 11 | 20 l., Prussian blue on bluish | | | | |

**(ii.) With figures, 6 mm. high, at back.**

| 12 | 5 l., green on greenish | 3.15 | 36 |
| 13 | 5 l., yell.-grn. ,, | 6.25 | 36 |
| 14 | 10 l., yellow-ochre on greenish blue | | |
| 15 | 20 l., Prussian blue on bluish | | |
| 16 | 20 l., steel-blue on yellowish | .. .. | |
| 17 | 40 l., violet on pale blue | 5.00 | 50 |
| 18 | 80 l., rose on cream .. | 7.50 | 62 |
| 19 | 80 l., carmine on cream | 10.00 | 12 |

In the 1 l. the lines of shading on the cheek and neck are continuous, but very fine; in all later printings the lines are thicker. In the 5 l. the body of the figure at the back is an upright oval in shape. The paper of the 80 l. is generally tinted the colour of the stamp, the figures at the back are in *vermilion*.

|   | | Un. | Used. |
|---|---|---|---|
| No. | | | |

### 1862–70.
*Same type. Printings made at Athens before the plates were cleaned in 1870.*

| 20 | 1 l., chocolate on cream | 50 | 50 |
| 21 | 1 l., brown ,, | 50 | 50 |
| 22 | 1 l., fawn ,, | 1.25 | 1.25 |
| 23 | 1 l., black-brown ,, | 36 | 36 |
| 24 | 1 l., pur.-brown ,, | 1.85 | |
| 25 | 1 l., red-brown ,, | 50 | 62 |
| 26 | 2 l., pale bistre on straw | 36 | 62 |
| 27 | 2 l., bistre-brown ,, | 62 | 62 |
| 28 | 2 l., deep yell.-brn. ,, | — | 25 |
| 29 | 5 l., green on greenish . | 62 | 2 |
| 30 | 10 l., orange on bluish .. | 1.00 | 4 |
| 31 | 10 l., red-orange ,, .. | 1.50 | 4 |
| 32 | 10 l., orange on blue .. | 6.25 | 3 |
| 33 | 10 l., red-orange on blue | — | 8 |
| 34 | 20 l., pale blue on bluish | — | 2 |
| 35 | 20 l., bright blue ,, | 1.00 | 2 |
| 36 | 20 l., blue ,, | 1.00 | 2 |
| 37 | 20 l., deep blue ,, | 1.85 | 4 |
| 38 | 20 l., blue on greenish .. | — | 25 |
| 39 | 40 l., deep violet on blue | 1.85 | 6 |
| 40 | 40 l., pale ,, ,, | 3.75 | 6 |
| 41 | 40 l., red-lilac ,, | — | 6 |
| 42 | 40 l., red-lilac on pale lilac | 8.75 | 12 |
| 43 | 80 l., rose on cream .. | 1.85 | 8 |
| 44 | 80 l., carmine on cream.. | 36 | 8 |

The figure at the back of the 5 l. has a circular body. To make the list as clear as it is possible to make it, several shades of the 2 l., 5 l., 20 l., and 80 l. have been grouped under one number. The later printings are generally much rougher than the earlier ones. In 1870 the first printings, after the plates were cleaned, show superior workmanship.

### 1870–77 (to 1883 for the 1 l., and to 1888 for the 2 l.).
*Printings made in Athens after the plates were cleaned.*
**A. Paper of medium thickness as in former printings.**
**(i.) Without figures at back.**

| 45 | 1 l., fawn on cream .. | 2.50 | |
| 46 | 1 l., red-brn. on cream | 4 | 4 |
| 47 | 1 l. ,, on buff.. | 3.15 | 62 |
| 48 | 1 l., brown ,, .. | 3.75 | 1.25 |
| 49 | 1 l., dark brown ,, .. | 3.75 | 1.00 |
| 50 | 1 l., grey-brn. on cream | 4 | 8 |
| 51 | 1 l., pale reddish brown on cream .. | 12 | 8 |
| 52 | 1 l., reddish bn. on crm. | 6 | 4 |
| 53 | 2 l., stone ,, | 18 | |
| 54 | 2 l., pale yell.-bistre ,, | 1.10 | |
| 55 | 2 l., bistre ,, | 6 | |

**(ii.) With figures at back.**

| 56 | 5 l., yellow-green on greenish | .. .. | |
| 56a | 5 l., sage-green | .. .. | |
| 57 | 10 l., red-orange on greenish blue | .. | — | 18 |

| No. | | Un. | Used. |
|---|---|---|---|
| 58 | 20 l., blue on bluish .. | — | 8 |
| 59 | 20 l., deep dull blue on | | |
| | bluish .. .. .. | 1.85 | 25 |
| 60 | 40 l., solferino on greenish | — | 50 |

In the 1 l., fawn, the lines of the shading on the cheek are shorter than in any other printing. The 20 l., blue, is generally known as the one "with worn spandrels," and the 20 l., deep dull blue, as that "with black spandrels," as it is often found oxidised. The so-called "solferino" 40 l., was originally printed in red-lake, as may be seen by the figures at back.

### B. Thin transparent paper.
#### With figures at back.

| | | Un. | Used. |
|---|---|---|---|
| 61 | 5 l., sage-grn. on greenish | 3.75 | |
| 61a | 5 l., yellow-green .. | 2.50 | 25 |
| 61b | 5 l., deep yellow-green | — | 50 |
| 62 | 10 l., bright red-orange | | |
| | on grey-blue.. .. | — | 1.25 |
| 63 | 20 l., indigo on bluish .. | 25.00 | 8 |
| 64 | 20 l., grey-blue ,, | — | 8 |
| 65 | 20 l., deep blue ,, .. | — | 8 |
| 65a | 20 l. ,, on blue | 12.50 | 18 |
| 66 | 40 l., pale violet ,, | 12.50 | 36 |
| 67 | 40 l., deep ,, ,, | 2.50 | 12 |
| 68 | 40 l., olive-gn. on greenish | | |
| 69 | 40 l., bistre on blue .. | 75 | 1.10 |
| 70 | 40 l., brown .. .. | 36 | 62 |

### 1862-77.
#### Errors of figures at back found in printings.

| | | Un. | Used. |
|---|---|---|---|
| 70a | 10 l., orange on blue | | |
| | ("0") .. .. | — | 5.00 |
| 70b | 10 l., orange on blue | | |
| | ("00") .. | | |
| 70c | 10 l., orange on blue | | |
| | ("01") .. .. | — | 75 |
| 70d | 20 l., blue on bluish | | |
| | ("80") .. .. | — | 12.50 |
| 70e | 20 l., blue on bluish | | |
| | ("oz") .. .. | — | 3.75 |
| 70f | 20 l., blue on bluish | | |
| | ("zo") .. . | | |
| 70g | 40 l., violet on pale blue | | |
| | ("4" on "20") .. | | |
| 70h | 40 l., violet on pale blue | | |
| | ("40" twice) .. | | |
| 70i | 80 l., rose on cream | | |
| | ("8" inverted) .. | — | 3.75 |

### 1876.
#### Without figures at back.
##### (i.) Paris print.

| | | Un. | Used. |
|---|---|---|---|
| 71 | 30 l., olive-bn. on cream | 12.50 | 1.50 |
| 72 | 60 l., dark green on green | 50 | 1.00 |

##### (ii.) Athens print.

| | | Un. | Used. |
|---|---|---|---|
| 73 | 30 l., black-bn. on cream | 3.75 | 8 |
| 74 | 30 l. ,, buff.. | 3.75 | 16 |
| 75 | 30 l., red-brn. on cream | 90 | 8 |
| 76 | 60 l., dark green on buff | 12.50 | 3.00 |

| No. | | Un. | Used. |
|---|---|---|---|

### 1876-78. With figures at back.

| | | Un. | Used. |
|---|---|---|---|
| 77 | 5 l., yell.-green on cream | 1.00 | 50 |
| 78 | 5 l., pale ,, ,, | 1.25 | 62 |
| 79 | 5 l., apple-green ,, | 3.75 | 50 |
| 80 | 10 l., bright oran.-red,, | 1.85 | 4 |
| 81 | 10 l., orange ,, | | |
| 82 | 10 l. ,, on buff | 6.25 | 62 |
| 83 | 20 l., deep blue on cream | 2.50 | 6 |
| 84 | 20 l., Prussian blue ,, | 6.25 | 8 |
| 85 | 20 l., dull blue ,, | — | 8 |
| 86 | 20 l., deep ultram. ,, | 2.50 | 4 |
| 87 | 40 l., rosy buff ,, | 36 | 62 |

#### Errors of figures at back.

| | | Un. | Used. |
|---|---|---|---|
| 87a | 10 l., bright orange-red | | |
| | ("1") .. .. | | |
| 87b | 10 l., bright orange-red | | |
| | ("oo").. .. .. | — | 75 |
| 87c | 10 l., bright orange-red | | |
| | ("o") .. .. .. | — | 1.25 |
| 87d | 10 l., bright orange-red | | |
| | ("10" twice) .. .. | — | 2.50 |
| 87e | 10 l., bright orange-red | | |
| | ("110") .. .. | — | 3.75 |
| 87f | 20 l., ultramarine ("zo") | — | 2.50 |

### 1879-81. Without figures at back.

| | | Un. | Used. |
|---|---|---|---|
| 88 | 5 l., deep green on buff | 2.50 | |
| 89 | 5 l. ,, on crm. | 62 | 6 |
| 90 | 5 l., green ,, | 36 | 2 |
| 91 | 5 l., pale green ,, | 36 | 2 |
| 92 | 10 l., bright oran-red ,, | — | 12 |
| 93 | 10 l., orange ,, | 50 | 2 |
| 94 | 10 l., orange-yellow ,, | 1.25 | 2 |
| 94a | 10 l., yellow ,, | 1.85 | 2 |
| 95 | 20 l., deep ultramarine .. | 2.00 | 50 |
| 96 | 40 l., mauve on cream .. | 1.25 | 18 |
| 97 | 40 l., deep mauve on crm. | 75 | 25 |

### 1882. Without figures at the back.

| | | Un. | Used. |
|---|---|---|---|
| 98 | 20 l., deep carm. on crm. | 6.25 | 6 |
| 99 | 20 l., deep rosine ,, | 62 | 2 |
| 100 | 20 l., rosine-pink ,, | 1.00 | 2 |
| 101 | 30 l., deep ultram. ,, | 3.00 | 75 |
| 101a | 30 l., ultramarine ,, | 5.00 | 75 |
| 101b | 30 l., grey-blue ,, | 5.00 | 75 |

### 1879-94. Athens print. Without figures at back. Pin-perf. or rouletted (unofficially).

| | | Un. | Used. |
|---|---|---|---|
| 101c | 1 l., No. 50 .. | .. | 2.00 |
| 101d | 1 l. ,, 51 .. | .. | |
| 101e | 1 l. ,, 52 .. | .. | 25 |
| 101f | 2 l. ,, 53 .. | .. | 1.25 |
| 101g | 2 l. ,, 54 .. | .. | |
| 101h | 2 l. ,, 55 .. | .. | 1.25 |
| 101i | 5 l. ,, 90 .. | .. | 1.85 |
| 101j | 5 l. ,, 91 .. | .. | |
| 101k | 10 l. ,, 94 .. | .. | 2.50 |
| 101l | 10 l. ,, 94a.. | .. | |
| 101m | 20 l. ,, 100 .. | .. | |
| 101n | 40 l. ,, 87 (with figs.) | | |
| 101o | 40 l. ,, 96 .. | .. | |
| 101p | 40 l. ,, 97 .. | .. | |

| No. | | Un. | Used. |
|---|---|---|---|

**1891.** *Athens. Without figures at back.*
*Perf.* 11½.

| 102a | 1 l., No. 46 .. .. | 36 | |
| 102b | 1 l. ,, 48 .. .. | 25 | |
| 102c | 1 l. ,, 51 .. .. | 25 | |
| 102d | 1 l. ,, 52 .. .. | | |
| 102e | 2 l. ,, 53 .. .. | 50 | |
| 102f | 2 l. ,, 55 .. .. | 36 | 62 |
| 102g | 5 l. ,, 90 .. .. | | |
| 102h | 10 l. ,, 94 .. .. | 1.25 | 1.25 |
| 102i | 20 l. ,, 99 .. .. | | |
| 102j | 40 l. ,, 87 (with figs.) | 1.50 | |
| 102k | 40 l. ,, 96 .. .. | 2.50 | 1.50 |
| 102l | 40 l. ,, 97 .. .. | 1.85 | |

2

**1886-91.** Type 2. *Belgian print.*
(i.) *Imperforate* (1886-88).

| 102 | 1 l., pale brown .. .. | 2 | 4 |
| 103 | 2 l., ochre .. .. | 12 | |
| 104 | 5 l., green .. .. | 12 | 2 |
| 105 | 10 l., dull orange .. .. | 12 | 4 |
| 106 | 20 l., carmine .. .. | 75 | 2 |
| 107 | 25 l., dull blue .. .. | 36 | 4 |
| 108 | 40 l., violet .. .. | 1.85 | 25 |
| 109 | 50 l., bronze-green .. .. | 30 | 4 |
| 110 | 1 dr., grey .. .. | 50 | 4 |

(ii.) *Perf.* 13½ (1889).

| 111 | 1 l., pale brown .. .. | 90 | 1.10 |
| 112 | 2 l., ochre .. .. | | |
| 113 | 5 l., green .. .. | | |
| 114 | 10 l., dull orange .. .. | — | 5.00 |
| 115 | 20 l., carmine .. .. | — | 4.50 |
| 116 | 25 l., dull blue .. .. | | |
| 117 | 40 l., violet .. .. | — | 6.25 |
| 118 | 50 l., bronze-green .. .. | 5.00 | 5.00 |
| 118a | 1 dr., grey .. .. | | |

(iii.) *Perf.* 11½ (1891).

| 119 | 1 l., pale brown .. .. | 36 | 36 |
| 119a | 2 l., ochre .. .. | | |
| 120 | 5 l., green .. .. | — | 1.00 |
| 121 | 10 l., dull orange .. .. | — | 1.85 |
| 122 | 20 l., carmine .. .. | — | 1.85 |
| 123 | 25 l., blue .. .. | — | 1.25 |
| 124 | 40 l., violet .. .. | 5.00 | 3.75 |
| 125 | 50 l., bronze-green .. .. | 18 | 6 |
| 126 | 1 dr., grey .. .. | 1.25 | 4 |

The Belgian-printed stamps may be distinguished from those of Athens by the impression being smoother and finer, and by the paper being more highly surfaced.

| No. | | Un. | Used. |
|---|---|---|---|

**1889-99.** *Athens print.* (i.) *Imperf.*

| 127 | 1 l., brown .. .. | 2 | 2 |
| 128 | 1 l., black-brown .. | 6 | 2 |
| 128a | 1 l., yellow-brown .. | 2 | 2 |
| 129 | 2 l., pale bistre .. | 18 | 25 |
| 130 | 2 l., ochre .. .. | 12 | 6 |
| 130a | 2 l., fawn .. .. | 6 | 6 |
| 131 | 5 l., yellow-green .. | 8 | 2 |
| 132 | 5 l., green .. .. | 8 | 2 |
| 132a | 5 l., emerald .. .. | 8 | 2 |
| 132b | 5 l., pale green .. | 8 | |
| 133 | 10 l., dull ochre-yellow. | 18 | 2 |
| 134 | 10 l., pale orange .. | 12 | 2 |
| 135 | 10 l., deep orange .. | 8 | |
| 135a | 10 l., yellow .. .. | 12 | 2 |
| 136 | 20 l., carmine .. .. | 18 | 2 |
| 137 | 20 l., rosine .. .. | 12 | 2 |
| 137a | 20 l., pink .. .. | 12 | 2 |
| 138 | 25 l., dull blue .. .. | 1.00 | 2 |
| 139 | 25 l., indigo .. .. | — | 2 |
| 140 | 25 l., ultramarine .. | 2.50 | 4 |
| 140a | 25 l., bright blue .. | 36 | 12 |
| 141 | 25 l., purple .. .. | 25 | 4 |
| 141a | 25 l., rosy purple .. | 16 | 4 |
| 142 | 40 l., purple .. .. | 1.50 | 1.50 |
| 143 | 40 l., blue .. .. | 12 | 4 |
| 144 | 1 dr., grey .. .. | 1.00 | 6 |

(ii.) *Perf.* 13½.

| 145 | 1 l., brown .. .. | 6.25 | 2.50 |
| 146 | 2 l., pale bistre .. | | |
| 146a | 2 l., fawn .. .. | 6 | 6 |
| 146b | 5 l., green .. .. | — | 3.75 |
| 146c | 10 l., orange .. .. | | |
| 147 | 20 l., rose .. .. | 3.75 | 1.25 |
| 148 | 20 l., carmine .. .. | — | 8 |
| 148a | 25 l., red-violet .. | | |
| 148b | 25 l., blue .. .. | | |
| 149 | 40 l., red-violet .. | 3.00 | 1.25 |
| 149a | 40 l., blue .. .. | | |
| 149b | 1 dr., grey .. .. | — | 3.15 |

(iii.) *Perf.* 11½.

| 150 | 1 l., brown .. .. | 2 | 2 |
| 151 | 1 l., black-brown .. | 2 | |
| 152 | 2 l., pale bistre .. | 12 | 8 |
| 153 | 2 l., ochre .. .. | — | 6 |
| 153a | 2 l., fawn .. .. | 4 | 2 |
| 154 | 5 l., green .. .. | 4 | 2 |
| 155 | 5 l., dark green .. | 8 | 2 |
| 155a | 5 l., emerald .. .. | 12 | |
| 156 | 10 l., dull ochre-yellow. | — | 2 |
| 157 | 10 l., pale orange .. | 25 | 2 |
| 158 | 10 l., deep orange .. | 36 | |
| 158a | 10 l., yellow .. .. | 8 | 2 |
| 159 | 20 l., rose .. .. | 12 | 4 |
| 160 | 20 l., carmine .. .. | 12 | 2 |
| 161 | 25 l., blue .. .. | 62 | 12 |
| 162 | 25 l., indigo .. .. | 1.00 | |
| 162a | 25 l., bright blue .. | 50 | |
| 163 | 25 l., purple .. .. | 25 | 2 |
| 163a | 25 l., rosy purple .. | 10 | 2 |
| 164 | 40 l., purple .. .. | 1.10 | 1.10 |
| 165 | 40 l., blue .. .. | 12 | 8 |
| 166 | 1 dr., grey .. .. | 75 | 4 |

| No. Type. | *Un.* *Used.* |
|---|---|

3

4

5

6

7

**1896.** *Olympic Games issue.*

*Perf.* 13½–14½.

| | | | | *Un.* | *Used.* |
|---|---|---|---|---|---|
| 167 | 3 | 1 l., ochre .. | .. | 2 | 2 |
| 168 | ,, | 2 l., rose .. | .. | 2 | 2 |
| 169 | 4 | 5 l., lilac .. | .. | 2 | 2 |
| 170 | ,, | 10 l., slate .. | .. | 4 | 2 |
| 171 | 5 | 20 l., brown .. | .. | 12 | 2 |
| 172 | 6 | 25 l., red .. | .. | 30 | 8 |
| 173 | 5 | 40 l., purple .. | .. | 18 | 8 |
| 174 | 6 | 60 l., black .. | .. | 30 | 18 |
| 175 | 7 | 1 dr., blue .. | .. | 50 | 6 |

| No. Type. | *Un.* *Used.* |
|---|---|

8

9

10

| | | | | *Un.* | *Used.* |
|---|---|---|---|---|---|
| 176 | 8 | 2 dr., bistre | .. | 1.00 | 50 |
| 177 | 9 | 5 ,, green | .. | 2.10 | 2.10 |
| 178 | 10 | 10 ,, brown | .. | 3.50 | 3.15 |

ΛΕΠΤΑ     ΔΡΑΧΜΑΙ

## 20     3

11     12

**1900.** *Provisionals.*

A. *Various stamps surcharged as
Types 11 and 12, in black.*

I. *On stamps of Type 2. Athens print.*

(i.) *Imperforate.*

| | | | *Un.* | *Used.* |
|---|---|---|---|---|
| 179 | 20 l. on 25 l., dull blue .. | | 6 | 4 |
| 180 | 20 l. on 25 l., indigo | .. | 25 | 4 |
| 181 | 20 l. on 25 l., ultramarine | | 50 | |
| 182 | 20 l. on 25 l., bright blue | | — | 12 |
| 183 | 1 dr. on 40 l., purple .. | | 25 | 8 |
| 184 | 2 dr. on 40 l.   ,,   .. | | 10.00 | |

*Double surcharge.*

| | | | |
|---|---|---|---|
| 184a | 20 l. on 25 l., dull blue | 1.85 | |

*Surcharge inverted.*

| | | | |
|---|---|---|---|
| 184b | 20 l. on 25 l., dull blue | 1.50 | |
| 184c | 20 l. on 25 l., indigo .. | 1.85 | |

(ii.) *Perf.* 11½.

| | | | *Un.* | *Used.* |
|---|---|---|---|---|
| 185 | 20 l. on 25 l., dull blue .. | | 6 | 8 |
| 186 | 20 l. on 25 l., indigo | .. | 36 | 25 |
| 187 | 20 l. on 25 l., ultramarine | | 50 | |
| 188 | 20 l. on 25 l., bright blue | | | |
| 189 | 1 dr. on 40 l., purple .. | | 25 | |
| 190 | 2 dr. on 40 l.   ,,   .. | | 6.25 | |

|  | | | *Un.* | *Used.* |
|---|---|---|---|---|
| **No.** | | | | |

*Double surcharge.*

| 190a | 20 l. on 25 l., dull blue | 1.85 |
| 190b | 20 l. on 25 l., indigo .. | 1.85 |

*Surcharge inverted.*

| 190c | 20 l. on 25 l., dull blue | 2.50 |
| 190d | 20 l. on 25 l., indigo .. | |

(iii.) *Perf.* 13.

| 191 | 2 dr. on 40 l., purple .. | 50 |

**II.** *On stamps of* Type **2,** *Belgian print.*

| 192 | 2 dr. on 40 l., violet (*imp.*) | 10.00 |
| 193 | 2 dr. on 40 l.,  ,,  (*perf.* 11½) .. .. .. | 12.50 |

**III.** *On stamps of* Type **1,** *Athens print.*
(a) *With figs. at back.* (b) *Without figs.*

(i.) *Imperf.*

| 194 | 30 l. on 40 l., lilac on cream (b) .. .. | 12 | 25 |
| 195 | 30 l. on 40 l., purple on cream (b) .. .. | 8 | |
| 196 | 40 l. on 2 l., stone on cream (b) .. .. | 10 | 12 |
| 197 | 50 l. on 40 l., rosy buff on cream (a).. .. | 16 | 4 |
| 198 | 3 dr. on 10 l., orange on cream (b) .. .. | 90 | |
| 199 | 3 dr. on 10 l., orange-yellow on cream (b) .. | 75 | |
| 200 | 5 dr. on 40 l., violet on blue (a) .. .. | 1.25 | |
| 201 | 5 dr. on 40 l., red-lilac on blue (a) .. .. | 2.50 | |

*Varieties.* "ΑΕΠΤΑ" *for* "ΛΕΠΤΑ."

| 202 | 30 l. on 40 l., lilac on cream (b) .. .. | |
| 203 | 30 l. on 40 l., purple on cream (b) .. .. | 3.75 |
| 204 | 40 l. on 2 l., stone on cream (b)   . .. | 3.15 |

(ii.) *Perf.* 11½.

| 205 | 30 l. on 40 l., lilac on cream (b) .. .. | 12 | |
| 206 | 30 l. on 40 l., purple on cream (b) .. .. | 18 | |
| 207 | 40 l. on 2 l., stone on cream (b) .. .. | 25 | 25 |
| 208 | 50 l. on 40 l. rosy buff on cream (a) .. | 18 | 6 |
| 209 | 3 dr. on 10 l., orange on cream (b) .. .. | 90 | |
| 209a | 3 dr. on 10 l., orange-vermilion .. .. | 1.50 | |
| 210 | 5 dr. on 40 l., violet on blue (a) .. .. | 1.50 | |
| 211 | 5 dr. on 40 l., red-lilac on blue (a) .. .. | 1.25 | |

*Varieties.* "ΑΕΠΤΑ" *for* "ΛΕΠΤΑ."

| 212 | 30 l. on 40 l., lilac on cream (b) .. .. | |
| 213 | 30 l. on 40 l., purple on cream (b) .. .. | 3.75 |

**B.** *Various stamps surcharged with* "A. M.", *and value as* Type **11** *or* **12.**

**I.** *On stamps of* Type **2,** *Belgian print, in* black.

(i.) *Imperf.*

| 214 | 25 l. on 40 l., violet .. | 18 |
| 215 | 50 l. on 25 l., dull blue.. | 50 |

(ii.) *Perf.* 11½.

| 216 | 25 l. on 40 l., violet .. | 25 |
| 217 | 50 l. on 25 l., dull blue.. | 90 |

**II.** *On stamps of* Type **1,** *Athens print, in* black. (a) *With figures at back.* (b) *Without figures.*

(i.) *Imperf.*

| 218 | 1 dr. on 40 l., brownish lake on blue (a) .. | 62 |
| 219 | 2 dr. on 5 l., green on cream (b) .. .. | 1.00 |

(ii.) *Perf.* 11½.

| 220 | 1 dr. on 40 l., brownish lake on blue (a) .. | 1.00 |
| 221 | 2 dr. on 5 l., green on cream (b) .. .. | 1.00 |

There are many errors of the above surcharges, such as double, inverted, etc.

**III.** *On Olympic Games issue, in* red.

| 222 | 5 l. on 1 dr., blue .. | 18 | |
| 223 | 25 l. on 40 l., mauve .. | 12 | 18 |
| 224 | 50 l. on 2 dr., bistre .. | 25 | 18 |
| 225 | 1 dr. on 5 dr., green .. | 36 | 36 |
| 226 | 2 dr. on 10 dr., brown .. | 75 | 1.00 |

*Double surcharge.*

| 227 | 5 l. on 1 dr., blue .. | 1.85 |
| 228 | 25 l. on 40 l., mauve .. | |
| 229 | 50 l., in *black*, and 25 l., in *red*, on 40 l., mauve | 1.85 |

| 14 | 15 |

**1901.** *Wmk.* Type **16.**

| No. | Type. | | *Perf.* 13½. | | |
|---|---|---|---|---|---|
| 230 | 14 | 1 l., brown .. .. | 2 | 2 |
| 231 | ,, | 2 l., grey .. .. | 2 | 2 |

| No. Type. | Un. | Used. |
|---|---|---|

**16**     **17**

| 232 | 14 | 3 l., orange | .. | 2 | 2 |
| 233 | 15 | 5 l., green | .. | 2 | 2 |
| 234 | " | 10 l.. carmine | .. | 4 | 2 |
| 235 | 14 | 20 l., lilac | .. | 4 | 2 |
| 236 | 15 | 25 l., blue | .. | 6 | 2 |
| 237 | 14 | 30 l., violet | .. | 6 | 4 |
| 238 | " | 40 l., dark brown | .. | 8 | 4 |
| 239 | " | 50 l., lake | .. | 10 | 4 |

Type 17. *Same wmk. Perf. 12½.*

| 240 | 1 dr., black | .. | .. | 18 | 6 |
| 241 | 2 ,, bronze | .. | .. | 36 | 36 |
| 242 | 3 ,, silver | .. | .. | 55 | 55 |
| 243 | 5 ,, gold | .. | .. | 95 | 95 |

**1901.** *Same types, wmk., and perf.*
*Thinner paper.*

| 244 | 1 l., brown | .. | .. | 2 | 2 |
| 245 | 2 l., grey | .. | .. | 2 | 2 |
| 246 | 3 l., orange | .. | .. | 2 | 2 |
| 247 | 5 l., green | .. | .. | 2 | 2 |
| 248 | 10 l., carmine | .. | .. | 2 | 2 |
| 249 | 20 l., lilac | .. | .. | 4 | 4 |
| 250 | 25 l., ultramarine | .. | 6 | 2 |
| 251 | 50 l., lake | .. | .. | — | 12 |

*Variety. Imperf.*

| 252 | 1 l., brown | | | | |

**18**

**1902.** Type 18. *No wmk. Perf. 13½.*

| 253 | 5 l., orange | .. | .. |
| 254 | 25 l., emerald | .. | .. |
| 255 | 50 l., ultramarine | .. |
| 256 | 1 dr., carmine | .. |
| 257 | 2 dr., brown | .. | .. |

Set of 5, unused, $1.10.

| No. | Un. | Used. |
|---|---|---|

UNPAID LETTER STAMPS.

**5¹**     **5²**

**1875.** Type 5¹. "ΛΕΠΤΟΝ" or "ΛΕΠΤΑ" *in small letters,* Type 5².

(i.) *Imperf.*

| 301 | 1 l., green and black | .. | — | 10.00 |
| 302 | 2 l. ,, | ,, | .. |
| 303 | 5 l. ,, | ,, | .. |
| 304 | 10 l. ,, | ,, | .. |
| 305 | 20 l. ,, | ,, | .. |
| 306 | 40 l. ,, | ,, | .. |
| 307 | 60 l. ,, | ,, | .. |
| 308 | 70 l. ,, | ,, | .. |
| 309 | 80 l. ,, | ,, | .. |
| 310 | 90 l. ,, | ,, | .. |
| 311 | 1 dr. ,, | ,, | .. |
| 312 | 2 dr. ,, | ,, | .. |

*Varieties with centre inverted.*

| 313 | 40 l., green and black | .. |
| 314 | 2 dr. ,, | ,, | .. |

(ii.) *Perf. 9 to 9½.*

| 315 | 1 l., green and black | .. |
| 316 | 2 l. ,, | ,, | .. | 8 |
| 317 | 5 l. ,, | ,, | .. | 6 | 8 |
| 318 | 10 l. ,, | ,, | .. |
| 319 | 20 l. ,, | ,, | .. | 50 | 25 |
| 320 | 40 l. ,, | ,, | .. | — | 50 |
| 321 | 60 l. ,, | ,, | .. | — | 50 |
| 322 | 70 l. ,, | ,, | .. | 1.00 | 1.00 |
| 323 | 80 l. ,, | ,, | .. |
| 324 | 90 l. ,, | ,, | .. | 50 |
| 325 | 1 dr. ,, | ,, | .. | — | 1.00 |
| 326 | 2 dr. ,, | ,, | .. |

(iii.) *Perf. 10½.*

| 327 | 1 l., green and black | .. | 2 | 4 |
| 328 | 2 l. ,, | ,, | .. | 2 |
| 329 | 5 l. ,, | ,, | .. | 2 | 2 |
| 330 | 10 l. ,, | ,, | .. |
| 331 | 20 l. ,, | ,, | .. | 25 | 18 |
| 332 | 40 l. ,, | ,, | .. | 1.00 | 50 |
| 333 | 60 l. ,, | ,, | .. | 25 | 18 |
| 334 | 70 l. ,, | ,, | .. | 25 | 25 |
| 335 | 80 l. ,, | ,, | .. | 30 |
| 336 | 90 l. ,, | ,, | .. | 36 | 36 |
| 337 | 1 dr. ,, | ,, | .. | 36 | 36 |
| 338 | 2 dr. ,, | ,, | .. | 75 | 75 |

*Varieties with centre inverted.*

| 339 | 1 dr., green and black . |
| 340 | 2 dr. ,, | ,, | .. |

| No. | | Un. | Used. |
|---|---|---|---|
| *(iv.) Perf. 13.* | | | |
| 341 | 1 l., green and black .. | 1.25 | |
| 342 | 2 l. „ „ .. | 1.25 | |
| 343 | 5 l. „ „ .. | — | 50 |
| 344 | 10 l. „ „ .. | | |
| 345 | 20 l. „ „ .. | | |
| 346 | 40 l. „ „ .. | | |
| 347 | 60 l. „ „ .. | — | 1.00 |
| 348 | 70 l. „ „ .. | | |
| 349 | 80 l. „ „ .. | 30 | 30 |
| 350 | 90 l. „ „ .. | | |
| 351 | 1 dr. „ „ .. | 30 | |
| 352 | 2 dr. „ „ .. | | |

*Perf. 10½ × 13.*

| 353 | 1 l., green and black .. | 12 | |
|---|---|---|---|
| 354 | 2 l. „ „ .. | | |
| 355 | 5 l. „ „ .. | 25 | 12 |
| 356 | 10 l. „ „ .. | — | 50 |
| 357 | 20 l. „ „ .. | | |
| 358 | 40 l. „ „ .. | — | 50 |
| 359 | 60 l. „ „ .. | | |
| 360 | 70 l. „ „ .. | 1.85 | |
| 361 | 80 l. „ „ .. | 1.25 | |
| 362 | 90 l. „ „ .. | 1.50 | |
| 363 | 1 dr. „ „ .. | | |
| 364 | 2 dr. „ „ .. | | |

*Perf. 11 × 9.*

| 364a | 20 l., green and black.. | | |
|---|---|---|---|
| 364b | 40 l. „ „ .. | | |

53

54

**1878.** Type 53. *Value in larger letters,* Type 54.

*(i.) Perf. 9 to 9½.*

| 364d | 20 l., green and black . | 1.25 | |
|---|---|---|---|
| 365 | 60 l. „ „ . | 1.85 | |
| 366 | 70 l. „ „ . | — | 1.85 |

*(ii.) Perf. 10½.*

| 367 | 1 l., green and black . | 2 | |
|---|---|---|---|
| 368 | 2 l. „ „ .. | 8 | 8 |
| 369 | 5 l. „ „ .. | 18 | 18 |
| 370 | 10 l. „ „ .. | | |
| 371 | 20 l. „ „ .. | 50 | 25 |
| 372 | 40 l. „ „ .. | 1.00 | 75 |
| 373 | 60 l. „ „ .. | 25 | 12 |
| 374 | 70 l. „ „ .. | 1.25 | 1.25 |
| 375 | 80 l. „ „ .. | 1.50 | 1.50 |
| 376 | 90 l. „ „ .. | 75 | 75 |
| 377 | 100 l. „ „ .. | 1.00 | |
| 378 | 200 l. „ „ .. | 1.85 | 1.85 |

| No. | | Un. | Used. |
|---|---|---|---|
| *(iii.) Perf. 11½ to 13.* | | | |
| 379 | 1 l., green and black . | 2 | 4 |
| 380 | 2 l. „ „ | 12 | |
| 381 | 5 l. „ „ .. | 12 | 12 |
| 382 | 10 l. „ „ .. | 25 | 12 |
| 383 | 20 l. „ „ | 8 | |
| 384 | 40 l. „ „ | 8 | |
| 385 | 60 l. „ „ .. | 25 | 6 |
| 386 | 70 l. „ „ .. | | |
| 387 | 80 l. „ „ .. | | |
| 388 | 90 l. „ „ .. | | |
| 389 | 100 l. „ „ .. | 36 | 36 |
| 390 | 200 l. „ „ .. | 62 | 62 |

*Error. Centre inverted.*

| 391 | 60 l., green and black .. | | |
|---|---|---|---|

55

**1902.** Type 55. *Perf. 13½.*

| 392 | 1 l., brown .. .. | 2 |
|---|---|---|
| 393 | 2 l., grey .. .. | 2 |
| 394 | 3 l., orange .. .. | 2 |
| 395 | 5 l., green .. .. | 2 |
| 396 | 10 l., carmine .. .. | 2 |
| 397 | 20 l., mauve .. .. | 4 |
| 398 | 25 l., ultramarine .. | 6 |
| 399 | 30 l., deep purple .. | 6 |
| 400 | 40 l., sepia .. .. | 8 |
| 401 | 50 l., brown-lake .. | 10 |
| 402 | 1 dr., black .. .. | 18 |
| 403 | 2 dr., bronze .. .. | 36 |
| 404 | 3 dr., silver .. .. | 55 |
| 405 | 5 dr., gold .. .. | 95 |

# GUATEMALA.

1   2

**1871.** Type 1. *Perf. 14 × 13½.*

| 1 | 1 c., bistre .. .. | 4 | 25 |
|---|---|---|---|
| 2 | 5 c., brown .. .. | 12 | 25 |
| 3 | 10 c., blue .. .. | 18 | 25 |
| 4 | 20 c., carmine .. .. | 12 | 25 |
| 5 | 20 c., blue (error) .. | 1.85 | |

|   | | *Un.* | *Used.* |
|---|---|---|---|
| No. | | | |

*Variety.  Tête-bêche (pair).*

| 6 | 5 c., brown | .. | .. | 3.75 | |
|---|---|---|---|---|---|

*Varieties.  Imperf.*

| 6a | 1 c., bistre | .. | .. | 50 |
|---|---|---|---|---|
| 6b | 5 c., brown | .. | .. | 62 |
| 6c | 10 c., blue | .. | .. | 62 |
| 6d | 20 c., carmine | .. | .. | 62 |

**1873.  Type 2.  *Perf.* 11½.**

| 7 | 4 reales, mauve | .. | 3.75 | 3.75 |
|---|---|---|---|---|
| 8 | 1 peso, yellow | .. | 3.75 | 4.50 |

3

4

5

6

**1875.  Types 1 *to* 4.  *Perf.* 12.**

| 9 | ½ real, black | .. | .. | 4 | 18 |
|---|---|---|---|---|---|
| 10 | ½ ,, green | .. | .. | 4 | 18 |
| 11 | 1 ,, blue | .. | .. | 6 | 18 |
| 12 | 2 ,, red | .. | .. | 8 | 12 |

The stamps of this issue are occasionally found imperf.

7

8

**1877.  Type 7.  *Perf.* 13½.**

| 13 | ½ real, green | .. | .. | 4 | 12 |
|---|---|---|---|---|---|
| 14 | 2 ,, carmine | .. | .. | 8 | 25 |
| 15 | 4 ,, violet | .. | .. | 12 | 16 |
| 16 | 1 peso, maize | .. | .. | 25 | 36 |

Reprints are known of the ½, 2, and 4 rls., perf. 12. The 1 p. probably also exists.

|   | | *Un.* | *Used.* |
|---|---|---|---|
| No. | | | |

**1879.  Type 8.  *Perf.* 12.**
Central design in second colour.

| 17 | ½ real, brown and green | 12 | 25 |
|---|---|---|---|
| 18 | 1 ,, black and green. | 25 | 25 |

## 1
## centavo
9

## 5
## centavos.
10

**1881.  Types 7 *and* 8 *surcharged as* Type 9**
No. Type.  *or* 10, *in* black.

| 19 | 8 | 1 c. on ½ rl., brown and green | .. | 12 | 18 |
|---|---|---|---|---|---|
| 20 | 7 | 5 c. on ½ rl., green.. | | 25 | 36 |
| 21 | 8 | 10 c. on 1 rl., black and green | .. | 25 | 36 |
| 22 | 7 | 20 c. on 2 rls., carmine | | 75 | 1.00 |

*Double surcharge.*

| 23 | 5 c. on ½ rl., green | .. |
|---|---|---|

*Errors of surcharge.*

| 24 | 8 | 1 centavo on ½ rl. | .. |
|---|---|---|---|
| 25 | 7 | 5 centavos on ½ rl. | .. |
| 26 | 8 | 10 ,, 1 rl. | .. |
| 27 | ,, | 1 ecntavo on ½ rl. | .. | 2.50 | 2.50 |
| 28 | 7 | 5 ecntavos on ½ rl. | .. | 1.50 | |
| 29 | 8 | 10 ecntavos on 1 rl. | .. | 2.50 | |
| 30 | ,, | 1 ccntavo on ½ rl. | .. | |
| 31 | 7 | 10 centavo on 1 rl. | .. | |

**1881.  Type 8.  *Perf.* 12.**

| 32 | 1 c., black and green | .. | 2 | 2 |
|---|---|---|---|---|
| 33 | 2 c., brown ,, | .. | 2 | 4 |
| 34 | 5 c., red ,, | .. | 2 | 2 |
| 35 | 10 c., violet ,, | .. | 4 | 8 |
| 36 | 20 c., yellow ,, | .. | 6 | 8 |

*Errors.  Centres inverted.*

| 37 | 2 c., brown and green.. | 7.50 | |
|---|---|---|---|
| 38 | 5 c., red ,, | .. | — | 25.00 |
| 39 | 20 c., yellow ,, | .. | 16.25 | |

11

**1886.  *Railway stamps of* 1 peso, Type 11, *surcharged, in* black, *as* Type 12, 13, *or* 14.**

| 40 | 25 c., vermilion | .. | 2 | 8 |
|---|---|---|---|---|

Lightning Source UK Ltd.
Milton Keynes UK
UKHW020616030323
417973UK00008B/796